Butterworths
Legal Research Guide

Butterworths
Legal Research Guide

Second edition

Guy Holborn MA LLB ALA
Librarian, Lincoln's Inn Library

With a foreword by the Rt Hon Lord Steyn

Butterworths
LexisNexis™

Foreword

The demands of courts for improvement in the depth and quality of legal research are becoming ever more exacting. Gone are the days when it was enough to muddle along with an *Archbold* or a *Chitty on Contracts*. The courts now expect, and are entitled to expect, careful research into statutory materials, contextual aids to construction, case law and legal literature.

But courts are entitled to even greater assistance. Cardozo wrote that the moulding forces of the law are 'logic, history, and utility, and the accepted standards of right conduct'. For example, practitioners must be able to deploy social data, economic materials and statistics relevant to what would be for the generality of cases the best answer to a question of law.

Another feature of modern research is the internationalisation of the required legal research. The multitude of treaties, which are part of our law, make an internationalist approach mandatory. But on the wider basis English courts expect practitioners to research comparative legal materials. An illustration of this process is the world-wide legal dialogue between the House of Lords and the Supreme Courts of other countries.

It is fitting that the Librarian of one of the Inns of Court should be the author of this valuable second edition of his *Legal Research Guide*. It is an indispensable tool to the development of skills in legal research. I unreservedly recommend this book to all who want to become adult lawyers in the broadest sense of that expression.

House of Lords   Johan Steyn
August 2001   A Lord of Appeal in Ordinary

Preface

The first edition of this book was written at a time when the teaching of legal research at undergraduate level and on the Legal Practice and Bar Vocational courses was beginning to take off. Legal research teaching has certainly matured, and this edition is once again largely aimed at those undertaking such courses. However, legal research skills are best learnt by practising them rather than reading about them. Accordingly, the first edition was also intended to be a practical work of reference to be used when the classes at law school were rather dim memories and the trainee solicitor or pupil barrister had a genuine problem (which the law librarian was not around to answer). It was also hoped that more experienced lawyers might find it useful as a reminder of the ever expanding range of research tools available and as a source of information on areas not encountered every day. This edition has been updated with all these constituent users in mind. But it is fair to say that it as a work of reference rather than as a course manual that the second edition has undergone expansion as well as mere updating.

The structure of the first edition has been adhered to. The work is divided into two main parts. The first half is a narrative text which is particularly aimed at those on taught courses, but which also gives more detailed guidance to others if needed. It necessarily covers topics that students on undergraduate or the vocational courses will have little need to worry about, for example local legislation or ecclesiastical law. On the other hand, the experienced lawyer may feel patronised by the basic offerings for new undergraduates, such as when to use square or round brackets in a citation. I am assuming that both classes of user will readily understand the implicit rubric at appropriate points, 'students can skip this bit' or 'what follows is teaching grandmothers to suck eggs'. The second half is a Quick Reference Guide, which in effect summarises the first half in a format that it is hoped can be used on the hoof when a research problem is encountered in practice. I would be glad if law librarians and information professionals also find it useful as an aide-mémoire in their day to day enquiry work.

The main structural change in this edition has been to drop, with some reluctance, the worked examples provided with the main text. They may have served a purpose, particularly while the work was new, but they do date very rapidly. Furthermore, perhaps selfishly, I came to the conclusion that the effort in contriving them, particularly the more elaborate examples, was disproportionate to their explanatory value. The main task in updating the work has been to take account of the enormous expansion of electronic sources and the advent of the Internet since the first edition. But the opportunity has been taken to rectify some omissions.

The second half of the first chapter on search strategies has been entirely rewritten, with the Internet in mind. The very last chapter of the first edition, 'Directories and subjects related to law', has been dropped, except that the section on legal directories will now be found at the end of Chapter 2. I was a little hesitant in writing about such areas as company and financial information in the first place. I now feel more than hesitant – it is bad enough trying to keep up to date with the legal sources proper. In Chapter 3, the section on Local and Personal Acts has been completely revised. Local legislation is inherently difficult material to deal with, and added experience of having to do so since the first edition has prompted a renewed attempt to unravel its mysteries. I have added for the sake of completeness a short section on Church Measures to Chapter 3. A more glaring omission from the first edition was any treatment of tracing derivations and destinations for consolidation Acts. It is a basic problem, particularly relevant to tracing judicial consideration of legislation. But its importance has been particularly brought home in the context of doing *Pepper v Hart* research. That decision of the House of Lords came just in time for some coverage at the end of Chapter 3 in the first edition, but its full impact was scarcely appreciated. Tracing Parliamentary debates and other background material on legislation accordingly now has a whole new chapter to itself, following on from Chapter 3 on legislation.

The policy of the first edition of treating EC materials alongside English materials, rather than consigning them to a chapter of their own, has been retained and now also extends to human rights materials. Chapter 5 on case law in particular reflects this change of emphasis. The section on style of case names was supposed in the first edition to include treatment of Social Security Commissioners decisions, but in a fit of amnesia was omitted. That has been put right, and decisions of the Commons Commissioners added for good measure. The decisions of the Social Security Commissioners also illustrate the benefits and drawbacks of the provision of case law on the Internet. It is marvellous to have free access to these primary materials, but there has to be some system to it. It is sincerely hoped that BAILII (the British and Irish Legal Information Institute), whose launch was greeted with enormous enthusiasm and goodwill, will deliver all that it promises. These matters receive a good deal of attention in Chapter 5. A short section on international case law has been added to the chapter on treaties. There was a case for substituting the whole of what is now the last chapter, on the law outside England and Wales, with the single sentence, 'Log on to the Internet and do a Google search'. But an attempt has been made to come to grips with the material on the Internet should a Google search not suffice. The section on the other jurisdictions in the British Isles has had to take account of devolution in Scotland and Wales, and the resumption of devolution in Northern Ireland, which now bring added intricacies in dealing with their legal materials.

A matter of style: addresses for websites have not been given in the text – some are mentioned quite frequently and they clutter up the text. Names of websites or web-based services are, however, given in Helvetica typeface. Where a product is available in hard copy or on CD-ROM as well as on the Internet the name is given in *Helvetica Italic* unless it is specifically the hard copy version that is being described, in which case it appears in conventional *italic*. Where a name appears in Helvetica, whether roman or italic, there should be an entry, with full web address, in the List and Index of Websites and Web-Based Services which is provided after the Quick Reference Guide.

Account has been taken of products and publications known to me as at 31 July 2001.

Guy Holborn
August 2001

Acknowledgements

I am most grateful to the following publishers for their kind permission to reproduce material in the illustrations:

Bowker Saur
Butterworths
EUR-OP
Her Majesty's Stationery Office (for Crown copyright and Parliamentary copyright material)
Incorporated Council of Law Reporting for England and Wales
John Harper Publishing
Martindale-Hubbell
The Stationery Office Ltd
Sweet & Maxwell

As with the first edition a number of people readily answered particular queries, including Jackie Elliott, High Court Librarian, Canberra, Australia, and the Worshipful Mark Hill, Chancellor of the Diocese of Chichester. A stimulating talk given by Avis Furness, Librarian of the European Parliament's UK Office, happily coincided with the revision of the treatment of European legislative procedures. Those law librarians who have heard the talks and read the articles by Valerie Stevenson (University of Aberdeen) on search engines will recognise the undisguised debt I owe to her. David Hart, University of Dundee, tactfully pointed out some egregious errors relating to Scottish materials in the first edition.

Jules Winterton, Librarian of the Institute of Advanced Legal Studies, University of London, kindly provided house room in the Institute, allowing a period, all too brief, of uninterrupted work on this edition, and it goes without saying that the book could not have been written without access to the resources of the Institute's Library.

The assistance and forbearance of all my colleagues at Lincoln's Inn Library are once again gratefully acknowledged. Catherine McArdle, Deputy Librarian, admirably fulfils her role – that is, she does the work while her putative superior writes books. Carolyn Malsher, Assistant Librarian, nobly gave up her free time to save an already delayed manuscript from further delay by indexing the websites mentioned in the text and finding and checking all the addresses (some 200) in the list.

My wife Sophie and children, Jack and Lucy, were not frightfully impressed at the recompense of seeing their names in print in the acknowledgements to the first edition. So there is little reason to suppose that mentioning them again will do much to make amends this time. But mentioned they most certainly must be.

Contents

6. Treaties and international materials   222

7. Other official publications   235

8. Law outside England and Wales   247

A. Legal research explained and illustrated

1. Introduction: aims and techniques of legal research

How to find a telephone number

1.1 I want to telephone an acquaintance who works at London University, but who is not at work. I remember he was staying at a hall of residence. How do I find its telephone number? Look in the phone book. Is the university in the business pages or is the hall of residence in the residential pages? Is it under London University or University of London? I find the number, and when I ring I am told he moved out a few months ago. So I ring Directory Enquiries, but then realise I do not know his new address and his name is John Smith. The phone books on the Internet are not going to be much help either. Pause for thought. Do I know someone else who would know his number? His girlfriend would. She works in a firm of estate agents, but I cannot remember their name. Ah, I think they were in Shaftesbury Avenue. They must have a website, or at least there must be listings of estate agents on the Internet. Get the Google search engine up on the screen and type in 'estate agents Shaftesbury Avenue'. Wade through a few hits for estate agents trying to sell property on Shaftesbury Avenue and an estate agent in Shaftesbury Avenue, Harrow, but only a few hits down I recognise the name. It gives the phone number and I speak to her. He has gone to visit relatives in New York, and she gives me the number of an uncle there who will know where he is. Start to dial the New York number, then realise my phone bill has recently been getting out of hand and I cannot afford a transatlantic call. Decide it is not that urgent, and send him an e-mail at his university department instead.

This story is contrived to illustrate some recurring themes in legal research. Indeed it could be said that if you can find a telephone number you can find the law – it merely requires the application of common sense and a little experience. However, the aims of this book are to make explicit the intuitive steps that may count as 'common sense' and to shorten the learning curve that may count as 'a little experience', and thereby place legal research among the essential skills to be gained early on by any lawyer or would-be lawyer.

Recurring themes in legal research

No single source is comprehensive

1.2 Like the London phone books, research tools cover different categories of materials or are designed to solve different sorts of problems. Even those tools that are multi-purpose and that aim at some degree of comprehensiveness – such as *Current Law*, which used to boast 'all the law from every source', or Lexis with its gigabytes of full text data – cannot be the last word. One reason for this is that there are bound to be time-lags – the information may have changed or been added to in the last few weeks, or days, or hours. But also, the quantity of information that might be of use to a lawyer is just not finite.

1.3 Two consequences flow from this. The first is the importance of being aware of the scope of particular sources, and not being misled by their titles. It is helpful when the sources themselves set out clearly their editorial policies. For example, the *Legal Journals Index* does this, explaining its coverage of all legal journals *published* in the UK. If you aware of that, you will realise that despite the mine of information to be found in it, there might be other articles in English on English law not indexed in it. Another example is *The Law Reports Index*. On its front cover it lists the series of law reports it indexes. These are neither just the 'official' law reports nor all the law reports there are, but only a selection of the major series. This makes it a very handy tool, but is not necessarily appropriate for in-depth research.

1.4 The other consequence is the converse: the importance of being aware of the overlap between different sources. Just as the phone book is not the only place to find a telephone number, there is more than one way of finding the law, and indeed the heading of this section could well have been another recurring theme of legal research: there is no single 'right' way to tackle a research problem. Although this flexibility is sometimes convenient, it can also mean that if you want to be thorough and squeeze the last pips out of a problem the research can be tedious and repetitive as you hunt through alternative sources hoping to find something the others have missed. But then there are plenty of other activities in the law that are tedious and repetitive.

Choosing a starting point

1.5 Given this variety of sources, an effective research strategy depends on choosing the best starting point. The most important step, dealt with below (paras **1.27–1.28**), is identifying the legal issues involved. Having got that, you still need to know, for example, whether the area is primarily statute-based or governed by common law cases. Date is very important too. For example, if you want to find cases on a particular subject it is sensible to try to find first the most recent case because it is likely that it will cite all the earlier cases of importance on the subject. On the other hand, the sources offering the greatest currency are not necessarily those offering the greatest coverage. For example, Lawtel, though offering excellent currency, would not necessarily be the best place to start unless you happen to know that there was a major case in the area in the last few weeks, which might not yet have been reported. It might be better to start with *Current Law*, then do a quick update.

1.6 Another factor in choosing a starting point is how comprehensive you need to be and how much time you have. If you are involved in a case in the House of Lords, then you are likely to want to pull out all the stops to track down an obscure Commonwealth case given among ten other authorities in fn 14 on p 1268 of *Rayden on Divorce*. On the other hand, if you are appearing before Highbury Magistrates' Court in five minutes, a scan of the 150 volumes of the *Canadian Abridgement* is not going to get your client off driving without due care and attention.

Choosing your words carefully

1.7 The success of a search depends on thinking through at the outset the relevant terminology. Whether the phone book chooses to use 'London University' or 'University of London' is an elementary illustration. Often there is no difficulty because much of the law is framed in specific technical language, but frequently there are synonyms or alternative expressions for the same legal concept or topic, for example, 'land law' or 'real property'; 'labour law' or 'employment law'; 'revenue law' or 'tax law'; 'conflict of laws' or 'private international law'; 'retention of title', 'reservation of title' or 'Romalpa clauses'; 'commercial lease' or 'business tenancy'. There may be alternative English and Latin expressions, for example, 'stare decisis' and 'precedent'. Awareness of synonyms is all the more important when using non-technical terms, especially in free text retrieval systems such as Lexis, for example, 'buyer and seller' as opposed to 'purchaser and vendor'. The last example also illustrates the need to think of antonyms as well as synonyms; other examples are debtor and creditor, legitimate and illegitimate.

1.8 Broader and narrower terms need to be thought of too. If you are looking for a specific term in an index it may entered directly or as a subdivision of a broader heading. Similarly, if you are looking for a book or article on a particular subject it may be dealt with in a book or article on a larger topic. Construct mentally a hierarchy of possible terms on the lines of the following two examples:

Remedies
    Equitable remedies
        Injunctions
            Freezing injunctions

Tort
    Negligence
        Professional negligence
        Clinical negligence
            Wrongful birth

1.9 As well as thinking through synonyms and a hierarchy of broader and narrower terms, one must bear in mind related terms and also disentangle different meanings that the same terms may have in different contexts. Examples of closely related, but not synonymous or identical, terms or subject areas are 'immigration' and 'nationality'; 'competition law' and 'monopolies'; 'consumer protection', 'product liability' and 'sale of goods'; 'mergers' and 'take-overs'. Some examples of the same terms being used in different contexts are: 'taxation', which will usually mean revenue law, but may well refer (in pre-Woolf language) to the taxation of costs; 'privilege', which may arise in the context of defamation or of discovery; 'caution', in the sense of a police caution or a caution on the land register; 'forfeiture', in the sense of criminal confiscation orders or in the context of forfeiture of leases (or forfeiture of an inheritance under the Forfeiture Act 1982); 'ultra vires', in administrative law or in company law.

1.10 The same terms, while not representing different concepts, may be applied in different areas of law, the most obvious examples being torts which may also be crimes, such as conspiracy, assault and nuisance. The same term may be used in a loose general sense or in a specific technical sense. For example, a 'settlement' may refer generally to a disposition of property, or specifically to a strict settlement under the Settled Land Act 1925 (as applies to settlements before 1997). A 'warranty' may be used loosely for any guarantee or assurance, or specifically as a contract term whose breach only gives rise to a right to damages not to rescission.

1.11 If your research takes you into materials or writings from other jurisdictions, it is also necessary to be aware of the possibility that terms may differ from their English usage. For example, in the US (and other jurisdictions) 'judicial review' will usually refer to the courts reviewing whether legislation is constitutional rather than the review of administrative action. Scots law is replete with its own technical terms, which should not be confused with their appearance in ordinary English usage, such as 'diligence' or 'irritancy'.

1.12 Change of terminology over time should be appreciated, especially if your research takes you into older materials. This may be the result of changes in fashion – for example, in contract law 'exclusion clauses' were often and may still occasionally be called 'exception clauses'. The umbrella term 'intellectual property' for copyright, designs, and patents is the preferred term, but 20 years ago it would have been 'industrial property'. It may be the result of changes in the boundaries and classification of subjects. It was only in 1966 that the first English textbook on the law of 'restitution' was written. Before then it would have been considered under the head 'quasi-contract' in contract books or dispersed in equity texts. The law, and so its terminology, may have mirrored changes in social conditions – the law of 'master and servant' and 'husband and wife' are now employment law and family law. Changes may also result from the intervention of legislation. Entire legal concepts may disappear as the result of legislation – since 1967 the student has not had to worry about the distinction between 'felonies' and 'misdemeanours', yet an appreciation may still be necessary for reading old cases. Or there may be a substitution of terminology – theft for larceny (Theft Act 1968), criminal damage for malicious damage (Criminal Damage Act 1971), personal insolvency for bankruptcy (Insolvency Act 1985), inheritance tax for capital transfer tax (Finance Act 1986), Jobseekers' Allowance for unemployment benefit (Jobseekers Act 1995), and employment tribunal for industrial tribunal (Employment Rights (Dispute Resolution) Act 1998). (The last example, incidentally, was unusual in having retrospective effect on the name of a previous Act – the Industrial Tribunals Act 1996, as it was called on its enactment, is to be cited as the Employment Tribunals Act 1996.) The Civil Procedure Rules 1998 (CPR) prescribed a raft of new terms with a view to importing plainer English into the language of litigation, for example, a Mareva injunction is now to be known as a freezing injunction and an Anton Piller order is a search order. Some of the new terms in the CPR, for example, clinical negligence for medical negligence, would seem rather neutral changes – one just has to remember to use both when searching databases. Others, however, in abolishing technical language, have removed precision. For example, discovery, a recognised stage in civil litigation, became 'disclosure', which is a wide general term used in all sorts of contexts and makes searching electronic sources much less precise. There are others still that, rather than removing mystery, add to it, for example, third-party proceedings are now 'Part 20 claims'.

1.13 These changes often present problems in using indexes, particularly to major works such as *Halsbury's*, produced over a period of time and serial works such as *Current Law*. Cross-references may be provided, but it is as well to prepare mentally one's own in advance. *Current Law* also exemplifies another problem that can occur with any serial publication – namely changes not in the terminology of the subject matter as such but in indexing policy. *Current Law*, together with the *Legal Journals*

Index and other databases in the Current Legal Information suite, follow an elaborate structured thesaurus for their subject indexing. This is constantly revised, not merely to add novel terms but to provide more specific terms warranted by the quantity of legal literature. Examples of the addition of more specific terms are 'fair comment', rather than using 'defamation' and 'defences'; 'knowing assistance' rather than just 'breach of trust'; 'just satisfaction' rather than 'human rights' and 'compensation'.

1.14 Although the emphasis on thinking through terminology has here been in the context of subject searching because that is where it is most pertinent, the same general advice applies to searching for names, whether as authors in catalogues, or as parties in cases or indeed as subject terms. Names of corporate bodies are the most likely to cause trouble. The London University problem of inversion is a common one: Commissioner of Police for the Metropolis or Metropolitan Police Commissioner, Secretary of State for the Environment or Environment Secretary, Law Reform Commission of Australia or Australian Law Reform Commission, Court of Justice of the European Communities or European Court of Justice. Changes of name, mergers and demergers are another common problem: Liberty was the National Council for Civil Liberties; the Stock Exchange has been variously known as the Stock Exchange, the International Stock Exchange and the London Stock Exchange; the Department of Trade and the Department of Industry merged to become the Department of Trade and Industry; the Department of Health and Social Security split into the Department of Health and the Department of Social Security. Acronyms and initialisms as opposed to the full name often occur. Occasionally a body may have a popular name and an official name, for example, the Ombudsman is formally known as the Parliamentary Commissioner for Administration. Policy in indexes and tables varies on the treatment of corporate bodies in the form of personal names, for example, Arthur Andersen or William Hill – they may be entered directly under the first element or inverted like a personal name.

1.15 Personal names do not present great problems – basic phone book skills are all that are needed. The unhyphenated double-barrelled surname versus the second (or third) forename is the standard problem: S A De Smith, Sir William Clarke Hall, E R Hardy Ivamy, T A Blanco White. For some reason, the surname of the author of the well-known work on personal insolvency is often assumed to be Muir Hunter, rather than just Hunter. Peerage titles that differ from the original family surname can occasionally confuse, though usually this arises in the case of old rather than modern writers: Charles Abbott or Lord Tenterden, Edward Sugden or Lord St Leonards, Quintin Hogg or Lord Hailsham of St Marylebone.

Currency

1.16 Each year nearly 4,000 new reported cases are digested by *Current Law,* over 3,500 statutory instruments (SIs) are made, and the *Legal Journals Index* adds over 30,000 records to its database. Taking these sources alone, 150 new items of legal information appear every working day. This rapid level of change makes it essential that your legal research is as up to date as possible.

Ensuring that the results of your research are as up-to-date as possible entails three elements: awareness of how particular sources are updated; awareness of which sources offer the greatest currency; and awareness at each stage of the precise date to which your research has taken you. In the course of this work many particular works will be examined and their updating mechanisms explained, but the basic principle when using any unfamiliar work is to ask oneself if and how it is updated – read any prefatory or explanatory matter. The tools offering the greatest currency for any particular problem will also be highlighted, but if in doubt ask someone, such as the law librarian or information officer, whether there is anything else more up-to-date. Most legal sources will say up to what date the law is stated – in textbooks look at the preface, in looseleaf works look at the latest filing instructions.

1.17 In the quest for currency it should not be overlooked that old law can sometimes help. A particular section of a statute hot off the Queen's Printer's press may in fact merely re-enact a previous provision. Old legal concepts may be resuscitated to meet novel problems – for example, the remedy of distress damage feasant, classically employed in the case of straying cattle, has been canvassed as a solution to the problem of private car-clamping.

Needles in haystacks

1.18 The John Smith problem is one quite often encountered in legal research. In the *Current Law Case Citator* for 1989–95 there are 40 cases with the name *Re F (a minor)*; in 2001 there were 70 SIs with a title starting 'Foot-and-Mouth Disease'. Sometimes there is no alternative but to plough through masses of material until you find what you want, but often the search can be approached from a different angle that yields a more specific result or can be narrowed in some way. One of the techniques of legal research is striking a balance between over-retrieval and under-retrieval. In the first example, if you knew the area involved you might do a full-text search on the *Family Law Reports* CD-ROM or go the relevant section of the *Family Court Practice* or a specialist work on child law. In the second example, if you only had manual sources at your disposal, you would probably be stuck, and even with all SIs available in a variety of electronic sources, you might instead go to the government department's foot and mouth website to see what orders were applicable to the locality in question.

Shortcuts: people sometimes better than books

1.19 'Ask the girlfriend' in the phone number illustration is by no means a flippant precept for legal research. In a law firm, barristers' chambers or law school there may well be someone else with expertise in the particular field you are researching who is able to say off the top of their head what the leading case is or what the best article is. Empirical research in the scientific research community has repeatedly shown that this form of informal networking comes ahead of libraries or databases as a source of information, and experience shows that this is the case in the law too. Even if there is no one of your immediate acquaintance who can help, it can often save a lot of time if you can go straight to the horse's mouth. If you are struggling with the EC regulation of seed varieties, telephone Legal Division A2 in the Ministry of Agriculture; if you are unsure whether the UK has ratified a treaty, phone the Treaty Department at the Foreign and Commonwealth Office; if you want to know whether a decision of the Court of Appeal has gone to the House of Lords, phone the Judicial Office of the House of Lords; if you think the regulations governing the disposal of land own by housing associations have been amended, phone the Housing Corporation, and so on. With large organisations and government departments try to find the number of the particular section or name of an individual rather than trying a general switchboard. Websites often help; in the case of government departments there is also the *Civil Service Yearbook*.

The half-remembered

1.20 As with finding the name of the girlfriend's firm, much legal research does not start completely cold. In fact what goes under the name of legal research is often no more than trying to find that case you saw in *The Times* a couple of weeks ago. The danger is that usually it turns out that it was not *The Times* but the *Independent*, it was not a couple of weeks ago but a couple of months ago, and that though 100% certain that the name of one of the parties was Ede, it was in fact Ravenscroft. Despite these pitfalls, if you do have some point of reference at the back of your mind to start from it can save considerable time in tackling a research problem. For this reason browsing journals and using current awareness services, be they published or in-house productions such as many large law firms and other organisations circulate, is a healthy exercise even if every item within your field of interest is not noted there and then. Not only lawyers but also the information professionals and librarians to whom this book is also addressed should make a point of scanning the legal press.

Lateral thinking

1.21 As with any research, speed and proficiency in legal research depend on a certain degree of luck and intuition as well as experience and knowledge. The ability to think round a problem and come up with alternative approaches when first attempts fail is probably not something that can readily be taught, though Edward De Bono's book *The Use of Lateral Thinking* ((1967) new edn 1990, Penguin), which coined the phrase, is relevant to research skills, and worth reading. All this book can do is elucidate the equivalent of the conventions that signal the presence of an anagram in a crossword clue – it cannot tell you in every case how to rearrange the letters to get the solution.

Knowing your sources and how they work

1.22 If lateral thinking cannot be taught, knowledge of the range of available sources is something concrete that can and should be assimilated, and indeed accounts for much of the content of this book. It should be emphasised though that familiarity with the materials is best gained from using them as much as from reading about them. Until that familiarity is gained, the best assumption to work on is that for most research problems there is a tool designed to solve it: if while tackling a problem you are thinking 'There must be an easier way of doing this', there usually is. The benefit of making the small effort to acquire the necessary knowledge is not just that you can go straight to the right place, but you will know when there definitely is no research tool designed for your problem before tackling it the hard way. Having a sound grasp of the available tools – tools which somebody has designed for a purpose – is also an antidote to the view 'well, we can just get it off the Internet, can't we?'. It is a fair thought-process nowadays to say 'there must be a website for this' – and the telephone number problem illustrated it – but there is good deal of difference between finding an estate agent, and finding an accurate and authoritative solution to a legal problem. Even where the Internet is the solution (using the Internet is discussed further below, paras **1.44–1.49**), some sound knowledge of what particular websites can and cannot do for you is a prerequisite – the admitted wonders of Google, or other search engines, are not a substitute for conventional legal research skills.

1.23 However, outside the mainstream tools dealt with in this book, there is a vast range of sources, some specialised or obscure and not necessarily widely available.

The range of tools is not static either. Even if you have access to a large and well-equipped law library, there is always a danger of forgetting that there might be better sources elsewhere. It should also be remembered that law librarians and information officers are not only paid to answer questions but actually quite enjoy being asked. Furthermore, apart from being trained, they have usually clocked up more 'flying hours' doing legal research than many lawyers, for whom research is necessarily only a small part of their work. So although this book aims to make the lawyer reasonably self-sufficient, asking for help is not a sign of failure, but often a sensible and timesaving move.

Costs, benefits and time

1.24 The decision whether to telephone the US or send an e-mail requires only a fairly basic application of cost/benefit principles. Applying the same principles to legal research does not require much greater sophistication, but is a necessary discipline. The classic illustration is the decision whether to use an on-line service, such as Lexis, which will cost money, or do a manual (or CD-ROM) search, which is free (ignoring, of course, the original purchase price of the materials). The variables are the quality of information required, the value of that information to you, the speed with which it is required and the cost (or value) of your time. It may be that the on-line source is in fact the only source – for example, for the transcript of an unreported case. Or the quality or quantity of information from the on-line source is better – for example, as with Lexis by retrieving many more references than the manual citators to statutes judicially considered. In those eventualities a judgment has to be made as to how badly you need the information. Depending on the context, the cost may seem cheap at the price, may be grudgingly met, or may be deemed too much because you can make do without the information. In many circumstances, the same information may be retrieved from manual sources but it takes much longer. If the matter is very urgent there may be no choice. If you are a solicitor using up billable hours it may well be cheaper to spend the money on an on-line search. Even if your time does not directly cost money, there may be better things you could be doing with it.

1.25 Another typical illustration of cost, benefits and use of time is delegation of research, be it to a trainee solicitor, to a pupil barrister, to a research assistant, or to a law librarian or information officer. Similar variables apply. As it is more likely that those categories of person – rather than the senior partner, silk or professor – will be reading this, the important point here, if the research is to be more cheaply done by you, is getting the research request absolutely clear. The assumption is often made by those delegating the task that what they really need is readily transmitted by telepathy. Sometimes a certain firmness of purpose is required to elicit what exactly is wanted. Find out why it is wanted, how much is wanted, and when it is wanted (usually yesterday).

Back to square one: approaching the problem from a different angle

1.26 As has emerged above, throughout the research process choices have to made – of starting points, of terminology, of sources, and so on. Frequently the wrong choice may be made and a dead end reached. Even where the problem has been tackled in the most efficient and elegant way, there is always the chance that a fresh approach will yield something more. If time allows double-checking is always a wise precaution – even the most reputable sources sometimes have errors or omissions. Illustrations of this will be given in the subsequent chapters, and the point is but one specific example of the general application of lateral thinking in legal research. At this stage it is just worth emphasising, however, that research tools that have one purpose can often be used in roundabout way for another purpose. *Halsbury's Statutes* can be used to find cases, both cases and legislation can be traced through the *Legal Journals Index*, information on government publications can be found in *Current Law Statutes*, and so on.

Getting off the runway: from fact to law

1.27 In practice the most difficult aspect of legal research, especially for the new practitioner, is not the grasping of such points as those listed above. Rather, the difficulty is conceptual. Legal problems as they arrive on the solicitor's or barrister's desk (or indeed in the student's examination paper), are not dressed as such, but usually come in the form of more or less complex fact situations. The first step in researching the problem has to be translating the fact situation into legal issues. The skills needed for spotting the relevant legal issues can only be acquired through experience and knowledge of the substantive law, and this book must assume such competence. Nowadays a good deal of emphasis is placed on fact management on the Legal Practice Course and Bar Vocational Course. The course manuals may include self-assessment practical exercises, where factual situations requiring identification of the legal issues are given. Or approaching it the other way, inventing facts to fit a legal issue, the following exercise, a sort of legal trivial pursuits, can be tried.

1.28 A brick comes through your window. Those are the facts of the case, what are the legal issues? On the basis of these facts alone, criminal damage may be the first thing that springs to mind. Inventing the fewest additional facts, use your legal imagination to raise other legal issues. Score highest for the most far-fetched legal topic arrived at with the addition of the fewest facts. For example, trespass or negligence would be fairly low scoring. An ecclesiastical law point might be higher. And indeed, a quick look at the ecclesiastical law title in *Halsbury's Laws* indicates that, if we suppose the window is a church window and you are a vicar conducting a service inside, the following possibilities might arise: riotous or indecent behaviour contrary to s 2 of the Ecclesiastical Courts Jurisdiction Act 1860; obstructing or assaulting a clergyman in the discharge of his duties contrary to s 36 of the Offences Against the Person Act 1861; and a common law offence of disturbing a priest in the performance of divine worship (*R v Parry* (1686) Trem PC 239). For a higher score try, say, copyright or *donatio mortis causa*. But register a minus score if you try human rights.

The research cycle summarised

1.29 Distilling what has been said so far, the following is the strategy to aim for:
(1)   identify the point of law;
(2)   choose your terminology – think of key words, broader terms, narrower terms, related terms, synonyms, antonyms;
(3)   choose a starting point – for example, textbooks, *Halsbury's*, case-finding aids, legislation-finding aids;
(4)   choose a starting date and work backwards;

(5)   bring yourself up to date – supplements, etc;
(6)   double-check using alternative sources;
(7)   start again from a different angle.

Using printed sources

1.30 Although the computer screen may often be the starting point, printed sources are far from being dispensable. For some types of research it is simply more convenient to use hard copy. If you are in a library and you need to look at an Act, why not just go the shelves of *Halsbury's Statutes* rather than work out how to log on to some electronic service. For some types of research, even where electronic sources exist, hard copy research is not merely more convenient but probably safer – *Pepper v Hart Hansard* research (see chapter 4) being a good illustration. There is much material, especially older material, which is simply not available in electronic form. There are also the not unfamiliar scenarios where the computer system has crashed, or where there are queues for the terminals, which are taken up with students composing lengthy e-mails to their boyfriends or girlfriends, playing solitaire or trying to find the cheapest flight to Bangkok. You need to know how to do it the old-fashioned way.

1.31 The main point to be aware of in using ordinary printed sources is the method, if any, of updating. Many standard hardbound and softbound books are simply reissued in new editions from time to time, without any intermediate supplementation. Some, like *Blackstone's Criminal Practice*, are reissued regularly on an annual basis to avoid the cumbrousness of supplements; it is also the standard way of issuing many tax handbooks after each Budget. But many practitioners' works have supplements between editions. Usually these are cumulative, but occasionally there may be more than one supplement to consult. In the past English legal publishers have occasionally followed the US practice of having 'pocket part' supplements that are physically inserted in a pocket inside the back cover, but usually they are kept (or lost) separately.

1.32 Looseleaf works have long been a solution to the updating of legal books. If properly maintained and organised, they are a great boon. But it is always essential to check when the last release of new material was inserted. Otherwise they can give a false sense of security as to their currency: the publishers may be tardy in issuing new releases, there may be a backlog of looseleaf filing in the library or office, the subscription may have lapsed or been cancelled. The pagination of looseleaf works is necessarily more complicated. Apart from making it sometimes difficult to find the relevant page, it can conceal the fact that some pages are missing or misfiled (which can all too easily happen after a trip to the photocopier). Apart from allowing updating proper, they also allow the publication of a work before it is complete. This does allow the publication of what is available more quickly, but can be a test of the scrupulosity of publishers in their marketing. It is also necessary to be aware that the looseleaf format is not proof against the need for supplements as well – special bulletins may be inserted in the front, pending the main text being amended, and some of the large looseleaf encyclopaedias do not consolidate their tables and indexes with every release but issue supplementary ones.

1.33 Large multi-volume works such as *Halsbury's* or *Atkin's Court Forms* may use a combination of the above methods of updating. Individual bound volumes are reissued from time to time, a cumulative supplement is published annually, and a looseleaf service contains new materials pending the reissue of a bound volume and provides a noter-up to catch developments between annual supplements.

1.34 Serial publications such as law reports and journals do not have any great problems. It is worth remembering, though, that while some only have indexes for each volume, others might have separate cumulative indexes, or, as can be easily overlooked, cumulative indexes covering several volumes bound in with one particular volume. An often unavoidable frustration is that the loose parts of serials have to go away to be bound up, though many series do have bound volume services whereby the publishers provide a bound volume as well as the loose parts. For finding aids and indexes issued in serial loose part format the pattern of cumulation should be noted. The entries in the body of the monthly parts of *Current Law* are only cumulated annually (into the *Current Law Yearbook*) but many of the tables and indexes cumulate each month.

Microforms

1.35 The use of microforms, whether in the form of roll film or fiche, may have dwindled, but they may still be encountered in law libraries for certain categories of material, particularly older bulky material for which there are no electronic surrogates, such as parliamentary papers, EC documentation and newspapers. They are also used as a cheap way of republishing out of print material, and as a preservation medium for old materials that in their original paper format are disintegrating. Microforms may use positive or negative images, but most reader-printers allow the printing out of negative microform in positive format like the photocopy of an ordinary page. If you have not used microfiche before and are struggling to insert them in the reader the right way round, follow the mortuary adage – face up, feet first.

Using electronic sources

Electronic formats

1.36 There are three main formats for electronic sources, the traditional on-line database, CD-ROMs and the Internet. The first, which involves dialling up via a modem a particular host database, is nearly redundant, though it remains an option with Lexis. CD-ROMs remain popular, though their use is likely to decline. They can be cheap to produce and buy, and avoid the vagaries of Internet connections. But the quantity of data they can hold is limited, and currency is an issue – usually only monthly updates at best. The Internet is now the preferred delivery method for most commercial on-line services, and is synonymous with the dissemination of free information. Commercial Internet services are usually paid for on a subscription basis, though some may have usage charges, and there is increasing availability of pay-as-you go using credit cards. Though not a distinct format as such, a fourth category to mention is Intranets, which are now very common in large law firms and other organisations. They use Internet technology to create in-house know-how databases of such materials as drafting precedents and counsel's opinions, which can be searched alongside externally provided services. The basic floppy disk is not used for research tools, but books on drafting quite often come with the precedents on diskette as well for ease of word-processing.

Types of data

1.37 Electronic sources fall into two broad categories according to the nature of the data they hold. The first are full-text systems. The entire text of law reports, legislation or other material is loaded wholesale on to the system. Any word, bar a very few words such as 'the' or 'and', wherever it occurs can be found. It is not thus an index – the user is the indexer. The only intervention by the suppliers of the database is to code segments of each item – for example, the name of the court, the head note, the names of counsel, in a law report – so that they can be searched individually without searching all the text in every item. The second category is indexing and abstracting services, which index the material, often with some form of abstract or summary; the full text then has to be gone to as a separate exercise. Full-text systems provide for one-stop shopping if required (though many users still tend to use them as a retrieval mechanism – having got the reference, they go away and read it in printed form, rather than on screen), but may require greater skill in searching. Indexing and abstracting services, on the other hand, may be more manageable to search, though the intervention of a third party, the indexer, between you and the raw data always entails some risk. Lexis is the traditional example of a full-text database, but there are many others. The Current Legal Information suite of databases is the paradigm of the indexing and abstracting service. There is also now a tendency towards hybrid systems. For example, Lawtel traditionally gave only summaries of cases – you had to order a hard copy if you wanted the full text of a transcript. Now it is putting on full-text as well. Likewise Westlaw UK, which takes much of its data from the Current Legal Information databases, but has some material in full-text as well. A further example is the parliamentary database, Parlianet, which is a traditional bibliographical database, simply indexing *Hansard* and so on, but now provides links to the free Internet versions of documents in full-text on the Parliament website where they exist.

Search strategies

1.38 If you are going to use a system such as Lexis that incurs usage charges (or are using the Internet on an ordinary phone line), it is sensible to have worked out in advance a search strategy, and alternative strategies should the first not work, before going on-line. Doing a preliminary search on a CD-ROM or other free database by way of experimentation may be a good idea. Even with systems that do not have usage charges, pause for thought before putting fingers to keyboard. The other general point to make, as with all sources, is that the currency should be checked, especially with CD-ROMs. Usually there is a screen somewhere that says when the data was last updated. The fact that the source is in electronic form is no particular guarantee that it is up-to-date.

1.39 Basic searching techniques are much the same whatever the format of the source and the type of data in contains. The main difference is that full-text systems require you to deploy the more sophisticated techniques more often than do indexing and abstracting services, simply because of the quantity of data to be searched. At the heart of successful electronic searching is striking the right balance between retrieving too much and too little. It is usually best to start with a broad search and then narrow it down as necessary.

1.40 The main ways of cutting down material are to use the Boolean AND, proximity (or adjacency) searching and field searching. Connecting two or more terms with

AND on most systems simply gets you the records containing all of those terms (a plus sign + may be used on many systems as an alternative, and is mandatory on one or two Internet search engines). On some systems AND is implicit if you just put in the terms as a string with no connectors (though on some no connectors signifies OR). AND is crude on full-text systems, since the terms may appear in entirely unrelated contexts in different parts of the document. Proximity searching retrieves occurrences of the terms only when they appear near each other. A connecting command, expressed in numbers of words or numbers of characters, will need to be entered. There may be a default 'near' command, or you may be able to confine the search to the terms appearing in the same paragraph. Field searching is also a very useful method of narrowing. When using full-text law reports you may wish to limit the search to the headnote field for example, so that only cases where the terms are in point are likely to found. Most systems tend to have a simple box for ordinary free-text searching on the front screen. Field searching is usually a separate option that goes under various names: 'advanced search', 'form search', 'focused search' and so on, which offer boxes to fill in. However, on some systems, and on Internet search engines, it is a matter of prefixing an ordinary free text with a field descriptor. The Boolean AND NOT is a way of getting rid of hits with the search word in the wrong context. If you are a criminal lawyer, rather than a shipping lawyer, 'arrest AND NOT ship' will save you a needless trip to *Lloyd's Law Reports*.

1.41 The main broadening techniques are the Boolean OR, truncation and wildcard characters. Use OR for synonyms, near synonyms, and for clusters of terms that are related, for example, 'intellectual property OR copyright OR patents OR designs'. Use truncation, often an asterisk, to search on various permutations of endings to word stems, for example, licen* for licences, licensing, licensed, licensee, licensees, etc. Some systems, such as Lexis, can cope with retrieving words both in the singular and plural without having to truncate but not all do. It seems obvious but material is often missed because the user has entered, for example, just 'contract' or just 'contracts', without either truncating or entering both with an OR. Wildcard characters do the same within words, for example, licen*es gets licences and licenses, wom*n gets woman and women.

1.42 If you create a long search string with different Boolean connectors, use parentheses to create a logical search order. If you were looking for sentencing cases for fraud or deception, and you simply put in 'sentenc* and deception or fraud' the system might be looking for '(sentenc* and deception) or fraud', which will include every case on fraud whether or not it is to do with sentencing, rather than what you want, which is 'sentenc* and (deception or fraud)'.

Problematic searches

1.43 Keep your wits about you in the following situations – if necessary look at the on-screen help or a manual. First, be aware how different systems treat phrases. Some will search for the phrase alone, others, unless the phrase is entered in inverted commas, will find occurrences of each word in the phrase as if there were a Boolean AND between them. Proximity searching is often safer than entering phrases, unless you are sure that an intervening word or expression will not orphan the parts of the phrase from each other. A 'demise charterparty' looks safe enough, but in fact might well appear as a 'charterparty by demise'. Most systems are not case sensitive – all occurrences will be retrieved whether or not you use lower or upper case. But some are – for example, if you enter words with capitals in the AltaVista Internet search engine only occurrences with capitals will be retrieved. Hyphenated words are another trap, both because of differences between systems – whether the hyphen is treated as a space or a character – and because of differences in editorial practice, for example, trade mark, trade-mark or trademark. If in doubt, use all permutations. Abbreviations and punctuation are other hazards. The inexperienced user looking for a case, or mentions of a case, may gaily type in 'Burnside v Emerson'. If they were using the *All England Law Reports* CD-ROM they would be in luck, but if the search were on the Justis *electronic Law Reports* they would not find it, simply because *The Law Reports* uses the style 'v.' with a stop, and the stop counts as a character in the phrase. So avoid 'v' – use AND or proximity searching. Likewise avoid 's.' or 'ss.' for section numbers of legislation – just enter the number alone. The presence or absence of a comma between the title of an Act and its date can also throw results. It is also sometimes useful to be able to search on a reference to a law report or journal. Again systems vary as to whether you need to enter 'W.L.R.' or 'WLR' or 'W L R'.

Using the Internet

1.44 The Internet may simply be the delivery mechanism for a commercial database. But accessing free databases and documents is what is usually in mind when the question is posed whether something can be found on the Internet. Throughout this book a number of useful websites are discussed (as explained in the Preface their addresses are given in a list after the Quick Reference Guide rather than here in the text), and the most important ones, like other research tools, will become familiar through regular use – you may well have them bookmarked. The difficulty arises where you do not know whether or not a legal research problem might be solved using the Internet. There are two basic approaches to finding legal material on the Internet from a cold start. One is a search engine, and the other is a gateway or portal. Each has its place.

1.45 A search engine can be useful for finding a known document that is likely to have been loaded onto the web, or for finding the websites of known organisations and bodies, when you do not know the address. As will be explained, they are not usually appropriate for general legal research. There are a number of different general search engines to choose from. The nature of search engines is such that they may get different results, so you may need to try more than one. At the time of writing Google is probably rated most highly for the number of web pages that it indexes, the speed of retrieval and relevancy of results. It has two other features that give it the edge. One is that it now indexes pdf (portable document format) documents. The standard format of ordinary web pages is html (hypertext mark-up language). It is more convenient for some providers of information to put material such as printed reports on the web as in effect images to be read or printed off – the layout, fonts, links and images of the original document remain intact. Such pdf documents cannot be read by an ordinary web browser, but have to be read with an Adobe Acrobat Reader (which is freely downloadable, and which most sites offering pdf documents will have links to). Conventional search engines cannot retrieve pdf documents. As pdf documents are very widely used for government publications, Google is particularly useful in the legal context. The other feature is that a version of the web page as it was when Google's web crawler originally found it is cached on the Google site. Thus if by the time of your search the direct link to a site given in the search results no longer works for some reason, at least you can look at the page that was there. Other popular search engines are AltaVista and Northern Light – the latter has a nifty way of organising search results by topics in folders on the left of the screen. There is a good deal of fluidity in the nature and structure of search engines. Some are combining the conventional search engine approach with the directory approach. Directories, of which the best known general example is Yahoo!, organise and index sites with human intervention. Three useful sites which give news of developments of search engines, review existing engines with comparative information on coverage and search syntax, and give excellent general tips on both basic and advanced web searching are Search Engine Watch, Search Engine Show Down and Websearch at About.

1.46 Even for basic searching, it is quite important to know how the search syntax of the particular search engine works – how they treat phrases, the format for Boolean connectors, capitalisation and what advanced features they support. Have a look at the search tips that they all provide. The equivalent of field searching is generally available and can be useful. If you confine a search to the title field, relevancy is likely to increase. A domain search confines the search to sites with, for example, .uk or .gov in the address, though that may miss .com sites. To find material from known sites that are very large and do not have their own search engine or an inadequate one, you can use a general search engine and confine its results to that site. On Google prefix the search with site: (other engines use host:). Searches can also be done on links (to see what other sites have provided links to a particular page) and urls, ie web addresses.

1.47 However, there are inherent drawbacks to search engines. Over-retrieval of irrelevant material is always a potential hazard. They are by nature hit and miss. Search results may include pages that are no longer there. But the greatest limitation is that there are very large quantities of material on the Internet that they are unable to access – the so-called invisible web. Apart from pdf documents, which Google can cope with, and other non-html formats, and sites that have been missed by web crawlers because there are no links to them, most of the invisible web is accounted for by databases of various kinds. Web crawlers can only get as far as the entrance to a database, even if it is free rather than a subscription service – they cannot index the content. The British Library Catalogue, containing millions of items, is freely searchable on the web, but a general search engine will not find a particular book in it. Likewise, the full report of a case from the European Court of Human Rights is freely available on the Strasbourg site, but would not usually be retrieved from a general search engine. Occasionally you can strike lucky if a document or record that originated in a database has been downloaded onto an ordinary web page by somebody, or you may retrieve other documents that mention what you are after, which enables you to find it. But generally speaking, for conventional legal research search engines, despite their familiarity to most students, are not usually the place to start.

1.48 Gateways, which provide organised sets of links, not only get you to material on the invisible web but also offer a structured approach to research which is usually more effective. Gateways are particularly helpful where the sites to which links are provided are described and the content critically assessed. The only drawback is the proliferation of gateways. Many university law libraries and other legal organisations, both here, but especially in the US, construct their own sets of links on their websites, which duplicate the same information. There is also a tendency towards self-perpetuation – the more gateways there are the more links to other gateways a particular site feels it ought to provide in case one has something that another does not. They also need to be actively managed. It is very frustrating to find seemingly useful links that no longer work because the site has moved. Perhaps the most useful legal gateways based in the UK are Sarah Carter's Lawlinks, hosted by the University of Kent, and Delia Venables' Legal Resources. You cannot go far wrong starting with just those. Other UK-based gateways worth mentioning are the SOSIG (Social Science Information Gateway) Law Gateway and Eagle-I, based at the Institute of Advanced Legal Studies. The Cornell Legal Information Institute is one of the leading American gateways. As resort to the Internet arises particularly in finding foreign and international materials, other useful gateways are mentioned in chapter 8, on the law outside England and Wales.

1.49 A very useful treatment to supplement this section, provided new editions appear as rapidly as the first two did, is Nick Holmes and Delia Venables *Researching the Legal Web: A Guide to Legal Resources on the Internet* ((2nd edn, 1999) Butterworths).

2. Starting from square two: textbooks and other secondary sources

Introduction

2.1 Later chapters of this book are devoted to finding the primary sources of the law – legislation, cases, treaties, and various other official publications. Certainly, it is necessary for lawyers to be able to find these materials for themselves from scratch in some circumstances, but in real life the first port of call in solving a legal problem is not usually the indexes to the law reports and statutes, but textbooks and other secondary sources. Someone has already done the research for you – why do it the hard way? It may then be wise to check for yourself the primary sources cited, and also to check for recent developments since the textbook was updated, but attacking the raw data of the primary sources completely cold is seldom necessary.

The range of secondary sources

2.2 The pre-eminent secondary source is *Halsbury's Laws of England*. You cannot go far wrong by starting virtually any legal research here. Arranged by topic in more than 50 brown volumes, it provides an authoritative statement of the law by experts. Some large topics may be covered in a more condensed fashion than in the equivalent practitioners' textbook, but there is always more than ample citation of authority. On the other hand, because it is completely comprehensive, it treats some topics not covered at all by the textbooks. For example, the law relating to barristers warrants a 165-page section, yet is not the subject of any current textbook. As well as being comprehensive and authoritative, *Halsbury's Laws* is also very current. A section below (paras **2.6–2.10**) is devoted to how to use it and get the most out of it. It is also available in electronic form as Halsbury's Direct, one of the Butterworths LEXIS Direct services.

2.3 Textbooks come in a variety of shapes and sizes. There are the large (and expensive) practitioners' works such as *Chitty on Contracts* or *Phipson on Evidence*. There are concise texts aimed at the practitioner in a hurry, with titles such as a 'Practical guide' to this or that. Major new Acts often elicit a rash of guides, such as those from Blackstone Press. Often produced very rapidly after the passing of a new Act, they can be of variable quality. Some may be potboilers, with the bulk of the book taken up with simply reprinting the text of the Act. Others may have been written by authors of particular authority in the field, and serve as a useful stopgap until the legislation has been assimilated into new editions or supplements to the major textbooks on the topic. Of books aimed at undergraduates, the nutshell type of guide is going to be of limited value for legal research, but some of the substantial academic texts, for example, *Megarry and Wade on Real Property*, *Treitel on Contract*, *Smith and Hogan on Criminal Law*, are highly regarded. They are used by practitioners too and have been cited in court. Not only for academic or comparative research, but also for the practitioner faced with a novel or doubtful point, textbooks from the other major common law jurisdictions should not be overlooked. The Americans, in particular, have a tradition of producing exhaustive treatments on a grand scale. The current editions of *Corbin on Contracts* and *Wigmore on Evidence* each run to many volumes, and the *Restatements* prepared by the American Law Institute, which if we had the equivalent would be analogous to *Halsbury's Laws* rewritten by the Law Commission, are occasionally cited in the English courts.

2.4 Although many practitioners' textbooks that would previously have been published in ordinary bound form are now appearing in looseleaf format, the traditional application of the looseleaf format is to subject encyclopaedias. Often multi-volume, they reprint in amended form all the primary materials, such as statutes and statutory instruments for a particular area (the term 'encyclopaedia ' in this context refers to their compendious nature rather than implying an A to Z arrangement). They also often contain introductory matter, substantive commentary and annotations to the primary materials. However, the ratio of such added value material to material merely reprinted varies. For example, the *Encyclopedia of Insurance Law*, while usefully bringing together the statutory material, has little by way of text, whereas the *Encyclopaedia of Banking Law* has two volumes of text which are as highly regarded as any of the bound textbooks on the subject. As emphasised in chapter 1, it is important to be aware of the date the law is stated to be at, whether the book is bound or looseleaf. Materials from looseleaf encyclopaedias may also be published in electronic form. For example, both Butterworths LEXIS Direct and Sweet & Maxwell's Westlaw UK have topic-based services, which incorporate material from their respective looseleaf services, together with law reports and journals. Or, publishers may offer CD-ROM versions instead of or in addition to the hard copy.

2.5 Articles in periodicals are the other main secondary source. There are over 400 legal periodicals published in the UK alone. Again, there is a wide range of form and substance. There are the long-established generalist heavyweights such as the *Law Quarterly Review*; there are the weeklies such as the *New Law Journal*, *Law Society's Gazette*, *Solicitors Journal*; and there is the ever-increasing number of specialist titles, which may offer substantial articles such as the *Construction Law Journal* or may be more in the form of a newsletter such as *Corporate Briefing*. The proliferation of journal titles (there are now perhaps twice the number that there were in 1993 when the first edition of this book was published) is partly attributable to specialist departments within the larger law firms offering, with an eye to the PR, their in-house bulletins to the wider world. Journals are generally valuable for current awareness and for catching recent developments since the last update to a textbook; they may be the only source of information for topics barely covered in the textbooks; and they may provide a depth of analysis for which there is not space in the textbooks. They may contain reports of cases in full or short form, as well as commentary on cases. As well as UK journals, there are English-language journals from other parts of the world to bear in mind, especially for academic and comparative research, or research involving an international element. The tradition of every law school in the US producing its own law review (the larger schools often producing ones in specialist areas, such as international law, as well the main one) accounts for the very large number of US titles.

Also covered in this chapter are legal dictionaries and sources for forms and precedents. The latter provide pro-forma examples as aids to drafting pleadings, particular types of contract, wills, trusts and all sorts of other legal documents. The chapter finishes with the small but practical matter of legal directories.

Using *Halsbury's Laws*

2.6 *Halsbury's Laws* is arranged alphabetically by broad topic. Large topics may occupy a whole volume, or even two volumes, while several smaller topics may be fitted into a single volume. Note that there is a separate index to each topic at the back of each volume; if there is more than one topic, there is more than one index. The numbered paragraphs, rather than the pagination, provide the principal reference system within volumes, and the numbering runs throughout each volume whether or not it contains more than one topic. All the references in the various tables and indexes are to paragraph, not page, numbers.

2.7 It is kept up to date in three ways. First, when the quantity and importance of new material warrants it, individual volumes are reissued in revised form. This does not usually create any difficulty – the spine will be marked 'reissue' and the date will be given on the title page. However, the current edition of *Halsbury's* started life almost 30 years ago and major changes in the law occasionally call for some restructuring of the arrangement and allocation of the broad topics. During a transitional period, it may be that a volume on the shelf contains the latest version of one topic, but that other topics in it have since been reassigned to another volume that has been reissued. A temporary label on the spine may cover the topics in it that are redundant. Occasionally where a volume, which is otherwise being revised, contains a topic that has not been revised but is awaiting reassignment to a different volume, the volume is reissued without that topic, and the text of the topic from the original volume is reprinted in the cumulative supplement or loose-leaf noter-up.

2.8 The second updating mechanism is the cumulative supplement, issued annually in two bound volumes. It mirrors the volume and paragraph numbering of the main work. Then, thirdly, there is a noter-up, arranged in the same format as the supplement, in one of the two looseleaf 'Current Service' volumes. Issued monthly, it provides updates between annual supplements. See figure 2.1, which illustrates a page from volume 28 (Reissue) under the title Libel and Slander. The cumulative supplement (figure 2.2) draws attention to a New Zealand case relevant to para 121. The looseleaf noter-up (figure 2.3) gives a further recent relevant English case.

2.9 The second of the two looseleaf 'Current Service' volumes contains *Halsbury's Laws Monthly Reviews*. These reviews, though flying the *Halsbury's* flag and having the same subject headings, are really a separate feature. Rather than relating directly to the text of the main work (though cross-references are given), they provide summaries of the latest cases and statutes and listings of selected journal articles. They are not dissimilar to the monthly digests of *Current Law*, issued by rival publishers, Sweet & Maxwell, though Butterworths launched in 2001 a separate publication, *Butterworths Legal Updater*, as a more direct competitor to *Current Law*. The *Monthly Reviews* can be used in the same way as the monthly parts of

Figure 2.1 Halsbury's Laws: *main work.*

---

1   See *Toogood v Spyring* (1834) 1 Cr M & R 181 at 193–194 per Parke B. Business communications are not to be beset with actions of slander: *Dunman v Bigg* (1808) 1 Camp 269n per Lord Ellenborough CJ, cited with approval in *Taylor v Hawkins* (1851) 16 QB 308 at 322 per Lord Campbell CJ. See also *Pittard v Oliver* [1891] 1 QB 474, CA, where the occasion was privileged notwithstanding the presence of reporters or persons other than guardians at the meeting of a board of guardians; and see at 477–478 per Lord Esher MR as to what the position would have been had the defendant called third persons into the meeting, and at 479 (criticism of *Purcell v Sowler* (1877) 2 CPD 215, CA).

2   *Taylor v Hawkins* (1851) 16 QB 308; cf *Somerville v Hawkins* (1851) 10 CB 583; and see *Toogood v Spyring* (1834) 1 Cr M & R 181; *Padmore v Lawrence* (1840) 11 Ad & El 380; *Parsons v Surgey* (1864) 4 F & F 247; *Davies v Snead* (1870) LR 5 QB 608; *Jones v Thomas* (1885) 53 LT 678, DC; *Pittard v Oliver* [1891] 1 QB 474, CA.

120. Answers to questions by the plaintiff in presence of third persons. A statement by the defendant to the plaintiff, although uttered in the presence of third persons, is a statement made on a privileged occasion if and in so far as it is an answer to a question put by the plaintiff[1]. Such a statement may also be protected by the defence of leave and licence[2]. However, in so far as the reply is not an answer to the question it is not made on a privileged occasion, and, unless the occasion is otherwise privileged, there is no need for the plaintiff to prove the existence of actual malice[3].

1   *Warr v Jolly* (1834) 6 C & P 497, considered in *Griffiths v Lewis* (1845) 7 QB 61 at 67; cf *Palmer v Hummerston* (1883) Cab & El 36.

2   See para 166 post.

3   See *Griffiths v Lewis* (1845) 7 QB 61; *Smith v Mathews* (1831) 1 Mood & R 151. An answer to an inquiry by a company as to a transfer is privileged: *Hesketh v Brindle* (1888) 4 TLR 199, DC. In *Davies v Snead* (1870) LR 5 QB 608, a statement as to the administration of a trust by A and B, two trustees, made on an occasion privileged as to A, was held to be made on an occasion privileged as to B also, since the statement concerning A could not be made without referring also to B.

(iii)   Communications to the Public Generally

➤ **121. Qualified privilege for communications to the press and public.** The common law principle that qualified privilege attaches to a communication made between parties who share a common and corresponding interest in the subject, or to one made pursuant to a duty to a person having a corresponding duty to receive, or interest in receiving, it, applies to communications to the public at large, as well as to communications to a limited class[1]. The courts have, however, applied a strict test of interest and duty in such cases and have, in particular, declined to recognise a duty or interest on the part of the press itself save in very clear cases[2].

1   As to the general principle see para 113 ante.

2   See *Blackshaw v Lord* [1984] QB 1, [1983] 2 All ER 311, CA; and paras 122–124 post.

122. Reply to attack. The clearest instance of a qualified privilege attaching to communications to the public at large is that of reply to a public criticism or attack. The person criticised has a sufficient common interest with the readers to confer privilege upon his reply to the same or substantially the same audience[1]. The attack may give rise to a duty upon others to reply on the victim's behalf[2] and to an ancillary privilege in the newspaper or other medium publishing the reply, especially if it carried the original attack[3].

1   See *Adam v Ward* [1917] AC 309, HL; *London Artists Ltd v Littler* [1968] 1 All ER 1075, [1968] 1 WLR 607 (on appeal [1969] 2 QB 375, [1969] 2 All ER 193, CA).

2   See eg *Adam v Ward* [1917] AC 309, HL (secretary of the Army Council held entitled to reply in defence of an army officer who had been attacked in Parliament).

Figure 2.2 Halsbury's Laws: *cumulative supplement.*

NOTE 1—See also *S v Newham LBC* [1998] 1 FLR 1061, CA (defence available to a local authority which, in accordance with ministerial guidelines, sent details concerning one of its social workers, to the Department of Health for inclusion in an index of persons unsuitable for child care work).

115 Statements at elections
TEXT AND NOTES—The 1952 Act s 10 has effect in relation to elections to the National Assembly for Wales (as to which see CONSTITUTIONAL LAW AND HUMAN RIGHTS vol 8(2) (Reissue) para 42A et seq ante): Government of Wales Act 1998 s 77(5).

117 Other occasions of qualified privilege
NOTE 1—1996 Act s 15, Sch 1 in force on 1 April 1999: SI 1999/817.
NOTE 3—See also *Regan v Taylor* [2000] EMLR 549, CA (statements made to the press by a solicitor, attacking a person who has attacked his client, are covered by qualified privilege notwithstanding that they have not been expressly authorised by the client).

121 Qualified privilege for communications to the press and public
TEXT AND NOTES—The New Zealand courts have held that the protection of qualified privilege should apply to claims for damages for defamation arising from political discussion: *Lange v Atkinson* [1997] 2 NZLR 22.

123 Public interest alone not sufficient
NOTE 3—1996 Act s 15, Sch 1 in force on 1 April 1999: SI 1999/817.

124 Publication to a section of the public sufficient
NOTE 1—1996 Act s 15, Sch 1 in force on 1 April 1999: SI 1999/817.

126 Effect of statutes
NOTE 4—Section 15, Sch 1 in force on 1 April 1999: SI 1999/817.

131 Statutory qualified privilege
NOTE 1—Section 15 in force on 1 April 1999: SI 1999/817.

132 Reports and statements protected by qualified privilege without explanation or contradiction
NOTE 2—Section 15, Sch 1 in force on 1 April 1999: SI 1999/817.
NOTE 3—The National Assembly for Wales (see CONSTITUTIONAL LAW AND HUMAN RIGHTS vol 8(2) (Reissue) para 42A et seq) is a legislature for these purposes: Government of Wales Act 1998 s 77(4).

133 Reports and statements privileged subject to explanation or contradiction
NOTE 3—Section 15, Sch 1 in force on 1 April 1999: SI 1999/817.
NOTES 19, 25, 27—As to commencement of Sch 1, see NOTE 3 supra.

150 Burden and standard of proof
TEXT AND NOTE 1—RSC replaced by the Civil Procedure Rules 1998, SI 1998/3132 ('the CPR'). For the destination of provisions see the table in PRACTICE AND PROCEDURE vol 37 para 1000A post.

157 Responsibility for publication
NOTE 4—An internet provider who fails to remove a posting on its news server upon becoming aware of its defamatory contents cannot satisfy the requirements of the 1996 Act s 1(1)(b) and (c), and therefore the defence under s 1 is not available to it: *Godfrey v Demon Internet Ltd* [1999] 4 All ER 342.

158 Authors, editors and publishers
NOTES 6–8—See *Godfrey v Demon Internet Ltd* [1999] 4 All ER 342 (internet service provider which received and stored a posting on its news server, and transmitted the posting to its subscribers who wished to download it, is a publisher at common law but not for the purposes of the 1996 Act s 1(2), (3)).

160 Offer to make amends
NOTE 3—Section 2 in force on 28 February 2000: SI 2000/222.

161 Accepting an offer to make amends
NOTE 3—Section 3(1)–(8), (10) in force on 28 February 2000: SI 2000/222.

162 Effect of acceptance on third parties
NOTE 1—Section 2 in force on 28 February 2000: SI 2000/222.

163 Failure to accept offer to make amends
NOTE 1—Section 2 in force on 28 February 2000: SI 2000/222.

164 Statutory defence of apology and payment into court
TEXT AND NOTE 7—RSC replaced by the Civil Procedure Rules 1998, SI 1998/3132 ('the CPR'). For the destination of provisions see the table in PRACTICE AND PROCEDURE vol 37 para 1000A post.
NOTE 10—Sections 2, 3(1)–(8), (10), 4 in force on 28 February 2000: SI 2000/222.

Figure 2.3   Halsbury's Laws: *looseleaf noter-up.*

<table>
<tr><td></td><td>Noter-up</td><td>Volume 28 (Reissue)</td></tr>
</table>

 121   **Qualified privilege for communications to the press and public**
NOTE 1—See *Loutchansky v Times Newspapers Ltd* [2001] EWCA Civ 536, [2001] EMLR 685, CA.

123   **Public interest alone not sufficient**
NOTE 2—See *Lukowiak v Unidad Editorial SA* [2001] All ER (D) 108 (Jul), (2001) Times, 23 July.

191   **Fair comment**
NOTES—See *Branson v Bowyer* [2001] All ER (D) 159 (Jun).

243   **Judge's duty where malice is in issue**
NOTE 4—See *Alexander v Arts Council of Wales* [2001] EWCA Civ 514, [2001] EMLR 27, CA.

246   **The jury's verdict**
NOTE 4—See *McPhilemy v Times Newspapers Ltd* [2001] All ER (D) 90 (Jun), CA.

250   **Gravity of the libel, manner of publication and extent of circulation**
NOTE 1—See *Baigent v British Broadcasting Corpn* 2001 SLT 427, IH.

301   **Functions of judge and jury**
NOTE 1—*Practice Note* [1995] 2 All ER 900 further amended: *Practice Note* [2001] 2 All ER 703.

LIBRARIES AND OTHER SCIENTIFIC AND CULTURAL INSTITUTIONS

416   **Books to be delivered**
NOTE 3—SI 1986/1081 reg 53(4) now the Representation of the People (England and Wales) Regulations 2001, SI 2001/341, reg 46(1).

608   **The National Lottery distribution fund**
TEXT AND NOTES 7–9—National Lottery etc Act 1993 s 22(3)(f) amended: SI 2000/3356.
NOTE 9—National Lottery etc Act 1993 s 30(1) amended: SI 2000/3355.

609B (Supplement)   **Joint schemes for distribution of money by distributing bodies**
NOTE 2—See the Sport and Arts Joint Scheme (Authorisation) Order 2000, SI 2000/3320.

613   **Transfer of objects or related documents between institutions**
NOTE 1—1992 Act Sch 5 Pt I amended: SI 2000/2955.

614   **Gifts to the nation**
NOTE 1—1992 Act Sch 5 Pt II amended: SI 2000/2955.

LIEN

No further updating since publication of the 2001 *Cumulative Supplement.*

LIMITATION OF ACTIONS

813   **Maritime claims**
NOTE 2—See *The Baltic Carrier* [2001] 1 Lloyd's Rep 689.

847   **Position where the remedy is barred but not the right**
NOTE 3—See *Lloyds Bank plc v Burd Pearce* [2001] All ER (D) 196 (Mar), CA.

851   **Pleading the statute**
NOTE 1—See *Lloyds Bank plc v Burd Pearce* [2001] All ER (D) 196 (Mar), CA.

859   **Action upon specialties and judgments**
NOTE 4—See *Re a Debtor (No 2672 of 2000)* (2000) Times, 5 December.

885   **The general limitation period**
NOTE 1—*R (on the application of Factortame)*, cited, reported at [2001] 1 WLR 942.

905   **Plaintiff's knowledge**
NOTE 1—*James v East Dorset*, cited, reported at (1999) 59 BMLR 196, CA.

908   **Factors to which court must have regard**
NOTE 1–9—*Long*, cited, reported at [2001] PIQR P18.
NOTE 13—See *Steeds v Peverel Management Services Ltd* [2001] All ER (D) 370 (Mar), CA.

912   **Time limit for claiming contributions**
NOTE 3—See *Hampton v Minns* [2001] All ER (D) 66 (Mar).

916   **Limitation periods**
NOTE 2—See *Times Newspapers Ltd v Chohan* (2001) Times, 1 August, CA.

977   **Meaning and effect of 'adverse possession'**
NOTE 4—See *Markfield Investments Ltd v Evans* [2001] 2 All ER 238, CA.
NOTE 6—See *Lambeth LBC v Bigden* (2001) 33 HLR 43, CA.
NOTE 7—*JA Pye*, cited, reversed: [2001] EWCA Civ 117, [2001] 2 WLR 1293, CA.

Halsbury's Laws Current Service   September 2001/Binder 2/Noter-up/63

Current Law to check for very recent material or to browse as a current awareness tool (they are in pamphlet form to facilitate circulation round the office or chambers before being filed in the binder). Their coverage is perhaps not as comprehensive as *Current Law*, but they are strong on some areas, such as summaries of unreported cases on quantum of damages for personal injuries. There is a looseleaf index, which cumulates with every issue during the year. The monthly reviews are then cumulated into the *Annual Abridgement*, which again are analogous to the *Current Law* yearbooks.

2.10 There are several ways of accessing the main work of *Halsbury's Laws*. Often all that is necessary is to browse along the shelf to find the appropriate volume and then to browse through the contents page for the particular topic. Otherwise you can approach it by using the subject indexes, or, if you know the name of a relevant case or statute, by using the tables of cases or statutes. Each volume has its own indexes (as mentioned, one for each topic in the volume) and tables, but at the end of the work volumes 53 to 56 comprise a consolidated table of legislation, a consolidated table of cases, and a consolidated index. Bear in mind that, though these are regularly reissued, they may pre-date a very recent reissue of a volume of the main work, in which case the precise paragraph references given may no longer be accurate. This will be apparent when you reach the volume of the main work – it is then simply a matter of readjusting the references using the volume's own index or tables. Having found the relevant section of the main work, always then check the cumulative supplement and looseleaf noter-up for any subsequent changes. The three-step process – main work/cumulative supplement/noter-up – should be an automatic routine whenever you use *Halsbury's Laws*.

Finding textbooks

2.11 The first step is naturally to be familiar with the way your law library organises its shelves and its catalogues, but you may well need to find out what might be available beyond your own library. Unfortunately there is no one comprehensive bibliography of all legal textbooks. The nearest to a one-stop tool is Donald Raistrick's excellent *Lawyers' Law Books: a Practical Index to Legal Literature*. The only caveat is that it is not supplemented and new editions are infrequent – the last was in 1997. It lists by subject all law books of current value, with an author index. It spreads its wings beyond UK textbooks, by including selected texts that might be of value to the English lawyer from other common law jurisdictions and on European and international law. Its selection of English textbooks usefully includes ancillary material such as Law Commission reports, and at the head of each listing of books the relevant volumes of *Halsbury's Laws* and *Statutes*, *Encyclopaedia of Forms and Precedents*, *Atkin's Court Forms*, are given along with the titles of any periodicals devoted to the subject.

2.12 Although not designed as bibliographies as such, the catalogues from the rival legal booksellers Hammicks and Books Etc Professional are very useful. They are in a similar format, listing most English legal books in print by broad subject, with an author and title indexes. They are prepared annually. A minor hazard is that, in the interests of currency, it does contain some titles not yet published but which are supposedly coming out within the lifetime of the catalogue, but they are usually marked 'NYP'. Fuller and more up-to-date information can also be found on-line in Hammicks catalogue.

2.13 Library catalogues on the web are also useful bibliographical tools. The Institute of Advanced Legal Studies, part of the School of Advanced Study in the University of London, has one of the largest law libraries in the country, so its catalogue (which is combined with other institutions from the School of Advanced Study) would be a good starting point. The library catalogues of the four Inns of Court, especially for older material, would be another specifically legal resource. But the British Library, the Library of Congress, or COPAC, the merged catalogue of over 20 of the largest research libraries in Britain and Ireland, are other possibilities.

2.14 Mainly of use for current materials, because it is not cumulated, is the annual *Bibliographic Guide to Law* published by G.K. Hall, which lists all the law material, both domestic and foreign, catalogued by the Library of Congress and the Research Libraries of New York Public Library. The *Index to Legal Periodicals* (see para **2.27**) has included coverage of books since 1993, and so its full title is now *Index to Legal Periodicals & Books*. It does pick up some UK books, but being a US product, only selectively.

2.15 Returning to domestic products, another source that may help is *Current Law*. Inside the back cover of each digest there is a list by author of legal books published that month; this list is not particularly useful as a finding aid as such, but it is interesting to browse through it as a current awareness exercise if you have time. These books, though, are listed within the monthly parts as the last entry of each subject under the heading 'Publications'; the cumulative subject index in the latest monthly part can save looking through each part – the entries are given under the subdivision 'publications' within each indexed subject. The same arrangement is mirrored in the yearbooks that cumulate the monthly parts – an alphabetical list by author at the back, under the main subject in the body of the work and entries in the subject index.

2.16 Apart from academic research in legal history, it is sometimes necessary to find older law books. There are a few treatises, such as *Coke's Institutes*, *Hale's Pleas of the Crown*, or *Blackstone's Commentaries* that rank as authorities in their own right and continue to be cited in court from time to time. For example, *Hale*, written in the 1670s, featured in the series of cases on marital rape that culminated in the House of Lords ruling in *R v R* [1992] 1 AC 599. These do not represent great difficulties – if the library does not have original editions they may have facsimile reprints. But you may need to follow up what the law used to be on some point, to make sense of an old reported case, for example, and this may require greater research. The standard bibliography is the *Legal Bibliography of the British Commonwealth* compiled by W Harold Maxwell and others, but generally known as 'Sweet & Maxwell' after its publishers. Volumes 1 and 2 cover English law. The first volume, published in a second edition in 1955, goes up to 1800 and is arranged by subject with an author and title index. The second volume covers 1801 to 1954 and is arranged by author with a subject index. More recently there have been the *Bibliography of Eighteenth Century Legal Literature* and the *Bibliography of Nineteenth Century Legal Literature* by J N Adams (note that the coverage of the latter is only up to 1870, though it is planned to complete the century). Neither are the easiest publications to use, though the latter incorporates some improvements and is available on CD-ROM. The first has a classified subject arrangement with an author index on microfiche; the primary arrangement of the second is by author. As well as being purely bibliographical tools, they also give locations for items in the major law libraries with historical collections. For books published before 1801 there is also the English

Short-title Catalogue (ESTC). Originally started as the *Eighteenth Century Short-title Catalogue*, it is now taking in the earlier period back to the start of printing. It is a vast database, based on the holdings of many libraries both here and in the US, and is not confined to law but aims to list all books printed in Great Britain, or printed in English during the period, with locations. It is available as a subscription service on-line and on CD-ROM.

Finding articles

Legal Journals Index

2.17 Probably the most popular research tool of them all (certainly with legal information professionals), *Legal Journals Index* (LJI) is an excellent place to start almost any legal research. For the reasons given above (para **2.5**) legal research requires frequent resort to journal articles both for very recent developments and for in-depth analysis. LJI does not provide the full text of the journal articles – it is an indexing and abstracting service. But just doing a search on LJI without even without going to the articles themselves can be helpful. If you retrieve entries for 25 different articles all commenting on the same case, you will be grateful to have a learnt of that case, as it is likely to be important. If you retrieve an article commenting on a bill currently going through Parliament, you will be alerted to an imminent legislative change. Conversely, if you find nobody has written anything on your problem, then, given the size of the database, either you have a genuinely novel point or you are barking up the wrong tree.

2.18 The above point is of some relevance when its coverage is considered. It indexes all legal journals, or journals regularly carrying legal items, published in the UK and Ireland from 1986 (over 400 titles) and English language legal journals published elsewhere in the EU from 1993 (over 85 titles). Thus it is extraordinarily comprehensive, but for that reason do not expect to find every article you retrieve in your law library (some hints on what to do if it is not in the library are given at para **2.34**). Newsletters merely digesting primary materials are not covered. Every article, law report, case note, book review and editorial are indexed. Generally, it is only news, or other ephemeral, items of less than a page that are not indexed. It may also be mentioned that since 1992 there has also been a sister database, Financial Journals Index, covering the fields of insurance, banking and pensions, which are of relevance to many practitioners, especially those in city law firms.

2.19 LJI is part of Sweet & Maxwell's suite of databases, Current Legal Information (CLI). The data from LJI has also been integrated into Sweet & Maxwell's premium on-line database, Westlaw UK. CLI comes in two main forms, a CD-ROM, updated monthly and using Folio Views search software, or as a subscription Internet service, updated daily. However, historically the data was supplied in a number of other formats to suit clients' needs, and for the time being some libraries may still have it in those forms – a popular one used to be the Blackwell Idealist search software. (Until recently there was a paper version as well – not surprisingly that ceased to be viable for both publisher and user.) If you are using the CD-ROM version, note that, because of the size of the database, it comes on two disks, covering 1986 to 1995 and 1996 to date. When you select LJI from the main list of databases on the front menu, it is the current disk you are searching. If you want to search older articles, you need to select the archive disk as a separate exercise.

2.20 The data provided consists of the author and title of the article, a brief abstract in amplification of the title, indexing terms, the reference to the journal, particular cases or legislation that are the subject of the article and the type of entry, for example, article, case comment, editorial, book review. These each form separate fields. Although most users generally just do a free-text search, looking for words anywhere they might appear in a record, it is worth having some grasp of the field structure of the records. Searching in a particular field may yield more specific results when too many hits are retrieved. It may also avoid false drops when the same word may be used in different contexts, for example, a common personal name that might be either a case name or an author. On the Folio Views CD-ROM simply select 'Search by field' as opposed to 'Free text search'. A revamp of the Internet version is in the pipeline, so the following description of field-searching on it may change. On the present Internet version scroll down below the 'Search text' box to the 'Go to Field Level Search' option. Although the content of the databases are exactly the same, a little confusingly at the moment, the fields available for separate searching are different, and slightly differently labelled and ordered, on the CD-ROM and on the Internet version. Currently, there is not a searchable case or legislation field on the Internet version.

CD-ROM	Internet
Subject	Title
Keywords	Author
Case	Subject
Legislation	Reference
Author	Keywords
Source	Entry type
Anywhere	

Taking them in the CD-ROM order, the subject field is a very broad topic, for example, Employment, Procedure, Torts. Its main use is for general searches, particularly for current awareness purposes or preparing bulletins, on a particular field of interest. The Keywords, in contrast, are very specific. They are assigned from a structured thesaurus using controlled and consistent vocabulary. Different words may be used in titles of articles or their abstracts to describe the same concept; the keywords should be all the same. Thus if you pick up the word you searched for in a title, have a look at the keywords, and if they are different repeat the search using those keywords instead – you may find some other articles where the terminology in the title is different. The thesaurus from which the keywords are drawn is constructed in a hierarchy of broader and narrower terms (see para **1.8**). Only the narrowest terms appropriate for the article will be assigned as keywords.

2.21 The case field is used for articles that are in the form of a case comment or for other types of article where discussion of a particular case features prominently. The field is also used for case *reports* that appear in journals. The item type field will distinguish a case *comment* from a case *report*. The latter are also distinguishable since no title or abstract is provided. On the CD-ROM version (and on Westlaw UK, but not on the CLI Internet version) where the case is within the scope of *Current Law* there are direct links to the digest of the case in Current Law Cases and to its entry in the *Current Law Case Citator*. Likewise if there are other articles on LJI on the same case, click on the name of the case for a hypertext link direct to those other articles.

2.22 The legislation field likewise is used for articles commenting on a particular statute or statutory instrument. The title and number of EU directives and regulations will also be entered in this field (and for this reason LJI is sometimes a shortcut to finding the number of a piece of EU legislation). As well as legislation proper, treaties and conventions are included here, as are Bills, which are frequently the subject of comment in the journals as they pass through Parliament. A consequence of the inclusion of the latter is that if you are searching for articles on a particular Act, do not type in the word 'Act', because otherwise you will miss any articles on it while it was still a Bill. Also be cautious about entering the date of an Act, because though it will be cited by the calendar year in which it was enacted, the Bill may have been introduced at the beginning of a parliamentary session at the end of the previous year (on parliamentary sessions see para **4.48**). Thus the legislation field will contain entries, for example, both for the 'Electronic Communications Act 2000' and the 'Electronic Communications Bill 1999'. An article, or case comment, may be focused on a particular section of an Act, regulation in an SI, or article of a treaty (for example, there is no shortage of comment on art 6 of the European Convention on Human Rights). In that case the particular section or other number will be entered in the field. But if you are after articles about a particular section it is best to start the search without the number, because there may be useful articles on the Act as a whole, and only narrow the search by adding the section number if too many hits are retrieved.

2.23 The author field is self-explanatory. It will be seen that the CD-ROM, a little oddly, does not have the title field on the search template. But if you want to combine a search of words from the title with another field, you can enter them in the 'Anywhere' box. There is, of course, no particular point in using the 'Anywhere' box unless you combine it with another field – otherwise you might as well do an ordinary free-text search. The source (reference on the Internet version) field contains the citation to the article. This is occasionally handy, for example, when you remember having seen an article in a particular journal, but not its exact reference. You need to enter the correct abbreviation of the title of the journal, and take care over spacing, etc. On the CD-ROM version you can check this from the separate Journals Indexed database. Incidentally, when *viewing* a record, if you do not recognise a journal abbreviation, on the CD-ROM version click on the abbreviation for an expanded version in full, or on the Internet version click on the link provided.

2.24 Apart from producing the index itself, the Yorkshire branch of Sweet & Maxwell also provide a document delivery service, DocDel, whereby photocopies of articles from most of the journals indexed can be supplied by post, fax or document exchange. A few journals are excluded from the service for copyright reasons. Sweet & Maxwell make a fixed charge, but also payable is a copyright licensing fee, which varies from publisher to publisher. Details of the DocDel service, together with an online order form, will found under Product Information on **Sweet & Maxwell**'s website. Copies of Butterworths/Tolley titles, which are excluded from the DocDel service, can be obtained from them. See also para **2.34**.

Other sources

2.25 Lawtel includes an articles index, which covers about 50 UK journals – most from 1998 onwards, with a few going back slightly earlier. Like LJI a brief summary is provided and relevant cases and legislation are separately highlighted, with hypertext links where they appear elsewhere in Lawtel databases. Copies of the full text of articles from some of the journals can be obtained from Lawtel's document delivery service, Transcripts Express. Clearly its coverage is not a patch on LJI, but if you have logged on anyway to do a case search, for example, it does no harm to search the articles index while you are at it. Butterworths' free service, Law Direct, also has an articles index, again with fairly limited coverage back to 1995, though the addition of a quite a number of journals in full text to Lexis (see para **2.28**) will be matched by an increase in the number of summaries on Law Direct.

2.26 Before the *Legal Journals Index* was founded in 1986, the only indigenous source was *Current Law*, which included selected articles from the mainstream English legal periodicals. However, indexing articles was subordinate to its main function of covering case law and statutory materials and, furthermore, there was no cumulation beyond the yearbooks. Indeed, it was the ineffectiveness of *Current Law* that led to the establishment of the LJI, which was originally produced by the independent company Legal Information Resources Ltd. In due course Legal Information Resources became a subsidiary of Sweet & Maxwell and was charged with revamping *Current Law*. *Current Law* continues to include selected journal articles, but since the provenance of the data is now LJI, it does not have a great deal of independent value, other than perhaps for current awareness purposes, where there is some merit in selection – even just one month's output from LJI is not a manageable quantity to browse.

2.27 Before 1986 researchers had to rely on the US-based *Index to Legal Periodicals*, published by H W Wilson since 1908 (since 1993 as *Index to Legal Periodicals & Books*). It covered all the main UK periodicals, as well as US and other English-language periodicals, and its coverage of UK periodicals was better than *Current Law* (though still not comprehensive); it also used to cumulate in larger chunks. Although no longer the preferred tool for UK periodicals other than for its retrospective pre-1986 coverage, *Index to Legal Periodicals* certainly continues to be of value for the English researcher. For example, there may be articles on English law published outside the UK, particularly in an academic or comparative context, which will not be in LJI, and it is extremely useful for articles on the law of other jurisdictions, particularly of course the United States. It is still published in hard copy, but it is also available (though only going back to 1981) on CD-ROM, as an Internet subscription service or on Lexis. Although *Index to Legal Periodicals* is the long-established product, since 1980 it has had a competitor in the form of *Current Law Index* (not to be confused *Current Law*), published by Information Access in California. This aimed to overcome certain perceived shortcomings of the Wilson product in terms of coverage, currency and arrangement. It is true that in face of this competition *Index to Legal Periodicals* has made a number of improvements, but the *Current Law Index* probably remains the superior, albeit more expensive, product. Because of its cost, it is not, however, as widely available in UK law libraries. Information Access, as well as providing its printed index to periodicals, has produced a larger database covering newsletters and newspapers, LegalTrac which is available on CD-ROM and on the Internet via Infotrac Web, though again its current availability in UK law libraries in this form may be limited. Another American product to be mentioned is the *Index to Periodical Articles Related to Law*. It has a 30-year cumulation covering 1958 to 1988, followed by five-yearly cumulations and current parts. It is useful for material, for example, of a criminological or sociological nature, which is not picked up by the main legal journal indexing services.

2.28 All the tools for finding journal articles mentioned so far are indexing services. There are an increasing number of journals available electronically in full text. For comprehensive research they are not a substitute for LJI and its US counterparts, but full-text searching gives the possibility of retrieval in ways not catered for in conventional indexes. Examples might be searching for individuals or companies mentioned in news items, or searching for cases or legislation, mentioned in articles but not sufficiently prominently to be indexed. Lexis used to have only a few English journals in full text, but has recently negotiated the addition of about 70 titles from other publishers (but not, unsurprisingly, Sweet & Maxwell titles). It also has very many US law reviews, though an increasing number of the latter are appearing free on the Internet through the University Law Review Project set up by the US legal portal FindLaw in collaboration with the main educational legal information providers. The University Law Review Project also has some non-US titles, either in full text or as abstracts. The subject modules on Butterworths LEXIS Direct and Westlaw UK include some journals from their respective sponsoring publishers. The *Journal of Information Law and Technology*, appropriately enough, was in this country the first example of a pure electronic law journal – one not published in hard copy at all; others may follow. Even if the full-text is not provided, contents pages or abstracts of many journals are now put on the web. The Electronic Law Journals Project at the University of Warwick, where the *Journal of Information Law and Technology* emanates from, provides a list of all UK legal journals with links to web-based material from them.

2.29 For historical research mention should be made of the *Index of Legal Periodical Literature*. The first volume by Leonard A Jones was published in 1888 and was a retrospective compilation going all the way back to 1786. As well as comprehensive coverage of all the then existing US and British legal periodicals, it also covered articles of legal interest in general periodicals. Two further volumes appeared taking its coverage up to 1907, when the *Index to Legal Periodicals* took over.

2.30 The above products are confined to English-language materials. The *Index to Foreign Legal Periodicals* covers foreign language material. This is only going to be needed rarely by the English practitioner, but its existence should be noted, especially as comparative materials, particularly on Europe, assume increasing importance.

2.31 So far it is general legal bibliographies and bibliographical tools that have been discussed. There may also be specialist subject bibliographies. The compilation of big subject bibliographies in book form is not as common as it once was (mainly because the general bibliographical tools such as LJI are so much better than they once were, making it easier for researchers to be self-sufficient without having to rely on the labours of others). But specialist journals sometimes carry regular listings of recent writings in their field, for example, the *Journal of Energy and Natural Resources Law*. One of the few examples of a specialist bibliography published in serial form is *Public International Law*, which is useful given the very wide catchment area of that subject, and does not necessarily duplicate what can found with general bibliographical tools.

2.32 For EU matters, access to a large body of literature is provided by SCAD, the documentation service of the European Commission. As well as indexing various classes of official documents (including one-off reports and the like) it covers a wide range (not just legal) of articles and documents received by the Commission library. Its coverage goes back to 1983, with some earlier material. There is a printed version, *SCAD Bulletin*, which is issued weekly. This can only sensibly be used as a current awareness tool; for other purposes an electronic version will need to be used. It is now available for free on the EU's Europa website, but much to be preferred, if you have it, is the version from Context, Justis European References, which is both on CD-ROM and on their web service, though the CD-ROM is only updated quarterly. Data from SCAD is also available on other CD-ROM products, for example, EC *Infodisk*. As well as the *SCAD Bulletin*, there are a number of other current awareness services, of which *European Access* published by Chadwyck-Healey in conjunction with the UK offices of the European Commission, probably provides the fullest coverage of recent secondary literature.

2.33 Apart from articles in journals and textbooks proper, collections of essays and papers should be briefly mentioned at the end of this section on secondary sources. Typically issued in honour of someone distinguished (*Festschriften*) or resulting from a conference, such collections are frequently fairly miscellaneous in scope and the contents may not be apparent from the standard catalogue entry for the book as a whole, which may only have the broadest of themes. A tool to solve this problem was once published – *Index to Legal Essays* covering the period 1975 to 1979, published in 1983 – but unfortunately was never updated. Unless they are cited in other secondary sources, one's only tool is thus serendipity.

Obtaining books and articles

2.34 The DocDel service for obtaining photocopies of articles indexed by the *Legal Journals Index* has already been mentioned (para **2.24**). Most academic libraries also operate an inter-library loan service, which enables photocopies and loans to be obtained via the British Library's Document Supply Centre (BLDSC). They have in stock at Boston Spa a wide range of English and foreign legal periodicals; if they do not have the title in stock they will pass it to back-up library. The BLDSC's holdings can be checked on the British Library's public catalogue on the Internet. The Institute of Advanced Legal Studies in the University of London once published a *Union List of Legal Periodicals*, which lists the holdings of all UK law libraries, but this is now only of use for old material, the last edition being in 1978. The Institute of Advanced Legal Studies also offer a document delivery service on a commercial basis to non-academic users, but to gain access to this an annual subscription must be taken out, though they permit access to personal callers on payment of a daily fee.

Theses

2.35 Doctoral and other theses are going to be needed primarily in connection with academic research (though the practitioner should not dismiss this possibility in an area devoid of other secondary literature). Because they are in their nature unpublished, they are usually only obtainable via inter-library loan from the British Library (which holds many in microform) or have to be consulted at the university concerned. As well as for their content, information on theses will be needed by prospective research students in order to see whether their projected topic has been covered already. The Institute of Advanced Legal Studies (who incidentally receive copies of all legal theses throughout the University of London) are currently developing a database of Current Legal Research, which will be published on their website and will list all British MPhil or PhD theses in progress; it may be expanded at a future date to cover wider research projects being undertaken at British law faculties. This website will be a long awaited replacement for an erstwhile publication of the Institute, the *List of Current Legal Research Topics,* last published in 1984. It may in due course also replace the other of the Institute's past publications in this field, *Legal Research in the United Kingdom,* which listed completed research since 1905, and which was the last published in 1984. Wider than law are Aslib's *Index to Theses* (also available on CD-ROM and on-line), which covers British and Irish theses accepted, and the social sciences volume of *Current Research in Britain,* which covers research projects (not just dissertations) in progress and is published by Cartermill International in association with the British Library. If you wish to research theses beyond British ones, the main tool, which covers all subjects not just law, is the vast *Dissertation Abstracts International* available on CD-ROM and on-line (the last two years can be searched without a subscription) .

Forms and precedents

2.36 There are two main general collections of forms and precedents, which set out standard or common forms of documents as aids to drafting. *Atkin's Court Forms* contains those that may be required in civil proceedings. It is arranged by topic in 41 volumes. It is kept up to date by the periodic reissue of individual volumes – the pace of reissue has accelerated markedly in order to take on board the effects of the Civil Procedure Rules – and a loose-leaf service volume containing a noter-up to the main work. Each volume has its own index but there is a consolidated index to the whole work, which is reissued annually. Each group of forms on a particular topic is preceded by a full commentary, covering the relevant substantive law as well as the procedure. The quantity and quality of the commentary can sometimes be overlooked – the work is not merely a collection of forms. A CD-ROM version was launched in 2000, which prompted a change in the system of numbering the text and forms, and thus the way the indexes to the printed version work. Until such time as all the pre-2000 volumes have been reissued, there is a rather confusing dual system in operation. For pre-2000 volumes the system was simple: the consolidated index gave the volume number followed by the *page* number; references to forms were distinguished from commentary by giving the page number in square brackets. Adopting the same system that has been used for the fifth edtion of the *Encyclopaedia of Forms and Precedents,* the volumes from 2000 are each paragraphed as a single sequence from beginning to end, with the paragraph number being given in square brackets on the right of the page and in the running head. These paragraph numbers are described as 'referential paragraphs' (as opposed to the conventional paragraph numbering used in the commentary for each topic). In the indexes for the new volumes, and in the consolidated index (where an asterisk precedes entries for the new volumes), references are now to these square-bracketed *paragraph* numbers. Square brackets can thus no longer be used to distinguish references to forms from those to commentary; instead references to forms, whether it be a page number for old volumes or a paragraph number for new volumes, are now given in italic (and in slighter larger font size).

2.37 The other major work is the *Encyclopaedia of Forms and Precedents* (*EF&P*), which contains the full range of documents and forms that may be needed by practitioners for all aspects of their work other than litigation. As in *Atkin's Court Forms,* there is a substantial amount of commentary as well as the text of the forms and precedents themselves. It is currently in its fifth edition, though, like *Halsbury's*, complete new editions will not now be prepared – individual volumes are reissued on a rolling basis. It also has a looseleaf service – it is rather larger than that for *Atkin's* and runs to five binders. It is also available on CD-ROM and an on-line version is being launched as a Butterworths LEXIS Direct module, and is available on Lexis itself.

2.38 The numbering system throughout is the same as that described above for the new volumes of *Atkin's*, ie paragraph numbers given in square brackets on the right of the page (see figure 2.4). The indexes to early volumes of the fifth edition, some of which are still on the shelves, used the convention of omitting the square brackets round the paragraph number for references to commentary – the idea being that references to forms and commentary could be distinguished. But this was a little confusing since it might have been thought that such unbracketed references were to the conventional paragraph numbers given at the start of the line on the left for the text of the commentary. In the more recently reissued volumes and in the consolidated index that practice has been dropped – all references are in square brackets and commentary and forms are not distinguishable. To remedy that disadvantage a separate annual Form Finder is issued. Although alphabetically arranged, its style is different from a conventional index. The forms are set out with their titles in full, rather as they would appear in the contents listing of a volume (see figure 2.5).

2.39 When using the consolidated indexes to either *Atkin's* or *EF&P*, bear in the mind the same hazard that occurs with the index to *Halsbury's*, namely that the volume referred to has been reissued since the index was prepared, in which case the paragraph number many have changed – recheck in the volume's own index.

2.40 Apart from *EF&P*, there is one other general collection of precedents, which should be mentioned, *Kelly's Draftsman*. This contains, in a handy one-volume format, the commonest forms and precedents needed by solicitors in general practice. There are, however, quite a number of specialist works with which to supplement the general collections above. On the contentious side, *Bullen and Leake* is devoted to pleadings. There used to be a separate work devoted to precedents in the county court, *Butterworths County Court Pleadings and Precedents*, since *Atkin's* originally focused on High Court proceedings. Post-CPR, it has been renamed *Butterworths Civil Court Precedents*. Although there is now no need to have a separate work on county court precedents, *Butterworths Civil Court Precedents* will continue to be a handy alternative to the 40-odd volumes of *Atkin's*, being at present in just two looseleaf volumes. In the early days of the CPR it also had material that had yet to be included in *Atkin's*. Textbooks on the practice and procedure in the various specialist courts, such as the Commercial Court, the Companies Court and the Admiralty Court, will often include relevant forms and precedents as appendices. On the non-contentious side, there are a number of subject collections – conveyancing naturally enough receiving particular attention. Sweet & Maxwell publish a useful series of looseleaf collections on various topics with the generic title *Practical . . . Precedents*, for example, *Practical Commercial Precedents* or *Practical Trust Precedents*. Standard textbooks, again, often include forms and precedents as appendices, as do many looseleaf encyclopaedias. Both *Atkin's* and *EF&P*, it has been noted, are available on CD-ROM; many of the other precedent books mentioned above come on CD-ROM or floppy disc for ease of word-processing. Most solicitors will also retain for future recycling any fresh precedents that they have had to draft, and the larger firms will have substantial precedent libraries on their know-how database or Intranet.

Figure 2.4   Encyclopaedia of Forms and Precedents:
index volume and main work (commentary).

13   VOL 16(1): FENCES, BOUNDARIES AND PARTY WALLS

4   *Bradbee v London Corpn (Governors of Christ's Hospital)* (1842) 4 Man & G 714.
5   *Voyce v Voyce* (1820) Gow 201; *Watson v Gray* (1880) 14 Ch D 192; cf *Cubitt v Porter* (1828) 8 B & C 257; *Jolliffe v Woodhouse* (1894) 10 TLR 553; *Hughes v Percival* (1883) 8 App Cas 443.
6   See 4(1) Halsbury's Laws (4th Edn Reissue) para 969.
7   See 4(1) Halsbury's Laws (4th Edn Reissue) para 970; *Jones v Pritchard* [1908] 1 Ch 630; *Phipps v Pears* [1965] 1 QB 76, [1964] 2 All ER 35, CA; *Brace v South East Regional Housing Association* (1984) 270 Estates Gazette 1286 (right of support acquired by prescription not lost under an agreement providing for demolition of adjoining building).
8   *Jones v Pritchard* [1908] 1 Ch 630.
9   *Jones v Pritchard* [1908] 1 Ch 630; *Bond v Nottingham Corpn* [1940] Ch 429, [1940] 2 All ER 12, CA.
10   See 4(1) Halsbury's Laws (4th Edn Reissue) para 971.
11   *Jones v Pritchard* [1908] 1 Ch 630; *Apostal v Simons* [1936] 1 All ER 207; *Upjohn v Seymour Estates* [1938] 1 All ER 614.
12   *Upjohn v Seymour Estates* [1938] 1 All ER 614; *Bond v Nottingham Corpn* [1940] Ch 429, [1940] 2 All ER 12, CA.

                                         [30]

20   **Effect of declaring a wall a party wall**

A declaration of a wall as a party wall in any disposition or other arrangement would have subjected such a wall to a tenancy in common before 1926[1] but now makes the wall subject to the Law of Property Act 1925[2]. However, the statute contains an inconsistency, for the wall is regarded as divided vertically and each half owned separately, although the respective owners are to enjoy such rights to support and user as confer rights corresponding to those that would have subsisted had a valid tenancy in common been created[3]. The inconsistency arises because the rights and duties of the adjoining owners where each half of a wall is owned separately are not in all respects the same as those of tenants in common of a party wall[4]. It is therefore recommended that a declaration should be accompanied by appropriate reservations or grants if it is intended that one or other owner may carry out work to the party wall that would constitute a trespass to that half in the absolute ownership of the other owner[5].

                                         [31]

1   *Watson v Gray* (1880) 14 Ch D 192.
2   See the Law of Property Act s 38(1) (37 Halsbury's Statutes (4th Edn) REAL PROPERTY).
3   See ibid s 38(1).
4   As to the rights of tenants in common see Paragraph 19 [29] ante.
5   For examples of such reservations and grants see Forms 6 [517]–8 [527], 10 [536], 11 [540] post. See also *Jones v Pritchard* [1908] 1 Ch 630; *Phipps v Pears* [1965] 1 QB 76, [1964] 2 All ER 35, CA.

                                         [32]

21   **Maintenance of a party wall**

Where a party wall is subject to the Law of Property Act 1925[1] the respective rights of support and use of the adjoining owners will not impose on either owner any positive obligations as to maintenance or repair, nor to contribute to any repairing expenses[2]. Covenants for maintenance, repair and, if necessary, weatherproofing[3] must therefore be imposed with any declaration of a wall as a party wall[4]. To the extent that such covenants are positive covenants, they are not, as such, binding on successors in title to a covenantor[5]. It is possible to reserve an estate rentcharge of a nominal sum, to which is annexed a right of re-entry, for the enforcement of positive covenants[6].

                                         [33]

1   Ie the Law of Property Act 1925 s 38(1) (37 Halsbury's Statutes (4th Edn) REAL PROPERTY): see Paragraph 18 [27] ante.
2   As to the rights and duties of adjoining owners see Paragraph 19 [29] ante.
3   See *Phipps v Pears* [1965] 1 QB 76, [1964] 2 All ER 35, CA.

Figure 2.5   Encyclopaedia of Forms and Precedents:
main work (forms) and Form Finder volume.

Forms and Precedents

1

Agreement for the erection and maintenance of a boundary fence (with variations for replacement and a maintenance contribution)[1]

THIS AGREEMENT is made the ...... day of .... BETWEEN:
(1)   *(first owner)* of *(address)* ('the First Owner') and
(2)   *(second owner)* of *(address)* ('the Second Owner')

WHEREAS

(1)   The First Owner is [[the registered proprietor *or* entitled to be registered as proprietor] with absolute freehold title of the property ('the First Property') registered under Title Number ... *(insert title number of first property) or if land unregistered* seised of the property known as ...... *(insert address or description of first property)* ('the First Property') for an estate in fee simple in possession [subject as mentioned below but otherwise] free from incumbrances]

(2)   The Second Owner is [[the registered proprietor *or* entitled to be registered as proprietor] with absolute freehold title of the property adjoining the First Property on the [north] side ('the Second Property') registered under Title Number ... *(insert title number of second property) or if land unregistered* seised of the property known as ...... *(insert address or description of second property)* ('the Second Property') for an estate in fee simple in possession [subject as mentioned below but otherwise] free from incumbrances]

(3)   The boundary between the First Property and the Second Property [between the points marked 'A' and 'B' on the attached plan] consists of [a fence ...... *(describe fence)* standing on and belonging to the First Property ('the Original Fence') *or* no marked physical feature *or as the case may be*] and the parties to this agreement have agreed that a fence shall be erected on the First Property along the said boundary on the terms set out below

➡️ **[501]**

NOW IT IS AGREED as follows:

1   Erection of new fence

The First Owner must within ... *(insert number)* months or within such longer period of time as may from time to time be agreed in writing between the parties [remove the Original Fence and in its place] erect [along the whole boundary between the First Property and the Second Property *or* between points 'A' and 'B' as marked on the attached~~
schedul~~

---

283   FENCES

Legal dictionaries

2.41 The materials under consideration in this section are adjuncts to the finding aids for statute and case law discussed in the following chapters, as well as to the textbooks and other secondary sources discussed in this chapter. There are tools that perform one or more of the following functions: explaining the meaning of technical terms; assembling the definitions given by the courts to words or phrases that have required construction be they in a statute or other document; assembling the definitions given in the statutes themselves; and translating foreign legal terms.

2.42 The leading 'explanatory' dictionary is *Jowitt's Dictionary of English Law*. Reference will be given to any statutory or judicial definitions, but this is the place to look if you wish to know what an advowson is or what the York-Antwerp rules are; in effect it is a mini-encyclopaedia of the law. It also performs a translating function for a wide range of Latin tags. However, at the time of writing, *Jowitt* is in sore need of updating – the main work in two volumes was published in 1977 and the last supplement was in 1985. Thus for reasons of currency, as well as convenience, recourse to the smaller one-volume paperback dictionaries may be needed. The main established examples are *Mozley and Whiteley's Law Dictionary* and *Osborn's Concise Law Dictionary*, but new ones appear on the market from time to time. The long-standing US publication, *Black's Law Dictionary*, is a valuable supplement to the English products – it has good coverage of Latinisms – as is the more recent *Butterworths Australian Legal Dictionary*.

2.43 A rather different kind of work in the 'explanatory' category is the *Oxford Companion to the Law* ((1980) Clarendon Press) by David M Walker. It is aimed at readers in other disciplines as well as at lawyers, but is none the less remarkably useful. It can be best described by quoting from the dust jacket: '[It] is neither a legal dictionary, nor an encyclopaedia of legal rules, still less a legal guide for laymen. It is a compendium of information about branches of legal science, legal systems, institutions such as courts and juries, notable judges and jurists, legal concepts and ideas, major legal principles and important documents and cases'. It is particularly useful for historical material (especially as there is no sign of a new edition) and for the explanation of terms and concepts from civil (including Scots) law which may not be covered in English sources. For a work of reference, the author's personal views are sometimes expressed with a surprising forthrightness (see, bearing in mind the work was published in 1980, the entry on trade unions).

2.44 There are also a few dictionaries confined to particular branches of law, such as insurance and banking. The *Oxford Encyclopaedia of European Community Law* by A G Toth was a promising project but seems to have ground to a halt. The first volume covering institutional law, published in 1990, has not been updated, and the further two planned volumes on substantive law and common policies have yet to appear. The intention was to elucidate the host of legal terms and concepts that either have no equivalent in national law or have acquired an entirely new and independent meaning in the context of a supranational Community law.

2.45 *Stroud's Judicial Dictionary*, published by Sweet & Maxwell, is the main work devoted, as it name implies, to the decisions of the courts that have interpreted the meaning of particular words and phrases. Originally the policy was not to include statutory definitions unless such definitions had themselves been subject to judicial interpretation, but in fact now quite a number of statutory definitions do appear. The current (sixth, 2000) edition has been reduced from the five volumes of its predecessor to three (admittedly larger) volumes, and for the fifth edition there was also substantial pruning of older cases and of Scottish, Irish and Commonwealth material. Thus, on an obscure point it may be worth consulting both the fourth and fifth editions too – if your library has had space to retain them. Between editions there are cumulative supplements.

2.46 A competitor to *Stroud* is *Words and Phrases Legally Defined*, published by Butterworths (3rd edn, 1988). As well as judicial definitions, it has always included definitions from statutory material. It also has extensive references to Commonwealth materials, to which in the latest (third) edition have been added selected references to US material. It is published in four volumes with a cumulative supplement. There are helpful cross-references to *Halsbury's Laws*. English lawyers, as well as Scottish, may also derive assistance from William J Stewart's *Scottish Contemporary Judicial Dictionary* ((1995) Green), which is modelled on *Stroud* and *Words and Phrases*. Although containing earlier references, it concentrates on cases since 1946 (the date of publication of the *Scottish Judicial Dictionary* by A W Dalrymple and D Gibb). It does not include statutory definitions unless judicially interpreted.

2.47 Words and phrases that have been judicially considered are also covered by *Halsbury's Laws Monthly Reviews* and by *Current Law*. Because of their frequency of updating, these will be more current than the supplements to *Stroud* and *Words and Phrases*. The index to words and phrases in the monthly reviews is filed in the looseleaf noter-up service volume to *Halsbury's Laws*, not in the binder containing the monthly reviews themselves. There is a table of words and phrases at the front of the *Annual Abridgement*, which cumulates the monthly reviews. The consolidated index to the main volumes of *Halsbury's Laws* has a separate listing of words and phrases at the back. In *Current Law* there is a cumulative table of words and phrases for the current year in the latest monthly digest, and this is incorporated into the yearbook in due course. *The Law Reports Index*, which covers mainstream cases, has an entry 'words and phrases' in its subject matter index.

2.48 Electronic sources that provide law reports in full text, such as Lexis or CD-ROMs of law report series, are another possibility for this kind of research. To find the mere occurrence of a particular word or phrase is of course straightforward; the trick is to limit the search to those cases where the term is actually analysed. You might start by entering the word or phrase just as free-text or possibly just in the headnote field. But if too many irrelevant hits are retrieved, a suggested strategy is to use a proximity search, so that the word or phrase appears near the words 'meaning', 'interpretation', or 'construction' and their equivalents in other grammatical forms. Thus to find any cases on the meaning of 'best endeavours', the search statement on Lexis would be: best endeavours W/15 meaning OR interpret! OR constru!. The same search using a Justis database would be: best endeavours within 75 of (meaning or interpret* or constru*).

2.49 There are quite a number of dictionaries that translate legal terms to and from English. Ordinary English legal dictionaries will cover many Latin words, but there is also *Latin Words and Phrases for Lawyers* by R S Vasan ((1980) Lewis Books), and the classic *Latin for Lawyers*, which was first published by Sweet & Maxwell in 1915, has had a facsimile reprint ((1992) Law Book Exchange). If you are tempted to follow up references to very old cases or treatises, remember that they may well turn out to be in Law French, which was the language of the courts before 1600 and continued to be used during the seventeenth century. If still undeterred, J H Baker's *Manual of Law French* ((2nd edn, 1990) Scolar Press) may assist. In the modern context, linguistic problems are most likely to be encountered in connection with EC materials. The Council Secretariat has a Terminology Office, which has produced glossaries translating terms between the Community languages. For other language dictionaries, and indeed for all kinds of legal dictionaries (only a small selection of the most useful have been mentioned by name in this chapter), consult the list provided in Raistrick's *Lawyers' Law Books* (under 'Dictionaries') and in the Hammicks catalogue (in the 'Reference' section).

Legal directories

2.50 There was a golden age, which lasted for 200 years until 1976, when for most practical purposes there was but one legal directory, *The Law List*; now there is a profusion. There is a vast and wasteful duplication of information, yet no one source is entirely self-sufficient. The only consolation is that many of them are now freely available on the Internet, if your law library, understandably, does not run to hard copies of them all.

Solicitors

2.51 The official directory is now that produced by the Law Society, *Directory of Solicitors and Barristers*. The publishers Waterlows used to have the official franchise, but continue to publish what is now called *Waterlow's Solicitors' and Barristers' Directory*. Both list solicitors geographically by firm and alphabetically by name of solicitor; the latter has a list alphabetically by firm. Date of admission of individuals and types of work carried out by firms are indicated. *Butterworths Law Directory* is an alternative giving much the same information, but it is probably fair to say that *Waterlow's* is better established. All are published annually and are available free on the Internet, except that *Waterlow's* only offers searches by names of firms, rather than individuals (though there is a full CD-ROM version). The Internet version of the Law Society directory is called Solicitors OnLine, the Butterworths directory is called Lawyer Locator (the .co.uk version, not the international one from Martindale-Hubbell) and the Waterlows directory is part of the parent ConnectingLegal service.

2.52 Alongside these purely factual sources are now two sources which offer more evaluative information: *The Legal 500* (Legalease) with its accompanying *Who's Who in the Law* and *Chambers Guide to the Legal Profession*. These aim to offer guidance on the specialisms and reputations of particular firms as well as giving factual information not found in conventional directories, such as number of staff, recruitment of trainee solicitors and history of the firm. Both, of course, are selective: qualification for entry is based mainly on size of firm, but the former includes editorial comment on smaller firms where appropriate and the latter includes smaller firms with notable expertise. In both the shorter entries are free, the longer entries are made on payment. Use as you would a *Good Food Guide*. Both are available free of charge on the Internet as well as in hard copy.

2.53 If you are interested in the current profile of particular firms or particular individuals, *The Lawyer*, *Legal Week* and *Legal Business* magazines often carry features. Many law firms and individual solicitors have their own websites. A particular strength of Nick Holmes' Infolaw site is links to these, but Delia Venables' Legal Resources also aims at extensive coverage.

2.54 If a solicitor cannot be found for some reason in a directory or if added information is required, such as details of when practising certificates were held or if there is a finding or order in respect of disciplinary proceedings, then it is best to contact the Law Society's Regulatory Information Service (in Redditch not at Chancery Lane), who for a charge can provide information.

Barristers

2.55 There has been an enormous boom in the production of directories of barristers, partly due to relaxation on advertising by barristers and partly due to the advent of direct professional access. Until recently even information on the type of work undertaken could be construed as advertising; and accountants, architects and other professionals can now brief a barrister without going via a solicitor, but do not necessarily have the traditional contacts that solicitors have.

2.56 The official directory is now the *Bar Directory*, published for the Bar Council by Sweet & Maxwell. The main listing is by chambers arranged geographically and within location alphabetically by name or address of chambers. All chambers have a basic entry giving members with their date of call, but chambers may opt for an expanded entry which gives details of the type of work undertaken and expertise of particular members. At the front there is an index of chambers by type of work undertaken. At the back there are three lists of individual barristers – barristers in private practice, barristers in employment and non-practising barristers – these include Inn and academic qualifications as well as date of call and address. It is now the only directory to include non-practising barristers. The *Bar Directory* can be searched free of charge on Sweet & Maxwell's website. There used to be a cheap and cheerful alternative to the *Bar Directory* – *Hazell's Guide the Judiciary and the Courts with . . . Bar List*; sadly it was discontinued in 1999. But there is another commercial rival to the official *Bar Directory*, intended particularly to provide information on areas of practice, which is *Havers' Companion to the Bar*. It is described – by itself – as 'the indispensable reference book for anyone instructing a barrister'.

2.57 There are a growing number of specialist bar associations (lists will be found in the *Bar Directory*) and some have produced their own directories, usually again with the aim of publicising areas of work undertaken. Examples are *The Chancery Bar* (Chancery Bar Association), *COMBAR: the Commercial Bar Associaton Directory*, and *The Planning and Environment Bar Association (PEBA) Handbook*. About a third of the bar practises outside London. Whether the Wales and Chester Circuit have set a trend remains to be seen, but they have recently published their own directory.

2.58 All of the sources mentioned above for solicitors cover barristers to a greater or lesser extent as well. The Law Society *Directory* only gives an alphabetical listing of barristers; *Waterlow's* lists by chambers as well but only includes barristers in practice; *Butterworths Law Directory* also includes barristers in employment (but not non-practising). *Chambers Guide* includes all chambers but all barristers in a set of chambers are not necessarily listed. The *Legal 500* includes only selected chambers. However, both works give comment on reputation and specialisms.

2.59 If there is a problem locating a barrister in a directory, then you can double-check, first with the Records Office of the General Council of the Bar, and then as a last resort the four Inns of Court (Gray's Inn, Inner Temple, Lincoln's Inn and Middle Temple) – to be a barrister in England and Wales, the person must have been called to the bar by one of the four.

Courts and judges

2.60 *Waterlow's* includes information on judges and courts, as does *Butterworths Law Directory*, but the fullest information on courts is to be found in *Shaw's Directory of Courts in the United Kingdom*, which as its title indicates covers Scotland and Northern Ireland as well as England and Wales. To be thoroughly recommended, especially to the newly qualified practitioner, is Andrew Goodman's *Court Guide* published annually by Blackstone. This gives all sorts of really practical information, such as nearest tube stations, parking facilities, canteen facilities and so on (though it currently only covers the South Eastern and Western Circuits). *The Lawyer's Remembrancer* includes lists of judges and courts together with a range of other useful information. The Court Service website has addresses for all the courts and tribunals, and also the daily cause lists for cases in the Royal Courts of Justice. The list of cases pending in Crown courts is available on the Sweet & Maxwell site. The Lord Chancellor's Department site has lists of the senior judiciary (High Court and above) with dates of birth and dates of appointment.

Legal services

2.61 *Waterlow's* includes a full section on legal services from accident investigation to shorthand writers, and there is the separate *Butterworths Legal Services Directory*. The Yellow Pages (also available on the Internet) has a heading 'Legal Services'. The *Law Society's Directory of Expert Witnesses* is available for free on the Sweet & Maxwell site, as well as being published annually in hard copy.

Scottish and Irish lawyers

2.62 There are now two directories for Scottish lawyers. The *Scottish Law Directory* is long established. In Scotland it is commonly called the 'White Book', hence the title of its recently started rival, *The Blue Book: the Directory of the Law Society of Scotland*. The Faculty of Advocates also has recently produced their own directory which, like their English counterparts, is particularly aimed at giving an idea of the type of work undertaken by the Scottish bar. Both the Law Society of Scotland and the Faculty of Advocates have lists of members on their websites. The Incorporated Law Society of Ireland publishes an annual *Law Directory*; it also includes a list of Northern Ireland solicitors; it is not yet available on the Internet. The Irish Bar Council are planning to put a list of members on their site.

Overseas lawyers

2.63 There are two, rival, one-volume worldwide directories of law firms: the *International Law List* and *Kime's International Law Directory*. Both are arranged by country. *Kime's* usefully includes brief notes (though of varying detail) on the legal system and legal profession of each country and also has an alphabetical index of all firms listed. Entries are made on payment. The *International Law List* is available free on the Internet; *Kime's* was on the Sweet & Maxwell site, but seems to have vanished for the moment.

2.64 However, often of more use than the above is the *Martindale-Hubbell International Law Directory*, the international section of the vast US directory. In hard copy it is in three volumes. The first two volumes list law firms and individual lawyers, with professional biographies, by geographical location. The third volume includes a complete alphabetical index to individual lawyers. It also has a short section, buried away near the back, of 'non-native' lawyers, for example, Spanish lawyers in London, or French lawyers in Madrid. Though it may sit on the reference shelves, the hard copy can be eschewed in favour of the splendid on-line version available free of charge, the Lawyer Locator. It also includes all the data from the US portion of *Martindale-Hubbell*, which otherwise occupies some 17 extremely fat volumes. Both the *Legal 500* and *Chambers* have regional or global counterparts on their free websites.

2.65 In the European context, though it is not a directory of lawyers, the *Cross-border Practice Compendium* prepared by the Conseil de barreaux de la Communauté Européene (published in this country by Sweet & Maxwell) should be mentioned. It gives details of professional regulation in each member state and on practice in the EC in general, together with addresses of the relevant professional bodies. *Kime's* gives contact details for local bar associations, law societies and professional bodies if it is necessary to pursue local information.

Solicitors' clients

2.66 Both solicitors, for marketing purposes, and prospective clients in choosing a solicitor are often interested to know which solicitors firm acts for a particular company or which companies are clients of a particular solicitors firm. There are at least three sources that provide this information via both permutations: *Crawford's Directory of City Connections*, the *PricewaterhouseCoopers Corporate Register* and the *Hemscott Company Guide*. These publications or the data in them are also available on the Internet – the first as Crawford's Online and the other two on Hemscott Net – but they are primarily subscription services with only basic information and searching available free of charge.

Law teachers

2.67 Both the Society of Public Teachers of Law and the Association of Law Teachers regularly issue directories to their members.

Law libraries

2.68 The main source is the *Directory of British and Irish Law Libraries*, published from time to time by the British and Irish Association of Law Librarians. The main sequence is by constituent countries of the British Isles and then alphabetically by town or city. Details of size of legal collection, opening hours, services and a contact name are given. There are separate indexes by name of organisation, type of organisation, contact name, and of special collections.

Bodies holding records and registers

2.69 A remarkably useful work, though in need of a new edition, is the *Directory of Registers and Records* ((5th edn by Bryan Abraham, 1993) Longman); its relative slenderness means it can easily be overlooked on the reference shelves. It contains a wealth of information on official records that may be needed in legal practice. As well as mainstream items such as birth certificates, wills, county court judgments and local land charges, it includes information on such diverse matters as the Bedford Level Deeds Registry, wartime debtors, closed burial grounds, registered residential homes, lotteries and Jersey companies.

Past lawyers

2.70 Useful sources of information on well-known legal figures from the past are the *Biographical Dictionary of the Common Law* ((1984) Butterworths) edited by A W B Simpson, the *Oxford Companion to the Law* by David M Walker, and A B Schofield *Dictionary of Legal Biography 1845–1945* ((1998) Barry Rose). There is in fact quite a body of material in this field; if research is needed, a full bibliography is given in Guy Holborn *Sources of Biographical Information on Past Lawyers* ((1999) British and Irish Association of Law Librarians).

3. Legislation

Forms of legislation

3.1 In the UK, as in most jurisdictions, there are two main classes of legislation. Primary legislation consists of the Acts – or statutes, the terms are interchangeable – passed by Parliament itself. The other class, usually published in the form of statutory instruments (SIs), is variously termed secondary, subsidiary, subordinate or delegated legislation. The last term most accurately reflects its nature, as this is legislation made under powers delegated by Parliament, typically to government ministers. It may (or may not) receive limited parliamentary scrutiny, but Parliament itself does not have time, even if it were desirable in principle, to enact all the rules, regulations and matters of detail required in the administration of the modern state. However, the power to make secondary legislation must derive from primary legislation – a section in an Act will set out by whom and how the secondary legislation may be made, for example:

> The Secretary of State shall by regulations make a scheme providing for payments to be made to a person to whom this section applies by their former registered employers . . . The power to make regulations under this section shall be exercisable by statutory instrument subject to annulment in pursuance of a resolution of either House of Parliament.

Apart from the difference in how they are made, there is another important constitutional distinction between primary and secondary legislation. In contrast to those countries with written constitutions and constitutional courts, for example, the US and its Supreme Court, the legality of primary legislation in the UK, subject to two new qualifications, cannot be challenged in the courts. Only secondary legislation can be subject to judicial review, if it is made in excess of its enabling powers (ultra vires). The qualifications to that traditional distinction arise from the Human Rights Act 1998 and the Scotland Act 1998. Even following the Human Rights Act, the distinction in essence remains valid. Although primary legislation may now be challenged on the ground that it conflicts with a Convention right, all the court can do is to make a declaration of incompatibility under s 4 of the Human Rights Act, which does not affect the validity of the legislation, nor the outcome of the case as far as the parties are concerned. Acts of the Scottish Parliament (see further paras **8.18** and **8.23**), on the other hand, despite otherwise having all the characteristics of primary legislation, are amenable to direct challenge under the procedure for determining devolution issues in Sch 6 to the Scotland Act, the Judicial Committee of the Privy Council having the final say.

3.2 As well as domestic legislation, there is also European legislation to consider, which will be treated separately. Another category of material that will be discussed in this chapter is not, strictly speaking, legislation, in that it is not directly legally enforceable, but it none the less may have legal consequences. It is highly miscellaneous, but is compendiously described as quasi-legislation, codes of practice being perhaps the most commonly cited example. Rather than starting with a description of how legislation comes into being, coverage of Bills, parliamentary procedure, proposals for legislation and other pre-legislative materials is left for the next chapter – an understanding of those topics is not necessary for the everyday use of legislation, and as far as the practitioner is concerned tends to come into play only when a problem of statutory interpretation arises.

Public General Acts

3.3 Primary legislation comes in two main forms, Public General Acts and Local and Personal Acts. The latter are encountered much less frequently and are dealt with separately below (paras **3.139–3.146**). (For the sake of completeness, it should also be mentioned that in ecclesiastical matters the General Synod of the Church of England – formerly the Church Assembly – pass Measures, which have a similar status to Public General Acts and are printed and issued with them: see further para **3.157**.) Public General Acts form the main body of statute law and as their name implies they are usually of general not merely local application and affect the community at large not just particular persons. They can be amended or repealed, either expressly or impliedly, only by another Act of Parliament (though some Acts do incorporate a power to amend by delegated legislation – a so-called Henry VIII clause). Otherwise an Act will remain in force indefinitely. The *Chronological Table of Statutes* published by the Stationery Office starts in 1235, and shows that many ancient provisions are still on the 'Statute Book', though various programmes of statute law revision have steadily removed obsolete material. It should also be borne in mind that not every new Act enacts new law. It may simply bring together for the sake of convenience and clarity a number of Acts on a particular area that have been passed over a period and which have progressively amended each other. Such Acts are called consolidation Acts (see paras **3.73–3.77**).

3.4 Currently about 50 or 60 Public General Acts are passed each year. Apart from identifying which statutes apply to a particular area, the two main tasks the legal researcher has to perform are establishing whether an Act or part of an Act is still in force on the one hand, or yet to come into force on the other. The latter exercise is necessary because, though some Acts come into force immediately on passing through the requisite stages in Parliament and receiving Royal Assent, many do not. The Act itself may specify a later commencement date, or it may contain a power for a minister subsequently to appoint a date. Usually this is only a matter of concern if one is dealing with recent legislation, but occasionally there can be long delays in bringing an Act into force, or wholly into force. The Easter Act 1928, which provides that Easter should fall on a fixed date, and which is neither repealed nor in force, is an often cited curiosity. Less of a curiosity is, for example, the Family Law Reform Act 1987, s 23 of which (allowing scientific tests of parentage other than blood tests) was only brought into force in 2001. And some Acts or parts of Acts are eventually repealed without ever being brought into force, as was the fate of s 9 of the same Family Law Reform Act 1987. There is also an important interplay between repeals and commencements. It is not sufficient to identify that an Act has been recently repealed. One must also establish that the repealing Act has itself been commenced.

Anatomy and citation

3.5 A typical modern Act in its official form is illustrated (figure 3.1); from 2001 there have been some small changes in layout that will be mentioned below. (1) is the short title, the official name of the Act. It only became the established practice to include a short title at the end of the nineteenth century. To facilitate the citation of earlier statutes with only long titles, the Short Titles Act 1896 retrospectively assigned short titles to over 2,000 Acts then in force, and the Statute Law Revision Act 1948 added a further list. Note that no comma appears between the title and the year – this has been the official practice since 1963, and should be followed even when citing earlier Acts. (2) A 'chapter' number, abbreviated as c (or sometimes ch) is assigned to each Act passed in a particular calendar year. The earlier practice was to assign chapter numbers according to the parliamentary session in which they were passed (see para **3.7**). The number is given in arabic numerals (before 1803 they were printed in capital roman numerals). (3) is the long title, which sets out in greater detail the purpose of the Act; in this case it is a consolidation Act, re-enacting three earlier Acts as one. (4) The date given beneath it in square brackets is the date of Royal Assent, which as already mentioned may or may not be the date of commencement into force. (5) is just a standard enacting formula. (6) Long Acts or ones covering separate areas may be divided for convenience into Parts, but the sections and subsections will be numbered consecutively throughout the Act. Later Acts sometimes amend earlier Acts by means of inserting new sections into the old Act. Such sections are identified by the addition of a letter, so that, for example, the new s 14A will appear between the old ss 14 and 15. The same procedure can apply to subsections. (7) The marginal notes are not technically part of the Act, but are a general convenience and may in some circumstances be used as aids for statutory interpretation. In the new style layout from 2001, marginal notes have been dropped. (8) An interpretation section, setting out definitions of particular terms used, is usually found near the end of the Act before the Schedules. (9) The last section of the Act usually provides for commencement and geographic extent. For commencement, one of three formulas is generally used: a specific date may given; a period after the passing of the Act may be specified, for example, three months (as here), whenever that should fall depending on the actual date of Royal Assent; or it is simply left to come into force on a day to be appointed by, for example, the Secretary of State. If the Act contains no commencement provision it comes into force at the beginning of the day on which it receives Royal Assent: Interpretation Act 1978 s 4(b). If the Act is not to apply to the whole of the UK, this will be stated; here the Act applies to England, Wales and Scotland but not to Northern Ireland. (10) Appended to the Act may be one or more Schedules which are referred to in the body of the Act – a Schedule must have a parent section (here s 15(2)). Schedules have equal force to the sections of the main Act but are a convenient means of setting out matters of detail such as procedural rules, tables of fees, and lists of various kinds. Repeals of earlier legislation will usually be given in Schedules, as here. The numbered parts within Schedules are referred to as paragraphs rather than as sections. Other than the dropping of marginal notes mentioned above, the changes to the layout of Queen's Printer copies of Acts from 2001 are cosmetic: a new style for the format and indentation of section numbers, a slightly different font and a change of style in the running heads.

3.6 Acts may properly be cited by either their short title (which includes the year), for example, Road Traffic Act 1991, or by their chapter number, 1991 c 40. The short

Figure 3.1

---

① # Protection of Badgers Act 1992

② **1992 CHAPTER 51**

③ An Act to consolidate the Badgers Act 1973, the Badgers Act 1991 and the Badgers (Further Protection) Act 1991. [16th July 1992] ④

⑤ **B**E IT ENACTED by the Queen's most Excellent Majesty, by and with the advice and consent of the Lords Spiritual and Temporal, and Commons, in this present Parliament assembled, and by the authority of the same, as follows:—

Offences ⑦

⑥ 1.—(1) A person is guilty of an offence if, except as permitted by or under this Act, he wilfully kills, injures or takes, or attempts to kill, injure or take, a badger.   Taking. injuring or killing badgers.

(2) If, in any proceedings for an offence under subsection (1) above consisting of attempting to kill, injure or take a badger, there is evidence from which it could reasonably be concluded that at the material time the accused was attempting to kill, injure or take a badger, he shall be presumed to have been attempting to kill, injure or take a badger unless the contrary is shown.

(3) A person is guilty of an offence if, except as permitted by or under this Act, he has in his possession or under his control any dead badger or any part of, or anything derived from, a dead badger.

(4) A person is not guilty of an offence under subsection (3) above if he shows that—

    (a) the badger had not been killed, or had been killed otherwise than in contravention of the provisions of this Act or of the Badgers Act 1973; or   1973 c. 57.

    (b) the badger or other thing in his possession or control had been sold (whether to him or any other person) and, at the time of the purchase, the purchaser had had no reason to believe that the badger had been killed in contravention of any of those provisions.

Figure 3.1 – *cont'd*

Interpretation. 1968 c. 27. 	**14.** In this Act— "ammunition" has the same meaning as in the Firearms Act 1968; "badger" means any animal of the species *Meles meles*; "badger sett" means any structure or place which displays signs indicating current use by a badger; "firearm" has the same meaning as in the Firearms Act 1968; "sale" includes hire, barter and exchange and cognate expressions shall be construed accordingly.
Short title, repeals, commencement and extent. ⑨	**15.**—(1) This Act may be cited as the Protection of Badgers Act 1992. (2) The enactments mentioned in the Schedule to this Act are repealed to the extent specified in the third column of that Schedule. (3) This Act shall come into force at the end of the period of three months beginning with the day on which it is passed. (4) This Act does not extend to Northern Ireland.

⑩   SCHEDULE

REPEALS

Chapter	Short title	Extent of repeal
1973 c. 57.	The Badgers Act 1973.	The whole Act.
1981 c. 69.	The Wildlife and Countryside Act 1981.	Section 73(4). In Schedule 7, paragraphs 8 to 12.
1985 c. 31.	The Wildlife and Countryside (Amendment) Act 1985.	Section 1.
1986 c. 14.	The Animals (Scientific Procedures) Act 1986.	In Schedule 3, paragraph 9.
1990 c. 43.	The Environmental Protection Act 1990.	In Schedule 9, paragraph 6.
1991 c. 28.	The Natural Heritage (Scotland) Act 1991.	In Schedule 2, paragraph 5.
1991 c. 35.	The Badgers (Further Protection) Act 1991.	The whole Act.
1991 c. 36.	The Badgers Act 1991.	The whole Act.
1991 c. 53.	The Criminal Justice Act 1991.	Section 26(3).

title, for practical purposes, is the more informative of the two elements, but for completeness there is no harm, and some virtue, in putting both, for example, Road Traffic Act 1991 (c 40). The chapter number, if it is cited, has since 1963 been assigned according the calendar year in which it was passed. When citing a particular section, the abbreviation s is used (or ss for sections in the plural).

3.7 For Acts before 1963, however, not only was the chapter number assigned by parliamentary session (in modern times usually running from November to October), rather than calendar year, but the parliamentary session was identified and described according to the regnal year or years in which the session was held. Each regnal year starts on the anniversary of the accession of the monarch to the throne. Thus 30 & 31 Vict c 27 refers to the 27th Act passed during the session of Parliament that straddled the 30th and 31st years of the reign of Queen Victoria (who acceded to the throne on 20 June). If the parliamentary session is unusually long then it might even straddle three regnal years, as happened in the parliamentary session of 1948–49. The date of accession to the throne of George VI was 11 December. When the session started on 26 October 1948 the regnal year was 12 Geo 6; by the time it was finished on 16 December 1949, 14 Geo 6 had been reached. Thus Acts passed in 1949 are cited as 12, 13 & 14 Geo 6. The same may happen when there is a change of monarch, as in 1952; Acts for that year are cited as 15 & 16 Geo 6 & 1 Eliz 2. Very rarely, the opposite may happen – if there are two successive exceptionally short parliamentary sessions (for instance caused by elections) they may both fall in the same regnal year, as happened in 1922. Acts passed in the latter part of 1922 will have chapter numbers assigned and cited as 13 Geo 5 (Sess 2). (Incidentally, the Act that effected the change of practice from the beginning of 1963, the Acts of Parliament Numbering and Citation Act 1962, necessarily had itself an old style chapter number, 10 & 11 Eliz 2 c 34.)

3.8 The terminology 'chapter' arises because the very earliest Acts were regarded as parts of a single statute passed at one meeting of Parliament. Such statutes are often referred to by the place where Parliament met. Thus the Distress Act 1267, which prohibits the seizing of goods without a court order, for example, for unpaid rent, and which is still in force and so to be found in *Halsbury's Statutes*, is c 1 of the Statute of Marlborough. Its short title was only retrospectively assigned to it, so the Distress Act would otherwise be cited as 52 Hen 3 c 1, or *Stat Marlb* c 1. Where more than one such overarching statute was passed in a regnal year, the chapter number may not uniquely identify a particular Act. Thus an Act concerning summonses to Parliament of 1382, again still to be found in *Halsbury's Statutes*, is cited as 5 Ric 2 Stat 2 c 4. By the beginning of the sixteenth century and the reign of Henry VIII, the modern status of 'chapters' pertained. One other complication with the chapter numbers (and sometimes section numbers) of old Acts is discrepancies between different published editions. The chapter numbering of the widely used, but privately published, *Statutes at Large* by Ruffhead, was not necessarily followed when the official *Statutes of the Realm* – based on exhaustive research in the original parliamentary rolls and records – was prepared (see para **3.32**). The official chapter number is as now given in the *Chronological Table of Statutes* (see para **3.37**), but at the beginning it has a table of variances from Ruffhead's edition – the statutes of Queen Anne are particularly troublesome in this respect.

3.9 Some older Acts were known by popular names taken from the name of the promoter of the Act or its subject matter. For example, the Marriage Act 1753 was known as Lord Hardwicke's Act and the Sunday Observance Acts were often called the Lords' Day Acts. A selective list of these giving their official references is in an appendix to *Craies on Statute Law* (7th edn, 1971) and the *Oxford Companion to Law* has entries for some. Probably the fullest list, though it may not be readily available, is the Table of Short and Popular Titles in volume 16 of *Chitty's Statutes of Practical Utility* ((6th edn, 1916) Sweet & Maxwell).

3.10 A modern manifestation of the same tendency is the use of acronyms, for example, PACE for the Police and Criminal Evidence Act 1984. The practice is perhaps more frequent in the case of statutory instruments, for example, TUPE for the Transfer of Undertakings (Protection of Employment) Regulations 1981, or the CDM Regs for the Construction (Design and Management) Regulations 1994. If such an acronym or abbreviation is not familiar to you, and the source where you found it has not had the courtesy to give it in full form at some point, then you will just have to use your initiative – Raistrick's *Index to Legal Citations and Abbreviations* (see para **5.60**) does not seem to stretch that far, or at any rate the above three examples are not in it.

Sources for the text of Acts

3.11 In most large law libraries you will be spoilt for choice if all you need is the unamended text of a recent Act. But, depending on the nature of your inquiry, you need to be aware of the pros and cons of the different forms of published Acts.

Halsbury's Statutes

3.12 This commercially published set is usually the best source: it prints the text of the Act as amended (or enables you readily to check whether the text has been amended), it is updated frequently, and has useful annotations, giving cross-references to other parts of the Act, to other Acts, to relevant SIs and to relevant case law. It is arranged in 40 or so bound volumes by broad topic. There is a softbound tables and index volume to the whole work, which is replaced annually. It is kept up to date in four ways. First, individual volumes of the main work are reissued from time to time when the quantity and importance of new material warrants it. Secondly, recent statutes are issued in looseleaf 'Current Statutes Service' volumes pending incorporation in a bound volume. For the sake of currency these may initially be issued in unannotated form and are then reissued when the necessary editorial work has been carried out. Thirdly, a cumulative supplement, arranged according to the same volume numbers of the main work, is issued annually in bound volume form. Fourthly, a looseleaf noter-up, arranged in the same way as the supplement, captures developments between annual supplements. The cumulative supplement and noter-up do not usually provide the full text of new Acts, but refer instead to the 'Current Statutes Service' volume. However, an expediency recently adopted for those titles that await a reissued main volume, but for which a substantial amount of material has accumulated in the looseleaf 'Current Statutes Service' volumes, is to issue softbound 'continuation' volumes to the main volume containing statutes passed since the bound volume was published in order to relieve pressure on space in looseleaf volumes. When using such continuation volumes, the cumulative supplement and noter-up still need to be used. Fortunately, the practice of issuing continuation volumes has so far been resorted to only sparingly. The fourth edition (in grey covers) of the main work is now complete, but earlier editions remain useful for legislation no longer in force, which sometimes needs to be referred to.

3.13 The annotations to each section of an Act give cross-references to other parts of the Act. For example, a particular term used in a section may be defined in an interpretation section elsewhere in the Act. Likewise, if a section confers a regulation-making power there may be a general section on the manner in which regulation-making powers are to be exercised. Where a section is printed as amended (apparent from text in square brackets or three stops as marks of omission), the annotations will give the source of the amendments. Where a section has been prospectively repealed, ie an Act repealing it has been passed but not yet commenced so that for the time being the section remains in force, it is printed in italic, and the annotations will again elaborate. Cross-references may also be given to other relevant statutes and to case law. The latter, though helpful, often amount to no more than what might be called stock references, ie references to cases which have interpreted common statutory words or phrases that crop up in the context of many different statutes, such as 'at all reasonable times', 'without reasonable excuse', 'forthwith', 'building'. There are also stock references to general words defined in the Interpretation Act 1978, for example, 'person' or 'writing'. The annotations in *Halsbury's Statutes*, in contrast to those in *Current Law Statutes Annotated* (see paras **3.20–3.21**), are thus very much in the nature of mechanical apparatus, rather than being discursive or offering commentary. However, slightly more general descriptive material, though still not really amounting to commentary, is offered; it will be found not in the annotations to the particular sections or at the start of each Act, but in the preliminary note that precedes each whole subject *title*.

3.14 One limitation to bear in mind is that, as its full title – *Halsbury's Statutes of England* – indicates, it does not cover statutes that apply to Scotland only. However, it does include Church Measures and, very selectively, some Local and Personal Acts, principally those relating to London. An occasional drawback is that because of its subject arrangement, the text of a particular statute may be split between different volumes if it covers separate topics. For example, the text of the Police and Criminal Evidence Act 1984 is split between vol 12 on Criminal Law and vol 17 which includes the title Evidence. To the newcomer *Halsbury's Statutes* may seem a little daunting, but a small effort early on to discover how it works will be amply repaid. How to use it for different types of research will be explained in detail at the appropriate points below. Although widely used throughout the legal profession, it is not, of course, an official text.

Queen's Printer copy

3.15 The official text of individual Acts is known as the Queen's Printer copy. They are printed and issued usually within a few days of Royal Assent (though occasionally longer delays can occur). They are subsequently reissued as annual bound volumes (the modern ones in red covers) which include tables and indexes. The loose prints are the only source for the text of very recent statutes that have not yet appeared in the commercially published series. If you have a citation that includes the year, it is straightforward to find them on the shelf. The obvious limitation to using the statutes in this form is that the text is only as it was on the date it was passed. However, for many purposes, if you know that it has not been amended, this is all that is needed. They are also a source if you need the text of statutes that are no longer in force.

3.16 Although nowadays many judges may be relaxed about it, you are generally expected to cite the Queen's Printer copy in court. This will avoid the embarrassment that arose in *R v Keriwala* (The Times, 4 January 1991), where the Court of Appeal observed that a crucial part of the text of Police and Criminal Evidence Act 1984 was incorrectly printed in *Current Law Statutes Annotated* and the first two editions of Zander's book on the Act. That is not to say that there are never misprints in the Queen's Printer copy. If the mistake is picked up straightaway a correction slip will be issued (for example, in 1995 correction slips were issued for three Acts), and the correction incorporated in the bound volume or before then if the Act is reprinted. Otherwise it is for the courts to say that there must have been a misprint – a rare occurrence, but see for example, *Green v Whitehead* [1930] 1 Ch 38 at 45, finding a misprint in s 23 of the Trustee Act 1925.

3.17 You buy Queen's Printer copies from what is now called 'The Stationery Office', but the Queen's Printer is in fact the Controller of 'Her Majesty's Stationery Office' (HMSO). The trading company, the Stationery Office Ltd, performs most of the functions of HMSO following its privatisation in 1996. But HMSO continues in being as the residual non-privatised part that performs statutory or quasi-statutory functions, of which the promulgation of the official text of legislation is one. This is merely to explain that the full text of the Queen's Printer copies are also available from 1988 on the HMSO website (though links from The Stationery Office website will take you there, as will those from the Parliament site). The Internet versions are an exact reproduction, but bear in mind the disclaimer that the authoritative text remains the hard copy.

3.18 From the beginning of 1999 for most Public General Acts – those that started life as government Bills, as opposed to Private Members' Bills – there are also officially prepared explanatory notes. (On their origin and use, see para **4.57**.) They are published by the Stationery Office, but have to be bought separately and are not incorporated into the official bound volumes of Public General Acts, though it is likely that libraries will keep them next to the Public General Acts. They are also on the HMSO website.

3.19 Some libraries may take the *Law Reports Statutes*, which are exactly the same as the official text but reprinted by authority for the Incorporated Council of Law Reporting and issued in a uniform binding to the *Law Reports*.

Current Law Statutes

3.20 *Current Law Statutes* are the commercially published added-value versions of the Queen's Printer copies; that is, they are arranged chronologically and the text remains as it was when originally passed, but they have the addition of explanatory annotations. They go back to 1949 (the first volume of 1948 is unannotated) and form part of the *Current Law* service published by Sweet & Maxwell (though they are available separately and may or may not be shelved in the library with other parts of *Current Law*). Individual statutes are issued soon after Royal Assent and are filed in a looseleaf service volume. For the sake of currency an unannotated version, printed on blue paper, may be issued in advance. Three or four blue bound volumes replace the looseleaf issues each year. The looseleaf service volume also contains a subject index, which is updated three times a year. At the end of the year this is incorporated at the back of the last bound volume. Since 1990 an index has also been supplied for each individual Act, which is a useful feature for long Acts. It includes all Public General Acts, including, unlike *Halsbury's Statutes*, Acts applying only to Scotland. From 1991, Local and Personal Acts, are also included, though they are seldom much annotated.

3.21 The main feature of the service is, of course, the annotations. Their extent varies according to the importance of the Act; it is also observable that the annotations in the more recent volumes have tended to be a little more discursive than they once were. The annotator for each Act is credited by name, so those with knowledge of writers in the field in question may gauge the value of the commentary. The general note at the start of a statute sets out the full legislative background – references are given to any preceding green papers, white papers, Royal Commission or Law Commission reports, any relevant case law that will be overtaken by the statute, and to the relevant parliamentary debates. There will then be further annotations at the start of each part of the Act, if it is divided into parts, and to each section, giving more detailed, and again often discursive, annotations, for example, highlighting potential difficulties in the operation or interpretation of the section. The main limitation of *Current Law Statutes* is that the information remains static. Some of the factual information, such as references to pre-legislative materials or to previous legislation replaced, may be of permanent value, but even if an Act is not amended or repealed, much of the material given in the annotations can date fairly rapidly. There are two, if not exceptions, at any rate qualifications to this ageing process, however. The first is where the material prepared for *Current Law Statutes* is recycled into a Sweet & Maxwell looseleaf subject encyclopaedia (see para **3.22**), which, reasonably enough, is sometimes done, particularly where the annotator and the looseleaf editor are one and the same. Consolidation Acts (see paras **3.73–3.77**) constitute the second qualification. With such Acts, the annotator has the opportunity of elaborating on the development of the law since all the statutes being consolidated were first passed. *That* information of course then remains static (unless another consolidation Act comes along).

Looseleaf encyclopaedias

3.22 Convenient sources for the text of legislation are subject-based looseleaf encyclopaedias. Often accompanied by expert commentary or annotations, they are as good a source as any. For some major subjects there may be more than one to choose from, produced by different publishers. Always check the date of the latest release. The main function of looseleaf encyclopaedias is to reproduce primary materials in convenient form, but of course standard bound textbooks may also reprint selected statutory materials as appendices.

Handbooks and subject collections

3.23 Statutes on a particular subject are often published in single volumes, usually softbound, as handbooks, as in the series published by Butterworths, or in collections of cases and materials designed for students. Convenience and portability (unlike the big looseleafs) are their virtues, though their date of publication should always be noted. Their availability, though, is confined to the major subject areas, for example, property law, company law, family law.

Justis Statutes

3.24 This electronic service from Context is available either on CD-ROM or on the Internet. It provides in full text every or almost every (see para **3.25**) Public General Act passed since 1235, whether in force or repealed. Although the text is provided as passed, whether an Act or section of an Act has been repealed is indicated, and there is a sophisticated and effective system of links between amending and amended statutes. As with other electronic versions of statutes the unit forming each record is an individual section of an Act, with the front listing of the arrangement of sections being also a record on its own. The consequence is that a large number of hits can be generated where the relevant Acts, even though there are not many of them, each have many sections. It may be useful if you are not near a library, but otherwise simply as a source of the text of an Act, this service, like other electronic versions, has nothing particular to commend it over conventional printed sources, unless it is old repealed legislation that you are after and your library does not have old sessional volumes or *Statutes at Large*. The benefits of electronic versions of Acts for certain types of research, on the other hand, are discussed below.

3.25 From 1870 the text is taken from the sessional volumes of Queen's Printer copies, and so every Public General Act from that date is included in full. The statutes from 1235 to 1869, however, are taken from *Statutes at Large* (see para **3.32**). Although *Statutes at Large* contains the full text of almost any Act that it likely to be needed, for some the full text is not provided, only the long title. For reasons explained more fully when Local and Personal Acts are described (see para **3.141**), before 1797 many Acts technically classed as Public Acts were in effect Local Acts, and it is the text of these that is usually omitted in *Statutes at Large*. The other class omitted in full text from *Statutes at Large*, even after 1797, is fiscal Acts in standard form, usually described as Supply Acts or Consolidated Fund Acts.

Lexis/Legislation Direct

3.26 Lexis contains the full text of all statutes in force as amended. As with the Justis Statutes each section of an Act rather than the Act as a whole is treated as a separate item. The text of each section of an Act is headed with the date it came into force, and at the foot is the annotations segment, which gives full details of derivations, commencement provisions and amending legislation. The data is also available as Legislation Direct, a module on the Butterworths LEXIS Direct Internet service.

Lawtel

3.27 This commercial service has the full text of Acts as originally passed from 1987, supplied by HMSO. Simply for the text of an Act, there is thus no advantage over the free HMSO site, unless you happened to be logged onto Lawtel anyway. But it does have a separate Statutory Status Table, giving a section by section listing of commencement dates and amendments and repeals.

Westlaw UK

3.28 This currently offers the consolidated text of statutes relating to major areas of practice, such as commercial law, company law, real property, intellectual property, tax, personal injuries and litigation.

Statutes in force

3.29 For the sake of completeness this is mentioned, in case you come across it and wonder what it is. If your library has it, it is likely that it will have been relegated to one of the more dusty corners of the library stacks. Acts as passed were added until the end of 1996, but any supplementation effectively stopped in 1991. Even when it was being actively published it was unloved. It was intended to be the official text, arranged by subject rather than chronologically, of all Public General Acts in force, including those covering Scotland, as amended, by way of replacement for the third edition of *Statutes Revised*, which was the official consolidation in bound volume form of all Acts in force in 1948. Though in looseleaf form – 100 or so dark brown binders – it had a separate system of cumulative supplements. It still has a small residual use. For heavily amended Scottish Acts (not in *Halsbury's*) it may save a little time by giving you the text as at the date of the last supplement.

Statute Law Database

3.30 *Statutes in Force* was suspended in order that official resources could instead be devoted to developing an official database of all statutes in force. Although it has been under development for a number of years, it is only currently available to government departments in a prototype version. A decision has long been awaited on how, and on what terms, it is to be made more widely available. Its content is all statutes that were in force on 1 February 1991 (when *Statutes in Force* was last properly updated) and all new statutes since that date. A particular feature of its design is that it will allow a 'freeze frame' to be viewed, showing the text of any statute as amended at any particular date after 1 February 1991.

Butterworths Annotated Legislation Service

3.31 Butterworths used to publish a service similar to *Current Law Statutes Annotated*, which published statutes as they came out in annotated form. Its arrangement was slightly different however. It consisted of bound volumes only; it did not have a looseleaf element. Major Acts had a volume to themselves, and shorter Acts were grouped in a miscellaneous manner. It had a cumulative index back to 1939, when the service started (under the name *Butterworths Emergency Legislation Service*). It lives on in name, but is really now a monographic series, with just two or three major Acts being covered each year. Issued in paperback, it is similar to guides to major new Acts put out by other publishers, such as Blackstone Press. Although still having 'Butterworths Annotated Legislation Service' on their covers, they are generally identified by the authors of each title.

Older Acts

3.32 Sessional volumes of Acts have been officially printed since 1483, but very few sets exist before the eighteenth century. However, there have been numerous unofficial compilations at various dates. The most widely used is *Statutes at Large*, which was originally compiled by Owen Ruffhead and hence is sometimes referred to simply as 'Ruffhead'. In the edition by Runnington it covers statutes from the Magna Carta to 1785 (25 Geo III). Continuation volumes go up to 1869. However, for statutes before 1714 the most authoritative edition (and recognised as such by the Interpretation Act 1978) is *Statutes of the Realm* prepared by the Record Commissioners and published in ten volumes, 1810–22. The drawback to using them is that they are extremely hefty folio volumes (though they have also been published on microfilm). Unless one is in weight training, *Statutes at Large* are sufficient for most everyday purposes (and certainly preferable for photocopying – with a volume of *Statutes of the Realm* if you do not damage it, it may well damage your photocopier!). Ruffhead's *Statutes at Large* are, however, only one edition of several with the same title published in the eighteenth and nineteenth centuries. The bibliography and interrelationship between the various editions is complex. If further guidance is needed, reference should be made to Sweet & Maxwell's *Guide to Law Reports and Statutes* (4th edn, 1962) pp 11–16. All these editions omit statutes passed during the Commonwealth. These are only going to be of historical interest, but they have since been published by the Statute Law Committee under the editorship of C H Firth in 1911, *Acts and Ordinances of the Interregnum 1642–1660*.

The range of finding aids

3.33 Most of the printed sources described above have their own tables and indexes. Full text electronic versions of course constitute their own finding aid. But there are one or two separately published finding aids. Probably the most useful is the *Current Law Statute Citator*. This is currently in four bound volumes going up to the end of 1999. The first volume, 1947–71, is called the *Current Law Statute Citator*. Subsequent volumes are called the *Current Law Legislation Citator*, of which the 'Statute Citator' forms a part. The current year is found in the looseleaf service volume to *Current Law Statutes*, and is issued in cumulative form six times a year. A paperback cumulation will cover the period between the last bound volume and the looseleaf current year. It covers all Acts that have been passed since 1947 and all earlier statutes amended or repealed since that date. (It also includes SIs made under those Acts and references to case law.) The *Current Law Legislation Citator* is also available on the Current Legal Information service on CD-ROM and the Internet, but only from 1989 at present.

3.34 *Is it in Force?* published by Butterworths is issued to subscribers to *Halsbury's Statutes*, but is also available separately. It is primarily a guide to commencement provisions for Acts passed in the last 25 years. Although it does give some information on repeals, that is not its function (see para **3.60**). It is arranged chronologically, but with the statutes listed alphabetically (not by chapter number) within each year. It is published annually. So that it does not expand indefinitely, the start date is brought forward by a year on each reissue; old editions, if they have been kept, are thus sometimes useful for historical information – it was first published in 1985 so coverage goes back to 1960. Between editions the equivalent information is given in the *Is it in Force?* section in the service volume to *Halsbury's Statutes*. Very usefully, it also available on Law Direct, the free part of Butterworths' Internet services.

3.35 A further adjunct to *Halsbury's Statutes*, new in 2001, is the *Halsbury's Statutes Citator*. This looks as if it may be a useful addition to the legal researcher's armoury, but as with other research tools its precise scope should be clearly understood. The main part of the volume (grey softback, like *Is it in Force?*) is a list of statutes arranged chronologically by year, and within each year alphabetically by title. Included in the list are all those statutes that have ever appeared in *Halsbury's Statutes* since it was first published in 1929 *and* that have been amended, repealed or otherwise affected. It thus excludes (a) statutes that were wholly repealed when *Halsbury's Statutes* started, (b) statutes outside the scope of *Halsbury's Statutes*, ie statutes applying to Scotland only, and most Local and Personal Acts, and (c) statutes that are still fully in force in the form in which they were originally passed. At the front is an alphabetical index by title of Act.

3.36 *Halsbury's Statutes Citator* would seem to have two purposes. One is as a quick reference source for details of amendments and repeals without having to delve into the main work. That is likely to arise when you have in front of you a mention or the text of a statute in a source other than *Halsbury's Statutes* – if you already looking at the statute in *Halsbury's Statutes* this volume will not be needed. The other is to provide a source of information for statutes no longer in the current edition – hitherto if a statute was not to be found in the current edition, you would know that it was no longer in force, but you could not readily tell, from *Halsbury's* itself at any rate, when and how it was repealed. Amendments and repeals are what it is about, but the introduction does rather reticently slip in the fact that 'Cases have also been noted to the relevant provision'. Indeed there are case references, but they turn out to be only to such cases as are reported in the *All England Law Reports*; it might have been better to have said so. It is not stated whether any interim supplementation between editions is to be provided, but a telephone hotline service is offered for any recent changes.

3.37 The *Chronological Table of the Statutes*, in two black volumes, is prepared by the Statutory Publications Office and published by the Stationery Office, so is an authoritative source. It lists every Public General Act passed since 1235, and for each indicates whether it has been amended or repealed. The limitations of the *Chronological Table* are that new editions no longer seem to be regular, and when they are issued there is still a considerable time-lag in coverage, though the new edition published in April 2001 was an improvement – it covered statutes up to the end of 1999. For the equivalent officially prepared information since the last edition, one needs to look at the Tables and Index volume for each year's official bound volumes of Public General Acts, which includes an 'Effects of Legislation' table.

3.38 Possibly still lurking on the library shelves next to the *Chronological Table* may be another pair of black volumes published by the Stationery Office, the *Index to the Statutes 1235–1990*. From 1870 there were regular editions of the *Index to the Statutes*. Being a subject index to Acts in force at a particular date it became in effect the subject index for *Statutes in Force* (see para **3.29**); hence the fact that it does not go beyond 1990, when that project began to grind to a halt.

3.39 Badger, one the Current Legal Information databases, indexes all legislation from 1993. Titles and catalogue information for statutes, SIs and Bills since 1980 are on the UKOP (United Kingdom Official Publications) service issued by the Stationery Office in conjunction with Chadwyck-Healey on CD-ROM and on the web. Statutes and Bills (but not SIs) are also included in the Stationery Office monthly and annual catalogues.

3.40 The *House of Commons Weekly Information Bulletin* is a useful source for recent legislation as it includes all Public Bills before Parliament in the current session, and will include date of Royal Assent and chapter number as soon as they are passed. It is also available on the Parliament website. Badger on CLI, the equivalent on Westlaw UK, Lawtel, and Law Direct from Butterworths all have similar Bill tracker services.

3.41 Most of the main journals, such as the *New Law Journal*, the *Solicitors Journal*, and the *Law Society's Gazette* summarise recent legislative developments either in current awareness sections or as the subject of separate articles in the case of important statutes. As already noted, for this reason, although it is not its main function, the *Legal Journals Index* can sometimes be a back door route to finding statutes.

Finding Acts by title

3.42 For statutes in force there are alphabetical lists in the tables and index volume of *Halsbury's Statutes*. Note that in *Halsbury's Statutes* the letter (S) following a volume number indicates the looseleaf 'Current Statutes Service' volumes, which mirror the arrangement of the main work. It can occasionally occur that a volume of the main work is reissued after the Tables and Index Volume was last issued. This might cause two small hiccups. First, the page number for the statute given in the Table and Index volume will no longer be accurate. However, the volume number will remain the same and when you get to it, it will be apparent that you have got a very recent reissue; it is then straightforward to relocate the item from the volume's own table. Secondly, if the statute is listed as being in a 'Current Statutes Service' (S) volume, it may in fact have since been incorporated in the reissued bound volume, so if the statute is no longer in the looseleaf binder, do not necessarily assume it has been stolen; check the equivalent volume of the main work. If the Act might have been passed since the last annual issue of the Tables and Index volume, check the alphabetical contents list at the front of the first volume of the looseleaf Current Statutes Service.

3.43 Volume 53 of *Halsbury's Laws* also contains an alphabetical list of statutes mentioned in that work, which is likely to be very comprehensive though it may not coincide totally with the contents of *Halsbury's Statutes*. There is an alphabetical table of statutes in the *Current Law Legislation Citator* volumes from 1972 (but not in the first volume of the *Statute Citator*, 1947–71). The tables include all statutes affected during the relevant period as well as those actually passed so their coverage is wider than might appear. The looseleaf service volume to *Current Law Statutes* also reprints the table from the last *Legislation Citator* – it is filed behind the Table of Statutes tab.

3.44 If the year of the Act is known it is a simple matter to go the annual volumes of Public General Acts or *Current Law Statutes*, which contain alphabetical tables for each year. To find the chapter number of very recent statutes not yet in *Halsbury's* or *Current Law Statutes*, you can use the table of Public Bills in the *House of Commons Weekly Information Bulletin* or electronic sources such as Badger and Lawtel, though it would not take much longer simply to browse along the shelf of Queen's Printer copies.

3.45 If a statute cannot be found in the alphabetical table to *Halsbury's Statutes* the implication is that it is no longer in force (or very recent or wholly Scottish or a Local Act). Try *Halsbury's Statutes Citator*. The Justis Statutes on CD-Rom or the web would then be the next place to go – if it were not found on that either, then the implication is that it is a Local Act , or not a UK Act at all, or, most likely, you have got the title wrong. If the Justis Statutes are not available, there is in fact no single printed alphabetical listing by short title of all Acts passed. Having checked on the off chance the tables, mentioned above, in *Halsbury's Laws* and the *Current Law Legislation Citators*, a search by subject matter would thus have to be the alternative approach. (see paras **3.47–3.50**).

3.46 Electronic versions other than Justis – Lawtel, Lexis, Westlaw UK, HMSO website – can of course also be used for statutes within their scope. On these it is usually best to do a field rather than free text search, for example, on Lawtel using the Focused Search template or on Lexis specifying the title segment. If the Act is since 1993, Badger, though it does not give the full text, is another straightforward alternative.

Finding Acts by subject

3.47 Subject-based looseleaf encyclopaedias, if there is one for the area in question, are often the most convenient source. Otherwise *Halsbury's Statutes* is the best place. There is a consolidated index to the whole work in the Tables and Index volume. Note that this index is in *two* sequences. The first and longest covers the bound volumes of the main work. The second sequence covers statutes in the looseleaf 'Current Statutes Service' volumes. The same problems as described in para **3.42** can occur if the relevant volume in the main work has been reissued since the index volume was last issued: the page references in the main sequence may not be accurate and the material referred to in the service sequence may have been incorporated into the main work. However, individual volumes of the main work also have their own indexes, so as long as you can get to the right volume there should be no problem. Having found the relevant matter in the main volumes and/or the 'Current Statutes Service' volume, always double-check the annual cumulative supplement and looseleaf noter-up for any more recent developments.

3.48 The *Index to the Statutes* published by HMSO used to be another possibility, but since it has not been updated since 1990, it should now be avoided, unless old legislation is relevant (see para **3.50**). It did cover Scottish Acts, and one of its useful features was that geographical extent within the UK was indicated by the abbreviations E, W, E & W, S, or L (for London).

3.49 The various full text electronic sources – particularly the Justis Statutes and Lexis or Legislation Direct – are well suited to subject searching, and in some ways searching statutes on them is more straightforward than searching for cases in that statutory language tends to be more consistent and formalised than the language used in judgments. However, as most standard research problems involving statutes can usually be answered satisfactorily and reasonably quickly by manual means, in practice resort to electronic versions tends to be confined to unconventional searches. They are particularly useful for tracing concrete entities that may treated in legislation covering entirely different topics. For example, a search on 'caravans' will not only retrieve the Caravan Sites Act and various statutes you might expect relating to housing, planning and rating, but also sections from the Timeshare Act, Norfolk and Suffolk Broads Act and the Public Order Act among others. Another similar application is finding a statutory phrase that might have been used in a number of disparate Acts. If you have a problem of statutory interpretation and there is little authority on your particular Act, you might wish to see if the same phrase has been used in another Act that has been judicially considered.

3.50 Usually one only needs to find statutes that are no longer in force by subject when tracing the history of a particular provision, in which case one can just look at the current statute and see what it repeals, and then see what that statute repealed and so on. But if research is otherwise required then since the advent of Justis Statutes it can be done relatively easily, though in formulating a search strategy bear in mind, if one is likely to be dealing with very old statutes, that the statutory language may be archaic. If the Justis Statutes are not available then superseded editions of *Halsbury's Statutes*, the first edition of which was published 1929–31, would be one suggestion. If one were doing 'time-slice' research, ie wanting to find the statutes in force on a subject at a particular date, then old editions of the *Index to the Statutes* would be one approach. It is arranged by broad heading, for example, Road Traffic, and at the start of the entry all the relevant statutes are listed by title and chapter number. Most topics are then broken down by subheading and by geographic extent, with detailed index entries to particular sections of Acts. In this part of the index the references are by chapter number only – the short title is not given. Within the detailed subheadings, cross-references are given to other headings. For statutes before 1786 *Statutes at Large* has an index volume, as does, for statutes before 1715, *Statutes of the Realm*. Old editions of standard textbooks would also be a practical way to approach this.

Finding amendments and repeals

3.51 Before discussing how to check whether an Act has been amended or repealed, it is worth outlining the usual methods of amendment and repeal so that you know what you might find if an Act had been amended or repealed. The whole of an Act may be repealed. This may be because the law in the Act is wholly redundant. It may be because piecemeal amendment would be too complex, and it is expedient to repeal it and then re-enact any relevant parts of it that are still to apply. An Act may be repealed in part, the part being several sections, a section, a subsection, a paragraph, or a mere word or phrase. In sources such as *Halsbury's Statutes* that reprint statutes as amended, the repealed parts will be indication by '…' as marks of omission. Acts being repealed are often listed in a Schedule at the back of the new Act. The Schedule will have a parent section in the body of the Act, but that section will just say something like 'The enactments mentioned in Schedule 3 are repealed to the extent specified in that Schedule'. As a consequence, where the authority for the repeal is given in the various sources discussed below, reference will be made both to a section number and a Schedule number. Amendment takes the form of either substitution or insertion. In either case, it again may be anything from a part of several sections to a single word. Where substitution occurs, there is no disruption to the structure and numbering of the original Act. However, where new matter is inserted and it occupies a whole subsection, section or larger unit, then it has to be numbered. The general practice is to use upper case letters in conjunction with the section number. So a new section to be inserted between ss 14 and 15 of the old Act, will be s 14A. New subsections that have to be inserted between existing subsections will be lettered in the same way: s 14(3A), etc. With very frequently amended statutes, such as the Income and Corporation Taxes Act 1988, multiple letters have to be used for successive insertions: so ss 257BA, 257BB, 257BC come between s 257A and s 257B (see figure 3.3). Where there have been substitutions or insertions *Halsbury's Statutes* will put them in square brackets (see figure 3.2). These techniques of partial repeal and amendment, which are the techniques most commonly used nowadays, are said to be direct and textual. If someone such as the publisher of *Halsbury's* has been kind enough to reprint the Act as amended, it can be read in one place. A different technique of altering statute law, used more frequently in the past, does not make direct textual amendments, but says in effect that the old Act should be read subject to the new one – both Acts have to be looked at and the combined effect understood. Bear in mind that Acts may be amended, and in the case of Deregulation Orders (see para **4.78**) even repealed, by statutory instrument.

3.52 *Halsbury's Statutes* or *Current Law Legislation Citators* are the printed sources to use for checking whether a particular statute has been amended or repealed. My own preference is to use *Halsbury's* first, then to check the statute citator in the *Current Law Statutes* looseleaf service volume, which is updated monthly, as a cross-check on the last noter-up to *Halsbury's*. Electronic sources are needed to check for amendments more recent still.

3.53 Find the statute in *Halsbury's* by looking either in the alphabetical list or the chronological list of statutes, which are both in the Table and Index volume. Having found the statute in the main work you will have the text as amended at the date that particular volume was issued. The source of any amendment, indicated by square brackets or marks of omission in the text, will be given in the notes (see figure 3.2). Check for later amendments first in the annual cumulative supplement under the same volume number and page as the main work, and then in the looseleaf noter-up service, which is arranged in the same way. The full text of amendments referred to in the supplement and noter-up may be in the Current Statutes Service volumes (see figure 3.3).

3.54 If you were unable to find the statute in *Halsbury's Statutes* in the first place, the implication is that it has been wholly repealed (or that it is a Local Act, or an Act applying only to Scotland, both of which eventualities will usually be apparent from the title). Look then at the *Halsbury's Statutes Citator* volume for details of what repealed it (and if still not found, look at the *Chronological Table of Statutes*: see para **3.59**). You could start with the *Halsbury's Statutes Citator* rather than the main work as described above, but there is no particular virtue in doing so, unless all that you need to know is the bare fact of whether a statute has been amended or repealed, not the text of any amendments.

3.55 The *Current Law Statute Citator* is arranged chronologically by chapter number. All statutes, of whatever date, that have been amended or repealed in the current year will be listed and the chapter number and section (but not the short title) of the amending or repealing statute (or SI) given. The appearance of the latest citator in the looseleaf service file is the same as the bound volumes (see figure 3.4). You can use the earlier bound volumes of the *Current Law Statute Citator* instead of *Halsbury's Statutes*, but since you just get a bald statement of the year, chapter number and section of the amending statute, which then have to be looked at as a separate exercise, it is usually much less convenient than starting with *Halsbury's Statutes*. But you would have to use the *Current Law Statute Citators* for the whole job, if you had an Act applying only to Scotland. You could also use them if you wanted to check how and when a statute no longer in force was amended or repealed, though for that job the *Chronological Table of Statutes* or *Halsbury's Statutes Citator* would generally be preferable.

3.56 The electronic version of the *Current Law Legislation Citator* does not generally, in the writer's opinion, have much to offer over the printed versions and indeed in some respects they are more difficult to use. But they are more current, and if for that reason you are going to use them anyway, you might wish to skip using the printed version at all (though the writer would still start with the printed version of *Halsbury's Statutes*). The drawbacks to the electronic version are that this type of information is not so easily viewed on a screen and you have to find the record for the particular section, and furthermore there is the hazard of separate records for the whole Act or parts of the Act as well for each section – where this arises it is much more easily spotted on the printed page. Note that at the moment the electronic version, unlike the case citator, only goes back to 1989.

3.57 Justis Statutes can be used. Though you are not given the text as amended, as you get in *Halsbury's Statutes*, you do have the full text of the amending statute, and the linking system works well. For currency, the Internet as opposed to the CD-ROM version is preferable. But as good as any of the electronic services is Lawtel,

Figure 3.2 Halsbury's Statutes: *main work.*

National Health Service Act 1977, s 43: *text as amended at date of reissue. Amended text is given in square brackets, and the notes give the source of the amendments.*

NATIONAL HEALTH SERVICE ACT 1977 s 43A

(3)(*d*), (*e*) shall have effect in relation to that determination or application as if the National Health Service and Community Care Act 1990, s 12(3), had not come into force; see the National Health Service and Community Care Act 1990 (Commencement No 1) Order 1990, SI 1990/1329, art 3(1).

---

43 Persons authorised to provide pharmaceutical services

(1) No arrangements shall be made by [a Family Practitioner Committee] (except as may be provided by [or under] regulations) with a medical practitioner or dental practitioner under which he is required or agrees to provide pharmaceutical services to any person to whom he is rendering general medical services or general dental services.

(2) No arrangements for the dispensing of medicines shall be made (except as may be provided by [or under] regulations) with persons other than persons who are registered pharmacists, or are persons lawfully conducting a retail pharmacy business in accordance with section 69 of the Medicines Act 1968 and who undertake that all medicines supplied by them under the arrangements made under this Part of this Act shall be dispensed either by or under the direct supervision of a registered pharmacist.

[(3) No arrangements for the provision of pharmaceutical services falling within section 41(*d*) above shall be made with persons other than those who are registered pharmacists or are of a prescribed description.]

NOTES

The words in the first pair of square brackets in sub-s (1) were substituted by the Family Practitioner Committees (Consequential Modifications) Order 1985, SI 1985/39, art 7(15).

The words in the second pair of square brackets in sub-s (1), and the words in square brackets in sub-s (2), were inserted by the Health Services Act 1980, s 21(2).

Sub-s (3) was added by the National Health Service and Community Care Act 1990, s 66(1), Sch 9, para 18(2).

Sub-s (1): Family Practitioner Committee. See s 10 ante and the note thereto.

Arrangements made under this Part. See s 41 ante.

Definitions. For "dental practitioner", "medical practitioner", "medicine", "prescribed", "registered pharmacist" and "regulations", see s 128(1) post; for "general dental services", see s 35(1), (1A) ante; for "general medical services", see s 29(1), (1A) ante; for "pharmaceutical services", see s 41 ante.

Medicines Act 1968, s 69. See Vol 28, title Medicine and Pharmacy (Pt 2).

Regulations under this section. The National Health Service (General Medical and Pharmaceutical Services) Regulations 1974, SI 1974/160, regs 29B, 30, 30A (as substituted for the original reg 30 by SI 1983/313), as amended by SI 1985/290, SI 1985/955 and SI 1990/1757.

See also SI 1974/160, Schs 3A, 3B, as inserted by SI 1985/290 and amended by SI 1985/540, SI 1986/381, SI 1986/1486, SI 1987/5, SI 1987/1425, SI 1988/1106, SI 1988/2297, SI 1989/1897, SI 1990/2513 and SI 1991/555.

For general provisions as to regulations, see s 126 post.

Savings. See s 129, Sch 14, para 7 post.

[Remuneration for services]

[43A Regulations as to remunerations

(1) Regulations shall make provision as to the remuneration to be paid to persons who provide general medical services, general dental services, general ophthalmic services or pharmaceutical services under this Part of this Act [and may include provision for the remuneration of persons providing those services in respect of the instruction of any person in matters relating to those services].

(2) Subject to sections 29(4) and 35(2) above, remuneration under the regulations may consist of payments by way of—

    (*a*) salary;
    (*b*) fees;
    (*c*) allowances;

Figure 3.3 Halsbury's Statutes.

VOLUME 30 (1991 Reissue)   NATIONAL HEALTH SERVICE

 Section 43

In sub-s (1), for the words "a Family Practitioner Committee" there are substituted the words "a Health Authority" by the Health Authorities Act 1995, s 2(1), Sch 1, Pt I, paras 1, 31, Vol 30, title National Health Service.

Sub-ss (2A)–(2C) are inserted and in sub-s (3) after the number "41(d)" there are inserted the words ", or additional pharmaceutical services provided in accordance with a direction under section 41A," by the National Health Service (Primary Care) Act 1997, ss 29(1), 41(10), Sch 2, Pt I, paras 3, 14, Vol 30, title National Health Service.

Annual Cumulative Supplement
Section 43 amended by insertion of new subsections, which are lettered.

NATIONAL HEALTH SERVICE (PRIMARY CARE) ACT 1997 s 30

 29 Authorised provision of pharmaceutical services by medical practitioners

(1) In section 43 of the 1977 Act, after subsection (2), insert—

"(2A) Regulations shall provide for the preparation and publication by a Health Authority of one or more lists of medical practitioners who undertake to provide drugs, medicines or listed appliances in the Authority's area.

(2B) In subsection (2A) "listed" has the same meaning as in section 41.

(2C) The regulations shall include provision for the removal of an entry from a list in prescribed circumstances."

Current Statutes Service volume
The full text of the amending Act.

VOLUME 30 (1991 Reissue)   NATIONAL HEALTH SERVICE

 National Health Service Act 1977 (c 49) — continued
Section 43

Sub-s (2A): for "in the Authority's area" substitute "under arrangements with the Authority" as from a day to be appointed (Health and Social Care Act 2001, s 43(5), Vol 30, title National Health Service).

 Sub-ss (2BA), (2BB): insert after sub-s (2B) as from a day to be appointed (Health and Social Care Act 2001, s 20(1), (7), Vol 30, title National Health Service).

Looseleaf Noter-up
Further amendments to s 43 by way of insertion, which are double-lettered. The text of s 20(1) of the Health and Social Care Act 2001 is again in the Current Statutes Service volume.

Figure 3.4 Current Law: *statute citator bound volume. The latest parts in the looseleaf service file to Current Law Statutes are similar in appearance.*

STATUTE CITATOR 1996–1999   **1982**

CAP.   CAP.

1982—cont.

45. Civic Government (Scotland) Act 1982— cont.
Sch.1, applied: 1996 c.58 s.33
Sch.1 para.4, see *Douglas v City of Glasgow DC* 1996 S.L.T. 413
Sch.2A, added: 1998 c.37 s.24, Sch.1
Sch.2A, referred to: SI 1998/2327 Art.4
Sch.3 para.3, amended: 1999 c.11 s.10, Sch.
Sch.3 para.3, repealed (in part): 1999 c.11 s.10, Sch.

46. Employment Act 1982
s.20, repealed: 1996 c.18 Sch.3 Part I
s.21, repealed (in part): 1996 c.18 Sch.3 Part I
Sch.2 para.1, repealed: 1996 c.18 Sch.3 Part I
Sch.2 para.2, repealed: 1996 c.18 Sch.3 Part I
Sch.2 para.3, repealed: 1996 c.18 Sch.3 Part I
Sch.2 para.4, repealed: 1996 c.18 Sch.3 Part I
Sch.2 para.5, repealed: 1996 c.18 Sch.3 Part I
Sch.2 para.6, repealed (in part): 1996 c.18 Sch.3 Part I
Sch.2 para.7, repealed (in part): 1996 c.18 Sch.3 Part I
Sch.3 para.1, repealed: 1996 c.18 Sch.3 Part I
Sch.3 para.2, repealed: 1996 c.18 Sch.3 Part I
Sch.3 para.4, repealed: 1996 c.18 Sch.3 Part I
Sch.3 para.6, repealed: 1996 c.18 Sch.3 Part I
Sch.3 para.7, repealed: 1996 c.17 Sch.3 Part I
Sch.3 para.8, repealed: 1996 c.17 Sch.3 Part I
Sch.3 para.9, repealed: 1996 c.17 Sch.3 Part I
Sch.3 para.15, repealed: 1996 c.18 Sch.3 Part I
Sch.3 para.21, repealed: 1996 c.18 Sch.3 Part I
Sch.3 para.22, repealed: 1996 c.18 Sch.3 Part I
Sch.3 para.23, repealed: 1996 c.18 Sch.3 Part I
Sch.3 para.25, repealed: 1996 c.18 Sch.3 Part I
Sch.3 para.26, repealed: 1996 c.18 Sch.3 Part I
Sch.3 para.27, repealed (in part): 1996 c.18 Sch.3 Part I
Sch.3 para.28, repealed: 1996 c.18 Sch.3 Part I
Sch.3 para.29, repealed: 1996 c.18 Sch.3 Part I
Sch.3 para.30, repealed: 1996 c.18 Sch.3 Part I
Sch.4, repealed: 1996 c.18 Sch.3 Part I

48. Criminal Justice Act 1982
see *R. v St Helens Justices Ex p. Jones* [1999] 2 All E.R. 73 (QBD), Brooke, L.J.
s.1, see *R. v Oldham Justices Ex p. Cawley* [1997] Q.B. 1 (QBD), Simon Brown, L.J.
s.1, amended: 1998 c.37 s.119, Sch.8 para.49
s.1, applied: 1997 c.43 s.40
s.1, restored (in part): 1996 c.25 s.44, Sch.5 para.1
s.1A, see *R. v Dover Youth Court Ex p. K* [1999] 1 W.L.R. 27 (QBD), Simon Brown, L.J.; see *R. v Secretary of State for the Home Department Ex p. J* Times, December 2, 1998 (CA), Lord Woolf, M.R.
s.1A, amended: 1997 c.43 Sch.4 para.11, 1998 c.37 s.119, Sch.8 para.50
s.1A, referred to: SI 1999/3426 Art.3, Art.4
s.1A, repealed (in part): 1998 c.37 s.119, s.120, Sch.8 para.50, Sch.10
s.1B, see *R. v AM (A Juvenile)* [1998] 1 W.L.R. 363 (CA (Crim Div)), Lord Bingham of Cornhill, L.C.J.; see *R. v Foran (James Victor)* [1996] 1 Cr. App. R. (S.) 149 (CA (Crim Div)), Hooper, J.; see *R. v O (A Juvenile)* [1999] 1 Cr. App. R. (S.) 35 (CA (Crim Div)), Ian Kennedy, J.
s.1B, amended: 1998 c.37 s.116
s.1B, referred to: SI 1999/3426 Art.3
s.1B, repealed: 1998 c.37 s.73, s.120, Sch.10
s.1C, see *R. v Accrington Youth Court Ex p. Flood* [1998] 1 W.L.R. 156 (QBD), Sedley, J.

48. Criminal Justice Act 1982—cont.
s.1C, amended: 1998 c.37 s.119, s.120, Sch.8 para.51, Sch.10
s.1C, applied: 1998 c.37 s.79
s.1C, referred to: SI 1999/3426 Art.3, Art.4
s.3, amended: 1998 c.37 s.106, s.119, s.120, Sch.7 para.33, Sch.8 para.52, Sch.10, 1999 c.22 s.24, s.106, Sch.4 para.25, Sch.15 Part I
s.3, referred to: SI 1998/2327 Art.2
s.8, applied: 1997 c.43 s.2, s.34, 1997 c.51 s.4, 1998 c.37 s.73
s.13, amended: 1998 c.37 s.106, Sch.7 para.34
s.13, applied: SI 1999/728 r.57
s.13, referred to: SI 1999/728 r.57
s.16, amended: 1998 c.37 s.106, Sch.7 para.35
s.16, applied: 1997 c.43 s.44
s.17, amended: 1997 c.43 s.36, 1998 c.37 s.68, s.70, s.106, Sch.5 para.5, Sch.7 para.36
s.17, applied: 1998 c.37 s.68, s.70, Sch.5 para.5
s.17, repealed (in part): 1998 c.37 s.68, s.70, Sch.5 para.5
s.18, amended: 1998 c.37 s.68, s.70, s.106, Sch.5 para.5, Sch.7 para.37, 1999 c.22 s.90, Sch.13 para.123
s.18, applied: 1998 c.37 s.68, s.70, Sch.5 para.5, SI 1999/2784 Sch. para.26
s.18, referred to: SI 1998/2327 Art.2
s.18, repealed (in part): 1998 c.37 s.106, s.120, Sch.7 para.37, Sch.10
s.19, amended: 1998 c.37 s.68, s.70, s.106, s.119, s.120, Sch.5 para.5, Sch.7 para.38, Sch.8 para.53, Sch.10
s.19, applied: 1998 c.37 s.68, s.70, Sch.5 para.5
s.19, referred to: SI 1998/2327 Art.2
s.66, referred to: SI 1998/2327 Art.2
s.66, repealed (in part): 1998 c.37 s.120, Sch.10
s.72, amended: 1999 c.23 s.67, Sch.4 para.10
Sch.3, repealed (in part): 1996 c.16 Sch.9 Part I, 1996 c.56 Sch.38 Part I
Sch.13 Part III, amended: SI 1996/3160 (NI.24) Sch.5 para.12
Sch.14, referred to: SI 1998/2327 Art.2
Sch.14 para.8, referred to: SI 1998/277 Art.3
Sch.14 para.28, repealed: 1998 c.37 s.120, Sch.10

49. Transport Act 1982
Commencement Orders: SI 1996/1943 Art.2
s.8, amended: 1999 c.12 s.7, Sch.para.1
s.10, amended: 1999 c.12 s.7, Sch.para.2
s.70, amended: 1999 c.10 s.1, Sch.1 para.6
s.76, enabling: SI 1996/1943

50. Insurance Companies Act 1982
see *DR Insurance Co v Central National Insurance Co* [1996] 1 Lloyd's Rep. 74 (QBD), Martin Moor-Bick Q.C.
applied: SI 1996/1669 Reg.21, SI 1996/2102, SI 1996/3127 Reg.6, SI 1997/2781 Art.2, SI 1998/2888 Reg.3
referred to: SI 1996/1669 Reg.2, SI 1997/1183 (NI.12) Sch.1 para.5, 1998 c.11 Sch.7 para.3
Class I, applied: SI 1998/1870 Reg.9
Class III, applied: SI 1998/1870 Reg.9
Part II, applied: SI 1996/546 Reg.10, SI 1996/943 Reg.2, Reg.22, SI 1996/946 Reg.4, SI 1996/3011 Reg.3, Reg.4, SI 1997/653 Reg.10, SI 1998/612 Reg.10, SI 1999/589 Reg.10, SI 1999/1082 Art.R1, Sch.6 para.5, Sch.6 para.8
Part II, referred to: SI 1996/2102 Art.3, Art.4, 1997 c.16 Sch.12 para.18, SI 1998/2842 Art.2, Sch. para.65

245

particularly for currency. Having retrieved the record for the Act in question, there is a 'Statutory Status Table' button. The table clearly sets out sections that have been amended with links to the full text of the amending statute. The main limitation of Lawtel is that it only covers Acts back to 1987.

3.58 Lexis or Legislation Direct, if you subscribe to either, are other possibilities. They have data in common with *Halsbury's Statutes*, but should be more up to date. They may be particularly useful where the text of an Act has been recently amended by more than one Act. What may require four steps in the printed *Halsbury's Statutes*, may be found in one step. The usefulness of Westlaw UK will depend on whether the statute is in a subject area currently covered.

3.59 If a statute was not in the main work of *Halsbury's Statutes*, and is also not in *Halsbury's Statutes Citator*, then the next place to look is the *Chronological Table of the Statutes*, which covers every statute from 1235. It should be there, in italic, indicating that it is wholly repealed, with the year and chapter number of the Act that *finally* repealed it. What are not given are any Acts that partly repealed it or amended it before it became completely extinct. Though for reasons of currency (see para **3.37**), it should not be used to establish the present status of an Act, if an Act was still in force in part (its title is given in bold) then set out are all the amendments and part repeals, as at the date of the edition. See, for example, the Royal Marriages Act 1772 (12 Geo 3 c 11) in figure 3.5. For the purposes of the Abdication Declaration Act 1936 (c 3 of the parliamentary session that spanned the first – and last – year of the reign of Edward VIII and first year of the reign of George VI), it was excluded. Section 2 was partly repealed by the Statute Law Revision Act 1888 and s 3 was repealed by the Criminal Law Act 1967. Otherwise, it was still in force. Being an official source, the information on amendments and repeals is authoritative, even if it is not up-to-date. Although for practical purposes it rarely arises – *Halsbury's Statutes* and so on are perfectly reliable – if you did want the reassurance of the equivalent authoritative information as is provided in the *Chronological Table* but of more recent date, you could see whether any annual official bound volumes of the Public General Acts have been issued since the last edition of the *Chronological Table*. The Tables and Index volume includes an 'Effects of legislation table'. That lists all Acts – both Public General and Local, of whatever date – that have been repealed, amended or otherwise affected by any legislation, including SIs, passed during that year.

3.60 In closing this section it perhaps ought to be emphasised that the tool *Is it in Force?* is *not* designed to answer the question 'Is it *still* in force?' which has been the subject of this part. Seeing *Is it in Force?*, with its title in large letters on the spine, sitting next to *Halsbury's Statutes* on the shelves, the new student hoping to check whether an Act has been amended or repealed, may think they have found the answer to their prayers, and may be fortified in that hope by seeing that some Acts or sections are indeed listed as 'repealed'. But this is simply because, being a guide to commencements, it has to be explained why no commencement information is given for those Acts or sections. Where this is so, what did the repealing is not stated, and of course nothing is said about any amendments to sections that are still in force.

Is it in force yet?

3.61 Of the three formulas generally used in the section of an Act that says when it is to come into force described in para **3.5** above, the commonest is the third, where

Figure 3.5 Chronological Table of the Statutes.

· 158   CHRONOLOGICAL TABLE OF THE STATUTES

1771 (11 Geo. 3)

c. 90	*Ayre and Lanark roads*—rep. 54 G. 3. c. ccii
c. 91	*Lancaster roads*—rep. 1-2 G. 4. c. xv
c. 92	*Worcester and Warwick roads*—rep. 59 G. 3. c. xlix
c. 93	*Liverpool and Preston road*—rep. 26 G. 3. c. 126
c. 94	*Sussex roads*—rep. 2-3 W. 4. c. lvii
c. 95	*Salop and Denbigh roads*—rep., 19-20 V. c. ciii
c. 96	*Pembroke roads*—rep. 48 G. 3. c. cxxxix
c. 97	*Berks. and Wilts. roads*—rep. 21-2 V. c. xlii
c. 98	*Sussex roads*—rep. 53 G. 3. c. ccviii; 3-4 W. 4. c. xliv
c. 99	*Sussex roads*—rep. 11 G. 4 & 1 W. 4. c. civ

1772 (12 Geo. 3)

cc. 1,2	*Exportations and importation*—rep. SLR 1871
c. 3	*Land tax*—rep. SLR 1871
c. 4	*Mutiny*—rep. SLR 1871
c. 5	*Marine mutiny*—rep. SLR 1871
c. 6	*Malt duties*—rep. SLR 1871
c. 7	*East India Company*—rep. SLR 1871
c. 8	*Plymouth: improvement*—rep. 5 G. 4. c. xxii
c. 9	**Bedford level***
`	am.- Methwold Drainage, 1854 (c.clxxxviii), s.32
c. 10	*Papists*—rep. SLR 1871
c. 11	**Royal Marriages**
	excl—His Majesty's Declaration of Abdication, 1936 (1 E. 8 & 1. G. 6. c. 3), s. 1 (3)
	s. 2 rep. in pt—SLR 1888
	s. 3 rep—Crim Law, 1967 c. 58 s. 13, sch. 4 pt. I
c. 12	*Mutiny in America*—rep. SLR 1871
c. 13	*Militia pay*—rep. SLR 1871
c. 14	*Great Yarmouth: improvement*—rep. 5-6 W. 4. c. xlix
c. 15	*Edinburgh: improvement*—rep. 11-2 V. c. cxiii
c. 16	*Port Glasgow Harbour*—rep. 27-8 V. c. cxl
c. 17	*London: streets*—rep. St. Pancras Improvement, 1812 (c.lxxiv), s.32; 5 G. 4. c. cxxv
c. 18	*Chatham: streets*—rep. Loc. Govt. Supplemental, 1860 (No. 2) c. 118
c. 19	*Crown lands in Fenchurch Street, London*—rep. SL(R) 1978 c. 45 s. 1 (1), sch. 1 pt. XIV
c. 20	*Felony and Piracy*—rep. SLR 1948
c. 21	*Municipal corporations (mandamus)*—rep. SLR 1887
c. 22	**Ayr Harbour***
c. 23	*Relief of insolvent debtors, etc*—rep. SLR 1871
c. 24	*Dockyards, etc., Protection*—rep. Crim. Damage 1971 c. 48 ss. 11 (2) (8) 12 (6), sch. pt. III; (I. of M.) SL(R) 1993 c. 50 s.1(1), sch.1 pt.1
c. 25	*Naval prize*—rep. Naval Prize Acts Repeal, 1864 c. 23 s. 1
c. 26	**Drainage: Cambridge, Isle of Ely***
	rep. in pt.—Huntingdonshire and Cambridgeshire Drainage, 1849 (c.xxiv), ss.1,2
	ext.—Huntingdonshire and Cambridgeshire Drainage, 1800 (c.xl), s.1
	restr.—Land Drainage (Benwick Internal Drainage District) Provisional O. Conf., 1941 (c. viii), sch. s. 3, schs. 1, 2
c. 27	**Drainage: Isle of Ely***
c. 28	**Watford Churchyard and Workhouse***
c. 29	*Spurn Point lighthouse*—rep. SLR 1861
c. 30	*Salaries of Justices of Chester, etc.*—rep. SLR 1861
c. 31	*Indemnity*—rep. SLR 1871
cc. 32,33	*Importation*—rep. SLR 1871
c. 34	*Workhouse, Westminster*—rep. S.R. & O., 1901/278
c. 35	*Crown lands at Richmond, Surrey*—rep. SL(R) 1978 c. 45 s. 1(1), sch. 1 pt. XIV
c. 36	*Richmond chapel, Lancs*—rep. 4 E. 7. c. c. s. 25, sch. 2
c. 37	**Market Weighton***
	saved in pt.—York and North Midland Railway (Canals Purchase), 1847 (c.ccxvi), ss.10,43
	am—S.I., 1983/52

a date is not given in the Act but will be set in due course. In its simplest form such a section will typically read:

> This Act shall come into force on such day or days as the Secretary of State may by order made by statutory instrument appoint, and different days may be appointed for different purposes.

There are a number of points to note. First the whole Act need not necessarily be brought into force on the same day. Frequently Acts are brought into force bit by bit. Secondly, the orders, known as commencement orders, are SIs (in modern times, there has only been one Act where the commencement orders were not made by SI: see para **3.70**). Thirdly, a section or sections of any Act may be brought into force on different days for different purposes. A section may be brought into force partially for a limited purpose on one date, and only be brought fully into force at a later date. One common example is where a section or part of an Act contains regulation-making powers, and it is necessary to allow the Secretary of State, or whoever, to get on and make them in advance of the substantive provisions in the same section or part coming into force. The operation of the Act might depend on the regulations, so there would be no point in bringing the substantive provisions into force unless the regulations had already been made. Another example of partial commencement is where the Act has a Schedule with a long list of repeals. If the substance of the Act is being brought into force in stages, then it is obviously necessary to wait until the new provision replacing the repealed Act has been brought in before effecting the repeal. Successive commencement orders will name the Acts in the Schedule whose repeal is to be effected at particular dates. The general parent section to the Schedule will likewise be partially commenced for the purposes of effecting the named repeals.

3.62 Often, however, the commencement section in an Act is more complicated than the example quoted. It may be provided that some sections of the Act come into force on the day it is passed, and others on a day to be appointed. An Act may have no commencement section at all – here the legislative draftsman is being economic, and is simply relying on the Interpretation Act, which says that unless the contrary is provided for in the Act, it comes into force on Royal Assent. Sometimes, however, the draftsman includes a commencement section but declines to say in it when or how every section in the Act is to be commenced, leaving those sections on which he is silent to come into force on Royal Assent by the presumption of the Interpretation Act – which seems a false economy. With devolution, there is a further nightmare. Acts may be commenced on different dates in relation to England or to Wales or to Scotland. In the case of Acts applying to Scotland, even if made at Westminster, the commencement order may not be an SI, but an SSI – a Scottish statutory instrument. An innovation used by some Acts of the Scottish Parliament, and also now at Westminster (for example, the Freedom of Information Act 2000) is the 'long-stop' commencement provision. The Act may be brought into force conventionally in stages by commencement order, but a date is set (2005 in the case of the Freedom of Information Act) when the Act will come into force even if the necessary commencement orders have not been made. Commencement orders thus have to be read carefully to see to which jurisdiction they apply and whether the sections are being brought in force fully or only partially for particular purposes. A further matter requiring careful perusal is whether the commencement provisions, in the Act or in the commencement order, are subject to any transitional or savings provisions. Especially with large new pieces of legislation, there may be complicated arrangements pending the old legislation going and the new coming in. Savings are where the old legislation is deemed to remain in force for certain purposes, notwithstanding its repeal. A typical such purpose is the making of regulations, so that secondary legislation made under the old Act can remain in force until there has been time to make secondary legislation under the new Act.

3.63 There are a number of tools for finding commencement dates. These can be useful, not only for letting you know whether a commencement order has been made, but also for 'translating' complicated commencement provisions in the order or in the Act. *Is it in Force?* is perhaps the best place to start – the commencement dates for every unrepealed Act of the last 25 years (except Finance Acts: see para **3.71** below) are clearly set out section by section. An Internet version is available as a free service on the **Butterworths Law Direct** website, which is continuously updated. But, depending when the Act was passed, you may wish to use the hard copy first and then log on to the Internet (or use alternative electronic sources) only if a commencement date has not yet been given in the hard copy and you wish to check the latest position. You will usually find the main work, one softbound volume reissued annually, next to *Halsbury's Statutes*. It is arranged by year and alphabetically within each year. In the example in figure 3.6, it will be seen that the Care Standards Act 2000 received Royal Assent on 20 July 2000. Commencement provisions are contained in s 122 of the Act, and five commencement orders have been made to date. One of the five is of general application, two apply to England only and two apply to Wales only. The date of entry into force of each section and whether the date relates to England or Wales is given with the authority – either the section number of the Act or the SI number of the commencement order. Some sections, for example, ss 42–53, are not in force at all. Others, for example s 54(1), are in force only for certain purposes, but not otherwise.

3.64 The looseleaf noter-up volume of *Halsbury's Statutes* contains a supplement to *Is it in Force?* It is in two parts. The first part adds commencement dates to the statutes listed in the main *Is it in Force?* volume that have been announced since it was last issued. The second part contains commencement dates for statutes passed in the current year.

3.65 The looseleaf noter-up to *Halsbury's Statutes* is issued six times a year. If your Act or section of your Act has not been commenced according to the noter-up, the best policy may be to go next straight to an electronic source, which could obviously be the web version of *Is it in Force?* An equally good alternative, which you could start with if you prefer, is **Lawtel**. If you find the Act from the Statutory Law part of the database, and access the 'Statutory Status Table' at the head of the Act, commencement dates will be given section by section. However, if you wanted to stay with hard copy, sometimes slightly more up-to-date than *Is it in Force?* in the *Halsbury's Statutes* noter-up volume is the table of Commencement of Statutes in the monthly parts of *Current Law*. It is cumulative through the year so it is only necessary to look in the latest monthly part, but remember that it only lists commencement dates announced during the current calendar year. Until about June each year, when the *Current Law Yearbook* for the previous year is issued and the monthly parts are replaced, the table of commencement dates in the December issue of the previous year's monthly parts can be referred to. The table is illustrated in figure 3.7. The layout is slightly different from *Is it in Force?*, but similar information is given, though where a section is brought into force partially for certain purposes ('part') you would need to look at the SI for the particulars. Likewise it does not indicate that dates differ for England and Wales. The references to 'C.L.' in the

Figure 3.6   Is it in Force?

2000   933

Carers and Disabled Children Act 2000 (c 16)—*cont*

s 9	1 April 2001 (E) (except in so far as it relates to the provision of vouchers) (SI 2001/510)
	Not in force (otherwise)
10, 11	1 April 2001 (E) (SI 2001/510)
	Not in force (otherwise)
12	20 Jul 2000 (RA)

Care Standards Act 2000 (c 14)

RA: 20 Jul 2000

Commencement provision: s 122; Care Standards Act 2000 (Commencement No 1) Order 2000, SI 2000/2544; Care Standards Act 2000 (Commencement No 1 (England) and Transitional Provisions) Order 2000, SI 2000/2795; Care Standards Act 2000 (Commencement No 1) (Wales) Order 2000, SI 2000/2992; Care Standards Act 2000 (Commencement No 2 (England) and Transitional Provisions) Order 2001, SI 2001/290[1]; Care Standards Act 2000 (Commencement No 2 and Transitional Provisions) (Wales) Order 2001, SI 2001/139[2]

s 1–38		*Not in force*
39		19 Feb 2001 (E) (for purposes of enabling an application for registration to be made under Registered Homes Act 1984, s 23(3)) (SI 2001/290)
		19 Mar 2001 (E) (otherwise) (SI 2001/290)
		Not in force (otherwise)
40		15 Oct 2000 (E) (for purposes only of enabling application for registration to be made under Children Act 1989, Sch 6, para 1(1), (2))
		1 Jan 2001 (E) (otherwise) (SI 2000/2795)
		1 Feb 2001 (W) (for purposes only of enabling application for registration to be made under the Children Act 1989, Sch 6, para 1(1), (2)) (SI 2001/139)
		28 Feb 2001 (W) (otherwise) (SI 2001/139)
41		1 Jan 2001 (E) (SI 2000/2795)
		28 Feb 2001 (W) (SI 2001/139)
42–53		*Not in force*
54	(1)	1 April 2001 (W) (so far as relates to Care Council in Wales) (SI 2000/2992)
		Not in force (otherwise)
	(2)	*Not in force*
	(3)–(7)	1 April 2001 (W) (so far as relates to Care Council for Wales) (SI 2000/2992)
		Not in force (otherwise)
55		1 April 2001 (W) (SI 2000/2992)
		Not in force (otherwise)
56–69		*Not in force*

authority column after the SI numbers are to the month and paragraph of *Current Law* where the SIs were originally digested. Another hard copy alternative to the monthly parts of *Current Law* is the Commencement of Statutes section in the looseleaf noter-up volume of *Halsbury's Laws* (as distinct from the *Statutes*), which is issued monthly, and so will state the position more or less at the same point in time as *Current Law* – you may want to check both.

3.66 If you had to check for any commencement orders since the last monthly issue of *Current Law* by manual means (for example, if the computers have crashed) there is a way to do it, which would probably be quicker and more reliable than simply looking at every single SI on the shelf, though still fairly tedious. The method would be to check every *Daily List* issued by the Stationery Office back to the relevant date. All SIs issued on a particular day are listed at the end. The process is not quite as time-consuming as it sounds because any commencement orders are given first in the SI section of each list – you do not have to read through the whole lot (see figure 3.8). The entry for the Criminal Justice and Court Services Act 2000 (Commencement No 7) Order 2001, which is illustrated, is also instructive for another reason. The entry appears in the *Daily List* on 4 July, having been issued according to the body of the entry on 2 July, yet it brings into force provisions of the Act for some purposes on 20 June, and even the substantive provisions had been in force for two days – it is one thing to expect lawyers to be assiduous in ensuring they are up to date; it is another to expect them to be psychic. (Some Welsh commencement orders made by the Welsh Assembly have provided even more extreme examples.)

3.67 The sources described above are usually more than sufficient to give you the answer. But as always there are further alternatives, which you might use, for instance if for some reason any of the tools above were not available or if you wanted to double-check. The electronic version of the *Current Law Legislation Citator* is one. All commencement orders made under an Act are listed at the top (you will then need to look at the orders to see what they say). Another is to use any of numerous sources which index or provide the full text of SIs (see paras **3.87** and **3.89**), for example, Badger, Justis SIs on the web, the HMSO site, Justis Parlianet, UKOP on the web. From the illustration already given from the *Daily List* (figure 3.8) it will be seen that SIs that are commencement orders simply have the name of the Act as their title. Thus they are easily found. If there are several commencement orders – very large Acts may eventually have ten or 15 – the trick is to look first at the most recent. Usually the explanatory note at the back summarises the effect of all the *preceding* commencement orders (but not the commencements made by the order you are looking at) – see figures 3.9 and 3.10. If the explanatory note does not give such a table, try the next most recent commencement order.

3.68 If you wish to check commencement dates before the current year using *Current Law* rather than *Is it in Force?*, you will need to use the *Statute Citators*. These will not give actual commencement dates, but the SI numbers for all commencement orders are given – the orders themselves have to be then consulted to establish the actual dates. It is the current practice for all the commencement orders to be given at the head of the entry for the Act, but for earlier Acts they are only listed under the relevant enabling section of the Act – you will thus need to know which section of the Act contains the commencement provisions. As well as in the statute citator section, the *Current Law Legislation Citator*s include an alphabetical list of all SIs; as the title of those that are commencement orders is the name of the Act they can be easily spotted there as well. An alternative to the table in current monthly parts of

Figure 3.7 Current Law: *monthly digest – table of commencement of statutes.*

DATES OF COMMENCEMENT–STATUTES

Statute	Commencement	Authority
Armed Forces Act 1996 (c.46)		
ss.3, 4, 35 (remainder), Sch.7 (remainder)	May 1, 2001	SI 2001 1519 (C.54)
Budget (Scotland) Act 2001 (asp 4)		
All provisions	March 15, 2001	Royal Assent
All provisions	March 15, 2001	Royal Assent
Budget Act (Northern Ireland) 2001 (c.7)		
All provisions	March 20, 2001	Royal Assent
Capital Allowances Act 2001 (c.2)		
s.579	March 22, 2001	Royal Assent
All provisions	April 1, 2001	s.579(1)(b)
All provisions	April 6, 2001	s.579(1)(a)
Care Standards Act 2000 (c.14) ◄		
s.6(3) (part), Sch.1 para.1 (part), 6 (part)	March 16, 2001	SI 2001 1193 (C.39) [2001] 5 C.L. 707
s.6 (part), Sch.1 (part)	April 9, 2001	SI 2001 1193 (C.39) [2001] 5 C.L. 707
s.23(1)-(3)	March 2, 2001	SI 2001 731 (C.26) [2001] 4 C.L. 602
s.39 (part)	March 19, 2001	SI 2001 290 (C.17) [2001] 3 C.L. 640
s.39 (part)	February 19, 2001	SI 2001 290 (C.17) [2001] 3 C.L. 640
s.40 (part)	February 1, 2001	SI 2001 139 (W.5) (C.7) [2001] 3 C.L. 639
ss.40 (part), 41 (part), 116 (part)	February 28, 2001	SI 2001 139 (W.5) (C.7) [2001] 3 C.L. 639
ss.79(1)-(4), 114, 115	March 16, 2001	SI 2001 1210 (C.41) [2001] 5 C.L. 708
s.98	April 1, 2001	SI 2001 1193 (C.39) [2001] 5 C.L. 707
Carers and Disabled Children Act 2000 (c.16)		
ss.1-2 (part), 4-6 (part), 7(1)-(3) (part), 8-11 (part)	April 1, 2001	SI 2001 510 (C.20) [2001] 4 C.L. 603
Child Support, Pensions and Social Security Act 2000 (c.19)		
s.11	February 15, 2001	SI 2000 3354 (C.112) [2001] 2 C.L. 523
ss.13-15, 22(1)-(3), 26 (part), Sch.3 para.11 (2)	January 31, 2001	SI 2000 3354 (C.112) [2001] 2 C.L. 523
ss.16, 17	April 2, 2001	SI 2000 3354 (C.112) [2001] 2 C.L. 523
ss.26 (part), 56 (part), 67, Sch.6 (remainder), Sch.3 para.13(1) (3), Sch.5 para.11, Sch.9 PartI (part), PartVI	April 2, 2001	SI 2001 1252 (C.45) [2001] 5 C.L. 683
ss.30-31 (part), 33(1) (2) (part), (3) (4) (remainder), 34-35 (part), Sch.4 (part)	January 25, 2001	SI 2001 153 (C.8) [2001] 3 C.L. 641
ss.30-31 (remainder), 33(1) (2) (remainder), 34-35 (remainder), Sch.4 (remainder)	April 6, 2002	SI 2001 153 (C.8) [2001] 3 C.L. 641
s.32 (remainder)	April 9, 2001	SI 2001 153 (C.8) [2001] 3 C.L. 641
ss.37, 42 (part), 51, 53, 73 (part), Sch.9 (part),	December 1, 2000	SI 2000 3166 (C.101) [2001] 1 C.L. 520

340   CLI - daily on the Internet and monthly on CD Rom. Tel. 0171 449 1111

Figure 3.8 TSO Daily List.

---

453 **Severn Bridges Act 1992 account 1998-99:**
accounts, prepared pursuant to section 28 (1) (b) of the Severn Bridges Act 1992, showing the income and expenditure account for the year to 31 March 1999 and statement of assets and liabilities as at 31 March 1999 together with the report of the Comptroller and Auditor General thereon. – Department of the Environment, Transport and the Regions – Tim Matthews (accounting officer, Highways Agency) – 14p.: 30 cm. – In continuation of HCP 825 of 1999-00. – 0 10 290934 2 £4.40

454 **Severn Bridges Act 1992 account 1999-2000:**
accounts, prepared pursuant to section 28 (1) (b) of the Severn Bridges Act 1992 showing the income and expenditure account for the year to 31 March 2000 and statement of assets and liabilities as at 31 March 2000 together with the report of the Comptroller and Auditor General thereon. – Department of the Environment, Transport and the Regions – Tim Matthews (accounting officer, Highways Agency) – 13p.: 30 cm. – In continuation of HCP 453 of 2000-01. – 0 10 290932 6 £3.75

506 **Minutes of proceedings:**
[Thursday 7 December 2000 - Wednesday 9 May 2001]. – Trade and Industry Committee – Martin O'Neill (chairman) – xvi p.: 30 cm. – 0 10 239101 7 £4.00

House of Commons papers – Session 2001-02

21 **House of Commons Members' Fund accounts 1999-2000:**
accounts, of the House of Commons Members' Fund, prepared pursuant to c. 49, s. 3 (6), of the House of Commons Members' Fund Act 1939 for the year ended 30 September 2000, together with the report of the Comptroller and Auditor General thereon. – John Butterfill (chairman, Managing Trustees) – 15p.: 30 cm. – In continuation of HCP no. 527 of 1999-00. – 0 10 291034 0 £4.40

Parliamentary Debates (Hansard)

House of Commons official report – [6th series] – ISSN 03098826 – Daily, unrevised
[Session 2001-02] Vol. 371. No. 12. Monday 2 July 2001 – iv, [1], cols. 1-124, 1WH - 40WH,. 1W - 80W: 30 cm. – 0 215 50011 3 £5.00. Available on annual subscription £825.00 (2001 rate)

Weekly Hansard – [6th series] – ISSN 02618303 – Weekly, unrevised
[Session 2000-01] Vol. 370. Issue no. 1896. 25th June to 28th June 2001 – cols. 365-900, 17W - 182W: 30 cm. – 0 215 60001 0 £12.00 Annual subscription £420.00 (2001 rate)

House of Lords official report – [5th series] – ISSN 03098834 – Daily, unrevised
[Session 2000-01] Vol. 626. No. 9. Monday 2 July 2001 – cols. 619-764, WA 29 - WA 34: 30 cm. – 0 10 700902 1 £3.00 Available on subscription £430.00 (2001 rate)

Statutory Instruments

This list is printed under the authority and superintendence of the Controller of Her Majesty's Stationery Office, being the Queen's Printer of Acts of Parliament and Government Printer for Northern Ireland.

Issued on 3rd July 2001

Commencement orders (bringing into operation an act or part of an act.) 2001

2232 **The Criminal Justice and Court Services Act 2000**
(C.75) **(Commencement No. 7) Order 2001**
– 4p.: 30 cm. – Enabling power: Criminal Justice and Court Services Act 2000, s. 80. Bringing into operation various provisions of the 2000 Act on 20.06.2001, 02.07.2001, in accord. with art. 2– Issued: 02.07.2001. Made: 19.06.2001. Laid: -. Effect: None. Territorial extent & classification: E/W. General. – 0 11 029621 4 £1.75

Statutory instruments 2001

2070 **The Housing Grants (Additional Purposes) (Wales) Order**
(W.142)2001
– 4p.: 30 cm. – Enabling power: Housing Grants, Construction and Regeneration Act 1996, ss. 12 (1) (i), 17 (1) (i), 27 (1) (i), 146 (2). – Issued: 03.07.2001. Made: 24.05.2001. Laid: -. Coming into force: 01.07.2001. Effect: None. Territorial extent & classification: W. General. – In English and Welsh. – Welsh title: Gorchymyn Grantiau Tai (Dibenion Ychwanegol) (Cymru) 2001. – 0 11 090249 1 £1.75

2262 **The Parental Responsibility Agreement (Amendment) Regulations 2001**
– 4p.: 30 cm. – Enabling power: Children Act 1989, s. 4 (2). – Issued: 03.07.2001. Made: 19.06.2001. Laid: 25.06.2001. Coming into force: 01.09.2001. Effect: S.I. 1991/1478 amended. Territorial extent & classification: E/W. General. – 0 11 029615 X £1.75

2301 **The Damages (Personal Injury) Order 2001**
– 2p.: 30 cm. – Enabling power: Damages Act 1996, s. 1. – Issued: 03.07.2001. Made: 25.06.2001. Laid: 27.06.2001. Coming into force: 28.06.2001. Effect: None. Territorial extent & classification: E/W/NI. General. – 0 11 029625 7 £1.50

Official
PUBLICATIONS

Environment Agency.

IPPC sector guidance note. Series 0 (S0)

S0.01 General sector guidance for use where there is no IPPC sector-specific guidance – Version 2, 2001 – iv, 51p., figs, tables: 30 cm. – IPPC = Integrated Pollution Prevention and Control. – This item is only available from the Stationery Office's on-demand publishing service. Previous versions of this document were not issued in hardcopy. – 0 11 310174 0 £20.00

Current Law for recent commencement dates is the Commencement of Statutes section in the looseleaf noter-up volume of *Halsbury's Laws* (as distinct from the *Statutes*). This is updated monthly, and unlike *Is it in Force?*, is arranged alphabetically regardless of year.

3.69 If you cannot find a commencement order, you may wish to know whether there are plans to issue one in the near future. Sometimes there may be a press release from the government department concerned, in which case you may want to check the sources that cover press releases, such as government websites or Badger. Also ministers sometimes announce their intention to bring out a commencement order by way of an answer to a parliamentary question. The Freedom of Information Act 2000 contains the novel provision that the minister must make an annual report to Parliament on progress and plans for bringing it into force. Parlianet would be the place to look (and since it indexes SIs as well as parliamentary questions, etc, it would be a double-check that a commencement order has indeed not yet been made). Otherwise you could try contacting the relevant government department. Rather than telephoning the main switchboard, try to identify the correct section in the department from the *Civil Service Yearbook*. The press office or library of the relevant department may also be able to put you on to the right official to speak to.

3.70 Because conceivably it could happen again, it is just worth mentioning the single example in recent times of commencement orders not being made by SI, which was alluded to at the start of this section. Due to a drafting error in its commencement section, the Competition and Service (Utilities) Act 1992 could not be brought into force by SI – the Department of Trade and Industry had to issue its own commencement orders. These were published by HMSO and attention was drawn to them in the *Daily Lists*; most libraries would have filed them with the SIs at the end of the numerical sequence for the year.

Commencement of Finance Acts

3.71 It was noted above that *Is it in Force?* does not cover the commencement of Finance Acts. This is because the date at which particular provisions are to take effect are usually stated in the body of the text of the particular provision of the Act, or otherwise simply come into force on Royal Assent. Some provisions may also be expressed to come into force on a date *before* Royal Assent. These will be in respect some of the measures announced by the Chancellor of the Exchequer in his Budget statement. There is a helpful note in the Preface to *Is it in Force?* on how effect is given to such measures before the relevant Finance Act is passed. However, some particular sections of Finance Acts may state that they are to take effect from an appointed day, and the day is appointed by means of an SI. These SIs are thus very similar to conventional commencement orders, but are usually called Appointed Day Orders and have the section of the Act to which they refer in their title, for example, Finance Act 1998, section 37, (Appointed Day) Order 1999. It is then simply a matter of using sources from which SIs can be found by title, as mentioned at para **3.67** above, and more fully described at paras **3.88–3.89** below.

Finding when repealed Acts were commenced

3.72 It is unusual, but occasionally it may be necessary to establish when an Act or section of an Act now repealed was commenced. The current edition of *Is it in Force?* will not help. If old editions are to hand, however, and the Act was passed since

Figure 3.9

S T A T U T O R Y   I N S T R U M E N T S

2001 No. 1498 (C. 53)

TRANSPORT

The Transport Act 2000 (Commencement No. 6) Order 2001

Made -   -   -   -   -   *9th April 2001*

The Secretary of State for the Environment, Transport and the Regions, in exercise of the powers conferred upon him by section 275(1) of the Transport Act 2000(a) hereby makes the following Order:—

Citation, and interpretation

   1. This Order may be cited as the Transport Act 2000 (Commencement No. 6) Order 2001.

Provisions coming into force on 1st May 2001

   2. Section 3 of the Transport Act 2000 shall come into force on 1st May 2001.

Provisions coming into force on 1st July 2001

   3. Section 265 of the Transport Act 2000 shall come into force on 1st July 2001.

Signed by authority of the Secretary of State for
the Environment, Transport and the Regions

Keith Hill,
Parliamentary Under Secretary of State
9th April 2001   Department of the Environment, Transport and the Regions

(a) 2000 c. 38.

[DOT 12416]

1

Figure 3.10

This Order brings section 3 of the Transport Act 2000 into force on 1st May 2001. That enactment makes it a criminal offence if a person provides air traffic services in respect of a managed area save where those services are excepted by that section or the subject of an exemption or a licence granted under Chapter I of Part I of the Act.

It also brings section 265 into force on 1st July 2001. That section extends to England and Wales only and amends the Public Passenger Vehicles Act 1981 to provide that a vehicle with no more than 8 passenger seats provided for hire with the services of a driver which carries passengers otherwise than at separate fares must, with certain exceptions, be licensed as a private hire vehicle.

NOTE AS TO EARLIER COMMENCEMENT ORDERS

(This note is not part of the Order)

The following provisions of the Transport Act 2000 have been, or will be, brought into force in accordance with commencement orders made before the date of this Order—

Provision	Date of Commencement	S.I. No
Sections 1 and 2	1st February 2001	2001/57
Sections 4 to 35	1st February 2001	2001/57
Sections 36 and 37	1st April 2001	2001/869
Sections 38 to 40	1st February 2001	2001/57
Sections 41 to 65	1st February 2001	2001/57
Sections 66 to 72	1st February 2001	2001/57
Sections 73 to 84	1st February 2001	2001/57
Sections 85 to 96	1st February 2001	2001/57
Section 97	1st February (in part) and 1st April 2001 (remainder)	2001/57 and 2001/869
Sections 98 to 107	1st February 2001	2001/57
Sections 108 to 113 (as respects England)	1st February 2001	2001/57
Section 119 (as respects England)	1st February 2001	2001/57
Sections 135 to 143 (as respects England)	1st February 2001	2001/57
Section 144 (in part) (as respects England)	1st February 2001	2001/57
Section 145 (as respects England)	1st January 2001 (in part), 1st February 2001 (in part) and 1st June 2001 (remainder)	2000/3229
Section 146 (as respects England)	1st January 2001 (in part), 1st February 2001 (in part) and 1st June 2001 (remainder)	2000/3229
Sections 147 and 148 (as respects England)	1st June 2001	2000/3229

2

1960, which was the start of the coverage of the first edition, then that would be the simplest solution. Otherwise, for statutes commenced since 1947, you could use the *Current Law Statute Citators*. All commencement orders are listed at the head of the entry for Acts passed from 1986. Before 1986 they are listed under the section containing the commencement provisions. Note that in the *Statute Citator* for 1947–71 the numbers given are *not* SI numbers, but paragraph numbers in the *Current Law Yearbook* where the SI is noted. Another possibility is old editions of *Halsbury's Statutes*, where notes to the commencement section will give the orders made. The *Index to Government Orders*, if old editions were available, would be an equally good route. Although principally arranged by subject, there is a table of enabling Act provisions at the front, which will take you to the right part of the *Index*.

Consolidation Acts: tracing derivations and destinations

3.73 From the latter part of the nineteenth century onwards, it has been found expedient from time to time to bring together in one new Act all the statutes on a particular subject, particularly where a principal Act has been amended piecemeal by a succession of later Acts. The essence of most such Acts, known as consolidation Acts, is that there is no intention to change the existing law, but merely to reorganise it into a more convenient form in a single Act. The wording of the previous enactments may simply be lifted and put into the new Act verbatim, or the drafting may be recast to some extent. The Consolidation of Enactments (Procedure) Act 1949 settled the parliamentary procedure for such Acts, and permitted, subject to controls, the incorporation of corrections and minor improvements. Usually, it is large and important Acts that warrant the effort of consolidation, for example, the Companies Act, the Highways Act, the Planning Act. But occasionally smaller topics are consolidated, as in the example illustrated as figure 3.1, the Protection of Badgers Act 1992. As will be seen from that example, whether an Act is a consolidation Act is apparent from its long title. Very occasionally, an Act both consolidates previous legislation and introduces new amendments, which will again be apparent from its long title. The Law Commission is often asked to do the groundwork for preparing consolidation Acts. They issue a report and draft Bill, before it goes through the requisite parliamentary procedure. Some consolidation Acts are not the result of a simple wish to tidy up the statute book, but are prompted by a major reform of the law. A pattern that sometimes arises is to have a major legislative change, which is not in fact brought into force, but is then almost immediately consolidated. A prominent example is the 1925 Property Acts, which though they introduced the new regime were technically consolidation Acts, the actual changes having been made by Acts in 1922 and 1924; likewise the Insolvency Act 1986 immediately followed the Insolvency Act 1985, which was never commenced. In important areas that have been the subject of long-standing legislation, there may have been successive consolidations. For example, the Companies Acts have been consolidated four times, in 1908, 1929, 1948 and 1985.

3.74 A novel form of legislation, to be contrasted with consolidation Acts, though having much in common with them, has arisen from the tax rewrite project. This has the aim of rendering all the main tax statutes more comprehensible, by rewriting them in plain English and providing a more logical structure. The first of such tax simplification bills, which was introduced in the 2000/01 parliamentary session, is the Capital Allowances Bill, for which various new parliamentary procedures have had to be devised, because it goes further than mere consolidation, but none the less does not aim to change the substance of tax law or policy.

3.75 Consolidation Acts throw up two research problems, one is tracing where a section in a consolidation Act derives from and the other is tracing the destination of a section in a previous Act in the new consolidation Act – in old-fashioned parlance, whence and whither. Finding derivations is not generally an end itself but rather a necessary preliminary for two other research problems. The first is finding case law on a particular section of an Act: when using statute citators and tables of statutes judicially considered, if you only look under the consolidation Act, you will miss any case law on its precursor Acts, which may well be relevant. As the *Legal Journals Index* grows, an analogous research problem would be finding older articles on an Act that has recently been consolidated. Secondly, as described more fully in chapter 4, if you want to find the relevant parliamentary debates on a section for *Pepper v Hart* research, you will need to find the debates on the Act which first introduced the section – such parliamentary materials as there are on the consolidation Act will generally be of no assistance. Researching destinations arises where you simply want to know what a familiar section number has become in a new consolidation Act. Or, it may be the reverse of the first circumstance: you are looking at a law report which contains statutory references, but which predates a consolidation Act, and you need to know if there is any later case law on the equivalent statutory provisions.

3.76 Tracing derivations and destinations is relatively straightforward for modern consolidation Acts. Since 1967 the Tables and Index volume of official annual volumes of Public General Acts have included derivation and destination tables for all consolidation Acts passed during the year. They list where each section comes from and has gone to – see figures 3.11 and 3.12. The separate Queen's Printer copy print of the Act now also includes a derivation table (but not a destination table) – the Powers of Criminal Courts (Sentencing) Act 2000, if not the first to do so, was certainly an example. Tracing derivations may equally easily be done using *Halsbury's Statutes* or *Current Law Statutes* – either the notes to a particular section will give the derivation or there will be a separate table of derivations at the end of the Act. Having found your derivation, it is vital not to overlook the next step: is the Act containing the derivation itself a consolidation Act? If so, then you need to repeat the process until you find the Act that first introduced the provision, which may take you outside the scope of the current materials described in this paragraph (see para **3.77**). *Current Law Statutes* in the past has occasionally provided destination tables, but issued with *Halsbury's Statutes* is a separate Destination Tables volume, especially designed for the task. The latest edition covers all consolidation Acts passed since 1983, with a selection of the more important Acts back to 1957. Look first for your Act in the table of legislation replaced at the back, which tells you the consolidating Act that covers it. (Sometimes an Act has not been consolidated wholesale – different parts may have arrived in different consolidation Acts, in which case more than one consolidation Act will be given in the table. You will need to follow through each in turn until you find the one covering your particular section.) Next find that consolidating Act in the body of the work, either by flicking through – they are arranged chronologically – or by using the alphabetical table of contents in the front. In the left column will be your original Act set out section by section, and in the right column the corresponding section in the new Act. As with derivations, the next step is to double-check whether the consolidation Act you found has not been itself replaced by a later Act. To do so, return to the table of legislation replaced at the back, and repeat the process.

3.77 You may need to trace the derivation of an old statute, particularly for *Pepper v Hart* research where there have been successive consolidations. If so, you may be in for a long haul. If the statute is no longer in force the current edition of *Halsbury's Statutes* will not help. If the statute is before 1948 nor will *Current Law Statutes* help. As a last resort all you can do is look at the Schedule of repeals in the consolidation Act, and then go to each Act listed, and peruse the table giving the arrangement of sections until you find a likely looking section. Sometimes an educated guess may be made as to which of the Acts listed in the Schedule of repeals is a likely candidate, simply from its title. However, one obvious alternative, if it is available to you, is to use the Justis Statutes on CD-ROM or the Internet. If there has been a verbatim re-enactment it ought to be straightforward to locate the original. But experience shows that it can often be quite tricky to formulate the search, especially where there has been substantial change in the statutory language, as is the case with modern provisions that have their origins in nineteenth century statutes. If you have difficulty getting a result with Justis Statutes, or you do not have it, another shortcut to bear in mind before tackling it the hard way, is old editions of standard treatises. For example, *Buckley on the Companies Acts* had fresh editions after each consolidation and gives derivations in the footnotes to the commentary on each section.

Statutory instruments

3.78 Statutory instruments (SIs) form the main category of subsidiary legislation. (For the few categories of subsidiary legislation not issued as SIs, see paras **3.159–3.167**.) The nomenclature of the different kinds of SI varies: rules, regulations and orders are the most common. The generic term, statutory instruments, and the rules for their promulgation and publication, derive from the Statutory Instruments Act 1946. Before that they were called Statutory Rules and Orders (SR & O), but they are a relatively modern phenomenon. Separately published annual volumes began only in 1890. There were some Statutory Rules earlier in the nineteenth century but their publication was entirely ad hoc. Those Statutory Rules made before 1890 that were still in force were included in the consolidated edition of Statutory Rules in 1896. Some legislation that is now made by SI was previously made by means of Schedules to the Act, as, for example, the original Rules of the Supreme Court, which were Scheduled to the Judicature Act 1875, and 'Table A' on memoranda of association which were Scheduled to the Companies Acts.

3.79 Over 3,000 SIs are made each year. They may be purely local in application, for example, authorising a bypass or trunk road. They may be very short, for example, substituting one sum for another in a social security regulation. They may be in force for only a brief period; for example, The Food Protection (Emergency Prohibitions) (Paralytic Shellfish Poisoning) Order 1998 came into force on 29 May was amended on 23 July, was partially revoked on 19 August and was completely revoked on 1 September. On the other hand, they may enact substantial bodies of law; the Insolvency Rules 1986, for example, run to 784 pages. Because of their number, they can be harder to track down than statutes. Apart from finding them by title or subject, there is the problem, as with statutes, of checking whether they have been amended or revoked (note the terminology, SIs are revoked, statutes are repealed). But with a rare exception (see para **3.106**) there is not the problem of finding commencement dates: they almost always bear this on their face. On the other hand, SIs have a research problem of their own, which is tracing them by enabling Act. Another occasional problem with SIs not encountered with the statutes is that not all of them are necessarily printed (see para **3.82**).

Figure 3.11 Public General Acts: *tables and index volume for the year. Table of derivations for consolidation Acts.*

---

xlviii   *Tables of Derivations and Destinations*

EMPLOYMENT RIGHTS ACT 1996 (c.18)

TABLE OF DERIVATIONS

(for Table of Destinations see page lxix)

Notes:

1. This Table shows the derivation of the provisions of the consolidation.

2. The following abbreviations are used in the Table—

BGLA	=	Betting, Gaming and Lotteries Act 1963 (c.2)
EP(C)A	=	Employment Protection (Consolidation) Act 1978 (c.44)
EA 1980	=	Employment Act 1980 (c.42)
EA 1982	=	Employment Act 1982 (c.46)
WA	=	Wages Act 1986 (c.48)
EA 1989	=	Employment Act 1989 (c.38)
TULR(C)A	=	Trade Union and Labour Relations (Consolidation) Act 1992 (c.52)
TURERA	=	Trade Union Reform and Employment Rights Act 1993 (c.19)
STA	=	Sunday Trading Act 1994 (c.20)
D&COA	=	Deregulation and Contracting Out Act 1994 (c.40)
PA	=	Pensions Act 1995 (c.26)
CRTUPER	=	Collective Redundancies and Transfer of Undertakings (Protection of Employment) (Amendment) Regulations (S.I.1995/2587)

Provision	Derivation
1(1), (2)	EP(C)A s.1(1); TURERA Sch.4.
(3) to (5)	EP(C)A s.1(2) to (4); TURERA Sch.4.
2(1)	EP(C)A s.2(1); TURERA Sch.4.
(2)	EP(C)A s.2(2)(a); TURERA Sch.4.
(3)	EP(C)A s.2(2)(b), (3); TURERA Sch.4.
(4) to (6)	EP(C)A s.2(4) to (6); TURERA Sch.4.
3(1)	EP(C)A s.3(1)(a) to (c); TURERA Sch.4.
(2) to (4)	EP(C)A s.3(2) to (4); TURERA Sch.4.
(5)	EP(C)A s.3(1)(d); TURERA Sch.4.
4(1)	EP(C)A s.4(1); TURERA Sch.4.
(2)	EP(C)A s.4(1), (2); TURERA Sch.4.
(3)	EP(C)A s.4(1); TURERA Sch.4.
(4)	EP(C)A s.4(3)(a); TURERA Sch.4.
(5)	EP(C)A s.4(3)(b), (4); TURERA Sch.4.
(6), (7)	EP(C)A s.4(5); TURERA Sch.4.
(8)	EP(C)A s.4(6); TURERA Sch.4.
5	EP(C)A s.5(2), (3); TURERA Sch.4.
6	EP(C)A ss.2(2)(a), (3), 3(1)(a), (c), 4(3)(a), (4); TURERA Sch.4.
7	EP(C)A s.6; TURERA Sch.4.
8	EP(C)A s.8.
9(1), (2)	EP(C)A s.9(1).
(3) to (5)	EP(C)A s.9(2) to (4).
10	EP(C)A s.10.
11(1)	EP(C)A s.11(1); TURERA Sch.8 para.10(a).
(2)	EP(C)A s.11(2).

Figure 3.12 Public General Acts: *tables and index volume for the year.*
Table of destinations for consolidation Acts.

EMPLOYMENT RIGHTS ACT 1996 (c.18)

TABLE OF DESTINATIONS

Notes:

1. This Table shows how the enactments and instruments proposed to be repealed or revoked are dealt with by the consolidation.

2. The following abbreviations are used in the Table—

EP(C)A	=	Employment Protection (Consolidation) Act 1978 (c.44)
EA 1980	=	Employment Act 1980 (c.42)
EA 1982	=	Employment Act 1982 (c.46)
EA 1989	=	Employment Act 1989 (c.38)
TULR(C)A	=	Trade Union and Labour Relations (Consolidation) Act 1992 (c.52)
TURERA	=	Trade Union Reform and Employment Rights Act 1993 (c.19)
P/T Regs	=	Employment Protection (Part-time Employees) Regulations 1995 (S.I.1995/31)
CRTUPER	=	Collective Redundancies and Transfer of Undertakings (Protection of Employment) (Amendment) Regulations (S.I.1995/2587)

Existing Provision	Subject matter	Provision of 1996 Act	Remarks
	BETTING, GAMING AND LOTTERIES ACT 1963 (c.2)		
31A	Betting workers	—	Unnecessary.
Sch.5A	Rights of betting workers		Inserted Deregulation and Contracting Out Act 1994 (c.40) Sch.8.
para.1		36(7), 45(4), 96(6), 210(1), to (3), 230(1), (2), (4), (5), 233(1) to (4), (6), 235(1)	Repealed in part P/T Regs Sch.; unnecessary in part.
para.2		36(1) to (4), 37(5), 38(3), 39(5), 45(9), (10), 101(4), 105(8)	Unnecessary in part.
para.3		36(5), (6), 37(3)	
para.4		40	
para.5		41(1), (2), 43(3), (5), 45(9), (10), 101(4), 105(8)	Unnecessary in part.
para.6		41(3)	
para.7		101(1) to (3), 197(2)	
para.8		105(1), (4)	
para.9		108(3), 109(2)	
para.10		45(1) to (8)	
para.11		42(1) to (3), (5), (6), 236(1), (2)	
para.12		37(1) to (4)	
para.13		43(1) to (4)	

Anatomy and citation

3.80 See figure 3.13. The year and the number of the SI in that year are given at the head. This is the main means of identification: in this case SI 2001/1412. There may also be another number in brackets after it preceded by an abbreviation, for example, (C 53) – see figure 3.9. These are subseries of particular classes of SIs. The two main general classes are C (Commencement Orders) and L (Legal: fees or procedure in the courts). The others are geographic series, NI (Northern Ireland), S (Scotland) and W (Wales) – how devolution has affected the publication of SIs is discussed below. The susbseries, however, with the exception of the NI series, are not necessary for identification or citation purposes and are mainly a convenience for those who do not wish to subscribe to all SIs from the Stationery Office. Beneath the number is a broad subject heading (here 'Patents'). The Stationery Office assigns these and are the headings used in their monthly and annual indexes of SIs. Then there is the title, which includes the year it was made. The title, with its year, will be unique, and is the form of citation specified in the SI itself, like the short title of an Act. Like Acts, SIs can be identified just by number or just by title, but in an ideal world both are given. Then there is the date it was made, the date on which it was laid before Parliament (if it was required to be laid – see para **4.77**) and the commencement date. The numbered parts of the SI are not called sections. If the SI is an 'Order' they are called paragraphs, but if the SI is in the nature of 'Regulations' or, as here, 'Rules', then they are referred to simply as regulation 1, 2, etc or rule 1, 2, etc, the usual abbreviations being reg and r respectively. As with the statutes, Schedules giving various detailed provisions, often in tabular form, may be included after the main body of the text. At the end an explanatory note is usually printed (see figure 3.14). It is not part of the instrument, but summarises, more or less helpfully, the purpose of the SI, and gives earlier SIs amended or revoked and any EC legislation that it implements.

3.81 Until 1999 SIs that applied only to Scotland had, as mentioned above, a number in the S series, as well as the main number. From 1999 subordinate legislation made by the Scottish Executive, either under pre-devolution UK Acts in respect of matters where the Scottish Parliament now has legislative competence, or under Acts of the Scottish Parliament, is issued as a separate series of Scottish statutory instruments (SSIs). In appearance SSIs are identical to UK SIs. There continue to be UK SIs with an S series number, but many fewer than before – they will be concerned with the Scottish application of legislation still reserved by Westminster. The National Assembly for Wales does not have power to make primary legislation, but legislates by subordinate legislation. The Government of Wales Act 1998 provides for the transfer of ministerial functions to the Welsh Assembly, and it is the functions of the Secretary of State of Wales that are the main ones to have been transferred. So any pre-devolution Act which gave the Secretary of State for Wales power to make SIs, is now to be read as giving the power instead to the Welsh Assembly. Post-devolution Acts will explicitly confer any appropriate power to make SIs on the Welsh Assembly. The resulting statutory instruments are issued in the main series of UK SIs, with a number in the W series in addition to the main number. Welsh SIs differ slightly in appearance to other UK SIs in that they are in both Welsh and English, set out in parallel text, and the explanatory note comes at the front rather than the back. The NI series of SIs, which appeared until the Northern Ireland Assembly resumed its legislative role in 2000, were rather different, however. These were SIs made under the Northern Ireland Act 1974 at Westminster, but equated in substance to primary legislation and would have been passed as Acts by the legislature in Northern Ireland

Figure 3.13

STATUTORY INSTRUMENTS

2001 No. 1412

PATENTS

The Patents (Amendment) Rules 2001

Made - - - - -	*9th April 2001*
Laid before Parliament	*9th April 2001*
Coming into force - -	*6th July 2001*

The Secretary of State, in exercise of the powers conferred upon him by sections 123 and 125A of the Patents Act 1977(a), after consultation with the Council on Tribunals pursuant to section 8(1) of the Tribunals and Inquiries Act 1992(b), hereby makes the following Rules:—

Citation and Commencement

1. These Rules may be cited as the Patents (Amendment) Rules 2001 and shall come into force on 6th July 2001.

Amendment of the Patents Rules 1995

2. The Patents Rules 1995(c) are amended as set out in rules 3 to 8.

3. In rule 17—
    (a) in the heading, for "Micro-organisms" substitute "Biological material";
    (b) in the rule, for "require for their performance the use of micro-organisms" substitute "involve the use of or concern biological material".

4. In rule 26(1)(b), after "paragraph 1(2)(a)(ii)" insert ", 1(2)(a)(iii)".

5. In rule 85(2), for "subparagraph (2)(a)(ii)" substitute "subparagraphs (2)(a)(ii) and (iii)".

6. In rule 110(2), for "paragraph 4(2) of Schedule 2" substitute "paragraphs 5(2) and 5(4) of Schedule 2".

7. Patents Forms 8/77 and 8A/77 in Schedule 1 are replaced by Patents Forms 8/77 and 8A/77 in Schedule 1 to these Rules.

8. Schedule 2 is replaced by the provisions of Schedule 2 to these Rules.

Kim Howells
Parliamentary Under Secretary of State
for Competition and Consumer Affairs
Department of Trade and Industry

9th April 2001

(a) 1977 c. 37.
(b) 1992 c. 53.
(c) S.I. 1995/2093 as amended by S.I. 1999/1092, S.I. 1999/1899 and S.I. 1999/3197.

1

Figure 3.14

EXPLANATORY NOTE

(This note is not part of the Rules)

These Rules amend the Patents Rules 1995 (S.I. 1995/2093 as amended by S.I. 1999/1092, S.I. 1999/1899 and S.I. 1999/3197 ("the 1995 Rules") in order to implement Articles 13 and 14 of Directive 98/44/EC of the European Parliament and of the Council of 6 July 1998 on the legal protection of biotechnological inventions ("the Directive"). Articles 13 and 14 of the Directive concern the deposit, access and re-deposit of biological material. Amendment is also made to the 1995 Rules to more closely align them with the parallel regulations on deposit of biological material under the European Patent Convention. The following amendments are made:

    (a) Rules 3, 4, 5 and 6 make consequential changes to references and terminology in the 1995 Rules,

    (b) Rule 7 substitutes updated versions of forms 8/77 and 8A/77 for those forms currently in Schedule 1 to the 1995 Rules,

    (c) Rule 8 substitutes a new Schedule 2 to the 1995 Rules.

Schedule 2 to the 1995 Rules contains detailed provisions dealing with the deposit, access and re-deposit of biological material.

A regulatory impact assessment is available, copies of which have been placed in the libraries of both Houses of Parliament. Copies of the assessment are also available from the Intellectual Property Policy Directorate of the Patent Office, Room 3B38, Concept House, Cardiff Road, Newport NP10 8QQ.

had there been one. Though UK SIs, they are Northern Ireland statutes, and are generally cited not by the SI number but by the NI number, which is thus in effect a chapter number. *Subsidiary* legislation for Northern Ireland, the equivalent of SIs in England, Wales and Scotland, is issued entirely separately by the Stationery Office in Belfast as Northern Ireland Statutory Rules. On Welsh, Scottish and Northern Irish devolved legislation, see further paras **8.16**, **8.18**, **8.23** and **8.30–8.34**.

Sources for the text of SIs

3.82 As with statutes, there is a wide choice. The official text is published by HMSO, who treat them in three categories: SIs of general application (which are all printed); SIs of only local application but of sufficient importance to be printed; and SIs of local application that are not printed. The first two categories are issued individually on a daily basis, and equate to the Queen's Printer copies of Acts. The SIs in the last category, which may, for example, merely provide for a one-way street in Nether Wallop, will in practice usually only be needed in connection with some local authority matter and the authority concerned should have access to the text. Otherwise the Statutory Publications Office (contact details in the monthly and annual lists of SIs) can provide copies. They hold a complete set, with one or two gaps, from 1922. There is no complete set before 1922. There are also sets from 1922 to 1960 at the Public Record Office and from 1922 to 1980 at the British Library's Official Publications Library. Unpublished SIs are assigned a number in the main series, so gaps in the numerical sequence of published SIs on the shelf will appear. They are included in the monthly and annual lists of SIs prepared by HMSO, but not in the *Table of Government Orders* (on which see para **3.104**). For further information on local SIs, see R J B Morris 'Finding and Using Local Statutory Instruments' (1990) 11 *Statute Law Review* 28–47.

3.83 The Stationery Office also publishes SIs in bound volume form (several pale blue volumes per year). These only appear some time in arrears. It is important to realise that the bound volumes do not include all the SIs that were originally published in individual form. Instruments revoked or spent within the year in which they were made are excluded as are, with a small qualification, all instruments classified as local (the second category above). The small qualification as to local SIs is that, starting with 1989, the bound volumes now include those SIs made under the Harbours Act 1964, the Pilotage Act 1987 and the Water Act 1989 (and later cognate legislation, for example, the Ports Act 1991, the Water Resources Act 1991 and the Land Drainage Act 1991). Some libraries may bind the loose SIs instead of taking the official bound volumes, or bind up as supplementary volumes those loose SIs not included in the official bound volumes. A further complication with the official bound volumes is that while excluding some SIs they also include a very few instruments that technically are not SIs. These pretty rare species of subordinate legislation are explained further below (paras **3.163–3.164**). Not being SIs, they do not have a number and appear at the back of the bound volumes by date. From 1961 the SIs in the bound volumes are arranged in numerical order. Before that date they are grouped by broad subject headings, with an index by number. As already mentioned the annual volumes go back to 1890, but there is an official consolidation, *Statutory Rules and Orders and Statutory Instruments Revised*, which includes the text of all instruments in force as amended at 31 December 1948 (there were two earlier consolidations, in 1896 and 1904). It is arranged by subject in 25 volumes.

3.84 As with Acts, it may be safest to use Queen's Printer copies in court (see para **3.16**) rather than the commercially published alternatives described below. And indeed s 2 of the Documentary Evidence Act 1868 provides for the production of the official copy as sufficient proof of the existence of a regulation, which, unlike an Act, would in theory otherwise have to be specifically proved. 'In theory', since it would seem that the courts do not regard failure to comply with s 2 as a valid ground of appeal in the case of a prosecution based on an offence contained in an SI (see *R v Koon Cheung Tang* [1995] Crim LR 813 and commentary thereon).

3.85 A companion to *Halsbury's Statutes* is *Halsbury's Statutory Instruments*. It is arranged and is used in a similar way, but unlike *Halsbury's Statutes* which offers the complete text of the statutes, not every SI is reproduced in full text, though the publishers, Butterworths, offer a telephone-ordering service to subscribers for the text of any SI not included. However, all SIs are listed and if not given in full text are summarised. It has 22 bound volumes arranged by topic, with instruments appearing chronologically within topics. The text, where it is given, is printed as amended and there are full annotations including case references, etc. A general introductory note giving an overview precedes each topic. Individual bound volumes are reissued from time to time. There are two looseleaf volumes, a service volume containing a chronological list of all SIs in the whole work and the monthly updating service and an 'Additional Texts' volume containing the full text of selected instruments made since the relevant bound volume was last reissued. The monthly updates in the looseleaf service volume are arranged by the subject titles of the main work. For each subject title the following information is given: a chronological list of SIs made since the bound volume was issued, a list of amendments and revocations since the bound volume, a noter-up by page number of the bound volume, and lastly summaries of relevant new SIs. Where the full text of a new SI has been included in the Additional Texts volume, a cross-reference is given from its summary. In addition to the two looseleaf volumes, there is a softback consolidated index volume reissued annually, which contains an alphabetical listing by title and a subject index. A new element to the service in 2001 is the *Halsbury's Statutory Instruments Citator*, the counterpart to the new citator for the statutes service.

3.86 Rather than using either of the above, subject-based looseleaf encyclopaedias or subject handbooks are often the easiest way to lay hands on a SI. Likewise, for court rules, which are published as SIs, the practitioner will invariably go the White Book, *Stone's Justices' Manual*, the *Family Court Practice*, and the like, rather than to the originals, unless they are extremely recent.

3.87 All SIs from 1987 are available in full text on the HMSO website, in the form that they were originally made. Though there is no reason to suppose that there will be any discrepancy, as with Acts the hard copy remains the authoritative version. Both Lawtel and the Justis SIs CD-ROM and Internet services also take the same HMSO data on licence, but give greater functionality than the free HMSO site. The Stationery Office has also recently launched its own commercial version, *SI CD incorporating SI Web*. Lexis and Legislation Direct have the full text of all SIs in force as amended.

Finding SIs by title

3.88 The main consolidated index to SIs arranged alphabetically by title is in the index volume to *Halsbury's Statutory Instruments*, reissued annually. The SI number is given together with the topic (but not page number) in the main work where it appears. There is also an alphabetical list in the looseleaf service volume for recent SIs made since the last consolidated index.

3.89 *Halsbury's Laws* also has an alphabetical table in vol 53, the consolidated tables volume, which can be a handy short cut. Though only including those SIs mentioned in the work, it is in fact pretty comprehensive. The alphabetical tables of SIs that are the front of the *Current Law Legislation Citator* bound volumes would be another print source. They will include not only all SIs from 1993, when the *Current Law Statutory Instrument Citator* started, but any SIs of earlier date affected since 1993. From 1990 *Current Law* has included an alphabetical list for the year. The list for the current year is cumulated in each monthly digest, so it is only necessary to look in the latest one. The list for the whole year then appears in the yearbook. Some publishers of looseleaf encyclopaedias (eg Butterworths) usually provide tables of the SIs included arranged alphabetically by title, though other publishers (eg Sweet & Maxwell) only provide tables arranged chronologically. However, using electronic sources may well be the preferred option. As well the full text electronic sources listed above (para **3.87**), there is Badger, which indexes all published SIs from 1993, UKOP which provides catalogue data back to 1980 (and covers unpublished local SIs), and Westlaw UK which covers SIs back to 1948. Finding SIs by title using electronic sources is usually straightforward, though resist the temptation to type in the full title unless it is very short – take a few keywords, and use if necessary Boolean connectors. If you were looking, for example, for The Education (Grant-maintained and Grant-maintained Special Schools) (Finance) (Wales) (Amendment) (No 2) Regulations 1996, there is ample scope for making a slip – even if you get the words right, search engines differ in their resilience to variations in the treatment of hyphens, brackets, capitalisation and spacing.

Finding SIs by subject

3.90 Of print sources, *Halsbury's Statutory Instruments* is usually the best starting place, or alternatively a subject-based looseleaf encyclopaedia. In *Halsbury's* look first in the consolidated index in the annual softback index volume. A reference to the volume number and page (together with the SI number) will be given. As with the *Statutes* there is always the possibility that an SI originally in the service volume has been incorporated into a bound volume of the main work reissued since the index was prepared. Having checked the main index, the most recent material can be found by looking in the looseleaf service volume. *Current Law* summarises SIs in the yearbooks and monthly digests under the relevant broad heading in the body of the work. Using *Current Law* is probably not the best method of finding SIs by subject unless one has a good idea of date.

3.91 Full-text electronic sources (see para **3.87**) are going to be particularly useful for this type of research. As with searching statutes, finding particular concrete entities, persons or places that might be mentioned in different contexts in a wide variety of SIs, is a particular strength of them. For SIs made after 1993 Badger is very good; although not giving the full text, the additional abstracting and indexing information should be sufficient to find most relevant SIs. Bear in mind also that the titles of SIs are generally very specific, so even without additional indexing terms they are readily retrievable. For example, if you have been told there might have been a recent SI to do with dangerous materials in batteries, it will be found straightforwardly since it bears the title, The Batteries and Accumulators (Containing Dangerous Substances) (Amendment) Regulations 2000.

3.92 Very occasionally it may be necessary to research SIs that are no longer in force. If there is a relevant SI that is in force, it may simply be a question of seeing what SIs it revokes, and taking it back from there. Superseded volumes and indexes of *Halsbury's Statutory Instruments* might be useful, if they have been kept. The main electronic sources based on HMSO data will include SIs made from 1987, even if revoked. Otherwise, you would need to use the *Index to Government Orders* that used to be published by HMSO. The last edition, in two volumes matching the blue of the official bound volumes of SIs, covered all SIs in force at 31 December 1991. It is arranged by broad headings with subheadings. Enabling powers are given at the top of each heading and the titles and numbers of the SIs made under them are listed. Where the enabling power has not been exercised a statement to that effect is given. The 1948 official *Statutory Rules and Orders and Statutory Instruments Revised* was arranged by subject matter.

Finding SIs by enabling Act

3.93 If you have a statute in front of you that contains a power enabling regulations or orders to be made, you may want to know whether the power has been exercised. An example of such an enabling power was given at the start of this chapter (see para **3.1**). When the power is delegated to a minister (eg 'the Secretary of State'), it is almost always stated expressly that the power is to be exercised by statutory instrument. In the example at para **3.1** it is so stated in the relevant section itself. Often, though, especially where an Act contains a number of regulation-making powers, to save repetition a general section on making regulations is given either at the end of the Act, adjacent to other general sections, such as those on commencement, extent, etc, or at the end of the relevant part of the Act, if it is divided into parts. However, some powers are not delegated to a minister but to the Crown itself. Such powers are usually expressed in the statute to be made by Order in Council – for example, 'Her Majesty may by Order in Council direct that the provisions of this Act apply to any relevant overseas territory' – with no mention of SIs. Do not be alarmed – such Orders in Council, because of the provisions of s 1(1) of the Statutory Instruments Act 1946, are in fact SIs like any other (though there can be Orders in Council which are *not* made under a statute and so are not SIs: see paras **3.163–3.164**).

3.94 The best manual approach is to use *Halsbury's Statutes* (not, incidentally, *Halsbury's Statutory Instruments*, which does not deal with this aspect, other than for SIs made in the current year in the service volume) and the *Current Law Statute Citators*. As with finding to amendments to Acts, the writer's personal preference is to do most of the job with *Halsbury's Statutes* and just use the *Current Law Statute Citators* to double-check for anything very recent. For one thing, *Halsbury's* gives you the title as well as the number of any SIs; it also will alert you to the presence of savings provisions, as discussed at para **3.99**. If you find the text of the particular section of the statute in *Halsbury's* as described in para **3.42**, any SIs will be given in a note 'Orders made under this section' or 'Regulations made under this section' – see figure 3.2. As always, then check the annual cumulative supplement under the volume number and page of the main work, and then the equivalent section in the looseleaf noter-up. Then verify your results in the looseleaf service volume of *Current Law Statutes*. Find the relevant statute by year and chapter number, and then look for the relevant section. From 1996 the *Current Law* statute citator has provided much fuller coverage of where statutory instruments refer to or relate to particular statutes, as well as showing the exercise of enabling provisions proper (and amendments to sections and case law). Thus the entries for each Act are longer and rather more intimidating (see figure 3.4). For these purposes ignore 'referred to', 'applied', etc and concentrate on spotting 'enabling' – for example, in figure 3.4, under Transport Act 1982 (c 49) s 76. The SI number is given.

3.95 As an alternative to using *Halsbury's Statutes* for the first step, you can use the bound volumes of the *Current Law Statute Citators*. In the two volumes covering 1972 to 1995 the entries appear as follows:

40. Education Reform Act 1988
  s.3, order 91/2567
  s.17, regs. 92/155-157

This shows that an order, SI no 2567 of 1991, was made under section 3 of the Education Reform Act 1988 (c 40), and that three sets of regulations, SIs 155, 156 and 157 of 1992, were made under section 17. If you need to go back to the first volume covering 1947–71, note that the numbers given are not SI numbers as in the example above, but paragraph numbers to the *Current Law Yearbooks*, which then need to be checked to find the SI number. If the Act in question is of long standing, working backwards, pausing to look at the SIs retrieved as you go, will ensure you do not have to bother with SIs listed in the earlier citators that in fact have since been revoked.

3.96 Another tip when doing hard copy research in this area is to bear in mind the table of SIs given at the front of each volume of *Halsbury's Statutes*, which consolidates in one list all the SIs mentioned in the annotations to each Act. It saves having to plough through the annotations to every section either if you want all the SIs made under a particular Act, especially since a particular SI may be made under several different sections, or if you are uncertain which sections of the Act contain enabling provisions.

3.97 Bearing in mind that it has not been updated since 1991, there is one other hard copy source, the *Index to Government Orders*. This is occasionally useful when a long-standing Act or Act now repealed is in issue, since its primary arrangement is by enabling power. On green pages at the front is a table of statutes, which gives references to particular subject headings in the body of the work where the particular enabling powers and details of the orders made under them are set out. One noteworthy feature is that it may include some orders (few in number) that are not made in the form of SIs.

3.98 Although you should be familiar with hard copy research, electronic tools nowadays are generally to be preferred for reasons of currency. The electronic version of the *Current Law Legislation Citator* is certainly an option here. However, Justis SIs, Lawtel, and Badger on CLI are suggested as being more convenient – the first two will give you the full text of any SIs found, and the latter will give you a title and some details, not just a number. Lexis or Legislation Direct are other possibilities, bearing in mind the start dates of other services. On all four the most efficient strategy is to use a field search. On Justis SIs there is an Enabling Act field on the form search. Enter the name of the Act, if necessary, with a Boolean AND, the bare number of the section (avoid 's.' etc and subsections). On Lawtel the problem can be approached either from the Act end or the SI end. Select statutes, find the Act, go to the Statutory Status table for it and click on the 'SIs enabled' button: you get a list of *all* the SIs made under the Act. But starting from the statutes end, you cannot limit your search to those made under particular sections (the notes to each section of the Act relate only to amendments, etc). If you select SIs, and then a focused search, which brings up the form, there is an enabling Act field. You can specify a section in that; if no section is specified you will simply get all the SIs under that Act. On Badger, use the Legislation field, where the number of the SI appears followed by 'm/u' the enabling Act, where 'm/u' stands for 'made under'. If you wish to specify a section on the Folio Views version, type it as for example, s.58, without spaces; anyone still using the Blackwell Idealist version, on the other hand, will have to put in 58 without the s. In the SIs library on Lexis, confine the search to the authority segment.

3.99 Having discussed the tools for the job as they usually apply, there is one quite important point to note, delayed to avoid muddying the basics above. That is the effect of amendment or repeal of enabling powers – have you been looking at the right Act? There are two main scenarios. The first is relatively straightforward. In the case of a new Act, especially a consolidation Act, there may be savings provisions, usually in the Act itself, with the other general sections at the end, but sometimes in 'transitional provisional and savings' orders made by SI under the Act, or very occasionally with very complicated legislation in a separate 'consequential provisions' Act. One of the things the saving provision may do is to keep in force for the time being SIs made under the earlier legislation being repealed. The notes to the section of the new Act in *Halsbury's Statutes* invariably point this out. For example, s 65 of the Land Drainage Act 1991 contains a general power to make regulations, and since 1991 only one SI has been made under it. Yet in fact ten other SIs going back to 1932, made under earlier legislation, remain in force, being deemed to have been made under s 65.

3.100 The second scenario is best explained by example. You have read or your lecturer told you that s 27 of the Access to Justice Act 1999 made important changes to the regime for conditional fee agreements, which is true. You want to find the new regulations. You go to say Lawtel or the *Current Law Statute Citator*, look under s 27 of the Act, and see no SIs enabled by it. Happy? What of course s 27 did was to substitute an entirely new version of s 58 of the Courts and Legal Services Act 1990, which first introduced conditional fee agreements. The relevant regulations are thus made not under the 1999 Act but under s 58 of the 1990 Act *as substituted*, and will be listed in the various tools under that Act and section. Take another very similar recent example. The Employment Relations Act 1999 introduced significant new provisions relating to maternity and parental leave, but it did so by substituting the new provisions for all of ss 71–80 of the Employment Rights Act 1996. The enabling power for The Maternity and Parental Leave etc Regulations 1999 is thus given as those sections of the 1996 Act, not s 7 and Sch 4 to the 1999 Act. The concealment of the correct enabling Act is most likely to arise where there is such substitution. Where amendment is made by insertion, the problem may be more apparent, but should none the less be borne in mind. Insertions of new sections in previous Acts are indicated by the addition of upper case letters to section numbers. For example, the new 'whistleblowing' provisions of s 1 of the Public Interest Disclosure Act 1998 were effected by inserting new ss 43A to 43L after s 43 of the Employment Rights Act 1996. Thus the Public Interest Disclosure (Prescribed Persons) Order 1999 was made under s 43F of the Employment Rights Act 1996, and will be so listed in citators, etc.

3.101 One other little teaser, though fortunately arising only very seldom, is where an Act retrospectively changes the title of a previous Act. The main recent example is again in the employment field. The Employment Rights (Dispute Resolution) Act 1998 not only said that the tribunals previously called industrial tribunals were to be called instead employment tribunals, but also that the Industrial Tribunals Act 1996 was to be renamed the Employment Tribunals Act 1996. The other well-known example that may be encountered is the Capital Transfer Tax Act 1984, which was renamed the Inheritance Tax Act 1984 by the Finance Act 1990. Using *Halsbury's Statutes* or hard copy *Current Law Statute Citators* to find SIs made under these Acts should not be problematic – the chapter number will not have changed. But you could conceivably get caught out using sources such as **Badger**, or full-text electronic SIs, if you did not think to search under both titles to get SIs made both before and after 1998.

Finding amendments and revocations

3.102 *Halsbury's Statutory Instruments* is the obvious hard copy source. Find the text or summary in the main work, either by looking up its title in the alphabetical list in the softback index volume or by looking up its number in the chronological table in the looseleaf service volume. The entry in the main work will give full details of amendments and revocations up to the date of its last reissue. Secondly, check the noter-up section of the relevant volume and topic in the monthly update in the looseleaf service volume. You can also use the *Halsbury's Statutory Instruments Citator* that is now provided. Like the new *Halsbury's Statute Citator*, what it does that was not previously possible is to enable you to find details of when and how SIs that are now longer in force, hence not in the main work, were revoked – for SIs that are still in force, if you are going to the main work in any event, you might as well go there. On the other hand, it is straightforwardly organised, and though only an annual publication, there is a hotline telephone number for updates. The first part is an alphabetical listing if you do not have the SI number. The second part is the numerical list with the amendment and revocation details. Mostly it is simply stated that the SI has been amended or revoked – details of which particular rules or regulations within the SI have been amended are not given. However, selectively, large heavily amended SIs are broken down into individual rules, regulations or paragraphs.

3.103 You may then wish to double-check in the latest *Current Law Statutory Instrument Citator* in the looseleaf service volume to *Current Law Statutes*. It is also updated monthly, but may not coincide with the last monthly survey of *Halsbury's SIs*. The *Statutory Instrument Citator* has been published as part of *Current Law* since 1993, and follows the format of the *Statute Citators*; it will be found with them in the bound volumes of the *Current Law Legislation Citator;* the data is also on the electronic version. It is particularly useful where you have a long SI, or an SI that has been heavily amended, since each article or regulation affected is set out separately – see figure 3.15. Other sources, such as **Lawtel** and **Justis SIs** discussed below, only say that an SI has been amended, not which bit of it, so that the SI in question then has to be checked. Another hard copy approach is to see if your SI has been reprinted in a looseleaf subject encyclopaedia or similar. If so, check that it incorporates amendments and if so up to what date, then do a check in say the *Statutory Instrument Citator* for any more recent changes.

3.104 Before 1993 *Current Law* did provide a numerical list of all SIs since 1947 that had been either amended or revoked. It will be found in the bound volumes of the *Legislation Citator*: the 1972–88 volume contains the table for 1947 to 1988 (it is the statute citator part of the volume that starts in 1972), and the 1989–95 volume contains the table for 1989–92. However, for amendments and revocations made before 1991 one is better off using the *Table of Government Orders*, unfortunately now defunct. This was the equivalent of the *Chronological Table of the Statutes* for SIs. It has official status and lists chronologically and numerically every SI that was in force in 1948 (and so in the revised edition of SIs) and those made since then up to the end of 1990, and states whether since 1948 they have been amended, revoked, spent or have otherwise ceased to be in force. Particular articles or regulations within an SI are separately set out, where there has been an amendment or partial revocation. Also included are those orders that are not SIs but which are included in the bound volumes of SIs (see para **3.83**), and any orders within its scope made before 1894, when the current position of numbered promulgation of subordinate legislation was introduced – these two classes of orders, having no number, appear by date in the relevant place. It does not include local SIs; hence the gaps in the numbers.

3.105 The main electronic tools are the same as those covered for finding SIs by enabling Act, except Badger, namely the on-screen versions of the *Current Law Legislation Citator* (for effects on SIs since 1993), Lexis and Legislation Direct (for the text of SIs in force as amended), Lawtel (for SIs since 1984) and Justis SIs (for SIs since 1987). The last two are probably the most useful. On any of them the number of the SI that may have been amended or revoked can be entered as a free text search, but again a field search may be the most efficient. On Justis use the Effect field. This gives the numbers of SIs that have been amended or revoked by an SI, so will retrieve all amending or revoking SIs. Lawtel has a similar Effect field using the focused search. However, from 1999 they have introduced an additional Status field. If you look at the record for the SI in question, it tells you straight away whether it has been amended or revoked. The focused search now has this as a field, but only use it for SIs made in 1999 or later, or which you are certain have not been amended before 1999 – it would seem safer to stick with the Effect field. When using both Justis SIs and Lawtel you will need to go via the link to the full text to see precisely what in the SI is being amended. Badger does not give amendment and revocation information as such, though this information may sometimes appear in the abstract, and many amending SIs have the same title as the principal SI, with the addition of 'Amendment', for example, 'The Importation of Bees (Amendment) Order'.

Commencements notified in the *London Gazette*

3.106 As already stated, it is the practice to print the date on which an SI comes into operation at its head, and indeed for SIs that are required to be laid before Parliament this is obligatory under s 4(2)(a) of the Statutory Instruments Act 1946. However, sometimes this is not possible because the operation of the SI is contingent on some future event of uncertain date. The commonest examples are SIs which implement in domestic law provisions of international treaties that are still subject to ratification, of which double taxation agreements probably form the most numerous class. An important recent example outside the field of double taxation was the Civil Jurisdiction and Judgments Act 1982 (Amendment) Order 2000 which extended the Brussels Convention to Austria, Finland and Sweden following their entry into the

Figure 3.15 Current Law: *legislation citator.*

1997   STATUTORY INSTRUMENT CITATOR 1996–1999

NO.   NO.

1997—cont.   *1997—cont.*

319. **Local Authorities (Capital Finance) Regu-**
lations 1997—*cont.*
Reg.16, revoked (in part): SI 1999/1852 Reg.4
Reg.16, substituted: SI 1998/371 Reg.4
Reg.24, amended: SI 1998/602 Reg.2
Reg.31, amended: SI 1999/1852 Reg.5
Reg.32A, added: SI 1999/1852 Reg.6
Reg.40, amended: SI 1997/848 Reg.4
Reg.40, substituted: SI 1999/3423 Reg.2
Reg.58A, added: SI 1998/1937 Reg.4
Reg.60, revoked: SI 1998/1937 Reg.12
Reg.64, amended: SI 1998/1937 Reg.5
Reg.64A, added: SI 1998/1937 Reg.6
Reg.65, amended: SI 1998/1937 Reg.7
Reg.66, amended: SI 1998/1937 Reg.8
Reg.66, revoked (in part): SI 1998/1937 Reg.8
Reg.66A, added: SI 1998/1937 Reg.9
Reg.68A, added: SI 1998/1937 Reg.10
Reg.70, revoked: SI 1998/1937 Reg.12
Reg.71, revoked: SI 1998/1937 Reg.12
Reg.73, revoked: SI 1998/1937 Reg.12
Reg.74, revoked: SI 1998/1937 Reg.12
Reg.75, revoked: SI 1998/1937 Reg.12
Reg.86, amended: SI 1997/848 Reg.5
Reg.87, amended: SI 1998/371 Reg.5
Reg.96, amended: SI 1999/1852 Reg.7
Reg.104, amended: SI 1999/501 Reg.3
Reg.104A, added: SI 1999/501 Reg.4
Reg.109, amended: SI 1999/1852 Reg.8
Reg.112, amended: SI 1997/848 Reg.6
Reg.130, amended: SI 1998/371 Reg.6
Reg.136, amended: SI 1998/371 Reg.6
Reg.138, amended: SI 1998/1937 Reg.11
Reg.153, amended: SI 1998/371 Reg.6

321. **Registration of Homeopathic Veterinary Medicinal Products (Fees) Regulations 1997**
revoked: SI 1997/1469 Reg.21
Sch.1 Part II, revoked: SI 1997/1469 Reg.21

322. **Registration of Homeopathic Veterinary Medicinal Products Regulations 1997**
applied: SI 1997/1349 Art.2, SI 1999/3142 Art.2
Reg.2, amended: SI 1999/3142 Art.5, Sch. para.3
Reg.2, referred to: SI 1998/2428 Reg.14
Reg.37, revoked: SI 1997/2884 Reg.4
Sch.6, revoked: SI 1997/2884 Reg.4

326. **Health Promotion Authority for Wales Constitution (Amendment) Order 1997**
revoked: SI 1999/807 Art.2
Art.2, revoked: SI 1999/807 Art.2

327. **Health Promotion Authority for Wales Regulations 1997**
revoked: SI 1999/805 Reg.2
Reg.2, revoked: SI 1999/805 Reg.2
Reg.3, revoked: SI 1999/805 Reg.2
Reg.4, revoked: SI 1999/805 Reg.2
Reg.6, revoked: SI 1999/805 Reg.2

328. **Housing (Change of Landlord) (Payment of Disposal Cost by Instalments) (Amendment) Regulations 1997**
revoked: SI 1997/1621 Reg.3 (with savings)
Reg.2, revoked: SI 1997/1621 Reg.3 (with savings)
Reg.3, revoked: SI 1997/1621 Reg.3 (with savings)

329. **Local Government Pension Scheme (Internal Dispute Resolution Procedure) Regulations 1997**
applied: SI 1997/1613 Reg.4, Reg.19, Sch.2 para.2
referred to: SI 1997/1613 Reg.3, Sch.2 para.6

347. **Merchant Shipping (Section 63 Inquiries) Rules 1997**
r.5, applied: SI 1999/678 Sch., SI 1999/1750 Art.2, Sch.1

348. **Merchant Shipping (Training and Certification) Regulations 1997**
applied: SI 1997/1320 Reg.4
referred to: SI 1998/1609 Reg.5, Reg.6, Sch., SI 1998/2771 Reg.4, Reg.5, Sch.1, Sch.2
Reg.2, amended: SI 1997/1911 Reg.2
Reg.3, amended: SI 1997/1911 Reg.2
Reg.5, amended: SI 1997/1911 Reg.2

351. **Waste Management (Miscellaneous Provisions) Regulations 1997**
Reg.3, revoked: SI 1998/607 Reg.3

358. **Occupational and Personal Pension Schemes (Contracting Out etc.: Review of Determinations) Regulations 1997**
amended: 1999 c.2 s.1, Sch.2
applied: SI 1999/527 Art.4

362. **Water Services Charges (Billing and Collection) (Scotland) Order 1997**
applied: SI 1997/363 Reg.2

363. **Domestic Sewerage Charges (Reduction) (Scotland) Regulations 1997**
applied: SI 1997/362 Art.9

368. **Education (Teachers) (Amendment) Regulations 1997**
revoked (in part): SI 1999/2166 Reg.2, Sch.1 Part I, SI 1999/2817 Reg.2, Sch.1 Part I
Reg.2, revoked (in part): SI 1999/2166 Reg.2, Sch.1 Part I, SI 1999/2817 Reg.2, Sch.1 Part I
Reg.3, revoked (in part): SI 1999/2166 Reg.2, Sch.1 Part I, SI 1997/2679 Reg.7, Sch.3, SI 1999/2817 Reg.2, Sch.1 Part I

371. **Motor Vehicles (Construction and Use) (Amendment No.2) Regulations (Northern Ireland) 1997**
revoked: SR 1999/454 Reg.126, Sch.19

371. **Register of Occupational and Personal Pension Schemes Regulations 1997**
Reg.1, see *Bus Employees Pension Trustees Ltd v Harrod* [1999] 3 W.L.R. 1260 (Ch D), Sir Richard Scott, V.C.
Reg.1, amended: SI 1998/600 Reg.3
Reg.3, amended: SI 1997/3038 Reg.11, SI 1998/600 Reg.3
Reg.4, amended: SI 1997/1405 Reg.2, SI 1998/600 Reg.3
Reg.5, amended: SI 1998/600 Reg.3
Reg.8, amended: SI 1997/1405 Reg.2, SI 1998/600 Reg.3

382. **Plant Breeders' Rights (Fees) (Amendment) Regulations 1997**
revoked: SI 1998/1021 Reg.7 (with savings), Sch.2 (with savings)
Reg.2, revoked: SI 1998/1021 Reg.7 (with savings), Sch.2 (with savings)
Sch., revoked: SI 1998/1021 Reg.7 (with savings), Sch.2 (with savings)

387. **Health and Safety (Young Persons) Regulations (Northern Ireland) 1997**
referred to: SI 1998/2411 Reg.3

389. **Bovine Products (Production and Despatch) Regulations 1997**
revoked: SI 1997/1905 Reg.20
Reg.3, referred to: SI 1997/1905 Art.6
Reg.3, revoked: SI 1997/1905 Reg.20
Reg.6, revoked: SI 1997/1905 Reg.20
Reg.10, revoked: SI 1997/1905 Reg.20
Reg.13, revoked: SI 1997/1905 Reg.20
Reg.14, revoked: SI 1997/1905 Reg.20

430

EC, but which only came into force on the date they ratified the Convention. In such cases it is the practice to notify their entry into force in the *London*, *Edinburgh* and *Belfast Gazettes*. This practice is apparently dictated by the Foreign and Commonwealth Office, without regard for the fact that few law libraries take the *London Gazette* and that it only has quarterly indexes. If you do use the indexes, look under 'Foreign and Commonwealth Office'. For issues since the last index look through each one in the 'State Intelligence' section at the front and keep an eye out for the 'Foreign and Commonwealth Office'. But it may be easier just to telephone the Treaty Section of the Records and Historical Department at the Foreign and Commonwealth Office. An alternative to notification in the *London Gazette* arose, whether by accident or design, in what seems to have been the unique example of the Antarctic Regulations 1995. That had a commencement provision like an Act – it was to come in to force on a day appointed by the Secretary of State. In the event, rather than there being a sub-delegated 'commencement order', an amending SI was subsequently issued substituting a date, 1 November, for what had been provided.

EC legislation

Introduction

3.107 A brief outline of the history of the European Union and its institutions may be helpful in understanding the legislation emanating from it. The first European Community was the European Coal and Steel Community (ECSC), formed in 1952. The treaty establishing it is due to expire in 2002, and is not likely to be renewed. The treaty establishing the European Economic Community (EEC), the Treaty of Rome, was signed in 1957 by the original six member states. At the same time the European Atomic Energy Community (Euratom) was established, making three European Communities. The European Communities, in the plural, continue to function under their respective treaties, though since 1965 they have shared common institutions in the form of the Commission and Council. The Single European Act signed in 1986 amended the EEC Treaty, and set the ball rolling for much wider harmonisation in order to extend the Common Market into a truly single internal market, with a deadline, largely met, of the end of 1992. In 1992, the Treaty of European Union was signed at Maastricht. This renamed the European Economic Community as the European Community (EC) and added economic and monetary union to its objects. It also created the wider concept of a European Union that would embrace political union, and specified two areas for joint action outside the purely economic sphere, foreign and security policy, on the one hand, and justice and home affairs, on the other. These two areas are said to form the second and third pillars which the European Union (EU), as created at Maastricht, comprises, with the first pillar being the European Communities (in the plural). Maastricht also reformed some of the decision-making procedures, and strengthened the role of the European Parliament (on which, see further paras **4.86–4.87**). This process was continued by the Treaty of Amsterdam signed in 1997, which further enhanced the role of the European Parliament, and also transferred one particular aspect of the third pillar, immigration and asylum of non-EU nationals, to the EC treaty, in the first pillar. The Treaty of Amsterdam also renumbered the articles of the EC treaty and EU treaty. The Treaty of Nice concluded in February 2001 will (when ratified by all member states – a referendum in Ireland rather awkwardly rejected it) make further changes to the voting structure, amend the functioning of the European Court of Justice, and allow for the transfer of the assets of the ECSC to the EC when the

ECSC treaty expires. The status of the Charter of Fundamental Rights of the European Union 'proclaimed' at Nice will be subject to a further intergovernmental conference in 2004.

3.108 Reform of the machinery of the EU has been particularly driven by enlargement. The UK, together with Ireland and Denmark, had joined with effect from the beginning of 1973. Greece joined in 1981, followed by Spain and Portugal in 1986, and Austria, Finland and Sweden in 1996, making 15 member states (and 11 official languages). Norway and Switzerland remain the main 'western' countries outside the EU. A queue is forming of eastern European states wishing to join.

3.109 The Council of the European Union consists of one representative of ministerial level from each member state. The same ministers, however, do not attend every meeting – the composition is dictated by the subject matter, and so the Council is a fluctuating body. It is the main decision-making and legislation-making body, though it is generally the Commission that initiates legislative proposals. Since Maastricht much legislation passes by the co-decision procedure, with the legislation being made jointly by the Council and the European Parliament, with the latter having a veto. The European Council, as distinct from the Council of the European Union, is the formalised structure for twice-yearly summits between heads of member states, which are intended to provide the political impetus to developments in the EU. In recent times it has also become the practice to have an informal meeting of the European Council as well as the two now stipulated in the treaty.

3.110 The Commission, whose formal title remains the Commission of the European Communities (not of the European Union), consists of 20 members from member states. It has three main functions: the initiation of legislative proposals; enforcement of EC law; and to provide the executive for the EC. In addition it makes legislation itself, either under powers delegated by the Council or in a few limited areas under powers given directly by the treaties. The 'civil service' of the Commission is organised into 23 directorates-general, and each commissioner has a 'ministerial portfolio' of one or more directorates-generals.

3.111 The European Parliament was originally only an advisory and consultative body. Since 1979 it has been directly elected, and its powers in the legislative process increased under successive treaties. Under the co-decision procedure it now plays a full part in performing the functions its name implies. This is discussed more fully at paras **4.84–4.87**. There remain, however, areas where the Council or the Commission can make legislation with no or only limited involvement of the Parliament.

Types of EC legislation

3.112 The terms primary and secondary legislation are sometimes applied to EC legislation, but they bear a slightly different meaning from those terms in the context of domestic legislation as described at the start of this chapter. Primary legislation refers to the treaty provisions contained in the treaties that established the three Communities, the subsequent treaties outlined above, together with the treaties of accession by subsequent member states. The treaty provisions can have direct effect and are capable of conferring individual rights enforceable in the UK courts without further enactment. Discussion of this form of legislation is deferred to chapter 6, where treaties in general are dealt with. Here we are concerned with secondary legislation, that is the legislation that emanates from the Council, the Council acting jointly with the European Parliament, and the Commission. In the following description of the types of legislation and their numbering and citation, it is legislation made under the EC treaty that is being referred to, which of course accounts for the vast bulk of the material. Legislation under the Euratom Treaty is exactly the same, but legislation under the ECSC Treaty, should you encounter it, has its own peculiarities, which will be mentioned separately (see para **3.116**). There are three main types: Directives, Regulations, and Decisions. The Council and the Commission also issue Recommendations and Opinions, but these are only a form of quasi-legislation and do not have binding force. Whether a particular piece of legislation takes the form of a Directive, a Regulation or a Decision depends on the 'legal basis' – ie which treaty article – it is made under. In most cases the Commission in formulating legislative proposals is free to choose which method would be most appropriate, but in some fields the relevant treaty article specifies that legislation must be by means of either a Directive or a Decision; only in a very few instances is legislation by Regulation mandatory.

3.113 A Directive, without more, does not have direct effect but requires all the member states to enact domestic legislation within a certain period of time. A Directive may, however, acquire direct effect and confer rights on individuals if it is not implemented in domestic law within the specified period or if the purported implementing legislation is contrary to the Directive. Most Directives are implemented in the UK by means of SIs, the enabling power for the making of the SIs being the European Communities Act 1972. Exceptionally, if its importance warrants it, a Directive may be implemented by means of an Act. The Consumer Protection Act 1987, which implemented the Product Liability Directive 85/374, and the Data Protection Act 1998, which implemented Directive 95/46, are two of the few examples. For the very rare occasions when implementation is by means of a Direction, which is not an SI, see para **3.138**.

3.114 Regulations, on the other hand, are directly applicable in that they do not require national implementing legislation. Indeed it can be contrary to EC law for a member state to enact its own legislation in an area provided for by a Regulation. This can give rise to the misconception that national legislation is of no relevance to Regulations. In practice many Regulations require additional national provisions in relation to, for example, procedure and enforcement, and such legislation is perfectly permissible as long as it does not impinge on the substantive effect of the Regulation. In 2000, although about 140 SIs or SSIs were issued in connection with the implementation of Directives, a further 70 or so were concerned only with Regulations.

3.115 Decisions, in contrast to Directives and Regulations, are not of general application but are addressed to particular member states or undertakings or individuals. They are binding on those to whom they are addressed. Decisions addressed to undertakings are particularly numerous in the competition field. Decisions addressed to member states may require national legislation, and where that is not forthcoming or defective, Decisions may have direct effect in the same circumstances as do Directives. Although particularity, rather than generality, of application is the hallmark of a Decision, where a Decision is addressed to all member states, it begins to take on the appearance of a Regulation. Decisions addressed to member states are less numerous than either Regulations or Directives. In the first edition of this book it was noted that in 1991 only seven SIs had to be issued in connection with Decisions. The BSE crisis has been responsible for a slightly larger number more recently – about 30 SIs were issued in 2000 in connection with Decisions.

3.116 There are two main types of ECSC legislation, Recommendations and Decisions. Each can either be 'general' or 'individual' in character. The latter distinction has legal significance, but for practical purposes if they are 'general' they are numbered like Regulations and appear in the 'obligatory' part of the *Official Journal* (OJ) (see para **3.123**); if they are 'individual' they are numbered in the style of Directives and appear in the 'non-obligatory' part of the OJ. An ECSC Recommendation, unlike an EC Recommendation, is binding, and is akin to an EC Directive, in that the choice of means of achieving the result is left to the addressee. They are different from Directives, however, in that they may be addressed to individuals as well as to member states. The ECSC equivalent of a Regulation is a 'general' Decision, whereas ECSC Decisions 'individual in character' roughly equate to an EC Decision. (Generally, see further the entries under Decision, General Decision, Individual Decision, and Recommendation in A G Toth *Oxford Encyclopaedia of European Community Law* (vol 1, 1990)).

Numbering and citation

3.117 An EC Regulation is illustrated (see figure 3.16). The format is similar for other types of legislation. All the Regulations passed in each year are assigned a running number in one sequence and all the Directives are assigned a number in another sequence. Decisions made up to the end of 1991 shared the same sequence as Directives. From the beginning of 1992 they were assigned their own sequence. To provide unique identification, the digits of the year are added to the number – originally just the last two digits of the year were used. From 1999 the full four digits have been used. Regulations can be distinguished from Directives and Decisions since the year is given after the number for the Regulations whereas the year is given before the number in the case of Directives and Decisions. For example, a Regulation passed in 1998 might be 534/98 and a Directive from the same year 98/143. Thus it is necessary to remain alert when dealing with those numbers in the annual sequence that could be mistaken for a year, for example, Regulation 90/91 or Directive 76/84. Although all legislation has since 1967 emanated from the joint bodies of the three European Communities, in a formal citation it is the practice to add the abbreviation for the relevant Community. It was also the formal practice to specify whether the legislation was made by the Council or the Commission. That practice continues, but a succinct way of describing legislation made by both the Council and the European Parliament under the co-decision procedure has not been arrived at. Some examples of citations of legislation of different dates are:

> Council Directive 76/149/EEC
> Council Directive 1999/20/EC
> Directive 2000/12/EC of the European Parliament and of the Council
> Commission Regulation 723/84/EEC
> Commission Regulation 1467/2000/EC
> Council Decision 89/176/Euratom
> Commission Decision 2030/82/ECSC
> Commission Recommendation 94/780/ECSC

3.118 In addition the date the legislation was made and the subject matter as it appears at the head of the text of the legislation may be given. As discussed below, the official text of legislation is published in the OJ L series. It is helpful and good practice to add the OJ citation. For the latter it is usually sufficient to specify the issue number and year, or the particular date on which the issue was published (which is not the same as the date the legislation was made), but for completeness both may be given. Thus a completely comprehensive citation would be:

Council Directive 82/471/EEC of June 30, 1982, Concerning Certain Products Used in Animal Nutrition (OJ No L213, 21.7.1982, p 8)

But for most practical purposes all that is needed is:

Dir. 82/471 (OJ 1982 L213)

Indeed, if all you had was 82/471, it would still be traceable, since before 1992 the numbers were unique. However, since Decisions were given their own separate sequence of numbers, a reference such as 1999/70 would refer to either of two documents unless 'Dir.' or 'Dec.' was specified. One other point on Decisions may be noted. You might come across one cited in this form: Commission Decision No. C(2000) 2046 of 24 July 2000. This is the number of the document notifying the decision to the recipient party. When published in the OJ a conventional Decision number will be given (and the number of the notification document cited). However, it would seem from examples that occasionally crop up in implementing SIs that they are not necessarily published in the OJ.

3.119 ECSC Recommendations and Decisions appear in the year/number sequence if they are 'individual'; if they are 'general' they appear in the number/year sequence. Speaking very loosely, the majority of ECSC Recommendations are in the year/number sequence together with EC Directives and Decisions; and the majority of ECSC Decisions are in the number/year sequence together with the EC Regulations.

3.120 The formal titles of EC legislation, in comparison with the titles of UK statutes and SIs, are usually the least used and least useful part of their citation on account of their length and unmemorability (eg Commission Directive on the Approximation of the Laws of the Member States Relating to Motor-Vehicle Headlamps which Function as Main-Beam and/or Dipped-Beam Headlamps and to Incandescent Electric Filament Lamps for such Headlamps). However, some legislation may be referred to colloquially or for convenience by some short title, especially if it is well known or important, for example, the Second Banking Directive. That particular Directive illustrates the hazards of colloquial titles. Its formal title is: Second Council Directive on the coordination of laws, regulations and administrative provisions relating to the taking up of the business of credit institutions. It will be seen that even with such prolixity the word 'banking' does not appear. Thus the use of colloquial titles without at some point giving a Directive number or OJ reference is to be deprecated (the Second Banking Directive, by the way, is Directive 89/646 OJ 1989 L386).

Celex document numbers

3.121 As using EC legislation will almost certainly take you to electronic sources, most of which derive from the official EU database, Celex, a simplified outline of

Figure 3.16

No L 205/2   Official Journal of the European Communities   22. 7. 92

COUNCIL REGULATION (EEC) No 2015/92

of 20 July 1992

amending Regulation (EEC) No 1432/92 prohibiting trade between the European Economic Community and the Republics of Serbia and Montenegro

THE COUNCIL OF THE EUROPEAN COMMUNITIES,

Whereas under Regulation (EEC) No 1432/92 (¹), trade between the European Economic Community and the Republics of Serbia and Montenegro is prohibited ;

Whereas the United Nations Security Council adopted on 18 June 1992 Resolution 760 (1992), which allows under certain conditions the export to the Republics of Serbia and Montenegro of commodities and products for essential humanitarian need ;

Whereas it is necessary to amend Regulation (EEC) No 1432/92 in order to allow under certain conditions the exports to the Republics of Serbia and Montenegro of commodities and products for essential humanitarian need ;

Having regard to the Treaty establishing the European Economic Community, and in particular Article 113 thereof,

Having regard to the proposal from the Commission,

HAS ADOPTED THIS REGULATION :

Article 1

Regulation (EEC) No 1432/92 is hereby amended as follows :

1. Paragraph (a) of Article 2 shall be replaced by the following :

'(a) the export to the Republics of Serbia and Montenegro of commodities and products intended for strictly medical purposes and foodstuffs notified to the Committee established pursuant to Resolution 724 (1992) of the United Nations Security Council, as well as the export to these Republics of commodities and products for essential humanitarian need, which has been approved by the said Committee under the simplified and accelerated "no objection" procedure ;'.

2. Article 3 shall be replaced by the following :

'*Article 3*

Exports to the Republics of Serbia and Montenegro of commodities and products for strictly medical purposes or for essential humanitarian need as well as foodstuffs shall be subject to a prior export authorization to be issued by the competent authorities of the Member States.'

Article 2

This Regulation shall enter into force on the day of its publication in the *Official Journal of the European Communities.*

It shall apply with effect from 19 June 1992.

This Regulation shall be binding in its entirety and directly applicable in all Member States.

Done at Brussels, 20 July 1992.

For the Council
The President
D. HURD

(¹) OJ No L 151, 3. 6. 1992, p. 4.

the mysteries of Celex document numbers is provided here. For almost all everyday purposes there is no need to use or understand them, but having a rough idea of what the strings of numbers cluttering you screen mean may make using the databases less daunting. A typical Celex document number, which uniquely identifies it on the system, looks like this:

31999LOO78

This is the number for Directive 1999/78. There are four elements to the number: Sector Number/Year/Document Type/Document number. A single digit represents the sector of the database the document is in. For example, 1 is for Treaties and 6 is for Case Law. Secondary legislation, as here, is 3. Then follows the year. This is now given in the full four digits, even for documents created before 1999 (though in the Directory of Community Legislation in Force on EUR-Lex, described further at para **3.127**, they display only two digits, even after 1999). A letter gives the Document Type. Letters have different meanings according to sector. For secondary legislation, ie sector 3, L stands for Directive, R for Regulation and D for Decision. Lastly there is the number of the Directive preceded by the requisite number of zeroes to make a four-digit number.

Sources for the text of EC legislation

Official Journal of the European Communities

3.122 Since 1967 the OJ has been published in two main series, Legislation (L series) and Information and Notices (C series, for 'Communications'), and it is the former which is the official vehicle for promulgating Community legislation. (There is also a supplementary S series for public procurement tenders.) It follows from the continental model of issuing legislation in the form of official gazettes. Both series are published in the 11 official languages. Most UK libraries will naturally only have the English version; one or two of the larger libraries, for example, the Institute of Advanced Legal Studies, may also have the French version, but all versions are equally authentic. They are extremely voluminous, being published almost daily. Although we are here concerned with the L series, it should be noted that because of the problem of volume from 1999 some material that is published in the C series is being made available in electronic format only (see para **4.85**).

3.123 When using them, two features can cause some puzzlement. First, some items are listed in bold with an asterisk, others are not; the latter are supposedly of lesser importance or short duration, usually on agricultural matters. Secondly, it is arranged in two sequences described as 'Acts whose publication is obligatory' and 'Acts whose publication is not obligatory'. The legal significance of this is that instruments in the first category take legal effect by virtue of publication in the OJ. Until the Maastricht Treaty, Regulations formed the main type of legislation to fall into this category; somewhat surprisingly Directives came in the second category. Since Maastricht, which put Directives into the first category, the second category mainly comprises Decisions – they take legal effect by virtue of notification to the state or undertaking affected, though it has always been the practice to publish most of them in the OJ.

3.124 As the OJ was not published in English before the accession of the UK, a special edition in several volumes was published in 1972 which translated all

Community legislation then in force into English. A further special edition, containing material not included in the first, was published in 1974.

Encyclopedia of European Community Law

3.125 This looseleaf work published by Sweet & Maxwell used to be published in three series. Series A contained UK legislation and Series B the treaties. Series A has gone and Series B has been revamped as the *Encylopedia of European Union Law: Constitutional Texts*. However, for the time being Series C continues on in its old format. Its ten or so volumes contain the text of much (though by no means all) EC secondary legislation in force. It is arranged by broad topic, with material filed chronologically within topics. Where a Regulation or Directive amends an earlier one, the original one is usually reprinted as amended. The first volume contains comprehensive tables of treaty provisions and secondary legislation by number. The last volume contains an index. As with some other very large looseleaf works, a hazard to be aware of is that the tables and index are not replaced in their entirety with every service issue but only consolidated from time to time. Separate supplementary tables and index will be found after the main sequence.

Other printed sources

3.126 Many looseleaf subject encyclopaedias will have an 'EC materials' tab, where will be found reprinted legislation relevant to the topic; likewise the subject 'handbooks' of legislation such as *Butterworths Employment Law Handbook* or the *E.C. Competition Law Handbook* from Sweet & Maxwell. Commercial publishers in other member states have produced works similar to Sweet & Maxwell's *Encyclopedia* in their own languages.

Electronic sources

3.127 Although the paper sources listed above continue to have their place, it is increasingly seldom that anyone will not go first to an electronic source. Electronic publishing of legislation by the EU itself is in a state of flux. Having overall responsibility is EUR-OP, the Office of Official Publications of the European Union. Until very recently it provided three different, but overlapping services, which are now reduced to two. First is Celex. This historically was the original official database, and contains the full text of all legislation, and much else besides. It remains the most complete and authoritative database, and provides much of the data to the other two services. It also remains a pay-for service, at any rate as a fully functional service (for limited free access, see para **3.128**). You can subscribe to the web version or CD-ROM versions direct from EUR-OP, but use of the data has been licensed to many other commercial suppliers, who offer different search facilities and interfaces and who also may add data of their own. On CD-ROM, the Justis version from Context is justifiably popular, but there is also OJCD from Ellis and Eurolaw from ILI. Both Context and Ellis offer web versions as well as the CD. Other online versions include Lawtel EU, EU Direct on Butterworths LEXIS Direct, Lexis itself and Westlaw. The second official service is EUR-Lex. This is the free website of European Law. The last 45 days' editions of the OJ are provided, just as they appear in paper. But much more useful is the *Directory of Community Legislation in Force*. This has a slightly odd appearance at first, since the primary arrangement is by subject matter, organised in a complex analytical directory. But embedded in it is the full text of the legislation itself (provided it is in force). This takes two forms. One is the legislation, as it was made. The other is consolidated legislation providing the text as amended. The consolidated texts do not have official status, but can be very useful. If a particular piece of legislation is retrieved, a link to the consolidated version is provided. It will thus be seen that unless you need legislation that is no longer in force (and there is a way round that, see para **3.128**) , you can at least get hold of the text of legislation even if you do not have access to any of the versions of Celex mentioned above. A third service used to be EUDOR. This was essentially a document delivery service, but with searchable catalogue data. External access to EUDOR was closed at the end of May 2001, but it continues to be provided as an internal service.

3.128 EUR-Lex and (if you subscribe) Celex are available on the main Europa server, but a number of other gateways will take you into them. Sarah Carter's Lawlinks points out that the University of California at Berkeley has a useful rearrangement of the Europa site, and also draws attention to the University of Mannheim's European Documentation Centre site. The latter gives limited free access to Celex. You can search for any legislation by OJ reference; in addition you can search for Regulations by number, and Directives by title or number. So provided you have a reference, you can access legislation no longer in force, which is not on EUR-Lex.

Finding known EC legislation

3.129 On electronic sources it should be straightforward to find a particular piece of legislation if you have a number or OJ reference. The Justis version of Celex on its Quick Search form has separate buttons to enter an OJ reference, a document number (ie Regulation, Directive or Decision number) and, very usefully, a colloquial title. If you search by Regulation or Directive number, the system is fairly robust as to form; for example, it will accept Directive 89/646 or Dir 89/646. If you are searching for a Decision, however, put in 'Decision' in full. If you do not have access to a commercial version, use EUR-Lex, which is reached from the Europa site: click on 'Official Documents' and then 'Legislation in force'. The 'Directory of Community legislation in force' is then displayed, with a link to an 'Alphabetical index' at the top. This is a *subject* index. Ignore this and click on the search button on the left (also at the bottom of the screen). Choose legislation in force (the OJ option is only for the last 45 days) and enter a number. If you prefer to use the Mannheim site, choose the 'Virtual Fulltext Library' option on the home page. The search options are then clearly laid out and include OJ reference if that is what you have.

3.130 If you are using paper sources and only have a Directive or Regulation number, the best place to look is Butterworths' *European Communities Legislation: Current Status*, which will give you the OJ reference. Another possibility is the tables at the front of the first volume of *Encyclopedia of European Community Law: C series*. The legislation you are after may well be reprinted there (reference in bold), but even if not it may be referred to, and the OJ reference given. For recent legislation remember to check the supplementary table. The monthly indexes to the OJ, which cumulate annually, also contain numerical lists. The consolidated tables volume of *Halsbury's Laws* also has very full numerical lists. The main point to bear in mind when using any of these tables is the order in which the different categories of legislation are listed. The Quick Reference Guide sets this out (QR3.18).

3.131 If all you have is a title, such as Fourth Directive on Company Law, you will probably need to use an electronic source. The various commercial versions will have full Boolean search facilities, but even EUR-Lex has a basic plain text search facility. A search in the legislation field on the *Legal Journals Index* or Badger is also quite often a handy short cut for legislation that is likely to have been commented on.

Finding EC legislation by subject

3.132 Electronic sources are again pretty much *de rigeur*. If you have to use manual sources, try the subject indexes to *European Communities Legislation: Current Status* and to the *Encyclopedia of European Community Law*. Also bear in mind looseleaf subject encyclopaedias, particularly on heavily Europeanised topics, such as *Butterworths Competition Law Service* or Miller's *Product Liability and Safety Encyclopaedia*. The EC produces its own indexes in the form of monthly indexes to the OJ and the *Directory of Community Legislation in Force and Other Acts of the Community Institutions*, which cumulates twice a year. But these are not particularly easy to use.

Finding amendments and repeals

3.133 On Celex separate 'modifies' and 'modified' fields for each piece of legislation list all amendments and repeals. The relevant documents are listed in Celex document number format. The Justis version is particularly good at checking amendments. You do not need to go to the amendments field. Having retrieved the legislation you are interested in, click on the Cross-ref button and all documents that have amended it or that it amends are displayed in either graphical form under J-View tab or in plain text under the 'amends' and 'amended by' tabs. Since Celex contains legislative proposals as well as legislation, there will almost always be something under the 'amends' tab. Even if the legislation amends no other legislation, a reference to the original proposal will be given there (a P in the middle of the Celex document number). In EUR-Lex, if you search legislation in force, the amendments are listed with hypertext links to each amending instrument. Alternatively, if it has been consolidated a link will be given to that. The text, which is in pdf format, will give at the start the amendments incorporated and then indicate by marginal notes where amending text has been inserted. If you want to double-check for any very recent amendments that have not been incorporated into the Directory of Legislation in Force, it is certainly worth searching the file of recent editions of the OJ. As most amending legislation contains the number of the legislation being amended as part of its title, for example, 'Commission Regulation 2788/98 Amending Council Directive 70/524 Concerning Additives in Feedingstuffs', select a plain text search, choose to search OJ summaries and then enter the number of the legislation in the search box. The summary of research results only displays the first item listed on the front of each issue of the OJ, so you will need to look through any hits in the L series to confirm that there is indeed some amending legislation there. Likewise, the same search, but selecting legislation in preparation, would alert you to any impending amendments. EUR-Lex does not contain legislation wholly repealed, so if you do not retrieve the legislation in question at all, the implication is that it has been repealed. If you wanted to double-check that without access to one of the commercial versions of Celex, go to the Mannheim site and search by Directive or Regulation number. The text should be there headed in red 'No longer in force', though it will not tell you directly what repealed it. Also on the EUR-Lex site you could do a search by putting the relevant number as a search term in the plain text search box, since amending legislation will almost always have the number the legislation being amended in the title.

3.134 If you are confined to hard copy sources, the best source is Butterworths' *EC Legislation: Current Status*, which lists all EC legislation chronologically by number and indicates whether it is still in force or whether it is has been amended (see figure 3.17). It is reissued every year in two bound volumes, with a softback index volume and quarterly supplements. In connection with this work and also the *Implementator* (see para **3.136**) there is a fortnightly newsletter *Butterworths EC Legislation Service* and also a telephone inquiry service. The *Encyclopedia of European Community Law* could also help. It either reprints the legislation incorporating amendments or indicates amending legislation in the annotations, though watch out for its currency. The hard copy version of the *Directory of Community Legislation in Force*, which is issued twice a year, is obviously intended for the task. The main difficulty is finding the legislation concerned in vol 1, which is arranged by broad subject. Volume 2 contains a numerical list, but in the form of Celex document numbers (see para **3.121**); otherwise there is an alphabetical index in vol 2.

Finding UK implementation of EC legislation

3.135 Celex has a national implementation field for Directives, but it is one part of the database that is notoriously out-of-date. It may be better than nothing if you wanted to find implementing measures in other member states. However, on the Justis version Context have supplemented the information on UK implementation with their own data, which should be reasonably up-to-date. Another very effective method is to search full text versions of UK legislation, using the number as a search term. Unlike the implementation field on Celex, which is only dealing with implementation in the strict sense of implementation of Directives, this will pick up UK legislation made in connection with the operation of Regulations. As most implementation is by means of SI, rather than Act, start with those (see para **3.87**), and then if necessary search statutes (see paras **3.17** and **3.24–3.28**). Lawtel is also a good source: their SI database now includes references to EC legislation being implemented. Alternatively, if you subscribe to Lawtel EU, and retrieve the record for the Directive or Regulation, the implementing SIs are listed with hypertext links to the text of them. Badger also gives implementation information in the abstract or scope fields for records for SIs, though if all SIs that may relate in any way to an EC Regulation are required, it may be as well to check a full text source as well as Lawtel and Badger.

3.136 There are paper sources too, notably *Butterworths EC Legislation Implemenatator*, which is issued twice a year – see figure 3.18. The main body of the work is arranged by Directive number against which details of UK implementation are given. If there is no entry for a Directive, then no implementing SIs have so far been noted. It also includes as an appendix the Commission's annual report on implementation in all member states, which lists those Directives that the Commission has taken action about during the year. *Current Law* also has a table of European Legislation Implemented by SI, cumulated in each monthly part, and then appearing in the bound volume of the *Legislation Citator*. Unlike the Butterworths *Implementator*, this covers Regulations as well as Directives, but does not include implementation by Act, in the few cases that that arises.

Figure 3.17 EC Legislation: Current Status.

86/104 [Cm Dec (EEC)]

86/104 [Cm Dec (EEC)]
(OJ L93 08.04.1986 p13)

on the implementation of the reform of
agricultural structure in Ireland pursuant to
797/85

86/105 [Cm Dec (EEC)]
(OJ L93 08.04.1986 p14)

amending 76/791, 78/436, 81/651

86/109 [Cm Dir (EEC)]
(OJ L93 08.04.1986 p21)

limiting the marketing of seed of certain
species of fodder plants and oil and fibre
plants to seed which has been officially
certified as basic seed or certified seed

2	r 89/424
2a	ad 89/424
3	r *89/424*, 91/376
3a	ad 91/376
4	am 89/424

86/110 [Cm Dec (EEC)]
(OJ L93 08.04.1986 p23)

on the conditions under which derogations
from the prohibition on the use of EEC
labels for the purpose of resealing and
relabelling packages of seed produced in
third countries may be granted

86/113 [Cl Dir (EEC)]
(OJ L95 10.04.1986 p45)

laying down minimum standards for the
protection of laying hens kept in battery
cages

86/114 [Cm Dec (EEC)]
(OJ L99 15.04.1986 p21)

amending 85/634 (see also Directive
88/166)

86/116 [Cm Dec (EEC)]
(OJ L99 15.04.1986 p25)

concerning zones referred to in 2616/80, art
2(3)

86/117 [Cm Dec (EEC)]
(OJ L99 15.04.1986 p26)

concerning animal health conditions and
veterinary certification for the import of
fresh meat from Greenland

86/121 [Cl Dir (EEC)]
(OJ L100 16.04.1986 p20)

amending 84/631

86/122 [Cl Dir (EEC)]
(OJ L100 16.04.1986 p22)

amending 79/409

86/125 [None Dec (EEC,ECSC)]
(OJ L86 31.03.1986 p1)

on the conclusion of the Third ACP-EEC
Convention

86/126 [None Dec (EEC,ECSC)]
(OJ L86 31.03.1986 p210)

Internal Agreement on the financing and
administration of Community aid

86/127 [None Dec (EEC,ECSC)]
(OJ L86 31.03.1986 p221)

Internal Agreement on the measures and
procedures required for implementation of
the Third ACP-EEC Convention

86/129 [Cm Dec (EEC)]
(OJ L101 17.04.1986 p32)

amending 75/271

86/130 [Cm Dec (EEC)]
(OJ L101 17.04.1986 p37)

laying down performance monitoring
methods and methods for assessing cattle's
genetic value for purebred breeding animals
of the bovine species

An   r 94/515

86/131 [Cm Dec (EEC)]
(OJ L101 17.04.1986 p40)

amending 83/471

450

3.137 If you find that implementation has not yet happened, you may wish to know how and when it will be implemented. Government consultation papers often precede implementation of major Directives. There may be comment in the legal journals. Press releases and parliamentary questions are other likely sources. Otherwise, see if you can find an official in the relevant government department from the *Civil Service Yearbook*.

Implementation by Direction

3.138 A number of statutes authorise the Secretary of State to give Directions to various bodies or agencies as to how they are to perform their functions. Such Directions are not generally SIs (see para **3.160**). In a few cases it is explicitly provided that such Directions may be made in order to implement the UK's obligations under the Community treaty. The main examples are Directions to the Environment Agency under s 40 of the Environment Act 1995 (and Directions to the Environment Agency's precursor bodies: to Her Majesty's Inspectorate of Pollution under s 7 of the Environmental Protection Act 1990, and to the National Rivers Authority under s 5 of the Water Resources Act 1991), Directions to local authorities under s 86 of the 1995 Act, Directions to regulators under Sch 1, para 3 to the Pollution and Prevention and Control Act 1999, and Directions to the Food Standards Agency under s 24(4) of the Food Standards Act 1999. Whether a particular Directive has been implemented by such means may not be all that easy to establish. There is a list of seven implementing Directions made under previous legislation in the annotations to s 40 of the Environment Act 1995 in *Current Law Statutes* (see also the annotations to s 5 of the Water Resources Act 1991 for comment on this means of implementation). Some may be reprinted in looseleaf works on environmental law. Directions that have been made to the Environment Agency have to set out in their annual report, which is laid before Parliament (s 52). Once a Direction implementing EC legislation has been made, it can only be varied or revoked if the conditions in s 122 are complied with, which include giving notice in the *London Gazette*. As stated in para **3.137**, with this problem you may be best off trying to speak to someone at the relevant government department or agency.

Local and Personal Acts

3.139 A separate parliamentary procedure is available to enact legislation that affects only a particular locality, person or body. A distinctive feature of this procedure is that rather than being initiated by a minister or an MP, as is public legislation, the Bill is promoted by the person or body interested (on the procedure, see further para **4.71**). The resulting Acts are known collectively as Local and Personal Acts (the terminology 'Private Acts', by which name they may also be known, is discussed below). Local and Personal Acts were very numerous in the nineteenth century; there were many more than the Public General Acts. They were used particularly in relation to boroughs, railway and canal companies, and the enclosure of common land. On the personal side, they were one important method of obtaining a divorce before it became available in the secular courts in 1857, and they were the only way of obtaining naturalisation before 1844. Their numbers have since declined, and the modern Local Acts have usually been employed in connection with the powers and constitutions of bodies such as local authorities, statutory companies and universities, and to enable works to be carried out for railways, light rapid transit systems, harbours and marinas. Their number has

Figure 3.18 EC Legislation Implementator.

Butterworths EC Legislation Implementator

Directive Number	Title/OJ Reference	Target Date	UK Legislation
82/319	Commission Directive (EEC) amending 77/541 OJ L139 19.05.82 p17	01.10.82 / 01.10.83 / 01.10.90	**SI 1982/1479** The Motor Vehicles (Designation of Approval Marks) (Amendment) Regulations 1982 **SI 1982/1623** The Motor Vehicles (Type Approval) (Amendment) (No. 2) Regulations 1982 (implement 77/541 as amended by 81/576, 82/319) **SI 1990/461** The Motor Vehicles (Type Approval and Approval Marks) (Fees) Regulations 1990 (implement 77/541 as amended by 81/576, 82/319) **SI 1991/820** The Motor Vehicles (Type Approval) (Amendment) Regulations 1991 (implement 77/541 as amended by 81/576, 82/319, 90/628) **SI 1998/2429** The Road Vehicles (Construction and Use) (Amendment) (No 6) Regulations 1998 (implement 77/541 as amended by 81/576, 82/319, 90/628 and 96/36)
82/368	Council Directive (EEC) amending 76/768 OJ L167 15.06.82 p1	01.01.83	**SI 1984/1260** The Cosmetic Products (Safety) Regulations 1984 **SI 1985/2045** The Cosmetic Products (Safety) (Amendment) Regulations 1985 (implement 84/415 which amends 82/368)
82/434	Commission Directive (EEC) on the approximation of the laws of the member states relating to methods of analysis necessary for checking the composition of cosmetic products OJ L185 30.06.82 p1	31.12.83	**SI 1983/1477** The Cosmetic Products (Amendment) Regulations 1983 **SI 1984/1260** The Cosmetic Products (Safety) Regulations 1984 **SI 1989/2233** The Cosmetic Products (Safety) Regulations 1989 **SI 1991/447** The Cosmetic Products (Safety) (Amendment) Regulations 1991 (implement 90/207 which amends 82/434)
82/471	Council Directive (EEC) concerning certain products used in animal nutrition OJ L213 21.07.82 p8	30.08.82	**SI 1994/499** The Feeding Stuffs (Amendment) Regulations 1994 **SI 1995/1412** The Feeding Stuffs Regulations 1995 **SI 1996/1260** The Feeding Stuffs (Amendment) Regulations 1996 (implement 95/33 which amends 82/471) **SI 1998/1049** The Feeding Stuffs (Establishments and Intermediaries) Regulations 1998 (implement 95/69 which amends 70/524, 74/63, 79/373 and 82/471) **SI 1999/1528** The Feeding Stuffs (Amendment) Regulations 1999 (implement 96/25 which amends 70/524, 74/63, 82/471 and 93/74)

declined even further since new procedures were introduced by the Transport and Works Act 1992 for authorising such works without the need for specific legislation. Whereas in 1899, 277 Local Acts were passed, in 1999 there were only four. On the personal side, these Acts have long been extremely rare. One vestigial use was to enable the marriage of persons within the prohibited degrees of affinity, for example, stepmother and stepson, but with the passing of the Marriage (Prohibited Degrees of Relationship) Act 1986 even for that purpose a personal Act is no longer necessary. The last personal Act to be passed was in 1987. Notwithstanding the decline in this form of legislation, very many Local and Personal Acts, often of considerable age, remain in force. Although of little concern to the student, the practitioner who regularly deals with matters connected with land, local authorities, utilities and transport may well have to grapple with them.

3.140 The current position, then, is that there are three separately numbered series of Acts of Parliament: Public General, Local and Personal, though the latter two will be found on the shelf bound together and share a common title page. Public General Acts have a chapter number in ordinary arabic numerals, Local Acts have lower case roman numerals and Personal Acts have arabic numerals in italic. How this position was arrived at and the history of the organisation of the printing and publication of this form of legislation is not altogether straightforward, but needs to set out for a full understanding of what is to be found on the shelves of those libraries that keep this material.

3.141 The first point to keep hold of is, as stated at the start, the difference between the procedure by which this legislation is enacted. And this gives rise to a particular terminological difficulty. Whereas Public General Acts start life as Public Bills and follow the procedure under the rules of each House for Public business, Local and Personal Acts start as Private Bills and follow the rules for Private business. Thus Local and Personal Acts are sometimes collectively described as 'Private Acts' simply because they both start as Private Bills. (Private Bills are not to be confused with private *members'* Bills, which are Public Bills introduced by a backbench MP as opposed to a government minister.) But as will become apparent from the following description, the term 'Private Act' is better confined to the narrower class of Act which is neither Local nor Public, and which is the precursor to the modern Personal Act. The distinction between Public Acts and Private Acts dates back to 1539, and from that date until 1797 there were just the two series of separately numbered Acts, Public and Private. Acts passed under the Private Bill procedure historically were different from Public Acts, not merely as a matter of classification and subject matter, but also juristically (and the formula for Royal Assent is accordingly different). Although having the endorsement of Parliament, a Private Act was in essence a private arrangement, like a contract or a deed. Two consequences flowed from this. First, for the purposes of the doctrine of judicial notice, the terms of a Private Act had to be expressly pleaded if it was being relied on in court. Secondly, Private Acts were not officially printed and promulgated by the King's Printer. Both consequences had perceived disadvantages, and so during the late seventeenth century the practice arose of inserting a clause in some Private Bills deeming the resulting Act to be a Public Act. Such an Act took effect as a Public Act and was published in the sessional volumes of Public Acts, with a Public Act chapter number, even though it was palpably only of local or personal application. At first such 'Local and Personal Acts declared Public' appeared in the sessional volumes indiscriminately intermingled with Public Acts proper. From 1753 (26 George II) the King's Printer, in view of the great increase in the number and length of such Acts (caused particularly by the widespread introduction of turnpike roads) adopted the ruse of printing the Public Acts in two volumes (though not numbered as such). The first volume contained the Public General Acts proper, numbered chapters 1 to say 39, and the second volume contained the Local Acts declared Public, numbered 40 to 95, or whatever. The first volume was distributed widely to those entitled by virtue of public service to King's Printer's copies; the second volume was printed in more limited quantities. The table at the back of the first volume which listed the Acts by chapter number was in two halves to reflect this arrangement, with the second half, beginning at chapter 40 or wherever the divide fell, headed 'Public General Acts *not* printed in this collection'. That arrangement continued for most of the century, its last year being 1796 (37 George III). Sets of the 'second half' Public Acts from 1753 to 1796 were bound and kept separately. They are generally called, and the volumes labelled, 'Road Acts', because many of the Acts in them, though by no means all, were to do with roads. (Note also that they are not included in the Justis Statutes, which otherwise includes all Public General Acts as passed from the earliest times.) From 1797 (38 George III), this arrangement was put on a more organised footing, and a separate series of 'Local and Personal Acts Declared Public' with its own chapter numbering was created. In the meantime there continued to be the series of Private Acts proper. So the introduction of the new series in 1797 made three: Public General, 'Local and Personal Declared Public' and Private.

3.142 Private Acts, if printed at all, were originally printed only by the parties themselves. However, in 1705 the rule was introduced that all Private *Bills* had to be printed, at the parties' expense. The consequence was wider circulation of this form of material, and the sets of early Private Acts that are to be found in libraries are often in fact made up of prints of the Bills. Whether a particular print is an Act or a Bill may not be entirely obvious since the parties would often entitle the Bill an 'Act' so that if it was passed without amendment it would suffice as a printed copy. Where a Bill was reprinted as an Act it will bear the date of Royal Assent either at the beginning or end. In 1815, however, the practice was introduced of some Private Acts being printed by the King's Printer, such printed copies 'whereof may be given in evidence'. Such Acts appear first in chapter number order; unprinted or privately printed Acts continue the chapter numbering in the same sequence. In 1850 (13 & 14 Victoria c 21) the requirement to insert a clause deeming an Act to be a Public Act in order to attract judicial notice was removed – all Acts were 'Public' and to be judicially noticed unless they expressly stated that they were Private. Notwithstanding this change the volumes of Local Acts continued to be called on their title page 'Local and Personal Acts declared public' until 1869 when they were renamed simply as 'Local Acts'; Private Acts were thenceforth in effect confined to Acts of a personal nature. From 1878 (41 & 42 Victoria) this was taken a step further and those Private Acts that were printed by the Queen's Printer (by this time most Private Acts) ceased to be published as separate sessional volumes and were included instead (though still with their own chapter number series) at end of the volumes for Local Acts. However, from the start of that arrangement until 1922, those Private Acts not officially printed, though listed, were not assigned any chapter number at all. From 1923 all Private Acts were officially printed, and in 1948 Private Acts were renamed Personal Acts.

3.143 A diagrammatic representation of all this is given at figure 3.19. The Quick Reference Guide also correlates the series of Acts in being with the sets of volumes you should be looking at on the shelves. If further help is needed reference should be made to the introduction to the Law Commission's *Chronological Table of Local*

Legislation (discussed further below at para **3.151**), Maurice F Bond *Guide to the Records of Parliament* ((1971) HMSO) pp 97–101, and Sheila Lambert *Bills and Acts: Legislative Procedure in Eighteenth Century England* ((1971) Cambridge University Press).

Acts arising from Hybrid Bills

3.144 Although it is usually apparent from its title whether you are dealing with a Local Act or Public General Act, occasionally an Act whose title suggests that it will be a Local or Personal Acts turns out to be a Public General Act after all. Some recent examples are the Museum of London Act 1986, the Channel Tunnel Act 1987, the Chevening Estate Act 1987, the Norfolk and Suffolk Broads Act 1988, the Severn Bridges Act 1992 and the Cardiff Bay Barrage Act 1993. Such Acts are usually in effect a cross between a Public and a Local Act. Where provisions in a Public Bill affect a particular private interest, as would a Private Bill, it is declared to be a Hybrid Bill. Those provisions then go through the equivalent of the Private Bill procedure first, before reverting to the ordinary Public Bill procedure and being passed as a Public General Act. Note, however, that while such Acts will be found in the official volumes of Queen's Printer's copies of the Public General Acts and in *Current Law Statutes*, they are not necessarily included in *Halsbury's Statutes* – none of the last three Acts given as examples above is there.

Figure 3.19 Schematic representation of Public/Private and Public/Local/Personal Acts.

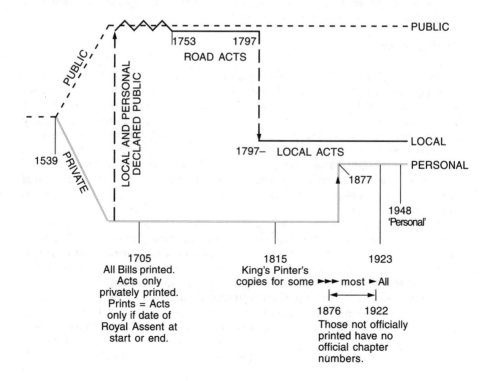

Provisional Order Confirmation Acts

3.145 In the mid-nineteenth century, this legislative procedure was adopted in order to deal with the implementation of general measures at local level without the need for individual Local Acts. A general Act empowered the making of provisional orders relating to particular localities, and then batches of such orders would be approved by a confirming Act, which was a Public General Act, but which had the various orders Scheduled to it. The main Acts to introduce this procedure were the Inclosure Act 1845 (see below), the Public Health Act 1848, which set up local boards, and the Turnpike Trusts Act 1851, which provided relief to trusts that were insolvent as a result of the collapse of the system of turnpike roads. The confirming Acts under this procedure were generally annual. The procedure was adopted more widely in later legislation, and the consequent proliferation of such Provisional Order Confirmation Acts led to them being reclassified from 1868 as Local Acts. The procedure continued to be widely used until 1945, when the Statutory Orders (Special Procedure) Act introduced a streamlined procedure, which bypasses primary legislation altogether (see para **3.165**). Provisional Order Confirmation Acts gradually declined as the general Acts containing provisional order powers were repealed; the procedure is now wholly obsolete, all such Acts having been repealed. The main types of Provisional Order Confirmation Act that might be encountered are Local Government Board and Ministry of Health Provisional Order Acts, the latter being in fact to do with the constitutions and financial powers of local authorities, much of local government organisation having its origins in nineteenth-century public health legislation, and Acts relating to electric lighting, water, gas, tramways, pilotage and piers and harbours. Although such Acts may confirm only a single order, or orders relating to a single place, in which case this is usually indicated in the title, many such Acts confirmed a whole raft of orders, relating to diverse localities. Thus there is not the advantage, that otherwise applies to most local legislation, of knowing simply from the title what or where is affected.

Enclosure Acts

3.146 The problem of classification again arises with Acts passed in connection with the enclosure of common land. These were very numerous in the late eighteenth century, when the agrarian revolution was in full swing, and during the first half of the nineteenth century; they still throw up problems for the practitioner, particularly in conveyancing matters. The preponderance of enclosure Acts were Private Acts, but after 1798 some may be found in the Local Acts. There were also three general enclosure Acts. The first of 1801 did not dispense with the need for an individual Private or Local Act for each area to be enclosed, but set out 'model clauses' so that there was greater uniformity and brevity in the Acts. The second of 1836, extended in scope in 1840, permitted the decision to be made by local commissioners without recourse to an Act of Parliament provided two-thirds of landowners affected agreed. The third of 1845 recouped parliamentary control, at first partially with respect to enclosure of waste but not open fields, and then on amendment in 1852 for all enclosures. This operated under the provisional order confirmation mechanism described above. Proposals for enclosure had to be approved, but instead of using Private or Local Acts, an annual Public General Act would authorise batches of enclosures, which were individually listed in a Schedule to the Act. The last of such annual Acts was in 1869. A reformed system was introduced by the Commons Act 1876, by which time the impetus for enclosure had largely passed and the power in the Act was exercised only sparingly. Thus enclosure Acts may be Private, Local or

Public General, and for the period 1836 to 1852 there may be no specific Act at all for a particular enclosure. Although the practitioner may need to refer to an enclosure Act, it may tell only part of the story. Most (though not all) enclosure Acts appointed bodies of commissioners who arbitrated on the ground between competing claims, and eventually made an award that formed the legal basis of the title to the various parcels of land affected. So it is often the award, which usually has large-scale plans attached, that is of more practical use than the Act. Awards are mostly preserved in the relevant County Record Office. The standard work listing enclosures and the whereabouts of the awards is W E Tate *A Domesday of English Enclosure Acts and Awards* ((1978) Reading University Library).

Local statutory instruments

3.147 The publication of SIs of local application has already been described (paras **3.82**–**3.83**). They are numbered and published (if printed) in the same series as general SIs. They are only mentioned again here lest, for understandable reasons, it was thought that they might have some connection with Local Acts. The enabling Act for even a local SI will invariably be a Public General Act. It might in theory be possible to have a Local Act containing powers for legislating by SI, but for delegated legislation to amount to an SI the power must be delegated to a minister (or the Crown), and it is local authorities, statutory undertakers, and so on, rather than ministers, who by the nature of Local Acts are concerned in their operation. On the other hand, what is very common is for Local Acts to contain powers to make bye-laws (on which see para **3.166**).

Anatomy and citation

3.148 Their appearance and citation are much the same as Public General Acts. The style of chapter numbers, which is the main difference, has already been mentioned (para **3.140**). Although that style, with Local Acts having lower case roman numerals, should be used when citing Acts of any date, the style of number as printed on the Act itself follows that form only from 1869. Before that date you will find Public General Acts with upper case roman numerals, Private Acts with arabic numerals, and all sorts of other variations (they are set in out in detail in Bond, cited at para **3.143**). Confusion can sometimes arise with nineteenth century Local Acts because well over a hundred were issued each year and the abbreviation 'c' for chapter can be mistaken for the roman numeral 'c'. Thus it is safer in this context to use the abbreviation 'ch.' for chapter.

Sources for the text of Local and Personal Acts

3.149 Sets of Local and Personal Acts will only be found in large university libraries or major public reference libraries. The *Chronological Table of Local Legislation* (see para **3.151**) helpfully sets out in its introduction a list of major collections in the UK. County record offices and the local studies centres of public libraries also often collect selected Acts connected with their locality. Such holdings of local importance are also given in the same source. The information on the major collections was partly gleaned from David Lewis Jones and Chris Pond *Parliamentary Holdings in Libraries in Britain and Ireland* ((1993) House of Commons Library), which may also be referred to (unlike the list in the *Chronological Table*, it provides contact details). The practitioner will find good collections at the Law Society Library and the libraries of the Inns of Court. For early unprinted Private Acts, seek the advice of the House of Lords Record Office – the only available text may be the original Act itself. The modern Local and Personal Acts are issued by the Stationery Office individually as Queen's Printer copies in the same way as Public General Acts, but there are no official annual bound volumes – tables, indexes and a title page are supplied for libraries to bind their own sets from the loose Acts. Queen's Printer copies are also available on the HMSO website from 1991 (slightly later than for Public General Acts, which start in 1988).

3.150 Other sources are few. *Current Law Statutes* have included Local Acts (calling them 'Private Acts') since 1991, though they are rarely annotated. *Halsbury's Statutes* includes most of those relating to London. Volume 26 is devoted to the title London, but some are placed in other titles; for example, the Port of London Acts are in the title Ports and Harbours in vol 34 and the Metropolitan Water Board Acts are in vol 49 in the title Water. The current edition of *Halsbury's Statutes* includes ten Local Acts, other than those relating to London (usually because they are amended by later legislation on the same topic that took the form of a Public General Act) and *Statutes in Force* contains 13 Local Acts. A list of the Local Acts in each of those works is given in the Quick Reference Guide (QR3.26). Lexis also includes Acts relating to London and also the Lloyds Acts. For the Lloyds Acts there is the looseleaf service *Lloyds Acts, Regulations and Bye-laws* (LLP); they are also are reproduced in the *Encyclopedia of Insurance Law*.

The range of finding aids

3.151 There are three main research tools for Local and Personal Acts which between them should satisfy most inquiries. First is the *Index to Local and Personal Acts 1801–1947*, with a supplement 1948–66 which until recently was the only official tool. It will be referred to below for convenience as the '*1801–1966 Index*'. It follows a classified arrangement by broad subject, for example, Bridges, Canals, Inclosures, etc. It covers all non-Public Acts, ie both Local Acts and Private Acts, and has occasional references to Public General Acts (eg annual enclosure Acts) and to a few Statutory Rules and Orders (eg gas supply). Complementing that index is now the *Index to Local and Personal Acts 1797–1849 and 1850–1995* (the '*Black Indexes*'), which has been prepared by the Private Bill Office in the House of Lords and is published by HMSO. These six volumes are an alphabetical index by title, but are also heavily cross-referenced by significant words in titles. It is important to appreciate the difference in coverage between the first two volumes covering 1797–1849 and the last four covering 1850–1995. The former does not include Private Acts, whereas the latter does. The third tool is the product of long labours by the Law Commission, and is the equivalent of the official *Chronological Table of the Statutes* for Local and Personal Acts. It is has two parts. The first, the *Chronological Table of Local Legislation 1797–1994* is in four volumes, and the second, the *Chronological Table of Private and Personal Acts 1539–1997* is one volume. There is an annual cumulative supplement to both parts. They are referred to below as the '*Red Tables*'.

3.152 There are a number of other works, which may be needed in particular for pre-1797 Acts. George Bramwell's *Analytical Table of Private Acts* is in two volumes covering 1727–1812 and 1812–34. It is arranged chronologically, but within each year by title rather than chapter number. There are separate alphabetical indexes, but only for enclosure and estate Acts. Although principally designed for Private Acts proper, some post-1797 Local Acts are included. Thomas Vardon's *Index to the Local and Personal and Private Acts 1798–1839* is arranged alphabetically by person or place. Except for the short period, 1789–1800, it is for most purposes superseded by the *1801–1966 Index*. William Salt's *Index to the Titles of the ... Private Acts of Parliament passed in the reign of Queen Anne [George I, and George II]* (1863), is in three parts for each reign, thus together covering 1702–59. For each reign there are four separate indexes: miscellaneous, persons, places alphabetically and places classified by county. It goes earlier than Bramwell, and even where it overlaps with Bramwell it may more readily answer some questions. Tait's work on enclosure Acts and awards has already been cited (para **3.146**). It is arranged by county, with a general alphabetical index. Only the year of Acts, not the chapter number is provided, it principally being a guide to enclosure awards. It is also confined to England and so does not cover Wales. For that reason there may some residual value in two official lists of enclosure awards (with date of authorising Act) published in the House of Commons Parliamentary Papers. The first (PP 1893-94, vol 71, p 485) is arranged alphabetically by place, and includes only those awards deposited with the Board of Agriculture. The second and fuller list (PP 1904, vol 78, p 545) is arranged by county. Sources for Public General Acts should also be borne in mind for pre-1798 Acts of local application that were not Private Acts, particularly 'Road Acts'. The problem here is that few libraries have early sessional volumes of Public General Acts, and rely on the standard compilation *Statutes at Large* in Runnington's edition (see para **3.32**). This generally does not print the text of those Public Acts that were in fact only local; just the title and chapter number are given at the appropriate point. If the text is not printed, then it is not mentioned at all in the general index. There are, however, other old indexes to the statutes that include the Road Acts, and other pre-1798 'local' Public Acts. One such – there may be others – is John Raithby's *An Index to the Statutes at Large from Magna Carta to the forty ninth year of George III inclusive* (1814). The *Statutes of the Realm* indexes all statutes, both Public and Private, up to 1714, but only prints the text of Public Acts. One other resource, though not widely available outside major research collections of parliamentary and official publications, is the *Journal of the House of Commons* and *Journal of the House of Lords*, which are the official minutes (not debates) of each House, and contain a wealth of information. There are cumulative indexes in 10–15 year chunks.

Finding by title

3.153 If you do not have a year or chapter number, the *Black Indexes* are the best place to start. There are no lists simply by title for pre-1797 Acts, and the *Black Indexes* do not include Private Acts 1797–1849. In either eventuality, use a subject/person/place approach. The relevant subject, person or place is almost invariably apparent from the title. There should be little difficulty in finding a very recent Local Act after the *Black Indexes* stop in 1995, since there are so few of them.

Finding by subject, person or place

3.154 Because it is so well cross-referenced, in most cases you can find a known Act in the *Black Indexes* by subject, person or place, even if you do not know the exact title, since the name of the person, subject or place is generally in the title (the main class of local Act that will not necessarily have the name of the place in the title is Provisional Order Confirmation Acts: see para **3.145** above). However, the main tool for the subject approach is the *1801–1966 Index* (you will, though, have to rely on the *Black Indexes* after 1966). Within each broad category there is an alphabetical listing, the entry element usually being the name of the place, person or company. If it is a pre-1801 estate or enclosure Act, use the alphabetical index in Bramwell. For Private Acts from 1702 to 1759 that are not estate or enclosure Acts, and for any Private Act from 1702 to 1726 (ie before Bramwell starts), use Salt.

3.155 The main gaps left are then (a) Private Acts that were not enclosure or estate Acts passed from 1760 to 1800 and (b) pre-1702 Private Acts. Probably the simplest thing to do would be browse through the 'Private and Personal' volume of the *Red Tables*, especially if you have a rough idea when the Act might have been. Alternatively for (a) you could use the cumulative indexes for the period in the *Journal of the House of Commons*, and for (b) use the subject indexes to *Statutes of the Realm*. If you are looking for an enclosure Act and you have not found it in the *1801–1966 Index* or Bramwell, obviously double-check in Tait. It may turn out that the enclosure was made under a general Act. If an Act is still proving elusive, you might want to double-check in Vardon, which covers both Private and Local Acts from 1798 to 1839. If you have exhausted all the above sources, then the implication is that it is a Public General Act. You could use the Justis Statutes, or for pre-1785 Acts the general index in vol 10 of *Statutes at Large*. But neither cover the 'Road Acts', which is the category that in these circumstances it is likely to be in; so you will need to use Raithby.

Finding amendments and repeals

3.156 The *Red Tables* are now the main source – see figure 3.20. It should cover all amendments and repeals, whether made by another Local Act, by a Public General Act or by an SI, though as explained in the introduction the effect of all *local* SIs is not guaranteed to have been covered. The introduction also explains that the effect of general 'cesser provisions', such as those in s 262 of the Local Government Act 1972, are not covered. Such provisions state in general terms that any local enactments that might otherwise impinge on the operation of the Act cease to have effect or are to be read as if amended by the Act (for example, so as to include references to the new county councils arising from the Local Government Act 1972). The *Current Law Statute Citator* has also covered amendments and repeals of Local Acts since 1996. The most recent volume and the current issue in the looseleaf service volume to *Current Law Statutes* can thus be checked for any very recent amendments since the last cumulative supplement to the *Red Tables*. The table of legislation affected in the Tables and Index volume in the latest annual volumes of Public General Acts, if it has appeared before the equivalent edition of the cumulative supplement to the *Red Tables*, is another source. Obviously if you looking at a London Local Act in *Halsbury's Statutes* you can use the usual updating apparatus. If you have recourse in any event to the *1801–1966 Index*, you will see that some amendments and repeals are noted. This did not purport to be comprehensive, though it attempted to note all repeals since 1900. If a complete repeal is noted, then you will have answered the question without going to the *Red Tables*.

Church Measures and other sources of ecclesiastical law

3.157 From the Reformation until 1920 legislation governing the Church of England, being the established Church, was made by ordinary Act of Parliament (generally Public, but also Local). The Church of England Assembly (Powers) Act

1919 devolved legislative powers to a new body, the Church Assembly, which from 1972 was renamed the General Synod. Primary legislation made by the Assembly and Synod, called Measures, remains subject to parliamentary approval (usually through scrutiny by the Ecclesiastical Committee) and to Royal Assent, and as with other more familiar forms of devolved legislation Parliament retains the right to legislate for the Church of its own accord. Measures have the force of an Act of Parliament and as mentioned at the start of this chapter are published with the official Queen's Printer copies of the Public General Acts. Those in force are also printed like other statutes in *Halsbury's Statutes*, in the title 'Ecclesiastical Law', and from 1949 in *Current Law Statutes* (though not annotated). They are not very numerous. In the past there may have been half a dozen a year. Nowadays there are usually one or two, occasionally none. The only qualification to the foregoing description is that no arrangement seems to have been made to include them with the annual volumes of Queen's Printer copies of Acts from 1920–25 – they only appear from 1926 (16 & 17 Geo V). However, all Measures as then in force were included as an accompanying volume to the third edition of the official *Statutes Revised* of 1948. Furthermore they were included in *Halsbury's Statutes* from its first edition of 1929. In the unlikely event of needing the original text of a Measure that is no longer in force but was amended or repealed before 1929, you might face a small difficulty. Where it is necessary for subordinate legislation to be made under a Measure, the enabling power is drawn so as to make the resulting legislation take the form of statutory instruments, which will be like any other SIs. However, the main exception is commencement orders. Where as in a conventional Act there is an enabling power to bring the Measure into force at a later date after Royal Assent, it is exercised by the Archbishops by means of notices, and such notices are not SIs. Archbishops' instruments only receive limited circulation. Fortunately, the editorial offices of *Halsbury's Statutes* are one such recipient, so *Is it in Force?* and its noter-up with *Halsbury's Statutes* extend to providing commencement information on Measures. If you needed to establish whether any commencement had occurred since the last update, or was likely to occur in the near future, you would be best advised to check with the Registrar at the Legal Office at Church House, Westminster.

3.158 The other main legislative source of law of the Church is canon law. Canons do not form part the general law of the land, and are binding only on ecclesiastical persons. They were made by the Convocations of the two provinces of Canterbury and York, and from 1920–71 concurrently by the Church Assembly. Since 1972 the General Synod makes them. The *Canons of the Church of England* are published in looseleaf form by Church House Publishing. A scholarly edition of earlier canons, with an extensive introduction, is *The Anglican Canons 1529–1947* edited by Gerald Bray ((1998) Boydell Press for the Church of England Record Society). 'Acts' of Synod and 'Acts' of Convocation, which are the most formal resolutions of those bodies, are not legally binding, but may have evidential value before the courts as to matters of doctrine and Church policy. Also not binding in the sense of judicial precedents, the legal opinions of the Legal Advisory Commission, appointed by the General Synod, are a valuable source of interpretation of ecclesiastical law. The Commission gives advice on matters referred to it by various ecclesiastical authorities, short of matters that are subject, or likely to be subject, to current litigation. Church House Publishing publish a looseleaf compilation, *Legal Opinions Concerning the Church of England*. Mark Hill's *Ecclesiastical Law* ((2nd edn, 2001) OUP) is not only a textbook but contains the full text of the current canons, Measures, rules and selected cases. There are now a number of other modern textbooks on ecclesiastical law. On ecclesiastical case law, see para **5.32**.

Figure 3.20 Chronological Table of Local Legislation (the 'Red Tables').

888

1871 (34 & 35 Vict.).

c.xv *continued*	36-39 r.- S.I.1989/2379(L), art.4, sch.2 pt.I. 40 am.- S.I.1981/1310(L), art.4, sch.2. 44 r.- S.I.1963/2128(L), art.5(1)(*b*), sch.3 pt.I. 48 r.- S.I.1981/1310(L), art.5. 49 ext.and appl.- Sutton Dist. Waterworks 1887 (c.lxxxix), s.36. 51 r.- S.I.1963/2128(L), art.5(1)(*b*), sch.3 pt.I. 52 r.- Sutton Dist. Waterworks 1915 (c.lvi), s.14. 53 r.- Sutton Dist. Waterworks 1929 (c.xxviii), s.50. 54 r.- S.I.1963/2128(L), art.5(1)(*b*), sch.3 pt.II. 55 r.- Sutton Dist. Waterworks 1929 (c.xxviii), s.50. 56-58 r.- S.I.1963/2128(L), art.5(1)(*b*), sch.3 pt.I. 59,61-69 r.- Sutton Dist. Waterworks 1929 (c.xxviii), s.50.
c.xvi	*Royal Exchange Assurance.* r.- Royal Exchange Assce. 1901 (c.x), s.3.
c.xvii	**Shotts Iron Company's.**
c.xviii	**Newport Pagnell Railway (Further Powers).** see: Newport Pagnell Rly.(Trans. and Dissolution) 1875 (c.cvi), s.4.
c.xix	**Westhoughton Gas.**
c.xx	**Rhyl District Waterworks.** r.in pt.- S.I.1965/2097(L), art.33, sch.6. s. 11 r.- Rhyl Dist. Water 1892 (c.cvi), s.13. 21-25 r.- S.I.1957/977(L), art.6, sch.2.
c.xxi	**Lloyd's.** ext.- War Risks Insurance 1939 (c.57), s.13(2); War Damage 1941 (c.12), s.69(2); 1943 (c.21), s.101(2). s. 10 r.and subst.- Lloyd's 1911 (c.lxii), s.4. 11 r.- Lloyd's 1925 (c.xxvi), s.4; 1982 (c.xiv), s.15(1)(*a*), sch.3. 12 r.- Lloyd's 1982 (c.xiv), s.15(1)(*a*), sch.3. 13-17 r.(prosp.)(saving) - Lloyd's 1925 (c.xxvi), s.4. 18-27,29 r.- Lloyd's 1982 (c.xiv), s.15(1)(*a*), sch.3 31 am.- Lloyd's 1911 (c.lxii), s.5. 32 r.and subst.- Lloyd's 1911 (c.lxii), s.11. 36-38 r.- Lloyd's 1911 (c.lxii), s.6. 39,40 am.- Lloyd's 1911 (c.lxii), s.5. sch. r.- Lloyd's 1982 (c.xiv), s.15(1)(*a*), sch.3.
c.xxii	**St. John's Church, Bradford.**
c.xxiii	**Huddersfield Waterworks.** excl.- Huddersfield Corpn. 1902 (c.cxxxvii), ss.15(2),17(2), sch.1. r.(exc. s.27)(West Yorks.)(saving) - Huddersfield Waterworks 1890 (c.cxv), s.7; Huddersfield Waterworks and Imprvt. 1876 (c.c), s.128; Huddersfield Imprvt. 1880 (c.xcix), s.111; West Yorks. 1980 (c.xiv), s.95, sch.5.
c.xxiv	**Dunstable Gas and Water.** r.(exc. ss.75,77,78) - Dunstable Gas and Water 1912 (c.xiv), ss.33,43,69; S.R.& O.1926/960(L), art.38; 1936/168(L), art.5; Dunstable Gas and Water 1937 (c.lxiii), s.44; S.I.1960/1515(L), art.7(3); 1972/1924(L), art.17(1), sch.4.

[see next page]

Subsidiary legislation not published as statutory instruments

3.159 The definition of an SI as provided by the Statutory Instruments Act 1946, which introduced the term, is wide and accounts for the vast bulk of subordinate legislation. However, there are some kinds that fall outside its ambit. They are generally encountered only rarely, but when they are they can cause disproportionate difficulty. They are of seven kinds: (1) those that can be described as anomalous exceptions; (2) sub-delegated legislation; (3) orders not made by the Crown or ministers; (4) prerogative or quasi-prerogative orders; (5) special procedure orders; (6) bye-laws; and (7) traffic regulation orders.

Anomalous exceptions

3.160 These were described in the first edition of this book as being 'perverse' exceptions, which may have been stating the matter too strongly. But from time to time enabling legislation is passed that for good reason, though that reason may not be apparent to the hapless legal researcher, provides that the subordinate legislation should not be promulgated by means of an SI. The best known example is the Immigration Rules made under the Immigration Act 1971, which are passed by way of a resolution of both Houses of Parliament and are published as House of Commons papers or Command papers. Other examples are the Parole Board Rules under the Criminal Justice Act 1991, Breath Test Device (Approval) Orders under the Road Traffic Act 1988 and Transport and Works Act 1992, Bus Lane Enforcement Camera Approval Orders, Postal Schemes under the Post Office Act and Lord Chancellor's Instruments under the Public Records Act 1958. As mentioned above (para **3.70**) commencement orders under the Competition and Service (Utilities) Act 1992 could not be issued as SIs simply because of a drafting error in the Act. The Regulations under the Statutory Instruments Act, with regard to Acts made before its commencement, made an exception for orders directed to particular persons, or orders in the nature of Private or Local Acts. And modern exceptions in enabling provisions tend to arise with delegated legislation of the same character. Thus orders of the Secretary of State authorising landowners to carry out drainage works under the Land Drainage Act 1991 are not SIs. A number of Acts authorise the Secretary of State to make Directions, which are usually of an administrative nature directed to particular persons or bodies and will likewise not be SIs, though sometimes they can be quite far-reaching, as in the case of those that implement EC Directives (see para **3.138**). Even with orders of a very local nature there is not a great deal of consistency. Stopping-up of highways orders under the planning Acts were until 1963 issued as SIs, albeit unpublished local ones, but then ceased to be and were published instead as an ad hoc series. On the other hand, the small specialist Somerset cheese-maker, Duckett, had in 1998 three full-blown SIs to himself, one of which even had to amend primary legislation (all because of the zealotry of food safety inspectors). The Stationery Office or the relevant body or government department may publish this kind of non-SI legislative material in an ad hoc fashion. By and large government departments and agencies have shown commendable commitment to publishing materials on the Internet, so a search on the web may be the first thing to do, provided the material is relatively recent. It is also always worthwhile to check any relevant looseleaf subject encyclopaedias. If difficulty is encountered it is probably best to try to speak to the relevant official in the government department, who may be identified from the *Civil Service Yearbook*.

Sub-delegated legislation

3.161 The Statutory Instruments Act 1946 only applies to powers conferred by an Act. Where, which is quite rare, an *SI* contains a power to make further orders – sub-delegation – the resulting order is, prima facie, not an SI. However, the power to sub-delegate must usually arise from the original enabling Act, which may specify that such sub-delegation is to be treated as if it did fall within the Statutory Instruments Act. Thus the Motor Vehicles (International Circulation) Regulations 1975, which were made under the Motor Vehicles (International Circulation) Order 1975, is an ordinary SI because the Motor Vehicles (International Circulation) Act 1952 provided that an Order under it may authorise the minister to make Regulations, and that the Statutory Instruments Act 1946 shall apply to such regulations as if they were made under an Act. The Civil Aviation Act 1982 achieved a similar result by a slightly different means, so that various Air Navigation Regulations may be made under an Air Navigation Order and be SIs. (That Act also, incidentally, provides another illustration of the first exception above: in a Schedule are listed certain sections containing order-making powers that are expressly not to be exercised by statutory instrument.) A new example of sub-delegation is subordinate provision orders under Regulatory Reform Orders (see para **4.78**). The Regulatory Reform Act 2001, s 5(10) once again deems such subordinate orders to have been made under an Act. None the less, examples arise, such as the Channel Tunnel (Security) Order 1994 which authorises the Secretary of State to make Directions, where there is no such deeming provision and so the resulting instruments are not SIs.

Orders not made by the Crown or ministers

3.162 The Statutory Instruments Act 1946 only applies to powers expressed to be delegated to the Crown or ministers of the Crown. Where it is expedient that the power should be exercised by some other official, the enabling Act will usually deem the official to be a minister for these purposes in order that the resulting regulations may be published and treated as SIs. The Chief Registrar of Friendly Societies, for example, made regulations under the Friendly Societies Acts as if he were a minister, and they were published as SIs. Sometimes, however, this is not considered appropriate. Perhaps the most familiar examples to lawyers are the various solicitors' practice rules made by the Council of the Law Society (with the concurrence of the Master of the Rolls) under the Solicitors Act 1974. Other examples are financial services regulations, that were made by the Securities and Investment Board, and the self-regulatory organisations, and will be made in future by the Financial Services Authority. Such substantial sets of rules as the solicitors' rules and financial services rules which are widely available to practitioners do not impose undue difficulty by not being published as SIs. Rather more irritating is the 'one-off' instrument not made by SI. An example is the Charities (Cy-près Advertisements, Inquiries and Disclaimer) Regulations 1993 made under the Charities Act 1993. Regulations made by the Secretary of State under the Act are SIs (of which there are quite a number), but these regulations are made by the Charity Commissioners under s 14(8), so are not an SI – s 14(9) simply says: 'Any regulations made by the Commissioners under this section shall be published by the Commissioners in such manner as they see fit.' Bye-laws and traffic regulation orders could be said to be another illustration of this category, but they are dealt with separately below.

Prerogative or quasi-prerogative orders

3.163 Where the enabling power in an Act is delegated to the Crown, rather than to a minister, the subordinate legislation under the Act is made by the sovereign in the Privy Council as an Order in Council. By virtue of the Statutory Instruments Act 1946 such Orders in Council are SIs like any other (with a very few exceptions contained in the regulations made under the Statutory Instruments Act, such as Orders in Council under the Naval and Marine Pay Pensions Act 1865, or in the enabling Act itself, such as Orders in Council under the Reserve Forces Act 1980, s 59). Very occasionally, usually in legislation connected with the medical professions, the enabling power is delegated directly to the Privy Council, and the resulting SIs, made without the presence of the sovereign, are called Orders *of* Council. However, the Privy Council does quite a number of other things by means of Order in Council, not under statute but under the remaining prerogative powers, and such Orders in Council are not SIs. Examples are approving amendments to charters of bodies incorporated by Royal Charter, amending the statutes of Oxbridge colleges, approving schemes of the Church Commissioners and discontinuing burial grounds. Of more interest to the legal practitioner are Orders in Council approving primary legislation made by the legislatures in the Channel Islands and Isle of Man, and constitutional orders affecting dependent states. Rare but important examples of prerogative legislation in the domestic sphere are Civil Service Orders in Council and Diplomatic Service Orders in Council, which regulate the conditions of employment of civil servants. Strictly speaking, Orders in Council made under prerogative powers are not 'delegated' legislation, and indeed it is noteworthy that for the purposes of the Human Rights Act 1998 Orders in Council 'made in exercise of Her Majesty's Royal Prerogative' are included in the definition of primary legislation (s 21).

3.164 The prerogative powers may still be exercised by species of instrument other than Orders in Council, for example, by Royal Proclamations and Royal Warrants, and such pure prerogative instruments will not be SIs. In some areas where such instruments were traditionally made, however, the power now derives from statute rather than the prerogative. For example, Proclamations as to the design and denominations of new coins are now made under the Coinage Act 1971. But such instruments, even though they are made under statute, are not SIs either. This is because the Statutory Instruments Act only applies (in the case powers delegated to the Crown, as opposed to ministers) where the enabling Act states that the power is to be exercised by means of an *Order in Council*. Thus, to summarise, there are two classes of this kind of 'not-SI' legislation:

(a) Prerogative orders: Orders in Council and other instruments that are not made under statute at all.

(b) Quasi-prerogative orders: Instruments made by the Crown (as opposed to ministers) under statute but by some form of instrument other than an Order in Council.

As mentioned above (para **3.83**) selected instruments that are not SIs are none the less published in the official *bound* volumes of SIs. For volumes before 1961, which are arranged by subject, they appear at the back of the last volume for the year after the SIs themselves and are arranged by date (they are not numbered). From 1961, when the bound volumes began to be arranged by number, you need to look in three volumes for each year – the volumes representing the last 'section' of each of the three 'parts' issued during the year. The title page of the last volume of the year will set out the contents of all the preceding volumes, if you are in doubt. A volume for

1972 illustrates the mixed bag one finds. It includes Royal Instructions concerning Hong Kong and the Cayman Islands, a Royal Warrant concerning war pensions and a Proclamation made under the Emergency Powers Act 1920 declaring a state of emergency during the dockers' strike. The Civil Service Orders in Council used not to be included, but the new principal order of 1995 is indeed there, which is helpful since they seem to have vanished from *Harvey on Industrial Relations and Employment Law* (Butterworths, looseleaf) which used to reprint them. Channel Islands and Isle of Man Orders in Council, mentioned above, resurface in the official printed editions of legislation of those jurisdictions. Other Orders in Council can be obtained direct from the Privy Council Office. Lists, but not currently the text, of all Orders of Council made at each meeting (approximately monthly) is posted on the Privy Council website.

Special procedure orders

3.165 Certain categories of order, usually relating to the compulsory purchase for certain purposes of land owned by local authorities or statutory undertakers, are not made by means of a Local Act or by means of an SI, but undergo a special parliamentary procedure and are subject to the Statutory Orders (Special Procedure) Acts 1945 and 1965. The notes to the 1945 Act in *Halsbury's Statutes* list those Acts containing provisions for orders to be made by the special parliamentary procedure. Because in most cases there are now much less convoluted ways of making compulsory purchase orders, they are very uncommon. The sessional returns for the House of Commons indicate that only one or two are made each year. The example given in the first edition of this book, The Great Yarmouth Outer Harbour Act 1986 (Extension of Time) Order 1991 was printed by HMSO as a one-off item, but they do not generally seem to be published in that way. The Joint Committee on Special Procedure Orders may make a report where objections are made, and so records relating to such orders may appear on Parlianet. Examples are the City of Stoke-on-Trent Tunstall Northern By-pass Local Government Act Compulsory Purchase Order 1997 and the Woodford Aerodrome (Control of Land by Directions) Order 1997. There may be entries in the House of Commons *Journal*, but if a question arises about such an order, it may be best to seek the advice of the Private Bill Office in the House of Commons. It is certainly not clear how you would find one if you did not know it already existed. If a minister wishes to proceed with an order that has been rejected by the Joint Committee, he or she would need to introduce a confirming Bill, and if passed the order would be a Local Act, though apparently there have only been two since 1945, the last being the controversial Okehampton By-pass (Confirmation of Orders) Act 1986 (see House of Commons Information Office Factsheet No 37).

Bye-laws

3.166 Bye-laws come in two varieties. On the one hand there are the bye-laws made by local authorities either under the general power in s 235 of the Local Government Act 1972 or under specific powers in a miscellany of statutes (lists of such powers are given as Appendix 6 in the *Encyclopedia of Local Government Law* and as Appendix 5 in *Cross on Local Government Law*). On the other hand, there are the bye-laws made by particular bodies, such as British Rail or London Transport, under their constituting legislation. For this material one is usually entirely reliant on the body providing the text in its accurate and up-to-date form. The extent to which local authorities are efficient in this varies. Because many bye-laws were subject to confirmation by a minister, particularly the Home Secretary, copies of bye-laws of historical interest may be found in departmental files held at the Public Record Office – one of their Records Information leaflets describes the scope of their holdings and the particular classes that may be most fruitful for such a search. Likewise local record offices may hold copies. Bye-laws in the City of London are made by Acts of the Common Council. Model bye-laws exist to cover common eventualities to enable provisions to be similar from authority to authority.

Traffic Regulation Orders

3.167 Responsibility for the regulation of roads and traffic is exercised by both the Secretary of State for Transport and by local authorities. Regulations made by the former will be in the form of SIs, albeit often local, unpublished SIs. But the plethora of minor rules and regulations – parking, bus lanes, bus stops, one-way streets, no right turns, etc – are made by the latter under powers delegated by the Road Traffic Regulation Act 1984. Outside London they come in the form of Traffic Regulation Orders, usually obtainable from the county council. Inside London, they used to be made by the GLC in the form of Traffic Management Orders, which came in a proper numbered series not dissimilar to SIs. With abolition of the GLC in 1986, each borough instead made orders separately. With the creation of the Greater London Authority in 1999, we have come, if not full circle, then a semi-circle to the former position – Transport for London, the executive body created under the 1999 Act, will make orders in respect of those roads that are designated 'GLA Roads'. As with bye-laws one is almost wholly reliant on the relevant local authority in providing an authoritative text (orders and proposed orders have to be available for public inspection). However, a notice (but not the text) may appear in advance in local newspapers. The placing of notices in the *London Gazette*, where they appeared in the quarterly indexes under 'Road Traffic Regulation Act 1984', has not been mandatory, except for certain London orders, since 1996. The procedure for making orders is now set out in The Local Authorities' Traffic Orders (Procedure) (England and Wales) Regulations 1996, SI 1996/2489, supplemented by guidance in Department of Transport Local Authority Circular 5/96.

Quasi-legislation

3.168 The legal effect of quasi-legislation, miscellaneous material falling somewhere between legislation proper and mere administrative rule-making, is illustrated by two well-known examples, the Highway Code and the Codes of Practice made under the Police and Criminal Evidence Act 1984. The breach of either does not give rise directly to any liability, but breach of the first can be used as evidence of negligence and breach of the second may render a confession inadmissible. There are many more examples of codes of practice, which may be made under statute or be purely voluntary agreements.

3.169 Government circulars are another common species of quasi-legislation. In some areas, such as planning law, they assume almost as much importance as subsidiary legislation proper. Home Office circulars impinge heavily on such matters as prison, police and the operation of magistrates' courts. From the wide range of other kinds of quasi-legislation, one particular example worth mentioning is extra-statutory concessions made by the Inland Revenue. Naturally enough these cannot override a statutory provision, but in practice a mass of detailed regulation of taxation is made in this way. Sweet & Maxwell publish a looseleaf *Inland Revenue Practice and Concessions* and recent information may be found in *Simon's Tax Intelligence*. Other examples of quasi-legislative materials are Building Regulations Approved Documents (until 1986 these details were published in the SIs themselves but are now separate), British Standards and Accounting Standards.

3.170 No particular rules can be laid down for finding and using quasi-legislation. The Stationery Office may publish the most important kinds, but mostly it will be issued by the government department or body concerned. Looseleaf subject encyclopaedias often include such material, as do some journals – the *Justice of the Peace*, for instance, often reprints Home Office circulars. A search on Legal Journals Index or Badger is often helpful – even if a source with the text is not found, it may at least confirm that the document exists. The Quick Reference Guide gives a few more examples.

4. *Pepper v Hart* research and the background to legislation

4.1 The need to research parliamentary materials and the background to legislation arises in two main situations. The commonest is when you are faced with a problem of statutory interpretation. The other is where you have to advise on proposed changes in the law that may be imminent. Traditionally, the courts declined to allow what was said in Parliament during the passage of a Bill to be referred to as an aid to statutory interpretation. (In other jurisdictions it has been otherwise – for example, in the US 'legislative history' is routinely referred to, and in Australia there is express provision in the Interpretation Acts of the Commonwealth and most of the states.) The furthest the English courts were prepared to go was to allow reference to reports, such as Law Commission reports, prepared before the legislation was introduced in order to identify the 'mischief' which the statute was intended to rectify. This was merely the application of one of the three traditional rules of statutory interpretation – the mischief rule. In 1992, while hearing a tax case, the House of Lords was invited to consider relaxing the exclusionary rule. Counsel for the taxpayer pointed out that during the passage of the relevant Bill the minister promoting it had made extensive statements on how the legislation was intended to operate and the exact circumstances of the taxpayer who was now appealing had been given as an example. The interpretation being pressed by the Inland Revenue was precisely what the minister had said would *not* be its effect. The hearing was adjourned and reconvened before a panel of seven Law Lords, instead of the usual five, to hear argument on the *Hansard* point. By a majority of six to one, the Lord Chancellor dissenting, the House of Lords held that in certain limited circumstances *Hansard* could now be referred to, and decided the case in front of them in favour of the taxpayer on the basis of what the minister had said in Parliament.

4.2 That case, *Pepper (Inspector of Taxes) v Hart* [1993] AC 593, has generated an enormous literature and in frequency of citation it joins the ranks of cases like *Donoghue v Stevenson* and *Associated Picture Houses v Wednesbury Corpn*. (Of the literature, apart from Bennion cited at para **4.10** for the detailed law, Geoffrey Marshall 'Hansard and the interpretation of statutes' in Dawn Oliver and Gavin Drewry (eds) *The Law and Parliament* ((1998) Butterworths) pp 139–154 is worth singling out as it gives in a brief compass an admirably readable assessment of the consequences of the case. An eye also ought to be kept on the future deployment of the arguments advanced extra-judicially by Lord Steyn in '*Pepper v Hart*: a re-examination' (2001) 21 *Oxford Journal of Legal Studies* 59–72, in which he suggests, if the question were to be revisited by the House of Lords, a basis for doing so – see paras **4.12, 4.57**

and **4.73**). Even before *Pepper v Hart*, practitioners and indeed judges, as Lord Denning openly confessed, would sometimes look at *Hansard* to gain reassurance and bolster their arguments, even though it could not be cited in court. And for many researchers, such as academics, *Pepper v Hart* is not directly relevant if citation in court is not in view. The task of understanding and using the materials of course remains the same whether or not you are destined for court. But *'Pepper v Hart* research' is now convenient shorthand for using *Hansard* and parliamentary materials for whatever reason.

Pre-legislative materials

4.3 Before proceeding with describing *Pepper v Hart* research proper, pre-legislative materials that provide background to legislation will be covered first. These may well be needed for *Pepper v Hart* research in order to understand the debates in Parliament, but they may also be needed independently either in connection with the mischief rule of statutory interpretation, as mentioned above, or for more general research.

Types of pre-legislative material

4.4 Typically, new pieces of government legislation are heralded by a Green Paper, so called because traditionally they had green covers (no longer necessarily so – they are as likely now to be glossy productions). They are consultation papers. Comments are invited from persons and bodies within a certain consultation period. These will be followed in due course by a White Paper setting out the government's firm policy in light of the consultation. If sufficiently important the White Paper may be considered in Parliament, either in a debate on the floor of the House, or more usually in a report from a select committee. The government may in turn produce a response to a select committee. A White Paper may also elicit parliamentary questions, written or oral. A new procedure, one of the products of the Labour government's modernisation programme, is the consideration of draft Bills by a Commons select committee or a joint committee of both Houses. This pre-legislative form of scrutiny was pioneered on the draft Pension Sharing Bill in 1998, and was further tested – nearly to destruction – on the Financial Services and Markets Bill in 1999. It has been used on a number of other Bills since, including the Freedom of Information Bill. Being before a select committee means that evidence can be received from outside bodies, while the input from members is less driven by partisan considerations than is the case when it comes to the committee stage proper.

4.5 Initial proposals for legislation, however, may not come directly from the government. The Law Commission is the official body charged with law reform, and their proposals go through the similar two-stage process of first being issued in a consultation paper (formerly working papers) and then in a final report. It is the modern practice for a draft Bill to be attached to the final report. Draft Bills are also sometimes nowadays attached to government Green or White Papers, or the initial consultation process may consist of issuing a draft Bill, with brief notes. The Law Reform Committee, which existed from 1952 to 1985, and the Criminal Law Reform Committee, which existed from 1958 to 1986, were important law reform bodies both before the Law Commission was set up in 1965, and after 1965 acting in parallel with it. Legislation may also have its roots in one-off reports, either emanating from a full-blown inquiry such as a Royal Commission (though these have fallen somewhat into disfavour in recent years) or from smaller departmental or inter-departmental committees. Occasionally reports from outside bodies may be relevant. Not all legislation, however, will have specific antecedents in the form of such reports. A matter may be non-controversial or too urgent.

Finding pre-legislative materials

4.6 The general note at the beginning of the Act in *Current Law Statutes* is the place to look first (see Figure 4.1). Details of Green Papers and White Papers and other reports are almost invariably given. Occasionally you may need to look further at the notes on a particular part or section of an Act. If no reports are cited in *Current Law Statutes*, you can double-check by looking at the second reading debate on the Bill in *Hansard*. The minister, in introducing the Bill, will almost always refer to the background to the Bill and how it arose. Another useful source, particularly where proposals have not yet reached the Bill stage, is *Law Under Review*, which used to be published in hard copy by the Law Commission, but which since 1997 has been provided on the Law Commission's website. It provides details of all law reform projects in progress throughout government, not only its own projects. The contact details of the official responsible are invaluable for getting the up-to-date position. Most government department websites have sections on current consultations in progress, and many archive those that have finished. The relevant papers and reports are usually downloadable free of charge. Otherwise, it is a matter of using the various tools for finding official publications in general described in chapter 7 – TSO catalogues, UKOP, Parlianet, Chadwyck-Healey CD-ROM, Badger, etc.

Pepper v Hart research

The decision in *Pepper v Hart* and its practical consequences

4.7 If you are going to court it is important to be aware of what the decision does and does not permit, especially since the House of Lords has subsequently threatened wasted costs orders on those who fail to abide by its terms. The most frequently cited passage from the judgments is the distillation of the new rule by Lord Browne-Wilkinson at 640. Reference to parliamentary material as an aid to statutory construction is permitted where:
(a)   the legislation is ambiguous or obscure, or leads to an absurdity;
(b)   the material relied upon consists of one or more statements by a minister or other promoter of the bill together if necessary with such other parliamentary material as is necessary to understand such statements and their effect; and
(c)   the statements relied upon are clear.

4.8 The first of these three criteria provides the initial threshold. Whether the threshold has been reached may be difficult to assess since lawyers are by nature and training adept at finding ambiguity. In a number of cases judges have not been convinced that the legislation is ambiguous, but have gone on, with half an eye on the case going to the Court of Appeal, to look at *Hansard* in any event. The second criteria means that you cannot rely, for example, on what an opposition MP says in moving an amendment, though what the minister says in response to the proposed amendment might be admissible. There is also the basic practical point of knowing

Figure 4.1 Current Law Statutes.

1990 *c.* 18 **18**

COMPUTER MISUSE ACT 1990*

(1990 c. 18)

ARRANGEMENT OF SECTIONS

Computer misuse offences

SECT.
1. Unauthorised access to computer material.
2. Unauthorised access with intent to commit or facilitate commission of further offences.
3. Unauthorised modification of computer material.

Jurisdiction

4. Territorial scope of offences under this Act.
5. Significant links with domestic jurisdiction.
6. Territorial scope of inchoate offences related to offences under this Act.
7. Territorial scope of inchoate offences related to offences under external law corresponding to offences under this Act.
8. Relevance of external law.
9. British citizenship immaterial.

Miscellaneous and general

10. Saving for certain law enforcement powers.
11. Proceedings for offences under section 1.
12. Conviction of an offence under section 1 in proceedings for an offence under section 2 or 3.
13. Proceedings in Scotland.
14. Search warrants for offences under section 1.
15. Extradition where Schedule 1 to the Extradition Act 1989 applies.
16. Application to Northern Ireland.
17. Interpretation.
18. Citation, commencement etc.

An Act to make provision for securing computer material against unauthorised access or modification; and for connected purposes.

[29th June 1990]

PARLIAMENTARY DEBATES
Hansard: H.C. Vol. 164, col. 390; Vol. 166, col. 1134; Vol. 171, col. 1287; H.L. Vol. 519, col. 230.

INTRODUCTION

Background to the Legislation
The Computer Misuse Act 1990 gives effect, with some modifications, to various changes to the law recommended by the Law Commission's Report No. 186, *Computer Misuse*, Cm. 819, published in October 1989. The Commission undertook an investigation of this area of law in the light of public concern over "the misuse of computers or computer systems by parties other than those entitled to use or control those computers, either by simply seeking access to the computers, or by going further and using the computers or amending the information in them for what may be a wide range of ulterior motives" (Law Com. No. 186, para. 1.1). The Report followed the publication of a Report by the Scottish Law Commission in 1987, which advocated the creation of a new offence in Scotland, of "obtaining unauthorised access to a computer": *Report on Computer Crime* (Scot. Law Com. No. 106, Cm. 174). During the period of the English Law Commission's deliberations, however, further urgency was given to the matter when the House of Lords confirmed the decision of the Court of Appeal quashing the convictions of the two defendants in *R.* v. *Gold*; *R.* v. *Schifreen* [1988] A.C. 1063, a case in which a freelance computer journalist and an accountant had taken advantage of slack computer security arrangements to gain unauthorised access to the Prestel system, a computerised public information service. They gained access to the system on numerous occasions, altered files, and left various messages in the

---

* Annotations by Martin Wasik, LL.B., Barrister, Senior Lecturer in Law, Manchester University.

18–1

when looking at *Hansard* whether the person speaking is indeed a minister, especially when using old debates or House of Lords debates where the names may not be familiar. In *Hansard* when a minister first speaks he or she is identified by office – Secretary of State, Under-Secretary, Economic Secretary to the Treasury and so on – with their name in brackets. Subsequent contributions are identified by name only. Bear in mind that different ministers may speak at different points during any one debate. For example, the senior minister, the Home Secretary or Lord Chancellor say, may introduce a Bill at second reading and then a junior minister may wind up the debate at the end. If in doubt a full list of ministers is given at the front of each bound volume of *Hansard*. The qualification 'or other promoter of the bill' is added to meet the case either of an Act that did not originate as a government Bill, but as a private members' Bill, or a Local Act which will have not have been promoted by an MP at all (see para **4.71**). In the first eventuality the identity of the promoter will generally be apparent (if not look at the beginning of the second reading or the Bill itself). The third criterion is designed to prevent the argument about what the statute meant developing into an argument about what the minister meant.

4.9 The House of Lords clearly envisaged that the combined effect of the three criteria would be to limit severely the occasions on which *Hansard* would be used, and so meet the concerns of Lord Mackay in his dissenting judgment about adding to the costs of litigation. As noted below, the Law Lords have subsequently had to fire a number of warning shots to try to ensure that that remains the case. Some would say that they have not been wholly successful. But even if keeping citation of *Hansard* within bounds may save the *court's* time, it will be apparent that rule does not necessarily save the *lawyer's* time. For once the first criterion has been met the research has to be carried out in any event simply to discover whether the other two criteria are met. And indeed, it might be regarded as negligent for an advocate not to carry out the research in nearly every case involving a point of statutory interpretation. As will become clear, carrying out *Pepper v Hart* research is time-consuming, even for the experienced. Those who have this task delegated to them – typically the pupil barrister or trainee solicitor – should beware. It is not something that can be done in the half hour between the library opening and the court sitting. It should also be appreciated that nine times out of ten nothing of even marginal assistance will be found, let alone something that will determine the outcome of the case.

The application of the decision by the courts

4.10 A full analysis of the decision and its subsequent application by the courts will be found in Francis Bennion *Statutory Interpretation* ((3rd edn, 1997 and cumulative supplement) Butterworths). But attention is drawn to three subsequent decisions of note. An opportunity arose for Lord Browne-Wilkinson to assess the impact of the decision in another tax case, *Melluish (Inspector of Taxes) v BMI (No 3) Ltd* [1996] 1 AC 454. It was here that he warned that a wasted costs order against an advocate personally might be necessary if the advocate failed to limit citation of *Hansard* to the strict circumstances laid down in the three criteria. He also added in effect a fourth criterion. In the case there were no relevant ministerial statements on the particular section of the Act in issue, but there were seemingly relevant statements made on another closely connected section. But that was not good enough – only statements directed to the specific provision under consideration are admissible. The usual circumstance for resorting to *Hansard* is to elucidate the meaning of a particular provision, often a very narrow point where the drafting is awry. The second case picked out for mention was different. Clarke J in *Three Rivers District Council v Bank of England (No 2)*

[1996] 2 All ER 363 (one of the many stages in the BCCI litigation) admitted *Hansard* in order to construe not a particular provision but the purpose of the statute as a whole, which was one implementing an EC Directive, and suggested in such circumstances a more flexible approach to the use of *Hansard* was permissible.

4.11 In the third case, *R v Secretary of State for the Environment, Transport and the Regions, ex p Spath Holme Ltd* [2001] 2 WLR 15, the House of Lords once again considered *Pepper v Hart* at length. Lord Browne-Wilkinson's three conditions were duly reiterated. But the divergent views expressed by the five Law Lords on how they were to be applied in the circumstances of the case do illustrate how matters can be far from cut and dried. The main problem in the case was, it is fair to say, novel. How was the first criterion to be applied where at issue was not the meaning of a statutory expression, but the scope of a statutory power, in this case one to make a statutory instrument (SI)? The majority thought that none of the words in the Act that gave the power were ambiguous – any ambiguity was as to the ambit of the power, so no *Hansard*. Lord Nicholls and Lord Cooke thought otherwise – there was a genuine problem of construction that *Hansard* might help to resolve. What was perhaps most illustrative of the difficulty in applying the rule in practice was the difference of opinion between Lord Nicholls and Lord Cooke on the third criterion. Lord Nicholls looked at what was said, but decided that the ministerial statements were not unequivocal. Lord Cooke, on the other hand, derived from them 'real help' if not 'decisive help'. As with the many other cases involving the application of *Pepper v Hart*, the case also illustrates the point that all the material had to be assembled by somebody and then looked at by their Lordships, whether or not they were prepared to use it in reaching their decision. The case is also relevant to *Pepper v Hart* research on consolidation Acts (see para **4.69**) and SIs (see para **4.73**).

4.12 The *Spath Holme* case is of interest for a further reason. It contains a hint on the way that the tide may possibly turn on the use of *Pepper v Hart* in general. Lord Hope at 48 says that the exception in *Pepper v Hart* is available to prevent the *executive* seeking to put a meaning on legislation which is different from that which the minister gave it when promoting it in Parliament. Subsequently, in *R v A (No 2)* [2001] UKHL 25 at [81], [2001] 2 WLR 1546 at 1575 (the case on evidence of previous sexual history in rape cases), Lord Hope referred to that passage, adding that 'strictly speaking' the exception is '*only*' available for that purpose. He goes on to acknowledge the debt he owed to the paper by Lord Steyn cited above (para **4.2**) for this view. Lord Steyn in his paper argues that a defensible and principled justification of *Pepper v Hart* would confine its application to a form of estoppel where, as in *Pepper v Hart* itself, the executive reneges on its undertakings. 'It is the argument that the executive ought not to get away with saying in a parliamentary debate that the proposed legislation means one thing in order to ensure the passing of the legislation and then to argue in court that the legislation bears the opposite meaning' – such an application of *Pepper v Hart* has nothing to do with searching for the 'phantom of Parliamentary intention' (at 67). Presumably, if *Pepper v Hart* were ever to be restricted in this fashion, it would rule out reference to *Hansard* in the circumstances of the case described next (and cause any need for reference to this chapter to arise more seldom).

4.13 One further case is worth describing quite fully. It is not on the scope of the *Pepper v Hart* criteria as such, for it applied them in conventional and strict fashion, but it is simply an illustration of a recent case where what was found in *Hansard* was indeed decisive of the outcome. The knowledge that such rarities can arise may boost morale as you contemplate the mountain of green and maroon volumes of *Hansard* in front of you. The facts of *A E Beckett & Sons (Lyndons) Ltd v Midland Electricity plc* [2001] 1 WLR 281 were straightforward. The claimants operated a poultry and egg business. There was a serious fire at their premises, caused by an electrical fault in the meter box installed by the defendants. The negligence of the defendants was admitted. The largest part of the damages claimed was for interruption to business. The defendants relied on an exclusion clause in their conditions of supply. That exclusion clause derived from s 21 of the Electricity Act 1989, the relevant part of which read:

> A public electricity supplier may require any person who requires a supply of electricity . . . to accept in respect of the supply . . . (b) any terms restricting any liability of the supplier for economic loss resulting from negligence which it is reasonable in all the circumstances for that person to be required to accept.

There was economic loss resulting from the defendants' negligence. Did any restrictions 'in respect of the supply' include the plant installed, as the defendants contended, or did they only relate to loss arising from the interruption or variation of the supply of the electricity itself, as the claimants contended? The Court of Appeal 'found these rival contentions based on textual analysis of the statute to be nicely balanced and inconclusive'. Furthermore, the court could not 'readily identify from the statute a purpose for the inclusion of s 21 that would illuminate its true interpretation'. So out with the *Hansard*. The clause that became s 21 had been introduced as a new clause at the report stage in the House of Commons (an illustration of the value of looking first at the Bills: see para **4.60**). The court found that the relevant passages in the debate 'immediately made clear what had previously been obscure'. The minister had said:

> . . . in some instances a couple of seconds of lost power could have highly significant effects, especially in these days when so much dependence is placed on computers . . . There might be little or no actual physical loss, but the economic consequences could be major, far outstripping the actual value of any supply. In cases in which the degree of sensitivity to the loss of supply is so much greater than normal, under the Bill as it stands the supplier would have to take on the role of the insurer for the consumer involved . . . For large computer companies or large companies owning computers – the type of consumer the new clause addresses – it would be surprising if they were not properly insured against such eventualities.

Allowing the appeal by the claimants, the court 'concluded that this a rare case where material admitted under *Pepper v Hart* has resolved an ambiguity in a statute being construed'. Section 21 permitted terms restricting liability for economic loss only in relation to the supply of the current; the exclusion clause did not extend to the negligent installation of equipment.

Putting extracts from Hansard *before the court*

4.14 The procedure to be followed for putting extracts from *Hansard* before the court was originally set out in the *Practice Direction (Hansard: Citation)* [1995] 1 WLR 192 – copies, taken from the *Official Report*, had to be served on the other parties and lodged with the court at least five working days in advance of the hearing. The substance, as far as the Court of Appeal was concerned, resurfaced in the consolidated practice direction for the Court of Appeal of 19 April 1999, issued with the early versions of the CPR. With the incorporation of the new Pt 52 on appeals, and its associated practice direction, explicit reference to citation of *Hansard* has disappeared from the CPR. *Blackstone's Civil Practice* (2001 edn, para 71.38) points out that for the Court of Appeal there is now the requirement to file the bundle of authorities 28 days before the hearing; as far as other courts are concerned it suggests that following the previous guidance would be a sensible approach. The original practice direction specified that copies should come from the official version of *Hansard* (which in practice is usually the only version there is). Not mentioned, but obviously sensible, is that copies should come from the official bound volumes, not from the daily or weekly parts, which are unrevised (see para **4.50**).

The parliamentary stages of a Bill: the basic pattern

4.15 A necessary preliminary to undertaking *Pepper v Hart* research is to have a clear grasp of parliamentary procedure in passing Bills. This section goes through the usual pattern for an ordinary Public Bill introduced by the government, and is what any law student should know. The section that follows it (paras **4.27–4.47**) goes into the various complications and exceptions that can arise. Some, for example, the splitting of the Committee stage between a Standing Committee and the floor of the House, are not unusual, but many are quite rare. That section is thus largely intended for reference rather than to be memorised. Later sections deal with procedure on consolidation Bills, on Private Bills (ie ones that become Local Acts) and on SIs. The bible on parliamentary procedure is *Erskine May's Treatise on the Law, Privileges, Proceedings and Usage of Parliament* ((22nd edn, 1997) Butterworths), but also very clear and useful are the Fact Sheets prepared by the House of Commons Information Office, which are also published on the Parliament website. The Information Office itself can also be very helpful.

Commons introduction and first reading

4.16 A Bill may be introduced in either House. The majority of government Bills are introduced in the House of Commons, the main exception being Bills for which the Lord Chancellor is the responsible minister. So Bills relating to the courts and administration of justice are generally introduced in the House of Lords. The House of Lords also usually takes first technical law reform Bills, such as arise from some Law Commission reports, and consolidation Bills. For reasons of timetabling, however, it is modern practice to give the Lords the first bite of the cherry on two or three major government Bills in other areas in each session. Whether introduced in the Commons or the Lords, there is no difference to the stages through which a Bill passes. The following description is based on a bill introduced in the Commons. Simply apply it mutatis mutandi to one introduced in the Lords. Bills that are introduced in the Lords have '[HL]' or '[Lords]' after their title, and are so cited in *Hansard* and other sources.

Introduction and first reading are a single, purely formal stage. The Bill is not yet printed. The various sources that give dates and *Hansard* references for the stages of Bills necessarily include the first reading, but there is no need to look them up. If you do, all you will find is as in the following example:

BILL PRESENTED
EDUCATION
Mrs Secretary Shephard, supported by the Prime Minister, Mr Chancellor of the Exchequer . . . presented a Bill to amend the law relating to education in schools . . . And the same was read the First time; and ordered to be read a Second time tomorrow and be printed. [Bill 8.]

The date set for the second reading may be, as here, fictitious. It will usually follow a week or two later, but unlike in the Lords there are no recommended minimum intervals between stages.

Commons second reading

4.17 The second reading consists of a general debate on the principles of the Bill. There are no amendments at this stage. The minister introduces the Bill, explains its purpose and background, usually mentioning any Green or White Papers that preceded it, and then outlines its main provisions. During the minister's introduction there may be interventions. He will finish with some formula such as 'I commend the Bill to the House'. There follows a general debate in which the minister will not usually intervene. Then at the end the minister, or frequently a different, junior, minister will wind up the debate and respond to some of the points made in the debate. Ministerial statements made at the end of the debate may be as fruitful as those made at the beginning, if not more so. In general, the value of the second reading debate very much depends on the prominence of your clause in the Bill. Small matters of drafting are unlikely to be addressed at this stage.

The start of a second reading debate appears in *Hansard* as in the following example:

Orders of the Day
Local Government and Rating Bill

Order for Second Reading read.
3.36 pm
The Secretary of State for the Environment (Mr. John Gummer): I beg to move, That the Bill be read a second time.

When we published our rural White Paper last year, we made clear our continuing commitment to . . .

At end of a second reading debate there may be a division (a vote) either on the question whether the Bill be read a second time, or on a 'reasoned amendment' which has the same effect. Otherwise, *Hansard* will simply state:

Question put and agreed to.
Bill accordingly read a Second time, and committed to a Standing Committee, pursuant to Standing Order No. 61 (Committal of Bills).

A second reading debate takes place on a single day.

Commons committee stage

4.18 Since 1907 the procedure has been for the committee stage of a Bill to be taken off the floor of the House in a Standing Committee, unless otherwise ordered. In practice the procedure did not become fully routine until after 1945. The expression 'Standing' Committee is something of a misnomer since a fresh committee is convened for each Bill. Standing Committees are also to be distinguished from Select Committees. The latter are also confusingly named, since most Select Committees, which include the departmental Select Committees, such as the Home Affairs Committee, are appointed for a whole Parliament. The other two significant differences between a Standing Committee and a Select Committee are first, that the former necessarily will include a minister, whereas the latter generally comprise only backbenchers, and secondly that the latter can take evidence, written or oral, from outside persons and bodies, whereas the former cannot (though see para **4.37**). The various Standing Committees sitting at one time are lettered, Standing Committee A, Standing Committee B, etc. The committee stage takes the form of detailed clause by clause consideration of the Bill and amendments. It is often the most fruitful stage for research, especially where the provision in question is a relatively minor one in the scheme of the Bill. The most important practical aspect is that the debates on Bills in Standing Committee do not appear in the main *Hansard*, but in their own separate series (see para **4.51**). Sittings of Standing Committees occupy a morning or an afternoon. On large Bills there may be 20 or more sittings, with the resulting debates occupying more than 500 pages.

Commons report stage

4.19 The Bill is reported back to the House. This is usually the final substantive stage in the Commons. It is sometimes also called the 'consideration stage'. The Bill is not gone through in its entirety again – only new amendments are considered. These amendments are often government amendments made on undertakings given at the committee stage. The opposition may have been unhappy about a particular point in Committee and tabled amendments, but agreed to withdraw the amendments on the minister undertaking to come back with his or her own amendments to meet the point at the report stage. There are greater restrictions on debate than in committee. In the Commons it is uncommon for the report stage to extend beyond one day.

Commons third reading

4.20 The third reading in the Commons is usually a purely formal stage that follows on immediately as soon as the report stage is concluded, without further debate. Occasionally on controversial Bills there may be a separate third reading debate, but no further amendments may be moved other than purely verbal corrections. The Bill is then ready to go the Lords, but it is usually not the last the Commons will see of the Bill, since there is one further stage later (para **4.26**).

Lords introduction and first reading

4.21 As in the Commons, this is purely formal. The Lords, unlike the Commons, observe minimum intervals between stages unless there are exceptional circumstances. Two weekends pass after first reading before second reading.

Lords second reading

4.22 This follows the same pattern as the second reading in the Commons. You will find that if you have read the minister's second reading speech in the Commons, what the minister in the Lords says often bears an uncanny resemblance – they will be reading from a very similar brief. However, the minister in the Lords will have the benefit of taking into account any changes in the Bill made during its passage in the Commons.

Lords committee stage

4.23 This comes at least two weeks after second reading. There is a major difference from the Commons. The committee stage is usually taken in a committee of the whole House on the floor of the House – so not really a 'committee' at all. Consequently, the debates are in the main Lords *Hansard*. Again there is detailed consideration, with each clause in the Bill having to be separately agreed, and again debate may be spread over more than one day. If you are looking at the entry for a Bill in the index to the House of Lords *Hansard*, you will see between the references for the second reading and committee stage, and again between the committee stage and the report stage, references to 'Motions for approval'. These do not involve substantive debate, but are simply the procedure by which the order of consideration of clauses in the Bill is approved in advance.

Lords report stage

4.24 On large Bills, there will again be gap of at least two weeks before taking the report stage. The procedure is similar to the Commons report stage, except that on large Bills the report stage more commonly exceeds a single day's debate.

Lords third reading

4.25 The Lords third reading, which comes at least three sitting days after the report stage, represents the second major difference from the Commons. This is a substantive stage where further amendments may be, and often are, moved. Commonly the amendments are to tidy up drafting, or consequential on government undertakings given at committee or report stages. But sometimes quite substantial clauses can find their way into a Bill at this stage. This means that a provision in an Act may turn out not to have been debated at all during the Bill's original passage through the Commons nor during most of its passage in the Lords, but only arrived in the Act at the eleventh hour. This is usually the last the Lords see of the Bill, which now goes back to the Commons.

Commons consideration of Lords amendments

4.26 The final stage is for the Commons to agree to the amendments made by the Lords. This stage will only be relevant to *Pepper v Hart* research if the Lords did indeed amend the clause in question. If you have established that your clause has emerged from the Lords in exactly the same state that it originally emerged from the Commons, then your task is done. Usually this stage is fairly brief, with the minister introducing each amendment, or block of amendments, and explaining why the government introduced or accepted them in the Lords. Occasionally, especially with relatively small technical amendments, you may find a snippet that adds to what was said in the Lords, but often not. Where matters are controversial, the Commons, of course, may not agree to the Lords amendments and may substitute their own further amendments. If that situation prevails, the particular amendments in dispute return once more to the Lords, where consideration is given to 'Commons Reasons for Disagreeing with Lords Amendments and Commons Amendments to Lords Amendments'. In theory, the Lords could once again reject them and the disputed amendments could yo-yo between the two Houses. As the Commons ultimately has the power under the Parliament Acts 1911 and 1949 to reintroduce a Bill in a subsequent session and pass it without the Lords' consent, in practice an accommodation is reached. Where a Bill was introduced first in the Lords, there is the equivalent final stage, Lords consideration of Commons amendments. The Bill then receives Royal Assent, which is of course purely formal, but is recorded in *Hansard*.

The parliamentary stages of a Bill: complications and exceptions

Commons introduction and first reading

PRIVATE MEMBERS' TEN-MINUTE RULE BILLS

4.27 One of the methods for a backbench MP to promote a Bill is under the 'Ten-Minute Rule'. Such Bills are an opportunity to air a topic of concern to the member – they are not introduced in any expectation that they will result in legislation. The procedural peg on which such debates are hung is a short debate on leave to introduce the Bill. However, very occasionally such a Bill does proceed further. Of 592 such Bills between 1983 and 1994, seven became Acts. In the unlikely event of such an Act being the subject of *Pepper v Hart* research, you would thus need to look at the original debate at introduction stage, as well the ordinary later stages.

Commons second reading

SECOND READING COMMITTEE

4.28 Occasionally, for small, uncontroversial Bills the second reading debate does not take place on the floor of the House, but in a Second Reading Committee, similar to a Standing Committee. A report in 1994 on the procedure of the House recommended that they be used more frequently, particularly for technical law reform Bills such as those emanating from the Law Commission. The main practical point to note is that the debates since the 1979/80 session are published with the Standing Committee debates. Before then they were in the main Commons *Hansard*.

SCOTTISH, WELSH AND NORTHERN IRELAND GRAND COMMITTEES

4.29 Before devolution Bills affecting Scotland or Wales only were considered by a Grand Committee consisting of all the Scottish and Welsh MPs. The principle of a Bill was debated in analogous fashion to a second reading debate. Their debates appeared with the Standing Committee debates. The Scottish and Welsh Grand Committees remain in existence, but are unlikely to have Bills referred to them. The Northern Ireland Grand Committee substantially enlarged its remit in 1997. Among its functions, it may consider draft Orders in Council that are still made at Westminster in lieu of primary legislation from Stormont (see para **8.32**).

MONEY RESOLUTIONS

4.30 If you are looking at the entry for a Bill in *Hansard* indexes, you will often see references to money resolutions and ways and means resolutions, immediately following the second reading. These are not directly relevant to *Pepper v Hart* research. The former authorise provisions involving expenditure and the latter taxation. The Bill cannot subsequently be amended so as to take any provision outside the scope of the resolutions. These are often formal, but are sometimes debated. Those on Finance Bills are taken after the Budget debate.

PROGRAMME MOTIONS

4.31 These may now also be encountered in *Hansard* indexes, but again do not need to be looked at. They are one of the upshots of the Labour government's programme for modernising Commons procedure, and were first used at the beginning of 1998. The idea is that after second reading the timetable for the passage of a Bill is agreed in advance, and provisions requiring more debate than others prioritised. They are now used on most government Bills, but remain experimental.

Commons committee stage

ALLOCATION OF TIME MOTIONS

4.32 Guillotine motions, formally known as allocation of time motions, are another procedural step that sometimes appears in the *Hansard* indexes. They most commonly arise when the government thinks the committee stage is going on too long. With a majority, it can impose a motion to curtail debate. These do have some relevance to *Pepper v Hart* research, in that if there has been a guillotine on a long Bill it can fall only a fairly short way through the Bill. Controversial parts of Bills often come in major clauses at the start, and the opposition may have spent most of the allocated time on those. The consequence is that a particular provision falling later on in the Bill may have received no detailed consideration in the Commons at all – it is very frustrating to wade though pages of Standing Committee debates trying to find when they reached your clause only to find that they never did. Fortunately, there is no equivalent procedure in the Lords.

PRIVILEGE AMENDMENTS

4.33 These are the technical means of the Commons sanctioning provisions involving taxation or expenditure in Bills that were introduced in the Lords, which are necessary since constitutionally the Lords do not have the power to introduce provisions levying taxes or laying out public expenditure. When the Bill emerges from the Lords, there is an extra clause tacked onto the very end of the Bill, which says that the Bill does *not* purport to levy tax or lay out expenditure. At the committee stage in the Commons an amendment is then passed to delete the clause. These are not relevant to *Pepper v Hart* research, but are mentioned to explain references to them in *Hansard* indexes and the presence of the clause in prints of the Bills where they are printed in bold and underlined.

COMMITTEE STAGE ON THE FLOOR OF THE HOUSE

4.34 Sometimes the committee stage of a Bill, or certain clauses in it, are taken by a committee of the whole House on the floor of the House, as the committee stage in the Lords is usually taken. This is the routine procedure for Finance Bills. It used to be the practice that the whole Bill was considered by a committee of the Whole House. In session 1967/68, as an experiment, the whole Bill was taken in an ordinary Standing Committee. From session 1968/69 it has been split, with the general clauses being taken on the floor of the House, and more specialised clauses being taken in Standing Committee. The consequence is that you may have to check both the main Commons *Hansard* and the Standing Committee debates. There are three other circumstances, where a committee of the whole House may be used. Bills, or parts of Bills, of major constitutional importance may warrant a committee of the whole House, as did, for example, the Human Rights Act 1998 and attempted amendments to reintroduce the death penalty during the passage of the Criminal Justice and Public Order Act 1994. 'Emergency' Bills requiring rapid passing and one-clause Bills not requiring detailed consideration are the other two categories.

SELECT COMMITTEES ON HYBRID BILLS

4.35 Sometimes Public Bills contain provisions affecting particular private or local interests, as would a Private Bill that leads to a Local Act. Examples of Acts resulting from hybrid Bills are the Channel Tunnel Act and Severn Bridge Act (see also para **3.144**). Hybrid Bills go through a hybrid procedure. The 'private' provisions are considered first by a Select Committee, which follows a similar procedure to that on a Private Bill. The proceedings do not appear in either *Hansard* or the Standing Committee debates, but are published as House of Commons papers (see paras **7.12–7.14**). After the Select Committee, the Bill is re-committed to an ordinary Standing Committee and proceeds like an ordinary Public Bill.

SELECT COMMITTEES ON NON-HYBRID PUBLIC BILLS

4.36 These are now only used routinely for Armed Forces Bills, which have to be renewed every five years. However, they were common in the nineteenth century before the current Standing Committee system was set up. Again, their proceedings are published as House of Commons papers.

SPECIAL STANDING COMMITTEES

4.37 Special Standing Committees were introduced in 1980. They are a cross between an ordinary Standing Committee and a Select Committee. Their distinctive feature is that outside persons or bodies can be asked to give evidence, as with Select Committees. The idea was that some Bills, particularly on non-controversial areas, would benefit from the additional scrutiny that outside experts could bring to bear. As originally introduced, however, they did not find much favour with government business managers, since they potentially increased the length of committee proceedings. Between 1980 and 1984 only five Bills went through this procedure, a notable example being the Bill that became the Criminal Attempts Act 1981, when Professor J C Smith and other academic lawyers were able to give evidence. They were briefly revived for certain Scottish Bills in session 1994/95, but for that purpose they were overtaken by events. The Modernisation Committee in Tony Blair's first government recommended that for appropriate Bills they should be tried again. A Special Standing Committee considered the Bill that became the Immigration and Asylum Act 1999. That Committee was also unusual in that for the first of its sittings it took evidence in private, and the proceedings of that sitting were not published.

RECOMMITTAL

4.38 This can arise in either House, though it possibly happens more often in the Commons. If at report stage there are important but late amendments that it is felt cannot be adequately dealt with within the confines of report stage procedure, then the Standing Committee (or in the Lords the Committee of the Whole House) can be reconvened to give them detailed consideration. It is fairly uncommon – amendments to complex or controversial Bills are the usual occasion. In theory the entire Bill can be recommitted, but that is rarer still. There is a further report stage after recommittal. Only amendments consequential on the amendments recommitted can be considered at it.

Lords committee stage

DELEGATED POWERS AND REGULATORY REFORM SELECT COMMITTEE

4.39 Consideration of Bills by this committee is in effect a new Lords stage that comes between second reading and the committee stage proper. The committee was originally called the Select Committee on the Scrutiny of Delegated Powers and was introduced in the 1992/93 session. Its original purpose, which it still retains, was as its title suggests to give greater scrutiny to provisions in Bills that enabled ministers to make regulations by means of SIs. For this purpose it examines two issues. The first is whether the power is one that is appropriate to delegate at all – whether the object of the provision should instead be achieved by primary legislation rather than by subordinate legislation. The second issue is whether, if there is to be a delegated power, the particular procedure specified for exercising it is appropriate. As described in paras **4.74–4.77**, there are various gradations of parliamentary scrutiny of the making of SIs, from the requirement of a positive vote by both Houses to none at all. The enabling Act has to specify which is to be followed. The Delegated Powers Committee may recommend a higher-level scrutiny procedure than that proposed in the Bill. With the passing of the Deregulation and Contracting Out Act 1994 by the Conservative government, scrutiny of Deregulation Orders was added to its remit, and with the passing of the Regulatory Reform Act 2001, which replaces the 1994 Act, the Committee's name has changed again (see further para **4.78**). The Committee's reports, which are published as House of Lords papers (see para **7.12–7.14**), appear by the time the committee stage of the Bill starts. It will be appreciated from the foregoing that their reports are most relevant to *Pepper v Hart* research that involves an SI whose enabling provisions need to be researched (see para **4.73**); they might also be relevant if a Deregulation Order or Regulatory Reform Order was, unusually, in the forensic spotlight.

NO COMMITTEE STAGE

4.40 The committee stage may be dispensed with altogether. This can happen in either House, but is mentioned under the Lords since it always happens there, as a matter of constitutional convention, with Finance Bills. The Lords have no say on such Bills. There is a second reading debate, which is in effect a general debate on the state of the economy. At the end the order for committal is negatived (OCN is the abbreviation in the *House of Commons Weekly Information Bulletin*). The other circumstance is where no amendments are tabled. The order for committal that had been made at the end of the second reading debate is subsequently discharged (OCD). If there is no committee stage then there is no report stage.

JOINT COMMITTEE ON CONSOLIDATION BILLS

4.41 The procedure on consolidation Bills is described more fully at para **4.68**. It is mentioned here since it replaces the ordinary committee stage. It is also mentioned under the Lords since, though a joint committee of both Houses, it is usually chaired by a peer, often a Law Lord.

SELECT COMMITTEES ON HYBRID BILLS

4.42 This is the same as for the Commons (see para **4.35**). Its proceedings are published as House of Lords papers.

SELECT COMMITTEES ON NON-HYBRID PUBLIC BILLS

4.43 This is procedure is still very occasionally used in the Lords. In the Lords there are no restrictions on the introduction of private members' Bills by individual peers. Controversial private members' Bills are sometimes sent first to a Select Committee after second reading, as a method, it might cynically be said, of booting them into touch. If the Committee recommends that the Bill should proceed, it is recommitted to a committee of the Whole House. The proceedings are again House of Lords papers, rather than being in *Hansard*.

SCOTTISH SELECT COMMITTEE

4.44 Introduced in 1996, this had only a brief life before devolution. Its novel feature was that it could sit in Scotland in order to take evidence. It could not amend a Bill, which was recommitted to a committee of the whole House.

PUBLIC BILL COMMITTEES

4.45 These are the equivalent of Standing Committees in the Commons. They were introduced in 1968, and although a report by Earl Jellicoe in 1992 on the procedure of the House recommended their more frequent use, they have not proved popular. Since 1968 only nine Bills have been passed using this method for the committee stage, the last being for the Trade Marks Act 1994. Resort to one for that Bill was necessitated by an imminent election. The main difference from a Commons Standing Committee is that, though it is off the floor of the House, any peer can participate, though only those nominated to the Committee may vote. Proceedings were issued to subscribers to the Commons Standing Committee debates in the same format.

SPECIAL PUBLIC BILL COMMITTEES

4.46 This form of committee was an innovation stemming from the Jellicoe report. They were modelled on the Special Standing Committees in the Commons (see para **4.37**), and were indeed initially so called. Oral and written evidence is taken before going through the Bill clause by clause. They were intended for non-controversial technical Bills, especially Law Commission Bills. They have not been as widely used as expected, perhaps because of one the early Bills to go through the procedure, the Private International Law (Miscellaneous Provisions) Bill 1995, had an inauspicious passage. An innocuous sounding Law Commission Bill, its provisions in respect of defamation proceedings had controversial and potentially far-reaching implications for the media in a global environment. The proceedings are published as House of Lords papers.

GRAND COMMITTEES

4.47 First used in the 1994/95 session, this is another of the recent experiments in Lords procedure. The original title before the more succinct name 'Grand Committee' was adopted in 1997 was a 'Committee of the Whole House off the Floor of the House', and this explains its nature. Like multi-screen cinemas, the idea is that proceedings can be carried on in two places at once. They often physically meet in the Moses Room, which is larger than an ordinary committee room. Hence they are also colloquially known as 'Moses Room committees'. The procedure is identical to the ordinary committee stage on the floor of the House, except that there are no divisions (votes). One very practical reason for this is that peers summoned from enjoying some refreshment by the division bells would not know where to go. If a matter necessitates a division it has to be postponed to the report stage. The procedure is proving quite popular – it was used for nine Bills in the 1999/2000 session, including the Electronic Communications Bill and the Transport Bill. The debates are appended to the daily parts of the main Lords *Hansard*, but with separate column numbering prefixed with 'CWH', for Committee of the Whole House. This convention means that when they are incorporated in the bound volumes, you need the *date* as well as the volume number. (A similar convention has been adopted in the Commons *Hansard* for the non-legislative debates that now take place in parallel session in Westminster Hall – the abbreviation 'WH', for Westminster Hall is used.)

Parliamentary sessions

4.48 The main materials that have to be used for *Pepper v Hart* research, which are described in the next section, are arranged according to parliamentary sessions. The usual pattern is that the session opens with Queen's Speech in November and continues through to the end of October or early November the following year, when Parliament is prorogued. The summer recess thus does not mark the end of a session – the session resumes for a short period in the autumn. The Lords, who often have to come back from their holidays earlier than the Commons, are particularly busy finishing off Bills that have accumulated from the Commons. The pressure comes because the traditional rule is that Public Bills cannot be carried over from one session to the next. If their passage is not completed, then they fail completely, and if reintroduced have to start all over again. That position is now qualified. The Modernisation Committee have introduced a 'carry over' procedure in limited circumstances where there is all-party agreement. It was first used to carry the Financial Services and Markets Bill over from the 1998/99 session to the 1999/2000 session. Occasionally the pattern is slightly altered – the start of the 2000/2001 session was delayed, somewhat controversially, to December. The usual reason for disruption to the normal cycle is a general election. The 2000/2001 session was very short, ending in May. The 2001/2002 session will be very long, running from June 2001 to November 2002. Acts are, of course, numbered and cited according to calendar year. Since no Bills are usually passed in an ordinary parliamentary session until after Christmas, finding the correct parliamentary session is not generally a problem – a 1999 Act will have been passed in the 1998/99 session. It soon becomes apparent if the year in question abnormally had two possible sessions. The only occasion where matters can get additionally confusing is where there are two Bills with the same name in the same session, which can arise sometimes with Finance Bills. Finance Bill No 1 may have been passed in a different calendar year from Finance Bill No 2 of the same session, in which case the Act resulting from the latter will be simply the Finance Act, not the Finance No 2 Act.

Parliamentary materials

Hansard

4.49 The formal title, though 'Hansard' also appears on them, is *Parliamentary Debates: Official Report*. They have been the 'official' report since 1909. Before that date they were published as a private enterprise, originally by Luke Hansard, though latterly they were subsidised from public funds. Since 1909 there has been a separate series for the Commons and the Lords and they have contained the near verbatim record of all proceedings on the floor of each House. They also contain written parliamentary questions and answers. Before 1909 there was only a single series, which was not necessarily full or accurately verbatim – the earlier one goes the patchier they are. *Hansard* itself goes back to 1803, but before 1841 there were a number of rival series, and also retrospective series (Cobbett's *Parliamentary History* ambitiously went back to 1066). Very occasionally researchers do want to go back to the early nineteenth century debates, either for statutes that are still lurking on the statute book or for pre-cursor statutes. Alternative versions to *Hansard*, such as the *Mirror of Parliament*, are worth checking. David Lewis Jones *Debates and Proceedings of the British Parliaments: a Guide to Printed Sources* ((1986) HMSO) is the standard bibliography.

4.50 *Hansard* is published in daily and weekly parts which are unrevised. Official revised bound volumes are then issued – in the Commons series they usually contain two weeks' worth. The revised volumes contain editorial corrections, not changes of substance, though MPs and – with full awareness of the implications of *Pepper v Hart* – ministers have been known on seeing the daily part to make a beeline for the editor's office, one trusts without success. The issues and volumes are numbered in columns rather than pages. Adjustments when printing the revised bound volumes means that the column numbers for a particular item may be slightly different from the numbers as they appeared in the daily and weekly parts. The written parliamentary questions and answers have a separate sequence of column numbers, which appears in the bound volumes at the back, not with each day's proceedings. In the Commons the written answer column numbers were distinguished only by being printed in italic. Very recently they have adopted the practice of suffixing the numbers with 'W' for greater clarity. The Lords have for some time *prefixed* the number with 'WA'. The full text of the daily parts and bound volumes of *Hansard* is available on the Parliament website. Currently the Commons go back to session 1988/89 and the Lords to 1996/97. There is a CD-ROM version of *Hansard* (Commons from 1988/89 and Lords from 1992/93, but not Standing Committee debates). This can be useful occasionally, for instance when you know that something was said by a particular speaker and for other types of research, but generally for *Pepper v Hart* research it really is easier to use hard copy. The type of flicking through required is not well suited to the screen, and you would need to be confident of your mastery of the search software to avoid missing anything.

House of Commons Standing Committee debates

4.51 These form a separate series, but are similar in appearance to the main *Hansard*. They are issued in parts covering a single sitting – a morning or afternoon. As well as the lettered Standing Committees on Bills, they include the proceedings of the other Standing Committees – Delegated Legislation, Scottish, Welsh, Northern Ireland and European. As mentioned above from 1979/80 they also include debates in Second Reading Committees. Eventually they are reissued in bound volumes, arranged by Standing Committee letter or title. The text is not revised as such, as with the main *Hansard* bound volumes, but a list of errata is included at the front, and indexes, including usefully a clause index, are provided. Some libraries may prefer to bind the loose parts themselves and arrange them by title of Bill.

4.52 Although the modern Standing Committee procedure was introduced in 1907, at first no verbatim record was kept. The printed series of Standing Committee debates only starts in 1919. Between 1907 and 1918 you are stuck – there are not even unpublished archival sources. Even after 1919 until 1945 the verbatim record was not necessarily ordered to be printed, particularly for private members' Bills. Typescript transcripts of proceedings on some such Bills, however, survive in the House of Lords Records Office. A list of the available transcripts is given in the Quick Reference Guide (QR4.6). If you are researching an old Bill and it is included in the printed debates, your difficulties are not over. Complete sets of the debates from 1919 are extremely scarce. Other than those held at the libraries of the House of Commons and House of Lords (which are only open to MPs and peers), there are only seven unbroken sets recorded in libraries in the entire UK, three of which are in London. Even for more recent debates, holdings at Lincoln's Inn Library (which holds the specialist parliamentary collection for the four Inns of Court) only start with session 1987/88 and the Law Society only has them from 1994, though they will advise barristers and solicitors where else to go. David Lewis Jones and Chris Pond *Parliamentary Holdings in Libraries in Britain and Ireland* ((1993) House of Commons Library) is the standard listing, but official publications librarians in university libraries and the large public reference libraries, or the House of Commons Information Office, will be able to advise others on the nearest library. The Standing Committee debates are available on the Parliament website from session 1997/98.

4.53 Not to be confused with the Standing Committee debates, are the *minutes* of Standing Committees. These are the official record of what was *done* rather than what was *said*, and equate to the *Journals* for the proceedings on the floor of each House. They are published as House of Commons papers. They are not generally needed for *Pepper v Hart* research, though they can be of peripheral assistance in confirming what changes were made to a Bill in committee where, as described above, the debates were not published (or where neither the debates nor the Bills are to hand).

Bills

4.54 The harassed pupil barrister marches into the library and asks where *Hansard* is kept. They may be clutching a copy of the Act from *Current Law Statutes*, which gives a string of more or less bewildering *Hansard* references. A couple of hours later they will be sat with an entire session's worth of *Hansard* volumes surrounding them, looking even more harassed and bewildered. As will be explained more fully in due course, it almost invariably saves time in the long run if you start with the Bills.

4.55 There are two series of Bills, one for the Commons and one for the Lords. In which House a Bill started is not relevant here. A Bill introduced first in the House of Lords will be printed in the Commons series like any other when it reaches the Commons. Bills are reprinted incorporating amendments at various stages during their passage. Commons Bills are usually reprinted once after the committee stage and Lords Bills twice, after the committee stage and again after the report stage. They are numbered in each session, and a fresh number is assigned to each print. The number on Commons Bills appears in round brackets. The numbers of Lords Bills used only to be distinguishable by being printed in square brackets; now 'HL Bill' is added before the number. Before session 1986/87 Lords Bills were not numbered separately from other House of Lords papers, but were intermingled with them. Those libraries holding complete sets of all categories of parliamentary papers may, before session 1979/80, have them bound according to the official arrangement of sessional sets (see para **7.13**). Bills arranged alphabetically by title will be found in the early volumes of each sessional set. There are separate sessional sets for the

Commons and Lords, but within each all the prints of the Bills will be found together. If Bills are kept separately in the library in numerical order, you will need to use one of the various tools described in chapter 7 to find the number – usually the annual HMSO catalogue is sufficient, and Bill numbers are given in the House of Commons *Sessional Information Digest* and *Weekly Bulletin* (see para **4.60** and figure 4.3). Any law library regularly fielding *Pepper v Hart* inquiries will have started arranging their Bills by title, if they did not do so already. The latest version of a Bill is available on the Parliament website, but previous versions of Bills are not kept up and when the Bill is finally passed it is replaced with the Act. So if you do not have access to a library, the admirable Parliament website is not of help on this occasion.

4.56 In the Lords the Bills are also very usefully accompanied by the lists of amendments to be tabled at each stage. The day before each day's proceedings on a Bill, these amendments are brought together as a marshalled list of amendments. These marshalled lists bear the same number as the print of the Bill they refer to. If a stage of a Bill lasts more than a day the marshalled list is reprinted, incorporating any new amendments and dropping those relating to clauses that have already been dealt with. So if a committee stage lasts say five days, there will be five marshalled lists of amendments each getting progressively shorter (see figure 4.2). Unfortunately, the same practice is not followed in the Commons. The amendments are not issued to subscribers to the Bills, but go in the 'Vote Bundle' issued daily to MPs. When it comes to the usual final stage of a Bill, Commons consideration of Lords amendments, the Bill is not printed in its entirety again, but a consolidated list of the all the amendments made at the various stages by the Lords is issued with the Commons Bills and given a Bill number. The amendments are organised with reference to the version first printed for the *Lords*. In the case of a Bill that was first introduced in the Lords, when the Lords usually have the last say, there is an equivalent list published with the Lords Bills, which refers the Bill as first printed for the *Commons*.

EXPLANATORY NOTES

4.57 These are a further innovation of the Modernisation Committee. Starting in the 1998/99 session all government Bills (except for annual Consolidated Fund Bills and the like) are accompanied by a separate set of explanatory notes, prepared by the government department sponsoring the Bill. They all start by stating:

> They have been prepared . . . in order to assist the reader of the Bill and to help inform debate on it. They do not form part of the Bill and have not been endorsed by Parliament. The notes need to be read in conjunction with the Bill. They are not, and are not meant to be, a comprehensive description of the Bill.

They are an amalgamation and replacement of two species of documents that were previously produced. One was an explanatory memorandum included in the first print of government Bills in each House. These were rather terse, and barely explanatory – not dissimilar to the explanatory notes on the back of SIs. The other was Notes on Clauses, prepared by the government department in order to brief the ministers steering the Bill through Parliament, and which were latterly also made available to MPs and peers generally, but which were not publicly available. The new explanatory notes give scope for expressing, in neutral terms, the purpose and content of the Bill in non-legislative language. A set of notes is produced more or less at the same time as the Bill is first printed for the first House, and then again when the Bill reaches the second House. A third version becomes the explanatory notes to the Act on the Bill

Figure 4.2

Countryside and Rights of Way Bill

FIFTH

MARSHALLED

LIST OF AMENDMENTS

TO BE MOVED

IN COMMITTEE

The amendments have been marshalled in accordance with the instruction of 30th June 2000, as follows—

Schedule 6	Schedule 9
Clauses 54 to 63	Clauses 68 to 71
Schedule 7	Schedule 10
Clauses 64 to 66	Clauses 72 to 76
Schedule 8	Schedule 11
Clause 67	Clauses 77 and 78

[Amendments marked ★ are new or have been altered]

Amendment
No.

Schedule 6

BY THE BARONESS BYFORD
THE LORD GLENTORAN

371   Page 62, line 26, leave out from ("authority") to ("the") in line 28

372   Page 62, line 30, leave out ("which would otherwise disrupt the life of the community")

BY THE BARONESS MILLER OF CHILTHORNE DOMER

372A   Page 63, leave out lines 1 to 5

BY THE BARONESS BYFORD
THE LORD GLENTORAN

373   Page 63, line 3, leave out ("high levels of")

374   Page 63, line 5, leave out ("persistent")
HL Bill 86—V   52/3

being passed. These are clearly of potential relevance for statutory interpretation. Lord Steyn took the view, in his paper cited at para **4.2**, that 'there is much concrete and valuable contextual information' in them, and that 'such documents may prove to be a more immediate and informative aid that earlier official reports' (at 71). At the time of giving the lecture on which the paper was based, the question of their use in court had not yet arisen. However, Lord Hope in *R v A (No 2)* already cited (para **4.12**), no doubt fortified by this suggestion as he was by the suggestions on the wider point already discussed, has now indeed referred to such explanatory notes on an Act. The case concerned the construction of s 41 of the Youth Justice and Criminal Evidence Act 1999 and its compatibility with the Human Rights Act 1998. The section sought to exclude evidence being adduced or questions being asked in cross-examination on behalf of the accused about any sexual behaviour of the complainant. One exception to such exclusion was where the sexual behaviour of the complainant took place 'at or about the same time' as the event that was the subject matter of the charge. The act of consensual sexual intercourse that the defendant wished to adduce in evidence took place one week before the alleged rape. The relevant explanatory note prepared by the Home Office said that it was expected that 'at or about the same time' would generally be interpreted no more widely than 24 hours before or after the offence. This was only a small slice of the interpretative picture and by no means determinative of a complex case, but it is instructive none the less. As Lord Steyn said in his paper 'if it is decided that in principle explanatory notes may be admitted, it is likely that the disinclination of judges to delve into *Hansard* will increase'.

Other parliamentary materials

4.58 The other classes of parliamentary materials are fully described in chapter 7. Those sometimes needed for *Pepper v Hart* research are House of Commons and House of Lords Papers, where proceedings relevant to a Bill (or as discussed later, statutory instruments) do not take place on the floor of the House or in a Standing Committee, as described above in the section on complications and exceptions. One other class of parliamentary publication which, though not directly relevant to *Pepper v Hart* research, is perhaps better dealt with here rather than in chapter 7 is the *Journals* of each House. As mentioned in connection with minutes of Standing Committees, they are the formal record of the business of each House. The modern *Journals* are based on the daily *Minutes of Proceedings* and are published as sessional volumes. Since in printed form they cover proceedings in the Lords from 1510 and in the Commons from 1547, they are a valuable source for parliamentary history and the historian generally. They are also the authoritative source for rulings on parliamentary procedure, and so references to them fill the footnotes to *Erskine May*. They may sometimes help in disentangling the procedural history of a Bill, particularly for old Acts where the debates are incomplete, and for Local or Private Acts, where proceedings are largely unpublished.

Finding the debates on a section of a Public General Act

Identifying the relevant Act

4.59 This step may seem self-evident but two points are easily overlooked. First, if you have been using a source for the Act that prints it as amended, such as *Halsbury's Statutes*, then your section or the relevant part of it, may have in fact been inserted by a later Act. As explained at para **3.51** such text will appear in square brackets, or the section may bear a lettered number. It is then simply a question of looking at the notes to identify the Act that made the amendment, and then concentrating your efforts, in the first place at any rate, on that Act. It sometimes turns out, due to the way the amending text interacts with the text of original Act, that you need to go back and find the debates on that too. The second eventuality is that you have a consolidation Act. Consolidation Acts, as described at para **3.73**, do not change the law. They go through a separate parliamentary procedure, and the substance of the Acts being consolidated are not debated. If you have a consolidation Act, which will be apparent from its long title, look at paras **4.68–4.70** before proceeding further.

Using the Bills

4.60 If it is available, a useful preliminary is to find the entry for the Bill in the House of Commons *Sessional Digest*, which has been published from the 1983/84 session (see figure 4.3), or for the current session the *Weekly Information Bulletin*. It sets out the dates of all the stages – you can see straightaway from the number of days spent in committee whether you have a short or long task on your hands. It gives the numbers of the Bills, and so how many prints to expect to find. It tells you whether or not it was a government Bill. The data from the *Sessional Digest* and *Weekly Information Bulletin* is available from 1993/94 on Badger on the record for the Act, and from 1995/96 on the Parliament website. It is obviously also helpful to have a copy of the Act to hand. The *Current Law Statutes* version is probably the most useful for this purpose. In recent volumes the notes to the section may already indicate relevant *Hansard* references (though this does not preclude doing your own research). The general note will also identify any Green Papers and White Papers, which you may need to refer to as well. You may also need the Act to compare it with the scheme of the various prints of the Bills, in order to find your clause in them.

4.61 Having assembled all the prints of the Bill, usually two for the Commons (plus the additional list of Lords amendments) and three for the Lords, work your way through them and compare your section with the clause in the Bills. If the very first print of the Bill has the clause in identical terms to the section of the Act, it generally presages the fact that the clause was not amended at any stage, which is usually bad news since it is most frequently amendments that generate relevant debate. But you need to press on: an amendment may have been inserted at one stage and removed at another, there may have been relevant debate when amendments were unsuccessfully moved, and there may be something in the second reading debates. However, if the clause in the first print is not identical to the section you need to identify, by comparing the prints of the Bills, at which stage the clause was inserted or reached its final form. This stage is likely to be the most fruitful. It does not preclude looking at the earlier or later debates – there may have been earlier similar amendments that were unsuccessful – but if you look at it first its provenance often becomes clear. For example, if it does not appear until the report stage in the Lords, you may find that the minister explains that it is introduced to meet concerns in committee, which you then know will be relevant too. Or if it went in at the Lords committee stage, it may be revealed that exactly the same amendment had been attempted in the Commons committee stage, and the government now relents. The other thing to be doing while you go through the prints of the Bill is to be noting the number of the clause at each stage. If you are lucky enough to have only a short Bill, or your section is s 1 of the Act, there may be no problem. But the clause numbers will change as the Bill progresses, and the number it started with will almost certainly not be the number of the section in the Act. When you come to look at the debates, it obviously helps to know what clause number they will be talking about.

Figure 4.3

Sessional Information Digest

Complete List of Public Bills

The following is a list of Public Bills which were before Parliament in session 1999-2000, with the exception of Order Confirmation Bills.
In order to save space, the list is in an abbreviated form. The title of the Bill is followed by a letter denoting the type of Bill (see Legislation - General Notes) and the name of the Member and/or Peer sponsoring it. This is followed by the Bill number (or Bill numbers if it has been reprinted as amended, with the original first and the latest reprinting last). Then follow the dates of the various stages (eg 20.6.2000 – 20 June 2000).

Government Bills are listed in bold type

AGE EQUALITY COMMISSION (T) Mr Lawrie Quinn
Commons: (159)   1R: 12.7.2000   Dropped

ANALYSIS OF COSTS AND BENEFITS (EUROPEAN UNION   Mr Michael Fabricant
MEMBERSHIP) (P)
Commons: (50)   1R: 20.1.2000 (not printed)   Order for 2nd Reading lapsed

ANALYSIS OF COSTS AND BENEFITS (NAFTA MEMBERSHIP) (P)   Mr Michael Fabricant
Commons: (67)   1R: 14.2.2000 (not printed)   Order for 2nd Reading lapsed

AREAS OF OUTSTANDING NATURAL BEAUTY [HL] (L)   Lord Renton of Mount Harry
Lords: (7)   1R: 23.11.99

ARMED FORCES DISCIPLINE [HL] (G)   Baroness Symons of Vernham Dean / Mr Geoff Hoon
Lords: (1,16,17)   1R: 18.11.99   2R: 29.11.99   Comm: 16.12.99   Rep: 18.1.2000   3R: 24.1.2000
    CA: 6.4.2000
Commons: (53, 89)   1R: 24.1.2000   2R: 17.2.2000   Comm (SC D): 29.2 - 14.3.2000   RS: 6.4.2000
Royal Assent: 25.5.2000 (Ch 4, 2000)   **ARMED FORCES DISCIPLINE ACT 2000**

ARMED FORCES (MINIMUM AGE OF RECRUITMENT) (T)   Mr Paul Stinchcombe
Commons: (127)   1R: 17.5.2000   Dropped

BROADCASTING OF RECORDED MUSIC IN PUBLIC PLACES (T)   Mr Robert Key
Commons: (90)   1R: 15.3.2000 (not printed)   Order for 2nd Reading lapsed

BUILDING SOCIETIES (TRANSFER RESOLUTIONS) (B12)   Mr Tony McWalter
Commons: (23)   1R: 15.12.99   2R: 19.5.2000 (Deb adj)   Dropped

CARE STANDARDS [HL] (G)   Lord Hunt of Kings Heath / Mr Alan Milburn
Lords: (11,18,52,103) 1R: 2.12.99   2R: 13.12.99   Comm: 10&13.1.2000   Comm: 18.1.2000
    Rep: 28.3.2000   3R: 4.4.2000   CA: 18.7.2000
Commons: (105,152) 1R: 5.4.2000   2R: 18.5.2000   Comm: (SC G):25.5&4.7.2000   RS: 12.7.2000
Royal Assent: 20.7.2000 (Ch 14, 2000)   **CARE STANDARDS ACT 2000**

CARERS AND DISABLED CHILDREN (B2) Mr Tom Pendry / Baroness Pitkeathley
Commons: (13)   1R: 15.12.99   P2R: 4.2.2000   Comm (SC C): 8-15.3.2000   RS: 5.5.2000
Lords: (62)   1R:9.5.2000   2R: 23.6.2000   OCD: 14.7.2000   3R: 20.7.2000
Royal Assent: 20.7.2000 (Ch 16, 2000)   **CARERS AND DISABLED CHILDREN ACT 2000**

CENSUS (AMENDMENT) [HL] (L)   Lord Weatherill / Mr Jonathan Sayeed
Lords: (15,29)   1R: 16.12.99   2R: 27.1.2000   Comm: 3.2.2000   Rep: 3.3.2000   3R: 14.3.2000
Commons: (92)   1R: 20.3.2000   Order for 2nd Reading discharged; returned to the Lords due to an error in the Bill
Lords: 3R: 28.3.2000   CA: 27.7.2000
Commons: (100)   1R: 28.3.2000   2R: 20.6.2000   MR: 26.6.2000   Comm (SC D): 5.7.2000 RS: 26.7.2000
Royal Assent: 28.7.2000 (Ch 24, 2000)   **CENSUS (AMENDMENT) ACT 2000**

CHEQUES (SCOTLAND) [HL] (L)   Viscount Younger of Leckie
Lords: (27)   1R: 1.2.2000   2R: 8.3.2000   OCD: 17.7.2000   3R: 19.7.2000*

CHILD CURFEW (SPECIFIED AGE) (T)   Vernon Coaker
Commons: (94)   1R: 22.3.2000 (not printed)   Order for 2nd Reading lapsed

CHILD SUPPORT, PENSIONS AND SOCIAL SECURITY (G)   Mr Alistair Darling/Baroness Hollis of Heigham
Commons: (9,83,167) 1R: 1.12.99   2R: 11.1.2000   Comm(SC F): 18.1-7.3.2000
    Rep: 29.3.2000   RS: 3.4.2000   LA: 24.7.2000
Lords: (54,70,92,110) 1R: 5.4.2000   2R: 17.4.2000   Comm: 8,15&22.5.2000   Rep: 22&27.6.2000
    3R: 19.7.2000   CA: 26.7.2000
Royal Assent: 28.7.2000 (Ch 19, 2000)   **CHILD SUPPORT, PENSIONS AND SOCIAL SECURITY ACT 2000**

Finding Hansard *references for each stage*

4.62 There is now quite an array of alternative methods of doing this, and it is to some extent a matter of personal preference. There is a lot to be said for simply using the sessional indexes to each series of *Hansard* itself (see figure 4.4 (a) and (b)). They look a little daunting, but you will have to have to go to the shelves where they are kept in any event. The length of the entries, and the fact that they are not altogether easy on the eye, is not only because the volume number, the column numbers and the date of each of the main stages is provided in a long string, but also because any other procedural matters such as ways and means resolutions, motions for approval and so on are given. Although references to these have to be disentangled from the references for the main stages, they are sometimes useful – for example, alerting you that there was a guillotine motion. The sessional indexes also indicate by means of an asterisk those stages that were purely formal without debate, such as the first reading. The sessional index for Commons *Hansard* forms a separate numbered volume in the series at the end of the session. The sessional index for Lords *Hansard* is not usually a separate volume, but is included at the back of the last volume of the session. Each bound volume also has it own index. The sessional indexes tend to be published a little in arrears, so if you have a very recent Act, you will need to use one of the alternatives below.

4.63 If you had the entry for the Bill from the *Sessional Digest* or *Weekly Information Bulletin* in front of you, you could simply use that to dive in. It does not give volume numbers or column numbers, but the date alone is sufficient to get you to the right place. Debates on Bills take up a fair chunk of a day's *Hansard*, and so are easily spotted. One small point to beware of, however. Lengthy debates are often interrupted by other business, particularly in the Lords at convenient times like 7.30 pm. In the *Hansard* indexes you will see the jumps in column numbering. If you have just dived in, and the debate seems to finish suddenly, check beyond the next item – which will be something like approving the Child Benefit and Social Security (Fixing and Adjusting of Rates) (Amendment) Regulations or an 'unstarred question' on dietary supplements – for resumption of the debate. As in the sessional indexes, stages that were formal only are given an asterisk in the *Sessional Digest*.

4.64 Many people use the *Hansard* references given at the start of the Act in *Current Law Statutes*. The drawback is that until 1998 they did not state which stage of the proceedings the references relate to. If you want to start, not at the beginning, but at a particular stage that you have identified from the Bills as being likely to be particulary important, they will not help. It is also much more conducive to a structured approach to have the stages with the references. Even after 1998, when stages are put in brackets, the format is not the clearest. The format provided in *Halsbury's Statutes* (for statutes passed since 1993) and in the new explanatory notes to Acts (from 1999), where stages, dates and references are set out in tabular form, is ideal if you are shy of the sessional indexes (see figure 4.4 (c)). The older volumes of *Current Law Statutes* are also not entirely reliable in this respect (and do not mention Standing Committee debates). Parlianet, based on the House of Commons own database, is another resource. The 'Bill Histories' section of the database gives all the references. If you do a free text search, you will get quite a lot of hits, since separate records are created for the references to individual speeches.

4.65 There are some short cuts. *Copinger on Copyright* was the first textbook to give a section-by-section table of *Hansard* references, in this case to the copyright

Figure 4.4

GENERAL INDEX—SESSION 1998–99
24th November 1998–11th November 1999

Employment Relations Bill 1998/99
  Debates etc.
1R (27.01.99) **324** 343
2R and Money res* (09.02.99) **325** 130–226
Rep (30.03.99) **328** 875–997
Rep and 3R (31.03.99) **328** 1110–203
Lords amendts (21.07.99) **335** 1244–91, (26.07.99) **336** 31–56, 85–8
Allocation of time motion (22.07.99) **335** 1359–407
Allocation of time motion* (26.07.99) **336** 57
Royal Assent (27.07.99) **336** 152
  Questions
325 206w, **330** 441w
Northern Ireland **326** 330w
Small businesses **326** 371w, 530

(a) Commons *Hansard* sessional index

24th November 1998–11th November 1999

Employment Relations Bill:
Brought from the Commons and 1R*, [599] (13.4.99) 625; 2R and Committed to a Committee of the Whole House, [600] (10.5.99) 964-87, 1001-46; Motion for Approval (Lord McIntosh of Haringey), [601] (26.5.99) 926;

Committee, (7.6.99) 1144-218, 1234-92; [602] (16.6.99) 288-361, 375-406; Motion for Approval (Lord McIntosh of Haringey), [603] (6.7.99) 724-5; Report, (8.7.99) 1037-143; 3R, Passed and Returned to the Commons with Amendments, [604] (15.7.99) 559-83; Amendments Considered, (26.7.99) 1360-8; Returned from the Commons with Lords Amendment in Lieu Agreed to (27.7.99) 1518; Royal Assent, 1420.

(b) Lords *Hansard* sessional index

These notes refer to the Employment Relations Act 1999 which received Royal Assent on 27 July 1999 (c.26)

Stage	Date	Hansard reference
House of Commons		
Introduction	27 January 1999	Vol. 324 Col. 343
Second Reading	9 February 1999	Vol. 325 Col. 130 - 226
Committee	16 February - 23 March 1999	Standing Committee E
Report and Third Reading	30 and 31 March 1999	Vol. 328 Col. 875 - 997 Vol. 328 Col. 1110 - 1203
House of Lords		
Introduction	13 April 1999	Vol. 599 Col. 625
Second Reading	10 May 1999	Vol. 600 Col. 966 - 1048
Committee	7 and 16 June 1999	Vol. 601 Col. 1144 - 1292 Vol. 602 Col. 288 - 406
Report	8 July 1999	Vol. 603 Col. 1037 - 1143
Third Reading	15 July 1999	Vol. 604 Col. 559 - 583
House of Commons		
Consideration of Lords amendments	21 and 26 July 1999	Vol. 335 Col. 1244 - 1291 Vol. 336 Col. 31 - 56
House of Lords		
Consideration of Commons amendment and reason	26 July 1999	Vol. 604 Col. 1363 - 1370
House of Commons		
Consideration of Lords amendment	26 July 1999	Vol. 336 Col. 85 - 88

(c) Explanatory notes to the Act

Acts. It would be admirable if other textbooks followed suit. Even if such a systematic table is not provided, the editors of textbooks will, of course, nowadays often make reference to *Hansard* in the footnotes. Guides to new Acts, such as those published by Blackstone Press, may include relevant extracts from *Hansard* as appendices. The many books on the Human Rights Act are particularly replete with such materials, but there is now an excellent section-by-section compilation of all the significant parts of the debates: Jonathan Cooper and Adrian Marshall-Williams *Legislating for Human Rights: the Parliamentary Debates on the Human Rights Bill* ((2000) Hart). A similar compilation, confined to ministerial statements, was prepared by Katie Ghose for the Immigration Law Practitioners' Association on the Asylum and Immigration Act 1996. If you want to pay for someone else to do the research for you, the fee-based Information for Business service run by Westminster Public Reference Library offers a 'clause search' service; other large public reference libraries may possibly do likewise.

4.66 Having assembled your references by any of the above means, you will typically have eight separate stages to look at: first, three stages in the Commons – the second reading, the committee stage, and the report stage; then, four stages in the Lords – the second reading, the committee stage, the report stage and the third reading; and finally, back to the Commons for consideration of the Lords amendments.

Order of consideration of clauses

4.67 If you have a large Bill and long debates at a particular stage – especially at committee which may occupy several days – it is helpful to be able to judge when they reached your clause in order to cut down on the quantity of material to be flicked through. It is here with the Lords stages that it is immensely helpful to have the marshalled lists of amendments that go with the Bills (see para **4.56** and figure 4.2). The order of consideration of clauses is printed on the front. Although by and large clauses will be considered sequentially, that is not always so. Schedules are often considered together with the parent clause, and for various reasons blocks of clauses may be considered out of sequence. Where the stage lasts more than one day, the marshalled lists will also tell you on what day they reached your clause, since the clauses already dealt with will have been dropped off the next day's marshalled list. The marshalled lists also contain the text of the amendments themselves, which are numbered in the margin. You can see straightaway whether there is to be amendment to your clause, and what it is, and furthermore the number of the amendment is given in *Hansard* – it is sometimes easier to follow through the amendment numbers rather than the clause numbers. If you did not have the marshalled lists to hand, look at the 'Motion for Approval' (indexed in the sessional indexes) a few days before the stage in question – it will at least give you the order of consideration of clauses. In the Commons you do not have the luxury of the marshalled lists. But again, there may be motions on order of consideration of clauses at the start of the stage. In Standing Committee look at the first day's sitting – such a motion will usually appear right at the start or towards the end of the sitting. There is one important difference between the Commons and the Lords on the way amendments are treated. In the Lords an amendment by way of insertion of an entirely fresh clause, rather than an amendment to a clause that is already in the Bill, is simply slotted in at the most convenient point – where if it is accepted it is likely to end up in the Act. The Commons, however, distinguish between amendments and new clauses when settling the order of consideration. At the committee stage, if the order is not otherwise varied by a specific motion, the usual order is as follows: each clause in the original Bill and amendments thereto, new clauses, then Schedules in the original Bill and amendments thereto, and finally new Schedules. Thus, if from inspection of the Bills you establish that your clause was inserted in its entirety at the committee stage, you will need to look towards the end of stage, when they have been through all the original clauses. The clause numbers under consideration are printed on the front of the debates for each sitting. New clauses will have an entirely separate number. At report stage in the Commons the 'default' order of consideration is the other way around: new clauses come first, then amendments to clauses, then new Schedules and finally amendments to Schedules.

Consolidation Acts

4.68 Consolidation Acts, which are made pursuant to the Consolidation of Enactments (Procedure) Act 1949, re-enact the existing law with corrections and minor improvements only. Existing words of the previous statute may be used, or the drafting may be recast. Some consolidation Acts are the result of recommendations from the Law Commission. In lieu of the committee stage, the Bill goes to the Joint Committee on Consolidation Bills. Its function is to scrutinise the Bill to ensure that it does indeed re-enact the existing law, and it takes evidence from the draftsman. The Bill will receive no debate, or only very limited debate on the floor of each House. Thus to find parliamentary debates on the substance of a section of consolidation Act there is no point at looking at the debates on the consolidation Bill – you need to look at the debates on the Act which first introduced the provision.

4.69 Before doing so, there is an important point of principle to bear in mind in light of the recent House of Lords decision in *Spathe Holme* (already cited at para **4.11**). It was held that it was ordinarily impermissible to construe a consolidating provision by reference to the enactments it replaced except where (a) the language of the provision was ambiguous, or (b) its purpose could only be understood by examining the context in which it had originally been used. The fact that either of the two exceptions applies does not give you carte blanche to embark on *Pepper v Hart* research on the original Act. The original Act itself has in turn to meet the ordinary *Pepper v Hart* criteria. If exception (a) applies, there may well be a likelihood, if the exact language has been recycled, that the original enactment is ambiguous too, in which case well and good, but it may not necessarily be so. Exception (b) certainly does not automatically lead to the need to go to *Hansard*. In *Spathe Holme* the Court of Appeal had been right to go back to the original enactments because of exception (b), but the majority in the Lords held that to go one step further and use *Hansard* as well had been wrong on *Pepper v Hart* principles – there was no ambiguity in the language of the original Act.

4.70 The first step is to trace the derivation of your section as described at paras **3.76–3.77**. As mentioned there, check that the derivation you find is not itself in a consolidation Act. When you have found the section as first enacted, compare it with the section in the consolidation Act. If they are identical or there is no material difference, then it is simply a question of proceeding with your research in the usual way. If, however, there is a difference that is relevant to your problem, then you will need to research the consolidation process to see how the difference arose. You will need to find the relevant report and minutes of the Joint Committee on Consolidation Bills – each report usually only covers a single Bill, though occasionally more than one Bill is considered in a particular report. They are published twice, both in the House of Commons papers and in the House of Lords papers, though libraries may only retain one copy. The annual TSO catalogue under 'Joint Committee' is the simplest method – the report has the names of the relevant Bills in its title – but any of the tools described in chapter 7 will do. If there is a Law Commission report, you will need that too. It will be referred to in the Joint Committee's report and also in the general note to the Act in *Current Law Statutes*. You should also check such debates as there are in the main *Hansard* – if there is anything it is usually only in the Lords.

Local and Personal Acts

4.71 Local and Personal Acts (in effect nowadays just Local Acts) start life as *Private* Bills, and go through a completely separate procedure from ordinary Public Bills. Such Bills are not promoted by a minister or even an MP, but by, for example, a local authority or statutory undertaker. The promoter will engage a parliamentary agent (there are specialist firms, which are usually also solicitors) to see the Bill through. Private Bills may start in either House and may be carried over from one session to the next. Progress and details appear, in a separate list from the Public Bills, in the *Sessional Digest* and *Weekly Information Bulletin*. The main proceedings take place at the committee stage. Where petitions from affected persons or bodies have been received, it goes before an Opposed Bill Committee. This is a quasi-judicial hearing with the promoter represented by counsel. Especially since many Private Bills are to do with infrastructure projects, the committee hearing closely resembles a planning inquiry, with evidence being given.

4.72 There are a number of practical limitations on doing *Pepper v Hart* research on a Local Act. First, the Stationery Office does not publish the Bills. For current Bills copies have to be obtained from the relevant parliamentary agent (these are given against the Bill in the *Weekly Information Bulletin*). The House of Lords Records Office also holds reference copies. Furthermore, the verbatim proceedings of the committee are not published at all. Transcripts are made, which are kept by the House of Lords Records Office. For current proceedings, copies of the transcripts are open to public inspection in the Private Bill Office of the relevant House (but may not be photocopiable), or can be purchased through the parliamentary agent. There are rarely any debates to be found in the main *Hansard*, the stages being taken formally only. If there is anything, it is usually a short third reading debate in the Lords.

Statutory instruments

4.73 Even before *Pepper v Hart* the House of Lords had held that in certain circumstances it might be permissible to look at parliamentary debates on an SI: *Pickstone v Freemans* [1989] 1 AC 66. That case, which had be concerned with an SI implementing an EC Directive, had a narrower ratio than *Pepper v Hart*. But certainly now the courts would not look on an SI any differently from an Act. After the rigours of researching a Bill, researching the passage of an SI will seem refreshingly straightforward. First of all most SIs receive no debate at all. If they are debated, there is very little to look at – a short debate, perhaps two or three pages, in each House. There are no amendments – the instrument stands or falls in its entirety. Since the cut and thrust of moving amendments tends to generate the useful *Pepper v Hart* fodder in the case of Bills, your chances of finding useful material on an SI are that much slimmer. Certainly Bennion, in setting out the rules that he considers can be extracted as to the professional duty of legal advisers and advocates as a consequence of the decision in *Pepper v Hart*, says:

> The duty extends to the construction of delegated legislation, and not only where it is debated in Parliament. The sponsor may have made a statement in debates on the Bill for the parent Act which indicates the way the delegated power was intended to be exercised. (*Statutory Interpretation* (3rd edn, 1997) p 482.)

But once again the decision in *Spath Holme* (cited at para **4.11**) needs now to be taken into account. As already noted, it was held that for *Hansard* to be admitted the 'ambiguity' in the first *Pepper v Hart* criterion had to relate to the statutory language of the parent Act, not to the scope of a discretionary power. Thus on the face of it if the language of the section in the enabling Act is plain, then there is no need to look beyond such parliamentary materials as there may be on the SI itself. However, Lord Bingham and Lord Hope did concede that an exception might arise if during the passage of the enabling Bill the minister gave a categorical assurance that exercise of the power would be restricted in some way. Such an eventuality may be remote. Since ministers and their advisers are fully aware of the potential use of their statements later in court, they would be very circumspect about giving such an assurance. The rationale of the exception would seem to derive from the narrower view of the purpose of *Pepper v Hart* as put forward by Lord Steyn (see para **4.12**) – restraining the executive rather than divining parliamentary intention. The difficulty, though, as is so often the case with *Pepper v Hart*, is that you would not know whether there had indeed been such a categorical assurance until you looked. If you did have an ambiguity of language in the enabling provision warranting conventional *Pepper v Hart* research on the Act, then particularly relevant might be, in addition to the debates, the report of the Lords Delegated Powers Committee (see para **4.39**) for Acts passed from 1993.

Parliamentary procedure on SIs

4.74 There are four procedures for making an SI (and a new fifth procedure in the case of Deregulation and Regulatory Reform orders, and remedial orders under the Human Rights Act, see paras **4.78–4.79**): affirmative resolution procedure; negative resolution procedure; simply laying; and no parliamentary stage at all. Which procedure is prescribed in the enabling legislation will determine whether there are likely to be any debates at all.

4.75 The affirmative resolution procedure requires the positive approval of both Houses of Parliament (or the House of Commons only for tax SIs). The instrument is laid in draft, and there is a short debate in each House to approve it. This procedure is reserved for only the most important SIs – perhaps one in ten. Only if the SI is an affirmative instrument will you be certain that there will be some form of debate. You can immediately tell whether an SI is an affirmative instrument, because the fact that it has been approved by a resolution of both Houses is printed at its head. But if you were to look at the relevant provision in the enabling Act it would typically read:

> No order shall be made under this section unless a draft of the order has been laid before and approved by a resolution of each House of Parliament.

There are minor variations on this formula. In the case of tax instruments consequent upon a budget, the SI may be made and become immediately effective, but will cease to be effective after a certain period, say 28 days, unless a resolution approving it is then made. The Parliament Acts, incidentally, do not apply to delegated legislation, so there has indeed to be approval of both Houses, though it is virtually unknown for the Lords to block an SI.

4.76 With a negative resolution instrument, the SI is made and is usually immediately effective, but may subsequently be annulled if a resolution to do so is passed within a certain period (the standard period provided for in the Statutory Instruments Act 1946 is 40 days). This procedure is quite common. The practical effect is that there may or there may not be a debate. Most commonly there is no debate since parliamentary time is rarely allocated for 'prayers' to annul. Whether or not you have a negative instrument can be determined from the enabling provision (cited in the SI). It will typically read:

> Any regulations made under this section shall be subject to annulment in pursuance of a resolution of either House.

There is a rare variant on this. The instrument is laid in draft and can only be subsequently made if there is no resolution against the draft within the time limit.

4.77 The simple laying requirement is the lowest form of check. The instrument is simply laid before Parliament *after* it is made (though, if the proper niceties have been observed, before it comes into force). In theory, members are thus alerted to its existence, and could raise questions with the minister about it. But if the instrument only has this requirement, you know there will be no debate. The enabling provision will typically read:

> Any Order in Council under this section shall be laid before Parliament after being made.

Many instruments are made under enabling provisions that do not even require laying.

DEREGULATION AND REGULATORY REFORM ORDERS

4.78 Orders made under the Deregulation and Contracting Out Act 1994 and its successor the Regulatory Reform Act 2001 go through what has been dubbed a 'super-affirmative' procedure. The 1994 Act was introduced by the Conservative government to cut legislative red tape, particularly as it affects businesses. Although there are fairly numerous examples of Acts being amendable by SI in minor respects, orders made under the 1994 Act are designed to amend substantially or to repeal primary legislation. Constitutionally, this is a very far-reaching power. Hence the need was felt to have an added level of scrutiny. About 50 orders were made under the 1994 Act, but there was a distinct tailing off of such orders after 1997. The Labour government in due course introduced the Regulatory Reform Act 2001. This has a very similar structure to the 1994 Act, but the range of legislation that will be subject to its provisions is significantly wider. The 1994 Act could only be applied if the resulting order reduced the burdens to those affected – it could not introduce new burdens, however small. The 2001 Act permits new burdens provided that there are countervailing benefits. It is thus anticipated that there will be rather more Regulatory Reform Orders than there were Deregulation Orders. The initial safeguard under both Acts is a requirement for widespread consultation on stipulated matters before a proposal for a Deregulation Order is even made. A *proposal* for a draft order then first goes, in the Commons, to the Deregulation and Regulatory Reform Committee. (This was formerly called the Deregulation Committee, and may possibly in future be called the Regulatory Reform Committee – its initial hybrid name is because for a short transitional period there are still proposals going through under the old Act.) This is a Select Committee, able to call for evidence. At the same time it goes to the Delegated Powers and Regulatory Reform Committee in the Lords. There is a period of 60 days for these committees (the 'Scrutiny Committees') to scrutinise the proposal – a period designed to ensure that such orders cannot be rushed through. At this point the committees can respond to their respective Houses in one of three ways: that the proposal should proceed; should not proceed; or should proceed in amended form. The government then goes away and finalises its draft Order. When that is laid the Committees have a further period to consider and report on it before a motion to approve the draft is put. In the Lords all draft orders are debated. In the Commons there is no debate if the Deregulation Committee recommended, without a division, that the order is approved. If the recommendation in favour was not unanimous, there is a short debate. If the recommendation was against, there is a longer debate, after which, as a matter of practice, the government will withdraw the draft order. Progress on Deregulation and Regulatory Reform Orders, with numbers of the relevant House of Commons and House of Lords papers for the committee reports, is given in the *Weekly Information Bulletin* and *Sessional Digest*. There is one novel aspect to orders made under the Regulatory Reform Act. There is now the facility to make 'subordinate provision orders', SIs made under an SI. The main order may contain enabling powers to amend certain designated parts of the order, expected to appear in Schedules, by an ordinary SI, without such SIs having themselves to go through the super-affirmative procedure. The Scrutiny Committees will look at the initial draft of the main order to ensure that such provisions, which are intended to deal with minor matters such as uplift of fees, are appropriately designated as such. The Scrutiny Committees will also be able to stipulate whether such SIs are affirmative or negative, or simply laying instruments. Furthermore, when made, such SIs will not go to the Joint Committee on Statutory Instruments (see para **4.80**), but to the Scrutiny Committees.

REMEDIAL ORDERS UNDER THE HUMAN RIGHTS ACT

4.79 Where either an English court has made a declaration of incompatibility under s 4 of the Human Rights Act 1998, or the Strasbourg court makes a ruling that cannot stand with English legislation, then a minister may make a remedial order, an SI, to amend the offending legislation. This route is not obligatory – amending legislation may be passed in the usual way. But it was thought necessary to have a route whereby matters could be put right more speedily. During its passage through Parliament, there was a good deal of concern over the powers to make remedial orders given in s 10 and Sch 2 to the 1998 Act, since amending Acts by means of an SI is inherently suspect. The procedure that had been adopted for the Deregulation Act 1994 was very much in mind. The result is that remedial orders have to go through a similar 'super-affirmative' procedure. It is not exactly the same as for Deregulation orders – for example, there is no power to amend the draft as there is with the first stage of Deregulation order scrutiny. But the Act provides a similar 60-day period to receive representations after the draft order is initially laid, and various explanatory materials have to be provided before the draft is approved. In cases of urgency an order may be made without initial parliamentary approval, but will lapse if not approved within 40 days. The first draft Remedial Order was laid in July 2001 in order to amend the Mental Health Act 1983 in the wake of *R (H) v Mental Health Tribunal for North and East London Region*

[2001] EWCA Civ 415, [2001] 3 WLR 512. A joint Select Committee of both Houses, the Human Rights Committee, has been set up which has scrutiny of any that do materialise among its functions.

JOINT COMMITTEE ON STATUTORY INSTRUMENTS

4.80 There is one additional form of scrutiny which applies to all SIs, except local SIs that do not have to be laid (and except for Deregulation and Regulatory Reform Orders). This is the Joint Committee on Statutory Instruments (or the Commons Select Committee on Statutory Instruments for tax instruments). Except for draft affirmative instruments, it considers SIs after they have been made – so the horse has bolted. But, none the less, its reports and minutes may very occasionally give assistance – they are worth checking, particularly if, as with most SIs, there has been no debate. The remit of the committee is not to examine the merits of the SI but draw the attention of Parliament to SIs that, for example, appear to have retrospective effect, or to be ultra vires the parent Act. In the context of *Pepper v Hart* research, the two most significant of its terms of reference are to draw attention to SIs that are defectively drafted and to those whose 'form or purport calls for elucidation'. The committee works in close collaboration with the government departments. Where there is concern on a particular instrument it may ask the department concerned to give written evidence. Such memoranda may be printed with the committee's report, and may or may not allay the committee's misgivings. If the committee does formally draw Parliament's attention to an instrument, nothing happens – the department just has to go away and consider whether it wishes to produce amending legislation. The committee now prepares annual returns from the departments on what action has been taken on its recommendations, for example, amending legislation to be made shortly, amending legislation to be made if a convenient opportunity arises, or simply disagrees with committee.

Finding debates and other parliamentary materials on SIs

4.81 If you have an affirmative instrument, simply go to the sessional indexes for *Hansard* for the session in which it was made. In the Commons index there may be either one entry or two under the title of the instrument. If there is only one entry the motion for approval will have been debated on the floor of the House. If there are two, then it will have been debated in the Standing Committee on Delegated Legislation (formerly on Statutory Instruments). Only the most important instruments are debated on the floor of the House. However, the formal motion to approve has to be made on the floor. So the first reference will be where the House refers it to a Standing Committee, and the second where it comes back from the Standing Committee for formal approval. The Standing Committee debates are issued with those on Bills in exactly the same format. A sitting may be devoted to a single instrument, or related instruments may be batched together. In the Lords there will be just a single entry under the title. With negative instruments you have to be a little careful. If there is going to be any debate it will have to be within 40 days of the date it was made, but the 40 days does not include when Parliament has been prorogued or adjourned, so does not include recesses. There is no requirement that the debate takes place in the same parliamentary session in which it was made. So an annulment debate for an instrument made towards the end of a session may have taken place in the following session – you need to check both sessional indexes. If the instrument is very recent and there is not yet a sessional index, you can use the Parlianet service, if you subscribe, try the free Polis version on the Parliament website or simply telephone the House of Commons Information Office.

4.82 Finding the relevant Joint Committee report can be a little tedious, since each report will cover dozens of SIs and they produce 20 or 30 reports a year. If you have an affirmative instrument, however, you are usually home and dry, since the Lords have the courtesy to wait for the Joint Committee's report on the draft before holding the debate on the motion to approve (not necessarily the case in the Commons) and print the number of the report at the start of the debate in *Hansard*. The reports of the committee for a particular session all bear the same main arabic House of Commons paper number, with an additional number in lower case roman numerals for each report. Look in the TSO annual catalogue under 'Joint' to find the main number, or use Parlianet and the other sources for parliamentary papers. At the end of each report but before any appendices there is a list of all the instruments, in numerical order, that were considered for that report. So it is usually a case of flicking through the pile of reports until you get to one fairly soon after the instrument was made. They do not necessarily go in strict order, but you can get close enough. Where attention has been drawn to an instrument its title is printed on the front cover, so readily spotted. But there may be a memorandum from the government department printed in it, even if in the event attention was not drawn to the instrument. It is important not to assume that the reports are only worth looking at if the title of your instrument is printed on the front cover. Of course, nine times out of ten, or even 99 times out of 100, you will find nothing, but if you have detected a drafting difficulty in an SI, the committee may well have done so too – they are very expertly advised.

4.83 The materials needed for Deregulation and Regulatory Reform Orders, in addition to the debates, are the reports of the respective Commons and Lords committees. The House of Commons and House of Lords paper numbers are given in the *Sessional Digest* and *Weekly Information Bulletin*.

Background to European legislation

4.84 Some background on the European institutions has already been given at para **3.107**. The further complexities of the European legislative process can only be covered superficially here. Full details will be found in the excellent book, Richard Corbett, Francis Jacobs and Michael Shackleton *The European Parliament* ((4th edn, 2000) John Harper). Timothy Bainbridge's *The Penguin Companion to European Union* (2nd edn, revised, 2000), as always in matters European, is very useful too. Of the main textbooks on EU law, particularly recommended in this context is Stephen Weatherill and Paul Beaumont *EU Law* ((3rd edn, 1999) Penguin). The European Information Association produces a number of valuable publications on EU documentation, and their website has a useful set of EU links.

Proposals for legislation

4.85 The Commission of the European Communities initiates legislation, though the Council may ask them to consider a matter, as may now the European Parliament. The most important species of pre-legislation documentation are the COM documents, which contain proposals for legislation together with an explanatory memorandum. They are identified by year and running number. When they come into the public domain the COM number is suffixed by 'final' to distinguish them from earlier drafts that may have circulated internally, for example, COM(80) 139 Final. COM documents are available at a number of libraries, which are designated European Documentation

Centres or Depositories (see para **4.91**); other libraries may take them on subscription. They can be ordered from the Stationery Office SCANFAX service, which prints them on demand. The text of the proposal, but usually without the explanatory memorandum, is published in the OJ C series (Information and Notices) – as opposed to the L series, which contains adopted legislation. Since 1999 some materials are only published in an electronic version of the C series, and proposals for legislation are one such category. The electronic version of the C series bears the same number as the paper copy published on the same day, with the addition of 'E', and so would be cited as, for example, OJ 2001 C103 E. The paper copy of C103 lists the texts that appear in C103 E. The text of the proposals can also be obtained from the official EUR-Lex website – the 'legislation in preparation' section includes the text of COM documents that have been adopted as well as those under active consideration. As mentioned at para **3.127** the OJ itself is only freely available for a limited period on this site, including it would seem the electronic C series, so there is not usually any point of choosing that option. Proposals for legislation are also included on Celex (see para **3.127**) – in sector 5. If you are looking at the record for the adopted legislation, the document number of the proposal will be given in the 'modifies' field – the Celex number starts with a 5.

Scrutiny by the European Parliament

4.86 The three main procedures that can be followed by the European Parliament are the consultation procedure, the co-operation procedure, and the co-decision procedure. The latter procedure, introduced by the Maastricht treaty in 1992 and greatly expanded and strengthened by the Amsterdam treaty in 1999, is now the normal legislative process whereby more than half of all EU legislation is made. However, there remain significant areas where legislation is still made by the earlier and weaker procedures. *Corbett, Jacobs and Shackelton* provide tables, showing the subject matter and treaty provisions applicable to each procedure. And indeed there are areas where the legal basis for legislation does not even require consultation with the European Parliament. Under the consultation procedure, the original procedure of the Parliament, the Commission proposes legislation, the Parliament give its *opinion* after consideration in a committee, the Commission then modifies its proposal taking into account the Parliament's opinion as it sees fit, and finally the Council adopts the legislation – usually by qualified majority, if no amendments, or unanimously if it is amended. It will be seen that there is only a single stage in the European Parliament under this procedure. Under the co-operation procedure, introduced by the Single European Act in 1987, there is an additional second stage. The proposal goes through as under the consultation procedure, but when it reaches the Council, the Council does not make a final decision but adopts a 'common position'. It returns to Parliament for a second reading where the common position may be approved, rejected or amended. Rejection or amendment can only be made by the Parliament by an absolute majority (not by a majority of members voting). If the proposal is rejected, the Council can only overrule Parliament with the agreement of the Commission and acting unanimously. If there are amendments, the matter is further considered by the Commission, which may or may not adopt them. The Council can then only modify the amendments adopted by the Commission if it acts unanimously. A table from *Corbett, Jacobs and Shackelton* (figure 4.5) sets out the *possible* steps in the co-decision procedure – most legislation will not follow the full gamut, but be adopted or dropped before all of the steps have been exhausted. The procedure is the same as the co-operation procedure as far as the second reading in the European Parliament. But now if the Parliament rejects the 'common position' at second reading, then that is final – the Council cannot overrule the

Figure 4.5   European Parliament co-decision procedure.

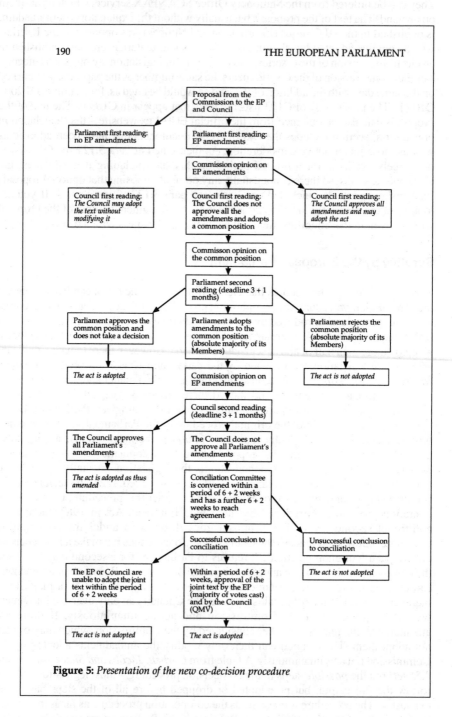

190   THE EUROPEAN PARLIAMENT

Figure 5: *Presentation of the new co-decision procedure*

Reproduced from Corbett, Jacobs and Shackleton *The European Parliament* (John Harper Publishing).

Parliament. Likewise, if Parliament approves the common position the legislation is adopted without further ado – it does not have to be formally approved by the Council. If there are amendments it returns to the Council. If they fail to agree to the amendments, the conciliation procedure comes into operation. A joint committee of members of the Council and the Parliament, with the Commission in attendance try to reach a compromise. If no compromise is reached the measure fails. If there is a compromise, it then has to be approved by the Parliament and the Council.

4.87 The European Parliament website is the best place to track materials. Its 'legal observatory' – slightly oddly named – provides 'legislative dossiers' on all legislation from July 1994. These provide very useful summaries of the stages, with links to much of the documentation in full text. On the site there is also the full text of the sessions of the Plenary meetings of the Parliament, and details of the committees who do most of the work. The Commission of the European Communities and the Council of the European Union meet in private, but information on their activities can be gleaned from press releases and the *Bulletin of the European Union*. There are links between all the main websites – the European Parliament, the Commission, the Council and the main EU site, Europa. Because of the large amount of European material received by the House of Commons Library and indexed on Polis, Parlianet, the commercial version of the database, can be very useful too, though, of course, it is only a bibliographical not full-text database.

Scrutiny at Westminster

4.88 A further area that may require research is consideration of proposed EC legislation at Westminster. While national Parliaments do not have a direct role in passing EC legislation, their scrutiny can have a strong influence on governments when the proposals come before the Council of Ministers. A resolution of the House of Commons of 1998, based on earlier resolutions, gives formal recognition to the understanding that ministers will not agree to EU proposals before parliamentary scrutiny is complete. Scrutiny of EU proposals differs somewhat between the House of Commons and House of Lords and, unlike consideration of Bills, is not a sequential and co-ordinated process. Although there may be co-operation between the two Houses, they largely proceed independently and may or may not consider the same legislation. In the House of Commons, the European Scrutiny Committee (so named since November 1998: previously the Select Committee on European Legislation), which like other Select Committees is composed primarily of backbenchers, considers proposed legislation first. Its role is not so much to consider the merits but to consider whether the proposals raise questions of legal or political importance and to recommend whether the House should consider them further. If further consideration is recommended, the matter will go to one of three European Standing Committees, though the Scrutiny Committee may press for a debate on the floor of the House if the importance warrants it. The reports of the Select Committee of which there are quite a number in each session are published as House of Commons papers and the particular documents considered in each report are usually listed in their titles. A frustrating feature of this is that documents under consideration are not identified by COM Doc numbers, but by a separate Council of Ministers reference number. Debates in the European Standing Committees (A, B and C according to subject matter) appear separately in the *Standing Committee Debates*.

4.89 In the House of Lords the relevant Committee has been called since 1999 the European Union Committee (previously it was the Select Committee on the European Communities); the distinction in its title from the Commons committee is indicative of its slightly different role. As well as considering particular documents, it also considers broader policy areas; and as well as mere scrutiny of documents, it fully investigates the merits of proposals. It is regarded as one of the most important Lords committees, and this is reflected in its manpower and expertise. Their reports, which can be quite substantial, are published as House of Lords papers, and almost always receive a full debate on the floor of the House. There is an excellent briefing on the Committee's role on the House of Lords website. As well as their full reports, regular bulletins, 'Progress of Scrutiny', are issued with the House of Lords Papers (they have their own species of House of Lords paper number – EUC-i, EUC-ii, etc).

4.90 Tracing whether a particular proposal has been considered, however, is not all that easy. House of Commons Select Committee reports are included in the main sources that index parliamentary papers. Electronic sources, such as Parlianet, offer the best chance: key words from the titles of the documents being reported on can be searched for, as these are usually included in the title of the report. Unfortunately, it is not usually possible to search on COM Doc number because, as mentioned above, the number for the document under consideration which is given in the title of the Committee report is a separate Council of Ministers reference number. But if the legislation has been adopted, search for the Directive or Regulation number on Parlianet – the record for the Directive or Regulation will give the original draft number as well, and then repeat the search on that number. Debates on the floor of the House can, with some perseverance, be traced through the indexes to *Hansard*; if the CD-ROM version is available so much the better. Finding particular Standing Committee debates is rather more difficult, unless you have Parlianet; without it, it would be a question of looking through the issues of the debates for a period after the Select Committee had recommended further consideration. In the House of Lords, consideration of particular documents may be buried in a report covering a wider topic, but the usual sources for parliamentary papers will retrieve what Select Committee reports there are. Debates on Select Committee reports are entered in the printed indexes to House of Lords *Hansard* under the title of the report.

Getting help

4.91 In this area more than most the simplest thing to do may be to get specialist advice. The European Parliament has a London office with its own website, and with a reading room for hard copy materials if they are unobtainable elsewhere. The European Commission's London Information Office tends to get rather busy, and Relay Centres have been set up to take the load off them. For solicitors, the Law Society Library is a designated Relay Centre and has specialist staff. Many university and public libraries that are European Documentation Centres will also have knowledgeable librarians. For a list of centres see the European Information in the UK website. Officials in the relevant government department may be able to help. The Department of Trade and Industry's Spearhead database, which gave full details of implementation of single market legislation including the name of the relevant official, was discontinued in June 2000 (though it is still available on the Justis version of Celex, and other products), but but there is the Department of Trade and Industry Single Market Legislation UK Contact List on its website. Or you could try the *Civil Service Yearbook*. Solicitors in some of the large firms will have the advantage of Brussels branch offices, which have their ears to the ground, to consult. The House of Commons Information Office will be able to help on the Westminster end, as indeed will the clerks to the respective committees in the Commons and Lords if necessary.

5. Case law

Introduction

5.1 Finding and using legislation, as chapter 4 indicated, may have its intricacies, but at least the extent of the material is reasonably finite. If you are looking for a statute in force, it is likely to be in the three or four shelves of books that comprise *Halsbury's Statutes*. Even the SIs, which seem to be published in daunting numbers, occupy only a few stacks in the law library. Law reports, on the other hand, represent a quantity of material of a different order of magnitude – only the largest law libraries contain anything approaching the complete corpus of published law reports. This fact puts effective legal research skills at a premium. The problem is compounded by the English common law doctrine that the force of a legal decision does not depend on it being reported. Hence this chapter is headed 'Case law', not simply 'Law reports', and a section below (paras **5.20–5.36**) is devoted to the problems of using unreported cases.

The doctrine of precedent

5.2 Case law acts as a source of law through the mechanism of the doctrine of precedent. This topic is catered for at length both in introductory works on the English legal system and as a matter of scholarly debate in academic books and journals, and a potted account will not be attempted here. But it does have two practical implications for legal research. The first is the importance of noting which court made a decision. This is not simply a matter of being familiar with the hierarchy of the courts and realising that a decision of the House of Lords is worth rather more than one from a county court. It is also important in assessing the chances of a particular court not following one of its own decisions, because the rules on the application of the doctrine of precedent on this point vary from court to court. The House of Lords *Practice Statement* [1966] 1 WLR 1234 and the Court of Appeal (Civil Division) guidelines in *Young v Bristol Aeroplane Co* [1944] KB 718 are only the most obvious examples. In the Divisional Court, for instance, there may be different practices depending on whether it is exercising its appellate jurisdiction or its supervisory jurisdiction. The problem also arises when using older cases decided by courts that no longer exist – in particular, the various different ways that appellate jurisdiction was exercised before the creation of the Court of Appeal in 1875 may need to be disentangled. Guidance on these matters will be found in *Halsbury's Laws* (under the title Judgments and Orders, vol 26, original 4th edn, paras 573ff, which at the time of writing is temporarily marooned in the cumulative supplement, the other material in vol 26 having been reissued). It should be added that, apart from the court, it is worth noting the judge, especially when faced with apparently conflicting decisions at the same level. The decisions of some judges, both from the past and sitting now, carry more weight than those of others, though assessing this factor can only be a matter of experience.

5.3 The second implication is the importance of obtaining the fullest report, where there is a choice. It is not always apparent what a case does decide – to use the jargon, what the *ratio decidendi* is – especially where there is more than one judgment. A notorious illustration of the sport 'Hunt the *ratio*' was provided by the five judgments of the House of Lords in *Chaplin v Boys* [1971] AC 356 (a reading of the headnote is sufficient to appreciate the problem). Reports in the newspapers or journals often cannot include all of the reasoning or all the judgments, and older reports vary greatly in their length. Even where it is clear what a case decides, there may be incidental arguments and reasoning that are of persuasive value. Using case law is not a matter of arithmetic, simply totting up the binding precedents on either side, but a fluid process of analysis and persuasion. Reliance on a short report may deprive you of valuable ammunition.

Which cases are reported?

5.4 It is worth looking briefly at how it is decided to report a case. The decision is in the hands of the editor of the series of law reports, not in the hands of the judge, though the judge, or indeed counsel, can suggest that a case is worth reporting. Carol Ellis QC, the former editor of *The Law Reports*, has described their policy:

> To merit reporting, a case must either introduce a new principle or new rule of law, materially modify an existing principle of law or settle a doubtful question of law. Also included are questions of interpretation of statutes and important cases illustrating new applications of accepted principles. Thus, a case which depends on its own particular facts is not reportable ((1975) 6 *Law Librarian* 5).

Because by their nature they more often meet the above criteria, and because of the weight accorded them by the doctrine of precedent, the decisions of the House of Lords and Court of Appeal feature most in the law reports as a percentage of cases heard. Virtually all of the 80 or so cases that the House of Lords hears each year are reported, while only a small proportion of the thousands of first instance cases in the High Court are reported. However, it should be realised that, apart from *The Law Reports*, most law reporting is in the hands of competing commercial publishers, and so the rigorous and apparently objective policy outlined above is not the end of the story. Economic limitations can determine whether a case, particularly one of only specialist interest, sees the light of day. Conversely, some series may include cases which in truth add nothing new, but which are included to give the impression of better coverage than their rivals. New series of law reports continue to start up, while others cease publication.

Citation of authorities in court

5.5 Although the doctrine of precedent entails the necessary proposition that any previous decision may be cited before the courts, there are now important practical limitations placed on advocates in using authorities in court. For a considerable time the courts have expressed concern at the overcitation of cases, which adds to the length and expense of litigation. Hitherto they have sought to tackle the perceived problem by issuing practice directions on the use of *unreported* cases, taking the view that such cases by their nature are unlikely to contain significant propositions of law not found in the reported cases. With the much wider circulation of unreported cases (see para s **5.22–5.29**), coupled with the proliferation of law reports series, it has at last been recognised that if there is indeed a problem it does not stem from whether the case is reported or not. On 9 April 2001 the Lord Chief Justice issued the *Practice Direction (Citation of Authorities)* [2001] 1 WLR 1001, which applies to all courts, except the criminal courts (which includes the Court of Appeal (Criminal Division)), and except the House of Lords which has its own practice directions (see para **5.35**). It is couched in terms of 'authorities', so applies to any case being cited whether or not it is reported. First it lists categories of judgment that generally may not be cited at all:

– Applications attended by only one party
– Applications for permission to appeal
– Decisions on applications that only decide that the application is arguable
– County Court cases except (a) personal injury quantum of damages (b) in the County Court itself if no higher authority is available.

Quantum cases are excluded from the ban because they are not precedents as such (see paras **5.129–5.130**), and their citation is necessary and routine. The cases that are generally to be banned would in fact have been cited relatively seldom – even the most desperate advocate would generally recognise their inherent weakness as authorities. But the ban is not total. Recourse to such a decision may be made, but only if it clearly states a new principle or extends the law. Although the occasions when that possibility arises will continue to be rare, there is the inherent difficulty of judging whether or not a case does meet the criterion. For cases decided before the Practice Direction was made, it will usually be a question of the advocate convincingly deducing from the judgment that the criterion is met. But for judgments given after the date of the Practice Direction to be cited, there will now be a higher hurdle still. That the case does stand for a new principle or extend the law may not be merely deduced – there must be an express statement to that effect. In other words, the judge will be to all intents and purposes certifying whether or not his judgment will be citable. Secondly, if any case, not just those in the above categories, includes an indication that the court was *not* extending or adding to existing law – that the court regarded itself as merely applying decided law to the particular facts – then its citation has to be expressly justified by the advocate. In any event, thirdly, the advocate in the skeleton argument or notice has to briefly state for each and every authority the proposition of law demonstrated by it. Moreover, the advocate is rationed to one authority for any particular proposition of law. A reason must be given for citing more than one authority on any point. Lists of authorities prepared for the court must carry the advocate's certification that these requirements have been met. The provisions above apply to citing English cases, European Court of Justice (ECJ) cases and European human rights cases. The Practice Direction goes on to make provision for citing cases from other jurisdictions (see para **8.2**).

The range of law reports

Modern series

General series

5.6 *The Law Reports*, already mentioned above, head the list. Although not a commercial publication, neither are they a government one (though the Stationery Office do publish one or two law reports, for example, *Reports of Tax Cases* and

Immigration Appeals). They are published by an independent body, the Incorporated Council of Law Reporting, which has charitable status (a fact that was itself the subject of a law report), and they are the nearest we have in England to 'official' law reports. They started in 1865, with funds from the Inns and the Law Society, at a time when law reporting had become an unmanageable free-for-all, a situation to which some might think we have come full circle. Their title, with its definite article, may falsely imply that there are no other law reports (and for that reason can cause confusion in speech), but correctly reflects their pre-eminence. They are the most authoritative reports because the judge is given an opportunity to check the text before publication. They are also the only reports to include a summary of the argument of counsel, which, though not a source of law as such, is a useful adjunct. For these reasons, and because of their consequent general availability, they should be cited in preference to other reports where there is a choice (certainly in court – *Practice Direction (Supreme Court: Judgments)* [1998] 1 WLR 825, reiterating earlier practice directions; if the case has not been reported in *The Law Reports*, a report either in the *Weekly Law Reports* or in the *All England Law Reports* should be cited, but if not in those either there are no further series identified by name as preferable in the practice direction, or merely any 'authoritative' series).

5.7 The organisation of *The Law Reports* follows the structure of the courts, and the different series within it mirror the rationalisation and amalgamations that have taken place since 1865, so today there is a series for each division of the High Court: Queen's Bench, Chancery and Family. Decisions of the House of Lords and Privy Council appear in the *Appeal Cases.* Decisions of the Court of Appeal, however, do not have a series of their own but appear in the series for the division in which the case originated. If the case is appealed to the House of Lords, publication of the report of the case in the Court of Appeal is sometimes delayed so that it can appear instead in the *Appeal Cases* alongside the judgment of the House of Lords. The table (figure 5.1) indicates the precursors of the modern series and how they evolved. It also indicates the modes of citation, which are subtly, but crucially, different for each series (citation in general is dealt with in more detail at paras **5.57–5.66**). Note that the loose parts of the *Chancery* and *Family* reports are issued together, and will only go into their separate series on the shelf on being bound. The full text of *The Law Reports* from their start in 1865 are available on the Justis CD-ROM and Internet services from Context under the name the electronic Law Reports, which was a joint venture with the Incorporated Council of Law Reporting. They are also available on Westlaw UK and from 1945 on Lexis. They have also been recently added as a separate module on Butterworths LEXIS Direct.

5.8 The Incorporated Council also publishes the *Weekly Law Reports* (WLR). The weekly parts form three volumes each year. The contents of vols 2 and 3 provide advance publication, for the sake of currency, of judgments that are destined to appear in *The Law Reports* proper. Volume 1 contains reports deemed to be of less importance and which are not subsequently included in *The Law Reports.* This arrangement means that each weekly part is in two halves, with separate pagination, the first half containing vol 1 cases, and the second half containing, depending on the time of year, either vol 2 or vol 3 cases. They are also available electronically as a Justis product, and are on Lexis, but not currently Westlaw UK.

5.9 The *All England Law Reports*, published by Butterworths, is the other major general series and like the *Weekly Law Reports*, with which it competes, it is published in weekly parts forming four (previously three) bound volumes a year. The overlap

Figure 5.1

Law Reports   39

TABLE OF THE LAW REPORTS

The mode of citation is given in brackets. In the first, second and third columns, dots (. . .) are put where the number of the volume would appear in the citation. In the fourth column square brackets([ ]) are put where the year would appear in the citation.

	1866–1875	1875–1880	1881–1890	1891–present
House of Lords. English and Irish Appeals (L.R. ... H.L.)				
House of Lords. Scotch and Divorce Appeals (L.R. ... H.L.Sc. or L.R. ... H.L.Sc. and Div.)	Appeal Cases (...App.Cas.)	Appeal Cases (...App.Cas.)	Appeal Cases (...App.Cas.)	Appeal Cases ([ ]) A.C.)
Privy Council Appeals (L.R. ... P.C.)				
Chancery Appeal Cases (L.R. ... Ch. or Ch. App.) Equity Cases (L.R. ... Eq.)	Chancery Division (...Ch.D.)	Chancery Division (...Ch.D.)	Chancery Division ([ ]) Ch.)	
Crown Cases Reserved (L.R. ... C.C., or, ... C.C.R.)	Queen's Bench Division (...Q.B.D.)			
Queen's Bench Cases* (L.R. ... Q.B.)		Queen's Bench Division (...Q.B.D.)	Queen's (or King's) Bench Division ([ ] Q.B. or K.B.)†	
Common Pleas Cases (L.R. ... C.P.)	Common Pleas Division (...C.P.D.)			
Exchequer Cases‡ (L.R. ... Ex.)	Exchequer Division (...Ex.D.)			
Admiralty and Ecclesiastical Cases (L.R. ... A. & E.) Probate and Divorce Cases (L.R. ... P. & D.)	Probate Division (...P.D.)	Probate Division (...P.D.)	Probate Division ([ ] P.) Since 1972 Family Division ([ ]Fam.)	

  * Note that there is also a series called Queen's Bench Reports in the old reports (113–118 E.R.).

  † After 1907 this includes cases in the Court of Criminal Appeal, later the Court of Appeal, in place of the previous Court for Crown Cases Reserved.

  ‡ Note that there is also a series called Exchequer Reports in the old reports (154–156 E.R.).

Reproduced from Glanville Williams *Learning the Law* (11th edn, Stevens, 1982).

of coverage with the *Weekly Law Reports* is considerable but by no means total. It also aims at greater timeliness in publication. They are also available on CD-ROM, as part of Butterworths All England Direct Internet service, and on Lexis.

Specialist series

5.10 Apart from these general series, there is a proliferation of subject-based reports. Some are long-standing, such as *Lloyds Reports* (which cover commercial and shipping law), *Reports of Tax Cases* and *Reports of Patent Cases*, and go back to the end of the last century. Others, such as the *Planning, Property and Compensation Reports* and the *Road Traffic Reports*, are of respectable middle age. The majority, though, have started in the last 15 years or so, and there are few areas not covered – *Community Care Law Reports*, *Immigration and Nationality Law Reports*, *Information Technology Law Reports*, *Professional Negligence and Liability Law Reports* and *Technology and Construction Law Reports* are just some that have started in the last three or four years, and at least three series have been launched to cover human rights cases. Not all, though, are destined for longevity. These reports often fill a need and may contain cases not reported elsewhere, but there is considerable overlap and duplication both with other rival specialist series and with general series. For legal research this can be both a boon and a bore. The more places in which a case can be found the better the chances of having available at least one report of it. On the other hand, if you wish to be thorough, you may need to check that you have the best and fullest report.

5.11 Many series are available on CD-ROM. Those available through the Justis services on CD-ROM, apart from the *Law Reports* and WLR, are *Lloyd's Law Reports*, *Criminal Appeal Reports*, *The Times Law Reports*, *Industrial Cases Reports*, and *Family Law Reports*. Some, but not all, are on the Justis web version. Several other series are available on CD-ROM, including *British Company Cases*, *British Tax Cases*, *Commercial Law Cases* and *Industrial Relations Law Reports*. The *Estates Gazette Law Reports* were also available on CD-ROM but in future will only be available on the EG Interactive website, a likely trend. The publishers Jordans are also putting some of their series on the web, sometimes initially free of charge as a 'taster'. Those series published by Sweet & Maxwell are generally available on Westlaw UK, and those published by Butterworths on the various Butterworths LEXIS Direct services. Nearly all series of law reports since 1945 are on Lexis itself (but see para **5.77**).

Journals

5.12 Many of the legal periodicals carry law reports. The general journals, such as the *New Law Journal*, the Law Society's *Gazette* and the *Solicitors' Journal* carry short reports, many of which will subsequently be reported more fully. The *New Law Journal* was formed in 1967 from the merger of two much older titles, the *Law Journal* and the *Law Times*, which go back to the nineteenth century. Their law report content can be a source of understandable confusion, because they both have separate law report and journal components, with the latter containing notes of cases as well as articles; furthermore, both have had old and new series. The original series of *Law Journal Reports*, which ran from 1822–31, is referred to as the old series and is cited as LJOS. The new series has two volumes for each year, one for common law and one for Chancery, and within each volume cases from the various courts are separately paginated, so are cited as LJKB or LJCh and so on. These volumes of reports are entirely separate from the journal, which does not start in its modern guise until

1865. The short reports of cases in it are cited as LJo. The *Law Times* (not to be confused with the *Times Law Reports*), which started in 1843, originally contained in the same volumes proper law reports and shorter notes of cases among the articles. In 1859 the law reports were hived off as a separate series, though notes of cases continued in the journal part. The new series of law reports is cited simply as LT. The law reports proper before 1859, which are found in a separate part of the volumes, are referred to as the old series and are cited as LTOS. Notes of cases in the journal are cited as LT Jo. The *Justice of the Peace*, which is still current, has a similar arrangement. Full reports appear as the *Justice of the Peace Reports*, cited as JP, while the periodical, the *Justice of the Peace*, carries briefer notes of cases, cited as JPN (though there is not always consistency – some sources may use JP for the journal and JPR for the reports).

5.13 The specialist journals also frequently carry reports, which can be very useful. Some, like those in the *Estates Gazette* on property matters and in the *Construction Law Journal*, are full-length reports, and are often not reported elsewhere. Others are briefer notes. The reports in the *Criminal Law Review* and in *Family Law* deserve special mention, though they are brief, because of the expert commentary given on each case. *Legal Action* is a source of unreported cases at county court level in housing and social welfare law. As mentioned in chapter 2, some journals are available in full text in electronic format, including, free of charge, the Law Society's *Gazette*.

Newspapers

5.14 The most up-to-date sources for law reports are the newspapers. *The Times* has been providing law reports since 1884 and for many years (except for a very brief excursion by the *Guardian* in the 1960s) had a monopoly. Indeed, it still leads the field and has the advantage that reporters from the Incorporated Council supply its reports. Their monopoly was first dented by the *Financial Times*, which started to carry reports, concentrating on commercial matters, in 1981, but stopped in 1992. Then, when the *Independent* was launched in 1986, it too carried reports, and continues to do so. This prompted the *Guardian* and the *Daily Telegraph* to follow suit. The *Daily Telegraph* fell by the wayside in 1991, but since October 2000 they have once again entered the fray, this time with a tie-in with the on-line service, Westlaw UK. Very brief summaries are given, but the full text from Westlaw may be viewed, for one week only, on the *Telegraph* website. The *Independent* also carries once a week a page of very brief 'Case summaries' prepared by the reporters of the *All England Law Reports*. There is a good deal of overlap between the newspaper reports, but the overlap does not necessarily occur on the same day. Many of the cases will get reported more fully, but many do not. Until 1950 this was not a problem as the reports in *The Times* were reissued in a proper series of numbered bound volumes, *The Times Law Reports*. We had to wait until 1990 for a Scottish publisher to reintroduce this sensible practice on a proper footing. They are issued in monthly parts and annual bound volumes, fully indexed, by A. & T. Clark. The *Financial Times*, in conjunction with the publishers Kluwer, attempted an even more ambitious project, which was not simply to reprint the reports as they had originally appeared in the paper, but to publish subsequently the full text of all the judgments. Unfortunately, this proved to be uneconomic and only ran from 1986 to 1988, with two retrospective volumes for 1982. Apart from the above, it is therefore necessary to use the collections of cuttings kept by most law libraries in various shapes and forms. If such a cuttings file is not available, reference will need to be made to the papers themselves. Large libraries may keep back files, often on microfilm or on

CD-ROM. For recent cases, you can use the newspapers' own websites, though they vary as to how searchable they are – for example, though *The Times* is fully searchable from October 2000, to find a law report before that date you would need the exact date of the issue. The full text of the newspapers is also available on some on-line services, such as Nexis, the other part of Lexis-Nexis, to give Lexis its trademarked name. The newspapers themselves are also occasionally needed for a case reported as a news item rather than as a law report proper. A pre-1950 reference to *The Times* cited by day of publication rather than a volume number in *The Times Law Reports* points to such a case.

Older reports

Nominates

5.15 Before the Incorporated Council of Law Reporting was founded in 1865, the pattern was for reports to be issued by commercial publishers under the name of a particular law reporter, who usually covered a particular court. Because these reports are known by the reporter's name, they are referred to as nominate reports. This form of reporting has its origins as far back as the sixteenth century, when the reports usually circulated in manuscript. The first reports were mostly printed retrospectively; it is only with Durnford and East's *Term Reports* at the end of the eighteenth century that contemporaneous reports published in serial parts, as we now know it, first began. Few libraries hold complete sets of all the various nominate reports that were published from 1571 until 1865. Instead, most libraries will have the *English Reports* which reprinted most of the nominate reports. The reports are collected together by court. The 178 volumes were originally published in 1900–32, but there has been a facsimile reprint since. As this is the form in which they are most commonly used, the pre-1865 nominate reports are often, if loosely, referred to as 'The English reports'. Another venture to make available the materials in the nominate reports in manageable form was the *Revised Reports*, published in 149 volumes from 1891–1917. They differ in three important respects from the *English Reports*. First, they only cover cases from 1785. Secondly, the arrangement is strictly chronological and only one report of a particular case appears. Thirdly, the reports are heavily edited to produce the 'best' report. The *English Reports*, in contrast, cover the full time-span (and even include some cases from the Year Books, on which see paras **5.17–5.19**), reprint the cases as they appeared and include collateral series covering the same cases. The consequence is that the *Revised Reports* are little used and are not acceptable as a formal citation. However, they do include cases from one or two series not in the *English Reports* and if the original nominates for those series are not available they may be better than nothing.

5.16 The *English Reports* have recently been issued in their entirety on CD-ROM. This is potentially an invaluable resource, though perhaps more for the legal historian than the practitioner. The text was reproduced by electronic scanning rather than re-keying, and there have been some quibbles about the quality of the data. (There were also quibbles about the data in the *English Reports* themselves, since they were reset from the original nominates, but the standard of compositors and proofreaders was in those days extremely high.) Even if the data has been faithfully reproduced, there are the problems when entering search terms if non-standard spelling or antique terminology has been used. Representing a substantial investment, and library budgets being what they are, the CD-ROM version may not be widely available.

Year Books

5.17 Pre-dating the nominate reports are the Year Books, so called because they are anonymous compilations arranged chronologically by regnal year and law term. Their function originally appears not to have been to record precedents as such, but to act as educational tools through which developments in the law were discussed. They date from early medieval times and the conventional date for their finish is 1535, though the onset of named law reports did not mark a distinct break in the nature of their content. They were among the earliest law books to be printed, but the standard edition, though arguably the least reliable, is the so-called Maynard edition, published 1678–80, which is available in a modern facsimile reprint. The Maynard edition and the early printed editions on which it is based did not cover by any means all the extant material. Modern scholarly editions by the Selden Society, the Ames Foundation, and in the Rolls series (*Rerum Britannicarum Medii Aevii Scriptores, or, Chronicles and Memorials of Great Britain and Ireland during the Middle Ages*) have put some of the earlier years into print, but some still remain in manuscript only. Modern scholarly editions will often also include the text or translations of the record of the case, as it appears in the court records preserved in the Public Record Office. These may fill in details lacking in the report in the Year Books, which may omit, surprisingly to modern eyes, significant aspects of a case, such as the names of the parties or even the outcome.

5.18 They are mainly of interest to legal historians, but from time to time cases from them are cited in the courts. For example, in *Midland Bank Trust Co Ltd v Green (No 3)* [1982] Ch 529 five Year Book cases were adduced on the point of whether the tort of conspiracy could apply to husband and wife. Some Year Book cases are referred to in *The Digest* (see para **5.69**) and as mentioned some are reprinted in the *English Reports*. Their use by the practitioner usually arises where the authority for a proposition has been diligently traced back to one of the authoritative treatises such as Coke's *Institutes* or Hale's *Pleas of the Crown*. Since the courts are usually content to accept such sources, in average circumstances the lawyer is more than happy to concede that the seventeenth century is far enough back to go. However, the curious, desperate or uncommonly industrious lawyer sometimes wants to know what Coke's or Hale's own sources were, and they will often be Year Book cases either cited directly, or as they appeared in abridgments such as Fitzherbert. If the Maynard edition is then referred to (because of the facsimile reprint it is in fact quite widely available in major law libraries) it will be found to be in Law French. However, there are two collections of translations of Year Book cases, designed for use by the student of legal history, which may help – since resort to Year Book authority tends to be confined to 'leading cases', these two books yield quite a good strike rate in practice. They are C H S Fifoot *History and Sources of the Common Law: Tort and Contract* ((1949) Stevens) and J H Baker and S F C Milsom *Sources of English Legal History: Private Law to 1750* ((1986) Butterworths). If the case is not translated, and for those who rate their historio-linguistic skills, assistance may be derived from J H Baker *Manual of Law French* ((2nd edn, 1990) Scolar Press).

5.19 Citation of law reports in general is dealt with below (paras **5.57–5.66**), but the citation of Year Book cases is best dealt with here. The parties to a case are sometimes identified and so it can be given a conventional case name, and some well-known cases acquired popular names through their subject matter, for example, *The Humber Ferry Case* or *The Miller's Case*. But many are anonymous. The early printed editions, as with many early printed books, did not have page numbers, but folio numbers – the front of each leaf was numbered but not the reverse, so that one folio referred to two pages. The printers also issued individual regnal years separately, which might later be bound up together. Each regnal year was separately foliated. The printers' foliation became standardised, so that a case can be identified simply from the regnal year and the folio number, for example, 5 Hen VII, fo 15. The Maynard edition, which was in a larger format than the early editions, could fit one folio onto a single page. So the page numbers in Maynard correspond to folio numbers in standard citations. An [A] and a [B] in the margin indicate where the page breaks occurred in the original editions. Each regnal year is divided into the four legal terms, Michaelmas, Hilary, Easter (Pascha in Latin in the originals and in citations) and Trinity. The cases in each term are separately numbered, with a plea or *placitum* number (pl), so that a citation with the plea number rather than the folio number will equally identify a case uniquely as long as its term as well as its year is given. However, it is generally helpful if all elements are provided. Thus a full citation would read *The Farrier's Case* (1372) YB Trin 46 Edw III, fo 19, pl 19. The only exception to the foregoing is references to the *Liber Assisarum*, an additional volume in the canon of printed Year Books containing cases on assize or circuit during the reign of Edward III (1327–77). These are not divided into terms and the plea numbers run through the whole regnal year. They are cited just by year of Edward III's reign and plea number thus: *Bukton v Tounesende (The Humber Ferry Case)* (1348) 22 Lib Ass, pl 41.

Unreported cases

5.20 Except in magistrates' courts, a record either on tape or in shorthand is made of proceedings in most cases. Where a judgment is given ex tempore, as often happens in cases at first instance, this will be the only record of the judgment. The recording of proceedings and preparation of transcripts is contracted out by the Court Service to private firms or handled by the Mechanical Recording Department in the Royal Courts of Justice, depending on the court. Even where judgments are handed down, and not given ex tempore, it is the shorthand writers who hold the 'official' transcript. The availability of transcripts is described below, but why might an unreported case be needed?

Why needed?

5.21 Usually, of course, transcripts are only of interest to the parties themselves, for example, if an appeal is being contemplated. Unreported cases have two main kinds of use for others. The first is where a case is needed as an authority but is not available in the law reports, either because it has simply been passed over – opinions on what is reportable can vary, and editors are not infallible – or because of a time-lag in reporting. The other type of application is where cases are sought not as authorities, but as illustrations of trends in judicial decision-making, especially in those areas where judges have wide discretion, such as quantum of damages, financial provision and other dispositions in family cases, and sentencing. Finding recent examples of what the courts have decided can give reassurance to advisers, even though the decisions are in no way binding precedents. Other applications include researching an unusual fact situation to see if any other cases like it have been heard, examining the track record of particular judges, barristers or solicitors, and checking what litigation a particular firm or individual has previously been involved in.

Availability

5.22 The development of Internet technology and the fact that, with some growing exceptions discussed below, judgments are not in the public domain have led to a proliferation of commercial services providing transcript coverage. Lawyers' natural lurking worry that they may have missed an important recent case makes for a ready market. As well as commercial electronic services and the free websites, there are permanent reference copies for limited classes of transcripts; otherwise there are the shorthand writers themselves. For reasons discussed below, however, there are unreported cases, referred to in other cases or textbooks, that cannot be obtained from any of these sources and are simply not available any more.

FREE SERVICES ON THE INTERNET

5.23 The major development in this area is the establishment of the British and Irish Legal Information Institute (BAILII), which is modelled on the Australian AustLII site. AustLII is neither a government nor a commercial site, but aims to provide an independent platform for mounting in a uniform format the full text of cases and legislation, accessible free of charge. Taking the view that the primary sources of law ought to be in the public domain, the judiciary and government have co-operated, with the consequence that the Australians are in the enviable position of having the full text of all judgments of the higher courts, state and Commonwealth, freely available. The BAILII site, which is still under development, has started with the more modest aim of providing a one-stop source for such case law as is currently available from the various separate free sites in the UK and Ireland. Having to go to only one site is not the only advantage; the data is automatically processed to provide hypertext links and other enhancements can be provided that are not necessarily available on the separate sites. The longer-term aim is to be able to take, as in Australia, a direct feed of all judgments directly from the courts, at any rate those judgments that are handed down, rather than given ex tempore (the Australians have the advantage that all judgments are written). At the time of writing an initial block of data has been taken as a pilot, but the only regular updates seem to have been for House of Lords cases. So for recent cases the individual sites may have to be used for the time being – but 'watch this space'. As well as the decisions of the courts from the sites mentioned below, BAILII covers cases from the Employment Appeal Tribunal and some from the Social Security Commissioners, but not so far from the other tribunals mentioned, though they may well be added. Its coverage of Scottish, Northern Irish and Irish cases is discussed in chapter 8.

5.24 The first cases to be put on the Internet were those from the House of Lords, which are available from November 1996 on the Parliament website. The Privy Council followed suit in 1999. The Court Service also started putting cases from the High Court and Court of Appeal on their website – the earliest dates from February 1996. At first there was only a handful of cases, more recently it has become a reasonably steady trickle – the database now contains about 750 cases. Whether a case is put on the site is at the instigation of the judge. There are no criteria or guidelines at all for what is and is not posted on the site – you just have to take potluck. In contrast, the scope of the free archive from Smith Bernal is clear. Smith Bernal have been the official shorthand writers for the Court of Appeal (Civil and Criminal Divisions) and what used to be called the Crown Office List, but which is now called the Administrative Court (ie judicial review, case stated, etc before the Divisional Court of the Queen's Bench Division), since April 1996. They operate their own fully searchable commercial service, Casetrack (see para **5.29**), but offer, free of charge, an archive of their transcripts from April 1996, currently to the end of 1999. The free archive, called Casebase, is searchable by name, date, case number and court, but not otherwise, so the service is mainly of use for laying your hands on the transcript of a case known to exist. Nor will it help with other High Court decisions that have recently been added to the commercial service. The Employment Appeal Tribunal has cases from 1999 on its website. Decisions of the Social Security Commissioners are currently available, rather confusingly on three sites, with different coverage (for an explanation of the different types of decision see paras **5.101–5.105**). The Commissioners own site is that currently maintained on a semi-official basis by Commissioner Howells. It is the site reached from Delia Venables' Legal Resources portal either from the topic list or the free case law list, and also from Sarah Carter's Lawlinks from the topics list (but not the case law list). This is the main resource for unreported decisions, a selection of which is available from 1995. It also has starred decisions from 1995, but for those there is fuller coverage on the Court Service site (under Tribunals), which has all starred decisions from 1990. Finally there is the Department for Work and Pensions site (the Department of Social Security as was), which under 'Information for professionals and advisers' has all the reported decisions from 1991. The Commissioners' site also has links to the Northern Ireland Department of Social Development site, which has Northern Ireland Commissioners' decisions. This proliferation of sites is the mischief that BAILII aims to cure, but currently it only has a small selection of unreported and starred decisions available. Recent decisions from the Special Commissioners of Income Tax, from VAT and Duties Tribunals, and from the Lands Tribunal are also available (there are links from the 'Tribunals' part of the Court Service site). Doubtless others will follow in due course. Butterworths' free service, Law Direct, gives access to the digests of unreported cases that appear on its All England Direct pay-for service (see below), but not the full text of the transcripts themselves (though transcripts can be ordered from Smith Bernal at a small discount if initially accessed from the Law Direct site).

COMMERCIAL SERVICES

5.25 Lexis, which has been available in this country since 1979, pioneered the provision of unreported cases, and until recently had a monopoly. Its transcript coverage starts in 1980 (its coverage of reported cases goes back to 1945, see para 5.77). It is comprehensive for the House of Lords, Privy Council, Court of Appeal (Civil Division) and certain defined categories of High Court case (for example, Crown Office list cases and Chancery Division revenue cases). Other first instance High Court cases were only included if they had already been noted in one of the journals that are scanned. But the coverage of High Court cases may be wider more recently. Unlike law reports, transcripts have no headnote or apparatus, so your search strategy may be different. You can if you wish confine a search to unreported cases only, or alternatively exclude them. If an unreported case is subsequently reported, the report is substituted for the transcript (unless the report is one of the few series that Lexis does not cover, for example, *British Company Cases*, in which case the citation is added but the text remains that of the transcript).

5.26 Somewhat confusingly Lexis is now branded as part of the Butterworths LEXIS Direct services. It continues to be a separately available database, but there is some overlap with the other main case service on Butterworths LEXIS Direct, namely All England Direct. This service covers cases back to 1995 and has three elements. The first is called the All England *Reporter* (as opposed to *Reports*) and provides digests updated daily of recent cases. These have the appearance of a law report with catchwords at the top, and are cited as, for example, [2001] All ER (D) 142, where the number is a case number rather than a page number. These digests have been freshly prepared from 1999. Earlier digests are taken from those prepared for *Halsbury's Law Monthly Reviews* and *Annual Abridgment*. As soon as the approved transcript is available, that is added with a link from the digest and also with the catchwords from the digest included. If the case is subsequently reported in the *All England Law Reports* the report is added too. Secondly, there are transcripts on the same basis as on Lexis (though only back to 1995). Not all these will have necessarily been provided with a digest. Lastly, there is a complete archive of the *All England Law Reports* back to 1936. As presently organised, on the search screen (accessed from 'Search Archive' option) scroll down to the databases option to pick transcripts – the default is otherwise just the All England Reporter, which, as explained, will not necessarily lead you to all the transcripts there are. If you have the name of a case and want to know if it is there, use the rather inaccurately labelled 'Noter-up' option. This is currently described as the way to find any case on the system by name, but in fact – unless this is a temporary fault – seems only to retrieve cases from the All England Reporter, not from the other two parts of the service.

5.27 Lawtel started life being a digesting service, for both reported and unreported cases. Quite full summaries were provided, updated daily. Where the case was not reported there was the option to order a hard copy of the full text from their Transcripts Express Service for a charge. They are now adding the full text of the transcripts to the main service with retrospective coverage, as far the transcripts are available, back to 1993 (their summaries of reported cases goes back to 1980). Lawtel now claim to include all handed down judgments of the High Court and above. Ex tempore judgments and judgments from other courts and tribunals are covered only selectively, so cases may be found on Lawtel that are not on All England Direct, and vice versa.

5.28 The newest entrant into the field is Westlaw UK from Sweet & Maxwell. This has transcripts of cases from 2000, as well as offering other case law services (see para **5.79**). In 2001 Sweet & Maxwell took over yet another transcript alerting service, which had been going for some time, New Law Online, latterly CCH-New Law Online. How that will fit in with Westlaw UK remains to be seen, but the result may be an increase in the retrospective coverage of transcripts. One would expect a good deal of overlap with All England Direct and Lawtel, particularly in the case of Court of Appeal transcripts, but as always it may well have first instance cases not on the other services.

5.29 Last but not least is Smith Bernal's Casetrack. As well as providing the full searchable database of its own transcripts from 1996, as described above, it includes most other High Court decisions from 1998. Unlike the other services, there is not a digesting or summarising element – it just provides the unadorned full text – but it may well be the most comprehensive of the services.

PERMANENT REFERENCE COPIES

5.30 Copies of unreported judgments are available for reference for only a limited number of courts. These are the House of Lords, Privy Council, Court of Appeal (Civil Division) from 1950, Court of Appeal (Criminal Division) from 1989, the Employment Appeal Tribunal, the Immigration Appeal Tribunal, the Technology and Construction Court (formerly the Official Referees) from 1991 (reserved judgments only), the Patents Court (part of the Chancery Division) from 1970 and the ecclesiastical courts from 1891. The Court of Appeal (Civil Division) transcripts from 1950–80 have also been published on microfiche by HMSO.

5.31 As virtually all House of Lords cases are now reported, access to the original judgments is usually only needed for extremely recent cases not yet reported or only reported in the newspapers (where they usually appear within a day or two), or for old cases that for some reason were not reported. The former are on the Internet as described. The main source for old materials arises from the fact that each side in an appeal to the House of Lords has to prepare in advance a written summary of their arguments, called the 'printed case'. These, together with other documents such as transcripts of the case in the courts below and documentary evidence, are produced in multiple copies for the use of the Law Lords, officials and the parties during the hearing. By a long-standing arrangement, each year surplus copies of these documents, together with the judgments, are deposited in a few libraries (such as Lincoln's Inn Library) which may have sets going back for a considerable period. The Privy Council operates a similar system. Otherwise, copies may be consulted by arrangement at the House of Lords Record Office and the Privy Council.

5.32 Cases from the Consistory courts, except for a handful in the main law reports series, were until the *Ecclesiastical Law Journal* started in 1987, generally unreported. Although there is now the excellent coverage in that journal, it is only in summary form. However, an archive of transcripts of such cases is kept at Middle Temple Library. The reasonably systematic collection of such cases started in about 1981, with one or two volumes per year thereafter, but there are three volumes covering the period 1891–1980: see Janet Edgell 'The Ecclesiastical Law Centre at Middle Temple Library' (2000) 5(27) *Ecclesiastical Law Journal* 455–459.

5.33 Except for the patent cases, the remainder of the transcripts mentioned at para **5.30** are kept at the Supreme Court Library (in the Queen Elizabeth Building in the Royal Courts of Justice). It is somewhat surprising that this practice is relatively recent. The retention of the Court of Appeal (Civil Division) transcripts was on the initiative of Lord Evershed, then Master of the Rolls, who had found himself in the unsatisfactory position of being bound by a decision of the Court of Appeal 15 years earlier which was unreported and for which only slender details could be unearthed – *Gibson v South American Stores* [1950] Ch 177. The usefulness of the material in the Supreme Court Library is limited in so far as it can only be consulted in person and there are no subject indexes. The HMSO microfiche edition has improved the availability of the Court of Appeal (Civil Division) transcripts, but that too has no subject index. However, from 1973 to 1989 summaries of the transcripts appeared in the *Current Law Yearbooks* (until 1986 as a separate section at the front, thereafter intermingled with the main entries). Some help in finding unreported judgments of the Court of Appeal (Criminal Division) by subject matter is the *Criminal Appeal Office Index*. This summarises selected cases on law, procedure and sentence, some of which may subsequently be reported but some of which may not. It is published three times a year as a supplement to *Archbold*. It cumulates through the year, the last issue of the year being permanent. The patent cases are kept in the Science, Business and Technology Collections at the British Library, and only cases more than six years old may be photocopied.

5.34 Having a transcript made specially is expensive, and even where one is already made, charges for copies can be high, though Smith Bernal, one of the main firms, now charge the relatively modest sum of £38 per case through their on-line Transcripts Direct service. To order a transcript, full details of the case will need to be known. Different firms cover different courts. Sittings of the High Court out of London will be covered by local firms, not those that cover the relevant Division sitting in the Royal Courts of Justice. The Supreme Court Library produced a booklet on where to obtain transcripts. The current edition is rather out of date, so you may need to seek their advice directly. The main point to note is that the shorthand writers generally only keep tapes for six years. If the case is more than six years old, and not on Lexis (or in due course the other commercial services), it is generally unobtainable – a slightly extraordinary state of affairs given that it potentially contains the law of the land. The only long shot is if the solicitors or counsel involved in the case retained a copy.

Use in court

5.35 A final word on transcripts concerns their use in court. The Lord Chief Justice's practice direction of 9 April 2001 on the citation of authorities has already been noted (para **5.5**). It was the culmination of a long line of judicial pronouncements and practice directions directed at the citation of unreported cases, which started with the comments from Lord Diplock in *Roberts Petroleum Ltd v Bernard Kenny Ltd* [1983] 2 AC 192 at 200–202. As a result of that case, which came shortly after the introduction of Lexis in this country, the House of Lords made a practice direction, as far as its own proceedings were concerned, on citing unreported cases. It is currently contained in the *House of Lords Practice Directions and Standing Orders applicable to Civil Appeals* (June 2001 edn) at para 15.6 (there is an equivalent provision for criminal appeals). It now reads:

> Transcripts of unreported judgments should only be cited when they contain an authoritative statement of a relevant principle of law not to be found in a reported case or are necessary for the understanding of some other authority.

This is slightly less proscriptive than earlier versions, in which there was a positive requirement to seek leave before citing an unreported case. In any case, counsel appearing at that level are conscious of what is and is not good advocacy, and the unnecessary citing of weak authority is poor advocacy. None the less, it remains a slightly anomalous provision since, as far as the other courts go, there is now no distinction between reported and unreported cases for the purposes of citation.

5.36 The only other point to note is that in *Hamblin v Field* (The Times, 26 April 2000), Peter Gibson LJ, while having a dig at the excessive citation of authority in general, made particular reference to the use of Lawtel *summaries*. What had particularly irked his Lordship, apart from the fact that the judge at first instance had clearly been misled by relying on a Lawtel summary rather than the full transcript, was that it was not clear whether the summary had been prepared by a professional lawyer or member of the bar. Lawtel may well have been stung by this criticism because their publicity since makes a point of emphasising that their court reporters are barristers, and as described above they are integrating transcripts into the on-line service, rather than making them available only to order. But the moral is clear: cite the full transcript, not the summary, whether it comes from Lawtel or another source such as All England Direct.

EC case law

5.37 EC law has long ceased to be a specialist area and, indeed, cases from the ECJ at Luxembourg are included selectively in the various English series described above (including from time to time *The Law Reports* themselves). But the official series is the *European Court Reports* (ECR), and for this reason they should be cited in preference where there is a choice. All cases are reported (in 1989 the practice was adopted of publishing some only in summary form, but that practice seems to have been quietly dropped after only a couple of years). Most libraries will only have the English version, but they are published in all the official languages of the EC (with the same page numbering in each). The authentic text is that of the language of the case. There are rules as to which language the language of the case is to be where more than one member state is involved, but it is stated on the report. Should you need the text in a language other than English, you will need to get it off the Internet (see para **5.38**). The publication of the ECR in paper form may be subject to delay, though there has been some improvement in timeliness recently. The longstanding commercially published series is the *Common Market Law Reports* (CMLR), which is indispensable, not only for filling the time-lag before the ECR appear, but also because it includes decisions of member state national courts (not just the UK), Commission decisions in competition matters and other materials, as well the judgments of the ECJ itself. It is currently published in five volumes each year, volumes 4 and 5 being devoted to antitrust (ie competition) cases and materials. Since 1989 there has also been the series *European Community Cases* (cited as CEC) published by CCH, which like CMLR includes Commission materials as well as ECJ judgments, but not national court decisions. Its precursor was the Court Decisions part of the *Common Market Reporter* published by CCH in its original American incarnation. In 1995 the *All England Law Reports* started a sub-series, *European Cases*. This now seems to be devoted exclusively to ECJ decisions, though in the early volumes one or two English cases were included. The *European Law Reports*, which started in 1997, are not an attempt to compete with these other series in coverage of ECJ cases; rather, the purpose of the series is to cover cases dealing with issues of EC law heard in the domestic courts throughout the UK and Ireland. As well as the ECR, the court does issue typescript versions of judgments in advance, which some libraries may take – if they are taken in French as well as English, a slight time advantage sometimes accrues. A fortnightly summary of proceedings, again in typescript format, is another source of information (and is indexed on Badger). The 'operative' part of the judgment, though not the full text, is also published in the OJ C series, as are various court notices.

5.38 ECJ cases are also widely available in electronic form. They are available free of charge on the ECJ's own website in searchable form from June 1997 onwards in all the official languages. That part of the website is described as 'Recent case law from Court of Justice and Court of First Instance'. You can also access the full text of cases before June 1997, but only if you know the case number, from the 'Numerical access to case law' option. This takes you to long lists by case number, which must be scrolled through. So a simpler option is to use the Mannheim site, which also gives free access by number but lets you type in a number to search for. The full text of ECR also forms part of the Celex database, so is available in the various versions of that (see para **3.127**). Cases for which the full text is not yet available appear with an ECR reference but just 'p 0000' as a page reference. The Justis version is again excellent. The CMLR are available on Justis, but only on the CD-ROM version, not on the Internet version. Being a Sweet & Maxwell title, the CMLR are on Westlaw UK (which has the ECR too, as does Lexis). ECJ cases from 1989 are on Lawtel's EU module. Butterworths EU Direct has the All ER (EC) which are also on the All ER CD-Rom.

5.39 When using EC cases it is useful to be aware of some differences from English cases and also of some aspects of procedure before the court. Cases may be heard by a full court, with up to 15 judges, or in a 'Chamber' with no fewer than three judges. As decisions are by simple majority, there is always an uneven number of judges. The most marked difference from English cases is that there is only a single judgment and there cannot be dissenting opinions; this can make interpretation of judgments, especially from a full court in a controversial case, somewhat fraught. One of the judges who will hear the case is appointed judge-rapporteur when the case is first registered, and he oversees preliminary matters and is also responsible for drafting the judgment.

5.40 The other aspect that is particularly foreign to the English lawyer is the role of the Advocate General. There are currently eight Advocates General appointed to the court, and one will be assigned to each case. To quote from Lasok *Law and Institutions of the European Union*, their function is threefold:

> ... to propose a solution to the case before the court; to relate the proposed solution to the general pattern of existing case law; and, if possible, to outline the probable future development of the case law.

The Advocate-General's submission is in the form of an 'opinion'. It is not binding on the court, but is highly influential and where the court adopt the reasoning they may only give a relatively brief judgment. The opinions are published in the ECR – before 1985 after the judgment, from 1985 in front of the judgment. They are also issued individually in advance in typescript form in the same way as the judgments. As well as opinions and judgments, the other species of document to appear in the ECR are orders of the court. These are decisions usually concerned with procedural matters or interim measures. Another feature that becomes apparent when using ECJ reports, is that the court frequently joins cases which relate to the same issue; several case numbers will then be attached to a single ECR reference. Although it does not affect use of the material, a further aspect of procedure before the court that is alien to the English way of doing things is that almost all of the proceedings are conducted on paper; the oral hearing plays only a small part.

5.41 Although the description above has been in terms of the European Court of Justice, since 1 November 1989 there has also of course been the Court of First Instance (CFI). This was created with the intention of lessening the load on the main court. It hears three main types of case: staff cases (ie disputes with employees of the EU bodies themselves), certain cases brought by undertakings under the European Coal and Steel Community Treaty, and certain competition cases brought by private parties. It does not currently hear references for preliminary rulings from national courts, nor cases brought by member states or the EC institutions themselves. Appeals on points of law only lie to the ECJ itself. The Treaty of Nice (2001) will make significant changes to the operation of the CFI and ECJ when it is ratified. The CFI will be able to hear cases on preliminary rulings in certain areas. Provision is also made for the introduction of a third tier of 'court', in the form of 'judicial panels', which may hear certain categories of first instance case, with appeals to the CFI. Cases from the CFI are reported in all the series mentioned above that cover ECJ cases and the ECR is now officially entitled *Reports of Cases Before the Court of*

Justice and the Court of First Instance. However, from 1993 staff cases were hived off into a separate series, *Reports of European Community Staff Cases* (ECR-SC) – now only staff cases of general importance are reported in the main ECR. Unlike ECR, ECR-SC does not publish the full text of all staff cases in all the official languages. English subscribers get English summaries of the all the cases (and French subscribers would get French summaries) in the first part, but the full text in the second part is simply in the language of the case.

European human rights case law

5.42 The European Convention on Human Rights was signed in 1950 and came into force in 1953. It was the product of the Council of Europe, which had been established in 1949 (at the risk of stating the obvious, it is entirely separate from the European Union). Then it had 15 member states; it now has 41. The UK first accepted the jurisdiction of the European Court of Human Rights in Strasbourg to hear applications from individuals claiming a breach of the Convention in 1966. Until the Human Rights Act 1998 was passed, the UK was among the minority of member states whose domestic courts could not give direct effect to the Convention. The Human Rights Act came fully into force in England and Wales on 2 October 2000 (its provisions had been given effect in Scotland by the Scotland Act 1998 which came into force in 1999).

5.43 Even before the 1998 Act came into force, the case law of the European Convention on Human Rights had long assumed considerable importance for the English lawyer. This was not just because of its interest to the academic lawyer or for the specialist practitioner involved in taking a case to Strasbourg, but because even while the Convention remained unincorporated the courts had increasingly made use of it in a number of guises. Murray Hunt's book *Using Human Rights Law in the English Courts* ((1997) Hart) gives a clear picture of the state of play as it had developed immediately before the passing of the 1998 Act (and also provides a valuable analysis of the principles of human rights adjudication, whether or not incorporated into domestic law). However, s 2(1) of the 1998 Act, which provides that a court in interpreting a Convention right *'must* take into account' Strasbourg case law 'whenever made', now means that every student and practitioner has to be as familiar with it as they are with the contents of say the *Weekly Law Reports*. The different classes of Strasbourg case law to be taken into account are enumerated in s 2(1). It is thus necessary to understand Strasbourg procedure in order to know how the particular types of decision are generated, to judge their likely value to the court, and to make sense of the documentation in which they appear and the associated research tools. By coincidence, only nine days before the Human Rights Act 1998 received its Royal Assent, Protocol 11 to the Convention came into force. This instituted a complete overhaul of the procedure by abolishing the Commission and creating a unified court (it also renumbered the relevant articles of the Convention). This new procedure has thus significantly altered the classes of material emanating from Strasbourg. The new procedure that has been in place since 1 November 1998, and the species of case law that it generates, will be described first. Then the differences in the old procedure will be highlighted. The European Court of Human Rights has never followed a strict doctrine of precedent as it is applied in the common law courts. Indeed, it has often emphasised the fluid nature of the Convention, which is a 'living instrument' that must be given a 'dynamic' interpretation. None the less, a considerable body of jurisprudence has accumulated and frequent recourse to decisions made by the Commission under the old procedure will still be needed.

Procedure since 1 November 1998

5.44 There is now a single judicial body, the European Court of Human Rights, which sits permanently. The only other body involved is the Committee of Ministers of the Council of Europe, which comprises the foreign ministers of each member state (though much business is conducted through deputies). The court transmits its judgment to the Committee, whose only remaining function with regard to the Convention is now to supervise the enforcement of judgments. A judge is appointed from each member state, so that there are currently 41 judges. The judges are divided into four 'sections', which thus each have 10 (or 11) judges. An application is initially assigned to a section, and one of the judges of the section is appointed 'judge-rapporteur'. The first matter to be decided is whether the application is admissible. To be admissible the application must satisfy a number of conditions, which include the facts that the applicant is a 'victim', that domestic remedies have been exhausted, that a Convention right has been violated and that it is not 'manifestly ill-founded'. Only a very small minority of applications is found admissible. The judge-rapporteur may first refer the application to a committee of three judges. The committee is designed to weed out at an early stage obviously defective applications. If they decide unanimously that the application is inadmissible, then that is the end of the matter. Their decision is not appealable. On the other hand, the judge-rapporteur may assign the case directly to a 'Chamber' of seven judges constituted for each case from the judges of the section. A Chamber will always include a judge from the member state concerned – if necessary from another section – though he may not act as President. A Chamber will also receive the case if the committee had been of the opinion that it was admissible or were not unanimous. The Chamber then proceeds in two separate stages. First, it must decide admissibility (even if the committee had been unanimous). If it is ruled admissible the Registry of the Court engages in negotiations to obtain a 'friendly settlement'. If one is not forthcoming, the Chamber then proceeds to consider the merits. The parties will make written submissions at various stages. There will usually be an oral hearing at the second stage, and there may be one at the first. The court will then make its judgment. If it finds in favour of the applicant it will also need to consider 'just satisfaction', ie whether compensation should be payable (the court has no other remedies, and may consider the declaration of a breach of the Convention sufficient 'just satisfaction' in itself). A ruling on just satisfaction may be included in the main judgment, or the matter may be adjourned and be subject to a separate judgment. The judgment is finally transmitted to the Council of Ministers, who may pass a resolution as to execution of the judgment. At any point during the Chamber hearing, the Chamber may decide, as long as neither party objects, to 'relinquish' the case to a Grand Chamber if they consider that the case involves an important question on the interpretation on the Convention or where their decision might conflict with existing case law. The Grand Chamber, which consists of 17 judges, follows the same procedure as an ordinary Chamber. An appeal to the Grand Chamber from the final judgment of a Chamber is also available in exceptional cases. A panel of five judges (rather like the Appeal Committee of the House of Lords) filters applications for such appeals. A request, which can be refused, may also be made within a certain period after final judgment for a Chamber to interpret its judgment if the operative part is unclear to the affected party or to revise a judgment if a fact crucial to the outcome unknown at the time comes to light. As well as the committees, the Chambers and the Grand Chamber, there is also the Plenary Court, which comprises all 41 judges. However, this no longer exercises a judicial function, but deals with administrative matters, including the election of Presidents and Vice-Presidents of the court and of each section.

5.45 Thus there are two main species of case law: *decisions* on admissibility and *judgments*, which may be on the merits, on just satisfaction, on a request for interpretation, or on a request for revision. Both decisions and judgments may emanate from either a Chamber or the Grand Chamber. In addition there are *resolutions* of the Committee of Ministers.

Procedure before 1 November 1998

5.46 The main difference under the old procedure was that a separate body, the European Commission of Human Rights, first considered an application, but there are a number of other differences. The Commission dealt with admissibility in the same way as the court does now – the grounds of admissibility have not changed. If the application was found to be admissible, the Commission then had to establish the facts and try to reach a 'friendly settlement', the function now carried out by the Registry of the Court. If a settlement was not reached, the Commission made a report giving an opinion on the merits of the case, and it is this stage, which was seen as involving duplication of effort, that has gone. The report on the merits was communicated to the Committee of Ministers. Within three months the case could then be referred – by the Commission, by the Committee of Ministers, or by a state (though not, until 1994, by an individual applicant) – to the European Court of Human Rights. Although not sitting permanently but in sessions, the case was heard as now by a Chamber. The Chamber could also relinquish jurisdiction as now, but until 1993 it was to the Plenary Court of all the judges. In 1993 the procedure of relinquishment instead to a Grand Chamber was introduced, but there remained the possibility of further relinquishment by the Grand Chamber to the Plenary Court. Although the court proceeded with further consideration of the merits, it considered itself competent to review the Commission's decisions on admissibility. Thus judgment might be given simply on the basis of preliminary objections to admissibility. If the case, having completed its Commission stages was not referred to the court, the final decision rested with the Committee of Ministers under the original art 32 of the Convention. The Committee would adopt a resolution, which usually accorded with the majority opinion of the Commission as there is no further investigation of the merits, and which contained no elaboration of reasons. This function of the Committee of Ministers has been abolished, since it served little purpose. The Commission generally only referred a case to the Committee rather than court if they found no violation or, if there were a violation, the state concerned indicated that it was willing to provide redress to the applicant. Another important difference was that the Commission proceeded in private, and indeed their report on the merits remained confidential to the parties until the case was brought before the court or disposed of by the Committee of Ministers.

5.47 Thus there were four main species of case law: *decisions* of the Commission on admissibility; *reports* of the Commission's opinion on the merits; *judgments* of the court; and *resolutions* of the Committee of Ministers, which included resolutions on violation as well as on execution of judgments. In addition, the Commission sometimes made reports in respect of friendly settlements, stating the facts and the outcome, which are principally of interest for the amount of compensation paid. The court also made *decisions* of two kinds. The first was 'relinquishment' to the Plenary Court or Grand Chamber. The second arose from Protocol 9, which came into force in 1994 but was repealed by the new Protocol 11 in 1998. This potentially gave individual applicants a route to have a case referred to the court, if the Commission or the state had declined to do so. Such applications were heard by a 'screening panel' of three judges, and were invariably dismissed. Both kinds of decision were purely formal and contain no reasoning. They are mentioned simply because they appear in the court's official series of reports, which explains their title of *Judgments and Decisions*, and because in the case of screening panel decisions they are an option on the search form on the European Court of Human Rights website.

5.48 The list of Strasbourg case law given in s 2(1) of the Human Rights Act is couched in formal terms. Section 2(1)(a) which refers to the judgments of the court is largely self-explanatory, but paras (b), (c), (d) can be translated in terms of the above description as follows:

  (b) opinion of the Commission given in a report under art 31 of the Convention
      = Commission *reports* on the merits
  (c) decision of the Commission in connection with art 26 or 27(2) of the Convention
      = Commission *decisions* on admissibility
  (d) decision of the Committee of Ministers taken under art 46 of the Convention
      = Committee of Ministers *resolutions*. (Article 46 is the equivalent of art 54 of the Convention before renumbering by Protocol 11, ie resolutions on the execution of judgments. This would seem to overlook resolutions on violation under old art 32. But s 21(3) of the Act provides that the reference to art 46 is to be taken to include old art 32 as well as old art 54. Thus this paragraph includes both kinds of Committee of Ministers resolution – execution and violation.)

The only part of para (a) of s 2(1) that may not be self-explanatory is the reference to 'advisory opinions' as well as judgments of the court. For reasons explained in Grosz, Beatson and Duffy *Human Rights: the 1998 Act and the European Convention* ((2000) Sweet & Maxwell) at para 2-18, these can safely be ignored – the court has never given, and is never likely to give, an advisory opinion.

Precedent value

5.49 A number of commentators on the Human Rights Act have discussed the likely use of Strasbourg case law by the English courts – the chapter on the subject in *Grosz, Beatson and Duffy* is particularly useful. Strasbourg case law is not *binding* on the English courts, but even if only persuasive not all cases will carry equal weight. The order in which they are set out in s 2(1) of the Act is a rough guide to the relative importance of each type of case. The judgments of the court are the most important and least numerous – up to 1998 they were only about 400 altogether, though the rate of output may be expected to accelerate somewhat. They are all published. Commission reports on the merits are of the next importance, and were also generally published, though as explained above not all were public. Decisions on admissibility are very numerous, and originally only a small selection was made generally available. Many decisions contain only brief reasoning. As Grosz, Beatson and Duffy point out, the most useful to the English courts are likely to be cases on the meaning of 'victim' and those finding an application inadmissible on the ground that it was 'manifestly ill-founded', since it is in those contexts that the scope of substantive Convention rights may have been explored by the Commission. The European Court in exercising its new function of deciding admissibility is doubtless going to make heavy use of Commission decisions generally. Committee of Ministers resolutions have never been widely referred to because they contain no reasoning, and that is likely to remain the case.

Reports of European human rights case law

5.50 The court has gone to admirable lengths to make its database of case law (HUDOC) freely available on its website. The current coverage of the database is as follows, though there remains the possibility of the addition of further retrospective material:

Court:	All judgments, and since 1998 all admissibility decisions *except* those made by a committee of three judges as opposed to a Chamber; all screening panel decisions (1994–98).
Commission:	All admissibility decisions from 1986 (though not necessarily all in English), and a selection of decisions before that date that were published; all reports on the merits from 1986 (if public).
Committee of Ministers:	Resolutions on execution 1972 to October 1997; resolutions on merits 1959 to March 1997.

The main tip when searching the site is to notice the boxes for each category of material at the top of the search form. The default is judgments only. You need to tick the other boxes to search other material – if in doubt tick all the boxes.

5.51 The official series of judgments published for the court was originally called *Publications of the European Court of Human Rights: Series A: Judgments and Decisions*. As with most of the other official publications described here, it is in French and English, the only two official languages, in parallel text (though its successor has now abandoned parallel text in favour of having each language version separately). Each case was issued as a separate part, which might amount to a whole volume, and assigned a number of its own, though occasionally subdivided as for example, no. 180-A and no. 180-B. Since *Series B*, discussed below, did the same, you sometimes have to mind your 'A's and 'B's. From 1995 *Series A* was renamed simply *Reports of Judgments and Decisions*. Though initially each case continued to have its own number (in a new series of numbers), the number ceased to be used for identification purposes and from November 1998 the numbering of each case was dropped altogether (see para **5.64**). There was also the accompanying series, *Series B: Pleadings, Oral Arguments and Documents*. They are numbered in the same fashion as *Series A*, but with the exception of the first few cases the *Series B* number does not match the *Series A* number for any particular case. *Series B* was discontinued with volume 104 for 1988 (not published until 1995). The decision to abandon publication, caused by a very large backlog, required a change of the rules of the court not adopted until 1995. As a result, *Series A* cases carried the note that 'the principal documents and pleadings are to be published in vol . . ., in *Series B*' until the end of 1993, by which time the number of putative *Series B* volumes had reached 259 – so the absence of series B vols 105–259 from the shelves does not indicate maladministration or kleptomania in your library. *Series B* included the full text of the Commission's report of its opinion on the merits. However, from about 1984 the practice was adopted of appending it, or the operative parts of it, to the judgment in *Series A*. Latterly all judgments appended the Commission's opinion on the merits. Advance copies of individual judgments were also issued as mimeographed typescripts in A4 format, but promulgation on the Internet now obviates the need to use these. Summaries of cases are also published as monthly *Information Notes*, which replace the former *Information Sheets* put out by the Council of Europe. The *Information Notes* are also on the Court's website, as are the Press Releases, which the Registry issues for every case as soon as a decision or judgment is made.

5.52 Probably more widely used and widely available than *Series A* and its successors is the commercially published *European Human Rights Reports*, if only for reasons of currency – the official series has always been pretty slow to come out. Although ostensibly it only started in 1979, the first two volumes were devoted to retrospective coverage and include all the judgments of the court back to its first in 1960. Thereafter it includes virtually every judgment – a cumulative table in each volume gives references by *Series A* number. Although judgments of the court form the bulk of its content, it does also include some selected Commission decisions and reports, other materials such as Rules of the court, and the odd UK case. Again there was some retrospective coverage – in vol 3 – and from 1993 material other than judgments has appeared in a separate section, paginated 'CD'. *Butterworths Human Rights Cases*, which started in 1997, also contains a few European Court of Human Rights judgments, but spreads it wings considerably wider than that, covering decisions of other international courts and tribunals, cases from a wide range of national courts, particularly from the Commonwealth, as well as UK cases. The European Court of Human Rights cases are also sometimes published in the ordinary English series, including the newspaper reports.

5.53 The official version of the Commission publications from 1975 was *Decisions and Reports* (cited DR); before then it was called *Collection of Decisions* (CD). This contains reports on the merits, a selection of admissibility decisions, and reports on friendly settlements. Committee of Ministers resolutions are also sometimes included, often appended to reports that have not been referred to the court. From 1994 for the last four years of its life, for reasons of currency, each volume was issued in two parts, A and B. Part A contains the texts in the original language in which they had been prepared – French or English – and Part B following later contained translations into the other language. Like the court judgments, the Commission reports were issued in advance (A4 with pale blue covers). The texts of selected admissibility decisions and of Committee of Ministers resolutions are included in the *Yearbook of the European Convention on Human Rights*, published under the auspices of the Council of Europe. It may contain, particularly in its early volumes, material not to be found in CD or DR. It also includes, though only in summary form, selected court judgments and Commission reports. The very first volume, cited as 1 YB, in fact covered three years, 1955–57, and was entitled *European Commission of Human Rights: Documents and/et Decisions*. The official *Digest of Strasbourg Case-law* as its name implies does not provide full reports, but its coverage of early case law does sometimes furnish the only published source of some Commission cases. The Council of Europe also published the *Collection of Resolutions Adopted by the Committee of Ministers in Application of Articles 32 and 54 of the European Convention on Human Rights, 1959–1989* (1993) with subsequent supplements.

5.54 All the main commercial Internet services now have human rights modules with a range of materials, including case law. Westlaw UK has the EHRR. Lawtel and Justis have the text of all ECHR judgments, and Butterworths LEXIS Direct has, as well as judgments, cases from its own report series including *Butterworths Human Rights Cases*. If you have access to these, the search software may be more to your taste than that offered on the Court's website, but bear in mind that they do not cover Commission reports and decisions (except in so far as they are included in EHRR), though of course they may have other non-case law materials of interest.

5.55 Section 2(2) and (3) of the Human Rights Act 1998 allude to rules for bringing before the court the case law mentioned in s 2(1). Those rules are to be found in the Practice Direction to Pt 39 of the Civil Procedure Rules. Paragraph 8.1 states that 'the authority to be cited should be an authoritative and complete report'. Reports from the EHRR would be regarded as authoritative – certainly they are widely cited in judgments on the Act. The Practice Direction goes on to say that the original texts from the court and Commission *'may'* be used, which is as you would expect, but the significant part of the subparagraph is that the texts may be paper-based *or* from the court's judgment database, HUDOC, on the Internet.

Anatomy of a law report

5.56 Most full law reports follow the pattern illustrated, which is taken from *The Law Reports* (see figure 5.2). (1) At the head are the names of the parties, the dates of the hearing and the judge or judges. (2) There follows catchwords, which are used for indexing, and (3) the headnote. The headnote is compiled by the reporter and is his most significant contribution. It has to summarise succinctly and accurately the issues in the case, what was *held* – the core of the case – and any statements on the law, not strictly necessary for arriving at the decision as *held*, but of significance. The latter appear after the rubric *'Per curiam'*, where it is the opinion of the whole court, or *per* the name of the relevant judge. (4) Lists of cases cited in the judgment and in *The Law Reports* cases cited in argument (and nowadays the written skeleton argument) are provided. (5) At this point a summary of the pleadings and of the facts may be given, or it may be that it is merely indicated where in the judgment the facts are to be found. (6) The names of counsel are given, and, in *The Law Reports*, a summary of their argument. (7) Preceding the judgment there may appear the words 'Cur. adv. vult.', which means that the judgment was reserved, as opposed to being given immediately in court at the conclusion of the proceedings (one technique sometimes used to play up the weakness of an unfavourable authority is to point out that is was unreserved). (8) After the judgments themselves and any consequent orders of the court, are (9) the names of instructing solicitors. (10) The final item is the name of the law reporter. Traditionally, for the case to be an authority that could be cited in court, a report had to be authenticated by a barrister, so this qualification appears after the reporter's name. Since 1 April 1991, when s 115 of the Court and Legal Services Act 1990 came into force, it may also be a solicitor. Although it is of small importance, the curious may wonder why in *The Law Reports* sometimes the full name of the reporter is given, and sometimes only initials. The answer is that full-time reporters of the Incorporated Council, whose appointment is approved by the court, have the privilege of using just their initials, whereas supernumerary reporters or those in training but not yet appointed give their full names.

Citations

5.57 The standard form of citing case references is: name of case (printed in *italic* or underlined); year; volume number; abbreviation for the series; page number; and, optionally, the court. For example:

Derry v Peek (1989) 14 App Cas 337, HL
Lloyd v McMahon [1987] 1 All ER 118, CA

Figure 5.2

① ROST v. EDWARDS and Others

[1989 R. No. 189]

1990 Jan. 22, 23. 29;   Popplewell J.
      Feb. 1

②
Parliament—Privilege—Proceedings in Parliament—Libel action by
Member of Parliament against newspaper—Newspaper article
alleging failure to register interests in Register of Members'
Interests—Member not appointed to committees of House—
Whether appointment of chairman and members "proceedings in
Parliament"—Whether evidence relating to registration of interests
privilege of Parliament—Bill of Rights 1688 (1 Will. & Mary,
sess. 2, c. 2), art. 9¹

The plaintiff, a Member of Parliament and a consultant to
two organisations concerned with energy, brought an action for
libel arising out of an article published in a national newspaper
which he alleged meant that he was improperly seeking to sell
privileged and confidential information obtained by him as a
member of the House of Commons Select Committee on Energy
to Danish companies. The plaintiff wished to call evidence that
as a result of the article he had been de-selected from
membership of the Standing Committee of the Electricity
Privatisation Bill and had not been appointed chairman of the
Select Committee on Energy. He further sought to adduce
evidence as to the criteria for registration in the Register of
Members' Interests, the nature of his consultancies and reason
why he had not registered his interest. The defendants, the
journalist, editor and publisher of the article in the newspaper,
wished by way of justification to rely on the failure to register.
    On the question whether the evidence related to proceedings
in Parliament:—
    Held, (1) that the appointment of a chairman and membership
③ of a committee of the House formed part of the proceedings of
Parliament; that even though the plaintiff merely wished to
adduce such evidence as evidence of fact without any critical
examination of the appointments, such evidence fell within the
privileges of Parliament and could not be adduced without the
authority of Parliament as they were matters that questioned
proceedings in Parliament within the meaning of article 9 of the
Bill of Rights 1688 (post, pp. 474ʜ—475ᴇ).
    Dingle v. Associated Newspapers Ltd. [1960] 2 Q.B. 405
and *Church of Scientology of California v. Johnson-Smith* [1972]
1 Q.B. 522 applied.
    Blackshaw v. Lord [1984] Q.B. 1, C.A. distinguished.
    (2) That since the Register of Members' Interests was a
public document, the court would not be astute to find a reason
for ousting its jurisdiction and, therefore, unless and until
Parliament enacted that the register was privileged, the court
would not rule against the admission of evidence of the practice
and procedure for the registration of members' interests in that
register; and that, therefore, the parties were entitled to adduce
evidence of whether the plaintiff should have registered an
interest therein (post, p. 478ᴀ–ꜰ).

The following cases are referred to in the judgment:

Attorney-General of Ceylon v. De Livera [1963] A.C. 103; [1962] 3 W.L.R.
    1413; [1962] 3 All E.R. 1066, P.C.
Blackshaw v. Lord [1984] Q.B. 1; [1983] 3 W.L.R. 283; [1983] 2 All E.R.
    311, C.A.
Bradlaugh v. Gossett (1884) 12 Q.B.D. 271
Church of Scientology of California v. Johnson-Smith [1972] 1 Q.B. 522;
    [1971] 3 W.L.R. 434; [1972] 1 All E.R. 378
Dingle v. Associated Newspapers Ltd. [1960] 2 Q.B. 405; [1960] 2 W.L.R.
    430; [1960] 1 All E.R. 294
Jay v. Topham (1689) 12 St. Tr. 821
④ *Parliamentary Privilege Act 1770, In re* [1958] A.C. 331; [1958] 2 W.L.R.
    912; [1958] 2 All E.R. 329, P.C.
Pickin v. British Railways Board [1974] A.C. 765; [1974] 2 W.L.R. 208;
    [1974] 1 All E.R. 609. H.L.(E.)
Reg. v. Paty (1704) 2 Ld. Raym. 1105
Reg. v. Secretary of State for Trade, Ex parte Anderson Strathclyde Plc.
    [1983] 2 All E.R. 233. D.C.
Stockdale v. Hansard (1839) 9 Ad. & El. 1
Williams v. Reason (Note) [1988] 1 W.L.R. 96; [1988] 1 All E.R. 262, C.A.

No additional cases were cited in argument.

Figure 5.2 – *cont'd*

ACTION.

⑤ By a writ dated 17 January 1989 and a statement of claim served on 17 February 1989 the plaintiff, Peter Rost M.P., claimed damages for libel contained in an article which appeared on the front page of the issue of "The Guardian" dated 15 February 1988, written by the first defendant, Robert Edwards, a journalist. The second defendant, Peter Preston, was the editor and the third defendant, Guardian Newspapers Ltd., was the publisher of the newspaper. In addition, the plaintiff sought an injunction to restrain the defendants from publishing ·or causing to be published the same or any similar libel of him.

During the trial, submissions were made to Popplewell J. for rulings on whether evidence of membership of committees of the House and the practice of Members of Parliament registering their interests in the Register of Members' Interests (H.C. 115) was inadmissible as being the subject of Parliamentary privilege. After the initial submissions were made, when it became clear that a question of Parliamentary privilege might be involved, the hearing was adjourned so that questions could be submitted to the Attorney-General and his assistance requested.

The facts are stated in the judgment.

⑥ *Sir Nicholas Lyell Q.C.,S.-G.* and *Philip Havers* for the Attorney-General. The basis of Parliamentary privilege is, first, the right of Parliament to be the sole arbiter of what is said and done in Parliament and secondly, the right of free speech in Parliament so that Members of Parliament may conduct themselves there without fear of legal consequences: see Article 9 of the Bill of Rights 1688. A Member of Parliament cannot be sued for what he says in Parliament or for what he does in the course of or in connection with proceedings in Parliament

Richard Hartley Q.C. and *Andrew Caldecott* for the plaintiff. The principles sought to be extracted by the Solicitor-General from the cases he cited have no application to the instant case because of the factual basis on which those cases depended. Although the courts appeared to have given a wide interpretation to the word "questioned", in fact it was used in the context of "attributing an improper motive" or "adversely questioning" and not used synonymously with "examining". If the Bill of Rights had intended to prevent any discussion about what was said in Parliament the word "impeach" would not have been used. All the cases cited involved some criticism either of individual Members of Parliament or the Houses of Parliament as a whole. Thus in *Bradlaugh v. Gossett*,

Cur. adv. vult. ⑦

1 February. POPPLEWELL J. read the following judgment. In this case the plaintiff is claiming damages for a libel arising out of an article published by "The Guardian" newspaper on 15 December 1988. The first defendant is a journalist, the second defendant is the editor and the third defendant is the publisher of the newspaper.

⑧ At the material time the plaintiff was a Member of Parliament and a member of the House of Commons Select Committee on Energy. He

In the result, I conclude that claims for privilege in respect of the Register of Members' Interests does not fall within the definition of "proceedings in Parliament," and accordingly I rule that it is open to the plaintiff to give the evidence that he seeks to do in relation to the registration of members' interests and it is open to the defendants to challenge that evidence.

Finally, may I say how grateful I am to all concerned for the very great assistance that has been given to the court.

Ruling accordingly.

 Solicitors: Peter `Carter-Ruck & Partners; Lovell White Durrant; Treasury Solicitor.

[Reported by MISS GERALDINE FAINER, Barrister-at-Law]

Square and round brackets

5.58 The above examples also illustrate the convention on the use of round and square brackets for the year. Some series adopt a volume numbering that runs consecutively throughout the series, so that the volume number can uniquely identify the volume on the shelf. The year is only given for added information and is given in round brackets. Other series either have no volume numbers or only use volume numbers within a year, in which case the year is the primary means of identification and appears in square brackets.

Technically, a round bracket date should refer to the date of judgment, not the date of publication of the report. This can cause confusion when a report is not published until some time later, particularly where the date of publication has been printed on the cover or lettered on the spine. The case of *B v B* decided in 1979 was reported in vol 3 of the *Family Law Reports*, and so is correctly cited as (1979) 3 FLR 187. On looking at the shelf, the reader might be a little puzzled to see that this series did not start until 1980 and vol 3 was published in 1982. In the case of square bracket dates (which necessarily have to reflect the date of publication), it is the practice (or should be) to add a round bracket date as well if there is a disparity. An extreme example was *Palmer v Young*, a case from the seventeenth century. It was only for a case in 1903 that counsel unearthed manuscript details of it. It was successfully relied upon and got included as a note to the case in question. The citation, correctly if curiously, is therefore (1694) [1903] 2 Ch 65n.

5.59 Unreported cases were usually cited just by name, court and date of judgment; for the sake of clarity 'unreported' may have been added:

> *Burke v Hare* 12 July 1990 ChD Patent Court (unreported)

However, as a consequence of the much wider availability of unreported cases from electronic sources, and because of electronic promulgation of law reports series, the Lord Chief Justice issued on 11 January 2001 the *Practice Direction (Judgments: Form and Citation)* [2001] 1 WLR 194. This introduced three matters: the provision of a court-assigned number for every judgment; paragraphing of judgments; and the authorisation of the citation before the courts of reported cases derived from an electronic version of the reports. The first two innovations together provide a so-called 'neutral citation', which uniquely identifies a case, and a passage in it, whether or not it is reported. This comprises the year, an abbreviation for the court, the number of the case, and then any reference to a particular paragraph in square brackets. Thus:

> *Smith v Jones* [2001] EWCA Civ 10 at [30]

This refers to case no 10 of the Court of Appeal (Civil Division) – EW for England and Wales – of 2001 and a passage at para 30. The *Practice Direction* initially applied to judgments of the Court of Appeal, Civil and Criminal Divisions, and the Administrative Court (Queen's Bench cases on judicial review, etc). It is to be extended in due course to the other Divisions of the High Court. The House of Lords has also adopted the practice – its abbreviation is UKHL, reflecting its wider jurisdiction.

Abbreviations

5.60 Law reports are universally cited by an abbreviation rather their full title. The standard guide for deciphering abbreviations is Donald Raistrick *Index to Legal Citations and Abbreviations* ((2nd edn, 1993) Bowker-Saur). A quotation from an experienced law librarian given in the foreword to this work strikes a chord: 'They cause more trouble than almost anything. They're supposed to save time. But they don't.' Raistrick has alleviated the problem, but they can still be a cause of aggravation even to the experienced lawyer. To minimise the aggravation, three things need to be borne in mind when using *Raistrick*. The first is to be aware of the context of an abbreviation. Many different series share the same abbreviation, but the application of common sense will usually point to the right one. For example, FLR, as well as standing for *Family Law Reports*, as in the previous paragraph, can equally stand for *Financial Law Reports*, the Australian *Federal Law Reports*, the Indian *Federal Law Reports*, the *Federal Law Review*, the *Fiji Law Reports* or the *University of Florida Law Review*. *Raistrick* gives coverage dates for particular series, and this is usually the main clue in distinguishing identical abbreviations. Secondly, at the time of writing the current edition of *Raistrick* is eight years old. It naturally suffers from creeping obsolescence, so do not be surprised if the abbreviation for a recent report is not in it (it is perhaps even more out-of-date for journal abbreviations since new journals proliferate at a greater rate than law reports). Lastly, one needs a grasp of the filing order of the abbreviations, which is not transparently obvious. A page is illustrated (see figure 5.3). There are two main sequences. First come initials on their own: A.A., A.B., A.C., etc. Then come part-words sharing the same root: Ab., Ab.Ca., Ab.Eq.Cas., etc. The added complication is abbreviations linked with an ampersand (&). These come at the end of the sequence with same initial letter or the same initial part-word, as the case may be: A.A., A.B., A.Z., A.& A., A.& B., Aa., Ab., Ab.& A., Ac., Ac.B., Ac.D., Ac.& A., etc. A useful feature of *Raistrick* is that for the nominate reports cross-references are given to the appropriate volumes of the *English Reports* and *Revised Reports* (see para **5.15**).

5.61 For abbreviations too recent to be included in *Raistrick*, the table of abbreviations in the monthly parts and yearbooks of *Current Law* are the best source. (If it is in fact a journal series rather than a law report series, use the list of abbreviations on the *Legal Journals Index*.) *The Digest* also includes a good list (in the front of vol 1(1) and in the cumulative supplement), as do *Halsbury's Laws* and Osborne's *Law Dictionary*. Many textbooks helpfully include tables of abbreviations of works cited. In the case of elusive citations it is worth checking the source. It may have simply been copied down wrongly, but also authors occasionally may cite non-standard sources and assign them their own abbreviation. For example, the abbreviation D.C.C. would be meaningless, unless one knew that it came from Gadsen's *Law of Commons*, where it is used to refer to a collection of Decisions of the Commons Commissioners that was held in the Arts and Social Sciences Library, University College Cardiff (now Cardiff University). The US equivalent of *Raistrick* is *Bieber's Dictionary of Legal Abbreviations* ((5th edn, 2001) Hein), but it has wide coverage of English abbreviations too, just as *Raistrick* has wide coverage of US abbreviations. There is also Igor I Kavass and Mary Miles Price (eds) *World Dictionary of Legal Abbreviations* ((1991–) 4 vols looseleaf) Hein).

5.62 *Raistrick* makes a point of including as many variant abbreviations for the same series as possible. It is therefore of no assistance if you are approaching the problem from the other end and wish to know what abbreviation to use if you yourself are citing a case. The problem is solved for many modern series of reports because

Figure 5.3 Raistrick *Index to Legal Citations and Abbreviations.*

K

K. Kammer (Ger.) Chamber, division
Kemble, Codex Diplomaticus Ævi Saxonici
Kenyon's Notes of Cases, King's Bench (96 ER) 1753–9
Keyes' Court of Appeals Reports (40–3 New York)
King
Kotze's High Court Reports, Transvaal (S.Afr.) 1877–81
Wetboek van Koophandel (Neth.) commercial code
KA Kammarrattens arsbok (Swed.) The annual Fiscal Court reporter. 1925–
K.B. King's Bench
KB 27 Public Record Office, Plea Rolls of the Court of King's Bench
KBA Kansas Bar Association
K.B.B. Kentucky Bench and Bar. 1975–
K.B.C. King's Bench Court
K.B.D. King's Bench Division
K.B.Div'I.Ct. King's Bench Divisional Court
K.B.J. Kentucky Bar Journal. 1971–4
Kentucky State Bar Journal. 1936–71
K.B.U.C. Upper Canada King's Bench Reports
KBr Kungl. brev (Swed.) Royal letter – decree
K.C. King's Counsel
K.C.L.J. Kings College Law Journal
K.C.R. Kansas City Law Review. 1932–8

Reports tempore King (25 ER) 1724–33
The University of Kansas City Law Review. 1938–63
The University of Missouri at Kansas City Law Review. 1964–8
KCirk Kungl. cirkular (Swed.) Royal circular – decree
KF Kungl. forordning (Swed.) Royal statute – law
K.F. Gold Coast Judgments and the Masai Cases, by King-Farlow (Ghana) 1915–17
KFC Kentucky Fried Chicken
KG Bundesgesetz über Kartelle und ahnliche Organisationen (Switz.) 1962
Kammergericht (Ger.) Appeal Court, Berlin
Kommandigesellschaft (Ger.) Limited partnership
Koninkijk Besluit (Neth.) Royal Decree
K.Ga.A. Kommanditgesellschaft auf Aktien (Ger.) Limited partnership on share basis
K.H.C.D. Kenya High Court Digest
KH.HC. Khartoum High Court
K.I.R. Knight's Industrial Reports. 1966–75
KK Kungl. kungorelse (Swed.) Royal regulation – decree
K.K. Kabushiki kaisha (Japan) Stock corporation
KKM Ministry of Foreign Trade (Hungary)
KL Konkurslag (Swed.) Bankruptcy Law. 1921
K.L.G.R. Knight's Local Government Reports. 1903–
K.L.J. Kentucky Law Journal. 1912–

K.I.R.
K.I.R. Kathiawar Law Reports (India)
Kenya Law Reports. 1919–
K.L.T. Kerala Law Times (India) 1948–
KMt Kungl. Majestat (Swed.) the King in Council or the Cabinet
KO Konkursordnung (Ger.) Bankruptcy
Konsumentombudsman (Swed.) Consumer Ombudsman
KPDR Korean People's Democratic Republic (North Korea)
KS Kungl. stadga (Swed.) Royal regulation – decree
K.S. King's Sergeant
K.S.C. Kenny, A Selection of Cases Illustrative of the English Criminal Law. 1901
KUVG Bundesgesetz über die Kranken– und Unfallversicherung (Switz.) 1911
KVO Kraftverkehrsordnung für den Guterfernverkehr mit Kraffahrzeugen (Ger.) Regulation of carriage of goods by motor vehicles
KWG Reichsgesetz über das Kreditwesen (Ger.) Law on credit operations
K.W.I.C. Keyword in context
K.& B. Kotze & Barber's High Court Reports (Transvaal, S.Afr.) 1855–88
K.& B.Dig. Kerford & Box, Victorian Digest
K.& E.Conv. Key & Elphinstone, Conveyancing. 15ed. 1953–4
K.& F.N.S.W. Knox & Fitzharding's New South Wales Reports. 1878–9
K.& G. Keane & Grant's Registration Appeal Cases. 1854–62
K.& G.R.C. Keane & Grant's Registration Appeal Cases. 1854–62
K.& Gr. Keane & Grant's Registration Appeal Cases. 1854–62
K.& J. Kay & Johnson's Vice Chancellors' Reports (69–70 ER) 1854–8
K.& O. Knapp & Ombler's Election Cases. 1834–5

K.& R. Kent & Radcliffe's Law of New York. Revision of 1801
K.& W. Kames & Woodhouselee's Dictionary of Decisions (Scot.) 1540–1796
K.& W.Dic. Kames & Woodhouselee's Dictionary of Decisions (Scot.) 1540–1796
Ka.A. Kansas Appeal Reports
Kahn Contract E. Kahn, Contract and Mercantile Law (S.Afr.)
Kahn Domicile E. Kahn, The South African Law of Domicile of Natural Persons
Kakyu minshu Kakyu saibansho minji saiban reishu (Japan) Lower court civil case reports
Kam. Kames & Woodhouselee's Dictionary of Decisions (Scot.) 1540–1796
Kam.Eluc. Kames, Elucidations of the Laws of Scotland
Kam.Eq. Kames, Principles of Equity
Kam.I.Tr. Kames, Historical Law Tracts (Scot.)
Kam.Rem. Kames' Remarkable Decisions, Court of Session (Scot.) 1716–52
Kam.Sel. Kames' Select Decisions (Scot.) 1752–68
Kam.Sel.Dec. Kames' Select Decisions (Scot.) 1752–68
Kames Kames & Woodhouselee's Dictionary of Decisions (Scot.) 1540–1796
Kames' Remarkable Decisions, Court of Session (Scot.) 1716–52
Kames' Select Decisions (Scot.) 1752–68
Kames Dec. Kames & Woodhouselee's Dictionary of Decisions, Court of Session (Scot.) 1540–1796
Kames Dict.Dec. Kames & Woodhouselee's Dictionary of Decisions, Court of Session (Scot.) 1540–1796

Published by Bowker-Saur (2nd edn, 1993).

they print the preferred form of citation on the reports themselves. For older series, the *Manual of Legal Citations*, published by the Institute of Advanced Legal Studies, provides some recommendations. Part I (1959) covers the British Isles, and part II (1960) the Commonwealth. Derek French *How to cite legal authorities* ((1996) Blackstone) gives general guidance, together with a list of recommended forms of citation. In these matters, however, there can be only recommendations and publishers have their own house style.

Citation of European Court of Justice cases

5.63 In same way that *The Law Reports* reference for a case should be cited in preference to references from other series, ECJ cases should be cited by the official *European Court Reports* reference, though as with English cases it is helpful to cite alternative references as well. The name of the case cited should be that which appears as the running head on the report in the ECR (though many publications follow various variants: see para **5.109** below), and the case number should be given as well. Each part and volume of the ECR is now printed in two sequences, with separate pagination distinguished by a roman numeral I or II, the first covering the ECJ itself, and the second the Court of First Instance. Examples of official citations would thus be:

> Case C-286/88 *Falciola v Comune di Pavia* [1990] ECR I-191
> Case T-38/89 *Hochbaum v Commission* [1990] ECR II-43

Since 1989 the case number for ECJ cases has been prefixed by 'C' and for CFI cases by 'T' (for 'Tribunal'). Case numbers are also sometimes suffixed with 'R', which signifies cases concerned with applications for interim relief, or 'A', which is added to the original case number if there are additional applications from the same applicant. Cases before the ECJ on appeal from the CFI are given a new 'C' number, with the suffix 'P'.

Citation of European human rights cases

5.64 The official reports of cases from the court bear the official form of citation as a footnote on the title page of each case. There are three different conventions depending on whether you are citing a case from *Series A*, from the *Reports of Judgments and Decisions* from 1995 when *Series A* stopped to 31 October 1998, or from the *Reports of Judgments and Decisions* from 1 November 1998. The first two include the date of judgment as part of the citation, and then either a *Series A* number or a *Reports* year and part number. The new system, since 1998, drops date of judgment, but includes the application number (the number assigned to it as soon as the case is logged at the Registry, which may be three or four years before the judgment). The new system drops the name of the series in favour of just the abbreviation for the court. It also adopts the practice of italicising case names, though many English sources citing European Court of Human Rights cases will italicise case names before 1998, as a matter of English practice or house style. Thus:

> Schiesser v Switzerland judgment of 4 December 1979, Series A no 34
> Zana v Turkey judgment of 25 November 1997, *Reports of Judgments and Decisions* 1997-VII
> *Hood v the United Kingdom* [GC], no 27267/95, ECHR 1999-I

The new system of citation also has other innovations. One, as illustrated, is to add '[GC]' if the decision or judgment is from the Grand Chamber. The other is to add a descriptor of the type of decision or judgment. The default, as in the illustration, is a *judgment* on the *merits*, where no descriptor is given. Admissibility decisions have 'dec.' and judgments other than on the merits have 'just satisfaction', 'revision' and 'interpretation' in brackets after the name. If you are citing a particular part of the judgment, the paragraph number should be cited as follows:

> *Nikolova v Bulgaria* [GC], no. 31195/96, § 24, ECHR 1999-II

5.65 Commission decisions and reports are identified by the names of the parties, the application number, date of decision, and the reference if there is one, in DR or CD. Of these elements, the application number is particularly important with admissibility decisions because the name of applicant was often confidential, so there are a very great many cases called *X v United Kingdom* which are otherwise indistinguishable (see para **5.110**). The court itself, when citing Commission decisions, tends to set them out in full:

> *X v Belgium*, application no. 9097/80, Commission decision of 13 October 1982, Decisions and Reports 30

In that case '30' is the number of the part, not the page number. Most English sources will in fact adopt conventional English practice, which is rather clearer:

> *X v Belgium* 9097/80 (1982) 30 DR 119

5.66 Committee of Ministers resolutions are identified by number, prefixed by 'DH' (for 'droits de l'homme') for example, DH (92) 8 – the eighth human rights resolution of 1992. The date of the resolution may be added for completeness.

The range of finding aids

Printed finding aids for English cases

5.67 Although an electronic source may be the first port of call, an understanding of the basic printed sources is essential too. For many basic questions they may be just as quick as an electronic source; also there may be a queue for the terminals or the computer system may have crashed.

Current Law

5.68 Although *Current Law* covers all sources of law, its particular strength is its coverage of case law. It is virtually comprehensive for reported case law. It also includes unreported cases on quantum of damages in personal injury cases, usually submitted by the barrister or solicitor in the case whose name appears with the phrase 'ex relatione'. There are also occasionally other 'ex rel' cases, usually cases from the county courts with unusual facts. From 1973–89 it also included summaries of Court of Appeal (Civil Division) transcripts of unreported cases. Already mentioned in chapter 3, there are the associated *Current Law Legislation Citators*, comprising the

Statute Citator and the *Statutory Instrument Citator* – these are relevant to case law research since they also pick up cases in which legislation has been judicially considered. And then there is the *Current Law Case Citator*, which will be described more fully below. As it name implies, *Current Law* is geared to recent materials, and this is reflected in its structure – monthly parts, which are cumulated into separate yearbooks. Although it does go back to 1947, and there are some cumulative subject indexes, nobody in their right mind would attempt retrospective research on any scale using the hard copy if they had access to the electronic version (see para **5.76**). From 1993 it has had an accompanying current awareness newsletter, *Current Law Week*. One feature of *Current Law* that used to cause some confusion was that until 1990 it was published in two versions. One, called *Current Law*, contained only English material; the other, called *Scottish Current Law,* included all the English material in the main version but with the addition of a supplement of Scottish materials. From 1991 the two versions have been integrated. A sister publication covering materials from countries throughout Western and Eastern Europe, *European Current Law*, started in 1992, though full coverage of EC law relevant to the UK is still to be found in *Current Law* itself.

The Digest

5.69 This provides access to the whole body of case law that might be still be of value, whatever its date. In approximately 100 volumes, arranged by subject, brief summaries are given not only of all relevant English case law but also of selected Scottish, Irish, Commonwealth and European cases (which appear in slightly smaller print). It is kept up-to-date in three ways. First, when there is sufficient new material to warrant it, particular volumes are reissued in revised form (hence it is important to be aware of the date of the volume you are using). Secondly, there is an annual cumulative supplement. Thirdly there are quarterly surveys. There are consolidated tables of cases and a consolidated index, both of which are reissued annually in soft cover. It was originally published as *The English and Empire Digest* from 1919–32 and has been through two complete editions prior to the current one. In preparing the new editions and reissued volumes, material that was obsolete was not generally removed on a case-by-case basis, so the work contains particular cases that may well have been overtaken by statute. But where whole *topics* became obsolete, for example, 'Land Tax', then these would be removed. Thus for very obscure old material it is occasionally necessary to refer to the old editions or replaced volumes.

5.70 The greatest strength of *The Digest* is its coverage of old case law. There are plenty of mainstream areas of law where the principles derive from cases decided long before *Current Law* started in 1947. There are also occasions when there is a dearth of modern authority and an old case may be better than nothing. Its coverage of old Commonwealth authority was also generally good – it was designed for use in the Empire. But for coverage of recent reported cases it is not as comprehensive as *Current Law*, and its coverage of Commonwealth cases is now pretty slender. It does though bring both the new and the old under one roof as it were, and for recent English cases it does give quite extended digests, often longer than the equivalent in *Current Law*. The other value of *The Digest* is that the entries are annotated, showing in which later cases the particular case has been considered, followed, overruled, etc. Although the *Current Law Case Citator* is generally to be preferred for modern cases, *The Digest* is the main source for finding whether a case has been judicially considered before 1947. The data from *The Digest* has very recently been made available in electronic format in Butterworths Case Search (see para **5.78**).

The Law Reports Index

5.71 *The Law Reports Index* is a widely used tool. Prepared by the Incorporated Council of Law Reporting, it is issued in pink parts three times a year, with an ongoing cumulation which eventually forms a permanent cumulation covering ten-year periods, bound in red. Its title was a little misleading: it is neither an index to just *the* (official) *Law Reports* nor to *all* law reports. The matter of the title has now been remedied since the latest cumulation is called *The Consolidated Index to Leading Law Reports 1991–1999: the 'Red Book'*. Apart from *The Law Reports*, the *Weekly Law Reports* and the *Industrial Cases Reports*, which are the reports prepared by the Incorporated Council, it covers: *All England Law Reports*, *Criminal Appeal Reports*, *Lloyd's Law Reports*, *Local Government Reports*, *Road Traffic Reports*, *Tax Cases* and *Tax Case Leaflets*. References to reports in these other series are only given in the main subject index if the case does not appear in one of the Incorporated Council's own titles, though parallel citations to them are provided in the tables of cases reported and considered. *The Law Reports Index* does, therefore, cover all the major series and often may be all that is needed. The structure of the cumulations is also in some ways easier to use than *Current Law* and some of its tables of particular materials judicially considered are not to be found in other publications. None the less, because there are so many series that it does not cover, it would be rash to rely on *The Law Reports Index* alone for any in-depth research. The precursor of *The Law Reports Index* was *The Law Reports Digest* with coverage back to 1865.

Halsbury's Laws

5.72 *Halsbury's Laws*, as we saw in chapter 2, is always a good starting point for any research. The main work, though not a digest of cases as such, will lead you to most of the relevant case law on a subject, and in the table of cases citations are sometimes found that are not in *The Digest*. But apart from the main work are the *Monthly Reviews*, which are filed in the service volume, and cumulated as the *Annual Abridgment*. These are similar to *Current Law*'s monthly digests, with which in many ways they compete. However, it is unusual to find cases in it that have not been picked up by *Current Law*, except for cases on quantum of damages in personal injury cases, where, particularly recently, it has made an effort to cast its net widely.

Butterworths Legal Updater

5.73 Launched in 2001 this is a print version of Butterworths' free Internet service, Law Direct. It is published in monthly parts arranged by broad subject, with a subject index. It covers all categories of legal materials, rather like *Current Law*. Its case coverage is based on the digests for All England Direct, which appear also on Law Direct. In the print version the summaries are generally even shorter than those in All ER (D). It would seem to be very much designed simply as a current awareness tool.

Indexes to particular series

5.74 Lastly, to be borne in mind are indexes and tables to particular series. The table of cases to the *English Reports* is particularly useful for finding pre-1865 cases by name and saves time battling with *The Digest*. The *All England Law Reports* regularly produce cumulated tables and indexes, as do some specialist series of reports. They are usually just a convenient shortcut and not a substitute for systematic research, but occasionally they can solve problems that the other sources described above cannot. For example, the *All England Law Reports* index is one of the few that list cases by defendant as well as by claimant.

Electronic finding aids for English cases

5.75 Some of the ground has been covered in describing electronic sources of unreported cases (paras **5.23–5.29**). The following are the main tools for finding reported cases.

Current Law Cases

5.76 Part of the Current Legal Information suite of databases from Sweet & Maxwell, this provides in electronic form all the digests of cases that appear in the monthly parts of *Current Law* and the *Current Law Yearbooks* back to 1947. As with the other CLI databases, it is available on CD-ROM or on the Internet. The data has also been included in the case law part of Westlaw UK (see para **5.79**). It is an excellent resource, and usually the best starting-point for any case law research. The associated *Current Law* citators are also available in electronic form as separate databases (though the electronic version of the *Legislation Citator* only goes back to 1989).

Lexis

5.77 Until recently it contained the full text of nearly all reported English decisions since 1945 (the *Reports of Tax Cases* go back to 1875), together with, as mentioned above, many unreported decisions from 1980. With the launch of Westlaw UK by rival publishers Sweet & Maxwell, licensing of their series was withdrawn from Lexis, leaving a significant gap in its coverage. However, Lexis are trying to fill that gap with retrospective enhanced transcript coverage to minimise the number of cases that it does not include. In addition, it has cases from many other jurisdictions, the US database being the most comprehensive. It is a subscription service, and generally trainee solicitors and others are not let loose on it until they have been trained. Though the web-based version will be preferably to many users, it is still available as a conventional on-line database, and since it has been going a long time, there is still a loyal customer base who prefer that.

All England Direct and Case Search

5.78 All England Direct has already been described (para **5.26**) in connection with its transcript coverage. Of course, many of the cases appearing as transcripts or digests on it will end up in various reported series. But, as explained, its coverage of reported cases as such is confined to those in the *All England Reports* themselves. Bear in mind that the digests are available free on Butterworths Law Direct. All England Direct also has a tie-in with Butterworths Case Search, launched in 2001. Case Search combines the data from *The Digest* with the All England Reporter part of All England Direct so contains summaries of more than 250,000 cases from the earliest times to today. Capitalising on the annotations feature of *The Digest* (see para **5.70**) it is being marketed principally as a citator. Using a traffic light system, of red, green and amber codes, it tells you whether a case is good law, bad law or should be used with caution. It remains to be seen whether in this aspect it competes favourably with the *Current Law Case Citator*. As both products depend on editorial judgment in deciding whether the depth of consideration given in a later case to an earlier case warrants its inclusion, there may well be differences in the results obtained from each. If the editorial effort being expended extends to highlighting where an unreported case in the All England Reporter has considered another unreported case in the All England Reporter, then there may be additional results using Case Search, but as explained in more detail at para **5.134**, for recent materials full text searching may be preferable to the citator approach. The undoubted benefit of Case Search, however, is the making available in electronic form such a large corpus of case law, albeit in summary form (but see further para **5.125**).

Westlaw UK

5.79 Westlaw used to be the big rival to Lexis in the US. Sweet & Maxwell have used the brand name to offer a rival service to Lexis in the UK, with access like Lexis to the data of the big American brother. Launched at the end of 1999, its case law content is a bit of a mish-mash. There is transcript coverage, for which it is a direct competitor of the other services described at paras **5.25–5.29**. There is the content of *Current Law Cases*, which otherwise remains available, perfectly satisfactorily, as a separate database on CLI, and of course is not full text, and then there is the full text of those series of law reports that Sweet & Maxwell itself publishes, with *The Law Reports* and *Lloyd's Law Reports* thrown in. So it is difficult to isolate the kind of research problem where Westlaw UK would be recommended as the preferred alternative, as far as case law goes anyway – there are other aspects to the service that may commend it to some users.

Lawtel

5.80 Although today it is very much geared to the transcript alerting side of the market (see para **5.27**) it has been around in various guises since 1980, and provides summaries of reported cases. Its coverage of report series is not as wide as that of *Current Law*, but it covers about 35 of the main series. It also has quantum cases, which by their nature will not necessarily be the same cases as covered by other sources.

Individual series of reports on CD-ROM or the Internet

5.81 The availability of the various series of law reports published in full text electronically has been described above (para **5.11**). They are in a sense their own finding tools. If you require full text searching, so that for example, *Current Law Cases* is not sufficient for your purposes, and you do not have access to Lexis, they may well be the next best thing. The Justis products are particularly useful, not just because the search software is generally excellent, but because you can search across more than one series at a time provided, in the case of the CD-ROMs, they have been networked or cached. CD-ROMs also come into their own in the case of the series before 1947 when *Current Law Cases* start, namely *The Law Reports*, *Lloyd's Law Reports* and the *English Reports*.

Legal Journals Index

5.82 Though not ostensibly a case-finding tool, as was described in chapter 2, it is useful for leading to cases, since those that have been commented on or reported in the journals are specifically indexed. If you are using *Current Law Cases* on CLI anyway it is not much bother to have a quick look at LJI while you are at it. Where a journal article comments on an unreported case it is particularly useful because (a) you would not have necessarily found the case using just *Current Law Cases* and (b) if it has been worth commenting on it may be of use despite being unreported (and may not have been easily found through the masses of transcripts on the various transcript services).

EC case law finding aids

5.83 The main printed source is *Butterworths EC Case Citator and Service*. It is issued in cumulative form twice a year, with a fortnightly news-sheet, and a telephone inquiry service. Despite its title, the one thing it does not do is tell you whether a particular case has been cited in a later case. But it does a number of other useful things. First is a numerical listing of all ECJ cases, with name and reference in the ECR, CMLR and All ER (EC). That is followed by an alphabetical listing by case name, giving the same information. Then, for the subject approach, the cases are given according to the legislation considered, by Treaty Article number, regulation number and directive number. There is a list by colloquial name, such as 'The Sugars Case'. Lastly, there is a listing by 'key phrase' or 'sector', which includes both broad headings such as 'copyright' and names of conventions such as the Brussels Convention. The ECJ itself issues in hard copy an annual index arranged numerically and alphabetically, with reference to the ECRs (but not other series). The only advantage over the Butterworths product is that it includes cases that have been registered, so have a number, but are still pending.

5.84 There are a number of other printed sources, but they are all now very out of date. There was the *Gazetteer of European Law*, which covered the contents of the CMLR up to 1983 by name, number and subject. A separate section called 'Case search' was in effect a citator. It was updated for a brief period from 1989 as a monthly and annual publication called *Case Search*. There was an official digest to EC law, *Digest of Case Law Relating to the European Communities*, in looseleaf form, but it did not cover cases beyond 1985. The T.M.C. Asser Institute published a *Guide to EC Decisions*, but that does not go beyond 1988.

5.85 Although the printed sources are useful for quick reference, not surprisingly, most research is going to mean using electronic sources, which have already been fairly fully described above (para **5.38**). A purely personal preference is to use the Justis on CD-ROM, then do an update on the court's website. One tip when using the cases on the Justis version of Celex is to select only the cases (not the legislation, treaties, etc as well). Otherwise you do not get the full functionality of the form search – you can only do a free text search, since the field structure of cases differs from the other sectors.

European human rights case law finding aids

5.86 The court's website and other electronic sources are described at paras **5.50** and **5.54**. Of printed sources, *Current Law* and *The Digest*, vol 26(2) cover European human rights cases to some limited extent, digesting cases from EHRR and newspaper law reports. Emanating from the Council of Europe, but not having official status, is the *Digest of Strasbourg Case-law Relating to the European Convention on Human Rights*. This collates all the case law, from both court and Commission, by Convention article number and has various alphabetical and numerical tables. The original five bound volumes covered 1955–82. There are looseleaf updates but at the time of writing they are still very behind – for most parts of the work, judgments and reports to the end of 1992, and decisions to the end of 1991. More up-to-date, but covering only court judgments, is Peter Kempees *A Systematic Guide to the Case Law of the European Court of Human Rights* (Nijhoff) in four volumes so far, covering cases up to 1998. It is again arranged by article number and provides key extracts. There was an earlier digest of court judgments, Vincent Berger *Case Law of the European Court of Human Rights 1960–1993* ((3 vols, 1989–95) Round Hall Press). This summarises each case in chronological order. A useful bibliography is given at the end of each case's entry, as well as there being a general bibliography at the end. It has indexes by subject and Convention article number. Two one-volume works aimed at the English lawyer trying to get to grips with the Human Rights Act are Keir Starmer *Blackstone's Human Rights Digest* (with accompanying CD-ROM) and Barbara Mensah *European Human Rights Case Locator 1960–2000* (Cavendish). The work by Starmer, who is also the author of a popular book on the Act, is the more substantial, and covers human rights case law of relevance from other jurisdictions. There are cumulative indexes covering vols 1–20, 21–40, 41–60 and 76–83 of the Commission's *Decisions and Reports*, which comprise indexes by subject, by state subdivided by application number, by application number and by Convention article number. The *Collection of Decisions* also had cumulative indexes for vols 1–30 and 32–43. The 1998 edition of the *Yearbook* has a handy supplementary volume, 41A, containing key extracts from a selection of court judgments and Commission decisions and reports during the whole history of the court.

Finding cases by name

5.87 A very common problem is that you can remember the name of case but not its citation. Or it may be that you have one citation but want to find out whether it is reported in another series of reports, either because the volume is not on the shelf (stolen from the library, on the senior partner's desk) or because it might be more fully reported elsewhere. Or it may just be that the citation you have proves to be inaccurate.

Variety and forms of case name

5.88 Although most cases are named in the form of *Smith v Jones*, it is worth being familiar with the other common and uncommon forms of case name for two reasons. First, it helps if you know under which element the name is entered in tables and indexes (though this is usually fairly apparent). Secondly, and more importantly, it can throw light on the subject and date of the case if you do not already know them. As discussed below, this is often useful in choosing the best place to start your search.

The following are examples of different forms of case name, with the usual entry element in bold.

5.89

***Donoghue** v Stevenson*

The usual form in civil cases, ie Plaintiff (or, as now called, Claimant) v Defendant (Pursuer v Defender in Scottish cases), or Appellant v Respondent. Names of firms looking like personal names can sometimes cause confusion: '**John** Fox v Bannister King' in *Current Law*, but '**Fox** (John) (a firm) v Bannister King' in the *All England Law Reports* index.

Cross-references from the names of defendants, if that is all you know, are only given in a minority of sources, which include *All England Law Reports* indexes.

5.90

R v Hunt

The usual form in criminal cases. There are two small pitfalls. In most modern tables of cases, this form of name comes at the beginning of the letter R, but in some older tables it is listed as 'Rex' or 'Reg', filing after cases beginning 'Ra'. Secondly, although 'R' is the filing element in most general sources, specialist criminal law works often use just the name of the defendant.

The new student or inexperienced librarian on hearing the name of the case in formal parlance, 'The Crown against Hunt', is advised not look it up under 'C'.

5.91

R v Secretary of State for the Home Department, ex parte Hosenball

The usual form of name for cases in the Divisional Court of the Queen's Bench Division by way of judicial review (as here) or by way of case stated from magistrates' or Crown Courts (in which case the name of the court will be given as defendant). The name given 'ex parte' is that of the applicant, and as these cases are often known by that name, some indexes provide cross-references from it.

The names of ministers can sometimes cause problems. In this case the name, quite reasonably, might be cited verbally or in print as 'R v Home Secretary', though that is not its official name. Since the practice directions under the Civil Procedure Rules relating to judicial review came into force, and with the abandonment of Latin expressions such as 'ex parte', the same case would now be cited as:

R (on the application of Hosenball) v Secretary of State for the Home Department

That form has indeed sprung up in various law reports. The Incorporated Council of Law Reporting, however, have intimated that they will rather more sensibly use the form:

R (Hosenball) v Secretary of State for the Home Department

5.92

Ex parte Rees

This form of name is usually where the report is on a point raised only at a hearing of one party in the absence of the other party, and the case does not proceed to trial between the parties, typically nowadays cases on application for leave to apply for judicial review. Although the name of the applicant is always used as the entry element, there is always the possibility of editorial error, as in the 1990 *Current Law* which has two cases under '**Ex** parte'.

5.93

Attorney-General, ex relator Tilley v Wandsworth Borough Council

The form of name in a relator action (a form of obtaining relief in public law matters through the Attorney-General, used before the introduction of the current form of judicial review in 1977, though not formally abolished). A case in this form is likely to be on administrative law before 1977.

5.94

Attorney-General's Reference (No 34 of 1992) (Oxford)

An Attorney-General's Reference is made to the Court of Appeal (Criminal Division) either where the prosecution wish to appeal an unduly lenient sentence or where the defendant was acquitted and the Crown wish to have the point of law on which he was acquitted clarified for the future. The number will be the primary element distinguishing one such reference from another. However, in the case of sentencing references, which are much more numerous than references on points of law, it is the general practice of the *Criminal Appeal Reports* and other sources to add the name of the defendant for ease of identification and recognition, as in the example. References on points of law do not generally carry the name of the defendant (who was acquitted), so one has to make do with the number alone.

5.95

Re Taylor

This form of name crops up most commonly, though by no means exclusively, in the area of wills and probate, where the name of the case is that of the deceased because the executors or administrators who have brought the case before the court are not parties as such. Likewise the three examples below.

In the goods of Parker
Re Potter's Will Trusts
In the estate of Potticary

5.96

Re a Company No 0003843 of 1986

There is no basic difficulty with such company law cases, other than the fact that they are a strain on the eye when perusing tables of cases (and a strain on the memory if one does not have a pencil immediately to hand).

5.97

Re S (A minor) (Care Proceedings: Wardship Summons)

In family cases, for reasons of confidentiality, the full name is often not given. The modern practice is to give the subject matter of the case in parentheses to help distinguish cases, but it can be an uphill struggle if one does not know the qualifying terms with precision. In older cases where they are not provided, one can only rely on a date to differentiate.

5.98

Practice Direction (Commercial Court: Urgent Matters)

These are not case reports as such, but are published in the law reports. As they are very numerous, the same problem of knowing the precise form of name arises. Although this species of report is most commonly in the form of 'Directions', to lure the unwary there are also 'Practice *Notes*', 'Practice *Statements*', and from the House of Lords '*Procedure* Directions'.

5.99

The Goring

This is the name of a ship, which is often the preferred form of name of shipping cases. Most indexes provide cross-references from the case in 'Claimant v Defendant' form to the name of the ship (or from the ship to the claimant if that is the entry point editorially preferred).

5.100

Bayer AG v Winter (No 2)

A case may be reported when the court decides a preliminary issue or interlocutory matter. If the same case is also subsequently reported on another point – the issue at trial or another interlocutory matter – then it will bear the same name but a number is added, as here, to distinguish the two. Numbers are not used to distinguish a case reported at first instance from the same case reported on appeal – if necessary, the abbreviation for the court, for example, QBD, CA or HL, is added after the name. Matters get complicated when separate interlocutory points and the substantive case each get appealed, possibly up to the House of Lords, in turn. The Spycatcher case and the International Tin Council litigation were notorious examples – tracing all the different reported points and stages in tables of cases will induce a headache.

Social Security Commissioners' Decisions

5.101 Decisions of the Social Security and Child Support Commissioners do not generally have a name, only a number. That the mysterious numerical reference you have in front of you is indeed a Social Security Commissioners Decision will usually be apparent from the context. But they are recognisable. There are three different classes of decision, with a different system of numbering – unreported, starred and reported decisions. All cases as soon as they are lodged are given a file number. The file number begins for all cases with 'C', and is then followed by an abbreviation for the particular benefit in question – CS for Child Support, IS for Income Support, M for Mobility Allowance and so on. There follows the number for the particular case and its year. Thus:

CCS/16904/1997
CIS/3749/1998
CM/936/1995

5.102 The social security legislation applies in Scotland as well as in England and Wales, and Commissioners sit in Edinburgh as well as in London. Northern Ireland has separate legislation, but as it is very similar the decisions of the Northern Ireland Commissioners are of relevance. If the case is Scottish, an 'S' appears after the C:

CSIS/701/1997

5.103 Copies of all individual decisions are available from the Commissioners, and some are available on the Internet (see para **5.24**), but if a case is not more widely promulgated by the following two methods, then the case is said to be 'unreported' and the file number is the means of citation.

5.104 Certain cases of greater importance that warrant circulation among the Commissioners themselves are 'starred'. About 100 decisions each year are starred. There is a separate series of starred numbers for each year, the year being the year it was selected for starring rather than the year of the decision (or the year of the file number). There is one sequence for all the different benefits, with the exception of Child Support, which had its own sequence until the end of 1998, distinguished by the letter 'C'. Also from 1999 starred decisions from the Northern Ireland Commissioners are included in the same sequence. Thus:

*15/01 – the fifteenth starred decision of 2001
*C3/96 – the third starred decision on child support of 1996

However, the general practice seems to be in tables of cases in the major social security works to stick with the case file number as the primary means of citation, even for starred cases. None the less, the inclusion of the starred number in the citation is helpful (a) to be make clear that it is indeed a starred decision, and (b) for ease of getting a copy off the Internet, where on the Court Service website they are listed by starred number. Such a citation would thus be:

CFC/2298/1995 (*40/97)

5.105 A smaller number of cases, which will usually have been starred cases, are then selected by the Chief Commissioner for full reporting and publication in *Reported Decisions of the Social Security and Child Support Commissioners.* These have a new number, prefixed by 'R' followed by the abbreviation for the benefit and a number of the decision for that benefit and a year. The year used to be the year it was selected; from 2000 it is the year it was published. Examples of three different reported decisions for 1999 would be thus:

R(DLA) 3/99
R(I) 3/99
R(IS) 3/99

The reported decisions include not only cases heard by the Commissioners but also cases heard on appeal from the Commissioners by the Court of Appeal (or on further appeal by the House of Lords) and cases from the EC J on reference for a preliminary ruling from the Commissioners (which are not uncommon). In the Court of Appeal and ECJ, such cases will have conventional case names, such as *O'Connor v Chief Adjudication Officer* or *Chief Adjudication Officer v Clarke and Faul*, and indeed if such cases are reported in the ordinary law reports, which they may be, then that is how they will be known. However, in the *Selected Decisions* the primary form of reference remains the number, for example, R(IS) 7/99 for *O'Connor v Chief Adjudication Officer*.

5.106 A list of the abbreviations for the various benefits appears in the *Selected Decisions*. There is also a useful note on citation of Commissioners' decisions in the standard work, *Ogus, Barendt & Wikely's The Law of Social Security* (Butterworths). It includes the practice for old pre-1951 cases, which differs from that described above. *Ogus, Barendt & Wikely* when citing cases heard by a tribunal of three Commissioners convened by the Commissioner to hear cases of special difficulty, add the suffix 'T' to the number.

5.107 Northern Ireland Commissioners' decisions are promulgated in a similar fashion. The reported decisions were hitherto in a separate series, but it is planned that in future they will be included in the bound volumes of English and Scottish decisions. The numbering of both unreported and reported decisions also follows a similar format, except that the abbreviation for the benefit comes after the number, not before it. There are also slight variations in the abbreviations of the benefits, and for recent decisions the style of file number references. For the avoidance of doubt it is helpful to prefix Northern Ireland cases with 'NI'. Thus:

NI C 069/97 (DLA)
NI C 001/99 (WB)
NI C 031/00-01 (IB)
NI R 001/92 (II)
NI R 002/00 (IB)

Decisions of the Commons Commissioners

5.108 If you come across a citation in the form 215/D/232 or 19/U/17, ie a two- or three-digit number followed by either 'D' or 'U', followed by a running number, you have a decision of the Commons Commissioners under the Commons Registration Act 1965, dating from 1965 to about 1990. These decisions remain important to conveyancers and others on rights to common land and village greens. The first number is a code for the county, which is a two-digit code before 1974, and then after the local government reorganisation of 1974, a three-digit number. 'D' is for Dispute and 'U' for Unclaimed Land. They were distributed in mimeographed typescript form, and are held by some law libraries, but are not indexed. The Commons Commissioners themselves have a bound volume set with place indexes which is open to public inspection. There is no general subject approach, but the main text on the subject, Michael Gadsen *The Law of Commons* ((1988) Sweet & Maxwell) cites many. The author compiled his own collection of decisions, which is deposited at the Arts and Science Library, University College Cardiff. See generally, Alec Samuels 'Decisions of the Commons Commissioners' [1997] *Conveyancer* 248–250. The offices of the Commissioners have moved (more than one once) since the article was written.

European Court of Justice cases

5.109 The names of ECJ cases can cause problems, which is why it is helpful to have the official ECJ case number as well, and in some sources cases are listed by number rather than name. But if name is what you have got, bear in mind the following. Where the case is solely a reference for a preliminary ruling under art 234 (ex art 177) from a national court of a member state, then the name is usually that of the case as it was in the national court. For references to the ECJ from the English courts, it may thus be in any of the forms above; for references from other national courts a wide of variety of often impenetrable-looking names will arise. In cases where the applicants or defendants are member states and the Commission of the European Communities, tables of cases vary as to the entry element and the form of the name of member states. There may be the following permutations, with the form used in the ECR themselves given first:

> **Commission** or **Commission** of the European Communities or **EC** Commission
>   or **European** Commission
> **Austria** or **Austrian** Republic
> **Belgium** or **Kingdom** of Belgium
> **Denmark** or **Kingdom** of Denmark
> **Finland** or **Finnish Republic**
> **France** or **French** Republic
> **Germany** or **Federal** Republic of Germany
> **Greece** or **Hellenic** Republic
> **Ireland** or **Republic** of Ireland
> **Italy** or **Italian** Republic
> **Luxembourg** or **Grand** Duchy of Luxembourg
> **Netherlands** or **Kingdom** of the Netherlands
> **Portugal** or **Portuguese** Republic
> **Spain** or **Kingdom** of Spain
> **Sweden** or **Kingdom** of Sweden
> **United** Kingdom or **UK** or **Great** Britain

Often, in addition to the parties, a popular name or name of the subject-matter is used, especially for cases between the Commission and member states where there are numerous examples under the same parties, for example:

> Re **Low-fat** cheese: EC Commission v Italy (C-210/89)

Or the subject matter may added after the name of the parties:

> **EC** Commission v United Kingdom: Re Tachographs

If you yourself are citing an ECJ case, as noted above (para **5.63**) you should use the form of name as it appears on the running head of the report in the ECR.

European human rights cases

5.110 As with ECJ cases, the form of country name is sometimes a problem, especially with admissibility decisions, which if given by name rather than number, often take the form of *X v Netherlands*. In one of the reputable new books on the Human Rights Act, the table of cases has a long list of cases under *X v Federal Republic of Germany*, followed by cases under *X v France*, followed by another long list under *X v Germany*. The application number is now a prescribed part of the citation of all cases from the court (see para **5.64**). In the past it tended only to be used with Commission cases, in particular admissibility decisions. Treatment in tables of cases varies. Some only have a list by name (without or without the number as well). Some have alphabetical tables for court cases, and numerical tables for Commission cases. Some have separate alphabetical tables containing both court and Commission cases, and a separate numerical table for Commission cases. Some have separate alphabetical tables for court and Commission cases, and a numerical table for Commission cases as well. *Lester and Pannick* has just one alphabetical table of cases, in which Commission cases as well as court cases appear under their name, but, cunningly, for Commission cases, it also has a numerical list in the alphabetical list by listing them under 'Application . . .'.

Choosing a starting point and following through

5.111 The best place to start looking for a case by name depends largely on how recent a case you think it is. If you know that, it can be an added advantage to know what it is about (which you usually will), because an obvious shortcut for cases that are not too recent is to look in the table of cases in a standard work: if you have a procedural point look in *The White Book*, if you have a landlord and tenant point look in *Woodfall*. Knowing the subject matter is also, of course, indispensable if you find there is more than one case with the same name. The form of name alone, as given in the examples above, can sometimes tell you immediately that you are dealing with say a shipping case or a family case. The names of the parties themselves can also help: an insurance company is likely to be involved in an insurance case, a construction company in a building case. The names may also be an early warning signal that you are not dealing with an English case at all. For example, a company name followed by 'Pty Ltd' points to an Australian case.

5.112 Assuming you have not been able to take advantage of the shortcut of looking in a textbook, the best way to illustrate a more systematic approach is to take the commonest eventuality: an English case reported in the last few years rather than the last few days. Undoubtedly the best starting point is the *Current Law Case Citator*, either in hard copy or on the screen. As well as all cases reported from 1947, you will pick up a pre-1947 case if it happens to have been cited since. If you are using the printed version, you will need to check the two bound volumes, the paperback supplements, and the cumulative table in the latest monthly digest. If you are using the electronic version, you might as well at this point also check the *Legal Journals Index* while you are at it, as explained above (para **5.82**). Otherwise, consider doing so at a later stage if you have not found the case. *The Digest* or its electronic equivalent *Case Search* is probably the next place to look. In hard copy it is slightly less satisfactory than *Current Law* as a starting point since it is a three-step process to arrive at the citation itself. On the other hand, *The Digest* provides much greater historical coverage and the initial search is limited to just two places, the consolidated table of cases and the table of cases in the cumulative supplement. If reasonably certain that the case is pre-1865, rather than looking in *The Digest* it is usually rather simpler and quicker to look in the table of cases to the *English Reports* (the reprint of the nominates).

5.113 *The Law Reports Index* is best spurned for this type of problem, unless it happens to be readily at hand and you are confident that you have a mainstream case. (The only cases to be found in *The Law Reports Index* that are not generally indexed in *Current Law* are the dismissals by the Appeal Committee of leave to appeal to the House of Lords, which are noted in the *Weekly Law Reports* – but all these contain is one line dismissing the petition.)

5.114 If you have not found the case in *Current Law* or *The Digest*, the likelihood is that the case is very recent or unreported. Then it is a question of working your way through those commercial services that you have access to: Lexis, All England Direct, Lawtel, Westlaw UK and Smith Bernal (see paras **5.25–5.29**). If you do not have access to any of these you can try your luck with the free sites (paras **5.23–5.24**). If by this stage you have still not found the case, you ought to be suspicious. Consider whether the spelling of the names could be wrong, whether the parties have been given the wrong way round, whether it is not an English case at all, or whether it might be an unreported case outside the scope of the electronic services. A double-check in *Halsbury's Laws* might be a precaution at this point. Look in the consolidated table of cases and the tables of cases in the cumulative supplement and current service. If you think it is not English, look at some of the sources suggested in chapter 8. If it might be an older unreported case, bear in mind the Court of Appeal transcripts in the *Current Law Yearbooks* from 1973–89 – these do *not* appear in *Current Law Case Citator* or in the electronic *Current Law Cases*. You would have to look through each *Yearbook*, where there is a separate table of transcripts – again they are not in the main table of cases for the volume. The other possibility, which will usually be apparent from the context, is that it is an old case that has somehow slipped the net of *The Digest*. Double-check in the table of cases to the *English Reports* and look in the tables of cases to superseded editions of *The Digest* (if they are available).

If you are sure that a case exists with a name *something* like the name you have, but you have failed completely to find it by name, the only course is do a subject search and hope you recognise it when you see it.

Using the printed version of the *Current Law Case Citator*

5.115 The illustration (see figure 5.4) shows a page from the 1977–97 volume. There is also a volume covering 1947–76, the paperback supplements since the last bound volume and the monthly digests.

A This case is one reported (and digested by *Current Law*) during the coverage period of the volume. Full citations to the reports are given, in this case to the *Weekly Law Reports*, *Solicitors Journal* and *All England Law Reports*.

References at the right-hand margin are also given to the paragraph numbers in the *Current Law* yearbooks where the case is digested and where it has been considered in later cases.

B This case has been *cited* during the coverage period. The full references are given to the original report. As it pre-dates *Current Law*, there is no reference to where it is digested.

C This is a House of Lords case which has also been reported both in the Court of Appeal and at first instance in the Queen's Bench Division. The references for alternative reports for the House of Lords are given first – HL comes after them before the semi-colon. The House of Lords affirmed the decision in the Court of Appeal, and again CA comes after the references and before the next semi-colon. The Court of Appeal had also affirmed the decision at first instance, references for which come last.

Figure 5.4 Current Law: *case citator.*

CASE CITATOR 1977–97   **PEA**

Peacock Homes v. Secretary of State for the Environment (1984) 48 P. & C.R. 20;
[1984] F.S.R. 729; 83 L.G.R. 686, CA . . . .   *Digested,* 84/**3431**

Peak v. Burley Golf Club; Harding v. Bramshaw Golf Club Ltd [1960] 1 W.L.R. 568;
[1960] 2 All E.R. 199; 53 R. & I.T. 277; 58 L.G.R. 191; 6 R.R.C. 73; 124 J.P. 296;
104 S.J.L.B. 426, CA; reversing 172 E.G. 849; 51 R. & I.T. 821; 4 R.R.C. 139;
[1959] J.P.L. 64, Lands Tr . . . .   *Digested,* 60/**2685**:
Applied, 80/2235: *Considered,* 88/2997

Peak v. Midland Commercial Services (Unreported, November 22, 1977), CC
(Banbury) . . . .   *Digested,* 77/**307**

Peak v. Stacey 195 E.G. 775; [1965] R.A. 363; [1965] R.V.R. 559; 11 R.R.C. 251;
[1965] J.P.L. 681, Lands Tr. . . . .   *Digested,* 65/**3325**:
Considered, 92/3680

Peak Construction (Liverpool) Ltd v. McKinney Foundations Ltd 69 L.G.R. 1; 1 B.L.R.
111, CA . . . .   *Digested,* 71/**999**:
Applied, 86/233: *Referred to,* 84/228

Peak Park Joint Planning Board v. East Midlands Electricity Plc (1997) 12 P.A.D. 525

Peak Park Joint Planning Board v. Secretary of State for the Environment [1991] 1 P.L.R.
98; [1991] J.P.L. 744 . . . .   *Digested,* 92/**4342**

Peak Park Joint Planning Board v. Secretary of State for the Environment and ICI (1980)
39 P. & C.R. 361; [1980] J.P.L. 114 . . . .   *Digested,* 80/**2678**:
Not followed, 80/2643

Peake v. Automotive Products Ltd; *sub nom* Automotive Products Ltd v. Peake [1978]
Q.B. 233; [1977] 3 W.L.R. 853; [1978] 1 All E.R. 106; [1977] I.C.R. 968; [1977]
I.R.L.R. 365; (1977) 12 I.T.R. 428; 121 S.J. 644, CA; reversing [1977] Q.B. 780;
[1977] 2 W.L.R. 751; [1977] I.C.R. 480; (1977) 12 I.T.R. 259; [1977] I.T.L.R. 105;
121 S.J. 222, EAT . . . .   *Digested,* 77/**1077**:
Applied, 78/1032: *Distinguished,* 79/944: *Disapproved,* 79/941:
Doubted, 80/967: *Considered,* 81/912

Peake v. Bradley CCRTF 95/1040/G, CA. . . . .   *Digested,* 96/**713**

Peake & Hall, Re [1985] P.C.C. 87, HC (IoM)   *Digested,* 85/**295**

A   Peal Furniture Co v. Adrian Share (Interiors) [1977] 1 W.L.R. 464; [1977] 2 All E.R. 211;
121 S.J. 156, CA . . . .   *Digested,* 77/**2382**:
Not followed, 84/186: *Disapproved,* 85/2704

Peara v. Enderlin [1979] I.C.R. 804, EAT . . . .   *Digested,* 79/**972**

Pearce v. Abraham Shaw & Co (Unreported, August 8, 1995), CC (Halifax) [*Ex rel.*
Allan Western, Solicitor] . . . .   *Digested,* 95/**1784**

Pearce v. Bastable [1901] 2 Ch. 122. . . . .   *Applied,* 84/3631

Pearce v. Chief Adjudication Officer, *Times,* May 10, 1990, CA. . . . .   *Digested,* 90/**4193a**

Pearce v. Croydon Justices (1977) 242 E.G. 207, DC . . . .   *Digested,* 78/**2459**

Pearce v. Diensthuber (1978) 81 D.L.R. 286, CA (Ont) . . . .   *Digested,* 78/**1593**

B   Pearce v. Foster (1885) 15 Q.B.D. 114 . . . .   *Followed,* 85/**1512**

Pearce v. Hampshire CC (Unreported, June 13, 1991), CC (Southampton) . . . .   *Digested,* 91/**1454**

Pearce v. Newham Cooperative Development Agency (Unreported, June 15, 1989),
CC (Bow) . . . .   *Digested,* 89/**1223**

Pearce v. Ove Arup Partnership Ltd [1997] Ch. 293; [1997] 2 W.L.R. 779; [1997] 3 All
E.R. 31; [1997] F.S.R. 641; (1997) 20(8) I.P.D. 20081; (1997) 94(15) L.S.G. 27;
(1997) 141 S.J.L.B. 73; *Times,* March 17, 1997, Ch D . . . .   *Digested,* 97/**901**:
Followed, 97/1046

Pearce v. Pearce (1979) 10 Fam. Law 209, CA. . . . .   *Digested,* 81/**712**:
Considered, 86/1089, 87/1727, 90/2294

C   Pearce v. Secretary of State for Defence [1988] A.C. 755; [1988] 2 W.L.R. 1027;
[1988] 2 All E.R. 348; 132 S.J. 699, HL; affirming [1988] 2 W.L.R. 144; (1988)
85 (7) L.S.G. 40; (1987) 137 N.L.J. 933; 132 S.J. 127, CA; affirming [1987] 2
W.L.R. 782; (1987) 131 S.J. 362; (1987) 137 N.L.J. 80; (1987) 84 L.S.G. 1334,
QBD . . . .   *Digested,* 88/**2417**

Pearce v. University of Aston in Birmingham (No.1) [1991] 2 All E.R. 461, CA . . . . . .   *Digested,* 91/**1578**

Pearce v. Woodall-Duckham [1978] 1 W.L.R. 832; [1978] 2 All E.R. 793; [1978] S.T.C.
372; 51 T.C. 271; [1978] T.R. 87; 122 S.J. 299, CA; reversing [1977] 1 W.L.R.
224; [1977] 1 All E.R. 753; [1977] S.T.C. 82; [1976] T.R. 303, Ch D . . . .   *Digested,* 78/**356**

Pearce Duff & Co Ltd, Re [1960] 1 W.L.R. 1014; [1960] 3 All E.R. 222, Ch D . . . .   *Digested,* 60/**428**:
Applied, 86/287

Pearl Assurance v. Shaw [1985] 1 E.G.L.R. 92; (1984) 274 E.G. 490 . . . .   *Digested,* 85/**1922**:
Considered, 88/2069, 91/203: *Referred to,* 90/2791

Pearl Carriers Inc v. Japan Line Ltd (The Chemical Venture) [1993] 1 Lloyd's Rep. 508 . .   *Digested,* 93/**3596**

Pearl Maintenance Services Ltd, Re [1995] 1 B.C.L.C. 449; [1995] B.C.C. 657, Ch D . .   *Digested,* 95/**2817**

Pearl Marin Shipping A/B v. Pietro Cingolani SAS see Pietro Cingolani SAS v. Pearl
Marin Shipping A/B (The General Valdes)

Pearl Mill Co v. Ivy Tannery Co [1919] 1 K.B. 79, KBD . . . .   *Applied,* 81/106

Pearlberg v. Varty (Inspector of Taxes) [1972] 1 W.L.R. 534; [1972] 2 All E.R. 6; [1972]
T.R. 5; 48 T.C. 14; 116 S.J.L.B. 335, HL; affirming [1971] 1 W.L.R. 728; [1971] 2
All E.R. 552; [1971] T.R. 5; 50 A.T.C. 4; 115 S.J.L.B. 388, CA; affirming [1970]
T.R. 25; 49 A.T.C. 30 . . . .   *Digested,* 72/**1701**:
Applied, 77/3

5.116 If you have not found the case in all the volumes of the *Case Citators*, you need next to check the cumulative table of cases in the latest monthly digest (and the previous December's issue, if you are in the early part of the year) in case it is very recent: see figure 5.5.

A This case is printed in capitals in the table of cases, indicating a case digested during the year rather than simply cited. A case reference is given together with the monthly issue and paragraph number where a digest of the case will found. Note that this case reference is simply to the *first* report of the case to be picked up by *Current Law* and the basis of the digest entry, in this case in *The Times*. Subsequent reports of the same case, which may be fuller, will only be found on the electronic version of the *Case Citator* or the electronic version of the digest on *Current Law Cases*, and indeed this particular case was already reported in the WLR and elsewhere. Any additional references will only appear in printed form, when the next annual supplement to the *Case Citator* itself is produced.

B The name for case B is printed in lower case, and so is a case cited rather than reported during the year. A case reference and the paragraph number of the *Current Law Yearbook* where it was originally digested are given. Again, only one case reference is given, though it is to the first report listed in the *citator* – not the first report of the case that appeared and was used in the digest. Since the citator lists cases in order of authority, with *Law Reports* or WLR references coming first, this single reference will usually be sufficient. But if you wanted alternative case references – this case also appears in the All ER – refer to the relevant volume of the printed *Case Citator*. The paragraph number of the relevant monthly part where the case is cited is given. Look in the body of the entry where it will say that the case was considered, followed, disapproved, etc.

Using *The Digest*

5.117 The consolidated table of cases will contain all the cases except those in the cumulative supplement: see figure 5.6. The consolidated table does not give you the case reference itself, but the volume of the main work where it will be found – in example **A** in vol 11. It also gives the title of the main topic that it is under in the main work. Example **A** is in the title Conflicts of Law, and example **B** is in Bills of Exchange. Each volume of the main work only has one table of cases even if it contains more than one title, so that it is not strictly necessary to know the title. But it is helpful, if you are looking for a known case with a common name, to know that you have picked out the right one. The abbreviations for the subject titles are reasonably self-evident, but there is a list at the beginning of the consolidated index. It also helpfully tells you whether the case is a Commonwealth case, as in example **B**, which is from New Zealand. Again, if you have a case with a common name that you know is English, this feature will help you to avoid a wild goose chase. Then it is simply a matter or turning to the table of cases in the volume given and looking it up again. The relevant paragraph number is given. If you have a Commonwealth case, you will find them intermingled in the same sequence of paragraph numbers – they just appear in slightly smaller print.

The cumulative supplement is arranged according to the volume numbering of the main work. From the table of cases go to the section covering the volume given (see figure 5.7). The paragraph numbers in each section are followed by the letter a, b, etc to distinguish them from the equivalent paragraph numbers in the main work. At the paragraph in the supplement the case with its reference is digested.

Figure 5.5 Current Law: *cumulative table of cases in monthly digests.*

374. Motor insurance – policy wordings – validity following disposal of vehicle – replacement vehicle

D appealed against an order that, upon the true construction of a motor insurance policy issued by ES and despite the sale of D's car during the currency of the policy period, D remained insured to drive any car belonging to third parties with their consent. D brought an action against his insurance brokers, PD, on the basis that they had negligently advised him that his insurance cover remained valid notwithstanding the fact that he had disposed of his vehicle. D contended that his cover under the policy depended upon his retaining either the insured car or a replacement for it. PD contended that (1) no general principle applied and the issue depended on the construction of the particular policy, and (2) "replacement" of the insured car was to be interpreted as meaning the purchase of another car at any time during the policy period, not necessarily immediately after disposal of the old one.

Held, dismissing the appeal, that the central issue was whether cover was conditional upon D's continuing ownership of his own car, the case turning upon the terms of the particular policy. D's submission that the policy had lapsed due to his failure to replace the car was unfounded, as ES had to be taken to have accepted the possibility of a replacement not being obtained at the moment of disposal of the old car and to have agreed nevertheless to provide cover on a continuous basis, given that this was undoubtedly a common situation. The presence of a clause concerning replacement vehicles was highly relevant to the policy in question, *Boss v. Kingston* [1963] 1 W.L.R. 99, [1963] C.L.Y. 3074 distinguished. It was more important to emphasise that insured persons were entitled to clearly worded policies and to the benefit of any ambiguity than to artificially construe the wording of the particular policy.

DODSON v. PETER H DODSON INSURANCE SERVICES, *The Times*, January 24, 2001, Mance, L.J., CA.

CUMULATIVE TABLE OF CASES

A

DISCAIN PROJECT SERVICES LTD v. OPECPRIME DEVELOPMENT LTD   [2000] B.L.R. 402 **Feb 98**
DISLEY v. LEVINE (T/A AIRTRAK LEVINE PARAGLIDING)   [2001] P.I.Q.R. P10 . . . . **May 599**
Ditta Estasis Salotti di Colzani Aimo e Gianmario Colzani v. Ruwa Polstereimaschinen GmbH (C24/
   76)   [1976] E.C.R.1831, [1977] C.L.Y.1242 . . . . **Jan 88**
DOBSON v. STANBRA   [*Ex rel*] . . . . **May 59**
DOCHERTY v. EDINBURGH CITY COUNCIL, 2001 S.L.T. 291 . . . . **Jun 710**
DODSON v. PETER H DODSON INSURANCE SERVICES   *The Times*, January 24, 2001 . . . . **Feb 374**
DOHERTY v. JAYMARKE DEVELOPMENTS (PROSPECTHILL) LTD (NO.1), 2001 S.L.T. (Sh Ct) 6 . . . . .
    . . . . **Apr 759**
DOMANSA v. DERIN SHIPPING & TRADING CO INC (THE SLETREAL), [2001] 1 Lloyd's Rep. 362 . . .
    . . . . **Apr 109**
DONNELLY (BRIAN) v. HM ADVOCATE, 2000 S.C.C.R. 861 . . . . **Apr 777**
Donoghue v. Stevenson   [1932] A.C. 562 . . . . **Mar 560**

B

Donovan v. Gwentoys Ltd   [1990] 1 W.L.R. 472, [1990] C.L.Y. 2960 . . . . **Jun 61**
Doorson v. Netherlands   (1996) 22 E.H.R.R. 330, [1996] C.L.Y. 3124 . . . . **Apr 764**

61. Limitations – personal injuries – discretion to disapply limitation period – effect of solicitors' default

[Limitation Act 1980 s.33; Civil Procedure Rules 1998 (SI 1998 3132).]

S, who had issued proceedings in his personal injury claim against PM seven weeks after the limitation period had expired, appealed against a decision upholding the refusal of the district judge to disapply the limitation period pursuant to the Limitation Act 1980 s.33.

Held, allowing the appeal, that the district judge had erred in (1) attributing the failure of S's solicitors to issue proceedings in time to S himself, *Thompson v. Brown Construction Ltd (t/a George Albert Brown (Builders) & Co)* [1981] 1 W.L.R. 744, [1981] C.L.Y.1618, *Das v. Ganju* [1999] P.I.Q.R. P260, [1999] C.L.Y. 470 and *Corbin v. Penfold Metallising Co Ltd* [2000] Lloyd's Rep. Med. 247, [2000] 6 C.L. 91 considered; (2) construing "delay" under the s.33(3)(a) and s.33(3)(b) of the 1980 Act. Delay for the purpose of those provisions meant the delay that had occurred after the primary limitation period had expired, *Donovan v. Gwentoys Ltd* [1990] 1 W.L.R. 472, [1990] C.L.Y. 2960 considered; and (3) purporting to apply the principles of the Civil Procedure Rules 1998. The 1998 Rules concerned the conduct of the proceedings that had been issued, not the issue of proceedings itself. In the circumstances, it would be appropriate for the court to exercise its discretion afresh. Given that no blame could be attributed to S himself, that PM had been notified of the claim 12 months after S's accident and that it had not been prejudiced by any delay, it would be equitable to allow the action to proceed. Any injustice suffered by PM were the claim to proceed was outweighed by the injustice that S would suffer were he to be compelled to sue his solicitors for negligence.

STEEDS v. PEVEREL MANAGEMENT SERVICES LTD *The Times*, May 16, 2001, Sir Christopher Slade, CA.

Figure 5.6 The Digest: *consolidated table of cases volume.*

GUTHRIC   416

Guthric v Muntingh (1829) (S AF) **42 Ship**
Guthrie, Re, Trustees, Exors & Agency Co of New Zealand Ltd v Gutrie (1925) (NZ) **50 Wills**
Guthrie, Re (1924) (CAN) **50 Wills**
Guthrie, ex p (1822) **4(2) Bkpcy**
Guthrie, ex p (1824) **4(2) Bkpcy**
Guthrie v Abool Mozuffer (1871) **16 Courts**
Guthrie v Abul Mazaffar (1871) (IND) **12(1) Contr**
Guthrie v Armstrong (1822) **1(2) Agcy; 29 Insce**
Guthrie v Baker (AUS) **17 Damgs**
Guthrie v Canadian Pacific Ry Co (1900) (CAN) **38 Rys**
Guthrie v Clark (1886) (CAN) **40 S Land**
Guthrie v Cochrane (1846) (SCOT) **34 Mines**
Guthrie v Crossley (1826) **5(2) Bkpcy**
Guthrie v Fisk (1824) **4(1) Bkpcy; 45 Stats**
Guthrie v G & SW Ry Co (1858) (SCOT) **3 Arbn**
Guthrie v Lister (1866) **12(1) Contr**
Guthrie v McCrindle (1949) **31 L&T**
Guthrie v Ogilvie, Dykes, etc (1830) (SCOT) **1(2) Agcy; 44 Solrs**
Guthrie v Stewart (SCOT) **31 L&T**
Guthrie v Walrond (1883) **11 Confl; 23 Exors**
Guthrie v Walroud (1874) **23 Exors**
Guthrie v WF Huntting Lumber Co Ltd (1910) (CAN) **36(1) Negl**
Guthrie v Wilson (SCOT) **30 Intox**
Guthrie v Wood (1816) **25 Fraud Conv**
Guthrie, Craig, Peter & Co v Brechin Magistrates (1888) (SCOT) **38 Pub Hlth**
Guthrie, R v (1870) **14(2) Crim**
Guthrie, R v (1877) (CAN) **22(2) Evid**
Guthrie, R v (CAN) **19 Eccl**
Guthrie & Co, Re, ex p Bank of Australasia (1884) (NZ) **35 Mtge**
B Guthrie & Co, Re, ex p Bank of NZ (1884) (NZ) **6 B of Exch**
Guthrie & Co, Re (1884) (NZ) **36(2) Prtnrs**
Guthrie's Case (1898) (NZ) **9(1) Coys; 9(2) Coys**
Guthrie's Exor v Guthrie (1945) (SCOT) **50 Wills**
Guthrie's Trustees v Ireland (SCOT) **30 Intox**
Gutieres, In the Goods of (1869) **11 Confl**
Gutierres, Re (1879) **4(1) Bkpcy**
Gutierrez, ex p (1879) **4(1) Bkpcy**
Gutierrez, ex p (1880) **4(1) Bkpcy**
Gutkin v Winnipeg City (1933) (CAN) **28(4) Infts**
Gutman, R v (1904) (AUS) **25 Gaming**
Gutsch, Re (1959) (CAN) **28(3) Infts**
Gutsch, ex p (1959) (CAN) **8(2) Comwlth**
Gutsch, ex p (1960) (CAN) **8(2) Comwlth**
Gutschmidt, R v (1939) (CAN) **14(2) Crim**
Gutsell v Reeve (1935) **32 Limit of A**
Gutsole v Mathers (1836) **3 Auct; 32 Libel**
Gutta Pecha Corpn, Re (1900) **10(2) Coys**
Gutta Percha & India Rubber Co of Toronto's Appln, Re (1909) **47(2) Trade Mks**
Gutta Percha & Rubber (London) Ltd (no 789,574) Appln, Re (1935) **47(2) Trade Mks**
Gutta Percha Corpn Ltd, Re (1899) **9(1) Coys; 10(1) Coys**
Guttenberg v R (1905) (S AF) **15 Crim**
Guttenberg v R (1906) (S AF) **14(2) Crim**
Gutter v Locrofts (1592) **31 L&T**
Gutter v Tait (1947) **3 Bailmt**
Gutteridge v Munyard (1834) **31 L&T**
Gutteridge v Smith (1794) **6 B of Exch**
Gutteridge v Stilwell (1883) **23 Exors**
Gutteridge, R v (1851) **15 Crim**
Gutteridge (Doe d) v Sowerby (1860) **1(2) Agcy**

A Guttierez, In the Goods of (1869) **11 Confl**
Guttridge, R v (1840) 9 C & P 228 **14(2) Crim**
Guy, Re (1887) **5(2) Bkpcy**
Guy v Brady (1885) (CAN) **1(2) Agcy; 3 Barr**
Guy v Brown (1600) **11 Comns**
Guy v Brown (1601) **19 Easmt**
Guy v Churchill (1887) **44 Solrs**
Guy v Churchill (1888) **5(1) Bkpcy**
Guy v Churchill (1889) **1(2) Agcy**
Guy v Ferguon Syndicate Co Ltd (1892) (NZ) **9(1) Coys**
Guy v Goudreault (1864) (CAN) **12(1) Contr**
Guy v Gower (1816) **44 Solrs**
Guy v Grand Trunk Ry Co, Re (1884) (CAN) **13 Corpns**
Guy v Gregory (1840) **32 Libel**
Guy v Guy (1840) **28(4) Infts**
Guy v Guy (1910) (NZ) **37(1) Perps; 50 Wills**
Guy v Guy and Foster (1900) **27(3) H&W**
Guy v Kearney (1842) (IR) **6 B of Exch**
Guy v Livesey (1618) **27(1) H&W**
Guy v M'Carthy (1886) (IR) **23 Exors**
Guy v Newson (1833) **17 Deeds**
Guy v Nichols (1694) **12(2) Contr**
Guy v Sharp (1833) **50 Wills**
Guy v Shulhan (1962) (CAN) **27(1) H&W**
Guy v Walker (1892) **37(2) Pract**
Guy v Waterlow Bros & Layton Ltd (1909) **9(2) Coys**
Guy v West (1808) **7 Bounds&F**
Guy (WJ) & Son v Glen Line Ltd (1948) **42 Ship**
Guy Butler (International) Ltd v Customs & Excise Comrs, Customs & Excise Comrs v Guy Butler (International) Ltd (1976) **49 VAT**
Guy Mannering, The (1882) **42 Ship**
Guy-Pell v Foster (1930) **12(2) Contr; 26 Guar**
Guyana and Trinidad Mutual Life Insurance Co Ltd v RK Plummer and Associates Ltd (1988) (TRINIDAD & TOBAGO) **12(2) Contr**
Guyer v R (1889) **25 Game; 45 Stats**
Guyer Oil Co Ltd, Golden Eagle Oil & Gas Ltd and Husky Oil (Alberta) Ltd v Fulton & Gladstone Petroleum Ltd (1973) (CAN) **47(1) Trade**
Guyer's Application, Re (1980) **26 Hghys**
Guyot v Thomson (1894) **12(1) Contr; 17 Deeds; 36(3) Pats**
Guyot, R v (1927) (CAN) **22(2) Evid**
Guyot & Vigouret & Award made by Gosselin, Re (1919) (CAN) **3 Arbn**
Guyot-Guenin & Son v Clyde Soap Co (1915) (SCOT) **2 Aliens**
Guyton & Rosenberg's Contract, Re (1901) **50 Wills**
Guzak and Guzak v McEwan (1965) (CAN) **27(1) H&W**
Guzerat Spinning & Weaving Co v Girdharlal Dalpatram (1880) (IND) **9(1) Coys**
Guzzala Hanuman v R (1902) (IND) **15 Crim**
Guzzo, R v (CAN) **21 Estpl**
GW Bates & Co v J & P Cameron & Co (1855) (SCOT) **8(1) Carr**
GW Golden Construction Ltd v Minister of National Revenue (1966) (CAN) **28(1) Inc T**
GW Murray & Co Ltd (1934) (CAN) **5(1) Bkpcy**
GW Ry Co, ex p, Re Foster v GW Ry Co (1882) **37(2) Pract**
GW Ry Co v Bater (1922) **37(2) Pract**
GW Young & Co Ltd v North British and Mercantile Insurance Co, GW Young & Co Ltd v Scottish Union and National Insurance Co (1907) **37(1) Pldg**

Figure 5.7   The Digest: *cumulative supplement.*

355

2619 Expld R v Pawlicki and another [1992] 3 All ER 902

**2619a Person having firearm with him —
Intent to commit indictable offence —
Whether firearms readily accessible**
The appellants P and S having allegedly agreed to
commit a robbery at the premises of an auctioneer,
P drove his car to the premises, where he parked it
outside and locked it, leaving three sawn-off shot-
guns and other items consistent with a planned
robbery inside, and then went into the premises,
where he met S. The appellants were then arrested
by the police, who had been alerted as to the possibility of a robbery. They were jointly charged with
and convicted of having with them firearms with
intent to commit robbery, contrary to s 18(1) of the
Firearms Act 1968. The appellants appealed on the
ground that a person could only "have with him" a
firearm within s 18 if the firearm was immediately
available to him which was not the case since at the
time of their arrest the guns were 50 yards away in
a locked car: *Held* In considering whether a person
"had with him a firearm" for the purposes of s 18(1)
of the 1968 Act it was necessary to consider the element of propinquity and the accessibility of the
firearm judged in a commonsense way in the context
of a criminal intending to commit an indictable
offence, rather than the exact distance between the
accused and the firearm. Accordingly, the separation
in terms of space of the appellants from the guns
which they had agreed to bring on a planned robbery
did not mean that they did not have the guns with
them. It was sufficient that the guns were readily
accessible to them at a time when they were about
to commit an offence. The appeals would therefore
be dismissed.
R v Pawlicki and another [1992] 3 All ER 902, CA

**2620a Firearms compensation scheme —
Claimant surrendering weapons and claiming
compensation under scheme — Claimant
bringing proceedings in county court alleging
entitlement to payment within reasonable
time — Whether scheme providing right to
payment if conditions met — Whether payments under scheme having to be made within
reasonable time — Whether proceedings
having to be brought by way of judicial review**
Acting under a power conferred by the Firearms
(Amendment) Act 1997, the Secretary of State introduced a scheme to compensate persons who, in
accordance with the Act's provisions, had surrendered
large-calibre hand guns. Claims had to be made to the
police who transmitted them for checking to the
Firearm Compensation Section of the Home Office
(FCS). Under the first two of the scheme's three

Using electronic sources

5.118 When searching for cases by name on electronic sources, it is best to use a field search rather than a free text search, particularly if the case has a common name. So for example, on Justis use the parties option on the Quick Search form, on Lawtel use the Focused Search facility, on Westlaw UK the party name box in the Case Locator, on All England Direct the title field, or on Lexis the name sector. Avoid typing in the whole name of the case. If there is a distinctive part of the name, just use that. For example, if you are after *Brown v Tiernan*, 'Tiernan' is obviously a better bet than 'Brown'. If you try to put in 'Brown v Tiernan', you will not necessarily get it (depending on the particular search software) if the case is in fact called 'Brown (Holdings) Ltd and another v J.G. Tiernan plc'. If you do need to put in more than one part of the name, link them with 'AND' or use a proximity search. For example, for a case like *Smith v London Borough of Lewisham*, put in 'Smith AND Lewisham'. For cases with very common names, you may need to combine it with another field, for example, date, if the search software allows it. For example, on Lexis to find *R v Johnson*, which you know to have been in the last ten years or so type: name(Johnson) and date aft 1990. If you fail to find the case using a field search, you can always try a free text search as the next line of attack. The case itself may not be on the particular database you are searching, but it may have been cited in one that is. If you need to put in more than one part of the name as a search term in a free text search, use a proximity search (simply 'ANDing' will not usually be sufficient). So on Justis 'Smith within 25 of Lewisham' or on Lexis 'Smith w/6 of Lewisham'.

Finding EC cases by name or number

5.119 This should be straightforward. *Butterworths EC Case Citator* is the printed source to use, or, bearing in mind it only gives ECR, not CMLR or other references, the court's *Index A-Z*. Electronic versions of the reports should, equally, present few problems. Since 1989 the *Current Law Case Citator* has also included separate tables, by both name and number, of EC cases that are digested in the main work. If it is the case number you have, on Justis Celex use the Document Number option on the Quick Search form. Incidentally, the Colloquial Terms option on Justis only applies to legislation, not cases. For a colloquial name use the separate index in *Butterworths EC Case Citator*.

Finding European human rights cases by name or number

5.120 Finding court judgments should not be too difficult. You can get them off HUDOC – the 'title' field on the search form is where you put the name of the applicant, if you have a name. HUDOC also gives the reference to the official series of *Judgments and Decisions* if you need it in printed form. If you want it in the EHRR, there is a cumulative chronological table in each volume, which will translate a *Series A* reference. EHRR are also included in *Current Law Cases* and *Citator*. *Kempees* also has a complete alphabetical list of court judgments with official reference. Finding Commission cases is sometimes more difficult. If it is on HUDOC, well and good. But HUDOC does not give references to the *Decisions and Reports* if you want it in printed form too. For cases before 1991, you can use the *Digest of Strasbourg Case-law*. For later cases you would need to browse the contents pages around the right time. For Commission cases too early to be on HUDOC, and if the *Digest of Strasbourg Case-law* is not available, you really need a rough idea of date, so if you have an application number it helps. Then you can use the cumulative indexes, which are provided at intervals in the DR, or browse the contents pages of the *Yearbooks*. Probably a sensible short cut would be simply to look in the tables of cases in the major texts, for example, *Lester and Pannick, Clayton and Tomlinson, Simor and Emmerson, Harris and O'Boyle* or *Van Dijk and Van Hoof.*

Finding cases by subject

5.121 The best way to tackle subject searching depends on your objective. You may be engaged on a major piece of research requiring an exhaustive list of authorities. You may, on the other hand, need only a quick overview of the leading cases. You may be familiar with the area and only want to check for any recent developments. Or, as often happens, you can remember a case but not its name. A pathway for an exhaustive piece of research is suggested here, but can be adapted as appropriate for these other needs. As discussed in chapter 1, before starting your search it is well worth while getting clear in your own mind the likely legal issues and areas of law involved, running through the possible terms that might be used and then considering broader and narrower terms and synonyms. Often, in practice you have gone to a textbook or *Halsbury's Laws*, looked up a few of the cases mentioned and then some of the cases cited in those cases, so that a preliminary list of authorities begins to build up. This is certainly a useful and practical approach because it gives a feel for what is likely to be relevant and clarifies the object of the search. But it tends to involve duplication of effort, and so, according to taste, it may be better to start on the systematic approach from the word go.

The systematic approach

5.122 The systematic approach has three stages, which usually proceed with diminishing returns. The initial stage is the main trawl, which will yield the bulk of the references. The second stage is to check for any very recent cases (in the last few days or weeks). And the last stage is to note up all the cases you have found so far to double-check whether they have been cited in any other cases you have missed. A fourth stage, either if you have found very little or if you have the time and resources to go to town, would be to repeat the whole process with sources from other jurisdictions – Commonwealth materials if the topic is a common law one, or possibly European materials if it is EC-related. If the subject is heavily legislation-based, it also might be worth considering starting instead with the tools specifically designed for that.

5.123 For stage one, the first edition of this book recommended using Lexis. If you have access to it, and cost is not an issue, it is certainly an option. But at that time there were not any other electronic sources, and the data contained in the *Current Law Yearbooks* could only be extracted by painfully slow and inexact means. Now, for most everyday purposes, the recommended starting point would be the electronic version of *Current Law Cases*, which will take to you the bulk of reported case law since 1947. If you find no or little reported authority, then you might consider using Lexis for unreported cases.

5.124 The general principles of subject searching on electronic sources have been described in chapter 1. Start with a broad term and narrow the search in stages. Think of as many synonyms as possible and 'OR' them. Truncate word stems, for example, COMPENSAT*. On full text systems, it is also generally recommended that you use a proximity search, rather either 'ANDing' terms or entering phrases. On *Current Law Cases*, since you are only searching summaries, you can usually get away with plain 'ANDing'. If you are searching in an area very heavily represented on the database, such as negligence, put in your main terms as keywords, using a field search, then add any more specific terms as free text. As with most systems, *Current Law Cases* will display the most recent hits first. If you have a fair number of hits, it is sometimes worth, having looked at the first few, pausing and looking at the full report of any that look particularly promising. It may help you to see if there any leading cases, which will then summarise the main authorities, and to gauge what further material might be relevant.

5.125 Having completed your search on *Current Law Cases*, the next thing to consider is whether older cases, decided before 1947, might be relevant, especially if you have found little or no modern authority. If so, it is off to *The Digest* or its electronic equivalent, Case Search. There is one point to note on using the latter for subject searching. Not every case in *The Digest* has a summary. Some lesser cases are simply listed under the relevant topic – these will not necessarily be picked up on Case Search using a keyword search. So if you were doing full-scale research it might be a wise precaution to see where in the hard copy any cases that you did get off Case Search are treated and just check that there no other, unsummarised, cases in the neighbourhood. *The Digest* is arranged by subject, and the contents pages for each title set out the matter in a systematic and full fashion. There are not indexes for each volume, but there is the consolidated index to the whole work. It most cases the simplest and most effective approach is simply to browse the contents pages, using the consolidated index not as a detailed guide, but simply to get you to the relevant volume if you are uncertain which it is. However, it is sometimes necessary to rely on the consolidated index, for example, where the subject might arise in a number of different legal contexts. If you do use the index, you will find that the policy is to use fairly specific headings, backed-up by copious cross-references. The contents page approach may be illustrated by an example. Suppose you wanted to find any cases where statements made about doctors have been found to be defamatory. Volume 32(1) contains the title Libel and Slander, which is broken down as follows:

1   THE CAUSES OF ACTION
   (3) Defamatory statements
      (ii) WHAT IS DEFAMATORY
         3   Libellous statements
            C   Statements reflecting on plaintiff in the way of his trade, profession or calling
            (b) Profession or calling
               iv Physicians and surgeons

Among the cases found in the relevant section are some in which it was held to be defamatory to call a doctor a 'quack'. The consolidated index approach is demonstrated by the fact that if you had wanted to know specifically whether it was defamatory to call a doctor a 'quack', then there is indeed an index entry simply under QUACK, which takes you straight to the particular paragraphs in vol 32(1). There is a cross-reference to QUACK under LIBEL and also an entry for PHYSICIAN AND SURGEON – Quack, though you might not find the latter if you had looked up

DOCTOR. Having searched *Current Law Cases* and *The Digest*, you then need to consider whether it is worth looking at any individual series of law reports in electronic form. This very much depends on the nature of the question, and whether full-text searching is likely to add to your results. A search on the electronic Law Reports is probably worthwhile as a double-check in most cases. Otherwise, recourse to these tends to be in circumstances where there is a particularly *factual* element that you are interested in. For example, you are au fait with the general legal principles of bailment, but has it ever been applied to a racehorse?

5.126 If you use the Internet version of *Current Law Cases,* which is updated daily, you will be as up-to-date as you can be, as far as reported cases go. As always, if you are using *Current Law Cases*, have a quick look at the *Legal Journals Index* as well. But for stage two, catching any very recent developments, you will need to check as many of the various transcript alerting services as you have access to, such as Lawtel, All England Direct and Westlaw UK.

5.127 Having completed stages one and two of your search, the final step is to check whether any of the cases you have found have been cited in other cases. Such cases are likely to be on the same subject (though not necessarily – the case may have been cited on an altogether different point) and it ensures that what you have found is still good law. The tools for doing this, citators, are treated in a separate section below (paras **5.133–5.139**) as their use is not confined to subject searching. The only other things then left to do, if necessary, are to research case law from other jurisdictions and if the subject involves specific legislation, use the legislation citators and related tools, described at paras **5.141–5.149**.

If time is short

5.128 The systematic approach above can be adapted according to how much time you have and how much prior knowledge of the subject you have. But if you do not need to be completely comprehensive and you have very little time, probably the two places to try are *The Law Reports Index* or the cumulated index to the *All England Law Reports*. The latter will cover all the mainstream case law from 1936 until the last year or so, while the former allows you to concentrate on just the last 10 or 20 years and will cover some specialist areas like industrial law or tax law. If there is a specialist series of law reports for the particular subject available in electronic form, then just stick with those, for example, *British Company Cases* if you have a company law point, or the *Family Law Reports* if you have a family law point. If it is in a general area of law, use the electronic versions of *The Law Reports* and the *Weekly Law Reports*. The advantage of these when you are in a hurry is that you have the full text in front of you, which can be printed off – you do not need to dash round the library to find the relevant volumes and then queue for a photocopier. If you are pressed for time and the above sources retrieve a lot of cases, do not try to look them all up. Pick one at the highest level of court which is also recent – nine times out of ten all the relevant authorities will already have been assembled there.

Finding cases on quantum of damages for personal injuries

5.129 In personal injuries cases, lawyers will need to advise their clients how much in damages they are likely to receive. Although there are general guidelines issued by the Judicial Studies Board, the matter is in the discretion of the court. Experienced personal injury practitioners will have a feel for what the 'going rate' is for a particular injury, say a broken leg or lost eye. But there are a number of sources that report the damages awarded in particular cases, which can be referred to, particularly by newly qualified lawyers or lawyers who do not frequently undertake such work. Such cases are not precedents and generally contain no 'law' – what is important is the particular facts. Thus they enumerate the nature and type of injuries, the age of the claimant, the part of the award attributable to loss of earnings and the part for general damages for 'pain and suffering'. Since these sources collect the cases largely on the basis of the barristers or solicitors involved sending them in, they do not by any means overlap with the same cases. Generally with quantum cases, as distinct from conventional law reports, the maxim is the more the merrier.

5.130 The basic tool is the looseleaf work *Kemp and Kemp: Quantum of Damages in Personal Injury and Fatal Accident Claims*, published by Sweet & Maxwell. Butterworths also publish a work, *Personal Injury Litigation Service* by Goldrein and De Haas, which gives full coverage of the substantive law and procedure, but also includes a section on quantum awards. There is also a newcomer to the field, Simon Levene *Damages Service* ((2001) EMIS Professional Publishing), a single volume book. If you buy the book you get free access to an on-line updating service. There are two other printed sources that should be consulted mainly, but not exclusively, for recent cases. First, there are the monthly parts of *Current Law*. There is cumulative table in the latest part, which is arranged by type of injury and gives brief details of the amount of the award. References are given to the relevant monthly part where full details of the case will be found. There is a similar table in the front of the *Yearbook*. The digests of quantum cases are of course included in the electronic version of *Current Law Cases*, but not the tables, so this is one area where the printed version is usually preferable. The other source is the monthly reviews which form part of the service to *Halsbury's Laws*, where the cases are found under the heading 'Damages'. But again there is a cumulative printed table by type of injury, which will be found in the looseleaf noter-up volume to *Halsbury's Laws*. The monthly reviews are cumulated as the *Halsbury's Laws Annual Abridgment*. There is a similar service in *Current Law*, though it may not necessarily cover the same cases. Of electronic sources, Lawtel is particularly good – there is a separate PI Quantum database on it. The PI Online service, one of the Butterworths LEXIS Direct services, also as a quantum database, as well as other materials such as the full text of Goldrein and De Haas. The *Personal Injuries and Quantum Reports*, which will be covered by *Current Law* and other sources, includes fuller reports of cases where quantum is in issue, as well as cases on the substantive law of personal injuries. The former are separately paginated with a Q.

Finding cases in which particular words or phrases have been judicially considered

5.131 See chapter 2, paras **2.45–2.48**.

Finding EC and European human rights cases by subject

5.132 Often the most precise way to find EC cases on a topic is to search by a particular treaty provision or legislative provision that might have been considered, rather than by subject terms. Likewise European human rights cases are often best searched by Convention article number. Sources that index cases by legislation are described below (para **5.148**). But if you do need to search by subject-matter, in the case of ECJ cases you really need to use an electronic source (see para **5.38**). There is no really satisfactory printed tool. For old cases there are the tools mentioned at para **5.84**. *Butterworths EC Case Citator* has a 'key phrase/sector' index, but this only covers selected cases that have 'substantially contributed to EC law'. The large looseleaf work the *Law of the European Communities* by David Vaughan used to be quite helpful in that at the end of each subject division there were lists of relevant cases, but the updating seems to have ground to a halt. For European human rights cases, the printed sources are somewhat better, at any rate for court judgments (see para **5.86**). The commercially available electronic sources mentioned at para **5.54** are largely confined to court judgments, so a search on HUDOC generally has to be attempted to find Commission material.

Finding whether a case has been cited

5.133 It is important to know whether a particular case you are using has been cited in a later case. Its authority may have been strengthened by being expressly approved by a higher court; on the other hand, it may have been overruled. Between these two extremes there are various gradations of citation. *The Digest* in the front of each volume sets out the terms it uses in its annotations with explanations of their meaning. A glance at them is instructive. The main terms are: applied, approved, considered, disapproved, distinguished, doubted, explained, extended, followed, not followed, overruled and referred to. The subtle distinctions in meaning between these terms epitomise the fluid way in which the doctrine of precedent is applied in practice. As has already been mentioned, following up citations is also an excellent way of doing a subject search if you already know of a leading case. The other question you may need to answer is whether a recent case has gone further on appeal.

5.134 There are two distinct approaches to this, and each has its pros and cons. One is searching on services that offer the full text of cases. The other is to use a citator or similar tool, whether in printed form or on screen. With the first approach there is no selection about it – you can retrieve every single mention, in that particular database, of the case that you are interested in, whether it is just mentioned in passing or considered in depth. It is then up to you to assess the significance or weight of what is said about the case. This approach is certainly the most comprehensive, and perhaps the safest approach, though you may need to repeat the search on a number of different databases. The drawback is where you are looking at a relatively well-known case – you may simply retrieve an unmanageable number of hits. If for example, you were rash enough to search for cases that cite *Caparo Industries v Dickman*, just the CD-ROM version of *The Law Reports* and the *Weekly Law Reports* would give about 140 cases, even though the case was decided barely ten years ago. In the case of electronic versions of law reports, this can be mitigated by confining the search to the headnote field, which will then only retrieve cases in which it has been substantially considered. But that option is not available if you are searching sources that include transcripts, and in any event slightly defeats the object of full text searching. Citators, on the other hand, are designed to pick up those cases in which a particular case has received substantial consideration. This has the advantage of directing you only to material that is likely to be relevant. The disadvantage, of course, is that unless the case is being expressly overruled or disapproved, it is a matter of subjective editorial judgment whether the consideration is sufficiently substantial to warrant inclusion. Confining full text searching of law reports to the headnote field, mentioned above as a strategy for dealing with too many hits, carries a similar danger – one is relying on the judgment of the law reporter who prepared the headnote. So it is horses for courses. For most everyday purposes, the best advice is probably to start with the citators and see what you get, and then move on to full-text sources if you get little or nothing. On the other hand, if you are embarking on a major research project or a big case where you going to have to be as absolutely comprehensive as possible, then you might as well start with the full text sources.

5.135 The *Current Law Case Citator* has already been described in connection with finding cases by name. The on-screen version is the most convenient not only because it consolidates all the information into a single entry and may be slightly ahead of the printed version, but also with the Folio View CD-ROM or Internet version, you have hypertext links to the *Current Law Cases* digests of the citing cases. But the data is the same as is to be found in the printed version. Depending on the date of the case, you may need to work your way through the two hardbound volumes, the softback supplements and the cumulative table of cases in the latest monthly digest. References are to paragraph numbers in the *Yearbooks*, which then have to be referred to find the citing case: see figure 5.4.

5.136 The *Current Law Case Citator* only goes back to 1947, though of course they cover earlier cases *cited* since then. The best source for earlier coverage is *The Digest* or in its electronic form **Case Search**. Find the case by name as described above. At the foot of the entry is a section 'Annotations' which gives other cases in which it has been cited. Further annotations will be given in the cumulative supplement. *The Law Reports Index* and its precursor *The Law Reports Digest* have tables of cases judicially considered (not to be confused with the separate tables of cases reported) which can be useful in addition or instead of *Current Law* and *The Digest*. There is a table of cases judicially considered in the consolidated tables to the *All England Law Reports* if that is all that is to hand, but it only covers citations in the All ER to other cases reported in the All ER.

5.137 Of the full-text systems, **Lexis**, simply because of its retrospective coverage, remains the most comprehensive source. Otherwise, it is very much a case of what is available to you – **Westlaw UK**, **Lawtel**, **All England Direct**, or individual series of law reports. Certainly, even a full-text search on just the *Weekly Law Reports* may well supplement what you get from the *Current Law Case Citator*. As explained at para **5.118**, when full-text searching for the name of a case, unless it has a single readily distinguishable element, put in two (or if necessary more) elements of the name using proximity searching – do not attempt to type in the whole name of the case exactly. So on **Lexis** to find cases citing *London and Blenheim Estates Ltd v Ladbroke Retail Parks Ltd*, put in 'Blenheim w/5 Ladbroke'. If proximity searching is not available, as on **Lawtel**, and you have a lengthy but unmemorable case name you may have to put quite a bit of the name and hope for the best. On **All England Direct** and the *All England Law Reports* CD-ROM, which do not currently have full proximity searching, you can configure the search so that the words 'ANDed' are in the same paragraph. If the case you are interested in is itself within the scope of the database you are searching, you have an in-built quality control. You should retrieve a minimum of *one* hit, ie the record for the case itself. If you get *no* hits, you know something must be wrong – perhaps you made a spelling mistake when keying in the name.

5.138 If you have been unable to find any cases in the above and you are doing in-depth research, you may wish to try your luck with Commonwealth authorities (on the citation of Commonwealth authority in court see now the Practice Direction, discussed at para **8.2**). English cases are often cited for example, in the Australian and Canadian courts. There are indigenous citators and full-text sources (see paras **8.89** and **8.95**), which will include any English cases. But a separate and useful tool is the *Australian and New Zealand Citator to UK Reports*, which is published at regular intervals. Its coverage is taken from English cases that appear in the headnotes of the main Australian and New Zealand series of law reports, excluding those referred to in the headnote as being merely 'cited' or 'referred to'. As originally compiled in 1972, it also only took in those English cases reported in *The Law Reports*, the *Weekly Law Reports* and the *All England Law Reports* (including the reprint series). Since then it has been wider. For Australian cases the *Australian Case Citator* may give wider coverage of Australian cases, but might not necessarily be available as well, and would not, of course, cover the New Zealand cases.

5.139　If any readers of this work frequent the Inns of Court libraries or the Bar Library in the Royal Courts of Justice, they may come across the system adopted before the *Current Law Case Citator* was invented. The pages of the law reports themselves are festooned with red ink. This is not the result of any proclivity of members of the bar to deface library books, but the fruits of the labour of the library staff, who carefully annotated the reports with references to later cases in which they are cited. This system of physical noting-up only stopped at Lincoln's Inn Library in 2000. Even in its heyday it had limitations, which was that the series of reports from which references were taken for noting-up were selective. None the less, particularly for older cases, it provides a record that is not replicated in any conventional printed source. *The Law Reports* used to have a similar system, whereby they issued sticky labels bearing the references for subscribers to stick into their own copies at the relevant point. That became truly redundant once the full-text of *The Law Reports* had been made available in electronic form.

Finding cases that cite EC and European human rights cases

5.140　The full text electronic sources are practically the only means (see paras **5.38** and **5.54**). Neither the *Butterworths EC Case Citator* nor the European section of the *Current Law Case Citator* perform this function for EC cases – they merely tell you where a case is reported. The main printed source at one time was the *Gazetteer of European Law*, but that only goes up to 1983. For human rights cases the EHRR have a table of cases judicially considered, but only on a volume-by-volume basis.

Finding cases on legislation

5.141　Even in those areas that are statute-based and not governed by common law, case law remains important as a source of interpretation and construction. As well as the statutes themselves, SIs are also often judicially considered. When searching for cases on statutes, an important preliminary is to check whether the statute is a consolidation Act (see paras **3.73–3.77**). If so, you may need to research the earlier case law on the statutes from which it derives.

5.142　As with searching for citations of cases, you have the choice of full-text searching, or using citators and other similar tools. There are similar pros and cons as described above, except that in the case of legislation the full-text problem of overretrieval due to the 'passing mention' phenomenon is sometimes magnified.

Legislation will frequently be referred to when its meaning is not in issue or under consideration. Quotations from two run-of-the-mill law reports taken more or less at random illustrate the point:

> On May 14, 1996 the appellant was arrested for conspiring to steal motor vehicles. He was later charged with 14 charges of handling stolen goods. The matter was adjourned for committal proceedings under section 6(1) of the Criminal Justice Act 1987. On October 14, 1996 the appellant was committed under section 6(2) of the Criminal Justice Act 1987 to Derby Crown Court on the charge of conspiracy
>   This is an application under section 288 of the Town and Country Planning Act 1990, relating to a large portal-framed building, currently in use in breach of planning control as car body repair shop, at Boxhedge Farm, Cranfield, Bedfordshire.

The Criminal Justice Act 1987 was not of relevance to the scope of the conspiracy to steal, nor the section of the Town and Country Planning Act as to whether the car body repair shop was for an agricultural purpose. As with cases, the general advice is start with the selective citator approach, and then go on to full-text searching if necessary.

5.143 The two main sources for statutes to start with are the annotations to *Halsbury's Statutes* and the *Current Law Legislation Citator*. The latter can be used either in hard copy or on screen. Although the on-screen version has some of the advantages of the on-screen *Case Citator*, described above, the hard copy in fact is often slightly safer. Each section of an Act forms a separate record on the electronic version, which is well and good if the case is on one particular section. But sometimes it is on several sections or on a whole part of an Act, or even the Act generally. In the printed version these appear, and are obvious, at the head of the entry for the Act. On the electronic version, you may miss them if it is a large Act and you do not look at every record for it. The electronic version also only goes back to 1989. *Halsbury's Statutes* is particularly useful when you have a consolidation Act, since cases on the earlier legislation may be referred to. On the other hand as mentioned at para **3.13**, some case references in the annotations turn out to be stock references, not necessarily relevant to the Act in question. As well as checking the main work, as always check the cumulative supplement and noter-up. There may well be some duplication of results with the *Current Law Statute Citator*, but it should be checked none the less. If you have a consolidation Act, you will need to check under the name and relevant section of earlier Acts. If you need to look at case law before 1947 (which will not be covered by *Current Law*) or for case law on statutes no longer in force (which will not be in the current edition of *Halsbury's Statutes*), there is a table of statutes judicially considered in *The Law Reports Digest*.

5.144 For full-text searching all the sources already mentioned in connection with case citations may be used. The main problems to be considered in formulating a search strategy are dealing with particular sections, the names of older Acts, and the problem of overretrieval mentioned above. If you are looking for cases on a particular section, you can start by using the name of the Act and not specifying a section. If it is an uncommon or short Act you may get a perfectly manageable hit list, which does not need narrowing further. If a section is to be specified, first of all avoid 's' or 'section', because editorial styles and the treatment of punctuation by search software vary. Just use a bare number. Likewise it is counterproductive to try to take the search down to the level of subsections. Secondly, where possible use proximity searching, preferably with quite a wide distance specified. The effect of using different values for the proximity connector is illustrated with a search of *The Law Reports* using the Justis software. If you were looking for cases on s 78 of the Police and Criminal Evidence Act 1984, you could enter 'Police and Criminal Evidence Act 1984 within 10 of 78', where '10' is the number of characters. That would get just five hits. Increase it to 15 characters and you get 18 hits. 20 characters gets 24 hits. You then need to go up to 50 characters to get just two more hits. Thereafter it is very much a question of diminishing returns, and increasing likelihood of false drops. At a distance of 150 characters, two more hits are retrieved, and one of them is simply referring to a paragraph 78 in some entirely unrelated document. The other extra hit, though, is instructive in showing how in the ordinary language of judgments the section number can get orphaned from the name of the Act. The relevant passage reads:

> ... proceedings to which the **Police and Criminal Evidence Act 1984** applied. In that case the question was whether the magistrate could in such circumstances apply the provisions of section **78**.

5.145 The name of the Act to be entered is not usually a problem for modern Acts. If it has a particularly long or complicated title, you can also use proximity searching of the main elements, rather than typing in the whole title. If you are searching sources that include old cases, such as *The Law Reports*, you need to bear in mind that the style of citing the names of Acts before 1963 was to include a comma between the name and year, for example, Regulation of Railways Act, 1873. If entered with a comma, the Justis software finds instances both with and without a comma, but if entered without a comma it does not find those with a comma. If there is only one Act by that name you can always omit the year. And in fact for very well-known Acts, you may find it cited without a year. If you search *The Law Reports* you get 21 more hits if you enter 'Offences Against the Person Act' than if you enter 'Offences against the Person Act, 1861'. That may be an unusual example and there are dangers in omitting the year. If you entered 'Police and Criminal Evidence Act' on Justis without putting it in double quotes, you will retrieve lots of cases on the Criminal Evidence Act 1898 in which the police are mentioned at some point. The other problem with the old reports is that statutes were quite often cited without the title at all – just by regnal year and chapter number. On *The Law Reports*, about 215 hits are retrieved with 'Offences against the Person Act'; 'OR' it with '24 & 25 Vict. c. 100' and you get another 58 hits.

5.146 If you get a large number of hits, and you want to narrow the search to those where there is some active consideration of the statute's meaning, then, as with looking for citations of cases, you can confine the search to the headnote field (if the database contains law reports). The other strategy is to put in some common words used by judges when construing a statute. Using a proximity connector (on Justis 'near' which stands for 40 characters might be suitable) add a string such as 'meaning or constru* or interpret*' (see also para **2.48**).

5.147 If you are looking for cases in which an SI has been judicially considered, full text searching, as with statutes is certainly an option, especially since the coverage of printed tools is not as extensive as it is for statutes. The SI will usually be referred to by name, but you can 'OR' the name with its number to be on the safe side. The main printed tool is the *Statutory Instrument Citator,* which forms part of the *Current Law Legislation Citator*. However, this has only been provided in addition to the main statute citator since 1993. The data is included in the on-screen version of the *Legislation Citator*, but as with statutes the printed version is generally more convenient. On the other hand, a search on the electronic version of *Current Law Cases* is worthwhile since it might catch some SIs mentioned in the abstract for cases before 1993. There are some case references in the annotations to *Halsbury's Statutory Instruments*. Otherwise, for pre-1993 cases (and as a cross-check on the *SI Citator* for cases since 1993) the main resource is *The Law Reports Index* and its precursor *The Law Reports Digest*, which includes a table of SIs judicially considered. *The Law Reports Index*, it may be noted in passing, has four other useful citators that are often overlooked: standard forms of contract judicially considered; overseas enactments judicially considered; European Community enactments judicially considered; and international conventions judicially considered. One other place to try is the consolidated tables to the *All England Law Reports*. Rather irritatingly, subsidiary legislation judicially considered is split between seven different tables: Rules of the Supreme Court; County Court Rules; Matrimonial Causes Rules; Bankruptcy and Insolvency Rules; Other Rules; Regulations; and Orders.

5.148 For finding EC cases by legislation, the main printed source is the *Butterworths EC Case Citator*. It includes full listings by treaty provision, regulations, directives and decisions. For recent cases, especially those from national courts in other member states, *European Current Law* could be checked: regulations, directives and decisions are in fact included in the table headed 'Treaty provisions referred to'. Otherwise, full-text searching on the various electronic versions of the ECR is the best bet. On Justis Celex, you can enter the directive or regulation number in the summary field, if you otherwise get too many hits. Treaty article numbers, which tend to be prolifically cited, could also be entered there. Bear in mind the problem of the renumbering of the treaty articles – it may be best to add some relevant terms as text as well. For European human rights cases, HUDOC has a specific field on the search screen for entering an article number of the Convention. There is an associated word wheel, which may assist with entering the subdivisions of articles, like 6(1), in the correct format. If you are looking at those articles of the Convention that deal with the procedure of the court, again bear in mind the renumbering effected by Protocol 11. The main printed digest of ECHR case law, *Kempees*, is arranged by article number, as is in effect *Starmer*.

5.149 If you need to find cases which consider a Local Act, you can use the full text sources already described for ordinary Public General Acts – Lexis would probably be the best, though it will not cover cases before 1945 and Local Acts are often of long standing, so earlier case law may be relevant. *The Law Reports Digest*, which goes back to 1865, has a separate table of Local and Personal Acts judicially considered. In *The Law Reports Index* Local and Personal Acts are interfiled in the main table of statutes judicially considered. In the consolidated tables to the *All England Law Reports*, there is a separate table, Table B, for Local and Personal Acts. However, the main printed source is now the *Current Law Statute Citator*, which resumed coverage of Local and Personal Acts in 1996, having previously covered them only in the first volume, 1947–71. Local and Personal Acts are listed before the Public General Acts for each year (in the 1947–71 volume they come after them). For the intervening period, as with SIs before the *Statutory Instrument Citator* started, you could try the electronic version of *Current Law Cases*. *Halsbury's Statutes* may have case references to Local Acts relating to London, which it includes.

6. Treaties and international materials

Reasons for researching treaties

6.1 In looking at how and why an English lawyer may use international treaties, it is necessary to appreciate the way in which English common law views them. The important distinction here is between treaties that have been expressly incorporated into domestic law and those that have not. In some jurisdictions, treaties (or some classes of treaty) can take effect in domestic law once they have been ratified without further legislation – they are said to be self-executing. In the UK direct or indirect parliamentary approval must be given by means of a statute or SI.

6.2 However, this is not to say than an unincorporated treaty can never have domestic legal consequences. For the purposes of statutory interpretation, it is assumed that Parliament would not pass legislation contrary to the obligations of the Crown under international law. If there is an ambiguity in a UK statute in an area covered by an international treaty that has been ratified by the UK, the courts can invoke the treaty provisions to resolve it. The European Convention on Human Rights before its incorporation by the Human Rights Act 1998 was perhaps the most prominent illustration. As is well known, before the Human Rights Act direct redress was only available via the European Court of Human Rights in Strasbourg. Yet the courts here were increasingly prepared to cite it, and quite a body of case law evolved.

6.3 The distinction between unincorporated and incorporated treaties, however, is heavily qualified in the case of the EU treaties. Under EU law treaty obligations are not only directly applicable in the sense of binding states without those states enacting domestic legislation, but also may (depending on the ECJ's view of the particular provision) have direct effect in the sense of conferring rights on individuals either vis-à-vis a state (so-called vertical direct effect) or vis-à-vis other individuals (so-called horizontal direct effect). The UK has coped with this novel regime by incorporating EC law in general into domestic law by means of statute – the European Communities Act 1972 – but, by that Act, permitting future treaty obligations to be given effect in the domestic law without further legislation.

6.4 International treaties, whether incorporated into domestic law or not, are also, of course, of interest to academics and students researching public international law, and to those practitioners who appear in disputes that come before international tribunals. Unincorporated treaties will also be of interest to practitioners in giving advice, in the same way that Bills and White Papers are, if there is a likelihood of their being adopted in the near future. Even if the UK has not incorporated a treaty, or indeed even if it has not signed it, the practitioner may be interested in it if an international transaction involves a country that has. For example, as more countries adopt it, the UN Convention on Contracts for the International Sale of Goods assumes increasing importance, even though the UK is not a signatory (yet).

Terminology and citation

6.5 Treaties may be bilateral, made between two states, or multilateral, made between several states. International organisations (depending on their constitution) may also enter into treaties with states – the EC, for example, does so frequently. Here the expression 'treaties' is being used generically to describe all international agreements. It is gratifying to find that a recent work on treaties written by an expert from the Foreign and Commonwealth Office states that 'one of the most mystifying aspects of treaty practice is the unsystematic way in which treaties are designated (named)' (Anthony Aust *Modern Treaty Law and Practice* (2000) Cambridge University Press). The documents themselves do indeed come with a bewildering range of labels. Generally speaking they are interchangeable and have no legal significance. 'Convention' is perhaps the commonest term in the multilateral sphere. On the other hand, many workaday bilateral agreements are called 'Exchanges of Notes' as this is how they are executed. Covenants, pacts, charters, concordats, agreements, declarations are other terms. 'Protocol' may also be encountered as a term for a treaty like any other, but nowadays it is used particularly for agreements that amend or supplement a principal treaty, as with the 12 protocols that have been added to the European Convention on Human Rights since it was originally made in 1950. The title of the document does not of itself confer treaty status. One of the ingredients of treaty status is an intention to create a legally binding agreement, and evidence of that within the document determines its status. As Aust helpfully makes clear, the difficulty arises most frequently with documents entitled 'Memorandum of Understanding' and 'Exchange of Notes'. The former are widely used in diplomatic transactions that are not intended to be legally binding – it may be sufficient and simpler to have a memorandum of understanding rather than a full-blown treaty. Yet the term is also to be found as the title of some documents which are unequivocally intended as treaties. Furthermore, both treaties and memorandums of understanding are frequently executed by means of Exchanges of Notes. If the Exchange of Notes is intended to be a treaty it may say that the exchange 'shall constitute an agreement between our two Governments'; if it is not it may say 'it records the understanding of our two Governments'. This will not usually present a problem with UK treaties, since they are either published as a treaty or not.

6.6 In using international legal materials another species that may be encountered are model laws prepared by international organisations. They are not treaties, but are mentioned here should they be confused with them. They may be drafted and agreed between participating members like treaties and have the similar aim of promoting international uniformity in the law, but they are not binding on states, merely offering a model to follow if states choose to enact them in their own law. The most well-known example is the UNCITRAL (United Nations Commission on International Trade Law) Model Law on International Commercial Arbitration, which, in the UK, has been adopted in Scotland but not in England and Wales.

6.7 Citation of treaties is not especially formalised. The main elements are the title, the date of signature, and, in the case of multilateral treaties, the place of signature. The formal titles of treaties that appear on their face are frequently abbreviated colloquially or for convenience. In some cases the popular title takes over from the title proper except in the most formal citations, as has happened with the European Convention on Human Rights, which is technically entitled the 'European Convention for the Protection of Human Rights and Fundamental Freedoms'. With such well-known treaties it is possible to get away without citing the date, but usually it is essential in order that they may be traced easily. The place of signature for multilateral treaties – usually the place where an international conference to draft and agree the treaty has been held – is not always a crucial element for identifying a treaty, but it assumes particular importance when, as often happens, it becomes transposed into the treaty's popular title. The Convention on Jurisdiction and Enforcement of Judgments in Civil and Commercial Matters, signed at Brussels on 27 September 1968, is widely known simply as the Brussels Convention. This is all very well if the context is clear (or in the few cases where it has virtually assumed official status, like the Treaty of Rome), but otherwise a reference to the Geneva Convention, the New York Convention, or the Hague Convention is as helpful as being referred to King Henry – there are rather a lot of them. The numbered provisions of a treaty – the equivalent of sections in an Act – are usually termed articles.

Sources for the texts of treaties

6.8 If the treaty has been incorporated into domestic law, the text is often going to be readily available because the modern practice is to append it, if possible, as a Schedule to the statute or SI. One-off treaties will usually be enacted by statute, but where there are frequent agreements in a particular area, for example, double taxation, an enabling statute will allow them to be given effect by SI. The title of the statute or SI may follow more or less closely the title of the treaty – for example, the Brussels Convention mentioned above is to be found in the Civil Jurisdiction and Judgments Act 1982. On the other hand, the only clue may be the broad subject matter of the Act: the Convention Relating to the Carriage or Passengers and their Luggage by Sea is to be found in the Merchant Shipping Act 1979. However, sometimes the treaty will be enacted merely by reference to the official text without incorporating it as a Schedule. This is usually on the grounds of length, which can be a problem, particularly where there is a multilingual parallel text. The Convention Concerning International Carriage by Rail 1980, for example, runs to almost 400 pages and so was not reproduced in the International Transport Conventions Act 1983 which gave effect to it.

6.9 The official text of treaties that the UK has ratified is the *United Kingdom Treaty Series*. They are published by TSO as command papers (on which generally, see paras **7.9–7.11**), and so bear a command paper number as well as a *Treaty Series* number. In libraries they may be kept together as a series or kept with other command papers. In the latter eventuality, as explained at para **7.13**, the command papers may be arranged by their number or by broad topic in sessional volumes of parliamentary papers. For citation purposes the command paper number is the most important element, but the *Treaty Series* number is helpful to have as well. An example is shown in figure 6.1. The command paper number is given in the bottom left-hand corner.

Figure 6.1

The International Convention was previously published as Miscellaneous No. 23 (1972) Cmnd. 5002.

INTELLECTUAL
PROPERTY

Treaty Series No. 63 (1990)

International Convention

further revising the Berne Convention for the Protection of Literary and Artistic Works of 9 September 1886

Paris, 24 July 1971 as amended on 2 October 1979

[The United Kingdom instrument of ratification was deposited on 29 September 1989 and the Convention and amendments entered into force for the United Kingdom on 2 January 1990]

Presented to Parliament
by the Secretary of State for Foreign and Commonwealth Affairs
by Command of Her Majesty
October 1990

LONDON : HMSO
£6·60 net

Cm 1212

6.10 As explained at para **6.27**, treaties often follow two separate stages. First they are signed, but may not be accepted as having binding force on a signatory until that signatory has ratified it. In the UK, under the so-called Ponsonby rule, which dates from 1924, it is the practice to lay before Parliament all treaties (with the exception from 1981of bilateral double taxation treaties) that will require ratification. Although treaty making is not a function of Parliament, the theory is that any concerns can be voiced before the treaty becomes binding. The treaties that are laid before Parliament are also command papers. They appear in the Foreign and Commonwealth Office 'Miscellaneous Series' if they are multilateral, or to particular country series if they are bilateral. These series have their own numbering, but it is almost invariably the command number that is used for citation purposes. When the treaty is subsequently ratified, which may be two or three years later in some cases, it is reissued in the *Treaty Series*. It will be seen that the treaty in figure 6.1 was previously published as Miscellaneous No 23 (1972), Cmnd 5002. That print will have stated on the front cover that it was not yet in force. Thus those libraries which subscribe to all the command papers are usually in the happy position of having two copies of many UK treaties. Since the beginning of 1997 treaties laid before Parliament in this way are accompanied by an explanatory memorandum, rather like that which now accompanies Bills. These are not published but are available on the FCO website.

6.11 The *United Kingdom Treaty Series* started in 1892. Before that date they appear as command papers among the sessional volumes of parliamentary papers and in the *British and Foreign State Papers*; there is considerable overlap between the two sources, but some treaties are only to be found in one of them. The latter series, compiled by the Foreign Office, began in 1812, and contained other international materials as well as treaties. It continued publication until 1968, and so for the period from 1892 until then there is also considerable duplication with the *Treaty Series* (for fuller details of its history and contents, see Nigel Smith 'British and Foreign State Papers' (1986) 17 *Law Librarian* 64–66).

6.12 If you do not have access to these primary sources, bear in mind that the text of important treaties may be reprinted as appendices to practitioners' works in the relevant field. There are also a number of subject collections of treaty materials. For example, CCH publish a looseleaf collection, *British International Tax Agreements* (also available on CD-ROM) and the *British Shipping Law* series published by Sweet & Maxwell (formerly Stevens) includes the four volumes of *International Maritime Law Conventions*, edited by Nagendra Singh. In the same field as the latter, is the US work *Benedict on Admiralty* and the *Ratification of Maritime Conventions*, published by Lloyds of London Press, which includes the full texts as well as the ratification information. The US-based looseleaf specialists Oceana have been especially active in publishing collections of materials of international interest in particular fields, such as commercial arbitration, telecommunications, multinational corporations, environmental law, law of the sea, human rights and terrorism. Diamond's *International Tax Treaties of all Nations* is an Oceana publication that deserves particular mention, as do, in the same field, the publications of the International Bureau of Fiscal Documentation, based in Amsterdam. For students of international law, there are Ian Brownlie's collections *Basic Documents in International Law* and *Basic Documents on Human Rights* (Oxford University Press).

6.13 Under art 102 of the United Nations Charter 1945 all treaties made by members of the UN are to be registered with its Secretariat 'as soon as possible' and published by it. But under the regulations that give effect to art 102, a treaty is not registered until it has come into force between at least two parties. This coupled with the bureaucratic inefficiency in the Secretariat means that the *United Nations Treaty Series* is lamentably in arrears. It is, however, the single most important source for treaties to which the UK is not party (if it is a party the *UK Treaty Series* is clearly preferable). The full text of all treaties registered with the UN is available from the United Nations Treaty Collection website, but regrettably now only on a subscription basis and even more in arrears than the printed version (for an evaluation see QR6.1). If you do have access to the website, one minor irritation is that the citation to the hardcopy version of *United Nations Treaty Series* is not given. Because of the delay in publication in the *United Nations Treaty Series*, *International Legal Materials* published in periodical form by the American Society of International Law is invaluable; it issues the text of many treaties very swiftly, though it cannot be comprehensive. The contents pages of recent issues are on the ASIL website; the full text from 1980 is available on Lexis.

6.14 The precursor to the *United Nations Treaty Series* was the *League of Nations Treaty Series*, founded in the hope that by means of registration and publication, secret treaties, which were seen as one of the evils leading to the First World War, would be eradicated. Before 1919, though there was no similar universal series, there were a number of compilations, commercial treaties naturally being covered most thoroughly. Hertslet and Martens are the two best-known compilers. However, a monumental work is the *Consolidated Treaty Series*, which aims to be as complete a collection as possible of treaties from all these disparate sources for the period 1648 until the foundation of the League of Nations in 1919. It is arranged by date, though there are some appendix volumes containing material omitted from the main work.

6.15 Many countries produce their own equivalents of the *United Kingdom Treaty Series* for treaties to which they are party. These are most likely to be needed for treaties which the UK has not ratified and which have not yet appeared in the *United Nations Treaty Series* and which are not of sufficient significance to be picked up by *International Legal Materials*, typically bilateral treaties.

6.16 There is an ever-expanding range of free sites on the Internet providing the text of treaties, particularly multilateral treaties, which may mitigate the fact that UN's own site (United Nations Treaty Collection) is no longer free. Research institutes, such as the Fletcher School of Diplomacy or the McGill Air and Space Law Institute put up some. Others are from international organisations, particularly those that act as depositaries or secretariats for particular multilateral treaties. For example, the Hague Conference on Private International Law site has all the conventions made under it. There may be also government sites, such as the US Department of State Private International Law Database, or other national sites such as the Australian Treaties Library (put up by AustLII). The latter, for example, has all Australian treaties since 1915, so if it is a multilateral treaty you are after and Australia happens to be a party, you are in luck. The American Society of International Law's website has good guide and links. Other portals worth trying are the Eagle-I service from the Institute of Advanced Legal Studies, the Cornell Legal Information Institute, AustLII World Law, as well as Sarah Carter's Lawlinks.

Texts of EC treaties

6.17 The treaties that established the Communities, the treaties of accession, and subsequent amending treaties are widely available from a variety of sources, apart from those already mentioned. The Official Publications Office of the EC produces a collection in two bound volumes, which are reissued from time to time. The English language version comes, as do all English language official publications of the EC, in distinctive purple covers. Sweet & Maxwell's *Encyclopedia of European Union Law: Constitutional Texts* contains the treaty material. The main treaties are also included in similar works produced by other publishers, often with substantial commentary, such as Smit and Herzog *The Law of the European Economic Community* ((1976–) Matthew Bender) and the *Common Market Reporter* published by CCH. There are also selections of treaty material designed for student use such as Rudden and Wyatt's *Basic Community Laws* (Clarendon Press). Any new provisions will be published first of all in the *Official Journal of the European Communities*. The texts of the main treaties are also on the main Europa website, and Celex.

6.18 Not to be confused with the treaties establishing and regulating the EC itself, are the treaties entered into *by* the EC. These are first published in the L series of the OJ, but there is also an official multi-volume compilation *Collection of the Agreements Concluded by the European Communities* – another purple manifestation. A third source, which may be more convenient, especially for recent treaties not yet in the latest edition of the purple *Collection*, is the Stationery Office version. All the EC treaties are published by TSO as command papers, but they are also numbered within each year in a 'European Communities' series which runs parallel to the *United Kingdom Treaty Series* and to the 'Miscellaneous series' already mentioned. The Council of the European Union has a website maintained by its Agreements Office, which lists the agreements and gives details of parties and status, but not the full text, for which, if wanted in electronic form, a commercial version of Celex will be needed.

6.19 With all European materials there is always the risk of confusing documentation relating to the European Communities with that relating to the Council of Europe; the Foreign and Commonwealth Office command paper 'European Communities' treaty series should not be confused with the *European Treaty Series*. The latter, which contains the fairly numerous treaties emanating from the Council of Europe – the European Convention on Human Rights is not its only claim to fame – is available on an excellent website as well as in hard copy.

Tracing treaties

6.20 For UK treaties the basic finding aid, though getting rather out-of-date, is the *Index of British Treaties*. Originally published by HMSO in 1970 in three volumes under the editorship of Clive Parry, it covered all treaties from 1101 to 1968 (or as nearly all as was practically possible given the time span and the inherent problems in defining a 'treaty'). A fourth volume, covering 1969–88 and updating the previous volumes, was published in 1991; the opportunity was also taken to reissue with it the first three volumes on microfiche, which is helpful for any library that originally failed to acquire them. The main form of arrangement of the index is chronological by date of signature. Exhaustive bibliographical references are given to virtually all possible sources, such as *United Kingdom Treaty Series* number, command number, volume and page number in sessional sets of parliamentary papers, *United Nations Treaty Series*. However, because it commenced publication after the *Index*, references are not given to the *Consolidated Treaty Series* for pre-1919 treaties. Understandably enough, it also does not go to the lengths of including references to statutes which have treaties annexed as Schedules or to books which are not ostensibly collections of treaties. Cross-references are given to later amending treaties, as are, for multilateral treaties, the parties at the time of publication of the index (supplemented to 1988 by vol 4). There are subject indexes in vols 3 and 4. These are each in three sequences: multilateral treaties arranged by subject; bilateral treaties by country subdivided by subject; and bilateral treaties by subject subdivided by country.

6.21 There are indexes produced from time to time to accompany the *United Kingdom Treaty Series*, but as they are not consolidated they are less useful. As the *United Kingdom Treaty Series* and the other related series issued by the Foreign and Commonwealth Office are published by the Stationery Office as command papers, they will also be listed in the various catalogues of government publications discussed in chapter 7.

6.22 For multilateral treaties, whether or not the UK is a party, Bowman and Harris *Multilateral Treaties: Index and Current Status* (originally published by Butterworths, with supplements issued by the University of Nottingham Treaty Centre) is the standard work (or was, at any rate – again, it is getting out of date). Although it does not claim to be absolutely comprehensive, it covers the vast bulk of treaties likely to be encountered in practice. The earliest treaty covered dates from 1856. The primary arrangement is again chronological. Full references to sources of the text and other apparatus are provided (see figure 6.2). After the main sequence is a separate table, easily overlooked, giving a chronological list of treaties that have not been provided with their own main entries but which are referred to in the notes, amendments or other sections of the main entries. At the back are a subject index and a word index. The main work was first published in 1984. There were then cumulative supplements, though unfortunately the last seems to have been published in 1995, covering treaties up to 1 January 1994. The supplement contains in its first half additional treaties (including some pre-1984 treaties originally omitted) and in the second half updating material arranged by the treaty number in the main work.

6.23 Although not dealing with parties and status in the same way as *Bowman and Harris*, there is now an even more comprehensive listing, Christian L Wiktor *Multilateral Treaty Calendar 1648–1995* ((1998) Nijhoff). The main listing is again chronological, with full listings of printed sources and other useful information, and there are various indexes. If it is available, it can certainly solve problems of tracing treaties that *Bowman and Harris* does not.

6.24 Not very widely available nor up-to-date, and less easy to use than either of the above two sources, but to be borne in mind in case of difficulty is the *World Treaty Index* by Peter H Rohn ((2nd edn, 1985) ABC-Clio Information Services,). Its coverage is from 1900–80, and it includes information on some post-1919 treaties that are not in the *League of Nations* or the *United Nations Treaty Series*.

6.25 The *United Nations Treaty Series* has its own indexes, which cumulate quite wide spans (as does the *League of Nations Treaty Series*). Each includes a chronological index and an alphabetical index. The UN also produce a monthly list *Statement of Treaties and International Agreements Registered or Filed and Recorded with the Secretariat*. An alphabetical index cumulates through the calendar year. Although produced in monthly issues, its publication is at least a year in arrears.

Figure 6.2 Bowman and Harris *Multilateral Treaties: Index and Current Status.*

1972

TREATY 592	CONVENTION FOR THE CONSERVATION OF ANTARCTIC SEALS
CONCLUDED	**11 Feb 72**, London
LOCATION	UKTS 45(1978), Cmnd 7209; 29 UST 441, TIAS 8826; 11 ILM 251; 77 RGDIP 555; Kiss 272
ENTRY INTO FORCE	11 Mar 78. Later acceptances effective 30 days after deposit: Art 13
DURATION	Unspecified. Denunciation permitted on 30 Jun of any year, by giving notice on or before 1 Jan of same year. Other parties may then withdraw on same date by giving notice to that effect within 1 month of notification of the first denunciation: Art 14
RESERVATIONS	No clause
AUTHENTIC TEXTS	E F R S
DEPOSITARY	UK
OPEN TO	States participating in the Conference on the Conservation of Antarctic Seals, and others invited to accede with consent of all parties: Arts 10, 12

PARTIES (11)   ARGENTINA* 7 Mar 78; BELGIUM 9 Feb 78; CHILE* 7 Feb 80; FRANCE 19 Feb 75; JAPAN 28 Aug 80; NORWAY 10 Dec 73; POLAND 15 Aug 80; SOUTH AFRICA 15 Aug 72; UK 10 Sep 74; USSR* 8 Feb 78; US 19 Jan 77

TERRITORIAL SCOPE	No clause. Declared applicable; UK - Channel Is, Isle of Man
SIGNATORIES	AUSTRALIA 5 Oct 72; NEW ZEALAND 9 Jun 72

NOTES   The present Convention regulates the killing of Antarctic seals by nationals or vessels of the parties' nationality or flag. See also the relevant measures agreed under the 1959 Antarctic Treaty (treaty 390) and the 1979 Conservation of Antarctic Marine Resources Convention (treaty 779). And see on the conservation of seals, the 1957 Interim Convention on Conservation of North Pacific Fur Seals, 314 UNTS 105, 8 UST 2283, TIAS 3948; 8 Ruster 3716, as amended and extended in 1963, 1969, 1976, and 1980. This establishes the North Pacific Fur Seal Commission. Parties: Canada 16 Sep 57; Japan 20 Sep 57; USSR* 14 Oct 57; US* 30 Aug 57. In force 14 Oct 57.

TREATY 593	CONVENTION FOR THE PREVENTION OF MARINE POLLUTION BY DUMPING FROM SHIPS AND AIRCRAFT
CONCLUDED	**15 Feb 72**, Oslo
LOCATION	UKTS 119(1975), Cmnd 6228; JOF 21 May 74; 1974 RTAF 38; 55 Vert A 725; 11 ILM 262; 78 RGDIP 901; 2 Ruster 530; Kiss 266
ENTRY INTO FORCE	7 Apr 74. Later acceptances effective 30 days after deposit: Art 23
DURATION	Unspecified. Denunciation permitted on 1 year's notice after the Convention has been in force for that party for 2 years: Art 24
RESERVATIONS	No clause
AUTHENTIC TEXTS	E F
DEPOSITARY	Norway
OPEN TO	States invited to participate in the 1971 Oslo Conference on Marine Pollution. Other states may accede by unanimous invitation of the parties: Art 22

PARTIES (13)   BELGIUM 28 Feb 78; DENMARK 28 Jul 72; FINLAND 2 May 79; FRANCE 7 Mar 74; GFR 23 Nov 77; ICELAND 27 Jun 73; IRELAND 25 Jan 82; NETHERLANDS 29 Sep 75; NORWAY 2 Jun 72; PORTUGAL 30 Jan 73; SPAIN 14 Jun 73; SWEDEN 13 Sep 72; UK 30 Jun 75

TERRITORIAL SCOPE	No clause
AMENDMENTS	

1983 Protocol, Misc 12(1983), Cmnd 8942 (amends Arts 8,19,22 and Annex IV). Not in force

NOTES   The parties to this regional Convention (applying to the North Sea and North East Atlantic) agree to harmonise their policies and introduce measures to prevent pollution of the sea by dumping from ships and aircraft. Poland and the USSR were invited to participate in the Convention but declined. A Commission (the Oslo Commission) based on London has been established to administer this Convention. See also the 1972 London Dumping at Sea Convention

358

Published by Butterworths 1984 Supplements issued by the University of Nottingham Treaty Centre.

6.26 Tracing pre-1919 treaties, especially non-British bilateral treaties, has been greatly simplified by the *Consolidated Treaty Series*. There are 12 volumes of indexes to the 231 volumes of the main work. There is a party index, subdivided chronologically within each country, and a general chronological index, which covers all treaties other than those dealing with colonial and postal matters; the latter, because they are particularly numerous and generally of less significance, have their own chronological index in order to make the main index easier to use.

Checking status and parties

6.27 Apart from tracing treaties by subject matter or date, as described above, the most usual research problem is finding out whether a treaty is in force yet and who the parties to it are. Some treaties become binding on the contracting parties as soon as they have all signed them, but the commonest method of entry into force is by subsequent ratification by the individual states. Which organ of state is empowered to ratify varies from state to state. In the UK, it is the Crown – treaty-making is a prerogative power, so is not a matter requiring parliamentary approval, though as a matter of practice treaties subject to ratification are laid before Parliament as least 21 days in advance under the Ponsonby rule. Treaty-making is also, of course, one of the prerogative powers that are beyond the jurisdiction of the courts (for an abortive attempt to prove otherwise, and an instructive legal analysis of treaty-making, see *R v Secretary of State for Foreign and Commonwealth Affairs, ex p Rees-Mogg* [1994] QB 552). In the US, in contrast, for some kinds of treaty the President requires approval of two-thirds of the Senate for ratification.

6.28 Ratification, though, may not be the end of the story. The treaty may provide, in analogous fashion to the commencement provisions of statutes, for a certain period to elapse after ratification before entry into force. Although, if there is no contrary provision, multilateral treaties only come into force when all the parties have ratified, many modern multilateral treaties provide for entry into force as soon as a certain number of parties (or certain specified parties) have ratified. Here it should be appreciated that it is in the nature of an international treaty that it can only bind those states that have actually ratified it; if they have not, it is immaterial that they were signatories and that it is otherwise in force.

6.29 A further complication is that, if the treaty so allows, a state may not ratify it in its entirety but may make reservations and derogations, ie limit or exclude particular articles from its undertaking. The parties to a treaty are not necessarily static either. States that were not original signatories may subsequently accede to it; and, if the treaty permits it, or if there exists one of the recognised grounds for termination, a state may withdraw from it. The duration of a treaty may not be indefinite. It may state on its face that it is to operate only for a limited period or a later treaty may expressly supersede it. Problems, analogous to the implied repeal of statutes, can also arise where a later treaty between the same parties is inconsistent with an earlier treaty. These problems can be exacerbated by changes in the constitutional or geographical identity of states – the reunification of Germany and the fragmentation of the rest of Eastern Europe provide ample contemporary illustration. This area is governed by the doctrine of state succession, for whose intricacies the reader is referred to standard works on public international law.

6.30 As it is in the context of multilateral treaties that the problems of status and parties usually arise, *Bowman and Harris* (see para **6.22** above) is the most useful work in this field (see figure 6.2). Among the annotations to each treaty there are sections covering entry into force, duration, reservations, depository, parties, and signatories. Either the date that the treaty came into force or the requirements for entry into force is given. 'Duration' will indicate any specific provisions as to expiry and also whether denunciation is permitted. Which articles, if any, may be derogated from by reservation are stated. The 'parties' are those that have 'accepted' the treaty, whatever the method of acceptance is, be it definitive signature, ratification, accession or otherwise. The 'signatories' section, however, lists only those parties that have signed but not ratified (or otherwise accepted). Under both headings an asterisk against the name of a country indicates that it has made a reservation; a double asterisk that it has withdrawn the reservation.

6.31 The *Index of British Treaties* gives similar information to *Bowman and Harris* and will cover bilateral treaties as well – provided of course that the UK is a party. Neither work, though, is much help with recent changes. There is the *Supplementary List of Ratifications, Accessions, Withdrawals, etc* prepared by the Foreign and Commonwealth Office issued with the *UK Treaty Series*. But it is quarterly and does not cumulate. So often the simplest thing to do is contact the Treaty Section of the Records and Historical Department at the Foreign and Commonwealth Office (details on the FCO website).

6.32 If you are dealing with a non-British treaty and *Bowman and Harris* does not help, there is the UN publication *Multilateral Treaties Deposited with the Secretary-General: Status as at 31 December . . .* . It is published annually in hard copy and even then is not entirely up-to-date. One useful feature, however, is that as well as information on date of entry into force and parties, it often includes the actual text of any reservations. If you access to the UN Treaty Collection website, it may be in a more up-to-date form there. Most multilateral treaties have official 'depositaries', which collate all subsequent ratifications, amendments, etc. Depositaries may be international organisations or states. The former, particularly those with extensive treaty depositary functions, such as the World Intellectual Property Organization, International Labour Organization, the Organization of American States, may have websites with status information (or published lists). If a state is the depositary, you can try the relevant foreign ministry. The UK is the official depositary for about 36 treaties, and full details of status and parties are on the FCO website. The status listing for EU treaties on the Council of the European Union website has been mentioned above; and the not-to-be-confused Council of Europe website gives full information on the status of all its treaties.

Preparatory materials

6.33 As well as the treaties themselves, preparatory materials – the equivalent of White Papers, Bills and *Hansard* – are often of particular interest. (A useful article amplifying some of the points discussed below is Richard Gardiner 'Treaties and treaty materials: role, relevance and accessibility' (1997) 47 *International and Comparative Law Quarterly* 643–662.) Minutes of negotiations, proceedings of international conferences and successive drafts of the treaty are often published, and are of use not only for the academic study of international law but also as aids to interpretation in the event of a dispute coming before an international tribunal such as the International Court of Justice, or even an English court. The principles for the interpretation of treaties are given in art 31 of the 1969 Vienna Convention on the Law of Treaties. As in statutory interpretation, the text of the treaty has primacy. But art 32 goes on to provide, in terms that were very much echoed in *Pepper v Hart* with regard to citing *Hansard* (see chapter 4), that preparatory work may be referred to if an interpretation resulting from art 31 leaves the meaning ambiguous or obscure, or leads to a result that is manifestly absurd or unreasonable. Such materials that constitute the 'preparatory work' (undefined in the Vienna Convention) are generally known as *travaux préparatoires*, and are in practice often liberally referred to. The leading case on the use of such materials by the *English* courts is *Fothergill v Monarch Airlines* [1981] AC 251. That case concerned the meaning of 'damage' to baggage under the Carriage by Air Act 1961, which gave effect to the Warsaw Convention of 1929, as amended by the Hague Protocol of 1956. Lord Wilberforce suggested that cautious use of the *travaux préparatoires* was permissible, provided two conditions were met. The second, again very much like *Pepper v Hart*, was that they should clearly and indisputably point to a definite legislative intention. The first suggested condition, however, is of particular interest – the material involved had to be public and accessible. And that is often where the rub lies in using or attempting to use *travaux préparatoires*. The form of their publication, if indeed they are published, is very disparate, and their availability in libraries often limited. In *Fothergill* the proceedings of the 1955 Hague Conference had been published by the International Civil Aviation Organisation and were available for sale through HMSO and 'so accessible to legislators, text-book writers, airlines and insurers'. In so far as there is a pattern, this instance was fairly typical. The main international organisations that sponsor treaty-making, particularly of course the UN, do have their own publishing programmes. The publications may not necessarily call themselves '*travaux préparatoires*' – more usually they are described simply as conference proceedings. Commercial publishers may reprint selections – Oceana often include this kind of material in their looseleaf collections, such as *New Directions in the Law of the Sea*.

6.34 There are also a number of instances of retrospective publication where the ongoing importance of the convention in question warrants disinterring the materials and giving them wider circulation. The publication of the *Collected Edition of the Travaux Préparatories of the European Convention on Human Rights* was only started in 1975 and not completed until an eighth volume was published in 1986. The complete record of the making of the Hague Rules, which date from 1924, was only published in 1990: Michael F Sturley *The Legislative History of the Carriage of Goods by Sea Act and the Travaux Préparatoires of the Hague Rules* (Rothman, 3 vols) (being an American work, the Act of the title is the US Act of 1936; the equivalent UK Act, which is briefly discussed, is the 1924 Act). Other examples are given in Gardiner's article: G Gaja *International Commercial Arbitration: the New York Convention* ((1978– , 4 vols) Oceana); R Horner and D Legrez *Second International Conference on Private Aeronautical Law: Minutes, October 2–12, 1929* ((1975) Rothman), which provides an English translation of materials on the Warsaw Convention, previously only published in French; and N Jasentuliyana and R S K Lee *Manual on Space Law* ((1979, 4 vols) Oceana), which includes the materials relating to the main multilateral treaties on outer space, which date back to the 1960s.

International case law

6.35 If treaties are the equivalent of legislation in the field of public international law, there is also the case law of international courts and tribunals, which apply and interpret them, to consider. The International Court of Justice at The Hague (also known as the World Court) is just the pinnacle of the international legal system. There are a plethora of other courts and tribunals. An extremely valuable guide to these is Philippe Sands (ed) *Manual on International Courts and Tribunals* ((1999) Butterworths). It goes through in turn the general bodies, such as the ICJ and the Permanent Court of Arbitration; trade and dispute settlement bodies, such as the International Centre for the Settlement of Investment Disputes; regional bodies, both well-known, such as the ECJ, and less well-known, such as the Court of Justice of the Andean Community; human rights bodies, of which there a number other than the ECHR; international criminal courts, which now comprise the new International Criminal Court set up in 1998 as well as the specific tribunals for Yugoslavia and Rwanda; the inspection panels of the multinational and regional development banks; and lastly the non-compliance procedure under the Ozone Layer Protocol. For each tribunal the *Manual* sets out in standard form its governing texts, composition, jurisdiction and procedure. There is also, most usefully, a section near the end of each entry giving the form in which the tribunal's case law is published and whether it is available on the Internet. The entries finish with a bibliography and, where relevant, a list of parties to the governing convention.

6.36 The decisions of the International Court of Justice (ICJ) are published in an official series, *Reports of Judgments, Advisory Opinions and Orders*, with an equivalent series for the precursor Permanent Court of International Justice. There was also the *Summaries of Judgments, Advisory Opinions and Orders of the ICJ, 1958–1991* ((1992) UN). The ICJ website has a complete list of cases from 1946, with the full text of recent decisions and the text of the summaries for older decisions. There have been several works summarising or digesting ICJ cases which include, E I Hambro *The Case Law of the International Court of Justice* (published on an ongoing basis from 1952 to 1976: Nijhoff); continued by R Berhardt *Digest of Decisions of the International Court of Justice 1976–1985* ((1990) Springer) continued in turn by R Hofmann *World Court Digest* ((1993) Springer). There are a number of other established series for other tribunals such as the *Reports of International Arbitral Awards* published by the UN. The main general, commercially published, series is the *International Law Reports,* which started in 1929 under the title *Annual Digest of Public International Law Cases*. The serial *International Legal Materials* includes the texts of decisions as well as treaties and other documents. That can be supplemented, particularly for current awareness, by summaries in the electronic newsletter International Law in Brief, also prepared by the American Society of International Law. For modern decisions, other than in the sources listed above, look at Sands's *Manual* if it is particular tribunal, or particular type of tribunal, that you are interested in. Otherwise, the promulgation of international decisions, as with international legal materials generally, is now heavily web-based. The portals suggested at the end of para **6.16** in connection with treaties are good places to start.

6.37 References will also be found in the major textbooks on international law, such *Oppenheim's International Law* ((vol 1, 9th edn, 1992; vol 2, 7th edn, 1952) Longmans) and Ian Brownlie's *Principles of Public International Law* ((5th edn, 1998) OUP), to earlier case law, particularly relating to individual international arbitrations, which pre-dates the setting up of the Permanent Court of Arbitration in 1899 and the Permanent Court of International Justice in 1922, and so pre-dating the series of reports deriving from them. They may have published in an ad hoc fashion but there are a number of collections of such decisions, notably John Bassett Moore's *Digest of International Law* (1906, 8 vols) and *History and Digest of the International Arbitrations to which the United States has been a Party* (1898, 6 vols). Records of early arbitrations to which the UK was a party may have been published in the Parliamentary Papers or *British and Foreign State Papers*.

7. Other official publications

When are official publications needed?

7.1 Legislation, case law and treaties are lawyers' primary sources: why should they need to look at other official publications? There are four main applications:

– legislation or quasi-legislation not issued as statutes or SIs;
– proposals for law reform and background to existing legislation;
– judicial or quasi-judicial material not published as law reports; and
– material relevant to research into government activities that impinge on the law or its administration.

The nature of the first two, which are probably the most important, have already been covered in chapters 3 (see paras **3.160–3.170**) and 4. In so far as treaties are the equivalent of legislation in the international sphere, the *travaux préparatoires* discussed in paras **6.33–6.34** can also be regarded as a species of the second category. The last two categories will be expanded on a little here.

Quasi-judicial material

7.2 'Quasi-judicial' denotes decisions that are a half-way house between full-blown judicial precedent and arbitrary administrative rulings. As with quasi-legislation they can most easily be defined by example rather than by any underlying principle, though the jurisprudence of natural justice in the context of judicial review has imported some order to this field. Examples at the top end of the scale, bordering on judicial decision-making, are ministers' and inspectors' decisions in planning matters, Lands Tribunal decisions on rating and valuation and Commissioners' decisions in the field of social security. Although on matters of law they are subject to the decisions of the higher courts and will often turn on their particular facts, they are of considerable importance to practitioners in ascertaining current practice and advising accordingly. Their affinity with case law is such that they have their own series of 'law reports' – the above three examples will found in, for example, the *Planning Appeal Decisions*, *Rating and Valuation Reporter* and *Reported Decisions of the Social Security and Child Support Commissioners*. For this reason these examples at the top end of the scale are really in the province of chapter 4 on case law – and indeed the above series are covered by such finding aids as *Current Law*.

7.3 Moving slightly down the scale we have, for example, the decision-making bodies who nowadays have wide-reaching powers in connection with the regulation of companies and commercial activity, and whose determinations are often of wider significance than the case in hand. Monopolies and Mergers Commission investigations and Office of Fair Trading reports come within this category. As well as the separately published full reports, summaries appear in the annual report of the Director of Fair Trading. Department of Trade investigations and the statements and rulings of the Panel on Take-overs and Mergers are important too.

7.4 Various public bodies, who are obliged to issue annual reports, take the opportunity to clarify their practice by highlighting particular cases they have had to deal with. Two that were traditionally referred to quite frequently by practitioners were the Charity Commissioners reports and the reports of the Criminal Injuries Compensation Board, though both have altered somewhat in format or content recently. Until 1993, the annual report of the Charity Commissioners contained decisions on charitable status – the 1991 report, for example, included the decision on whether the objects of the Margaret Thatcher Foundation were educational in the charity law sense. These annual reports continue to be referred to since the principles applied in the decisions have not changed. From 1993 the case law part of the annual report was hived off as a separate publication, *Decisions of the Charity Commissioners*. They have gone if not the way of all flesh then the way of much paper – from 1998 they are only published on the Charity Commission's website. The practice and policy of the Commission is important to practitioners, since charities by their nature are often reluctant to spend their funds on having points determined in the courts. The annual reports of the Criminal Injuries Compensation Board used to summarise awards made for different kinds of injury. Since under the Criminal Injuries Compensation Scheme, prior to its replacement by a tariff system under the Criminal Injuries Compensation Act 1995, the Board awarded compensation in the same way that damages for personal injuries were calculated at common law, its reports acted as a kind of *Kemp & Kemp* in this field, and indeed criminal injuries awards were cited in conventional personal injury cases. Because of a backlog of outstanding cases, the old Board continued in being until 31 March 2000, and issued its last annual report in 2001. These annual reports, unlike the Charity Commissioners' reports, are now redundant and the annual reports of the successor body, the Criminal Injuries Compensation Authority, only contain the usual statistics and accounts. However, under the 1995 Act there is now an independent Criminal Injuries Compensation Appeals Panel, which issues its own annual reports, the first being for the year 1 April 1996 to 31 March 1997. Although with the fixed tariff system the quantum of awards is not directly in issue, the Panel's annual reports do contain a section of 'Hearing Procedures – Case Summaries' illustrating how it approached and decided a variety of issues, which will be of value to the practitioner.

7.5 The reports of the Ombudsman, or to give him his formal title, the Parliamentary Commissioner for Administration, are another important source. When the office was first set up reports of all cases investigated were published; nowadays select cases only are published (four times a year), but they continue to provide valuable guidance on what may amount to maladministration and when redress may be available. As well as the reports themselves, useful supplementary information can also be obtained from the reports of the House of Commons Select Committee on the Parliamentary Commissioner for Administration which monitors his activities (and also now those of the Health Services Commissioner). As well as the original Ombudsman, parallel offices have been set up, either under statute or voluntarily, as watchdogs on various non-governmental public services, such as banking, insurance, building societies and legal services. Their annual reports can similarly offer guidance in the event of a dispute in these fields.

7.6 As well as these regular publications, reports of one-off inquiries may be of wider interest than just to those involved. Official reports into air, sea or rail accidents, for example, may give valuable background information on safety standards and procedures in the event of a lawyer having to act in similar circumstances. Another example is the guidelines in child abuse cases set out by Dame Elizabeth Butler-Sloss in the Cleveland Report (Cm 412) – though now dating from 1988, they continue to be widely referred to in the courts.

7.7 Although current materials are the most needed, from time to time older items may have to be consulted. Two illustrations indicate that the scope of materials of possible relevance is not narrow. The decisions of the Industrial Assurance Commissioner dating back to the 1920s continue to be cited in the footnotes to *MacGillivray and Partington on Insurance Law*. Such footnotes tend to cause difficulty since 'I.A.C. Rep' is not a series of law reports but refers to the Commissioner's annual reports, which were published in the House of Commons papers (or even, if you are exceedingly unlucky, in the papers of the old Northern Ireland Parliament). The other illustration is the Royal Commission on Market Rights and Tolls, whose reports were published from 1889 to 1891, collected a vast range of material on ancient franchises and other matters that are still referred to in the current edition of *Pease and Chitty's Law of Markets and Fairs*.

Research into law-related government activities

7.8 The kinds of material in this area are those likely to be used more in connection with academic research than as aids to the practitioner. One obvious example would be statistical information, such as the *Criminal Statistics* and *Judicial Statistics*. The police, the Crown Prosecution Service, prisons, the probation service, the administration of the courts and immigration are all areas where various official publications are produced, whether in the form of annual reports, particularly studies, or statistics. The House of Commons Home Affairs Committee is particularly active in producing material in these kinds of areas. In chapter 4 the use of *Hansard* in connection with the background to Bills was discussed, but it serves also as a repository of factual information because it contains ministers' answers to parliamentary questions, both written and oral, which may be of value to the researcher, as may be general non-legislative debates. If only for prurient rather than scholarly reasons, the reports of the Review Body on Top Salaries, which include judicial salaries, are often asked for.

Types of official publications

Parliamentary papers

7.9 Bills, *Hansard* and the *Journals* were described in chapter 4. There are three other types of parliamentary publication that are usually what is meant by 'parliamentary papers': command papers; House of Commons papers; and House of Lords papers. Command papers are presented to Parliament by ministers, technically by command of Her Majesty. Typical examples are government White Papers and reports of Royal Commissions. House of Commons and House of Lords papers, while naturally enough covering material emanating from Parliament itself – such as reports and minutes of Select Committees – are wider than that. For example, many quangos and other external bodies are required to present annual reports or accounts to Parliament, and these may be House of Commons papers. But the distinctions between the series are not very meaningful to the average user, and so predicting which materials will be found in the command papers, which in the House of Commons papers, and which will not be parliamentary papers at all, can be done with little precision. The Quick Reference Guide gives examples of the most commonly encountered publications and which category they fall into (QR7.5). In the case of annual reports of quangos (or NDPBs – non-departmental public bodies), the directory *Public Bodies*, prepared by the Cabinet Office and published annually by the Stationery Office used to tell you (among other things) whether they are published by the Stationery Office, by the body itself or are not published at all. It seems to have stopped doing so, but web addresses are given for most.

7.10 Command papers began in 1833 and have been published in six separately numbered series since then, the new series being started to avoid the numbers exceeding four digits. To distinguish the six series, a different form of the abbreviation for the word 'Command' has been used, the very first series having a number only. It thus essential to note and cite the precise form of the abbreviation. The coverage of the six series is as follows:

1833–1869	1 – 4222
1870–1899	C 1 – C 9550
1900–1918	Cd 1 – Cd 9239
1919–1956	Cmd 1 – Cmd 9889
1957–1986	Cmnd 1 – Cmnd 9927
1986 to date	Cm 1 – [Cm 5000 in 2001]

7.11 Command papers are not currently available on the Internet as a class, but quite a number, especially Green or White Papers, are put up on the relevant government department's website. Selecting six recent command papers fairly much at random, the following five were all available on the Internet: Cm 4404 FCO *Human Rights Annual Report*; Cm 4413 Home Office *The Funding of Political Parties* (White Paper); Cm 4783 Lord Chancellor's Department *Judicial Appointments Annual Report*; Cm 5060 Department for Education and Employment *Schools: Building on Success* (Green Paper); Cm 5066 Home Office *Proceeds of Crime: Consultation on Draft Legislation*. The sixth, Cm 5014 Competition Commission *Report on the Acquisition of Interbrew SA of the Brewing Interests of Bass PLC*, was not available in full text, but there was a summary. All Law Commission reports, which are usually command papers, are now published on the Internet, and go back to about 1997.

7.12 House of Commons and House of Lords papers are separately numbered in each parliamentary session, which in modern times, unless disrupted by a general election that year, runs from November. It is thus necessary to cite the years of the session, not merely the calendar year of publication. The following is the correct form:

HC 129 (1974–75) or HL 174 (1984–85)

7.13 Libraries which take a complete set of parliamentary papers will usually keep the recent ones filed as the three separate series. However, traditionally a set of sessional volumes for each House would be bound up, with the material rearranged according to subject matter rather than numerically. Title pages and indexes were officially prepared and pagination assigned to each volume. Some libraries may have physically added the pagination or may have allowed it to remain merely notional. The order of the material in these sets, which amounted to anywhere between 30 and 100 volumes for each session, would be: bills, accounts and papers, and the reports from committees, etc. The index volume for each session translated command paper or House paper number into the appropriate volume and page numbers. As all command papers and many of the other papers are presented to both Houses of Parliament, the sessional sets for each House contain much of the same material, though they are not identical. If there is no reference to the contrary, a citation to a sessional set will be to the House of Commons version. A citation to a sessional set would look like:

PP (1894–1895) XXIV, 247

The roman numerals are the volume number, and the arabic numerals the page number, ie the notional page number within the whole volume. Difficulty is sometimes caused when citing a particular page within an item since it will bear the printed page number of the individual item. Citation by means of numbered paragraphs, if the item has them, is one way to avoid confusion. The House of Commons paper number or command number may cited too.

7.14 House of Commons and House of Lords papers, as with command papers, are not published in blanket form on the Internet. The current policy is to make available, on the Parliament website, Select Committee reports and minutes (which are generally the most sought after category), and these go back in most cases to the beginning of session 1997/98. A small selection of the papers of general interest is also put up on the site.

7.15 It should be mentioned that as well as the hard copy version, the parliamentary papers are published on microfiche by Chadwyck-Healey. As well as the current papers issued monthly (so a little in arrears of the printed version), all of the papers from 1801 onwards are available in this form and, especially for early nineteenth-century papers, is more bibliographically complete than many printed sets. A project to reprint the nineteenth-century papers rearranged by subject was started by the Irish University Press but never completed; some libraries may have the papers in this form (large dark green volumes).

Non-parliamentary publications

7.16 As mentioned, there are no hard and fast rules for knowing whether a governmental document is published in the parliamentary papers or not. Even major reports which one expects always to appear as command papers can catch one out – for example, the Woolf report *Access to Justice*, which led to the Civil Procedure Rules, was simply a one-off item published by HMSO, as was the earlier Roskill Fraud Trials Committee report. The Stationery Office is responsible for publishing many departmental items as well as parliamentary papers, but there is an increasing trend for government departments to publish their own material themselves, and there are also starting to be examples of materials published only on the web, not in hard copy at all (unless you download it and print it off yourself). But again there is no way of predicting whether or not an item will be a Stationery Office publication. The Nugee Committee report, which the Landlord and Tenant Act 1987 was based on, was not a command paper nor an HMSO publication, but was issued by the Department of Environment.

Since 1980 Chadwyck-Healey have been archiving non-Stationery Office government publications as part of their *Catalogue of Government Publications not Published by TSO* service. Originally it was by means of microfiche. Now it is also in electronic form on the Internet, as part of the UKOP service (see below). What is particularly valuable is that some documents not originally published in electronic form are digitised for inclusion.

Tracing official publications

Electronic sources

7.17 There are quite a variety of electronic sources, some free, others not. Perhaps the most comprehensive service, but which is only available on subscription, is UKOP, which combines the data from the Stationery Office's own catalogues with Chadwyck-Healey's *Catalogue of Government Publications Not Published by TSO*. The web version now includes links to a large number of documents in full text. It also continues to be available for the time being on CD-ROM. Its coverage starts in 1980. The *Not Published by TSO* product also continues separately in hard copy with CD-ROM keyword indexes.

7.18 As well as UKOP, Chadwyck-Healey also produces a CD-ROM index covering the House of Commons parliamentary papers, ie command papers, House of Commons papers and House of Commons Bills. Although it has no particular advantage over UKOP, it is issued free to the subscribers of the microfiche edition of the papers. However, the data from this has been combined with an electronic version of Peter Cockton's mammoth subject index to the nineteenth-century parliamentary papers, and the digitisation of earlier twentieth century official catalogues of parliamentary papers to produce a consolidated *Index to House of Commons Parliamentary Papers on CD-ROM* from 1801 to date. Although only updated annually, it is an enormously powerful tool for retrospective searching. House of Lords papers, however, are outside its scope. Another retrospective service, BOPCRIS, has just been launched – it is selective, but free (see QR7.1).

7.19 Polis, the parliamentary on-line information service, is created by the House of Commons Library. Not only does it index such material as *Hansard* and the parliamentary papers, for which coverage goes back to 1979, but also the contents of the House of Commons Library itself. As this naturally includes a very wide range of official publications other than parliamentary materials as such, it is a useful resource. A free version is available on the Parliament website. A more sophisticated version, Parlianet, is available on subscription as one of the Justis Internet services from Context. Parlianet replaces the *Parliament* CD-ROMs from Context. Although it is a bibliographical indexing service, it provides links to full text sources, where they are available, such as recent *Hansard*. Polis is updated daily, and it is for current material that it is most useful, but it is now a very large database – dates of coverage of the various categories of material indexed on it are given in the Quick Reference

Guide (QR7.1). The availability of the full text of *Hansard* on the Internet and on CD-ROM has already been discussed at para **4.50**.

7.20 The Badger database on Current Legal Information (and the equivalent data on Westlaw UK) indexes parliamentary papers and other selected official publications from May 1993. Its coverage of government press releases is also a useful indirect route to tracing official publications, since publication is invariably heralded by an official press release. Lawtel covers command papers.

7.21 The Stationery Office website has a searchable catalogue of all its publications available for sale, and also the *Daily Lists*. It also maintains a separate Official Documents website, which is very useful. It lists all Stationery Office publications that have been published on the Internet either in full text or in summary form, so it is a good place to check whether, for example, a command paper is available free of charge (though rather irritatingly there is not a simple numerical listing of them, and a free text search on the number produces unpredictable results). It also tries to collate other official documents published on the Internet by government departments. The general ukonline site should also take you to relevant departmental sites if necessary. But a Google search is often the quickest way to find official documents on the Internet.

Manual sources

7.22 The Stationery Office produces monthly catalogues of its publications, including parliamentary papers, Bills and Acts (but not SIs), and these are cumulated into annual catalogues. Before 1966 the annual catalogues were collected together in five-year groups with continuous pagination and a consolidated index. The publications issued by the Stationery Office (and by certain bodies for which it acts as agents) each day appear in the *Daily Lists*. These are a source of information between monthly catalogues, though it is necessary to browse through each list to locate a particular item. (Unlike the monthly and annual catalogues, they also include SIs and draft SIs.)

7.23 In the monthly and annual catalogues, parliamentary papers and Bills are listed first in their respective numerical sequences. There then follows a list arranged alphabetically by body responsible. Parliamentary papers are included here as well as in the numerical sequence. Publications from parliamentary committees are entered in the alphabetical sequence strictly by title, for example, under 'Select Committee on European Legislation' (the House of Commons committee) or 'Select Committee on the European Communities' (the House of Lords committee). The monthly catalogues have indexes, which cumulate through the year. They include the names of chairmen of committees as well as subjects (as have the annual catalogues in recent years). The monthly catalogues have page numbers that run from issue to issue, and it is these that are referred to in the index, rather than the particular month.

Figure 7.1 shows an entry from a Stationery Office annual catalogue with entries in both the numerical sequence of House of Lords papers and in the alphabetical sequence under the name of the Committee. Figure 7.2 shows that both entries are indexed under 'Medicinal products: patent protection', 'Oliver' (the chairman of the committee) and 'Patent protection: medicinal products'. Figure 7.3 shows the title page of the report itself; the paper number is in the bottom left-hand corner.

Figure 7.1 HMSO Annual Catalogue.

10 *House of Lords papers. Session 1991-92*

House of Lords papers. Session 1991-92

Her Majesty's most gracious speech to both Houses of Parliament: delivered on Thursday, 31st October 1991. – [2], 4, [2]p.;30 cm: 0 10 499992 6 *£1.45*

(ECC-i) Progress of scrutiny, 12 November 1991. – Select Committee on the European Communities. –17p.; 30 cm. – 0 10 497892 9 *£3.95*

(ECC-ii) Progress of scrutiny, 26 November 1991. – Select Committee on the European Communities. –14p.; 30 cm. – 0 10 497992 5 *£3.95*

(ECC-iii) Progress of scrutiny, 17 December 1991. – Select Committee on the European Communities. –18p.; 30 cm. – 0 10 498092 3 *£3.95*

(1) Roll of the Lords spiritual and temporal. – 44p.;30 cm. – 0 10 401192 5 *£7.00*

(3) Social security, Northern Ireland: consolidation of certain enactments relating to social security in Northern Ireland: Lord Chancellor's memorandum. – House of Commons papers 10. – 12p.;30 cm. – 0 10 400392 8 *£2.35*

(4) 1st report, session 1991-92. – Committee of Selection. – The Lord Aberdare (chairman). – 4p.;30 cm. – 0 10 400492 4 *£1.30*

(5) 1st report [session 1992-93]: patent protection for medicinal products with evidence. – Select Committee on the European Communities. – The Lord Oliver of Aylmerton (chairman of Sub-committee E). – 22, 25p.;ill.;tables;30 cm. – Evidence taken before Sub-committee E [Law and Institutions]. – 0 10 400592 0 *£8.00*

(6) Amendment made on 11th November 1991 to the standing orders relating to public business. – 2p.; 21cm. – Relates to Standing Order 82. – 0 10 400692 7 *£0.60*

(9) 2nd report, session 1991-92. – Committee of Selection. – 4p.; 30 cm. – 0 10 400992 6 *£1.30*

(13) 1st report from the Select Committee on the House of Lords' Offices: session 1991-92. – Select Committee on the House of Lords' Offices. – 4p.; 30 cm. – 0 10 401392 3 *£1.30*

(15) 3rd report, session 1991-92. – Committee of Selection. – 2p.; 30 cm. – 0 10 401592 6 *£0.70*

(17) Special report from the Select Committee on the Severn Bridges Bill. – Select Committee on the Severn Bridges Bill. – The Lord Ampthill (chairman). – [6]p.; 30 cm. – 0 10 401792 9 *£1.90*

(18) 1st report from the Select Committee of the House of Lords on Procedure of the House, session 1991-92. – Select Committee of the House of Lords on Procedure of the House. – 2p.; 30 cm. – 0 10 401892 5 *£0.70*

(23-I) 1st report, session 1991-92: Social Security Contributions and Benefits Bill [H.L.], Social Security Administration Bill [H.L.], Social Security (Consequential Provisions) Bill [H.L.], Social Security Contributions and Benefits (Northern Ireland) Bill [H.L.], Social Security Administration (Northern Ireland) Bill [H.L.], Social Security (Consequential Provisions) (Northern Ireland) Bill [H.L.]. – 1: Report. – Joint Committee on Consolidation Bills. – House of Commons papers 140-I. – [8]p.]; 30 cm. – 0 10 480192 1 *£1.90*

(24) Radioactive substances: consolidation of certain enactments relating to radioactive substances: Lord Chancellor's memorandum. – House of Commons papers 148. – 7p.; 30 cm. – 0 10 402492 5 *£1.90*

(25) 2nd report from the Select Committee on the House of Lords' Offices session 1991-92. – Select Committee on the House of Lords' Offices. – [7]p.; 30 cm. – 0 10 402592 1 *£1.90*

(30-i) Minutes of evidence taken before the Select Committee on Science and Technology. Sub-committee I: safety aspects of ship, design & technology: Thursday 7 November 1991: United States Coast Guard. – Select Committee on Science and Technology. Sub-committee I. – The Lord Carver (chairman). – p. 235-245: 30 cm. – 0 10 480292 8 *£4.50*

(30-ii) Minutes of evidence taken before the Select Committee on Science and Technology. Sub-committee I: safety aspects of ship design and technology: Thursday 14 November 1991: the Nautical Institute. – Select Committee on Science and Technology. Sub-committee I. – The Lord Carver (chairman). – p. 246-260: 30 cm. – 0 10 480392 4 *£4.50*

---

340 *Select Committee on the Armed Forces Bill*

6th report from the Select Committee on Statutory Instruments, session 1990-91. – 6p.: 30 cm. – House of Commons papers 27-vi. – 0 10 029169 4 *£1.90*

Minutes of proceedings, session 1990-91: [Tuesday 13th November 1990 - Tuesday 15th October 1991]. – Bob Cryer (chairman). – 12p.: 30 cm. – House of Commons papers 700. – 0 10 270091 5 *£3.75*

Select Committee on the Armed Forces Bill

Special report from the Select Committee on the Armed Forces Bill, session 1990-91: together with the proceedings of the Committee, minutes of evidence and memoranda. – John Wilkinson (chairman). – xxvi, 179p.: 30 cm. – House of Commons papers 179. – The Bill relates to disciplinary procedures in the Services. – 0 10 217991 3 *£21.00*

Select Committee on the Avon Light Rail Transit (Bristol City Centre) Bill [H.L.]

Special report from the Select Committee on the Avon Light Rail Transit (Bristol City Centre) Bill [H.L.]. – The Lord Elibank (chairman). – [2], 10p.: ill.: 30 cm. – House of Lords papers 43. – 0 10 404391 1 *£3.10*

Select Committee on the British Waterways Bill [H.L.]

Special report from the Select Committee on the British Waterways Bill [H.L.]. – 20p.: 30 cm. – House of Lords papers 73. – 0 10 407391 8 *£5.25*

Select Committee on the Darlington Borough Council Bill [H.L.]

Special report from the Select Committee on the Darlington Borough Council Bill [H.L.]. – The Lord Quinton (chairman). – 8p.: 30 cm. – House of Lords papers 60. – 0 10 406091 1 *£1.45*

Select Committee on the European Communities

1st report [session 1991-92]: patent protection for medicinal products with evidence. – The Lord Oliver of Aylmerton (chairman of sub-committee E). – 22, 25p:ill.: tables: 30 cm. – House of Lords papers 5. – Evidence taken before Sub-committee E [Law and Institutions]. – 0 10 400592 0 *£8.00*

3rd report, [session 1990-91]: a new structure for Community railways. – Report. – The Lord Shepherd (chairman Sub-committee B), The Lord Ezra (chairman Sub-committee B). – 34p.: 30 cm. – House of Lords papers 11-I. – Evidence was taken before Sub-committee B [Energy, Transport and Technology]. – 0 10 400991 4 *£7.95* [Vol. 2: Evidence]. – The Lord Shepherd (chairman Sub-committee B), The Lord Ezra (chairman Sub-committee B). – 34, 167p.: 30 cm. – House of Lords papers 11. – Evidence was taken before Sub-committee B [Energy, Transport and Technology]. – Incorporates paper 11-I. – 0 10 401191 0 *£19.80*

4th report, session 1990-91: working time: with evidence. – The Baroness Lockwood (chairman of Sub-committee C). – 16, 83p.: 30 cm. – House of Lords papers 12. – Evidence given before Sub-committee C [Social & Consumer Affairs]. – 0 10 401291 9 *£13.50.*

5th report, session 1990-91: Conference of Parliaments of the European Community: report. – 11p.: 30 cm. – House of Lords papers 20. – 0 10 402091 1 *£3.80*

6th report [session 1990-91]: correspondence with ministers. – The Baroness Serota (chairman)[The Lord Shepherd (chairman Sub-committee B). – 43p.: 30 cm. – House of Lords papers 21. – Correspondence October 1990 to January 1991. – 0 10 402191 8 *£8.70*

7th report [session 1990-91]: non-food uses of agricultural products: with evidence. – The Lord Middleton (chairman of Sub-committee D). – 51, 219p.:ill.; tables: 30 cm. – House of Lords papers 26. – Evidence taken before Sub-committee D [Agriculture & Food]. – 0 10 402691 x *£22.75*

8th report, session 1990-91: European agreements with Poland, Hungary and the Czech and Slovak Federal Republic: with evidence. – The Lord Aldington (chairman of Sub-committee A). – 128p.: tables: 30 cm. – House of Lords papers 35. – Includes written & oral evidence submitted to Sub-committee A (Finance, Trade & Industry & External Relations). – 0 10 403591 9 *£18.45*

9th report [session 1990-91]: conduct of the Community's external aviation relations: with evidence. – The Lord Oliver of Aylmerton (chairman of Sub-committee E). The Lord Lowry (chairman). – 128p.: 30 cm. – House of Lords papers 39. – Evidence submitted to Sub-committee E [Law & Institutions]. – 0 10 403991 4 *£19.65*

Figure 7.2 HMSO Annual Catalogue.

Media: Cross media promotion: Standards 140, 253
Medical & related professions: Statutes in force 354
Medical devices: Sterile: Systems requirements 226
Medical equipment: Systems requirements 226
Medical qualifications 20, 21, 23, 134, 164
Medical research: Treaties 144, 363
Medical staffing 180
Medicinal products: Italy: Treaties 154, 374
  Patent protection 10, 340
Medicine: General: Staffing 180
  Professions allied to medicine 139, 324
Medicines: Names: Approved 303
Medieval finds from excavations in London 309

Oil prices 53, 251
Oil resources 213
Oils: Mineral: Carcinogenicity: Guidance notes 261
  Mineral: Rates of duty 121
Oil wells: Technical data 214, 215, 216, 217, 218, 219, 220, 221, 222
OLD R.A. 179
OLIVER Peter Raymond 4, 6, 7, 9, 10, 340, 341
Opencast coalmining: Future 155, 380
  Future: Wales 42, 378
Operating departments 314
Operating theatres: Use: National Health Service 66, 80, 206, 311
Operation Granby: Preliminary lessons 65, 209
Ophthalmology: Staffing 180
Options for change: Royal Navy 63, 208
Orange badge scheme: Disabled persons: Transport: Circulars 244
Orders: Government: Indexes 356
Ordinary deposits: National Savings Bank: Accounts 94, 313
Ordnance Survey: Accounts 52, 321
  Trading accounts 87, 321
Ordovician: Snowdonia 179
Organic peroxides: Storage & handling 261

Particleboard: Manufacture: Processes: Guidance notes 238
Partnership teaching 210
PARTRIDGE A.D. 314
Part time punishment 295
Patent Office: Annual reports 77, 321
Patent protection: Medicinal products 10, 340
Patents: Treaties 142, 363
Patents, designs & trade marks: Annual reports 77, 321
PATERSON I.B. 179
Pathogens: Vaccination: Laboratory workers 172
Pathology services: Accommodation: Health buildings: Design notes 314
  Management: Reviews 176
Patient data: Computer readable: Care card: Exmouth project 314
Patients: HSS trusts: Working guides: Northern Ireland 386
  Younger & older: Separation 96, 226

Figure 7.3

HOUSE OF LORDS   SESSION 1991–92
1st REPORT

SELECT COMMITTEE ON
THE EUROPEAN COMMUNITIES

PATENT PROTECTION
FOR MEDICINAL PRODUCTS

WITH EVIDENCE

Ordered to be printed 12 November 1991

LONDON: HMSO
£8.90 net

(HL Paper 5)

7.24 As many committee reports are best known by the name of the chairman, TSO also produce a separate quarterly and annual listing by chairman. To find any government publication (not just HMSO ones) before 1982 by chairman, the place to look is the four volumes of *British Government Publications: an Index to Chairmen and Authors* compiled by Stephen Richard ((1974–82) Library Association), whose coverage goes back to 1800.

7.25 The Stationery Office *Daily Lists* and the monthly catalogues include a selection of material from international organisations, such as the European Communities, the UN, and the Council of Europe, which the Stationery Office sells on an agency basis, though not published by them. These materials do not reappear in the annual catalogue, but have their separate annual catalogue, the *Agency Catalogue*, formerly called the *International Organisations Catalogue*.

7.26 Although the sources mentioned above are suitable for finding recent parliamentary papers, there are separate indexes to these, which may need to be consulted, especially for older papers. There are three consolidated indexes covering 1801–52, 1852–99 and 1900–49 respectively; thereafter two decennial consolidations of the annual sessional indexes have appeared. However, the two nineteenth-century indexes have now been superseded by the subject catalogue produced by Peter Cockton in connection with Chadwyck-Healey's microfiche edition of the nineteenth-century papers. Although these printed indexes, as mentioned, have been consolidated into one CD-ROM, they remain useful for many basic inquiries if you have a rough idea of the date of the publication.

7.27 Finding material from *Hansard*, such as parliamentary questions and non-legislative debates, using the sessional indexes is no different from finding debates on Bills as described in chapter 4, so nothing further will be added here, except a reminder that written questions and answers have their own sequence of column numbering.

7.28 Material published by departments rather than by TSO was notoriously difficult to trace until Chadwyck-Healey started to publish their work, accurately, if somewhat awkwardly, entitled *Catalogue of Government Publications Not Published by TSO*. Though now more sensibly consulted on UKOP, the basic listing continues to be produced in hard copy.

Obtaining official publications

7.29 Individual Stationery Office publications, if they are not available on the Internet, can of course be purchased through them if they are in print (or a photocopy obtained if out of print), and individual microfiche of non-Stationery Office publications can be bought from Chadwyck-Healey. Practitioners will have access to the resources available through firm libraries, the Law Society and the Inns. Among the latter, Lincoln's Inn Library has a complete set of parliamentary publications from 1801, with the exception of House of Commons Standing Committee debates before session 1987/88. Most university libraries will have extensive holdings of official publications, whether in special collections or arranged with other materials. Large public libraries may also stock them. In London, Westminster Central Reference Library and the Guildhall Library are particularly well equipped. The Official Publications and Social Sciences Service of the British Library is the major national resource and is now housed in the main British Library building near St Pancras. Although access arrangements vary, the libraries of the government departments themselves, on the principle of going to the horse's mouth, should not be overlooked. The House of Commons and House of Lords libraries themselves are not open to the public, though the House of Lords Record Office which contains the archives (including printed records) of both Houses has a public search room. The place to check on government libraries and many other sources of information on official publications is the *Guide to Libraries and Information Units in Government Departments and other Organisations* prepared and reissued at frequent intervals by the British Library Science Reference and Information Service. On specifically parliamentary materials, there is David Lewis Jones and Chris Pond *Parliamentary Holdings in Libraries in Britain and Ireland* ((1993) House of Commons Library), or the Information Office at the House of Commons will be able to advise.

8. Law outside England and Wales

When non-English law might be needed

8.1 There are three main types of research that might involve non-English law, and each may entail a different approach. The first is the not uncommon situation where the practitioner encounters a matter involving a foreign element. International trade, international financial transactions, offshore trusts, international commercial arbitration and so on are the staple of City lawyers. Procedural matters are important too: forum shopping and the reciprocal enforcement of judgments being examples. But any practitioner may get a case involving perfectly everyday circumstances where the only complication is that they occur to a British citizen abroad, or to a foreign citizen in the UK: having an accident, buying and selling property, getting divorced, dying, committing a crime, paying tax. And of course in this context abroad may, depending on the circumstances, mean Scotland, Northern Ireland, the Channel Islands or the Isle of Man. Unless an English lawyer happens also to have the relevant legal qualifications, it will often be necessary to instruct a local lawyer. But even if that is done, the English lawyer may well want background information and clarification to make best use of any local advice; or, it may be that the information sought is only incidental and can be found without the need to go to a local lawyer.

8.2 The second application is in using cases from other jurisdictions that may have persuasive authority in the English courts. Although not binding on English courts, the decisions from the other common law countries – the US, Canada, Australia and New Zealand being the most important – can be cited, though the content of the new *Practice Direction (Citation of Authorities)* [2001] 1 WLR 1001 (see also para **5.5**) must now be taken into account. Such US and Commonwealth cases were typically used where English authorities on a point were controversial, contradictory, weak or lacking altogether. For this reason such cases tended to assume greater importance in argument before the appellate courts. This is likely to continue to be the case. The *Practice Direction* under the heading 'Authorities decided in other jurisdictions' acknowledges that 'Cases decided in other jurisdictions can, if properly used, be a valuable source of law in this jurisdiction'. It continues: 'At the same time, however, such authority should not be cited without proper consideration of whether it does indeed add to the existing body of law'. As well as complying with the general provisions of the *Practice Direction*, there are two further conditions. An advocate seeking to cite an authority from another jurisdiction must:

(ii) indicate in respect of each authority what that authority adds that is not to be found in authority in this jurisdiction; or, if there is said to be justification for adding to domestic authority, what the justification is;

(iii) certify that there is no authority in this jurisdiction that precludes the acceptance by the court of the proposition that the foreign authority is said to establish.

As already noted the *Practice Direction* does not apply to criminal courts. Nor does it apply to the House of Lords, and indeed the House of Lords, though as averse to the over-citation of authority as any other court, expects counsel to have undertaken the widest research where comparative legal material might be of assistance (see Lord Steyn, extra-judicially, [1999] PL 51 at 58). Like English authorities, the weight attached to a US or Commonwealth case will depend on the level of the court and the reputation of the judge or judges. To the traditional canon of common law case law, now also have to be added decisions of national courts from member states in matters of EC law. Although for this kind of research the primary materials needed are the law reports themselves, legislation, textbooks and journal articles from the relevant jurisdiction may be needed to make sense of the law surrounding the reported decision, and, importantly, to ensure that the decision does not turn on a statute or precedent that expressly departs from English law.

8.3 The third application is what can be described as pure comparative research. This will usually be in the nature of academic research, where comparative law has a rich and long tradition. But it may impinge on the practitioner in so far as law reform proposals, particularly from the Law Commission, are often based on research into the law of other countries.

8.4 For the sake of completeness, two further scenarios should also be mentioned. The first is appeals from Commonwealth courts to the Judicial Committee of the Privy Council. English lawyers are less likely to get involved in these than they once were for two reasons. First, the number of countries that still retain this means of final appeal is steadily diminishing. New Zealand (for the time being) and the Commonwealth Caribbean islands now provide the bulk of the business. Australia and Malaysia for instance have only relatively recently abolished such appeals, while other countries, such as Canada, did so long ago. Secondly, lawyers from their own countries increasingly conduct the appeals. None the less, English firms of solicitors may act in such cases and English counsel may be instructed. A number of English lawyers voluntarily act in death penalty cases from the Caribbean, especially Jamaica, which has a notoriously high number of prisoners awaiting execution on death row. Clearly, in such cases the English lawyer would need to be acquainted with the relevant law, which may or may not be the same as English law. The other possibility is that English lawyers are instructed to act before a court in another jurisdiction because of a lack of suitably qualified local counsel. For example, the Baron Thyssen litigation in Bermuda, which recently achieved some notoriety, involved swathes of solicitors from the City firms and top-notch English silks.

8.5 This chapter can only give a brief outline of materials that may be of use if you are in any of these situations, and only covers those jurisdictions most likely to be encountered by the English lawyer. For many of the larger jurisdictions detailed legal research manuals exist to which reference can be made.

General comparative sources

8.6 Before looking at particular parts of the world, it is worth bearing in mind that there is quite a range of general materials comparing the law in a number of jurisdictions, though much of it relates to business and commercial law because that is where the biggest market for such publications lies. The *Statesman's Yearbook* (Macmillan) is a useful general reference book, particularly if you are dealing with a far-flung or volatile part of the world and need to know the latest position on its government and constitution.

Books and periodicals

8.7 For the quick inquiry into the nature of a particular foreign legal system the entries in the *Oxford Companion to Law* are often a useful starting point, though it is now a little dated. There are also academic works on comparative law in general, such as Rene David, *Major Legal Systems in the World Today* ((3rd edn, 1985) Sweet & Maxwell), Konrad Zweigert and Hein Kotz (translated by Tony Weir) *An Introduction to Comparative Law* ((3rd edn, 1998) Clarendon Press) and Peter de Cruz *Comparative Law in a Changing World* ((2nd edn, 1999) Cavendish). There are numerous academic monographs on the comparative law of particular topics. Geared more to the practitioner is the multi-volume looseleaf work *Modern Legal Systems Cyclopedia* (W Hein).

8.8 Remarkably useful for basic factual inquiries is the international law digest volume of the huge US annual law directory *Martindale-Hubbell*. It covers about 64 countries of the world. Each country only gets about 10 to 15 pages, but they are in small print and a lot of information, in the form of A to Z topics, is crammed in (see figure 8.1). Canadian law, both federal and provincial, gets much fuller treatment, and a whole separate volume is devoted to the digest of US law.

8.9 A major looseleaf publication is the *International Encyclopaedia of Laws* (Kluwer). It is published in separate modules covering particular topics, such as Family Law or Transport, and then summarises the law for a variety of jurisdictions. The main limitation is knowing, before going in search of a set, whether the particular subject, and for that subject the particular jurisdiction, has been dealt with. The *International Encyclopedia of Comparative Law* ((1971–) Mohr) started publication 30 years ago and is still not yet complete. Its scholarly approach and lack of any updating mechanism makes it likely to be of most use for academic research.

8.10 More practical are looseleaf compilations of the law of various countries on various topics, such as those produced by the US-based publishers Oceana. They have full coverage of business law, for example, *Digest of the Commercial Laws of the World*, but they cover other areas, for example, *Transport Laws of the World*. J O von Kalinovski's vast *World Law of Competition* ((1979–) Matthew Bender) is another US product, but English publishers produce similar comparative compilations in some fields: for example, *Butterworths Offshore Service*; *International Trust Precedents* (Sweet & Maxwell); *International Corporate Procedures* (Jordans). The International Bar Association is active in producing works on procedural matters; for example, *Trial and Court Procedures Worldwide*, *Pre-trial and Pre-hearing Procedures Worldwide*, and *Enforcement of Foreign Judgments Worldwide*. The latter topic is also the subject of one of the numerous works edited by Dennis Campbell

Figure 8.1 Martindale-Hubbell.

SWITZERLAND LAW DIGEST

Revised for 1999 edition by

PESTALOZZI GMUER & PATRY, of the Zurich and Geneva Bars.

(C.C. indicates Civil Code; C.O. indicates Code of Obligations.)

INTRODUCTION

CURRENCY:

Basic monetary unit is franc of 100 centimes. Bank notes are legal tender. See also categories Business Regulation and Commerce, topic Banks and Banking; Foreign Trade and Commerce, topic Exchange Control.

Liechtenstein uses Swiss franc currency and subjects its banks to supervision of Swiss National Bank. See Currency Agreement of June 19, 1980.

GOVERNMENT AND LEGAL SYSTEM:

Position within Europe: see category Treaties and Conventions, topic Treaties. (Federal Constitution of the Swiss Confederation of May 29, 1874, as am'd.)

Switzerland (Swiss Confederation) is federation of 26 states called cantons. Six cantons (called half cantons) send only one senator to Senate instead of two and have only one-half of vote in federal referenda requiring not only majority of voters but also majority of cantons. Each canton has its own cantonal constitution. Cantons are competent in all matters not reserved by Federal Constitution to Confederation.

Every Swiss male and female over 18 years can participate in federal, cantonal and local elections and referenda. Swiss cantons and municipalities extend right to vote to foreign residents.

Total revisions of the Constitution and constitutional amendments must be submitted to popular referendum and require majority of voters and of cantons (mandatory constitutional referendum). With respect to popular referenda of federal statutes, etc. (optional and mandatory legislative referendum), see subhead Legislative Power, infra. One hundred thousand voters have right to request total revision of Constitution, or constitutional amendments (Initiative).

Human Rights.—Switzerland is party to European Convention on Human Rights. Basic rights of individual are set forth in Constitution. Governing principle in Art. 4: "All Swiss are equal before the law." Based on that provision Swiss Federal Supreme Court (see subhead Judicial Power, infra) has developed extensive practice for protection of individuals, including foreigners, against arbitrary measures by cantonal authorities which also execute most federal statutes. Men and women have equal rights and right to equal pay for equivalent work. *Note:* Implementing statute in force since July 1, 1996. Switzerland has joined international convention on elimination of all forms of racial discrimination (1965).

Constitution guarantees special freedoms of individuals: freedom of trade and industry; of settlement; of religion, conscience and religious cult; of marriage; of the press; of association; of petition to authorities. Various constitutional amendments since 1947 permit certain restrictions of freedom of trade and industry and State interventions for economic and social reasons by federal (and under some conditions also by cantonal) legislation, and federal legislation for peaceful labor relations.

Suits against solvent debtor must be brought before court at Swiss domicile (by 1999, this must be changed to comply with Lugano Convention). Court must have jurisdiction according to rules on conflict of jurisdiction. Court cannot accept or deny jurisdiction arbitrarily. Exceptional courts are not permitted.

German, French, Italian and Romansch are national languages. The first three are official languages in which all amendments to Federal Constitution, all federal statutes, and certain decrees of Federal Assembly, Federal Government and its departments, and Federal Supreme Court are published. Three published texts are equally authentic. International treaties concluded in one of three official languages are published with translations into two others; only original text is authentic, provided treaty itself does not stipulate otherwise.

As a general rule the organization of the federal authorities is built on the principle of separation of powers. The independence of courts is safeguarded by provisions of Constitution and statutes.

Legislative Power.—Legislative power is vested in Federal Assembly, consisting of two chambers: (a) House of Members (Nationalrat, Conseil National, Consiglio Nazionale) of 200 members and (b) Senate (Staenderat, Conseil des Etats, Consiglio degli Stati) of two members for each canton and one member for each half canton. There are four ordinary sessions per year, extraordinary sessions as necessary.

Certain matters, mainly elections, are deliberated and voted in joint session of both chambers. For all other matters separate approval of both chambers is required. Resolutions are passed in form of federal statutes or federal decrees.

Federal statutes and federal decrees must be submitted to popular referendum if requested by 50,000 voters or eight cantons. Majority of voters decide on acceptance or rejection. Same applies to federal decree approving certain international treaties, unless Federal Government concludes treaty based on prior authority by Federal Assembly. Federal decrees may be enacted at once for limited time by majority of members in each of two chambers. Such decrees, however, cease to be in force after one year, if not accepted by popular referendum if referendum was requested by 50,000 voters or eight cantons. If such decrees are not based on Constitution, popular referendum requiring majority of voters and of cantons is mandatory within one year, otherwise validity expires.

Executive Power.—Seven member Federal Government (Bundesrat, Conseil Fédéral, Consiglio Federale), elected for four years by House and Senate in joint session. Each member of Federal Government heads one department of federal administration. Every year another member acts as president and another as vice-president of Swiss Confederation with largely ceremonial powers.

Judicial Power.—The members of the Swiss Federal Supreme Court (Bundesgericht, Tribunal Fédéral, Tribunale Federale) are elected by House and Senate in joint session. See category Courts and Legislature, topic Courts.

HOLIDAYS:

Provisions for legal holidays are set by Confederation and by each individual canton. In Zürich, following are legal holidays: New Year's Day, Good Friday, Easter Monday, May 1, Ascension, Whitsun-Monday, Aug. 1, Christmas Day, and Dec. 26. If holiday falls on Sun., next day is usually not holiday. For legal purposes Sats. and Suns. are considered to be equal to legal holidays. Transactions on Sats., Suns. and holidays are legally valid.

Switzerland adheres to European Convention on the Calculation of Time Limits dated May 16, 1972.

OFFICE HOURS AND TIME ZONE:

Switzerland is in the Central European (GMT + 01:00) time zone. Office hours are generally from 8 a.m. to 5 p.m.

BUSINESS ORGANIZATIONS

AGENCY:

Swiss law makes distinction between power of attorney and its underlying legal basis. Power of attorney is unilateral authorization by principal to representative to perform legal acts on behalf of principal. (C.O. 32.) Underlying legal basis of power of attorney may be ordinary mandate, or other contract.

Ordinary Mandate.—Agent is responsible to principal to carry out mandate faithfully and carefully. Compensation is due if agreed or if customary. Principal is required to reimburse agent for outlays and expenses incurred in duly carrying out mandate, plus interest thereon, and to discharge agent from any obligations which agent contracted. Mandate may at any time be terminated by revocation or notice by any party. Where it is terminated at unreasonable time, terminating party is required to indemnify other party for damage caused. (C.O. 394-406).

Contracts kindred to mandate with partly special provisions are: Letters and Orders of Credit (C.O. 407-411); Brokerage (C.O. 412-418); Commercial Agency (C.O. 418a-418v); Commission (C.O. 425-439); Shipping Contract (C.O. 440-457). See category Property, topic Powers of Attorney.

ASSOCIATIONS:

Associations for noneconomic or economic purposes may be created in various forms either by agreement or incorporation.

Associations by agreement include various forms of partnerships. See topic Partnerships. Corporate bodies are legal entities (juristische Personen, personnes morales, persone giuridiche). Legal entities are entitled to all rights and subject to all liabilities, except those arising out of human nature, such as sex, age, family relationship. As general rule, corporate bodies for economic purposes acquire legal capacity upon their entry in Register of Commerce. Those not needing registration acquire legal capacity as soon as organized according to law. (C.C. 52-59).

Legal entities include membership association, foundation, share corporation, limited liability corporation, cooperative corporation, and corporate bodies under federal, cantonal or local public law. See topic Corporations.

CORPORATIONS:

Share Corporation.—(Aktiengesellschaft, société anonyme, società anonima). Swiss Code of Obligations applies. Amended Share Corporation Title in force since July 1, 1992.

Legal entity with fixed capital divided into shares. No personal liability of shareholders beyond share capital. (C.O. 620).

Purpose.—Any defined lawful purpose, mostly business. (C.O. 620).

Corporate Name.—Chosen freely; must designate legal nature only if names of living persons are included. (C.O. 950).

See also category Business Regulation and Commerce, topic Firm and Corporate Name.

Duration of Corporate Existence.—Perpetual (or limited if provided in articles).

Incorporators.—At time of incorporation there must be at least three shareholders. (C.O. 625). No restrictions as to nationality of shareholders, but see catchline Alien Shareholders, infra.

Capital.—Minimum capital SFr. 100,000. (C.O. 621).

If shareholder pays for shares in kind, or purchase of assets by corporation from shareholders or third parties is planned, details of transaction must be given in articles. Same for privileges granted to incorporators or other persons. (C.O. 628).

Articles must state corporate name, seat of registered office, purpose of enterprise, capital and contributions made thereto, par value and type of shares issued, manner of calling meetings, voting rights of shareholders, organization of management and internal auditing, and form of announcements by corporation. (C.O. 626).

Articles may provide for regulations (by-laws) specifying powers of different bodies in charge of management.

Incorporation.—Resolutions of organizing meeting must be embodied in publicly authenticated deed with basic documents attached. Same for any amendment of articles, especially any increase or reduction of capital, and for resolution of dissolution. (C.O. 637, 638, 647, 650, 736).

See Topical Index in front part of this volume.

SWZ – 1

collecting together the laws of various countries, either in looseleaf works or in conventional hardback – put him in as an editor on a bibliographical database and you are likely to find something on the subject in question. The Law Library of the Library of Congress produces a number of valuable reports on foreign law.

8.11 The indexes to periodicals described in chapter 2 can be used. Comparative articles from British journals picked up by *Legal Journals Index* are likely to be of particular use as being written from an English perspective, but the *Index to Foreign Legal Periodicals*, briefly mentioned in chapter 2, will give a much fuller range of material, though most of the articles will not be in English. The other leading work, which has the advantage of being confined to material in English, is the *Bibliography of Foreign and Comparative Law Books and Articles in English* ((1955–) Oceana) originally edited by Charles Szladits. The leading comparative law journal published in this country is the *International and Comparative Law Quarterly*, issued by the British Institute of International and Comparative Law.

Legislation

8.12 Finding the legislative sources of foreign countries has been revolutionised by the multi-volume looseleaf work *Foreign Law: Current Sources of Codes and Basic Legislation in Jurisdictions of the World* ((1989–) Rothman) by Thomas H Reynolds and Arturo A Flores. It lists each country's codes, main compilations of laws, official gazettes and court reports, and then gives a subject listing of the main laws operative in a particular area, together with any sources of English translations of the particular laws. A general introduction to the legal system of each country is also given and major English language works on its law are mentioned. Being an American work it omits the US. It is also available as a subscription Internet service, Foreign Law Guide, which has the advantage of numerous direct links.

8.13 One of the problems of using foreign legislation, if you can get access to it, is that of course it will not necessarily be in English. Some of the looseleaf works described above may give extracts of legislation in translation, but there are a number of works that reproduce the full text as well as, or instead of, providing commentary. Oceana Publications, for example, have a series of *Commercial, Business and Trade Laws* of various countries in addition to their *Digest of Commercial Laws of the World*. Graham and Trotman in this country have produced translations of business laws from Middle East countries. Rothman publish the *American Series of Foreign Penal Codes*, though be careful of their date. The International Labour Office publish a *Legislative Series* covering labour laws. Blaustein *Constitutions of the Countries of the World* (Oceana) in a large number of looseleaf volumes is the definitive source for constitutional material. Blaustein may now also be supplemented by sources on the Internet – for many jurisdictions the constitution if nothing else is put up. AustLII's World Law (see para **8.15**) is generally good at picking them up but two other specialist sites are the International Constitutional Law site at the University of Würzburg and the Constitution Finder at the University of Richmond.

Law reports

8.14 Apart from the Commonwealth and Europe, dealt with below, there are relatively few sources that bring together decisions of the courts of different countries. *World Intellectual Property Reporter* (BNA, Washington), *Lloyds Arbitration Reports* and

International Litigation Procedure (Sweet & Maxwell) are the main examples that come to mind.

Primary sources on the Internet

8.15 Legislation, case law and other primary sources from around the world appear on the Internet in ever increasing quantities on both official and unofficial sites. You can of course simply try a Google search, but there are number of gateways that might get you there in a more structured fashion. World Law on the AustLII site is particularly valuable, as it is not merely a set of links. The data is harvested onto its site and can be searched uniformly with its own search engine. The Global Legal Information Network (GLIN) project at the Library of Congress Law Library likewise aims to gather from official sources primary materials into a self-contained database. Material is in the original language with summaries in English where possible. The Library of Congress as an adjunct to the GLIN project produces a useful set of links Guide to Law Online, which includes a 'Nations of the world' section. Links to foreign material will also be found on the other main gateways, such as Cornell, and in this country the IALS's Eagle-I service and SOSIG. As always, the simple uncluttered short lists of links on Sarah Carter's Lawlinks may be the best place to go if you are starting completely from scratch. Some other general foreign law gateways are mentioned at paras **8.102** and **8.110**. For constitutions, see those mentioned at para **8.13**.

Other jurisdictions in the British Isles

Wales

8.16 In revising this chapter for this edition, the heading 'Law outside England and Wales' was retained only with some hesitation. England and Wales remain, of course, for most purposes a single jurisdiction. Indeed the Lord Chief Justice recently made a point of styling his office 'Lord Chief Justice of England and Wales', not just 'of England', while at the same time setting up permanent sittings of the High Court in Cardiff. Primary legislation affecting Wales continues to be made at Westminster. But as we have seen (para **3.81**), the National Assembly for Wales now exercises many powers to make subordinate legislation for the principality. Since those powers can only be exercised within the framework of the enabling Act, which will usually apply to England too, it is unlikely that much substantive difference in the law will arise. But on points of detail, the assumption can no longer be made that the law will be identical. The areas where a weather eye on Welsh legislation may be most needed are local government, social services, education and agriculture. However, since devolution in Wales did not follow the pattern of Scotland whereby competence was given in particular subject areas, the powers of the Welsh Assembly have to be ascertained on a case-by-case basis, depending on the terms of each enabling Act. Fortunately some help is at hand, since the Cardiff Law School, in conjunction with the Welsh Governance Centre at Cardiff University, have a Wales Legislation Online website, which digests each Act for its Welsh implications. The Law Society Office in Wales has also produced a leaflet for solicitors. There is another important consequence of the devolved legislative powers, which is the question of timing. As noted when discussing commencement provisions in general in chapter 3, even where the legislation is substantially the same in both England and Wales, it may come into force on different dates. The convolutions of commencement orders now have to be unravelled with even greater care. Likewise, the implementation of EC directives in Wales may be ahead of or behind the English process.

Scotland

8.17 Historically, the Scottish legal system developed separately from the English common law, taking its roots instead from continental Roman-based civil law. However, it has been heavily anglicised because since 1707 its legislation has emanated from Westminster and its final Court of Appeal in civil cases has been the House of Lords.

8.18 As far as legislation is concerned, the Scotland Act 1988 has radically altered the legal landscape. Even before devolution there were legislative complications. Some Acts of Parliament, or parts of Acts, applied to the whole of the UK, while others applied to Scotland only. Even where Scotland had separate legislation, its provisions may have been very similar to the equivalent statute for England and Wales, except for translating technical terms or making adjustments for differences in procedure. Many statutes applying to Scotland only bore the same title as the related English statute simply with the addition of 'Scotland' in parentheses; for example, there was a Housing Act 1988 and a Housing (Scotland) Act 1988. On the other hand, they sometimes appeared in another guise; for example, parallel provisions to the Courts and Legal Services Act 1990 were applied to Scotland, together with a whole range of other unrelated measures, by the Law Reform (Miscellaneous Provisions) (Scotland) Act 1990. There will continue to be Westminster Acts that apply to Scotland as part of the UK as a whole – those dealing with 'reserved matters' outside the legislative competence of the Scottish Parliament, as elaborately set out in the Scotland Act. Section 28(7) of the Act expressly preserves the power of the Westminster Parliament to make laws for Scotland (though on a conventional view of the doctrine of parliamentary supremacy such a provision might seem strictly speaking unnecessary). But clearly it is expected to be the convention that Westminster will not legislate on devolved matters. Such Westminster Acts applying to Scotland only as there may continue to be are likely to concern mixed devolved and reserved matters, passed at Westminster as a matter of convenience. The Acts of the Scottish Parliament then add another tier.

8.19 The adoption of a strict doctrine of precedent in Scotland was only a nineteenth-century development made under English influence. But now case law is treated in Scotland as a similar source of law. The decisions of the House of Lords in Scottish appeals (which only lie in civil matters, not from the criminal courts) are binding on the Scottish courts. As no Scottish judges were appointed to the Judicial Committee of the House of Lords until 1866 and they have only been in a small minority since, the influence of English legal principles has been strong. As a result the same law may apply in Scotland as in England, even where there is no statutory provision. *Donoghue v Stevenson* after all was a Scottish appeal, as was, to take a more recent example in the law of negligence, *McFarlane v Tayside Health Board* [2000] AC 59 (vasectomy and the unwanted child). The decisions of the other English courts are not binding in Scotland but may be highly persuasive, and the reverse applies in England, particularly where an identical statutory provision has to be construed. Scottish decisions on quantum of damages in personal injury cases and on sentencing, as in England, do not operate as binding precedents but may provide useful illustrations for the English lawyer as much as for the Scottish lawyer.

8.20 If further background is required reference can be made to David M Walker *The Scottish Legal System* ((7th edn, 1997) W. Green; 8th edn forthcoming 2001); Robin M White and Ian D Willock *The Scottish Legal System* ((2nd edn, 1999) Butterworths); and Hector MacQueen *Studying Scots Law* ((1999) Butterworths). The *Scottish Legal Tradition* by M C Meston and others ((new edn, 1991) The Saltire Society and The Stair Society) remains useful too. David M Walker is also the author of the *Oxford Companion to Law*, so due weight is given to Scottish entries in it. If an English practitioner is consulting this section because he or she has been confronted with a matter that crosses the border, they may also benefit from R E Aird and J N St C Jameson *The Scots Dimension to Cross-Border Litigation* ((1996) W Green), especially if fresh editions appear. As well as dealing in some detail with the application of the Brussels Convention, it has useful material on the Scottish legal system and practices of the Scottish courts written for the non-Scottish lawyer. Before outlining materials relevant to Scottish legal research, attention is drawn to fuller treatments elsewhere:

> David R Hart 'Scotland' in Jules Winterton and Elizabeth M Moys (eds) *Information Sources in Law* ((2nd edn, 1997) Bowker Saur) pp 575–601.
> David R Hart 'Researching the law of Scotland' (chapters 9–13) in Peter Clinch *Using a Law Library* ((2nd edn, 2001) Blackstone Press).
> David R Hart 'Scots law' in Jean Dane and Philip A Thomas *How to Use a Law Library* ((3rd edn, 1996) Sweet & Maxwell; 4th edn forthcoming 2001)
> James W Colquhoun *Finding the Law: a Handbook for Scots Lawyers* ((1999) T & T Clark).
> Valerie Stevenson *Legal Research in Scotland* ((revised edn, 1997) Legal Information Resources).

Textbooks and journals

8.21 Walker's *Scottish Legal System*, cited above, although not containing a formal bibliography is a source for a wide range of bibliographical information on Scottish books. There has recently been a marked increase in the output of Scottish legal textbooks and up-to-date treatments of many subjects are available. Both the publishers Butterworths and the Scottish arm of Sweet & Maxwell, W Green, have been particularly active, and the list of the Scottish publisher T & T Clark has expanded. The major event in Scottish legal publishing in recent years, however, has been the production of *The Laws of Scotland: Stair Memorial Encyclopaedia* by the Law Society of Scotland in conjunction with Butterworths. It is the equivalent of *Halsbury's Laws* for Scotland, the last similar venture, Green's *Encyclopaedia of the Laws of Scotland*, not having been updated since 1952. The main work of 25 volumes was originally published between 1986 and 1996. Like *Halsbury's Laws* there is an annual bound cumulative supplement and looseleaf service volume. The volume of material accumulating in the supplement has meant that the fate of the bound volumes of the main work has had to be faced up to. The policy adopted for the time being is to reissue particular titles, rather than whole volumes. These come as booklets filed in looseleaf binders. So care is needed in using the bound volumes, which may contain a mixture of superseded and unsuperseded topics. An on-line version is available as part of Butterworths Scotland Direct suite of databases on the Internet. As well the *Stair Encyclopaedia* and textbooks proper, the reports of the Scottish Law Commission can provide valuable expositions of the existing law in areas where reform is under consideration.

8.22 The first edition of this book listed six current Scottish journal titles. As with legal journals generally, there have been a number of newcomers since then. The following are the current titles, all of which are indexed in *Legal Journals Index*:

> *Edinburgh Law Review*:
> *Journal of the Law Society of Scotland* (full text also on Lexis from 1990)
> *Juridical Review*
> *SCOLAG* (Scottish Legal Action Group)
> *Scots Law Times*
> *Scottish Constitutional and Administrative Law and Practice*
> *Scottish Law and Practice Quarterly*
> *Scottish Law Gazette*
> *Scottish Licensing Law and Practice*
> *Scottish Parliament Law Review*
> *Scottish Planning Law and Environmental Law*

In addition, W. Green publishes a number of current awareness bulletins on particular subject areas, such as business law, criminal law and property law.

Legislation

8.23 As pointed out in chapter 3, *Halsbury's Statutes* does not cover Acts or parts of Acts applying to Scotland only, nor does Lexis include UK statutes applying wholly to Scotland. One of the few virtues of the dreaded brown binders of *Statutes in Force* (see para **3.29**) used to be as a source of the text of Scottish Acts in amended form. Since, as already explained, there has been no updating since 1991, it now only has residual use – it may be better than nothing as a starting point for an oldish Act still in force. The lawyers and citizens of Scotland have more reason than most to be waiting with bated breath for the Statute Law Database. On the other hand, *Current Law Statutes*, also described in chapter 3, except for its very first volume has always included UK statutes applying to Scotland, and also includes Acts of the Scottish Parliament. Until 1991 there was a separate edition, *Scottish Current Law Statutes Annotated*, but its content was identical to the English edition except for the addition of Acts of Sederunt and Acts of Adjournal (not Acts in the sense of statutes, but SIs containing the rules of procedure for the Court of Session and the criminal courts respectively). The unannotated text as passed will of course also be available in the official HMSO edition of Public General Acts. The Acts of the Scottish Parliament are officially published in the same form, and are likewise available, in unamended form, on the HMSO website, the Scottish part of which also has links to those UK statutes (from 1996) and SIs (from 1997) that apply wholly or mainly to Scotland. An Act of the Scottish Parliament is almost identical in appearance to a Westminster Act. The principal difference is that in place of the enacting formula – (3) in figure 3.1 – and the date of Royal Assent at the right margin beneath it, there is a statement in the form 'The Bill for this Act of the Scottish Parliament was passed by the Parliament on 8 February 2001 and received the Royal Assent on 15 March 2001'. The Bill only becomes an Act when it has been both passed and given Royal Assent. The gap between being passed and receiving Royal Assent is to allow for the operation of the mechanisms in ss 33–35 of the Scotland Act 1988 for reviewing the legislative competence of the Bill. Acts of the Scottish Parliament are cited in the form '2001 asp 4', rather than having chapter numbers. Acts of the Scottish Parliament are also published in *Butterworths Scottish Legislation Service* (also available on-line as part of Butterworths Scotland Direct Internet service), are included in the Justis Statutes CD-ROM and Internet services, and are listed with status information and with links to the HMSO text on Lawtel. A useful looseleaf compilation of statutory materials of use to the practitioner and arranged by subject is the *Parliament House Book*. It is one of the components of Westlaw UK's Scots Law module, which also contains consolidated Scottish legislation from both Westminster and Holyrood. *Is it in Force?*, despite bearing the colours of *Halsbury's Statutes* and often shelved with it, does include Scottish statutes and Acts of the Scottish Parliament – the latter are simply inter-filed in the alphabetical sequence for each year. The *Current Law Statute Citator*, on the other hand, has asps in a separate sequence at the front. Bear in mind that there has been a Scottish Parliament before. Pre-1707 Acts of the Parliaments of Scotland have a separate table in the second volume of the *Chronological Table of Statutes* – if the text of such statutes is needed reference should be made to one of the detailed guides already listed. Scottish Statutory Instruments (SSIs) made by the Scottish Executive under Acts of the Scottish Parliament or under Westminster Acts under devolved powers are covered by all the sources mentioned at paras **3.82–3.87**, except *Halsbury's Statutory Instruments*. There are two additional services: *Greens Scottish Statutory Instruments Service* is based on the summaries that appear in the monthly digests of *Current Law* but with the addition of annotated copies of the full text of important SSIs; and *Butterworths Scottish Legislation Service* includes summaries of SSIs.

Law reports

8.24 The main series of reports, equivalent to *The Law Reports,* is the *Session Cases* (some Scottish appeals to the House of Lords will also be in the English *Appeal Cases*). However, they suffer from a time-lag in publication. To give greater timeliness and wider coverage, two major series are published under the auspices of the Law Society of Scotland, *Scottish Civil Law Reports* and *Scottish Criminal Case Reports*. The case reports in the *Scots Law Times* are also more timely. They are roughly equivalent to the *Weekly Law Reports*: they are proper, authoritative, full-length reports appearing weekly. There are also now three subject series from W Green: *Family Law Reports, Housing Law Reports* and *Reparation Law Reports*. *The Times* in its law reports section carries occasional cases from the Scottish courts, a practice that was briefly emulated by *The Scotsman* from 1988 to 1996. Unlike in England, in Scotland there has always been greater regard for preserving transcripts of unreported cases – collections are maintained at the Advocates' Library, the Signet Library and the library of the Society of Solicitors in the Supreme Courts. Since 1986 *Green's Weekly Digest* has performed the valuable service of digesting nearly all the decisions of the higher courts and selected decisions from sheriff courts. The entries give the length of the judgment should a full transcript be wanted. Again in a much more organised fashion than their English counterpart, the Scottish Court Service has since 1998 mounted the full text of transcripts of most cases from the higher courts on its website. These will, it is hoped, also be available through BAILII – the pilot had an initial tranche of such cases. For older series of reports reference should be made to one of the specialist guides, but there is a pattern similar to English nominate reports – and in fact before 1907 the *Session Cases* are divided into, and cited by, series identified by reporter.

8.25 Finding Scots case law in the English law library has been made simpler by the inclusion since 1991 of Scottish material in *Current Law*. From 1948 to 1990 there was a separate edition *Scottish Current Law* (with associated *Scottish Current Law Yearbooks* and *Scottish Current Law Case Citators*). This contained all the material in the English edition, but with the addition of digests for Scottish materials in a separate section. The Scottish section of the *Yearbooks* had its own subject index, but the tables of cases and SIs at the front of the volume covered both parts. Another minor variation from the English edition was that there was not a Scottish equivalent of the consolidated edition of the 1947–51 *Yearbooks*. *Scottish Current Law* was not as widely available as the standard edition in English libraries. In the monthly digests and the yearbooks under the current arrangement, the Scottish material in the body of the work is still listed separately, coming at the end after Northern Ireland material. In the cumulative index to the monthly digests and in the index to the yearbooks 'S' suffixes the paragraph numbers of the Scottish entries. There is also a separate section for Scotland in the *Current Law Case Citator*, which usefully has included from 1997 the names of all the cases in *Green's Weekly Digest* as well as those in law reports proper.

8.26 The other main manual source available in English law libraries, particularly for older cases, is the *Digest* and its electronic spin-off, Butterworths Case Search, described in chapter 5; Scottish cases are among the small-print sequences. There are number of digests and indexes to older Scottish cases, such as the *Scots Digest*, the *Faculty Digest* and, going back to 1540, *Morison's Dictionary of Decisions*.

8.27 Lexis, though limited for legislation, is useful for Scots case law, especially if your library does not run to holding the reports in printed form; unreported cases are included too. They are in the CASES file in the SCOT library (not the ENGGEN library). The full text of the reports in the *Scots Law Times* from its start in 1893 has been available on CD-ROM for a while. The recently launched Scots law module of Westlaw UK includes the cases from 1930, and the Butterworths Scotland Direct service includes digests of recent Scottish cases.

8.28 When using Scottish cases, it is useful to have an idea of the various courts. In outline the following are the main courts. The superior civil court is the Court of Session which is divided into the Inner House, which is roughly equivalent to the Court of Appeal (Civil Division), and the Outer House, which hears cases at first instance and is roughly equivalent of the High Court. The Inner House sits in two Divisions, usually of three judges, though the full complement of each is four. An Extra Division may also be convened, and nowadays often is. The Divisions, unlike in the Football League, are of equal standing. Cases in the Outer House are heard before a single judge. In criminal matters the superior court is the High Court of Justiciary. It sits both as an appellate court equivalent to the Court of Appeal (Criminal Division) and on circuit with a single judge to try serious crimes similarly to Queen's Bench Division High Court judges hearing serious cases on circuit at Crown Courts. The main inferior court is the sheriff court which has a civil jurisdiction similar to county courts, and in criminal matters tries less important cases on indictment before a jury as in Crown Courts before circuit judges or recorders, and also summarily. In the towns or cities that are burghs there are also the equivalent of magistrates' courts. One other small point: 'judgments' are generally called, and so headed in law reports, 'opinions'. However, in the *Sessions Cases* and *Scots Law Times* you may also see in the headnote to some cases, following the section on what was *held*, a further '*opinion*'. This equates to the section of the headnote to an English law report '*per curiam*' (see para **5.56**).

Northern Ireland

8.29 Very useful for general background is Brice Dickson *The Legal System of Northern Ireland* ((3rd edn,(1993) SLS Publications; 4th edn forthcoming 2001). The same publishers, which were set up with the support of the profession and Queen's University Belfast to make better provision for legal works in this small jurisdiction, did at one time promise a book *Finding the Law: a Guide to Legal Research in Northern Ireland*. Pending that materialising, there is some coverage in other sources:

> George Woodman 'Northern Ireland' in Jules Winterton and Elizabeth M Moys (eds) *Information Sources in Law* ((2nd edn,1997) Bowker Saur) pp 557–574.
> 'Northern Ireland Law' (chapter 9) in Jean Dane, Philip A Thomas and Catherine Cope *How to Use a Law Library* ((3rd edn,1996) Sweet & Maxwell; 4th edn forthcoming 2001).
> Thomas O'Malley *The Round Hall Guide to the Sources of Law: an Introduction to Legal Research and Writing* ((1993) Round Hall Press) chapter 2.

As well as books from SLS some books published in Dublin, for example, those by Wylie on land law and conveyancing, cover both Northern Ireland and the Republic. The *Northern Ireland Legal Quarterly* is the main periodical and of high quality. Articles from this and other British journals will be picked up by the *Legal Journals Index*. For earlier periodical literature reference should be made to the *Bibliography of Periodical Literature Relating to Irish Law* by Paul O'Higgins ((1966; Supplements 1973, 1983) Northern Ireland Legal Quarterly). The general current awareness tool covering both recent cases and legislation is the *Bulletin of Northern Ireland Law*.

8.30 The complexity of legislation for Northern Ireland reflects the complexity of the constitutional arrangements. The position, which, except for a brief period between 1973 and 1974, prevailed from the end of March 1972 until December 1999, and again for a brief period between February and the end of May 2000, was that most statutes that applied to Northern Ireland only were made by Order in Council under the Northern Ireland Acts and were issued as UK SIs: they took the form of and were passed as delegated legislation at Westminster, but were in substance the equivalent of primary legislation. They bore an SI number but were not included in the official bound volumes of SIs; instead they were filed by a separate NI number (the equivalent of a chapter number for an ordinary statute) in binders labelled 'Northern Ireland statutes'. They were also distinguishable from ordinary UK SIs by being issued not in A4 format but in a smaller size.

8.31 In addition to the Northern Ireland statutes there were some UK statutes that extended to Northern Ireland in the same way that some extended to Scotland; in the absence of any provision to the contrary an Act passed by the Westminster Parliament was presumed to extend to Northern Ireland, but in practice an express provision at the end of the Act indicated whether or not it so extended either wholly or in part. Usually such statutes were ones that applied to other parts of the UK as well, but some applied to Northern Ireland only; these will have 'Northern Ireland' in their title (*before* the word 'Act'), for example, the Social Security (Northern Ireland) Act 1975 or the Judicature (Northern Ireland) Act 1978. The reason these were not made by Order in Council as Northern Ireland statutes is that even before 1972 there were certain matters solely within the province of the Westminster Parliament and not within the legislative competence of Stormont, and it is those matters that were subject of Westminster statutes – the Westminster Orders in Council only replaced the Stormont statutes.

8.32 Under the Northern Ireland Act 1998, the matter is slightly more complicated. There are three categories of legislation, according to subject matter. First are excepted matters, listed in Sch 2, which remain solely at Westminster, and which will continue to be subject to conventional Westminster legislation, whether Act or SI. The third category is transferred, ie devolved, matters which are the responsibility of the Assembly, and which will be covered by Acts of the Assembly. In between is the second category, reserved matters. Reserved matters, which are set out in Sch 3, are matters that potentially may be devolved, but for the time being remain at Westminster, albeit with legislation only being made in consultation with the Assembly. A reserved matter may be designated a transferred matter (and vice versa) by order of the Secretary of State by SI. The mechanism for legislating at Westminster on reserved matters is contained in s 85. In practical terms, it is the same as prevailed from 1972 to 1999. Such legislation under s 85 will made by Order in Council, and will be UK SIs, but will not appear in the bound volumes of UK SIs. They will carry an NI number. As they go through the affirmative procedure for making SIs (see para **4.75**), they are first laid before Parliament in draft. The draft of the first one to be made, the Financial Investigations (Northern Ireland) Order 2001, came in the smaller format in which the Northern Ireland 'Statutes' were issued from 1972 to 1999, though oddly the final version was published in the ordinary A4 format for SIs. Since like Orders in Council under the old regime they may be omitted from the official bound volumes of SIs (see s 85(11) of the 1998 Act), it may well be that on the library shelves they will live with, if not be bound with, the Acts of the Northern Ireland Assembly, and will be treated in official tables and indexes as primary legislation, as were the Northern Ireland 'Statutes' 1972–99. There is also in s 5(6) the counterpart of s 28(7) of the Scotland Act 1988 (see para **8.18**), reserving the power of Westminster to make law for Northern Ireland generally. Its presence, like s 28(7), is largely symbolic.

8.33 Statutes were passed at Stormont by the Parliament of Northern Ireland from 1921 to 1972, and Measures (only four) were passed there between 1973 and 1974 during the brief legislative life of the (first attempted) Northern Ireland Assembly. Following the direct elections in June 1998, powers were finally transferred to the new Northern Ireland Assembly on 2 December 1999. It managed to pass one Act – the Financial Assistance for Political Parties (Northern Ireland) Act 2000 – before it was suspended on 11 February 2000. Three Acts were passed under the Northern Ireland Act 2000 under the previous method of legislating, until the Assembly's powers were reinstated on 29 May 2000. The titles of Acts that emanate from Stormont under both its old and new guises are distinguishable from those that emanated from Westminster: the former all have the word 'Northern Ireland' *after* the word 'Act', for example, the Land Registration Act (Northern Ireland) 1970. In addition some statutes passed by the Parliament of Ireland at Dublin before 1800 are still in force, as are of course some statutes passed at Westminster from 1800 to 1920. The *Statutes Revised, Northern Ireland* contain all the above material as at 31 March 1981 *except* UK statutes passed at Westminster since 1920 that extend to, or apply only to, Northern Ireland. The latter are included in the Public General Acts and *Current Law Statutes*. *Halsbury's Statutes* gives annotations as to the extension of UK statutes to Northern Ireland, but only includes the full text of selected UK statutes that apply only to Northern Ireland. HMSO Belfast produce indexes and chronological tables to the Northern Ireland statutes from time to time, and there is an annual cumulative supplement to the *Statutes Revised, Northern Ireland* issued in A4 format (the work itself, though in looseleaf binders, has not been updated so far). Northern Ireland statutes from 1972 to 1999 will be covered by those sources that cover UK SIs. The full text of the *Statutes Revised* is available on BAILII. Acts of the new Northern Ireland Assembly are available on the HMSO website, and on the Justis statutes service. The Quick Reference Guide sets out all the various categories of primary legislation that affect Northern Ireland described above, and where they are to be found (QR8.8).

8.34 Some UK SIs made under UK Acts that extend to Northern Ireland will likewise extend to Northern Ireland, but the vast bulk of subsidiary legislation for Northern Ireland is issued as an entirely separate series, *Northern Ireland Statutory Rules* by HMSO Belfast (before 1973 *'Statutory Rules and Orders'*). The full text of all Statutory Rules from the beginning of 1998, and selected ones from 1991, is available from the main HMSO website. There is an officially published index to the Statutory Rules in force, reissued from time to time. They are also indexed from 1995 on Badger on CLI. *Current Law* has included digests of Northern Ireland legislation, both primary and secondary, since 1958.

8.35 The counterpart of *The Law Reports* in England is the *Northern Ireland Law Reports*, prepared by the Incorporated Council of Law Reporting for Northern Ireland. These used to suffer from delay. To remedy this the *Northern Ireland Judgments Bulletin* appeared. Although this started in primitive form in 1971, it only became more widely available outside the province in 1985. It in turn suffered from production and distribution problems, with the series grinding to a halt in the early 1990s. The situation was salvaged by Butterworths taking over publication of both the *Judgments Bulletin*, with retrospective coverage back to 1994, and the *Law Reports*. In the earlier years of the province decisions of the Northern Ireland courts were also published in series of law reports emanating from Dublin, such as the *Irish Law Times Reports*. The *Appeals Cases* will contain Northern Ireland cases that reach the House of Lords. Some other English series, for example, the *Tax Cases* may contain Northern Irish decisions. The availability of Northern Ireland Social Security Commissioners decisions has already been noted (para **5.24**). In another fruitful collaboration between the Incorporated Council and Butterworths there has now been published an *Index to Northern Ireland Cases 1921 to 1997*, which covers cases from all the above sources. It is very much along the lines of the *Law Reports* 'red book' indexes: a list of all the cases reported, a subject index based on catchwords, and tables of legislation and cases judicially considered. The *Northern Ireland Law Reports* are also covered in the *Irish Digest* (now available on CD-ROM,: see para **8.57**). Although *Current Law* does digest Northern Ireland cases, its coverage, especially for cases from the *Judgments Bulletin* during its rocky era, seems a little patchy. The *Northern Ireland Law Reports* from 1945 and unreported cases from 1984 are on Lexis in the NILAW library. At the time of writing the Northern Ireland Court Service has put only a single judgment on its website. A greater number of cases, from both the Court of Appeal and High Court, starting in 1999 were obtained by BAILII for its pilot.

Isle of Man

8.36 The practitioner is most likely to encounter Manx law in the context of companies, trusts and financial services on account of the island's status as a tax haven. Much of the legal literature will accordingly be found in specialist books and journals on offshore jurisdictions and tax planning, rather than in specific works devoted to the law of the Isle of Man – see, for example, the following looseleafs: Giles Clarke and Barry Spitz (eds) *Butterworths Offshore Service*; John Glasson (ed) *International Trust Laws* (Jordans); David Harvey (ed) *Offshore Financing: Security and Insolvency* (Sweet & Maxwell); and Withers *International Trust Precedents* (Sweet & Maxwell). Stephen Netherway et al *Limited Liability for Professional Partnerships* ((1998) Jordans) includes chapters on the Isle of Man. Books on the law of the Isle of Man alone are few, but two recent books are noteworthy additions to the literature. Peter W Edge's *Manx Public Law* ((1997) Isle of Man Law Society) comprises three parts. The first is a valuable account of the legal system in general. The second deals in more detail with the Manx constitution, while the third, whose presence is perhaps not immediately apparent from the title of the work, is a very full treatment of Manx criminal law. The other, which is not aimed solely at lawyers, is Mark Solly *Government and Law in the Isle of Man* ((1994) Parallel Books). The same author and publisher have also produced a series of guides to tax, banks, company and partnership law. Two other monographs, now getting a little dated, are *Trusts, Tax and Estate Planning Through the Isle of Man* by John Glasson and others ((1989) Key Haven Publications) and Jane Bates *Isle of Man Companies Act* ((1992) Sweet & Maxwell). For earlier Manx legal literature a bibliography is included in W Twining and J Uglow *Law Publishing and Legal Information: Small Jurisdictions of the British Isles* ((1981) Sweet & Maxwell) (see also *Chloros*, cited at para **8.45**). To be thoroughly recommended as an adjunct to this section is the chapter on the Isle of Man (and Channel Islands) by George Woodman in Jules Winterton and Elizabeth M Moys (eds) *Information Sources in Law* ((1997) Bowker Saur).

8.37 Practitioners using the Isle of Man (or indeed the Channel Islands) as an offshore financial centre will be aware of the Edwards Report (Home Office *Review of Financial Regulation in the Crown Dependencies*, Chairman Andrew Edwards, Cm 4109-I to 4109-IV, Stationery Office, 1998). The last three of its four parts each comprise 'A guide to the International Finance Centre' for Jersey, Guernsey and the Isle of Man respectively. These guides are a useful starting point for the financial law of the islands, though it should be appreciated that the main report has generated some legislative activity since. The Isle of Man Financial Supervision Commission publishes a number of regulatory guides in looseleaf format, which may also help. However, the guides with the Edwards Report and the main Report itself also have wider interest in giving general background to the legal systems of each of the jurisdictions.

8.38 The island is able to pursue in its own fiscal policies because it is not part of the UK and has its own legislature, the Tynwald, which has a long history. None the less, it is a dependency of the UK, which acts on behalf of the island in external matters such as foreign affairs and defence, and Acts of Tynwald receive Royal Assent. Tynwald, however, does not make all legislation. Many Acts of the UK Parliament extend, with the consent of Tynwald, to the Isle of Man. The normal procedure for this is different from the way UK statutes are extended to Scotland and Northern Ireland. Instead of simply incorporating an extension provision directly into the statute, an enabling power is inserted under which an Order in Council can be made (often incorporating certain local adaptations and modifications) after the consultative process has been completed. Such Orders in Council are UK SIs. The Isle of Man is not a member of the European Communities as such but has a special arrangement under Protocol 3 of the UK's Treaty of

Accession so that it is treated as part of Europe for the purposes of customs and the free movement of goods. The Isle of Man is subject to the European Convention on Human Rights, though its application went through, to put it politely, a sticky patch on account of its laws relating to birching and homosexual activity. The Convention has now been incorporated into the island's own law by Act of Tynwald, the Human Rights Act 2001. Although it has its own indigenous legal traditions based on Norse customary law, modern Manx law largely follows English common law as well statute law.

8.39 Individual Acts of Tynwald are officially printed. From 2001 they are also available on the Isle of Man Government website. For a long time there was no modern consolidation, but that situation has now been remedied by the publication of *Juta's Statutes of the Isle of Man*. This is published in regular new editions in hard copy with interim annual noters-up, but the whole text is also published annually on CD-ROM. It is arranged by broad subject and the noter-up has tables, but the separate annually produced *Subject Guide to the Acts of Tynwald including Alphabetical and Chronological Lists of the Acts* is a necessary additional finding tool. G V C Young *Subject Guide and Chronological Table relating to the Acts of Tynwald 1776–1975* ((1975) Shearwater Press) remains of residual value, particularly the chronological table, which includes all Acts whether or not in force (with details of amendment or repeal), unlike the chronological tables in the current annual *Subject Guide*. The *Chronological Table of Acts of Parliament Extending or Relating to the Isle of Man* is produced from time to time (4th (last) edn, 1998). Orders in Council extending UK Acts will be available in the English law library among the ordinary SIs, but there is a consolidated edition *Isle of Man Orders in Council* (3rd edn, 2001). Subordinate legislation is published in the form of Statutory Documents, formerly Government Circulars. There is a *Subject Guide and Chronological Table to Subordinate Legislation*, but it was last revised in 1981. Inquiries on obtaining copies of primary materials, particularly subordinate legislation, which is not widely available outside the island, should be directed to the Central Reference Library, Government Buildings, Douglas, Isle of Man. The Attorney-General's Chambers may also be able to offer advice. The Isle of Man Government website has some other materials of possible use, such as consultative papers and draft bills. The annual policy review, loaded on it, contains the government's legislative programme. Tynwald has its own website, which includes progress of Bills (not the text at the moment), *Hansard* (somewhat in arrears) and other materials.

8.40 The *Manx Law Reports* (Law Reports International) began publication in 1985 with a volume covering 1981–83. Since then as well covering new cases, it has been steadily going backwards with retrospective coverage. So far it has got to 1952. There are cumulative tables and indexes from time to time. Earlier unreported judgments are only available at the Manx Law Society and Attorney-General's Chambers. There is also A *List of Constitutional and Privy Council Judgments Affecting the Isle of Man from 1523 to 1991* (2nd edn, 1992) prepared by the Attorney-General's Chambers.

8.41 Finally, an indispensable tool for all aspects of the law of the Isle of Man is the *Manx Law Bulletin*, prepared by the Attorney-General's Chambers since 1983. It contains case notes and summaries of Acts of Tynwald (together with bills and questions in Tynwald), subordinate legislation and applicable UK statutes, all with their commencement dates; occasional articles are included too.

Channel Islands

8.42 The Channel Islands have a similar constitutional status to the Isle of Man and similar importance as tax havens. However, their legal systems derive from Norman law, the islands having originally been part of the Duchy of Normandy. As a consequence the customary law adapted from the old Norman *coutumes* is still a source of law, together with legislation and the decisions of the courts. There is also the consequence that much of the materials, especially the older ones, are in French. The Channel Islands comprise the two bailiwicks of Jersey and Guernsey, each with their own legislatures, courts, and government. Alderney and Sark are dependencies of Guernsey, but are distinct jurisdictions with their own legislatures and legal customs.

8.43 The name of the body that is both legislature and government is 'The States' in three of the four jurisdictions; in Sark it is 'The Chief Pleas'. The position of the islands vis-à-vis the European Communities is similar to the Isle of Man: they are not member states but are treated as being within the Communities for the purpose of customs and the free movement of goods (but not the free movement of persons and services).

8.44 As in the Isle of Man, the usual means nowadays of extending UK statutes to the Channel Islands is by Orders in Council issued as UK SIs. But whereas the Acts of Tynwald receive Royal Assent, the primary legislation of the States is sanctioned by Her Majesty by Orders in Council; these orders are made in the exercise of the prerogative power and so should not be confused with Orders in Council that are UK SIs (see paras **3.163–3.164**). The States can also legislate in certain areas without Royal sanction, either under general powers given by Order in Council (for example, the power given to the Jersey States to make 'Regulations' of no more than three years' duration) or in Guernsey under a residual common law power to legislate.

8.45 George Woodman's contribution to *Information Sources in Law*, cited above (para **8.36**) is again invaluable. The Channel Islands are not covered by *Twining and Uglow*, but some general guidance on the earlier legal literature may be found in the *Bibliographical Guide to the Law of the United Kingdom, the Channel Islands and the Isle of Man*, edited by A G Chloros ((2nd edn, 1973) Institute of Advanced Legal Studies). Butterworth Tolley's publish an annual *Taxation in the Channel Islands and the Isle of Man*. The accountants KPMG Peat Marwick, who have offices on both of the main islands, regularly issue booklets on such matters as banking, finance, investment and insurance in the islands. Again, it should be emphasised that one must bear in mind comparative works, such as those mentioned at para **8.36**, and journal articles rather than assume there is no secondary literature to speak of on the islands. There is also the Edwards Report described above (para **8.37**).

Jersey

8.46 The Solicitor-General of Jersey, Stéphanie Nicolle, has recently produced the first modern general account of Jersey law and its history, *The Origin and Development of Jersey Law: an Outline Guide* ((revised edn, 1998) States' Greffe), and 1997 saw the launch of *The Jersey Law Review* (now also available on the Internet: see para **8.50**), so a small general literature is growing. The standard work on Jersey's constitution is F de L Bois *A Constitutional History of Jersey* ((1972) States' Greffe). Otherwise, other than the general works cited at para **8.36**, the available monographs are from Key Haven, the offshore specialist publishers: Paul Mathews and Stéphanie Nicolle *The Jersey Law of Property* (1991); Paul Mathews and Terry Sowden *The Jersey Law of Trusts* (3rd edn, 1994); and Anthony Dessain and Michael Wilkins *Jersey Insolvency Law in Practice* (2nd edn, 2001). These do, however, include general introductory matter as well as covering the subjects in their titles.

8.47 The *General Index of Legislation* is an index to all Jersey legislation, both primary and secondary, issued annually in a looseleaf binder. The primary legislation has been issued as 'Laws' since 1979, before which the series was entitled *Recueil des Lois*. The Income Tax (Jersey) Law 1961 is reprinted as amended in looseleaf form. The other series, which has been published since 1939, is called Regulations and Orders.

8.48 This series contains four species of legislation: (1) regulations of three years' duration made under general powers; (2) regulations (or sometimes 'rules') of indefinite duration made by the States under powers in particular laws; (3) acts of the States which are the form of instrument used, for example, for commencement orders and for incorporation of treaty provisions; and (4) orders made by committees of the States (ie ministries) under powers in laws. Unlike the laws, which are numbered only within each year, regulations and orders have a reference number that runs from year to year. By 1999 the reference number was heading for five digits, so a new sequence of numbering has been started afresh from 2000, and will continue to run from year to year. The full text of Jersey legislation is available from 1997 on the Jersey Legal Information Board website (see para **8.50**).

8.49 Before 1950 the Royal Court of Jersey gave no reasoned judgments in the English style, so there are no proper law reports before that date. The only published guide was a *Table des Decisions*, which acted as a kind of digest of unreported decisions filed at the Royal Court. From 1950 a more English approach to precedent was adopted and reports appeared as *Jersey Judgments*, published locally until 1984 when they were superseded by the *Jersey Law Reports*, published by Law Reports International in Oxford. The index and tables volume of the *Jersey Law Reports*, reissued in cumulative form from time to time, now also cover the *Jersey Judgments* from their start in 1950. The *Table des Decisions*, already mentioned, began in 1884 and continued to 1963. It was resuscitated for one further volume covering 1964–78 published in 1980; unlike its predecessors this volume was mostly in English and its purpose was simply to note decisions *not* reported in the *Jersey Judgments*.

8.50 Only in operation for a short time, the Jersey Legal Information Board website promises to be a useful resource as it develops. It currently contains the full text of Laws and Regulations and Orders from 1997. It also has pre-legislative materials for Laws: consultation drafts, drafts, and Laws adopted (ie those approved by the States and waiting confirmation by Order in Council; when so confirmed they are described as Laws registered). A consolidated version of the main court rules, the Rules of the Royal Court, is provided, as are practice directions back to 1979. Issues of the *Jersey Law Review* more than 12 months old are there and there is a directory of Jersey law firms. The only disappointment is that though a list of unreported judgments with a brief indication of subject matter is available for cases from 1997, the full text of the judgments is only available at the moment to registered users. The Jersey Financial Services Commission also has a website.

Guernsey

8.51 See again generally Woodman (para **8.36**), offshore looseleafs and the Edwards report. There are two booklets on its constitution, *The Constitution and Law of Guernsey* by Sir John Loveridge ((1975) La Société Guernesiaise) and *A Guide to the Constitution of Guernsey* by David Ehmann and Paul Le Pelley ((1993) Guernsey Press). Sark also has a small booklet devoted to it: J M Beaumont *The Constitution and Administration of Sark* ((1993) Guernsey Press). An article, G Rowland 'The Bailwick of Guernsey' (1992) 23 *The Law Librarian* 181–188, is also useful. The Guernsey Financial Services Commission produced in 1991 the *Guernsey Company and Trust Law Handbook* (edited by D E Thompson). The only full-length monograph is Raymond Ashton *An Analysis of the Guernsey Law of Trusts* ((1998) Key Haven), though another work by the same author is promised, *Guernsey Company Law* ((forthcoming 2001) Key Haven).

8.52 The primary legislation is called 'laws' though the series on its spine and covers is called *Orders in Council* (formerly *Recueil d'Ordres en Conseil*) because that is how they are enacted; an example of a formal title is thus: 'Order in Council ratifying a Projet de Loi [ie a Bill] entitled The Conditions of Employment (Guernsey) Law, 1985'. The other main series of legislation is called 'ordinances of the States' (formerly Ordonnances), which include original legislation made by the States not requiring Royal sanction and delegated legislation made by the States under laws. Before 1948 the Royal Court of Guernsey also had legislative powers. These were transferred to the States except in the case of defence regulations and rules of the court itself, which continue to appear in a series *Orders of the Royal Court*. In addition, the committees of the States make delegated legislation in the form of statutory instruments. Both Alderney and Sark similarly have their own *Orders in Council* and *Ordinances*. In certain areas Guernsey applies its legislation to Alderney, for example, The Alderney (Application of Legislation) (Supplementary Benefit) Ordinance 1990, which is Guernsey Ordinance No XXXVI of 1990 applying Ordinance No XXXV.

8.53 Since 1965 judgments of the Court of Appeal of Guernsey and some other judgments have been printed. Since 1985, however, the main source of information on cases has been the *Guernsey Law Journal* which provides summaries, as it does of all legislation (including Alderney and Sark); occasional articles also appear in it. This publication makes finding Guernsey material considerably easier than it is for Jersey. Copies of the materials summarised are available from The Greffe. It is to be hoped that Guernsey follows Jersey's lead in putting primary materials on the Internet – there are none at the time of writing.

Other common law jurisdictions

Republic of Ireland

8.54 The main research guide is O'Malley, already cited (para **8.29**) for its chapter on Northern Ireland. That is now getting a little out of date; it can be supplemented by John Furlong's chapter in *Winterton and Moys* and the chapter in *Dane and Thomas* (also cited at para **8.29**). Raymond Byrne and J Paul McCutcheon *The Irish Legal System* ((3rd edn, 1996) Butterworths Ireland; 4th edn forthcoming 2001) will provide general background. Both Sweet & Maxwell, which took over the indigenous

Round Hall Press, and Butterworths have Irish arms, and there is now a reasonable range of modern textbooks devoted to the law of the Republic. Blackstone Press also publishes a range of manuals for the Law Society of Ireland. Though aimed at apprentice solicitors studying for Law Society exams, their up-to-date coverage of the main areas of practice make them useful resources generally. The Republic is of course also a full member state of the EU so its law is of interest from that point of view as well as being another common law jurisdiction. The Centre for European Law based at Trinity College Dublin produces a valuable series of publications.

8.55 The *Legal Journals Index* covers Irish legal journals from 1993. The *Gazette of the Incorporated Law Society* (the text of which is also available from 1999 on the Law Society's website) and the *Irish Law Times* are the two main professional journals. The *Irish Jurist* is the leading academic journal, though it also contains material of use to the practitioner such as an annual digest of decisions and a list of legislation. Other specialist journals are also appearing. The periodical literature up to 1981 is covered by the bibliography by O'Higgins, already cited (para **8.29**).

8.56 The official edition of the statutes, the *Acts of the Oireachtas*, are published in loose parts as they are passed and in annual bound volumes. There is no current consolidation of the text and the last consolidated index was published in 1986. A chronological table of the statutes is slightly more up-to-date, having last been published in 1995. Since 1984 the official edition has been supplemented by the commercially produced *Irish Current Law Statutes Annotated*, which is similar to its English counterpart though in looseleaf format, and includes a statute citator. Secondary legislation is in the form of SIs as in England. There are official indexes to these, but they are neither cumulative nor very up-to-date. The *Irish Current Law Monthly Digest*, which has been published since 1995, is similar to its UK counterpart, so includes summaries of recent legislation. A CD-ROM of all legislation as enacted since 1922 (currently up to 1998) was officially published at nominal cost. The data is also available on BAILII and the Attorney General's Office website.

8.57 The two main current law reports series are the long-standing official *Irish Reports*, which emerged out of the previous Irish series produced by the Incorporated Council of Law Reporting, and the more recently established *Irish Law Reports Monthly* (1976–). The Incorporated Council, like its English counterpart, has recently struck a deal with Context to provide the full text of their reports on CD-ROM in the same format as the other Justis products. The CD, as well as including the reports themselves from 1919, includes the *Irish Digest* from the same date. Published by the Incorporated Council in volumes usually covering ten-year periods, the *Irish Digest* summarises cases reported in all the other main series of reports as well as the *Irish Reports*, namely the *Irish Law Times*, *Irish Law Journal*, *Irish Jurist*, *Irish Law Reports Monthly* and the *Northern Ireland Law Reports*. The nine volumes of the hard copy, 1894–1993, have been reprinted by Butterworths Ireland. Selected Irish cases also appear in the English *Digest* – as with the Commonwealth coverage of *The Digest*, older cases are more fully represented than recent ones. The *Irish Current Law Monthly Digests* are now the main current printed tool.

8.58 However, in Ireland there has always been considerable reliance on unreported cases. A commercial service giving access to the full text of all recent reserved judgments from the superior courts is offered by First Law's electronic Irish Weekly Law Reports Internet service. From 1976 all the written judgments of the superior courts have been distributed to various libraries and bodies. Indexes to these, known as 'pink lists', were issued about three times a year. The pink lists stopped in 1996, but have been revived by First Law with effect from May 2001 and are being distributed free of charge by the Law Society and Bar Council to their members. The Irish Association of Law Teachers prepared a consolidation of the pink lists, *Index to Irish Superior Court Written Judgments 1976–1982*, to which were subsequently added a retrospective volume for 1966–75 and a continuation by Jennefer Aston for the Bar Council up to 1989. The pilot data for BAILII included the decisions of the Supreme Court and the High Court from 1999 – it is to be hoped they will continue to be updated. The Irish content of the BAILII project was facilitated by John Mee at University College Cork; the Irish Law website maintained there is a good general starting point for Internet research on Irish law.

United States

8.59 Not surprisingly, given the size of the legal literature, the size of the legal profession and the emphasis traditionally placed on legal research in US legal education, there are a large number of US legal research manuals. An annotated bibliography of such works will be found on the Cornell Law Library website (as opposed to the Cornell Legal Information Institute site) under 'Finding the law', which also has much other useful information on American legal research. Three selected for mention are:

> Morris L Cohen and Kent C Olson *How to Find the Law in a Nutshell* ((7th edn, 2000) West).
> Robert C Berring and Elizabeth A Edinger *Finding the Law* ((11th edn, 1999) West).
> J Myron Jacobstein, Roy M Mersky and Donald J Dunn *Fundamentals of Legal Research* ((7th edn, 1998) Foundation Press).

8.60 The complexity of US legal literature is a consequence of the federal legal system: the researcher has to cope not only with the mass of federal law but also the law of each individual state. While the law may often be similar from state to state because their courts follow similar common law principles (disregarding the anomalous position in the mixed jurisdiction of Louisiana) and their legislatures may adopt model laws such as the Uniform Commercial Code, variations, sometimes quite radical ones, do occur.

8.61 For the English lawyer there is also the problem of access to the material. Many academic libraries take basic materials and there are major collections in Oxford and Cambridge, and in London at the Institute of Advanced Legal Studies and the Middle Temple Library. But no English library has a collection in printed form that could match the resources that would be available to a US lawyer. For this reason electronic sources often represent the only practical means of proceeding. Both Lexis and Westlaw are in origin US systems and the vast bulk of federal and state legislation and case law (and many law reviews) are available in full text, and accessible in just the same way as the English materials. They are of course commercial services, with the advantages that the material is organised, reliable and available in very substantial retrospective libraries. The US version of Lexis can be searched on a pay-as-you-go basis or for a fixed charge for short periods using a credit card, and Westlaw also has a credit card Westdoc service. But US attitudes to placing primary legal materials in the public domain also means that there is a very great deal available free of charge on the Internet. The drawbacks are variations in availability, particularly for material other than the relatively recent, and ease of access. There is also quite a proliferation of gateways to legal resources on the Internet – many US law school libraries will have sets of links on their websites – making the choice of starting place quite difficult. Probably coming top of the list are the Cornell Legal Information Institute and FindLaw. The latter comes from Westlaw but has much free material. The American Association of Law Libraries website simply gives links to 13 of the major gateways or resources, which is a reassuringly short list with the imprimatur of legal information professionals. Likewise the American Bar Association's Lawlink, constructed by the ABA Legal Technology Resource Centre, has a manageable list, with the advantage of annotations. Annotations and appraisal are also a feature of the UK SOSIG Law site – the section on the US has a number of useful links. As well as a proliferation of gateways, primary sources such as cases and legislation are often available on alternative sites, with not merely different search engines or interfaces but with different date coverage.

8.62 Although it does not normally present great difficulties, the English researcher should bear in mind differences in spelling and usage in both legal and ordinary American English. The spelling point is particularly pertinent to electronic searching, where, for example, to search for the word OFFENCE instead of OFFENSE might derail a search strategy. *Black's Law Dictionary* ((7th edn, 1999) West) and Bryan A Garner *A Dictionary of Modern Legal Usage* ((2nd edn, 1995) Oxford University Press) are helpful here.

Textbooks and journals

8.63 The main US tools for finding books and journal articles were described in chapter 2 because the coverage of many includes English material, but an additional tool which is useful is Francis R Doyle *Searching the Law* ((2nd edn, 1999) Transnational). This follows a subject arrangement and under each subject are listed the leading texts, journal, treatises and bibliographies. A companion work by the same author is *Searching the Law: the States: a Selective Bibliography of State Practice Materials in the 50 States* ((3rd edn, 1999) Transnational). The University Law Review Project, mentioned at para **2.28**, should be particularly borne in mind.

Legislation

8.64 Acts of Congress are officially issued in loose form and bound volumes as *Statutes at Large* in the same way as Queen's Printer copies of Public General Acts, but for most purposes the preferable source is the *United States Code* which is a compilation by topic, each topic being called a 'title', of the main legislation in force. It comes in three versions, the official version published by the government printer, and two versions published by rival commercial publishers, *United States Code Annotated* (West) and *United States Code Service* (Lawyers' Co-operative). The latter two, because of their extensive annotations, are to be preferred. The bound volumes have pocket part supplements and are reissued from time to time. Subordinate legislation is published daily in the *Federal Register*, and is consolidated in the *Code of Federal Regulations*. The *United States Code, Federal Register* and *Code of Federal Regulations* are all available on the Internet on GPO Access, the government printer's website.

8.65 State legislation follows a similar pattern with sessional laws and consolidations in the form of codes. The codes may cover the whole body of law or a part, such as a criminal code. Alongside the official versions, there are often commercially produced annotated versions. The codes of some states are more important than others because they have acted as models which other states have followed; for example, the Delaware Corporations Code. The National Conference of Commissioners on Uniform State Laws, which has an official website maintained in association with the University of Pennsylvania Law School, also produces model laws which may be widely adopted, such as the Uniform Commercial Code. Many state codes are available on the Internet.

Law reports

8.66 Like the United States Code, the reports of the Supreme Court are available in an official series and two rival annotated commercially published series. The official *United States Supreme Court Reports*, cited simply as US, go all the way back to 1790. The early volumes, like other early US reports, which followed the English pattern, were known by the names of their reporters and may be still so cited. But when in 1875 simple sequential volume numbering was introduced, those volumes were retrospectively numbered as part of the main series in addition. The official bound volumes of the *US Reports* are the definitive text. As explained on the Supreme Court website, the bound volumes are the fourth generation in printed form. They are three earlier generations, which are successively revised – bench opinions, slip opinions and preliminary prints. Incidentally, what we would call court judgments or decisions are referred to generally as court 'opinions'.

8.67 The *Lawyers' Edition*, cited L Ed, covers the entire series and is published by Lawyers' Co-operative. The *Supreme Court Reporter* (S Ct), published by West as part of its *National Reporter System*, starts in 1882. These two each have their own volume numbering system, but on both the equivalent volume number for the official series also appears. The full text of the *US Reports* back to 1893 is available free of charge on the FindLaw site; from 1990 they are also available from Cornell and the Supreme Court website (and some other sites). Cornell also offers a selection of the most important historical decisions before 1990. Lexis and Westlaw will have the complete run.

8.68 Until 1880 there were numerous nominate reports covering the other federal courts. These were collected together in a reprint, *Federal Cases*. Since 1880 there has been the *Federal Reporter*, again part of the *National Reporter System*. Decisions of the district courts, the lowest level of federal court, were hived off in 1932 to another series, the *Federal Supplement*.

8.69 Reports of state courts were originally published as nominates, and in many states there continues to be an official state series, but virtually all English libraries that collect US reports will have them in the form of the *National Reporter System*. This is published in seven series covering geographic groups of states, the *Atlantic Reporter*, the *North Western Reporter* and so on. State decisions are also published in the *American Law Reports*. This series is not intended to be comprehensive like the *National Reporter System*, but provides in-depth annotations and commentary on selected cases. Before 1969 it also covered federal cases, but these are now separately covered by *American Law Reports Federal*. Most Federal and state appellate court decisions from the 1990s onwards are available on the Internet. Earlier retrospective coverage varies – look at both Cornell and FindLaw.

8.70 There are a number of reports covering specialist tribunals or particular subjects, but because the coverage of the general series is much less selective than in England (*all* decisions of the final appellate court, and a very large number at intermediate appellate level, in each state are included in the *National Reporter System*), less reliance on them is needed.

8.71 American citation practice follows the English pattern except for date: the use of volume numbering rather than year as the preferred means of identification is universal so the square bracket/round bracket convention on dates does not arise, and the date is given at the end of the citation not at the beginning. In the case of voluminous series the Americans have a predilection for starting new series of volume numbering every so often; the abbreviation used for second series, third series, etc, which may momentarily perplex the English eye, is 2d, 3d, etc. It is the proper practice to cite first the reference in the relevant state reports and then the reference to the *National Reporter System*, which makes for long citations: the English lawyer should concentrate on the second citation. If only a state report citation is given, it can be translated into a *National Reporter* citation using the *National Reporter Blue Book* (in the unlikely event of needing to translate a *National Reporter* citation into a state report citation use *Shepard's Citations*, mentioned at para **8.73**). Thus a typical American citation may look like:

> *Hill v Bowen* 8 Ill 2d 527, 134 NE 2d 769 (1956)

This 1956 decision is reported in vol 8 of the second series of *Illinois Reports* at p 527 and in vol 134 of the second series of the *North Eastern Reporter* (in the *National Reporter* system) at p 769.

Abbreviations for US series of reports are fairly fully covered by *Raistrick*, but a US equivalent is *Bieber's Dictionary of Legal Abbreviations* ((5th edn, 2001) Hein).

8.72 The sheer volume of US case law means that Lexis or Westlaw are unquestionably the best finding tools. But there are printed sources. The *American Digest*, consolidated up to 1896 and thereafter in decennial, and more recently five-yearly chunks, is the main way to find cases by name or subject. Between consolidations it is kept up to date by the *General Digest*, issued monthly and cumulated into bound volumes issued three times a year. *Corpus Juris Secundum* and *American Jurisprudence 2d*, published by West and Lawyers' Co-operative respectively, are more in the nature of encyclopaedias, but their copious citation of authorities means that they are used largely as an entry into case law.

8.73 *Shepard's Citations* provides an elaborate means of identifying subsequent citations of a particular case. In US parlance, to 'Shepardize' means to note up. It performs the same function as the *Current Law Case Citators* but its appearance is different because it operates entirely on the reference for the case not its name. Taking the example above, you would look up '134 NE 2d 769' to see if *Hill v Bowen* had been subsequently cited. A further system of notation indicates whether the case was followed, distinguished, or otherwise treated. You can 'Shepardize' on-line on Lexis.

Commonwealth in general

8.74 Before looking at some of the major Commonwealth jurisdictions, it is worth mentioning some general comparative sources. Sir William Dale *The Modern*

Commonwealth ((1983) Butterworths), though no longer 'modern' is still quite useful. Apart from describing the legal development and the constitutional position of the Commonwealth as a whole it has sections on each member country giving brief details of their legal system, constitution, courts and so on. Recent political and constitutional developments and other factual information on particular countries can be found in the *Commonwealth Yearbook* (Stationery Office). Although legal literature on the Commonwealth in general is not published at the same rate as it used to be when it had a higher profile, comparative works on particular subjects continue to appear from time to time. The complex legal history of many of the jurisdictions quite often takes one into older material. The classic work *A Legal Bibliography of the British Commonwealth*, published in a second edition (for most of the volumes) from 1955–64 and generally known as 'Sweet & Maxwell', thus remains of use. It may now be supplemented by Jerry Dupont *The Common Law Abroad: Constitutional and Legal Legacy of the British Empire: An Annotated Bibliography of Titles Relating to the Colonial Dependencies of Great Britain Held by Twelve Great Law Libraries* ((2001) Rothman), which is an adjunct to a major project to preserve and make accessible the material listed in microform. Its detailed introductory sections for each jurisdiction provide very valuable historical background.

8.75 Raistrick's *Lawyers' Law Books* (see para **2.11**) includes Commonwealth textbooks selectively. *International Legal Books in Print* (Bowker Saur) the last edition of which was 1993–94 aimed to cover all English language law books published outside the US. Even when current it had shortcomings, but it may still be of residual value. There used to be published an *Index to Commonwealth Legal Periodicals*, but unfortunately it has stopped, so national legal periodical indexes where they exist, or *Index to Legal Periodicals* will have to be used.

8.76 *The Law Reports of the Commonwealth* (not to be confused with the well-known Australian series, *Commonwealth Law Reports*) published by Butterworths provides wider access to the major decisions of Commonwealth courts. It started in 1980 and originally had three volumes a year covering commercial law, criminal law, and constitutional and administrative law respectively. The subject arrangement has been abandoned, but it does now run to five volumes a year. It is worthwhile resource covering cases that are not necessarily in national series. This series does include a few Privy Council cases. The *Appeal Cases* of course report many Privy Council cases, but some appear only in the law reports of the country concerned. As was mentioned at para **5.31**, full sets of Privy Council judgments and related appeal documents are deposited in a number of libraries.

The *Commonwealth Legal Bulletin* prepared by the Commonwealth Secretariat provides valuable information on legal developments throughout the Commonwealth and includes notes of cases and summaries of legislation. Hart is launching a new journal, the *Commonwealth Law Journal*, in 2001.

8.77 As was mentioned in the introduction to this chapter, the main Commonwealth materials of use to English lawyers are law reports. Tracing these has been greatly facilitated by the publication of the *Bibliography of Commonwealth Law Reports* edited by Wallace Breem and Sally Phillips ((1991) Mansell). It is arranged by jurisdiction with, in federal jurisdictions, the federal material coming first followed by individual states. General series are listed alphabetically within each group and reports covering particular subjects are listed under broad subject headings. There are title and subject indexes to the whole work. The coverage, incidentally, is broad and includes both present and former members of the Commonwealth (so, for example, South Africa and the Republic of Ireland are covered); England and Wales, Scotland, Northern Ireland, the Channel Islands and the Isle of Man are also fully covered. A useful feature is that as well as bibliographical details of the printed version, availability of the reports on on-line systems is indicated. It is now getting a little out-of-date, and the major jurisdictions such as Australia and Canada have unfortunately spawned quite a number of more recent series.

8.78 Useful as the bibliography is, it does not extend to providing locations for the material listed, and gaining access to Commonwealth legal materials in general can sometimes be problematic for the English lawyer. The *Union List of Commonwealth and South African Law* ((2nd edn, 1963) IALS) which covers legislation, law reports and digests of cases is still of some residual use for old materials. Many academic law libraries will hold material, particularly law reports, and their catalogues will be searchable on the Internet, either individually or through co-operative schemes such as COPAC or the University of London Union List of Serials. There are major collections at Oxford and Cambridge, and, in London, at Inner Temple, Lincoln's Inn, the School of Oriental and African Studies and the Institute of Advanced Legal Studies. The latter's already strong collection has been enhanced by the transfer of the Foreign and Commonwealth Office Legal Library, which, through official channels, had been able to build up an especially comprehensive collection of Commonwealth legislation. For those without ready access to the printed versions, Lexis includes a small range of law reports from Australia, New Zealand and Canada. These can be searched separately or simultaneously (together with all the English, Scottish and Irish material on Lexis) in the COMCAS library.

Australia

8.79 The long-established guide to Australian legal research is Enid Campbell *Legal Research: Materials and Methods* ((4th edn, 1996) LBC). But there have a been a number of newcomers to the field:

> Surendra Dayal *E-law Research: Your Guide to Electronic Legal Research* ((2000) Butterworths).
> Deakin University School of Law Research Staff *Researching Australian Law* ((1997) LBC).
> Andrew D Mitchell and Tania Voon *Legal Research Manual* ((2000) LBC).
> Irene Nemes and Graeme Cross *Effective Legal Research* ((1998) Butterworths).

Textbooks and journals

8.80 The three main Australian legal publishers, Law Book Company (LBC), Butterworths Australia, and CCH Australia, have long lists of current books and looseleaf services covering federal and state law and, in common with legal publishing elsewhere, often produce competing works on the same subject. There are two major Australian general encyclopaedias, *Halsbury's Laws of Australia* from Butterworths and *Laws of Australia* from LBC. Large and expensive (and looseleaf), they are not widely available in English law libraries. In London the IALS and Lincoln's Inn are two libraries to have the *Halsbury's*. The Bodleian Law Library in Oxford is one of the few libraries, if not the only one, to run to the LBC title as well. They do mean, however, that there is some update coverage on the whole span of Australian law, if there is no Australian textbook on a particular topic available.

8.81 The leading periodical is the *Australian Law Journal*, published monthly. Other specialist titles and university law reviews exist. The *Journal of Contract Law* and the *Tort Law Review*, though published in Australia, have relevance throughout the common law world and are of a very high standard. The main indigenous index to legal journals is AGIS – the Attorney-General's Information Service. It is available on a variety of Australian commercial legal services; access here would probably have to be through Lexis. But the *Index to Legal Periodicals and Books* will cover the main journals.

Legislation

8.82 Primary federal legislation is passed as *Acts of the Parliament of the Commonwealth of Australia*. A consolidation in bound volume form up to 1973 was published. Thereafter, as well as the individual Acts as passed which will be bound up into annual volumes, there are also reprints in pamphlet form of individual Acts as amended. The same arrangement applies to subsidiary legislation, which is passed as statutory rules: there is a consolidation to 1956, annual volumes and reprint pamphlets of particular statutory rules as amended. There is not a direct equivalent of *Halsbury's Statutes*, but works similar to the *Current Law Statute Citators* are *Federal Statutes Annotations* from Butterworths and *Commonwealth Statutes Annotations* from LBC. The great advantage of the Australian way of doing things is the frequent consolidation of amended Acts as reprints, which as well as being printed are fed directly to the AustLII website. The AustLII site includes all the statutes in the 1973 consolidation and all Acts passed since then, as well as the consolidated reprints. The official Australian site, Scaleplus, run by the Attorney-General's office includes much of the primary materials that are also available through AustLII, though AustLII generally has more. In the case of legislation, the main material on Scaleplus but not on AustLII is superseded reprinted consolidations of Acts, which allows you to do point-of-time research. Being an official site, it may be worth double-checking having done an AustLII search, especially for anything very recent.

8.83 The states all have their own primary and secondary legislation in the form of consolidations of varying degrees of currency with subsequent annual volumes. Again, individual Acts are reprinted in amended form. In some cases, for example, the Corporation Acts, the substance of the legislation follows the equivalent federal legislation, in order, as in the US, to achieve uniformity across the states. AustLII has at least the consolidated reprints of statutes of all the states, and for one or two also the 'numbered' Acts as passed. Again, Scaleplus has some archived consolidations of state legislation.

8.84 Recent legislative developments in both the Commonwealth and the states are given in two rival publications, *Australian Legal Monthly Digest* (LBC) and *Australian Current Law* (Butterworths), both of which resemble our own *Current Law* (though the current parts of the second one are in looseleaf format).

Law reports

8.85 The Australian court system is one of some complexity. The supreme federal court is called, somewhat confusingly for the English lawyer, the High Court of Australia. It also hears appeals from state Supreme Courts. Beneath the High Court in the federal system is the Federal Court, but state courts also have federal jurisdiction in certain areas. There are also the federal Family Court and specialist tribunals.

Australia is probably one of the most advanced jurisdictions in respect of promulgation of judgments of the courts in an organised fashion on the Internet. The judges take a relaxed attitude to the citation of cases derived from the Internet, and indeed there is an officially sanctioned form of neutral citation on which the recent innovation in the UK has been modelled (see para **5.59**). Though some retrospective conversion has been done, it naturally tends to be only recent judgments that are available on the Internet, but that is still an enormous help to the English lawyer, given that few English law libraries have the full range of Australian law reports, which continue to be produced in conventional printed form. AustLII is of course the site to go to for the judgments, though Scaleplus has quite a lot of the same materials.

8.86 The authorised reports of the High Court are the *Commonwealth Law Reports* (CLR) (ie the Commonwealth of Australia). Advance reports of High Court cases are published as the *Australian Law Journal Reports*, issued with the journal but paginated and bound separately. The full text of High Court cases back to 1947 is available on AustLII. The database is rightly headed '1947– ', but it also includes in effect a list of all CLR cases back to 1903. The only text attached to the case name contains the judges and the list of cases cited in the judgments – there is not even the headnote. The pre-1947 High Court material is thus limited to checking a CLR citation, or noting-up an old case that might have been cited between 1903 and 1947. Since 1984 the authorised reports of the Federal Court have been the *Federal Court Reports* (FCR). Before that date decisions of the Federal Court were included in *Federal Law Reports* (FLR). The *Federal Law Reports* no longer cover the Federal Court itself, but report cases decided by state courts exercising federal jurisdiction, courts of the two territories, the Family Court of Australia, and federal tribunals. Federal Court decisions on the Internet go back to 1976.

8.87 Roughly equivalent to the *All England Law Reports*, are the *Australian Law Reports* (ALR) which report cases from all the courts covered by the series mentioned above, namely the High Court, the federal courts, and state courts exercising federal jurisdiction – not state reports. As with the *All Englands* vis-à-vis other series, there may be duplication, but there may also be differences in coverage and timeliness. Although ALR does not include state reports and is not an authorised series, it contains in addition to the federal material listed above reports from the courts of the two territories, Australian Capital Territory and Northern Territory. In the case of the Australian Capital Territory the reports are revised by the judges, and there is no independent series. In the case of the Northern Territory they were likewise the authorised reports until 1992, when a separate series of authorised reports, the *Northern Territory Law Reports* started up, though the ALR continues to carry *Northern Territory Reports*. Somewhat confusingly to the uninitiated, the territory reports, which have their own separately paginated sections at the end of most volumes, are not cited as ALR, but as ACTR and NTR respectively. Moreover, the volume numbering of NTR, and from 1993, of ACTR, differs from the volume numbering of ALR. Thus, for example, (1999) 162 ALR includes 137 ACTR and 129 NTR.

8.88 Each of the states has its own series of authorised reports. In New South Wales there was from 1960 to 1970 also a collateral series published commercially by Butterworths which sometimes causes confusion. The Butterworths series was called *New South Wales Reports* (NSWR); the official series was called *New South Wales State Reports* (NSWSR) until 1970 and *New South Wales Law Reports* (NSWLR) thereafter. AustLII has all state Supreme Court decisions from varying dates in the late 1990s, though one or two go back to the 1980s. There is also some coverage of Australian case law on Lexis, but it is not as comprehensive as the UK or US libraries.

As in England there are also numerous specialist subject reports. Care is sometimes needed to differentiate series on the same subject from rival publishers.

8.89 Although our own *Digest* includes many, particularly older, Australian cases, the indigenous aid for finding cases by subject is the *Australian Digest*, published by LBC. It is now in its third edition, which is looseleaf. The *Australian Legal Monthly Digest* covers recent cases and there is a noter-up table that cross-refers these to the main *Australian Digest*. For finding cases judicially considered the main printed tool is the *Australian Case Citator*, also published by LBC. It covers 1825–1959 in two bound volumes, followed by more frequent, non-cumulative, bound volumes. A looseleaf volume cumulating quarterly covers recent cases. As with most of the research tools mentioned in this section, it is also available on CD-ROM. The rival product, apparently rated by some as having fuller coverage, is *CaseBase* from Butterworths. This, however, is only available in electronic form, either on CD-ROM or on-line; the IALS in London is currently a subscriber. As mentioned above in connection with legislation, there is also *Australian Current Law*, which digests cases and in the current binder has a table of cases judicially considered. It is cumulated in annual bound volumes. A particularly useful aid for the English lawyer, because it gives immediate guidance on whether Australian cases are likely to be relevant, is the *Australian and New Zealand Citator to UK Reports*, which gives references to Australian cases that have considered UK cases. Its coverage before 1972 is confined to cases reported in *The Law Reports*, *Weekly Law Reports* and *All England Law Reports* and the only pre-1865 cases included will be those in the *All England* reprint volumes. From 1973 it is wider in scope and includes some cases from other English series, and indeed some Canadian, American and other overseas reports. It is based only on cases that appear in the headnotes as having been actively considered – cases not mentioned in the headnotes and cases in the headnotes that are merely cited or referred to are not included.

Canada

8.90 Like Australia there are both federal and provincial materials to cope with; an added complication is that the legal system of Quebec is a mixed one, following civil law adapted from French law in some private law matters but following common law in other matters. The position in Quebec has also resulted in an official policy of bilingualism throughout the country. Detailed manuals for Canadian legal research are:

> Douglass T MacEllven *Legal Research Handbook* ((4th edn, 1998) Butterworths).
> Margaret A Banks *Banks on Using a Law Library* ((6th edn, 1994) Carswell).
> Jacqueline R Castel and Omeela K Latchman *The Practical Guide to Canadian Legal Research* ((2nd edn, 1996) Carswell).

Textbooks and journals

8.91 There is a large legal literature in Canada. A wide range of textbooks is published by the leading law publishers, Butterworths, Carswell, Canada Law Book, and, in Quebec, Walter Lafleur; likewise there is a full complement of legal periodicals in the form of university law reviews, professional publications and specialist subject journals. Fortunately, there is a comprehensive tool for finding both textbooks and articles: the *Index to Canadian Legal Literature*, which is issued as part of the *Canadian Abridgment,* published by Carswell. There is a bound volume consolidation supplemented by loose issues of *Canadian Legal Literature*, part of the *Canadian Current Law* service. An alternative publication (though not covering textbooks) is *Index to Canadian Legal Periodical Literature*. The main Canadian journals are also covered by the US products *Index to Legal Periodicals* and *Current Law Index*.

Legislation

8.92 A consolidation of federal primary legislation, *Revised Statutes of Canada* was published in 1985 in bound volume and looseleaf format – oddly only the former had official status – and most of the provinces also publish looseleaf consolidations of statutes. Acts as they are passed are issued in the *Canada Gazette* and there are official annual bound volumes. Subordinate legislation in the form of regulations is published in part II of the *Canada Gazette*, but the last hard copy consolidation, the *Consolidated Regulations of Canada*, was back in 1978. There are commercially published annotated collections of statutory materials; the Canadian Criminal Code is produced in a number of rival formats, and individual codes from Quebec are published on the continental model. These hard copy sources are likely to be available in up-to-date form in few English law libraries, so for practical purposes the researcher will go to the Internet, though even official websites tend to have prominent disclaimers that the version is not 'official'. In emulation of AustLII, there is now a CanLII, but so far it only has federal legislation, in the form of consolidated statutes and regulations and annual volumes of statutes back to 1995. Some provincial legislation is promised, but in the meantime there are official sites, either from the legislature or government printer, for most of the provinces and territories, which offer consolidated versions of legislation, of varying dates of currency, and also on some annual legislation as passed, again with varying degrees of retrospective coverage. The LexUM site at the University of Montreal is the probably the most convenient place to find the relevant links. The *Canada Gazette* is available in pdf format from the beginning of 1998. The main Canadian on-line database Quicklaw includes legislation as well as case law (see para **8.96**).

8.93 The *Canada Statute Citator*, published by Canada Law Book, covers federal (but not provincial) statutes and includes amendments and dates in force as well as cases in which statutes have been judicially considered. As part of their *Canadian Current Law* service, Carswell publish in loose parts *Legislation*, which are consolidated as the *Legislation Annual*. This covers both federal and provincial legislation and is in three sections: progress of bills; statutes amended, repealed or proclaimed in force (arranged by jurisdiction and alphabetically by title); and regulations (arranged by jurisdiction and title of enabling statute).

Law reports

8.94 Publication of law reports in Canada is prolific, and there is considerable duplication of coverage. The commercially published *Dominion Law Reports* is the main general series covering both Federal and provincial courts. There are official series for the Supreme Court and Federal Court, series for each of the provinces, regional series covering cases from groups of provinces, and an increasing number of subject-based reports. The decisions of the Supreme Court are available on the Internet from 1985, of the Federal Court from 1993, and of most provincial superior courts from various dates in the late 1990s. It is to hoped than CanLII, as with AustLII, will become the standard home site for all them. At the moment, rather as with BAILII, you may still need to check out individual court sites as well, either for earlier cases or very recent cases not yet available through CanLII. Again, the LexUM site will provide links.

8.95 Although there is quite a range of digests and finding aids, many devoted to particular provinces, the most comprehensive and most widely available in this country is the *Canadian Abridgment*, a vast multi-volume work. As well as its own complex updating mechanisms in the form of replacement volumes, permanent supplements and looseleaf supplements, it is supplemented by the loose parts of *Jurisprudence* and *Canadian Citations* which form part of the *Canadian Current Law Service*. The first of these provides summaries of recent cases from all the Federal and provincial courts. Quite a large proportion of the cases summarised are unreported or not yet reported, but the publishers, Carswell, offer a photocopy delivery service for these. *Canadian Citations* covers both cases and legislation judicially considered. If you do not have access to the *Canadian Abridgement*, remember that selected Canadian cases appear in *The Digest*.

8.96 As with Australia, Lexis coverage is limited. Quicklaw is the main Canadian commercial on-line full-text service, covering both reported and unreported cases. Context, the suppliers of the Justis databases, has recently struck a deal to make this more widely available in this country – hitherto the IALS in London was one of the few English subscribers.

New Zealand

8.97 New Zealand now has a welcome legal research guide written by a law librarian and two academics: Margaret Greville, Scott Davidson and Richard Scragg *Legal Research and Writing in New Zealand* ((2000) Butterworths). Being a smaller jurisdiction and being a unitary rather than federal state, New Zealand has a less complex legal literature than Australia, but none the less, as with most of the major jurisdictions of interest to the English lawyer, there is considerably more to grapple with than there was once. Butterworths, Brooker's and CCH are the three main legal publishers, and *Greville* usefully includes as an appendix a bibliography of the main current legal texts. A major event in New Zealand law publishing is *The Laws of New Zealand* (Butterworths), a multi-volume looseleaf providing the equivalent of *Halsbury's Laws*. There are now quite a number of periodicals (again listed in *Greville*), the *New Zealand Law Journal* being the leading general series.

8.98 Legislation is now published in a similar fashion to Australia: rather than attempting a global consolidation (the last of which was in 1957) particular Acts are reprinted from time to time, though these are produced in numbered bound volumes containing several Acts rather than as individual pamphlets as in Australia. There is an annual *Table of New Zealand Acts and Ordinances and Statutory Regulations in Force* from the government printer and a looseleaf *Index to the New Zealand Statutes* (Butterworths). *Butterworths Annotations* performs roughly the same functions as the *Current Law Statute Citators,* covering both amendments and case law.

8.99 The main series of law reports is the *New Zealand Law Reports*, but there are also now getting on for 20 series of specialist subject reports. The *Abridgement of New Zealand Case Law* is the main retrospective finding tool for cases. But, though it has periodic supplements, these only covers cases in the NZLR. For recent cases there are two publications, *Butterworths Current Law*, which also cover legislative developments, and Brooker's *New Zealand Case Law Digest*. There are electronic versions of some of the printed research tools, and other commercial electronic services, but none are likely to be available to the English lawyer. The *New Zealand Law Reports* from 1970 are on Lexis (the CASES file in the NZ library).

8.100 Primary materials available free of charge on the Internet are currently very limited. The decisions of the New Zealand Court of Appeal are available from 1995 on the Brooker's site (also from 1999 on AustLII). There are also the decisions of one or two other tribunals or bodies, such as the Human Rights Commission, Commissioner of Patents, Designs and Trademarks, and the Refugee Status Appeal Authority. Unconsolidated versions of the statutes are available in browsable, but not searchable, form on the Knowledge Basket site. A very good set of links to New Zealand legal sites is provided by the Auckland District Law Society – they will take you to all of the above.

Other Commonwealth countries

8.101 This section is even more cursory than the foregoing, and can only give a few hints and tips as to possible sources.

Africa

8.102 Legal materials from Anglophone Africa are notoriously hard to get, though for some countries such as Nigeria they are quite prolific. The *Journal of African Law*, published for the School of Oriental and African Studies (SOAS) in the University of London, is a general source of secondary materials. (The library at SOAS is one of the main sources of African legal materials in this country.) South Africa has a well-developed and organised legal literature. Although its legal system is mainly based on Roman-Dutch law, it has imported many common law principles, so its law reports are sometimes cited in an English context, though less frequently than those from the countries already covered. Cases from its Constitutional Court have also attracted attention. Websites for some African countries, providing legislation and case law in varying degrees of completeness and currency do sometimes exist – the ForInt-Law gateway from Washburn University, as well as the gateways mentioned at para **8.15**, might be worth a try. For South Africa, the Wits Law School has an archive of Constitutional Court judgments and has judgments from the Supreme Court from 1999. The Parliament of South Africa site provides the full text of all Acts passed from 1993.

India and Pakistan

8.103 India has a vast, if somewhat disorganised, legal publishing output. The single most useful source is the *All India Reporter*, which covers both cases and legislation from the central and separate state courts and governments. Old Indian cases are quite often encountered in old English cases because of the volume of Indian appeals dealt with by the Privy Council, and indeed *The Law Reports* used to have a special separate series *Indian Appeals. All Pakistan Legal Decisions*, cited as PLD, is the source most likely to be encountered from Pakistan.

Malaysia, Singapore and Brunei

8.104 Malaysia, Singapore and Brunei follow English common law in many matters. Recently started publications are *'Halsbury's Laws'* for both Malaysia and Singapore, which will be of enormous assistance. *Halsbury's Laws of Malaysia*, which is in bound volume form, has adopted the slightly unusual policy of assigning volume numbers to each volume as published, notwithstanding that the titles in each are not being published in alphabetical order. Thus vol 5, containing 'Tort' and 'Trusts' precedes vol 6 containing 'Bankruptcy', while vol 4 contains both the titles 'Insurance Law' and 'Wills'. *Halsbury's Laws of Singapore*, which is also in bound volume form, has adopted the more conventional policy of settling on a scheme of titles for the whole work, and publishing volumes as and when ready even though for the time being they do not form a continuous sequence of volume numbers. The long-established *Malayan Law Journal* was the main vehicle for case reports (as well as articles) from these jurisdictions until 1991. From 1992 it continues to be the main source for Malaysia, but it no longer carries Singapore cases which now have their own series, *Singapore Law Reports*. Since 1992 it has also had a competitor from Sweet & Maxwell Asia, *All Malaysia Reports*. Appeals to the Privy Council from Malaysia were abolished in 1989. Finding aids for Malaysian and Singapore case law are well developed. *Mallal's Digest of Malaysian and Singapore Case Law* is in its fourth edition with the cyclical reissue of volumes. Although primarily a digest of cases, it does list the main relevant legislation at the start of each topic. It has consolidated indexes and a case citator; the *Malayan Law Journal* also has consolidated indexes and tables of cases and legislation judicially considered. Since 1987 there has also been a comprehensive monthly publication which in content and appearance is very similar to English *Current Law*, covering both recent cases and legislative developments. After various changes in title it is in fact now called *Mallal's Current Law*. A complete official reprint of the federal statutes of Malyasia in booklet form in looseleaf binders with the title *Laws of Malaysia* is underway, and there is the recent *Annotated Statutes of Malaysia*, available in either looseleaf or bound volume form, which seeks to emulate *Halsbury's Statutes*. There is also an official looseleaf consolidation of Singapore legislation. There appears to be very little available by way of cases or legislation on free Internet sites – the main Malaysian service, CLJ Legal Network, is for subscribers only.

Hong Kong

8.105 Hong Kong both as a UK dependency and as a commercial centre was traditionally an area of interest to English lawyers. English barristers were sometimes appointed as judges of the High Court, and English barristers were instructed to appear there. The Privy Council also heard a good number of appeals from Hong Kong. With effect from 1 July 1997 Hong Kong became the Hong Kong Special Administrative Region (HKSAR) of the People's Republic of China, but continues to be of importance to English lawyers as a commercial centre. Much of its pre-existing legal system has been retained, and indeed English Law Lords serve as non-permanent judges (NPJ) on its supreme court, the Court of Final Appeal. There is now quite an extensive secondary legal literature due to the activities in particular of Butterworths Asia and Sweet & Maxwell Asia. The former, as in other jurisdictions mentioned above, has produced a *Halsbury's Laws of Hong Kong*. The main journal is the *Hong Kong Law Journal*.

8.106 Legislation is promulgated by means of the official *Hong Kong Gazette*, but there is also an official looseleaf consolidation, the *Laws of Hong Kong*, which contains both primary legislation (ordinances) and subsidiary legislation in English and Chinese parallel text. Resort to a library that is masochistic enough to house and file these particularly unwieldy volumes is fortunately not now necessary since commendably the whole work is available free of charge as the Bilingual Laws Information Service (BLIS) on the Hong Kong Department of Justice website. As well as being fully searchable (not merely browsable like many official sites), admirable features are its currency and the availability of point-of-time research. Currency is achieved not merely by incorporating amendments into the text pretty quickly, but by marking up on the same day that each *Gazette* is published all affected legislation with a 'pencil' tick, so that you know that there is an amendment pending incorporation and, if there is no pencil tick, that what you have is current to within one day. A view option allows to you display all versions of a particular section, which given that the print version is looseleaf is very helpful. Notes give commencement information. There is also a commercially published looseleaf service *Annotated Ordinances of Hong Kong*. It is a Butterworths product modelled on *Halsbury's Statutes*, though its coverage is limited to 150 of the most important and frequently referred to ordinances.

8.107 Until 1997 the main law reports were the *Hong Kong Law Reports*. From 1985 until 1996 there was also the separately commercially published *Hong Kong Law Digest*, published in monthly parts and yearbooks in analogous fashion to *Current Law* (it was in fact originally called *Hong Kong Current Law*). From 1997 these have merged to form a single authorised publication, *Hong Kong Law Reports and Digest* (HKLRD). It is published in loose parts twice a month. The first part of the month contains reported cases only. The second part contains both reported cases and digests of additional cases, together with digests of legislation and cumulative tables. The parts are consolidated into annual bound volumes, the first two or three of which contain the reports and the last a yearbook of the digests. The whole series of HKLR and HKLRD from 1903 are available electronically on CD-ROM or on-line. Sweet & Maxwell Asia, the publishers of HKLRD, also offer an on-line transcript service for unreported cases – Latest Judgments Alert Service (LJAS). HKLR, HKLRD and LJAS are now also available through Westlaw International. Although HKLRD contains Court of Final Appeal cases, the headnotes are reviewed by the court and the reports issued as a separate authorised series, *Hong Kong Court of Final Appeal Reports*. From 1991, with retrospective coverage back to 1946, there has also been a rival, though not authorised, series to HKLRD, *Hong Kong Cases*, published by Butterworths Asia and also available on Lexis.

Caribbean

8.108 Finding out what legislation is in force for the various Caribbean islands has been revolutionised by the regular and timely publication of consolidated indexes for each one by the West Indian Legislation Indexing Project based at the Faculty of Law in the University of the West Indies on Barbados. The problem is that the index is sometimes more up-to-date than the holdings, in UK law libraries at any rate, of the actual texts. Legislation is often published as supplements to government gazettes and consolidations of varying degrees of currency exist for most jurisdictions. There is a one general series of law reports, the *West Indian Reports* (now also available as a module on Butterworths LEXIS Direct), and relatively current individual series for the Bahamas, Cayman Islands and Jamaica. Cases for those islands that promote themselves as tax havens may also get reported in series covering offshore jurisdictions generally, such as the cases portion of the looseleaf *Butterworths Offshore Service*, *International Tax Law Reports*, and *Wills and Trusts Law Reports*. Most of the islands retain the Privy Council as a final Court of Appeal. Cases, particularly on constitutional matters, may reach the *Law Reports of the Commonwealth*. The *Caribbean Law Review* carries notes of unreported cases as well as articles. Cavendish have published some student textbooks on Caribbean law; but there is very little in the way of published textbooks, other than what appears in offshore looseleafs. A useful modern study of the region from the constitutional point of view is Elizabeth W Davies *The Legal Status of British Dependent Territories: the West Indies and North Atlantic* ((1995) Cambridge University Press). The availability of primary materials on the Internet is currently very limited. For some of the jurisdictions, such as Anguilla, the Cayman Islands, St Christopher and St Vincent, there is some company and financial services legislation available from either official sources or offshore firms that operate in the region (AustLII World Law will find them). There is virtually no case law. The Supreme Court of Jamaica has a nascent site, which promises judgments, and also some general legislation (including the consolidated rules of the court) is already there. The Supreme Court of Trinidad and Tobago seems to be the most advanced, with recent judgments apparently being loaded. The biggest collection of hard copy resources in the region, including copies of unreported judgments, is at the Faculty of Law, UWI at Cave Hill, Barbados.

Pacific

8.109 Although not all are Commonwealth or common law jurisdictions, the various Pacific islands are mentioned here. Except in the context of tax havens, the English lawyer does not very frequently encounter them. A pioneering work, published in Australia (where the area is naturally of greater significance), was Jacqueline D Elliott *Pacific Law Bibliography* ((2nd edn, 1990) Pacific Law Press). The English law publishers Cavendish have also recently published two works prompted by the establishment in 1994 of a Department of Law of the University of the South Pacific and a LLB programme: Jennifer Corrin Care, Tess Newton and Don Patterson *Introduction to South Pacific Law* (1999) and Jennifer Corrin Care *Contract Law in the South Pacific* (2001). They give very useful background on constitutional matters and on the application of common law. The jurisdictions covered are: Cook Islands, Fiji Islands, Kiribati, Nauru, Niue, Samoa, Solomon Islands, Tokelau, Tonga, Tuvalu and Vanuatu. AustLII in conjunction with the School of Law of the University of the South Pacific on Vanuatu are developing resources available on the Internet. The University currently holds the live system, but a prototype PacLII is under development. Some recent decisions of the courts are available. There is little full text legislation, but there are indexes to legislation for many of the islands.

European countries

8.110 For the English lawyer the law across the Channel may pose greater difficulties than the law, discussed above, across the Atlantic or across the globe. Few undergraduates study Roman law nowadays, which traditionally would have given some insight into civil law systems, and few English lawyers have a knowledge of European languages of the standard necessary to read legal texts. None the less, the law of European countries is assuming ever-greater importance, and an increasing amount of material is available on the Internet in English. For example, there is quite a lot of translated legislation from the Scandinavian countries. As well as using the general foreign law gateways mentioned at para **8.15**, two further gateways based in Europe are worth mentioning, the Maastricht Internet Law Library and the Law-Related Internet Project at Saarbrücken University.

Books and periodicals

8.111 One immediate difference from common law systems is the importance attached in civil law systems to authoritative commentary on the law published in textbooks and scholarly journals. Such writings, *doctrine* in French, are regarded as a source of law comparable to the decisions of the courts. There is a variety of legal bibliographies produced in most European countries (for an overview of traditional printed sources see Thomas Reynolds 'Secondary sources for research in European law' (1992) 20 *International Journal of Legal Information* at 41–53), but for the English lawyer the best places to start are sources already mentioned: *Index to Foreign Legal Periodicals*, *Bibliography of Comparative and Foreign Law*, and *Reynolds and Flores*. The on-line catalogues of libraries that collect European law are another obvious practical step. The coverage of the *Legal Journals Index*, which is otherwise limited to journals published in the UK, extends to journals published elsewhere in Europe in English.

Legislation

8.112 A distinctive feature of civil law systems is that much of their legislation is codified. Virtually all European countries will have a civil code, a criminal code, a code of civil procedure, a code of criminal procedure and a commercial code. Many other more specialised areas may have codes – France has over 50 separate codes. Usually they are available from commercial publishers in annotated form. These may be small pocket-sized books, like the well-known French series *Petits codes Dalloz*, or vast impenetrable tomes like those of Staudinger's *Kommentar zum Bürgerlichen Gesetzbuch*. Some of the more important codes have been translated into English as individual publications, for example, the French civil code, the Dutch civil code, the Swiss code of obligations and several criminal codes in the *American Foreign Criminal Codes* series, but these one-off publications rapidly become out of date. Bear in mind the translations that may be available in general comparative looseleaf works.

8.113 New legislation is usually issued in official government gazettes – the *Official Journal of the European Communities* has made this format more familiar – such as the *Journal officiel* in France and the *Bundesgesetzblatt* in Germany. Consolidations of legislation, apart from codes, on the common law model, are rare, but exist for example, in Switzerland.

An important source for the text of current legislation in English is *Commercial Laws of Europe*, published monthly by Sweet & Maxwell. Access to the legislation (and court decisions) of European countries has been radically improved by the launch of *European Current Law* in 1992; it should be appreciated that this is not confined to coverage of member states of the EC. Like *Current Law*, to which it is a companion, it is a digesting service and does not provide the full text. It had a precursor in the form of the *European Law Digest* which goes back to 1973, but this was notoriously difficult to use, not least because the monthly parts were not consolidated in the annual bound volumes.

French legislation is available on Lexis. It includes the full text of the *Journal officiel* since 1955, all the codes, and many administrative regulations from various dates. The text of course is entirely in French.

8.114 In most European countries the principle identifying feature of legislation other than codes is the date it was passed rather than, as in England, the title. There may also be given a reference number or citation to an official gazette; in German-speaking countries acronyms are widely used in place of titles.

Law reports

8.115 Although it is often said that civil law systems do not accord the decisions of the courts the same importance as do common law systems, in practice law reports are as indispensable to the continental lawyer as they are to the English lawyer, even though they may not be used in quite the same way. The French term for this source of law, and there are cognate terms in most other European legal languages, is *jurisprudence*, not to be confused with its English usage meaning the philosophy of law.

Most reports of cases are commercially published rather than being official. There may be series covering particular courts, but the publication of cases in legal journals is widespread. Apart from the *Common Market Law Reports* which reports cases relevant to EC law from national courts as well as from the European Court of Justice itself, there are two sources for the text in English of decisions of European courts. One is *European Commercial Cases*, which started publication in 1978 and is now issued by Sweet & Maxwell. Its coverage is quite wide and includes areas such as intellectual property, broadcasting, product liability, as well as more narrowly commercial fields like agency and restrictive practices. The other is *International Litigation Procedure*. Although its coverage is wider than Europe, it is particularly strong on cases relating to the Brussels Convention of Civil Jurisdiction and Judgments. Its title suggests that it is merely a conventional journal, but while it contains some news items and summaries of legislation, it is principally a case reporting service. The Brussels Convention, which we will now have to get used to calling the Brussels Regulation (Council Regulation 44/2001 of 22 December 2000 on jurisdiction and the recognition and enforcement of judgments in civil and commercial matters, OJ 2001 L12 p 1, in force 1 March 2002), is a frequent cause for English practitioners getting embroiled with European case law. A helpful digest is *European Case Law on the Judgments Convention* edited by Peter Kaye ((1998) Wiley). Summaries in English of European cases in general are also available, as mentioned above, in *European Current Law*.

The above sources, for the benefit of the English reader, report and cite European cases by the names of parties, but this is not the normal practice in Europe, where generally the official citation is simply by name of court and date.

8.116 Lexis includes the full text of several series of French reports as from various dates since 1959. They are arranged in two libraries, PRIVE covering private law cases and PUBLIC covering public law cases. The journal *Public Law* has long carried a regular column 'Recent decisions of the French Conseil d'Etat'.

B. Quick Reference Guide

Contents

QR4 *Pepper v Hart* research and the background to legislation   329

QR5 Case law   344

QR6 Treaties and international materials   365

QR7 Other official publications   373

QR1 Search engines: a checklist of features

QR1.1 Know your search engine or search software

Listed below are the common features of search engines. Before entering a search consider whether the particular search engine or system you are using supports them, and if so how they are treated.

— read any on-screen help or search tips

— ask an experienced user, eg your law librarian

— for features of the general Internet search engines, see the excellent Search Engine Features Chart by Greg R. Notess on Search Engine Showdown

QR1.2 Case sensitivity

— Does it matter whether or not you enter words in lower case or capitals?

    — most systems are not case sensitive; if in doubt enter everything in lower case letters

    — but some are sensitive to capitals, eg Alta Vista will find everything if only lower case is used, but will only find occurrences with capitals if capitals are used

QR1.3 Boolean logic

— AND, OR, AND NOT are the three connectors supported by almost all systems

— How are they to be entered?

    — in upper or lower case or does not matter (eg upper case only on Butterworths Books on Screen CD-ROMs) or only as a + sign (eg Lycos)?

— What is the default if no connector is entered between two words?

    — as if there was an AND, an OR or the two words are together as a phrase?

— Can more than one type of Boolean connector be used in a search string?

    — if so, can they be nested using parentheses?

QR1.4 Phrases

— How do you search for an exact phrase?

    — is phrase searching the default or do you have to put the phrase in double quotes, as on many Internet search engines such as Google?

QR1.5 Truncation and wildcards

— How can you truncate word stems to retrieve different grammatical endings, or cater for alternative spellings?

    — many databases allow for simple truncation, with a symbol standing for any number of characters at the end of the word, usually an * (but ! on Lexis, and a $ sign on some systems)

    — wildcards within words are also often provided

        — are there different symbols for multiple character or single character wildcards?

        — does the truncation symbol double up for a multiple character wildcard?

        — is there a minimum number of characters that must appear before a truncation symbol (eg four characters on Northern Light)?

    — does the system automatically search for singulars and plurals without having to truncate (eg Lexis, Northern Light)?

    — does the system automatically truncate and find all words beginning with the search string (eg Lawtel)?

QR1.6 Proximity searching

— Can you search for words appearing near each other?

    — by number of words in between (eg Lexis), by number of characters (Justis one of the few examples), by a general 'near' command (eg equals 10 words on Alta Vista, 40 characters on Justis), or only if in the same paragraph (eg All England Direct)?

    — what is the command, eg product w/10 liability (Lexis), product within 40 of liability (Justis), "product liability"@10 (Folio Views software)?

    — can you specify whether the words only appear either before or after each other, eg product within 40 before liability (Justis)?

QR1.7 Fields

— Can you confine a search to a particular field within a record?

    — often done by means of filling in a form with the various searchable fields set out, frequently called 'advanced search' but also 'form search' (Justis) or 'focused search' (Lawtel)

    — or a field descriptor has to be added to the search (eg with Blackwell Idealist search software, case=samuels for the case name field)

    — the same concept applies on many Internet search engines, where putting eg title: before the search term will only search the title of documents, not content

QR1.8   Search limits

— Can you limit the search, for example by date range?

    — search forms often come with boxes to select particular categories of material on the database or a range of dates

    — many Internet search engines allow you to specify language or parts of domain names, eg .uk

QR1.9   Stop words

— Are there words that are not searchable?

    — almost all systems have stop words, such as 'the', which are not searchable, but some, especially Internet search engines such as Google allow you to override stop words to make them searchable

QR1.10   Displaying search results

— Can you specify how you wish the results to be displayed?

    — before executing the search

        — is there a limit on the number of hits that will be displayed unless you specify otherwise?

        — can you change the settings so that you get, for example, oldest first, rather than latest first?

    — after executing the search

        — are there display options on the results screen?

        — most Internet search engines limit the number of hits displayed from any particular site (usually only one or two pages per site): can you display further pages from that site, for example, with a 'more pages like this' option?

— How are the search terms found within the displayed records?

    — on full text systems with long records it may not be obvious where the search terms occur in each hit

        — usually highlighted, but not necessarily (eg Lawtel)

        — some display page with first occurrence of term, but some display top of the record

            — can you go to the first (or next) occurrence of the term (eg the 'term' function on Justis)?

            — can settings for display of search terms within hits be changed (eg Blackwell Idealist)?

— Can search results themselves be searched?

    — many Internet search engines have a 'search within these results' option, but also available on other databases (eg the 'find' function on Justis)

QR2 Textbooks and other secondary sources

QR2.1 *Halsbury's Laws* [2.6–2.10]

Getting into it
— Consolidated index (volumes 55 and 56)
— Indexes to individual volumes
— Consolidated table of cases (volume 54)
— Tables of cases in individual volumes
— Consolidated tables of statutes, SIs and European Communities material (volume 53)
— Tables of statutes and SIs in individual volumes
— Tables and index in annual cumulative supplement
— Electronic version: Halsbury's Direct

Updating it
— Volumes of main work
— Annual cumulative supplement (two bound volumes)
— Noter-up (looseleaf 'Current Service — Noter-up' volume)

QR2.2 Books on a subject? [2.11–2.15]

— Raistrick *Lawyers' Law Books*
— *Hammicks Law Book Catalogue* (annual bookshop catalogue) and Hammicks online
— Library catalogues on the Internet, eg
    — Institute of Advanced Legal Studies
    — Inns of Court
    — British Library
    — Library of Congress
    — COPAC (Consortium of British and Irish research libraries)
    — Eagle-I – World-wide library catalogues

— *Current Law*: in the body of main entries in the monthly digests; separately at the back in the yearbooks

QR2.3   Old books [2.16]

— Sweet & Maxwell's *Legal Bibliography of the British Commonwealth*
  Vol 1: English law to 1800
  Vol 2: English law 1801–1954
— J.N. Adams *Bibliography of Eighteenth Century Legal Literature*
— J.N. Adams *Bibliography of Nineteenth Century Legal Literature*

QR2.4   Finding articles in UK journals [2.17–2.32]

— *Legal Journals Index* 1986–
  *   **The main source**
— Lawtel (mostly 1998–)
  *   **If LJI not available, better than nothing**
— Law Direct 1995–
  *   **Limited coverage, but free**
— *Index to Legal Periodicals and Books* (American but main UK titles); hardcopy 1908– , electronic 1981–
  *   **Especially for pre-1986 articles**
— *Current Law Index* (American but main UK titles) or LegalTrak 1980–
— *Current Law*: in body of the main entries in the monthly digests; separately at the back in yearbooks
— *Current Law Case Citator*: 1947–76 bound volume only: case comment
— Lexis: full text of about 70 journals
— Westlaw UK: full text of some Thomson titles
— Electronic Law Journals project: details of contents lists, abstracts or full-text available on the web
— *Index of Legal Periodical Literature* (ed Leonard A. Jones) 1786–1907

QR2.5   Finding articles in foreign journals [2.27–2.32] (See also QR8.23 and QR8.27)

— *Index to Legal Periodicals and Books*: English language only
— *Current Law Index* or Legaltrak: English language only
— *Index to Foreign Legal Periodicals*: mainly foreign language
— University Law Review Project: mostly US law reviews
— *Index to Periodical Articles Related to Law*: mainly US
— SCAD: European references

QR2.6   Where to get books and articles [2.34]

— Local union lists of serials, eg University of London Union List of Serials, Inns of Court
— Inter-library loan
— DocDel service from Sweet & Maxwell (Yorkshire office) for journal articles indexed in LJI
— Institute of Advanced Legal Studies distance services (subscribers only)
— *Union List of Legal Periodicals* (but last edn 1978)

QR2.7   Forms and precedents [2.36–2.40]

— *Atkin's Court Forms*
    * **The main source for civil litigation**
— *Butterworths Civil Court Precedents*
    * **Handy alternative to** *Atkin's***, particularly pending the whole of** *Atkin's* **being CPR-friendly**
— *Encylopaedia of Forms and Precedents*
    * **The main source for non-contentious matters**
— *Kelly's Draftsman*
    * **One volume for general practice**
— Subject collections, eg *Practical Commercial Precedents*

Legal directories

QR2.8   Solicitors [2.51–2.54]

— Law Society *Directory of Solicitors and Barristers* or Solicitors On-line
    * **The official directory of solicitors**
— *Waterlow's Solicitors' and Barristers Directory*, also on ConnectingLegal
    * **Well used**
— *Butterworths Law Directory* or Lawyer Locator (.co.uk)
    * **An alternative**
— *The Legal 500*
    * **Evaluative guide to the leading firms**
— *Chambers Guide to the Legal Profession*
    * **Evaluative guide to the leading firms**
— Law Society's Regulatory Information Service at Redditch
    — for details of eg practising certificates held, disciplinary findings, etc
    — searches charged for

QR2.9   Barristers [2.55–2.59]

—   *The Bar Directory*
     *   **The official directory**
         —   includes, selectively, details of work undertaken, expertise etc
         —   only directory to include non-practising barristers
         —   by chambers and alphabetically
—   *Havers' Companion to the Bar*
     *   **Designed especially to provide information on areas of work undertaken, though not included for every barrister**
         —   by chambers and alphabetically
—   All the directories listed above for solicitors
         —   not all both by chambers and alphabetically
         —   *The Legal 500* includes only selected chambers
         —   *Chambers Guide* (as in the firm Chambers and Partners, not barristers' 'chambers'!)lists all chambers but not all barristers; evaluates only selected chambers
—   Specialist bar association directories, eg
         —   *The Chancery Bar*
         —   *COMBAR: the Commercial Bar Association Directory*
         —   *The Planning and Environment Bar Association (PEBA) Handbook*
—   Records Office of the General Council of the Bar

QR2.10   Courts and judges [2.60]

—   *Waterlow's Solicitors' and Barristers Diary*
—   *Butterworths Law Directory*
—   *Shaw's Directory of Courts in the United Kingdom*
     *   **The most detailed guide**
—   Andrew Goodman *Court Guide*
     *   **A practical guide to facilities, etc for the court user (SE and Western circuits only)**
—   *The Lawyer's Remembrancer*
—   Court Service website
—   Lord Chancellor's Department website: list of senior judiciary

QR2.11   Legal services [2.61]

—   *Waterlow's Solicitors' and Barristers' Directory*
—   *Butterworths Legal Services Directory*
—   *Yellow Pages*
—   *Law Society's Directory of Expert Witnesses*

QR2.12 Scottish and Irish lawyers [2.62]

— *Scottish Law Directory*
— *The Blue Book: the Directory of the Law Society of Scotland*
— Law Society of Scotland website
— Faculty of Advocates website
— *The Law Directory* (Incorporated Law Society of Ireland)
— Irish Bar Council website: list of members forthcoming

QR2.13 Overseas lawyers [2.63–2.65]

— *Martindale-Hubbell* and Lawyer Locator
   — *International Law Directory*
   * **The most detailed source other than indigenous directories**
     — Volumes 1–2 by location, volume 3 index to individual lawyers
     — 'non-native' lawyers in volume 3
   — Law Directory
   * **The main part of the work devoted to US lawyers**
— *Kime's International Law Directory*
   * **Probably the most useful alternative**
     — separates local lawyers and foreign lawyers under each country
     — includes brief notes on professional regulation etc for each country
— *International Law List*
   * **An alternative**
— *The Legal 500* and *Chambers Guide* websites: regional and global guides
— *Cross-border Practice Compendium* (Sweet & Maxwell)
   * **For details of professional regulations for lawyers practising in EC member states**

QR2.14 Solicitors' corporate clients and companies' solicitors [2.66]

— *Crawford's Directory of City Connections* (annual) and Crawfords Online
— *PricewaterhouseCoopers Corporate Register* (twice yearly)
— *Hemscott Company Guide* (quarterly) and Hemscott Net

QR2.15 Law teachers [2.67]

— Society of Public Teachers of Law and Association of Law Teachers directories

QR2.16 Law libraries [2.68]

— *Directory of British and Irish Law Libraries*

QR2.17   Bodies holding records and registers [2.69]

—   Bryan Abraham *Directory of Registers and Records*

QR2.18   Past lawyers [2.70]

—   A W B Simpson *Biographical Dictionary of the Common Law*
—   *Oxford Companion to the Law*
—   Guy Holborn *Sources of biographical information on past lawyers* (1999)

QR3 Legislation

Public General Acts

QR3.1 Alternative sources for the text of Public General Acts [3.11–3.31]

— *Halsbury's Statutes of England*

    * **Best source for most purposes**

        — arranged by subject, annotated, kept up to date

        — only statutes still in force

        — not official

        — excludes wholly Scottish Acts

— Queen's printer copy (HMSO)

    * **For very recent Acts, citing in court, Acts no longer in force; otherwise only use if certain Act or section has not been amended or repealed**

        — arranged by date

        — official text, as originally passed

        — first text to appear

        — on HMSO website from 1988

— *Current Law Statutes Annotated* 1947–

    * **Useful for: recent Acts, Acts no longer in force, commentary and finding green papers, white papers, debates etc preceding Acts, Scottish Acts; otherwise only use if certain Act or section has not been amended or repealed**

        — arranged by date, annotated, text not amended

        — includes Scottish Acts from 1991 (previously in separate Scottish edition)

— Lexis and Legislation Direct

    * **Useful for: heavily amended Acts, access to text when printed versions not available (eg home or office), finding statutes when printed indexes and tables inadequate**

        — full text of statutes in force as amended, with some annotations

        — not official

        — remember that each section of an Act is retrieved as a separate item

— Looseleaf subject encyclopaedias

 * **Useful for: most everyday purposes, expert commentary, finding statutes by subject**

  — various arrangements, often annotated, kept up to date

— Handbooks and subject collections

 * **Useful for: personal purchase, carrying around, most everyday purposes, finding quickly statutes in mainstream subject areas**

  — various arrangements, often annotated, kept up to date only by new editions

— Justis Statutes

 * **Useful for: full text searching, especially of legislation no longer in force; older statutes if not available in hard copy**

  — all statutes as passed since 1235 (excluding only some pre-1797 public Acts of a local nature)

— Lawtel

 * **No particular advantage to HMSO website for just the text but has Statutory Status Table**

— *Statutes in Force* (HMSO)

 * **Not updated beyond 1991, now of little use**

QR3.2 Old Acts [3.32]

— *Statutes of the Realm*

 — up to 1714

 — official

— Ruffhead's *Statutes at Large* (ed Runnington)

 — up to 1785 (with continuations to 1869)

 — not official

 — used for pre-1869 texts in Justis Statutes

— Other editions of *Statutes at Large* (see Sweet & Maxwell *Guide to Law Reports and Statutes* (4th edn, 1962) pp 11–16)

— *Acts and Ordinances of the Interregnum 1642–1660* C H Firth (ed) (HMSO, 1911)

QR3.3 Finding Acts by title – year and chapter number unknown [3.42–3.46]

— *Halsbury's Statutes*: alphabetical list in Tables and Index volume (softbound)

 * **The main source**

 — gives volume and page number in main work

 — NB volume numbers prefixed with 'S' refer to the looseleaf 'Current Service' volumes

 — if not found, then the statute is no longer in force, or very recent, or not a Public General Act, or applies only to Scotland

— Justis Statutes

 * **A title search on the Quick form should get it if not in *Halsbury's Statutes***

— Hard copy alternatives

    — *Halsbury's Statutes Citator*: alphabetical list at front, if amended or repealed since 1929

    — *Current Law Statute Citators*: alphabetical table of statutes in front, if passed or affected since 1972

    — *Halsbury's Laws* (as opposed to *Statutes*): alphabetical list in volume 53

— Electronic alternatives

    — Lexis or Legislation Direct: if in force

    — *Current Law Legislation Citator*: if passed or affected since 1989

    — Lawtel or HMSO website: if passed since 1988

    — Badger: if passed since 1993

    — Parlianet or Polis: if passed since 1979

    — Westlaw UK

QR3.4 Finding Acts by chapter number and year – title unknown

— Annual volumes on the shelf of

    — Public General Acts (HMSO, Queen's Printer copies), or

    — *Current Law Statutes Annotated*: from 1947

    * **If this is the preferred version of text**

— *Halsbury's Statutes*: chronological table of statutes in Tables and Index volume (softbound)

    * **If this is the preferred version of text**

— Justis Statutes

    * **If hard copy annual volumes not available**

        — Reference option on Quick form

— *Chronological Table of the Statues* (TSO, two black bound volumes)

    * **An alternative to find what title is if actual text not needed**

        — covers all statutes from 1235 to about two years ago

— *Current Law Statute Citator*

    * **An alternative to find what title is if actual text not needed**

        — all statutes from 1947; only pre-1947 statutes affected since 1947

QR3.5 Finding Acts in force by subject [3.47–3.50]

— *Halsbury's Statutes*: Tables of Statutes and General Index volume (softbound)

    * **Best hard copy starting point**

        — NB two sequences:

            — Volume index: to the main bound volumes

            — Service index: to the looseleaf 'Current Statutes Service' volumes

— Looseleaf encyclopaedias, subject handbooks, textbooks, *Halsbury's Laws*

*   **Shortcut for mainstream topics**

— Lexis or Legislation Direct

*   **At their best when searching for specific technical terms or concrete entities**

— Justis Statutes

*   **But check status of results with 'cross-ref' function**

— Badger

*   **For very recent statutes**

— *Current Law*: monthly digests

*   **For very recent statutes**

    — use cumulative index in latest part or browse through main body of entries in each part

QR3.6   Finding Acts no longer in force by subject [3.50]

— Justis Statutes

*   **At its most useful**

— Look at a relevant statute in force and see what it repeals

— *Halsbury's Statutes*: indexes to 1st–3rd editions

— Old editions of standard textbooks

— *Statutes at Large*: index (volume 10)

    — to 1786

— *Statutes of the Realm*: index

    — to 1715

QR3.7   Finding amendments and repeals [3.51–3.60]

— *Halsbury's Statutes*

*   Best starting point (but should be supplemented by latest *Current Law Statute Citator,* Legislation Citator or Lawtel)

    — **Main work**: text as at date of issue of the volume. Look at notes to each section for details of amendments and repeals incorporated

    — **Cumulative supplement** (annual bound volume): under same volume and page number of main work. If actual text of any amendment not given in full, a reference to the looseleaf 'Current Statutes Service' volumes (or another volume of the main work) will be given. NB Includes annotations to statutes in looseleaf 'Current Statutes Service' volumes (statutes awaiting incorporation in a reissue of a bound volume). These appear at the end of each topic title within the sequence for a particular volume number and have '(S)' after the volume number

— **Noter-up** (thin looseleaf volume): under same volume and page number as main work or 'Current Statute Service' volumes. NB Not always as up to date as the statute citator in the latest monthly part of *Current Law*, which should be checked next

— *Current Law Statute Citators*

  * **An alternative hard copy approach, but only references to year and chapter numbers of amending Acts given – not title or text of amendments. The latest issue can be a cross-check on *Halsbury's Statutes* noter-up. Includes Scottish statutes**

    — find statute by year and chapter number

    — Statute Citator 1947–1971 (bound volume)

    — Statute Citator in Legislation Citator bound volumes 1972–88, 1989–95, and 1996–99

    — Statute Citator in Legislation Citator 2000– previous year (softbound)

    — Statute Citator for current year (and, depending on time of year, previous year) in *Current Law Statutes* looseleaf service volume

— *Current Law Legislation Citators*

  * **Internet version for greatest currency; otherwise no particular advantage over hard copy**

— Lawtel

  * **Recommended electronic source, having used hard copy *Halsbury's Statutes*, for statutes passed since 1984**

    — look at 'Statutory Status Table' for the Act

    — links to HMSO text of amending statutes (1988–)

    — can also be used for pre-1984 Acts amended since 1987: do a free text search on its name, but finding where mentioned in hits may be difficult

— Justis Statutes

  * **Internet version best; if using CD-ROM version essential to update using the above sources**

    — use cross-ref facility on particular section

    — if it is an *inserted* section, eg Housing Act 1985 s 11A, look through all amendments using cross-ref facility on the whole Act from arrangement of sections page

— Lexis or Legislation Direct

  * **Most useful for heavily amended text**
    Lexis search examples:

      TITLE(Income w/5 1988) and SECTION(434) will retrieve section 434 of the Income and Corporation Taxes Act 1988 as amended

      TITLE(Vehicles Excise w/5 1971) and SECTION(Sch 4) will retrieve Schedule 4 to the Vehicles (Excise) Act 1971

— *Halsbury's Statutes Citator*

  * **Use first if statute no longer in current edition of *Halsbury's Statutes*, then go to next**

— *Chronological Table of the Statutes* (TSO, two black volumes)

* **Best source for finding when and how old Acts not included in any of the above were *finally* repealed. Otherwise because of lack of currency of limited use. Includes Scottish Acts**

QR3.8 Finding commencement dates [3.61–3.72]

— Lawtel

* **Best source: updated daily**

— find Act and look at 'Statutory Status Table'

— if necessary for complicated provisions use links to full text of commencement order

— *Is it in Force?*

* **Best printed source to start with; current edition covers last 25 years**

— Grey softbound volume, often shelved with *Halsbury's Statutes*, then latest issue in looseleaf noter-up to *Halsbury's Statutes*

— Arranged by year and alphabetically by title within year

— Repeals noted (but without authority for repeal); commencement dates not given for repealed Acts or sections

— Free online version on Law Direct: check details on screen for currency – under redevelopment in 2001

— *Current Law*: Dates of Commencement Table in latest monthly part

* **Usually the most up-to-date printed source and a cross-check on *Is it in Force?* in noter-up, but only covers commencement orders issued in the current calendar year**

— Arranged alphabetically by title

— *Halsbury's Statutes*: main work, cumulative supplement and noter-up

* **No particular advantage over a combination of above two sources where the information is more readily accessible. Source of commencement dates for statutes more than 25 years old but still in force**

— Look at the annotations to particular sections or the section containing the commencement provisions

— *Halsbury's Laws*: Commencement of Statues division in looseleaf Noter-up Current Service volume

* **An alternative to the above and to Current Law monthly parts, but again not usually quite as up-to-date**

— Covers commencements since the last annual cumulative supplement to *Halsbury's Laws*

— Arranged alphabetically by title

— Full text of SIs on HMSO website

* **A bit cumbersome, but a way of updating printed sources if Lawtel is not available**

– Use the search engine to search on name of Act and 'Commencement Order', then look at text of latest, and its explanatory note

— Justis Statutory Instruments

 * **The Internet version for the full text of commencement orders; the CD-ROM version will have no particular advantage over other sources**

— *Current Law Statute Citators*

 * **An alternative to *Is it in Force*? and other printed sources listed above, but less straightforward to use for this purpose. A source for commencement dates of Acts passed from 1947 that have since been repealed. Includes Scottish Acts**

 — For recent Acts commencement orders listed at start of entry; for older Acts check also for orders made under the particular section containing the commencement provisions

 — Only the SI number is given; refer to the SI itself for details of date and extent

 — If several commencement orders found, look at the latest first: effect of previous orders usually given in a note

— Lexis

 * **Probably an expensive approach unless other sources not available**

 — If only one or two sections relevant find the text of sections themselves in the STAT file: the commencement date is given at the head of each

 — If a whole Act or large part of one relevant, find the relevant commencement orders in the SI file

— TSO *Daily List*

 * **Last resort for finding by manual means commencement orders issued since the last monthly part of *Current Law***

 — Details of commencement orders are given at the start of the section listing SIs that appears at the end of each *Daily List*. If not stated, refer to the SI itself to find which provisions of the Act have been brought into force

— Parlianet for Parliamentary questions; contact an official in relevant government department (identifiable from *Civil Service Yearbook* or departmental website)

 * **For information on possible timetable for implementation when no commencement order yet issued**

Consolidation Acts

QR3.9 Finding derivations [3.73–3.77]

— Public General Acts annual volumes: table of derivations in Tables and Index volume

 * **Best source for Acts passed since 1967**

— *Current Law Statutes*

 * **Best source for Acts 1947–66; an alternative 1967–**

 — derivations given in notes to sections or separate table of derivations

— *Halsbury's Statutes*

    * **An alternative for most statutes in force**

        — derivations usually, though not invariably, provided in notes to sections

— Justis Statutes

    * **Especially for pre-1947 statutes no longer in force**

        — free text search on words from section in consolidation Act that are likely to have been used previously

— Old editions of standard textbooks, eg *Buckley on the Companies Acts*

    * **Shortcut for pre-1947 statutes no longer in force if Justis Statutes not available or not getting results**

— Schedule of repeals in consolidation Act

    * **The hard way as a last resort**

        — examine each Act listed as being repealed until you find the equivalent provision

QR3.10   Finding destinations [3.77]

— *Halsbury's Statutes Destination Tables* (softbound volume)

    * **The most handy source**

        — covers all consolidation Acts from 1983, plus selected earlier ones from 1957

        — table of legislation replaced at back tells you name of new Act

        — go to that Act in main work for section by section listing of destinations

— Public General Acts annual volumes: table of destinations in Table and Index volume

    * **Need to know name and year of consolidation Act, but otherwise equally good alternative for statutes passed 1967–**

— *Current Law Statutes* or *Halsbury's Statutes* (main work)

    * **Tables of destinations often, but not always, provided with consolidation Acts**

— Justis Statutes

    * **Could be used, but unlikely to be necessary except possibly for old consolidation Acts not in the above sources**

Statutory instruments

QR3.11   Alternative sources for the text of SIs [3.82–3.87]

— HMSO individually printed SIs

    — arranged by year and number

    — official text, as originally made

    — first text to appear

    — includes all SIs of general application and *some* of local application; but some SIs of local application not published at all (see below)

- — may subsequently be bound, or may be replaced by official bound volumes
- — the only source for SIs not included in any of the sources below
- — on HMSO website from 1987
- HMSO official bound volumes
  - — go back to 1890
  - — from 1961 arranged by year and number
  - — before 1961 arranged by year and subject-matter (with tables to numbers)
  - — official text, as originally made
  - — do not include *any* local SIs nor short-lived SIs spent or revoked within the year
  - — include some non-SI subsidiary legislation (unnumbered at the back of the last volume for the year)
- *Statutory Rules and Orders and Statutory Instruments Revised*
  - — official text, as amended, of all instruments (other than local ones) in force as at 31 December 1948
  - — arranged by subject-matter (with tables by number)
- *Halsbury's Statutory Instruments*
  - — covers all SIs (other than local and wholly Scottish ones) in force
  - — only selected SIs in full text, others summarised
  - — full text of summarised SIs available to subscribers from the publishers on demand
  - — arranged by subject
  - — fully annotated, indexed and updated
- Looseleaf encyclopaedias and subject handbooks
  - — sometimes annotated
- *Civil Procedure* (the White Book), *Civil Court Practice* (the Green Book), *Stone's Justices' Manual*
  - — for SIs containing court rules
- Justis Statutory Instruments
  - — Internet or CD-ROM versions
  - — full text of published SIs from 1987 (catalogue data only from 1980)
  - — catalogue data for unpublished SIs from 1987
  - — excludes some graphics
- Lawtel
  - — Links to the HMSO text from 1987
- SI CD incorporating SI Web
  - — The Stationery Office's commercial version
- Lexis or Legislation Direct
  - — full text of all SIs in force (other than local ones)
- Unpublished local SIs

—   available from:

Her Majesty's Stationery Office
Statutory Publications Unit
4 Central Buildings
Matthew Parker Street
London SW1H 9NL

*   **From 1922 (except 1942, 1950, 1951 and up to SI 940 of 1952)**

Reader Information Services Department
Public Record Office
Kew
Richmond
Surrey TW9 4DU

*   **As above up to 1960**

Official Publications and Socials Sciences Service
British Library
96 Euston Road
London NW1 2DB

*   **As above up to 1980**

—   otherwise try your luck with relevant local authority or body

QR3.12   Finding SIs by title – year and/or number unknown [3.88–3.89]

—   *Halsbury's Statutory Instruments*:
    *   **The only alphabetical listing of all SIs in force (except the most recent)**
        —   index volume (softbound)
        —   gives SI number and topic in main work (but not page number)
        —   then alphabetical list in looseleaf service volume for more recent SIs
—   *Halsbury's Statutory Instruments Citator*
    *   **Check here if not found in *Halsbury's SIs* main work (because now revoked)**
        —   alphabetically listing in first half
        —   only covers those in the citator itself, ie only those that have been amended or revoked during the lifetime of *Halsbury's SIs*
—   *Halsbury's Laws*: consolidated table of SIs (in volume 53)
    *   **Likely to cover most SIs in force; next best printed source to *Halsbury's SIs* index volume**
—   *Current Law*: alphabetical table of SIs in latest monthly part
    *   **A cross-check for very recent SIs**
        —   cumulative for the current calendar year
        —   refer to December issue of monthly parts or the yearbook for the previous calendar year

— *Current Law Legislation Citators*

    *   **An alternative for SIs made or affected since 1993**

        — alphabetical tables in front of bound volumes, or electronic version

— Full text electronic sources

    *   **As good a method as any except for old SIs not in force, and gets you the text; for coverage see QR3.11**

        — HMSO website, Justis SIs, Lawtel, Lexis, Legislation Direct

        — where possible, do a field search on the title field

— Badger

    *   **OK for SIs made since 1993**

— Westlaw UK

    *   **Should get SIs from 1948**

— Looseleaf encyclopaedias: alphabetical tables of SIs

    — included in some but not all looseleafs (usual in Butterworths publications but not in Sweet & Maxwell's)

— UKOP

    *   **For unpublished local SIs; otherwise if none of the above available, eg in a non-law library**

        — catalogue data 1980–

— Parlianet or Polis

    *   **An option**

        — catalogue data for *laid* SIs 1982–

QR3.13   Finding SIs by year and number – title unknown

— Annual volumes on the shelf

    — from 1961 official HMSO volumes arranged by number within each year

    — before 1961 look at numerical table at front of first volume for the year

    — NB if official HMSO volumes taken, local and temporary SIs may have been bound by the library separately

— *Halsbury's Statutory Instruments*: chronological list of instruments

— *Halsbury's Statutory Instruments Citator*

    — but only if amended or revoked

— *Current Law Legislation Citators*

    — for SIs made or affected 1993–

— *Table of Government Orders* (HMSO, pale blue bound volume)

    — for pre-1991 SIs only

    — arranged by year and number

    — omits unpublished local SIs

    — for SIs that were in force in 1948 references to the volume number and page of *SR & O and SIs Revised* are given

— *List of Statutory Instruments* (TSO, monthly and annual): numerical list
   — gives the subject heading in the main list where details will be found
   — includes unpublished local SIs
— *Statutory Rules and Orders and Statutory Instruments Revised*: numerical table in tables volume (volume 25)
   — covers SR & Os (equivalent of SIs before 1946) and SIs in force in 1948, and SIs for 1949–1951
— *Current Law Yearbooks* (1947–): numerical table of SIs
   — gives paragraph number in yearbook where full details of the SI will be found
— Electronic sources: see QR3.12
   — HMSO website (primary arrangement by number), Justis SIs, Lawtel, Lexis, Legislation Direct, Badger, Westlaw UK, UKOP, Parlianet, Polis
— Looseleaf encyclopaedias: chronological tables of SIs
   — included in some but not all looseleafs (usual in Sweet & Maxwell publications but not in Butterworths)

QR3.14   Finding SIs by subject [3.90–3.92]

— *Halsbury's Statutory Instruments*
   * **Best printed starting point**
      — consolidated index in annual softbound index volume
      — index in looseleaf service volume
— Looseleaf encyclopaedias
   * **Shortcut for mainstream topics**
— Full text electronic sources
   * **Generally ideal, but at their best when searching for specific technical terms or concrete entities; for coverage see QR3.11**
      — Justis SIs, Lexis, Legislation Direct, Lawtel, HMSO website (but search engine for latter a bit crude)
— Badger
   * **Not full text, but generally effective, though 1993– only**
— UKOP
   * **Titles only, so limited; will include unpublished local SIs; 1980–**
      — limit the search to SIs using the 'categories' facility
— Parlianet or Polis
   * **An option; some indexing terms as well as titles**
— *Index to Government Orders in force at 31 December 1991* (HMSO, two pale blue volumes)
   * **For old SIs only**
— *Current Law*: monthly digests
   * **For very recent SIs not yet in other printed sources**
      — cumulative index to latest monthly part or browse through body of main entries in each monthly part

— *Current Law*: recent yearbooks

* **An alternative printed source for recent SIs. Not worth the effort for older SIs**

— *List of Statutory Instruments* (HMSO, monthly and annual): list by subject heading

* **Only printed source for unpublished local SIs. A shortcut if you know subject and year but not number**

QR3.15 Finding SIs by enabling Act [3.93–3.101]

Halsbury's Statutes

* **The best printed source, but may need to be updated for the most recent SIs by electronic sources**

— look in the notes to particular enabling section of the Act in the main work

— check annual cumulative supplement (bound volume) under same volume number and page

— check looseleaf noter-up under same volume number and page

— if particular enabling section is not known, all SIs made under an Act are listed at the front of the volume of the main work containing the Act

— *Current Law Statute Citator*: latest issue in *Current Law Statutes* looseleaf service volume

* **A cross-check on noter-up to *Halsbury's Statutes* – may be more up to date**

— find Act by year and chapter number

— SI number, but not title, of orders, regulations, etc given against each section of the Act

— Lawtel

* **Probably the most up-to-date and convenient source for SIs made since 1984. Includes Scottish SIs**

— either go to record for *Act*, and in the Statutory Status Table click on 'SIs enabled' for all SIs under the whole Act

— or do a focused search on the enabling Act field in the *SI* search options, adding eg 's.4(5)' if necessary

— Lexis or Legislation Direct

* **Fast and effective. Unlike Lawtel will include all SIs made under statutes in force**

— Lexis search example:

AUTHORITY(Merchant Shipping w/6 1983) will retrieve all SIs made under the Merchant Shipping Act 1983

— Justis Statutory Instruments

* **Internet version preferably; if CD-ROM used essential to update from other sources**

— use 'Enabling Act' field on form search

— Badger

    * **A good alternative for SIs made since 1993**

        — search in legislation field, where 'm/u' means 'made under'

— *Current Law Legislation Citator*

    * **An alternative, particularly in the Internet version, for checking recent SIs; otherwise no particular advantage over other sources**

— *Current Law Statute Citators* printed volumes

    * **A possible manual alternative to *Halsbury's Statutes*, but more long-winded. A way of finding, if they were ever needed, revoked SIs by enabling provision, or SIs that were made under an enabling provision now repealed**

        — 1947–71 volume; 1972–88, 1989–95; 1996–99 and any softbound supplements thereafter in Legislation Citator volumes

        — find Act by year and chapter number

        — work backwards from the most recent citator; if several SIs given look at the most recent first before proceeding further: it may have revoked the earlier ones listed

        — from 1972 the number given (there are no titles) is of the SI itself; for the 1947–71 citator the number given is the paragraph number in the *Current Law* yearbook where the SI is digested *not* the SI number

— TSO *Daily Lists*: list of SIs

    * **As a last resort. A tedious plod, but the only safe way to check by manual means for very recent SIs made since the last statute citator in the *Current Law Statutes* looseleaf service volume**

        — read through the entries for every SI listed: the enabling power is given after the title

— *Index to Government Orders in force at 31 December 1991* (HMSO, two pale blue volumes)

    * **For old SIs only; also covers non-SI orders**

        — look at the table of statutes on the green pages at the front of volume 1, which refers to the relevant subject heading in the main work

        — under each subject heading the text of the enabling power is set out and below, under the heading 'Exercise', the SIs are listed, or, if none as at 1991, 'Power not yet exercised'

QR3.16   Finding amendments and revocations [3.102–3.105]

— *Halsbury's Statutory Instruments*

    * **One of the main methods using printed sources, but will need to be supplemented by electronic sources**

        — check volume in main work; will include amendments and revocations up to date of reissue

        — check noter-up in the looseleaf service volume

— *Halsbury's Statutory Instruments Citator*

    *   **Look here next if not in main work because revoked**

       — covers all SIs amended or revoked during the lifetime of *Halsbury's SIs*

       — large and important SIs broken down by regulation, etc number

— *Current Law Statutory Instrument Citator*

    *   **Perhaps the simplest printed source for SIs passed or affected 1993–; latest issue a cross-check on noter-up to *Halsbury's SIs;* but will need to be supplemented by electronic sources**

       — in *Legislation Citator* 1989–1995; 1996–1999 bound volumes; any softbound supplement; current year (and, depending on time of year, previous year) in *Current Law Statutes* looseleaf service volume

       — all SIs broken down by regulation, etc number

— *Current Law Legislation Citators*

    *   **The on-screen version includes the data from the above but, particularly Internet version, more up-to-date; on large SIs comprising many records take care**

       — a separate record for effects on whole instrument (eg revocation) and for each numbered regulation, etc

       — search first for all records on the SI, look at general ones first, then if necessary narrow search by regulation, etc number

— Lawtel

    *   **Very good and current; often the best first port of call; but for large and/or heavily amended SIs does not break down by regulation, etc number – every amending SI has to be looked at**

       — put number of SI in Effect field in focused search option – will get all amending and revoking SIs from 1984

       — note that the status information on the record for the SI itself (whether it has been amended or revoked) has only been provided with effect from 1999

— Justis Statutory Instruments

    *   **Internet version good; but as with Lawtel for large and/or heavily amended SIs; CD-ROM version must be supplemented by other more current sources**

       — either use Effect field search, or find record for SI and use cross-ref facility

— Lexis or Legislation Direct

    *   **Most useful for getting heavily amended text as is; said to be current to within about four working days; Lawtel may be two or three days ahead**

— Badger

    *   ***Not* its main function; but data on Internet version may be very slightly ahead of *Legislation Citator***

       — search on similar words in title of SI (amending SIs often have the same name) and as widely as possible on subjects

— Looseleaf encyclopaedias

   *   **Often a convenient shortcut to get heavily amended text as a starting point, but will need to be supplemented by other sources**

      — if text printed as amended check notes for latest SI incorporated, or if not stated date of last release in filing record, then use above sources for anything since then

— TSO *Daily List*: list of SIs

   *   **As a last resort. A very tedious plod, but the only safe manual way to check for very recent amendments or revocations made since the last issue of the *Current Law Statutory Instrument Citator* if no electronic sources available**

      — read through the entries for each SI listed (likely ones can usually be spotted by their titles): the numbers of SIs amended or revoked are given in the body of the entry under 'effect'

Table of Government Orders 1671–1990 (HMSO, pale blue bound volume)

   *   **The authoritative source for amendments and revocations before 1991.**

      — includes all SIs, Statutory Rules and Orders, and other orders in force or partly in force as at 31 December 1948, and all SIs made since then until the end of 1990

      — arranged numerically

      — SIs in force in bold

      — SIs revoked, spent or expired in italic

      — am. = amended; **r.** = revoked

      — amendments broken down by regulation, etc number

      — for SIs in force at 1948 only post-1948 amendments indicated: for earlier amendments reference is given to *SR & Os & SIs Revised*

      — includes pre-1890 government orders

      — omits local unpublished SIs

— *Current Law Legislation Citator*: tables of SIs affected 1947–1992

   *   **A less useful alternative to the *Table of Government Orders* for old SIs – amendments not broken down by regulation, etc number**

      — **1947**–88 table in **1972**–88 *Legislation Citator*; 1989–**92** table in 1989–**95** volume

      — covers SIs of whatever date affected since 1947

      — arranged purely numerically; the SIs on the shelf will need to be consulted to find the text and title

      — if more than one amending SI listed, look at the most recent first

      — the effects of Scottish SIs issued in 1986 were omitted in error from the 1972–88 volume, but are included in the 1989–95 volume

      — superseded by the *Current Law Statutory Instrument Citator* 1993–

QR3.17 Finding commencement dates of SIs [3.106]

— Text of SIs themselves (hard copy, Justis SIs, HMSO website, Lawtel etc)

     — commencement date almost always given at head

— Badger

     — if text not available or not needed; 1993–

List of Statutory Instruments (TSO, monthly and annual)

     — if text not available or not needed: find SI in subject listing, commencement date given in entry details

— *London Gazette*

     * **Very rare: needed only for SIs whose commencement is dependent on the ratification of an international treaty by another state. Safer and easier to ask the Treaty Section of the Records and Historical Department at the Foreign and Commonwealth Office (contact details on FCO website)**

     — if *London Gazette* attempted, look in quarterly indexes under 'Foreign and Commonwealth Office' and then in each issue in the State Intelligence section at the front again under 'Foreign and Commonwealth Office'

EC legislation

QR3.18 Types of legislation and numbering [3.112–3.119]

EC, Euratom

Directives	Need implementation	Year/Number
ECSC		
Recommendations (Individual)	Need implementation	Year/Number
Recommendations (General)	Need implementation	Number/Year
EC, Euratom		
Regulations	Direct effect	Number/Year
ECSC		
Decisions (General)	Direct effect	Number/Year
EC, Euratom		
Decisions	Need implementation	Year/Number
ECSC		
Decisions (Individual)	Need implementation	Year/Number
EC, Euratom		
Recommendations	Not binding	Year/Number
EC, Euratom, ECSC		
Opinions	Not binding	Year/Number

QR3.19 Alternative sources for the text of EC legislation [3.122–3.128]

— *Official Journal of the European Communities*: L series
  * **Main printed source provided that you first have a full OJ reference**
    — official text
    — published daily
    — cited as OJ
    — in English since 1973 (also published in all official languages)
    — special editions 1972 and 1974 provide English translation of legislation in force at the time of UK accession
    — last 45 days only available for free on EUR-Lex
— *Encyclopedia of European Community Law*: C volumes (Sweet & Maxwell, 10 black looseleaf binders)
  * **Convenient for most everyday purposes**
    — full text of much (though by no means all) of the legislation in force, usually as amended
    — arranged by broad subject and chronologically within subjects
— Subject looseleafs and handbooks
  * **Sometimes a shortcut**
    — eg *Butterworths Competition Law Service, Encyclopaedia of Banking Law, EC Competition Law Handbook*
— Celex
  * **The official EU database containing all legislation (and much else); not a free service, but widely available in libraries in a variety of forms**
    — via the Internet, from Justis (Context), Lawtel EU, EU Direct (Butterworths LEXIS Direct services), Lexis, Westlaw, Lovdata, or EUR-OP (Office of Official Publications of the EU) itself
    — on CD-ROM from Context, OJ Online (Ellis), ILI, EUR-OP

— EUR-Lex: *Directory of Community Legislation in Force*
  * **On the EU's free website, this gives all legislation in force, as passed and often in (unofficial) consolidated form**
— University of Mannheim European Documentation Centre: Virtual Fulltext Library
  * **Limited free access to legislation on Celex, including legislation no longer in force**
    — searchable by OJ reference, Regulation number, Directive title or number

QR3.20 Finding EC legislation by number [3.130–3.131]

— Celex
  * **Should be straightforward depending on search software**
    — on Justis version, use the document number on the Quick Search form, and enter OJ reference, or number of Directive, Regulation or Decision prefixed with 'Dir' or 'Directive', or 'Regulation' or 'Decision' (last two in full)

— EUR-Lex
  * **If you do not have access to Celex; fairly straightforward; only for legislation in force**
    — from main Europa site, select 'Official Documents', then 'Legislation in force': the 'Directory of Community of Legislation in Force' is displayed. Find the search button at left of screen or bottom of page, and enter the number
— Mannheim
  * **An alternative free site**
— *Official Journal*: methodological index (annual and monthly)
  * **If you are planning on using hard copy anyway; as the number includes the year, straightforward to find the right annual index**
    — in two sequences: (1) number/year material and (2) year/number material (see QR3.18 above)
    — from 1992 Directives listed first in the year/number sequence
— *European Communities Legislation: Current Status* (Butterworths, two bound volumes + supplement)
  * **An equally or more convenient printed source**
    — bound volumes reissued annually
    — telephone enquiry service
    — covers all legislation in the special editions 1972 and 1974 and everything in OJ since (so excludes legislation repealed before 1972)
    — arranged by year and within each year in two sequences: (1) number/year material; (2) year/number material (see QR3.18 above)
    — gives full OJ references and title or subject-matter of main acts
— *Encyclopedia of European Community Law*: Table of Community Secondary Legislation (at front of binder CI)
  * **If OJ not available**
    — two sets of tables: main table, and, for recent legislation since the last consolidation of the main table, a supplementary table
    — each table arranged in three sequences: (1) Regulations; (2) ECSC Decisions and Recommendations; (3) EEC/Euratom Decisions and Directives
    — gives just references to paragraph number in the encyclopaedia where text (and OJ reference) is to be found (the first part of the number is the division number not the binder number)
— *Halsbury's Laws* volume 53: tables of European Communities materials
  * **Possible shortcut**
    — legislative material arranged in two sequences: (1) year/number material; (2) number/year material
    — a third sequence of other materials, eg notices, resolutions, and non-ECSC recommendations
    — gives full OJ references as well as paragraph numbers of where referred to in main work

— *Directory of Community Legislation in Force*: chronological index in volume 2

    * **Only if you are familiar with Celex version of Regulation and Directive numbers**

        — separate sequences for different categories of legislation within each year arranged in Celex format

        — gives page number in volume 1, where full details given

— *Official Journal*: L series: recent issues

    * **Only if stuck with hard copy; for very recent legislation since the last monthly index**

        — browse through the contents list at the front of each issue

QR3.21   Finding EC legislation by title – number unknown [3.131]

— Celex

    * **The usual recourse**

        — beware of Eurospeak in official titles, eg the Second Banking Directive is the Second Council Directive on the coordination of laws ... on credit institutions

— EUR-Lex

    * **If Celex not available; only fairly basic text searching facility**

— *Legal Journals Index* and/or Badger

    * **Sometimes a shortcut for recent or important legislation that is likely to have been commented on**

        — search in the legislation field if reasonably confident of title; otherwise a subject search

— SCAD

    * **An unlikely but possible alternative for most legislation since 1983**

        — omits the minor legislation listed in light type in the OJ L series

        — bibliographic details only not full text

QR3.22   Finding EC legislation by subject [3.132]

— Celex

    * **The usual recourse**

        — search on free text: there is a system of subject headings but best ignored

— EUR-Lex

    * **If Celex not available**

        — the primary arrangement of the *Directory of Community Legislation in Force* is an elaborate subject structure, but again a plain text search is best tried first

— SCAD on CD-ROM

    * **Convenient for most legislation since 1983**

        — omits legislation listed in light type in OJ L series

        — various subject descriptors available, but search also on key words from the title

        — bibliographical details only, not full text

— *Encylopedia of European Community Law*: C volumes: indexes at back of last binder

    * **A convenient manual source for most legislation in force**

        — two sequences of index: main index and supplementary index (for recent material)

        — references are division numbers not binder numbers

— *European Communities Legislation: Current Status*: subject index

    * **Equally good manual source**

        — gives Directive or Regulation number in main volumes

        — numbers printed in italic refer to legislation no longer in force

        — numbers printed in bold (which may or not also be in italic) refer to originating Acts; numbers in ordinary type to amending Acts

— Looseleaf subject encyclopaedias

    * **Shortcut for mainstream materials**

— *Legal Journals Index* and/or Badger

    * **A possible shortcut, especially for important new legislation**

— SCAD

    * **Could be used**

        — most legislation since 1983; omits the minor legislation listed in light type in the OJ L series

        — bibliographic details only not full text

— *Directory of Community Legislation in Force* (twice yearly, two volumes)

    * **Only as a last resort, if electronic sources not available.**

        — volume 1, the analytical register, arranges the legislation under 17 broad topics headings

        — volume 2 contains an alphabetical index to the analytical register

— *Official Journal*: alphabetical index in monthly indexes

    * **For very recent legislation since last edition of the *Directory* above if electronic sources not available; annual indexes could be used for known to exist legislation**

QR3.23 Finding amendments and repeals of EC legislation [3.133–3.134]

— Celex

    * **The usual starting point**

        — look at the 'modifies' and 'modified' fields

        — the cross-ref facility on the Justis version particularly useful

— **EUR-Lex**

    * **Provision of consolidated texts makes this useful in addition or instead of Celex; also for very recent changes in OJ**

        — find the relevant legislation in the *Directory of Community Legislation in Force*, and follow through links to amending texts, or to consolidated version

        — as a cross-check put in document number as a free text search

        — go to the part with the last 45 days' OJs and do a search on the number as a plain text search

— *European Communities Legislation: Current Status*

    * **The most convenient printed source, and can be updated with telephone service**

        — bound volumes reissued annually

        — quarterly supplements

        — covers all legislation in the special editions 1972 and 1974 and everything in OJ since (so excludes legislation repealed before 1972)

        — arranged by year and within each year in two sequences: (1) number/year material; (2) year/number material (see QR 3.18 above)

        — where *part* of act affected the following abbreviations are used:

            ad = added

            am = amended

            d = deleted (or repealed)

            r = replaced (or substituted)

        — where *whole* act no longer in force number printed in italic and the following abbreviations are used:

            consld = consolidated

            rpld = repealed

            spent = spent

            ssd = superseded

— *Encyclopaedia of European Community Law*: C volumes

    * **Not usually as up-to-date as the above, but better than nothing**

        — amended legislation either reprinted as amended or amendments noted in annotations

— *Directory of Community Legislation in Force*

    * **Manual source of last resort, if you can find the entry for the legislation you are looking for**

        — reissued twice a year

        — main entries arranged by broad topic in volume 1 (analytical register) list amending acts

        — either find main entry by subject via the alphabetical index in volume 2 to the analytical register

        — or find main entry by number in chronological index to volume 2; but these are Celex numbers, so you need to know how to translate from ordinary Regulation or Directive number (see 3.121)

QR3.24 Finding UK implementation of EC legislation [3.135–3.138]

— *Butterworths EC Legislation Implementor*

    * **Very convenient and, with telephone enquiry service, very up-to-date, but only covers Directives**

        — twice yearly

        — arranged by Directive number (with title, OJ reference and target date)

        — omits repealed or spent Directives

        — if only specific articles implemented these are only indicated if they are mentioned in the explanatory note to the implementing SI

— Electronic full text of SIs (Justis SIs, Lawtel, Lexis, Legislation Direct etc)

    * **A very good approach. Will capture all SIs relating to, not just implementing, EC legislation, but remember the possibility of implementation by Act for major Directives**

        — do a free text search on the number of the Directive or Regulation

        — full details of relevant EC legislation given in explanatory note at end of each SI

— Lawtel EU

    * **Implementation information now given on record for Directive or Regulation**

— Celex

    * **Only if using a version, such as Justis, with enhanced data; implementation field on Celex itself can be very out of date**

— Badger

    * **A possibility, especially if a full text SI service not available**

        — records for SIs usually give implementation information in abstract or scope field

— *Legal Journals Index*

    * **Possible shortcut, especially for recent material, as implementation often prompts articles**

        — search in legislation field

— *Current Law*: table of 'European Legislation Implemented by Statutory Instruments'

    * **A possible manual alternative for SIs from 1996**

        — after *Statutory Instrument Citator* in bound volume of *Legislation Citator* 1996–99, and any softbound supplements

        — cumulative table in latest *Monthly Digest* (and if necessary, December issue of previous year)

— See para **3.138** of main text for (very rare) implementation by Directions to the Environment Agency and other bodies

Local and Personal Acts

QR3.25 Classification and arrangement of sets of sessional volumes of Acts [3.140–3.143 and figure 3.19]

Public General Acts

— Content of this series on the shelves:

— Until late seventeenth century, and from 1797 just Public General Acts proper

— From late seventeenth century to 1752 may include, intermingled indiscriminately, Acts which are of a local or personal character that originated as Private Bills, but contain a clause deeming them to be Public Acts

— From 1752 to 1796 Acts numbered in each year as chapters 1 to say 50 are Public General Acts proper

— In that period Acts numbered say 50 to 100 are in separate volumes, which may be shelved separately and labelled as 'Road Acts', and comprise Acts of a local or personal character that originated as Private Bills, but contain a clause deeming them to be Public Acts

— Modern chapter numbers in the form c 1, 2, 3, etc

Private Acts

— Content of this series on the shelves:

— Private Acts proper from 1539 (though very rare in print before eighteenth century) to 1877

— Official prints only for some and only after 1805

— Prints even if called 'Act' may be of the Bill (all Bills printed from 1705)

— Only an Act if date of Royal Assent printed at beginning or end

Local and Personal Acts

— Content of this series on the shelves:

— From 1797 to 1877 a single series of 'Local Acts Declared Public' (from 1869 just 'Local Acts')

— From 1878 to 1947 two separately numbered series bound together, 'Local' and 'Private', the latter being much less numerous than the former

— From 1878 to 1922 not all Acts in the 'Private' series officially printed; if not printed *no* chapter number

— From 1948 the 'Private' series renamed 'Personal'

— Last Personal Act passed in 1987; from then in effect a single series of Local Acts

— Modern chapter numbers in the form: Local c i, ii, iii, etc; Personal, *c 1, 2, 3,* etc

QR3.26 Alternative sources for the text of Local and Personal Acts [3.149–3.150]

— *Local and Personal Acts* (HMSO, Queen's Printer copies)
  * **Virtually the only source**
    — arranged chronologically in unamended form
    — also on HMSO web site from 1991
— *Current Law Statutes*
  * **From 1991 only**
    — arranged chronologically in unamended form
— *Halsbury's Statutes*
  * **Most of those relating to London and the following**
    — British Railways (Pensions Schemes) Act 1981, British Waterways Act 1985, Gun Barrel Proof Acts 1868 and 1950, Imperial Institute Act 1925, National Trust Acts 1907 to 1971
— *Statutes in Force*
  * **The following 13 Acts (asterisked titles also in *Halsbury's Statutes*)**
    — City of London (Union of Parishes) Act 1907*, Dean Forest Act 1906, Dean Forest (Mines) Act 1904, Derbyshire Mining Customs and Mineral Courts Act 1852, Greater London Council (General Powers) Act 1974*, Gun Barrel Proof Acts 1968 and 1950*, Imperial Institute Act 1925*, New Forest Acts 1877 and 1879, Tweed Fisheries Acts 1857, 1859 and 1969
— Lexis
  * **Most of those relating to London and the Lloyds Acts**
— *Encyclopedia of Insurance Law* (Sweet & Maxwell) or *Lloyd's Acts, Regulations and Bye-laws* (LLP) looseleaf services
  * **Lloyds Acts only**

QR3.27 Finding aids for Local and Personal Acts [3.151–3.152]

— *Index to Local and Personal Acts 1801–1947* and supplement 1948–1966 (HMSO), the '*1801–1966 Index*'
— *Index to Local and Personal Acts 1797–1849 and 1850–1995* (HMSO, 6 volumes), the '*Black Indexes*'
— *Chronological Table of Local Legislation 1797–1994* (4 volumes) and *Chronological Table of Private and Personal Acts 1539–1997*(1 volume) and cumulative annual supplement to both (TSO), the '*Red Tables*'
— George Bramwell *Analytical Table of Private Acts 1717–1834* (2 volumes)
— Thomas Vardon *Index to the Local and Personal and Private Acts 1798–1839*
— William Salt *Index to the Titles of the …Private Acts of Parliament passed in the reign of Queen Anne [George I, and George II]* (1863)
— W E Tate *A Domesday of English Enclosure Acts and Awards* (Reading University Library, 1978)

— *Statutes of the Realm* [to 1714] index volume

— *Journal of the House of Commons* and *Journal of the House of Lords*, cumulated indexes

— John Raithby *An Index to the Statutes at Large from Magna Carta to the forty ninth year of George III inclusive* (1814)

QR3.28   Find Local and Personal Acts by title – year and chapter number unknown [3.153]

— *Black Indexes*

    *   **Best starting place; for Acts outside its scope use subject/person/ place approach**

        — will not cover pre-1797 Acts, nor Private Acts 1797–1845, nor Acts since 1995

QR3.29   Finding Local and Personal Acts by subject, person or place [3.154–3.155]

— *1801–1966 Index*

    *   **The best starting place, if within the period**

— *Black Indexes*

    *   **Not a subject index as such but heavily cross-referenced; use for Acts since 1996 and as a cross-check on the *1801–1966 Index***

        — will not pick up Provisional Confirmation Order Acts (or other Acts) without the subject/locality/person in the title

— *Bramwell*: alphabetical table

    *   **Only for estate and enclosure Acts that are earlier than *1801–1966 Index*, and later than 1727**

— *Salt*

    *   **For any Private Acts that are not estate or enclosure Acts 1701–59; for any Private Act 1701–26**

— *Red Tables*

    *   **For Private Acts that are not estate or enclosure Acts 1760–1800**

        — would have simply to browse through the entire contents of the Private legislation volume for the period

— *Journals of the House of Commons* and *Lords*: relevant cumulated indexes

    *   **An alternative approach for Private Acts that are not estate or enclosure Acts 1760–1800**

— *Statutes of the Realm*: index

    *   **For Private Acts before 1702; an alternative to *Salt* for Private Acts of Queen Anne**

— *Tait*

    *   **For enclosure Acts; should have been found by above means, but a cross-check or alternative**

— *Raithby*

    * **If Act might not be a Local Act but a Public General Act in the 'Road Acts' 1753–96**

QR3.30 Finding amendments to and repeals of Local and Personal Acts [3.156]

— *Red Tables*

    * **The main source, except for any very recent changes since the last annual cumulative supplement**

— *Current Law Legislation Citator*

    * **The main source for checking any changes since the last supplement of the *Red Tables*; an alternative for effects 1996–**

        — Local Acts listed first before Public General Acts for each year in the hard copy *Statute Citator*; data also on electronic version

        — in hard copy bound volume + latest issue in *Current Law Statutes* looseleaf service volume

— Public General Acts annual volumes: Tables and Index volume: effect of legislation table

    * **If latest bound volume published ahead of the last cumulative supplement to the *Red Tables* could be used as a cross-check on *Current Law Legislation Citator* (which should be checked too)**

— *1801–1966 Index*

    * **Not comprehensive for repeals, so not a substitute for the *Red Tables*, but if using anyway most repeals since 1900 noted**

— *Halsbury's Statutes*

    * **If using for London Acts; but double-check with *Current Law Legislation Citator***

        — the usual updating mechanism: main work + cumulative supplement + looseleaf noter-up

— Electronic full text services for Public General Acts and SIs

    * **Could be used to double-check for any very recent amendments made by Public General Act or SI (which is common)**

        — enter the chapter number and year (provided the system does not use automatic right hand truncation, which otherwise causes problems with roman numerals) as free text

— Text of any very recent Local Acts issued since above sources updated, in hard copy on the shelves or on HMSO website

    * **All that can be done as a final check; the small number of Local Acts nowadays does not make this difficult**

        — hope that any possibly relevant Act is apparent from its title

— The horse's mouth

    * **If there is an extant corporate body affected by a Local Act, enquire (especially if they have a legal department) whether they can tell you what is in force**

Church Measures

QR3.31 Sources for the text of Church Assembly and General Synod Measures [3.157–3.158]

— *Halsbury's Statutes*
  * **Main source for current Measures in force**
    — in the title 'Ecclesiastical Law'
    — treated like ordinary statutes, with the usual updating mechanism, etc
— *Current Law Statutes*
  * **Unamended text as passed 1949–**
    — but not annotated
— Public General Acts and Measures
  * **Official text as passed**
    — loose prints and official bound volumes as for ordinary Public General Acts
    — on HMSO website 1988–
    — series starts in 1920, but not printed in official volumes 1920–25
— *Halsbury's Statutes* 1st edn (1929)
  * **Source of text of Measures 1920–25 (if not amended or repealed before 1929)**
— *Statutes Revised* 3rd edn (1948): accompanying Measures volume
  * **Source of official text of Measures 1920–25 in force as at 1948**
— Mark Hill *Ecclesiastical Law* (OUP, 2nd edn, 2001)
  * **Handy source for most current Measures and other materials**

QR3.32 Subsidiary legislation not published as SIs: examples and availability [3.159–3.167]

— Immigration Rules
  — published as House of Commons papers or Command papers
  — reprinted in *Butterworths Immigration Law Service*
— Solicitors' Practice, Accounts, etc Rules made by the Law Society under the Solicitors Act 1974
  — reprinted in *The Guide to the Professional Conduct of Solicitors*, *Cordery on Solicitors*
  — *Law Society's Gazette* for information on recent changes; or the Law Society itself
— Financial services rules
  — Financial Services Authority CD-ROM and website
  — looseleaf services, eg *Encyclopedia of Financial Services* (Sweet & Maxwell), *Financial Services: Law and Practice* (Butterworths), Robin Ellison *Pensions Law and Practice* (Sweet & Maxwell), Macfarlanes *Collective Investment Schemes* (Sweet & Maxwell)

— Parole Board Rules

    — Appendix to Stephen Livingstone and Tim Owen *Prison Law* (OUP, 2nd edn, 1999)

— Orders in Council (that are not SIs), Royal Proclamations, Instructions and Warrants

    — some in back of official HMSO bound volumes of SIs

    — check with Privy Council Secretariat

— Miscellaneous materials

    — try the government department concerned

— Bye-laws

    — ask the local authority or body concerned

— Traffic Management and Traffic Regulation Orders

    — in London ask the borough concerned, or for GLA, Transport for London

    — outside London ask the county council

QR3.33 Quasi-legislation: codes of practice, government circulars, regulatory materials: possible sources [3.168–3.170]

— Government department websites (see ukonline) and other websites, looseleaf subject encyclopaedias, specialist textbooks, journals. Check Badger and *Legal Journals Index*

    * **The following is a very selective listing intended only to give an idea of the possibilities: this kind of material is easily overlooked**

— ACAS codes of practice:

    — Sweet & Maxwell's *Encyclopedia of Employment Law*

— Rules of various arbitration schemes:

    — Ronald Bernstein *Handbook of Arbitration Practice*

— Department of Health medicines and poisons circulars:

    — *Butterworths Law of Food and Drugs*

— Department of the Environment circulars:

        Encyclopedia of Compulsory Purchase

        Encyclopedia of Environmental Health

        Encyclopedia of Planning Law

        Journal of Planning and Environment law

— Finance Houses Association code of practice:

        Encyclopedia of Consumer Credit

— Home Office circulars:

    — *Justice of the Peace*

— Trade association codes of practice:

    — C J Miller *Product Liability & Safety Encyclopaedia*

QR4 *Pepper v Hart* research and the background to legislation

QR4.1 Types of pre-legislative materials [4.4–4.5]

— Green Papers (consultation papers)
— White Papers (government policy)
   — Parliamentary consideration of Green/White Papers
      — debates
      — Parliamentary questions, written or oral
      — select committee reports
         — government response to select committee reports
— Law Commission consultation papers and reports
— Royal Commission and other inquiry reports
— Law Reform Committee reports (1952–85)
— Criminal Law Revision Committee reports (1958–86)
— Draft Bills
— Select committees (Commons, Lords or Joint) on draft Bills
   — government response to select committee reports

QR4.2 Finding pre-legislative materials [4.6]

— *Current Law Statutes*
   — general note at start or notes to particular part or section of Act
— Second reading debate in *Hansard*: minister's introduction
— *Law Under Review* (published quarterly in hard copy by the Law Commission 1987–97; from 1997 on the Law Commission's website)
— Indexes to official publications: TSO catalogues, UKOP, Parlianet or Polis, Badger, etc

QR4.3 The parliamentary stages of a Bill: the basic pattern [4.15–4.26]

Commons introduction and first reading
— no debate, purely formal
— Bill not yet printed: ordered to be printed

Commons second reading

— debate on the principle of the Bill

— useful for mischief aimed at and background to Bill, eg Green/White Papers, court decisions etc.

— possible explanation by minister of major clauses

— at start of debate

— at end in winding up (may be different minister)

— no amendments at this stage

[Print of Bill: as first printed for the Commons]

Commons committee stage

— detailed clause by clause consideration of Bill and amendments

— since 1907 automatically referred to a Standing Committee off the floor of the House (Standing Committee A, B, C etc.) unless otherwise ordered

— usually the most fruitful stage for research

— debates in Standing Committee since 1919 published as separate series not in *Hansard*

[Print of Bill: as first printed for the Commons]

Commons report stage

— sometimes called (esp older sessional indexes to *Hansard*) consideration stage

— new amendments, especially government amendments made on undertakings in committee

— but not repetition of debate in committee

— more restrictions on speaking than in committee

[Print of Bill: as amended in Standing Committee]

Commons third reading

— usually purely formal and taken without a gap immediately after report stage

— no further amendments, other than purely verbal corrections

— report stage and third reading = 'RS', ie Remaining Stages, in *Weekly Information Bulletin* and *Sessional Digest*

[Print of Bill: as amended in Standing Committee]

Lords introduction and first reading

— as in Commons

Lords second reading

— as in Commons

[Print of Bill: as first printed for Lords, ie as amended after third reading in Commons]

Lords committee stage

— clause by clause consideration as in Commons

— but usually taken by a 'Committee of the Whole House', ie on the floor of the house, so debates in main Lords *Hansard*

[Print of Bill: as first printed for the Lords]

Lords report stage

—   as in Commons

[Print of Bill: as amended in Committee]

Lords third reading

—   separated from report stage

—   substantive amendments frequently moved, especially on government undertakings at committee and report stages

[Print of Bill: as amended on Report]

Commons consideration of Lords amendments

—   Bill returns to the Commons: usually the last stage

—   brief explanation by minister of reasons for Lords amendments

—   but Commons can disagree with Lords amendments and can amend them or substitute their own amendments

[Print of Bill: whole Bill not reprinted, but list of amendments, printed in the *Commons* series of Bills, which refers to Bill as *first* printed for *Lords*]

Lords consideration of Commons reasons and amendments

—   only if Commons have disagreed with Lords amendments

—   possible to have Lords amendments to Commons amendments to Lords amendments ...

—   Parliament Acts 1911 and 1949 if Lords do not agree

[Print of Bill: whole Bill not reprinted, but 'Commons Reasons for Disagreeing with Lords Amendments and Commons Amendments to Lords Amendments' printed in the *Lords* series of Bills, which refers to Bill as first printed for the Lords]

Royal assent

—   recorded in *Hansard* but purely formal

QR4.4   The parliamentary stages of a Bill: complications and exceptions [4.27–4.47]

Commons introduction and first reading

—   private members' Bills under the 'Ten-Minute Rule'

    —   short debate on leave to introduce the Bill

    —   Bill rarely proceeds further

Commons second reading

—   second reading committee off the floor of the House

    —   uncontroversial Bills, especially those started in Lords

    —   before 1979/80 debates published in main *Hansard*, subsequently with Standing Committee debates

—   Scottish and Welsh Grand Committees

    —   Bills that affected Scotland or Wales only

    —   consideration of the principle of the Bill, analogous to second reading

— debates published with Standing Committee debates

— though formally retained, legislative function gone with devolution

Commons financial resolutions

— money resolutions authorising expenditure and ways and means resolutions authorising taxation

— usually taken immediately after second reading (for Finance Bills taken after budget debate)

— no subsequent amendments outside the scope of the resolutions

— sometimes debated but often formal

— privilege amendments

— formal method of Commons sanctioning expenditure/taxation powers in a Bill that started in Lords, taken at Commons committee stage

Commons allocation of time or 'guillotine' motions

— usually used by government to curtail prolonged debate in Committee or on Report

— stage cut short, and remaining stages strictly timetabled

— means some clauses not debated at all

— only in Commons: no formal method of curtailment of debate in Lords

Commons committee stage

— Committee of the Whole House (on the floor of the House)

— debates in main *Hansard*

— used for:

— Finance Bills

— before 1967/68 the whole Bill

— 1967/68 not used, whole Bill in Standing Committee

— from 1968/69 split: 'specialist clauses' in Standing Committee, 'general clauses' on floor of House

— 'Emergency' Bills needing rapid passing

— 'One clause' Bills not requiring detailed examination

— Bills or parts of Bills of major constitutional importance

— Select Committees on Hybrid Bills

— public Bills of general application, but including provisions affecting private interests as would a private Bill (eg Channel Tunnel Bill)

— evidence taken from interested parties, proceedings akin to committee stage of a private Bill

— after Select Committee recommitted to a Standing Committee to proceed as an ordinary public Bill

— proceedings published in House of Commons papers (not in *Hansard* or Standing Committee debates)

— HC paper numbers given in *Weekly Information Bulletin* and *Sessional Digest* (otherwise, TSO Catalogues under 'Select Committee' , CD-ROMs etc)

— Select Committees on [non-hybrid] Public Bills
  — now very rare (used for five-yearly Armed Forces Bills)
  — common in 19th century
  — can take evidence
  — proceedings published as above
— Special Standing Committees
  — written and oral evidence taken from outside parties
  — used for only five Bills 1980–84
  — more use in the future, eg Immigration and Asylum Bill 1999

Recommittal

— occasionally needed after Report stage (in either House) to deal with late amendments requiring detailed consideration
— same procedure as at ordinary Committee stage

Lords Delegated Powers and Regulatory Reform [Deregulation] Committee

— for all Bills from 1992/93–
— scrutiny of provisions in Bills enabling subordinate legislation
  — appropriateness of delegating the power
  — appropriateness of method of Parliamentary scrutiny
— scrutiny of Regulatory Reform (formerly Deregulation) orders
— reports, sometimes including memoranda from government departments, published (as House of Lords papers) after second reading and before committee
— HL paper numbers for reports on Regulatory Reform or Deregulation Orders given in *Weekly Information Bulletin* and *Sessional Digest*

Lords committee stage

— no committee stage
  — Finance Bills (order for committal negatived)
  — no amendments tabled (order for committal discharged)
  — if no committee stage, no report stage
— Joint Committee on Consolidation Bills
  — see QR4.8
— Select Committee on Hybrid Bills
  — as for Commons
  — proceedings published as House of Lords papers
— Select Committee on [non-Hybrid] Public Bills
  — used very occasionally, especially for controversial private members' Bills
  — may be used at any time between second and third readings
  — evidence taken, and recommends whether Bill should proceed
  — proceedings published as House of Lords papers
  — thereafter recommitted to a Committee of the Whole House

— Public Bill Committee
  — equivalent of a Commons Standing Committee
  — off the floor of the House
  — procedure introduced in 1968, but used for only nine Bills since:
     > 1967–68 Gaming Bill; 1968–69 Development of Tourism Bill; 1970–71 Highways Bill, Civil Aviation Bill; 1974–75 Lotteries Bill; 1986–87 Pilotage Bill; 1991–92 Charities Bill; 1993–94 Law of Property (Miscellaneous Provisions) Bill, Trade Marks Bill
  — hitherto proceedings not published in main Lords *Hansard* but in separate prints (supplied by TSO to subscribers to Commons Standing Committee debates)
— Special Public Bill Committee
  — oral and written evidence, then clause by clause consideration off the floor of the House
  — for non-controversial, technical Bills, especially Law Commission Bills
  — proceedings and debates published as House of Lords papers
— Grand Committee
  — Committee of the whole House off the floor of the House (and originally so-called, renamed 'Grand Committee' from Jan 1997)
  — 'Moses Room Committees'
  — same as a Committee of the Whole House except no divisions
  — first used 1994/95
  — debates published in main Lords *Hansard* with the day's proceedings on the floor of the House but with separate column numbering 'CWH'

QR4.5 Categories of parliamentary materials [4.49–4.58]

Hansard

— *Parliamentary Debates: Official Report*
— 'Official Report' from 1909
— earlier series, back to 1803, unofficial and not necessarily full or verbatim
— only general series from 1841, but other series before then, see: David Lewis Jones *Debates and Proceedings of the British Parliaments: a guide to printed sources* (HMSO, 1986)
— two main series, Commons and Lords (before 1909 one series)
— both issued in daily and weekly unrevised parts
— then official revised bound volumes (containing editorial corrections but not changes of substance)
— contain near verbatim record of all proceedings on the floor of the House + written questions and answers
— numbered in columns in two sequences: main and written answers (latter in italic, Commons, WA, Lords)
— written answers at back of bound volumes, but after each day in weekly parts
— free on Parliament web site, Commons 1988/89– and Lords 1996/97–

NEEDED FOR:

All stages except (usually) Committee stage in Commons

House of Commons Standing Committee debates

— from 1919 (none published 1907–18)
— pre-1945: debates on some Bills (especially private members' Bills) not published, but some typescripts 1926–33 preserved in House of Lords Record Office (see QR4.6)
— proceedings on Bills, and certain other proceedings in Standing Committee off the floor of the House
— issued in loose parts, one per sitting (am and pm)
— full text available free on the Parliament web site from 1997/98 session
— TSO bound volumes arranged by Committee letter or name (include errata slips but not revised like *Hansard* bound volumes)
— comprise Commons:
  — Standing Committees A, B, C etc on Bills
  — Second Reading Committees 1979/80–
  — Standing Committees on Delegated Legislation (formerly on SIs)
  — European Standing Committees
  — Scottish Grand Committee, Welsh Grand Committee, Northern Ireland Committee
  — Special Standing Committees (including written evidence)
— Lords debates in Public Bill Committee issued in similar format (but not in bound volumes)

NEEDED FOR:

Commons Committee stage for most Bills
Commons Second Reading when taken off the floor of the House (1979/80–)
Commons debates on SIs when taken off the floor of the House
Commons debates on European legislation off the floor of the House

Bills

— two series, Commons and Lords (not to be confused with which House the Bill starts in)
— reprinted, incorporating amendments, at various stages during the passage
— numbered each session
— fresh number for each print
— HC Bills, number in round brackets
— HL Bills, number in square brackets (now also 'HL Bill')
— HL Bills before 1986/87 not a separate series but intermingled with HL papers
— amendments (and marshalled lists of amendments) issued with Lords Bills (and bear relevant Bill number)
— amendments to Commons Bills only issued in the 'Vote Bundle' not to subscribers to the Bills

- used to include an explanatory memorandum; instead explanatory notes issued (as separate publication) with first print for each House for government Bills from 1998/99 onwards
- Bills on Parliament web site, but not much use for *Pepper v Hart* research because
  - just the latest version of Bills for the current session
  - lists of amendments just relating to latest stage
  - removed when passed (replaced with link to Act)

NEEDED FOR:

Finding at what stage a clause was inserted or amended if not in the Bill from the beginning

Finding the number of the relevant clause at each stage

Making sense of the debates

Explanatory memorandum

Command papers

- see QR 7

NEEDED FOR:

Background to legislation, eg White Papers, Royal Commission reports etc

Sometimes understanding what a Minister is saying about a particular clause

House of Commons papers

- See QR7

NEEDED FOR:

Reports and minutes of (departmental) Select Committees on Green Papers, White Papers, other proposals for legislation, or investigations that result in legislation as background to a Bill

Reports and minutes of Select Committees on draft Bills

Reports and minutes of Select Committees on Hybrid Bills

Reports and minutes of Select Committees on Public Bills (especially nineteenth century)

Reports and minutes of Joint Committee on Consolidation Bills

Reports and minutes of Joint (or Select) Committee on Statutory Instruments

Reports and minutes of Deregulation and Regulatory Reform Committee

House of Lords papers

- See QR7

NEEDED FOR:

Reports and minutes of (subject) Select Committee when relevant as background to a Bill

Reports and minutes of Select Committees on Hybrid Bills

Reports and minutes of Select Committees on Public Bills

Reports and minutes of Special Public Bill Committees

Reports and minutes of Delegated Powers and Regulatory Reform (Deregulation) Committee

Journals of each House

— published each session, based on Minutes of Proceedings printed daily
— formal record of what was done (as opposed to said)
— source on points of Parliamentary procedure, historical source
— not generally needed for *Pepper v Hart* research, except occasionally for tracking proceedings on very old Acts

QR4.6   Typescript copies of Standing Committee debates 1926–33 held at the House of Lords Record Office if not in published debates [4.52]

1926–27	Diseases of Animals Bill (Lords)
	Wild Birds Protection Bill
1927–28	Destructive Insects and Pests Bill
	Stabilisation of Easter Bill
	Rating (Scotland) Amendment Bill
	Petroleum Amendment Bill
	Rubber Industry Bill
	Administration of Justice Bill (Lords)
	Registration (Births, Deaths and Marriages) Bill
	Public Rights of Way Bill
	Merchant Shipping (Line-throwing Appliance) Bill
	Rag Flock Act (1911) Amendment Bill
1928–29	Appellate Jurisdiction Bill
	Superannuation Diplomatic Service Bill
	Overseas Trade Bill
	Reconstituted Cream Bill
	Fire Brigade Pensions Bill
	Police Magistrates Superannuation (Amendment) Bill
	Salmon and Freshwater Fisheries (Amendment) Bill
1929–30	Arbitration (Foreign Awards) Bill
	Children (Employment Abroad) Bill (Lords)
1930–31	Metropolitan Police (Staff Superannuation & Police Fund) Bill
	Colonial Naval Defence Bill (Lords)
	Ancient Monuments Bill (Lords)
	Marriage (Prohibited Degrees of Relationship) Bill
1931–32	Universities (Scotland) Bill (Lords)
	Rights of Way Bill
	Public Health (Cleansing of Shell Fish) Bill
	Marriage (Naval, Military and Air Force Chapels) Bill (Lords)
	Gas Undertakings Bill (Lords)
	Rating and Valuation (No 2) Bill (Lords)
1932–33	Visiting Forces (British Commonwealth) Bill (Lords)
	Assurance Companies (Winding Up) Bill (Lords)
	False Oaths (Scotland) Bill
	Cotton Industry Bill
	Protection of Birds Bill (Lords)

Information taken from: Maurice F Bond *Guide to the Records of Parliament*. London: HMSO, 1971, pp 220–221.

House of Lords Record Office: By appointment: Tel 020 7219 3074

QR4.7 Finding the debates on a section of a Public General Act [4.59–4.67]

STEP 1: Are looking for debates on the right Act?
   (a) Has your section or part of section been inserted by a later Act?
      — words in square brackets or lettered section numbers, eg 24A
      — if using eg *Halsbury's Statutes* look at notes to section
   (b) Is it a consolidation Act?
      — if in doubt look at long title, or *Sessional Digest* (see step 2 below) where Consolidation Bills marked 'C' (from 1997/98 – previously 'B')
      — if yes, see QR4.8 before proceeding

STEP 2: If you have it, it is useful to have to hand the entry for the Bill in the House of Commons *Sessional Digest* (first published for session 1983/84) or, for the current session, the latest issue of the *Weekly Information Bulletin*

STEP 3: Find all prints of the Bill for both Commons and Lords
   — Usually two complete prints for the Commons and three for the Lords
   — If arranged numerically, Bill numbers given in *House of Commons Weekly Information Bulletin* and *Sessional Digest*, TSO Catalogues, UKOP, etc
   — Have Act to hand as well to see position of clause in scheme of Act
      (a) note whether clause is present and in identical form to section throughout and if not, at what stage it was inserted or reached its final form
      (b) note number of clause at each stage

STEP 4: Find *Hansard* references for each stage

Acts more than two or three years old
   — Go to sessional index for *Hansard* for first House, then for second House. Sessional indexes are usually a separate volume for the Commons and bound with the last volume of the session (usually November) for the Lords. Under the title of the Bill, all stages are given. Ignore those with an asterisk – these are formal only without debate
      — stage at which clause reached final form likely to most useful
      — but possibility of debate on unsuccessful amendments before or after
      — index will usually say whether in Commons committed to a Standing Committee, if not look at end of second reading debate
      — TSO bound volumes of Standing Committee debates include an index by clause for each Bill

Acts in the last two or three years
   — If sessional index not yet available, use, for current session, latest issue of *House of Commons Weekly Information Bulletin* or, for earlier sessions, *House of Commons Sessional Digest*
      — gives all stages with dates (asterisk no debate)
      — but not actual column numbers

Alternatives:
- — Official *Explanatory Notes* to Acts, 1999–
- — *Halsbury's Statutes*
  - — full details given on Acts passed 1993 onwards
- — *Current Law Statutes*
  - — *Hansard* references given at start (but before 1998 stages not specified); also consolidated table in looseleaf Current Service volume
- — Parlianet
- — Badger 1993–
  - — records for Acts have dates of the stages, and full *Hansard* references

Shortcuts:
- — Copyright Acts: full section by section table in *Copinger on Copyright*
- — Human Rights Acts 1998: Jonathan Cooper and Adrian Marshall-Williams *Legislating for Human Rights: the Parliamentary Debates on the Human Rights Act* (Hart, 2000)
- — Asylum and Immigration Act 1996: Katie Ghose *The Asylum and Immigration Act 1996: a Compilation of Ministerial Statements* (Immigration Law Practitioners' Association, 1996)
- — detailed annotations to the particular section in *Current Law Statutes*, especially recent volumes (but full research as above may still be needed)
- — references in footnotes, or appendices of *Hansard* extracts in textbooks, especially 'guides' to new Acts
- — House of Commons Information Office (hcoinfo@parliament.uk tel: 020 7219 4272)
- — Pay someone else, eg 'Clause Search' at the Information for Business service, Westminster Reference Library (020 7976 1285)

STEP 5: Find the debates on your clause at each stage

Typically, you will have found references to eight stages where there might be debate: *Commons*: second reading (1), committee (2), report & third reading (3); *Lords*: second reading (4), committee (5), report (6), third reading (7); *Commons*: Lords amendments (8)

Leaf through relevant stage until clause number found, but if order of consideration of clauses not obvious:

Commons committee stage
- — look at first sitting in the debates for any motions on order of consideration of clauses (at beginning or sometimes towards end of sitting)
- — otherwise, usual order: each clause in the original Bill and amendments thereto, new clauses, schedules in original Bill and amendments thereto, new schedules
- — clause numbers printed on front cover of each sitting of Standing Committee debates
- — new clauses under consideration at Committee stage will have an entirely separate number until agreed and incorporated

Commons report stage

— look at start of first day's debate
— otherwise, usual order: new clauses, amendments to clauses, new schedules, amendments to schedules

Lords committee, report and third reading

— unlike Commons generally no distinction between new clauses and amendments: treated together
— look at marshalled lists of amendments with relevant print of Bill
— order of consideration of clauses given on front cover
— if stage lasts more than one day marshalled list reprinted each day: from this you can tell on which day the clause was considered
— or, look at 'Motions for Approval', when the order of consideration is formally approved in advance, which are listed under the Bill in the sessional indexes to *Hansard*

STEP 6: If researching a very recent Act and copies taken from daily or weekly unrevised parts, and needed later for court, check whether an official revised bound volume has subsequently been produced

QR4.8   If the Act is a consolidation Act [4.68–4.70]

STEP 1: Trace derivation of section in previous Act (see also QR3.9)

— annotations to section (or sometimes separate table of derivations) in *Halsbury's Statutes* or *Current Law Statutes*
— or, table of derivations in index volume of official annual volumes of Public General Acts (provided from 1967)
— if not given in above, look at Acts listed in schedule of repeals in the consolidating Act
— or consider using Justis Statutes to find previous use of similar wording

STEP 2: Check that the previous Act from which the section derives is not itself a consolidation Act

— if so, repeat step 1 until the Act which first enacted the provision is found

STEP 3: Compare the wording of the provision in the original Act and the consolidation Act

— if identical, proceed with your research on the original section as described in QR4.7
— if not identical, and difference material, research the consolidation process:
  — Report and minutes of Joint Committee on Consolidation Bills (printed identically in both House of Commons and House of Lords Papers: has numbers for both series on it)
  — Any Law Commission report on the Bill (will be referred to in Joint Committee report or *Current Law Statutes*)
  — Any debates in *Hansard* on the consolidation Bill

QR4.9 *Pepper v Hart* research and Local and Personal Acts [4.71–4.72]

— Local and Personal Acts start as *Private* Bills (not to be confused with private *members'* Bills)

— Bill not promoted by government or member, but by eg local authority, statutory undertaker etc

— Bills seen through by private firms of Parliamentary agents

— Bills may be carried over from one Parliamentary session to the next if not completed

— progress and details in *House of Commons Weekly Information Bulletin* and *Sessional Digest*

— Bills not published by TSO

    — reference copies held by House of Lords Record Office

    — copies of current Bills obtainable from relevant Parliamentary agent (given in *House of Commons Weekly Information Bulletin*)

— proceedings in Committee not published at all

    — copies of transcripts (of proceedings in both Houses) held by House of Lords Record Office

    — copies of current proceedings open to public inspection in the Private Bill Office of the relevant House (but not usually photocopiable)

    — copies of current proceedings available from Parliamentary agent for a charge

— rarely much to be found in *Hansard*: except for sometimes a Lords third reading debate, proceedings on the floor of each House usually purely formal

QR4.10 Finding Parliamentary debates and materials on statutory instruments [4.73–4.83]

STEP 1: Establish type of SI

— look at preamble to SI

    — if eg 'whereas a draft of the following order was laid before Parliament in accordance with section ... of the ... Act and approved by resolution of each House of Parliament' = affirmative instrument

    — otherwise look at the enabling provision of the parent Act cited in the preamble (or any general section on the making of regulations) to see if a negative instrument

— if affirmative or negative instrument go to Step 2, otherwise go to Step 4

STEP 2: Find *Hansard* references

— if affirmative instrument must be debate; if negative instrument *may* be debate (but only rarely)

SIs more than two or three years old

— go to sessional indexes for each House

— NB debates on annulment of negative instruments made late on during a session may be in following session

SIs in the last two or three years

If sessional index not yet available:
— Parlianet
— look at indexes to individual volumes of *Hansard*; for affirmative instruments shortly before the SI was *made*, for negative instruments for at least forty sitting days' worth after the SI was *laid*
— ask House of Commons Information Office (hcinfo@parliament.uk tel: 020 7219 4272)

STEP 3: Look at any references found. If in Commons referred to Standing Committee, the main *Hansard* will contain no debate, only two formal mentions: motion to refer to committee, and formal resolution to approve the instrument after committee

STEP 4: Consider whether to research debates on the enabling provision in the parent Act, and, for Acts from 1993, Lords Delegated Powers Committee report on the Bill

STEP 5: Is the SI made under the Deregulation and Contracting Out Act or Regulatory Reform Act?
— if yes, consider looking at reports of Commons Deregulation (and Regulatory Reform) Committee and of Lords Delegated Powers and Deregulation (Regulatory Reform) Committee (HC and HL paper numbers given in *Weekly Information Bulletin* and *Sessional Digest*)
— if no, consider looking at reports of the Joint (or Select) Committee on Statutory Instruments
  — each report through session bears same main HC paper number with addition of running roman numeral 12-i, 12-ii etc
  — a Parlianet search by name or number of SI, or looking at TSO catalogues etc under the Committee, will find the relevant report if the SI is in the title of the report because special attention was drawn to it
  — *but* possibility of reports containing departmental memoranda on SIs to which attention is not in fact drawn; leaf through reports published shortly after SI made: a list of SIs considered for each report appears at the end of the report before any appendices

QR4.11 Background to European legislation [4.84–4.91]

— Proposals for legislation: COM Docs
  — Hard copy from Libraries designated as European Documentation Centres; TSO Scanfax service
  — Published, without explanatory memorandum, in C series of *Official Journal*
  — CELEX (sector 5, proposals for legislation)
  — EUR-Lex: 'Legislation in preparation'
  — websites of individual Commission Directorates-General

— Scutiny by European Parliament
    — European Parliament website: 'Legal Observatory' July 1994–
    — Hard copy *Official Journal: Annex*: debates of the European Parliament in plenary session; and European Parliament reports: Series A (committee reports)
    — press releases from Commission and Council websites
— Scrutiny at Westminster
    — House of Commons European Scrutiny Committee
        — reports on European Documents published as HC papers
— Debates on European Documents on the floor of the House of Commons
    — Commons *Hansard*
— Debates on European Documents in the European Standing Committee
    — *Standing Committee Debates*
— House of Lords Select Committee on the European Union
    — reports published as HL papers; plus separate 'Progress of Scrutiny' bulletins
— Debates on the reports of the Select Committee on the floor of the House of Lords
    — Lords *Hansard*
— Getting help
    — European Parliament London Office
    — EU Relay Centres, eg Law Society Library, university libraries designated as European Documentation Centres and public libraries designated as European Public Information Centres (see European Information Network in the UK)
    — DTI Single Market Legislation UK Contact List
    — House of Commons Information Office

QR5 Case law

QR5.1 Sources for reported English case law [5.6–5.19]

— general series of law reports
  — *The Law Reports* 1865–
    — published by the Incorporated Council of Law Reporting, non-profit organisation
    — to be cited in court in preference to any other series
    — full text in electronic form from Context (Justis) on CD-ROM or via the Internet, on Lexis, as a separate module on Butterworths LEXIS Direct, and Westlaw UK
  — the *Weekly Law Reports*
    — published by the Incorporated Council
    — cases in volumes 2 and 3 reissued, having been checked by judge, in *The Law Reports*
    — to be cited in preference to other series if not in *The Law Reports*
    — full text in electronic form on CD-ROM or via the Internet, and on Lexis
  — *All England Law Reports*
    — main commercially published general series
    — to be cited in preference to other series if not in *The Law Reports* or the WLR
    — full text in electronic form on CD-ROM, All England Direct, and Lexis
— specialist subject series
— journals
— newspaper law reports
— the nominate reports
  — pre-1865 series edited by named reporters
  — most reprinted in *The English Reports*
— Year Books
  — pre-1535 cases arranged by regnal year and term
  — in Law French; translations of selected leading cases in: C H S Fifoot *History and Sources of the Common Law* (Stevens, 1949) and J H Baker and S F C Milsom *Sources of English Legal History* (Butterworths, 1986)

QR5.2   Sources of unreported English case law: free services on the Internet [5.23–5.24]

— BAILII
  — under development 2001, aims to have all unreported cases that are available free of charge on the Internet; pending full development use separate sites below for recent cases; earliest coverage 1996
  — excellent search engine, with eg 'Noter-up' facility
— House of Lords, November 1996–
— Privy Council, 1999–
— Court Service, 1996–
  — selected judgments only, High Court and Court of Appeal, and links to certain tribunals, eg Special Commissioners of Income Tax, VAT and Duties Tribunal, Lands Tribunal
— Casebase
  — free part of Smith Bernal service
  — April 1996 to, at the moment, 1999
  — Court of Appeal, and QB Divisional Court
  — limited searching – not free text
— Employment Appeal Tribunal, 1999–
— Social Security Commissioners
  — different categories of material on three different sites
— Law Direct
  — not full text, but digests from All England Direct, 1995–

QR5.3   Sources of unreported English case law: commercial services on the Internet [5.25–5.29]

— Lexis
  — all HL, PC, CA (Civil), Divisional Court and certain other categories of High Court cases, other selected High Court first instance judgments, 1980–
— Casetrack from Smith Bernal
  — all CA and Divisional Court cases April 1996–, + most other High Court cases 1998–
— All England Direct
  — includes full text of a wide range of official transcripts from October 1997–
— Lawtel
  — originally summaries only online, full text transcripts being added to go back to 1993; hard copy transcripts can be ordered
— Westlaw UK from Sweet & Maxwell
  — includes a wide range of transcripts from 2000– ; CCH New Law online service, with older transcript coverage taken over by Sweet & Maxwell in 2001, still running as a separate service, but may possibly merge

QR5.4   Sources of unreported English case law: permanent reference copies [5.30–5.33]

— House of Lords
    — copies of judgments + parties 'printed case' and other documents, deposited annually at certain libraries, including Lincoln's Inn Library; otherwise at House of Lords Record Office
— Privy Council
    — as for Lords; otherwise at Privy Council Judicial Committee office
— Court of Appeal (Civil Division)
    — Supreme Court Library, Royal Courts of Justice, 1951– (photocopying not permitted)
    — published on microfiche by HMSO, 1951–1980 only
— Court of Appeal (Criminal Division)
    — Supreme Court Library, 1963–1989
— Chancery Division
    — Patent Court cases only, 1970– British Library, Science, Business and Technology collections
— Technology and Construction Court (formerly Official Referees Business)
    — Supreme Court Library, selected handed down judgments, 1991–
— Employment Appeal Tribunal
    — at the Tribunal by appointment
    — Supreme Court Library, 1979–
— Immigration Appeal Tribunal
    — Supreme Court Library
— Consistory and other ecclesiastical courts
    — Middle Temple Library 1891–
— if available through none of the above, pay for a copy of the transcript from the shorthand writers, but generally only last six years available

QR5.5   Sources of EC case law [5.37–5.38]

— *European Court Reports*
    — the official series; includes all cases before the ECJ and the Court of First Instance in all the official languages, except for staff cases, which are in separate ECR-SC from 1993, with full text only in the language of the case; unrevised typescripts of Advocate Generals' opinions and judgments issued in advance of inclusion in ECR
    — also part of the Celex database (available through a wide variety of vendors – see QR3.19), and available on Lexis, Westlaw, and from 1989 Lawtel EU
— ECJ website (free)
    — fully searchable from June 1997; earlier cases accessible by number
— University of Mannheim website
    — searchable by number, but more easily than on the ECJ site

— *Common Market Law Reports* (Sweet & Maxwell)
  — main commercially published series
  — includes member state national court decisions, Commission materials as well as ECJ decisions
  — available on Justis CD-ROM (but not Justis via the Internet); and on Westlaw UK
— *All England Law Reports: EC cases* 1997–
  — almost exclusively ECJ decisions
  — available on CD-ROM and on Butterworths EU Direct
— *European Community Cases* (CCH)
  — ECJ decisions, some Commission materials, but not national court decisions
— *European Law Reports* 1997–
  — UK and Irish national court decisions only, not ECJ decisions

QR5.6   Categories of European human rights case law [5.44–5.48]

— European Commission of Human Rights, for cases lodged before 1 November 1998
  — decisions on admissibility
  — reports on the merits
  — reports on friendly settlements
— European Court of Human Rights
  — judgments
    — on the merits, on just satisfaction, on a request for interpretation, on a request for revision
  — decisions on admissibility, for cases lodged after 1 November 1998
  — decisions on relinquishment from a Chamber to a Grand Chamber or (pre-November 1998) the Plenary Court: formal only
  — screening panel decisions: 1994–1998: formal only
— Committee of Ministers of the Council of Europe
  — resolutions under art 32: decisions where case not referred to the Court, before 1 November 1998 only
  — resolutions under art 46 (ex art 54): execution of judgments of the Court

QR5.7   Sources for European human rights case law [5.50–5.54]

— *European Human Rights Reports*
  * **Main commercially published series**
    — includes virtually all Court judgments; vols 1–2, 1979–80 contain retrospective coverage back to first judgment in 1960
    — included selective Commission materials; retrospective coverage in vol 3; and separately paginated 'CD' section, 1993–
    — also available on Westlaw UK

— *Publications of the European Court of Human Rights: Series A: Judgments and Decisions*, renamed 1995 *Reports of Judgments and Decisions*

    * **The official reports but publication in arrears**

      — as well as all Court judgments, Commission report on the merits usually appended 1984–98

      — also *Series B: Pleadings, Oral Arguments and Documents*, which included Commission report on the merits before 1984; ceased publication with vol 104 for 1988

— HUDOC database on ECHR website

    * **The most up-to-date source, and acceptable for court use; now with substantial retrospective coverage as follows**

      — *Court*: all judgments, and since 1 November 1998 all admissibility decisions, other than those made by three judge committee rather than a Chamber; screening panel decisions 1994–98

      — *Commission*: all admissibility decisions 1986– (though not all in English); selected pre-1986 decisions if previously published; reports on the merits 1986– (if public)

      — *Committee of Ministers*: resolutions on execution 1972 to October 1997; resolutions on the merits 1959 to March 1997

— European Commission of Human Rights *Collection of Decisions* (CD, 1960–74) and *Decisions and Reports* (DR, 1975–98)

    * **The official source for reports on the merits, and selected admissibility decisions and other materials**

— Lawtel Human Rights, Justis Human Rights, and Human Rights Direct on Butterworths LEXIS Direct

    — include all Court judgments, but not Commission materials

— Keir Starmer *Blackstone's Human Rights Digest*: accompanying CD-ROM

    — the CD accompanying the book has the full text of Court judgments and selected Commission decisions

— *Information notes* (monthly) and press releases on ECHR website: summaries only

— *Butterworths Human Rights Cases*

    — only a selection of ECHR cases; mostly cases from other jurisdictions and human rights bodies

    — also available on Human Rights Direct

— *European Human Rights Law Review*

    — includes occasional reports of cases as well as articles

— Committee of Ministers resolutions

    — individual prints, and *Collection of Resolutions Adopted by the Committee of Ministers in Application of Articles 32 and 54 of the European Convention on Human Rights, 1959–1989* (1993) + supplements

    — Cited by DH number

— *Yearbook of the European Convention on Human Rights*

    *   **Full text of only a selection of Commission admissibility decisions, Commission friendly settlement reports and Committee of Ministers resolutions; summaries of Court judgments and Commission reports on the merits**

    —   Volume 1, covering 1955–57, called *European Commission of Human Rights: Documents and/et Decisions*

    —   Supplementary volume 41A for 1998 contains a retrospective collection of key extracts from Court judgments and Commission decisions on the merits

—   *Digest of Strasbourg Case-Law Relating to the European Convention on Human Rights*

    *   **Includes summaries of admissibility decisions, especially earlier ones, not in any other published source; as a general digest of case law not up to date**

—   cases from time to time in general and specialist series of English law reports, including *The Times Law Reports*

QR5.8   Deciphering abbreviations [5.60–5.62]

—   Donald Raistrick *Index to Legal Citations and Abbreviations* (2nd edn, 1993)

    *   **Best source**

    —   remember filing order

    —   includes references to reprints of nominate reports in *English Reports* and *Revised Reports*

    —   for abbreviations to *journal* references derived from *Legal Journals Index* use its own list of abbreviations

—   *Current Law*: monthly parts and yearbooks: table of abbreviations

    *   **For new series since last edition of *Raistrick***

—   *The Digest*: table of abbreviations in front of volume 1(1)

    *   **Covers nominates and all the main series, if *Raistrick* not to hand**

—   *Halsbury's Laws*: list of reports in front of volume 1(1) and in cumulative supplement

    *   **As above**

—   *Bieber's Dictionary of Legal Abbreviations* (5th edn, 2001)

    *   **American equivalent of *Raistrick***

—   *World Dictionary of Legal Abbreviations* (eds Kavass and Price, 4 volumes looseleaf)

    *   **If not in *Raistrick*, and may be not English but from somewhere exotic**

QR5.9   Finding English cases by name – citation unknown [5.111–5.118]

—   *Current Law Case Citator*

    *   **Best starting point unless case very recent and not yet reported or old**

- — will include both cases reported and cases cited during the coverage period
  - — electronic version covering the whole period 1947 to date most convenient and up to date;
  - — hard copy: bound volumes 1947–76, 1977–97; and softbound supplements to previous year, then
  - — cumulative table of cases in latest *Current Law* monthly digest for whole of current calendar year (and December issue for previous year if necessary): references are to monthly issue and paragraph number. NB at this stage only reference to the first report to appear given; references to later (and possibly fuller) reports only on electronic version
- — Case Search on Butterworths LEXIS Direct
  - * **Will pick up most cases not in *Current Law Case Citator* because before 1947 (from its data based on *The Digest*) and some recent cases not in the *Citator* because unreported (from its data based on All England Direct)**
- — *The Digest*
  - * **If Case Search not available; the most comprehensive source for old cases; a cross-check on modern cases up to about a year ago; may help if not an English case**
    - — consolidated table of cases to find right volume number
    - — table of cases at front of volume of main work will give paragraph number: citation at foot of entry at that paragraph
    - — check table of cases in annual cumulative supplement for more recent cases
- — *The English Reports*: table of cases
  - * **For pre-1865 cases not in the current edition of *The Digest***
    - — covers virtually all nominate reports for which references given as well as ER references
    - — will not pick up pre-1865 cases not reported in the nominates but only in *Law Journal, Law Times, Jurist* etc
- — *The Digest*: superseded editions
  - * **Long shot for old cases not in the current edition of *The Digest* nor in the *English Reports***
    - — would pick up cases on obsolete topics deleted from *The Digest* that were pre-1865 and not in the nominate reports or post-1865
- — commercial services on the Internet: Lexis, All England Direct, Lawtel, Westlaw UK, Casetrack
  - * **Especially if very recent and may be unreported**
    - — work your way through those you have access to
    - — usually best to use a field search on case name or title where available, especially if a common name; but free text searching will pick up mentions even if not on service in question; use proximity searching where available if more than one element of name has to be entered

— free services on the Internet: see QR5.2

    *   **For recent unreported cases, if commercial services unavailable**

        — note that for most courts only a small selection of judgments are currently available on free websites

— *Legal Journals Index*

    *   **A double-check for recent unreported cases**

        — will confirm the existence of a recent unreported case if it has been subject to comment

        — search in the case field

— *Halsbury's Laws*: consolidated table of cases, and tables in cumulative supplement and looseleaf noter-up

    *   **A double-check for cases not found in *Current Law Case Citator* or *The Digest***

— *Law Reports Index*: table of cases reported and table of cases judicially considered

    *   **A shortcut for mainstream cases, if it is all that is to hand**

— Tables of cases in textbooks

    *   **Often the quickest way if subject-matter known**

— Tables of cases in indexes to particular series

    *   **Sometimes a shortcut if likely series known**

— Finding aids for cases from other jurisdictions (see QR8)

    *   **Bear in mind the possibility, if difficulty is encountered, that the case may not be English at all**

QR5.10   Printed sources listing English cases by name of defendant, as well as claimant or first party

— *All England Law Reports*: consolidated table of cases (1936–)

— *Daily Law Reports Index*: parties index (1988–97)

— *Legal Journals Index*: case index (1986–99)

— *Index to the Times Law Reports* (Professional Books, 1982–88): index of cases

— *Times Law Reports* (W & T Clark, 1990–): table of cases reported

— some other individual series that issue cumulative tables of cases, eg *Estates Gazette Law Reports*, *Industrial Relations Law Reports*

QR5.11   Finding EC cases by name [5.119]

— electronic full text sources: see QR5.5

— *Butterworths EC Case Citator and Service*: alphabetical list

    *   **Probably the most convenient printed source for ECJ cases**

        — by applicant only, but separate 'Nickname' table if another part of the name better known

        — ECR references only, not CMLR

— Court of Justice of the European Communities *Index A–Z: Numerical and Alphabetical Index*

    * **Being annual, not as up to date as above, but otherwise equally convenient**

        — includes listing by both parties

        — ECR references only, not CMLR

        — includes cases pending

— *Current Law Case Citator*

    * **Electronic version will get non-ECJ cases reported in *Common Market Law Reports*, *European Commercial Cases* and *International Litigation Procedure* and for ECJ cases give CMLR reference**

        — hardcopy version will only get those digested in *Current Law* itself, which does not include all those in the above sources

QR5.12 Finding European Court of Justice cases by number [5.119]

— full text electronic services: see QR5.5

— *Butterworths EC Case Citator*: numeric list

    * **The most straightforward approach**

— Court of Justice of the European Communities *Index A–Z: Numerical and Alphabetical Index*

    * **An alternative, not quite as up to date, but includes cases pending**

— *Halsbury's Laws*: consolidated table of cases and table in cumulative supplement

    * **Not comprehensive, but a useful shortcut, or if above not available**

        — chronological table of ECJ decisions at back of consolidated table of cases (vol 54)

        — chronological table of ECJ decisions after alphabetical table of cases at front of cumulative supplement

— Typescript advance ECJ judgments themselves

    * **Especially for very recent cases not in the above; but only possible if shelved in library in case number order!**

QR5.13 Finding European human rights cases by name or number [5.110 and 5.120]

— HUDOC on the ECHR website

    * **Gets you the text as well, so as good a place to start as any**

        — search form has a field for application number; or put name of applicant in 'title' field

        — but for Court only gives official series reference not EHRR if you want hard copy (though cumulative chronological table in EHRR will translate the reference for you)

        — for Commission does not give DR references if you want hard copy

— *Current Law Case Citator*

    *   **Covers EHRR so will get you most Court judgments (and cases in English series of reports)**

— *Digest of Strasbourg Case-Law*

    *   **Especially for old Commission case law not on HUDOC; otherwise very out of date**

— *Decisions and Reports*: cumulative indexes

    *   **For Commission case law not on HUDOC, if *Digest of Strasbourg Case-Law* not available**

        —   available for CD 1–30, 32–43; DR 1–20, 21–40, 41–60, 6–83

— tables of cases in standard textbooks

    *   **Often a quick shortcut**

        —   eg *Lester and Pannick, Clayton and Tomlinson, Simor and Emmerson, Harris and O'Boyle, Van Dijk and Van Hoof*

— *Legal Journals Index*

    *   **Another shortcut, given the volume of comment generated by human rights cases**

        —   search in the case field

— Barabara Mensah *European Human Rights Case Locator 1960–2000* (Cavendish)

    *   **An alternative for finding EHRR references to Court judgments**

        —   main listing alphabetically, with separate chronological, country and convention article listings

        —   only Court, not Commission; only EHRR references given

QR5.14   Finding English cases by subject [5.121–5.128]

— *Halsbury's Laws* and textbooks

    *   **Although not case-finding aids as such, often the best way to start a subject-based research problem if you need to get your bearings**

        —   in *Halsbury's* use consolidated index and/or browse contents pages of each topic

        —   check cumulative supplement and looseleaf noter-up under same volume number and paragraph number as main work

— Current Law Cases

    *   **Should do most of the job, unless pre-1947 cases relevant; supplement with sources covering recent unreported cases**

— LEXIS

    *   **Will get most reported cases since 1945, and has the best historical coverage of unreported cases; best source when full text retrieval preferred**

— *The Digest* and/or Case Search on Butterworths LEXIS Direct

    *   **For in-depth research, where older cases likely to be relevant; also for selected Commonwealth authorities**

— in *The Digest* either go straight to relevant volume and then browse through table of contents for each topic or use consolidated index to get you to the right spot and then browse through table of contents; check annual cumulative supplement

— on Case Search do a keyword search; if you find relevant cases see where they are treated in *The Digest* if you have it as well (using consolidated table of cases): there may be further adjacent cases on the same point not picked up by the keyword search because no summaries provided for them

— Lawtel, All England Direct, Westlaw UK, Casetrack

* **Especially for very recent unreported cases; work your way through those you have access to**

— unreported cases on free websites

* **May be better than nothing, if commercial services not available**

— BAILII will be the place to go when its content is sorted: it has a good search engine; search engines on other sites variable

— electronic full text versions of particular law reports series on CD-ROM or the Internet

* **Where full text searching preferred and Lexis etc not available; when time is short for mainstream case law or where a particular subject series likely to be relevant**

— eg *The Law Reports, Weekly Law Reports, All England Law Reports* for mainstream case law

— eg *Criminal Appeal Reports, Estates Gazette Law Reports* for particular subject areas

— *Legal Journals Index*

* **Always worth a look for any research problem**

— the number of articles commenting on a particular case gives some idea of its weight or importance

— may pick up unreported cases that have been the subject of comment

— *Law Reports Index*

* **A shortcut for mainstream cases, if it is all that is to hand**

QR5.15 Finding cases on quantum of damages for personal injuries [5.129–5.130]

— Kemp & Kemp *Quantum of Damages in Personal Injury and Fatal Accident Claims* (4 volumes looseleaf)

* **The basic bible**

— Goldrein and de Haas *Butterworths Personal Injury Litigation Service* (5 volumes looseleaf)

* **Wider than just quantum but includes in binder 2 quantum summaries and in binder 3 quantum judgments**

— *Current Law*: table of damages for personal injuries or death

    *   **Especially for very recent awards not in above**

        — cumulative table in latest monthly part and in each yearbook summarises the awards; the cases themselves digested in the main entries under Damages

— Current Law Cases

    *   **If free text searching preferred as a means of accessing the digests of quantum cases in *Current Law***

— *Halsbury's Laws*: monthly reviews and annual abridgments

    *   **Quantum cases a particular strength**

        — cumulative table to quantum cases in current monthly reviews filed in the 'Personal Injury' divider in looseleaf noter-up volume to *Halsbury's Laws* (not in the monthly review binder); also separate table in annual abridgment

        — cases themselves digested in the main entries under Damages

— Lawtel

    *   **Good coverage; use as well as the above sources if you have access to it**

— PI Online on Butterworths LEXIS Direct

    *   **Includes a quantum database derived from other Butterworths sources**

— Simon Levene *Damages Service* (EMIS, 2001)

    *   **A new rival to the established services**

        — handy one-volume book + access to online updating service

QR5.16   Finding cases in which a particular word or phrase has been construed [2.45–2.48]

— *Stroud's Judicial Dictionary*

    — main work and cumulative supplement

    — superseded 3rd and 4th editions still of use for old and Commonwealth cases

— *Words and Phrases Legal Defined*

    — main work and cumulative supplement

— *Current Law*: table of words and phrases in yearbooks and monthly parts

    *   **Especially for recent cases not yet in the supplements to the above**

        — cumulative for the year in the monthly parts

— *Halsbury's Laws*: table of words and phrases in noter-up and annual abridgments

    *   **An alternative to, or cross-check on, Current Law**

        — table in looseleaf noter-up volume of current service refers to monthly reviews filed in the other current service volume

— *Law Reports Index*

    *   **An alternative for mainstream cases**

        — under 'Words and Phrases' in the subject-matter index

— electronic full text case law services

    * **Can be very effective as long as word not too common in ordinary usage**

        — Lexis search example:

        emergency w/10 meaning or defin! or constru! or interpret!

        will retrieve cases on the construction of the word 'emergency'

— William J Steward *Scottish Contemporary Judicial Dictionary* (Green, 1995)

    * **Worth a look by English lawyers, if nothing much in *Stroud* or *Words and Phrases*, especially of course if English and Scottish law the same**

QR5.17 Finding EC cases by subject [5.132]

— Celex and other full text electronic services carrying EC cases: see QR5.5

    * **The main approach**

— *Butterworths EC Case Citator and Service*: key phrase/sector index

    * **Only selected cases that have 'substantially contributed to EC law' included in this part of the work**

— *European Current Law* (1992–)

    * **Covers all of Europe not just member states and not just EC law, but useful for recent decisions of national courts**

— the sources listed above for English cases

    * **For decisions of English courts relevant to EC law, though some ECJ cases covered by, for example, *Current Law* and *The Digest***

— a search on treaty provision, Directive or Regulation often more effective than a general subject search, see QR5.23

QR5.18 Finding European human rights cases by subject [5.132]

— full text electronic sources: see QR5.7

    * **The main approach**

        — bear in mind that the human rights modules on Lawtel, Justis, and Butterworths LEXIS Direct contain little or no Commission materials

— Keir Starmer *Blackstone's Human Rights Digest* (Blackstone Press, 2001)

    * **Handy one volume work; includes coverage of cases from other jurisdictions and human rights bodies**

        — accompanying CD-ROM for ECHR judgments and selected Commission decisions only

— Council of Europe *Digest of Strasbourg Case-Law Relating to the European Convention on Human Rights*

    * **Very out of date, but comprehensive for period covered**

— Peter Kempees *A Systematic Guide to the Case Law of the European Court of Human Rights* (Nijhoff, 4 volumes)

    * **Excellent summaries of all Court judgments**

        — currently covers all judgments to 1998, but further volumes may appear

        — does not cover (directly) Commission decisions

— Vincent Berger *Case Law of the European Court of Human Rights 1960– 1993* (Round Hall, 3 volumes)

    * **An alternative to *Kempees* for the period covered; useful bibliographical references to case comment**

    — again just Court judgments

— *Decisions and Reports*: cumulative indexes

    * **For Commission case law not on HUDOC, if *Digest of Strasbourg Case-Law* not available**

    — available for CD 1–30, 32–43; DR 1–20, 21–40, 41–60, 6–83

— *Yearbook of the European Convention of Human Rights* volume 41A for 1998

    * **'Key extracts' from judgments and decisions: convenient access to the leading cases**

— Current Law Cases

    * **Covers cases in EHRR from about 1992, with a few earlier ones**

— *The Digest* and/or Case Search

    * **Covers selected cases mostly, though not exclusively, from EHRR, BHRC, and English law report series**

    — 'Human Rights' in volume 26(2) of *The Digest* + cumulative supplement

QR5.19 Finding cases in which a particular English case has been cited [5.133–5.139]

— *Current Law Case Citator*

    * **Usually the most convenient starting point for cases cited since 1947; should get the bulk of cases with substantial consideration**

    — electronic versions using Folio Views or the Internet have hypertext links to the digest of the citing cases

    — hard copy: two bound volumes 1947–76, 1977–99 and subsequent softbound supplements: references in the right hand column are to yearbook paragraph numbers where the citing case will be found

    — then cumulative table of cases in latest monthly part (and if necessary December issue of previous year): cases in lower case are those that have been cited during the year and references are to monthly part and paragraph number

— Lexis

    * **For the most comprehensive results**

    — free text search on the name of the case

    — will need other sources for (a) pre-1945 cases (b) very recent unreported cases that may be on rival transcript services or (c) if unmanageable number of hits, in which case revert to the citator approach

— Case Search on Butterworths LEXIS Direct

    * **For cases cited before 1947, for very recent unreported cases, and as a cross-check on *Current Law Case Citator* for reported cases 1947–**

— data derived from the annotations to cases in *The Digest* and editorial scrutiny of cases on All England Direct (1995–)

— system of 'traffic lights', green, red and amber, for good law, bad law, and proceed with caution

— *The Digest*

* **The printed alternative to Case Search (without the All England Direct data); main printed source for cases cited before 1947; and a cross-check for cases thereafter**

   — find the digest entry for the case in the main work via the consolidated table of cases and the table of cases in the volume

   — at the foot of the entry in small print the ANNOTATION section shows later cases in which it was cited

   — check the annual cumulative supplement under the same volume number and paragraph number as the main work

— commercial transcript services on the Internet: Lawtel, Westlaw UK, All England Direct, Casetrack

* **For any citations in recent unreported cases; a cross-check in so far as they include reported cases**

   — where no proper proximity searching facility, eg Lawtel take care in entering the name of the case if more than one element of the name has to be entered

— transcripts on free websites (see QR5.2)

* **May be better than nothing for recent unreported cases if commercial services not available and website supports free text searching**

   — on BAILII use the 'Noter-up' facility

— individual series of law reports in full text on the Internet or CD-ROM

* **Often a useful 'top-up' to *Current Law Case Citator* if Lexis not available; the electronic Law Reports (1865–) and the *English Law Reports* (to 1865) on CD-ROM also useful as supplements to *The Digest* for old cases**

   — of the CD-ROMs, the Justis products from Context particularly recommended because of ability to search across several CDs and search software

   — free text search to start with; if too many hits field search in the headnote field

— *Law Reports Digest* (1865–1950): tables of cases judicially considered

* **A cross-check on *The Digest* for older cases if the electronic Law Reports not available**

— *Law Reports Index* (1951–): table of cases judicially considered

* **A shortcut for mainstream cases**

— *All England Law Reports*: table of cases reported and considered in consolidated tables

* **Better than nothing, but limited coverage**

   — coverage of cases considered confined to those that were themselves originally reported in All ER or appeared in the All ER Reprint

— *Index to the Times Law Reports* (Professional Books, 1982–88) and *Times Law Reports* (W & T Clarke, 1990–): tables of cases judicially considered

   * **Scraping the barrel if CD-ROM of *Times Law Reports* (and Lexis) not available; may net material not in *Current Law Case Citator***

— *Australian and New Zealand Citator to UK reports*

   * **For in-depth research or where above sources yield few or no English citations**

      — before 1973 confined to Australian and New Zealand cases that cite those cases that were originally reported in *The Law Reports*, the *Weekly Law Reports*, the *All England Law Reports*, or the *All England Law Reports Reprint* series; from 1973 covers a wider range of UK reports

— citators from other jurisdictions, eg *Australian Case Citator*, *Canadian Case Citations*; full text electronic law reports of other jurisdictions, eg on Lexis

   * **For in-depth research or where above sources yield few or no English citations**

QR5.20 Finding cases in which a particular EC or European human rights case has been cited [5.140]

— free text search of full text electronic versions of the case law (see QR5.5 and QR5.7)

   * **Just about the only feasible way**

      — *Butterworths EC Case Citator* and the European cases section of the *Current Law Case Citator* do *not* perform this function

— *Current Law Cases*

   * **Worth a search**

      — will pick up cases mentioned in the digests of those EC and ECHR cases that are included

— *European Human Rights Reports*: table of cases judicially considered in each volume (pending the publication of consolidated tables)

   * **A plod that is easier the more recent the case in question**

— *Gazetteer of European Law* (1953–83) volume 2 case search table

   * **For ECJ cases during the period**

      — arranged by ECJ case number

      — only gives number of citing case: refer to main numerical sequences for details of the case

      — includes decisions of national courts that cite ECJ cases

      — importance of citation graded: cases in bold indicate substantial consideration, cases in italic indicate a mere mention; other cases are in normal type

— The sources above at QR5.19

   * **For decisions of the English courts that have cited EC or European human rights cases cases**

QR5.21 Finding cases on Public General Acts [5.141–5.146]

— Is it a consolidation Act? (Look at long title)

    * **If yes, trace derivation (see QR3.9) to find case law on predecessor Act as well**

— *Halsbury's Statutes*

    * **Together with *Current Law Statute Citator* the most convenient starting point**

        — find the statute in the main work from the alphabetical or chronological tables in the annual softback index

        — check notes to particular section for any case references

        — check annual cumulative supplement under same volume and page number as main work

        — check looseleaf noter-up volume under same volume and page number as main work

        — will often include references to case law on earlier Acts for consolidation Acts

— *Current Law Statute Citator*

    * **May be slightly more up to date than *Halsbury's Statutes*, and may get additional references**

        — hard copy is safe and simple; but electronic *Current Law Legislation Citator* can be used if preferred (see **5.143**), though only back to 1989

        — statute citator 1947–71, statute citator in legislation citator 1972–88, 1989–95, 1996–99 and any softbound supplement, then latest issue (and if necessary previous year) in looseleaf service volume to *Current Law Statutes*

        — arranged chronologically by year and chapter number

        — any case references given under each section number

— Lexis

    * **For the most comprehensive results**

        — search on name of Act and if necessary section number; avoid searching on 'section', 's' or subsection numbers

        — search example: employment w/4 1990 w/15 7 for cases on s 7 Employment Act 1990

        — add 'meaning or defin! or constru! or interpret!' to search string if too many hits retrieved

        — will need other sources for (a) pre-1945 cases (b) very recent unreported cases that may be on rival transcript services or (c) if unmanageable number of hits, in which case revert to the printed sources above

— commercial transcript services on the Internet: Lawtel, Westlaw UK, All England Direct, Casetrack

    * **For any citations in recent unreported cases; a cross-check in so far as they include reported cases**

— where no proper proximity searching facility, eg Lawtel, take care in entering the name of the Act if more than one element of the name has to be entered

— transcripts on free websites (see QR5.2)

* **May be better than nothing for recent unreported cases if commercial services not available and website supports free text searching**

— individual series of law reports in full text on the Internet or CD-ROM

* **Often a useful 'top-up' to *Halsbury' Statutes* and *Current Law Statute Citator* if Lexis not available**

— of the CD-ROMs, the Justis products from Context particularly recommended because of ability to search across several CDs and search software

— free text search to start with; if too many hits field search in the headnote field or add terms as suggested for Lexis

— *Law Reports Digest* (1865–1950): tables of statutes judicially considered

* **For cases on statutes no longer in force and for pre-1947 cases**

— arranged by regnal year and chapter number of Act

— *Law Reports Index* (1951–): table of statutes judicially considered

* **A shortcut for mainstream cases**

— arranged by year and chapter number

— *All England Law Reports*: table of statutes considered in consolidated tables

* **A shortcut for mainstream cases**

— arranged alphabetically by title

— *Index to the Times Law Reports* (Professional Books, 1982–88) and *Times Law Reports* (W & T Clarke, 1990–): tables of statutes judicially considered

* **Scraping the barrel if CD-ROM of *Times Law Reports* (and Lexis) not available; may net material not in *Halsbury's Statutes* and *Current Law Statute Citator***

QR5.22   Finding cases on SIs [5.147]

— The full text electronic sources as for Acts

* **Even more useful than for Acts, since other sources for SIs more limited**

— search on name of the SI 'ORing' the number

— *Current Law Statutory Instrument Citator*

* **The main tool, but only from 1993**

— in hard copy 1993–95 in the **1989**–95 legislation citator; 1996–99 a separate volume; any softbound supplements for subsequent years; then latest issue (and if necessary previous year) in looseleaf service volume to *Current Law Statutes*

— or on screen in *Current Law Legislation Citator*

— *Law Reports Index* (1951–): table of Statutory Instruments etc judicially considered

* **The most useful feature of this tool and the main source before 1993; a cross-check after 1993**

   — Rules of the Supreme Court listed first followed by other SIs by title

— · Current Law Cases

* **For cases before 1993**

   — a free text search should pick up any SIs mentioned in the digests; for cases from 1993 should duplicate results of *SI Citator*

— *Halsbury's Statutory Instruments*

* **Case annotations not a prominent feature but some cases may be found in introduction to topic and annotations to SI**

— *Law Reports Digest* (1891–1950): table of statutory rules and orders of court judicially considered

* **For older cases; no table in 1865–90 volume**

   — arranged alphabetically by title

— *All England Law Reports*: tables G–M in consolidated tables volume

* **Might possibly catch some cases not in *Law Reports Index*, but remember how the material is divided into different tables**

   — six different tables:

     G Rules of the Supreme Court
     H County Court Rules
     I Matrimonial Causes Rules
     J Bankruptcy and Insolvency Rules
     K Other rules
     L Regulations
     N Orders

   — each table arranged alphabetically by title

— *Index to the Times Law Reports* (Professional Books, 1982–88) and *Times Law Reports* (W & T Clarke, 1990–): legislation index

* **Scraping the barrel if CD-ROM of *Times Law Reports* (and Lexis) not available; may net material not in above sources**

QR5.23   Finding cases on EC legislation [5.148]

— if searching on a treaty provision, bear in mind the renumbering following the treaty of Amsterdam 1997

— free text search on full text electronic sources of the case law (see QR5.5)

* **The most comprehensive approach**

— *Butterworths EC Case Citator*

* **The main printed source**

   — separate tables by treaty provision, Regulation, Directive, and Decision

— Current Law Cases

* **Worth a search**

   — will pick up legislation mentioned in the digests of those ECJ cases included, as well as English cases in which EC legislation has been considered

— free text search on Directive or Regulation number; but can confine to legislation field, which may be easier for numbered treaty provisions

— *European Current Law* (1992–)

    * **A cross-check for recent material**

    — Table 'Treaty provisions referred to' in fact includes Regulations, Directives and Decisions

— *Law Reports Index* (1971–): European Community enactments judicially considered

    * **Mainstream cases only**

    — mostly English cases or English referrals to ECJ, but a few non-English ECJ cases reported in English series (mostly from ICR)

QR5.24   Finding European human rights cases by Convention article

— bear in mind the renumbering of Convention articles 19–66 after Protocol 11 in 1998 if a procedural point is in issue

— HUDOC on the ECHR website

    * **The main resource**

    — article number field on search form, with word wheel for format of subdivided articles

— Other full text electronic services covering the case law (see QR5.7)

    * **Search software may be more to your taste, but primarily for Court judgments; little or no Commission material**

— Current Law Cases

    * **Worth a search**

    — will pick up legislation mentioned in the digests of those ECHR cases included, as well as now the numerous English cases in which have considered the Convention

    — best to confine to legislation field, putting the article number in as a bare number rather with 'art' or whatever

— Keir Starmer *Blackstone's Human Rights Digest* (Blackstone Press, 2001)

    * **Largely arranged by substantive Convention rights; but see also specific article numbers in the 'Table of International Instruments'**

    — accompanying CD-ROM for full text searching of ECHR judgments and selected Commission decisions only

— Council of Europe *Digest of Strasbourg Case-Law Relating to the European Convention on Human Rights*

    * **Arranged by Convention articles (very out of date but comprehensive for period covered)**

— Peter Kempees *A Systematic Guide to the Case Law of the European Court of Human Rights* (Nijhoff, 4 volumes)

    * **Arranged by Convention articles**

    — currently covers all judgments to 1998, but further volumes may appear

    — does not cover (directly) Commission decisions

— Vincent Berger *Case Law of the European Court of Human Rights 1960–1993* (Round Hall, 3 volumes)

    * **An alternative to *Kempees* for the period covered; arranged chronologically but index to article numbers**

    — again just Court judgments

— *Decisions and Reports*: cumulative indexes: 'index related to the articles'

    * **For Commission case law not on HUDOC, if *Digest of Strasbourg Case-Law* not available**

    — available for CD 1–30, 32–43; DR 1–20, 21–40, 41–60, 6–83

— Barbara Mensah *European Human Rights Case Locator 1960–2000* (Cavendish)

    * **Court judgments only; has table by article number**

QR5.25   Finding cases on Local and Personal Acts [5.149]

— the full text electronic case law sources as for Public General Acts (see QR5.21)

    * **For the most comprehensive results**

— *Current Law Statute Citator*

    * **The main printed source from 1996; also coverage 1947–71 but *not* covered 1972–95**

    — Local Acts after Public General Acts for each year 1947–71; before Public General Acts 1996–

    — from 1996 can also use the electronic version of the *Current Law Legislation Citator*

— *Law Reports Index* (1951–): table of statutes judicially considered

    * **The main printed source 1972–95; a cross-check on the *Statute Citator* before and since**

    — by year and chapter number interfiled with Public General Acts

— *Law Reports Digest* (1911–50): Local and Personal Acts judicially considered

    * **Only printed source before 1936; only available from the 1911 volume**

    — separate table after Public General Acts and before Dominion statutes, arranged by year and chapter number

— *All England Law Reports*: statutes considered table B in consolidated tables volume 1936 to date

    * **Might catch cases not in *Law Reports Index***

    — separate table after Public General Acts, arranged alphabetically by title

— *Times Law Reports* (W & T Clarke, 1990–): legislation table

    * **If not available on CD-ROM**

    — at back of annual volume, and cumulative in monthly parts

    — separate table after Public General Acts, arranged by year and chapter number

QR6 Treaties and international materials

QR6.1 Alternative sources for the text of a treaty [6.8–6.16]

— *United Kingdom Treaty Series* (1892–)

    * **Main source for treaties ratified by the UK**

      — issued by TSO as command papers, but also bear own series number

      — may be shelved as a series, by command paper number, or in sessional volumes of Parliamentary papers

      — will have been previously issued as a different command paper before ratification in a Foreign and Commonwealth Office series (see below)

— *United Nations Treaty Series*

    * **Main printed source for all treaties from 1946, but publication several years in arrears**

      — should include all treaties entered into by members of the United Nations

— United Nations Treaty Collection website

    * **The online version of the *United Nations Treaty Series*, but (at the moment) less up to date than the print version**

      — on subscription only unless you strike lucky with the free 'Sample Access'

      — currently loaded retrospectively from the printed volumes, so up to a year behind printed version

      — for a detailed evaluation of this site see Wiltrud Harms 'United Nations Treaty Collection' (2001) 29 *International Journal of Legal Information* 501–510

— *International Legal Materials*

    * **Especially for important recent multilateral treaties which UK has not signed**

      — issued in periodical form by the American Society of International Law

— selected treaties and other materials
— cumulative indexes from time to time
— contents pages available on ASIL website
— available on Lexis and Westlaw
— *League of Nations Treaty Series* (1920–46)
  * **Main source for all treaties before 1946**
— *Consolidated Treaty Series* ed Clive Parry (1648–1919)
  * **Main source for all treaties before 1920**
— *British and Foreign State Papers* (1812–1968)
  * **An alternative to *UK Treaty Series* for many treaties after 1892; contains some pre-1892 treaties not in the command papers**
— Command papers in sessional volumes of Parliamentary papers (1800–92)
  * **An alternative for UK treaties before 1892; some not also reprinted in the above**
— Old compilations of treaties
  * **An alternative if available and *Consolidated Treaty Series* is not**
    — eg *Hertslet's Commercial Treaties* (1820–1925, 31 volumes), G.F. de Martens *Recueil de traités* (1791–1943)
    — See also on old treaty series Clive Parry 'Where to look for your treaties' (1980) 8 *International Journal of Law Libraries* 8–18
— National treaty series
  * **For non-UK treaties not yet in *United Nations Treaty Series* and not in *International Legal Materials***
    — some may be available on the Internet, eg Australian Treaties Library (1915 to date)
— Foreign and Commonwealth Office *Miscellaneous Series* (multilateral) and country series (bilateral)
  * **An alternative source for selected treaties not yet ratified by the UK**
    — issued by TSO as command papers, and usually shelved by command paper number or in sessional volumes of Parliamentary papers rather than by Miscellaneous (or country) number
— The Internet in general
  * **Why not just do a Google search on the name of the treaty; never ceases to amaze**
— Websites of sponsoring international organisations
  * **Often the simplest solution, if there is such a body; often full text and free**
    — eg Hague Conference on Private International Law, WIPO (World Intellectual Property Organisation)
— Websites of international law research institutions or government foreign ministries
    — eg Fletcher School of Diplomacy, McGill Air and Space Law Institute, US Department of State Private International Law Database
— Specialist gateways
    — eg links on the American Society of International Law website

— The general legal gateways

    — eg Eagle-I, Cornell Law Institute, AustLII World Law, Sarah Carter's Lawlinks

— Looseleaf subject compilations of international legal materials, appendices to textbooks, etc

    * **Often a convenient shortcut**

— Public General Acts and SIs

    * **For some treaties incorporated into UK domestic law, provided you know the title of the relevant legislation**

        — text of treaty sometimes printed as a schedule, but sometimes only referred to

        — if you do not know title of relevant Act, use an electronic source containing full text legislation, eg Justis Statutes and SIs (see QR3.1 and QR3.11)

— Lexis and Westlaw

    * **A wide range of materials, particularly of American interest, in their international libraries**

        — also may be treaties in subject libraries, eg on Lexis Double Taxation Agreements in the UK Tax library

Alternative sources for the text of EC treaties

QR6.2   Text of treaties establishing the EC, accession treaties etc [6.17]

— Celex (see QR3.19) and EUR-Lex

— *Treaties Establishing the European Communities [etc]* (Office for Official Publications of the European Communities, two purple volumes)

    * **Official hard copy edition reissued from time to time**

— *Encyclopedia of European Union Law: Constitutional Texts* (Sweet & Maxwell, looseleaf)

— *Halsbury's Statutes* volume 50 (+ volume 50 section in Current Statutes service volume)

— Smit and Herzog *The Law of the European Economic Community* (New York: Matthew Bender, looseleaf)

— *Common Market Reporter* (CCH, looseleaf)

— Various compilations of EC materials for students, eg Rudden and Wyatt *Basic Community Laws* (OUP)

— for help following the renumbering of the main Community treaties see the following:

    — Treaty of Amsterdam: Annex: Tables of equivalences (1997 OJ C240 p 85)

    — Explanatory report from the General Secretariat of the Council on the simplification of the Community treaties (1997 OJ C353)

    — *The Rome, Maastricht & Amsterdam Treaties: Comparative Texts* (Euroconfidentiel, 1999)

QR6.3 Text of treaties entered into by the EC [6.18]

— Celex (see QR3.19)

— *Collection of the Agreements Concluded by the European Communities*

    — (Office for Official Publications of the European Communities, several purple volumes)

— Foreign and Commonwealth Office *European Treaty Series*

    * **Especially for recent treaties not yet in the above**

        — issued by HMSO as command papers and shelved by series number, or command paper number or in sessional volumes of Parliamentary papers

— *Official Journal of the EC*: L series

    * **For very recent treaties**

QR6.4 Finding treaties by date or subject [6.20–6.26]

— Clive Parry and Charity Hopkins *An Index of British Treaties 1101–1988* (HMSO, 4 volumes)

    * **The main source up to 1988 for treaties ratified by the UK**

        — volumes 1–3 cover 1101–1968

        — volume covers 1969–1988 and updates volumes 1–3

        — main sequence with full details arranged by date

        — three subject indexes:

            — multilateral treaties by subject

            — bilateral treaties by country subdivided by subject

            — bilateral treaties by subject subdivided by country

        — full references to different sources of the text, *except* for the *Consolidated Treaty Series*

— M J Bowman and D J Harris *Multilateral Treaties: Index and Current Status* (bound volume and cumulative supplement)

    * **Probably the most widely available source for multilateral treaties (though does not cover every single multilateral treaty there is)**

        — may not include recent treaties: in 2001 last supplement published in 1995 covering treaties to end of 1993

        — main sequence with full details arranged by date

        — bound volume goes up to June 1983

        — cumulative supplement in two parts:

        Part A: Additional treaties (ie some pre-1983 treaties omitted from bound volume and post-1983 treaties)

        Part B: Noter-up to treaties in bound volume

        — table of other multilateral treaties after main sequence in bound volume lists treaties referred to but not detailed in full

— Christian L Wiktor *Multilateral Treaty Calendar 1648–1995* (Nijhoff, 1998)

    * **Now the most comprehensive source for multilateral treaties**

        — main sequence by date, with a general subject index

— Peter H Rohn *World Treaty Index*

    *   **For treaties 1900–80 not found in the above; includes many treaties not in UN or League of Nations treaty series**

        — main sequence chronological by date of signature

        — party index covers both bilateral and multilateral

        — key word index

— Indexes to government publications (see QR7)

    *   **An alternative for treaties published by HMSO as command papers in the United Kingdom Treaty Series and the FCO 'European Communities' and 'Miscellaneous' series. Especially for recent treaties**

        — search by subject and/or party

— Indexes to the *United Kingdom Treaty Series*

    *   **Possible shortcut for recent treaties**

        — recent indexes issued annually

        — by subject

— *International Legal Materials*

    *   **For recent treaties not in UK Treaty Series or *Bowman and Harris***

        — look through recent parts

        — cumulative indexes

        — also on Lexis and Westlaw

— United Nations Treaty Collection website

    *   **Especially for non-UK bilateral treaties from 1945**

        — subscription only

— *United Nations Treaty Series*: cumulative indexes

    *   **A long haul, but a source for non-UK bilateral treaties from 1945**

        — cumulative indexes covering 50 volumes each

        — in two sequences, chronological and alphabetical

— *League of Nations Treaty Series*: cumulative indexes

    *   **A source for treaties 1919–45 especially non-UK bilateral treaties**

        — indexes covering 20–40 volumes: look in each unless approximate date known

        — each index in three sequences:

            — chronological index of all treaties

            — chronological index of general international agreements (ie multilateral treaties) only

            — alphabetical index under both country and subject for bilateral treaties and under subject only for mulitilateral treaties; within each heading arranged chronologically

— *Consolidated Treaty Series*: indexes

    *   **Main source for treaties before 1919, especially non-UK bilateral treaties**

        — three indexes:

— general chronological list
 — excludes colonial, postal and telegraphic agreements
 — arranged by date with full details of treaty
— special chronological list
 — as above for colonial, postal and telegraphic agreements
— party index
 — by country (with former territories grouped with their modern equivalents)
 — within country arranged chronological
 — title of treaty not given; only name of other party, date, and volume reference
— Looseleaf subject compilations of international materials, appendices to textbooks etc
 * **Often a shortcut**

QR6.5 Checking parties and status of treaties [6.27–6.32]

— Treaty Section of the Records and Historical Department, Foreign and Commonwealth Office
 * **The safest option for a UK treaty if there are likely to have been recent changes**
 — contact details (but not data) on the FCO website
— M J Bowman and D J Harris *Multilateral Treaties: Index and Current Status*
 * **The main printed source, with caveat as to date (see above)**
 — find treaty in main work and then check cumulative supplement
— *Index of British Treaties*
 * **Only up to date to 1988, but may help**
 — find treaty in main chronological sequence and then check volume 4 for any additional information
— *Supplementary List of Ratifications, Accessions, Withdrawals, etc*
 * **For recent information, but tedious to use**
 — issued four times a year as part of the *UK Treaty Series* (command papers published by HMSO)
 — arranged by subject-matter
 — plough through each list
— United Nations *Multilateral Treaties Deposited with the Secretary-General: Status as at ...*
 * **Online version on the United Nations Treaty Collection website is apparently up to date; annual printed version may now be better, pending it being updated, than *Bowman and Harris***
— Council of the European Union Agreements Office
 * **For status and parties (not text) of treaties entered into by EU**

— Websites of sponsoring international organisations or official depositaries, eg Council of Europe, GATT, International Labour Organisation, Organisation of American States, World Intellectual Property Organisation, FCO (multilateral treaties for which UK is official depositary)

　　* **Status information often given, even where texts not also available**

— Rohn *World Treaty Index*

　　* **Only up to date to 1980, but may help with retrospective information**

　　　— full details of parties, entry into force etc in main chronological sequence

QR6.6　Tracing *travaux préparatoires*

— usually published as ad hoc publications in the form of international conference proceedings, or as official documents of the sponsoring international organisation, eg UN

　　— try on-line catalogues of the major libraries holding international legal materials, or the international law websites and gateways mention at QR6.1

— for major treaties sometimes reprinted in retrospective collections, for example the following

　　— *New Directions in the Law of the Sea* (Oceana)

　　— *Collected Edition of the Travaux Préparatoires of the European Convention on Human Rights* (Nijhoff, 1975–86, 8 volumes)

　　— Michael F Sturley *The Legislative History of the [US] Carriage of Goods by Sea Act and the* Travaux Préparatoires *of the Hague Rules* (Rothman, 1991, 3 volumes)

　　— G Gaja *International Commercial Arbitration: the New York Convention* (Oceans, 1978– , 4 volumes looseleaf)

　　— R Horner and D Legrez *Second International Conference on Private Aeronautical Law: Minutes, October 2–12, 1929* [the Warsaw Convention] (Rothman, 1975)

　　— N Jasentuliyana and R S K Lee *Manual on Space Law* (Oceana, 1979, 4 volumes)

QR6.7　Sources for international case law [6.35–6.37]

— Phillipe Sands (ed) *Manual on International Courts and Tribunals* (Butterworths, 1999)

　　* **An indispensable guide**

　　　— lists every current international court and tribunal from the International Court of Justice to the Ozone Layer Protocol mechanism

　　　— for each includes how their case law is published with website addresses if available on the Internet

— International Court of Justice *Reports of Judgments, Advisory Opinions and Orders*

    *   **The official series for the ICJ**

        —   recent judgments in full text, and earlier judgments in summary form back to 1946 also available on ICJ website

        —   three series of digests of ICJ judgments 1952 to 1993 with varying titles edited respectively by E.I. Hambro, R. Berhardt and R. Hofman

—   *International Law Reports* 1929–

    *   **The main commercially published series**

—   *International Legal Materials*

    *   **For recent cases not yet in the above**

        —   contents pages on American Society of International Law website

        —   see also summaries of cases in ASIL's electronic newsletter International Law in Brief

—   international law websites and portals mentioned at QR6.1

QR7 Other official publications

Sources for finding official publications

See also sources mentioned at QR4.2 on finding pre-legislative reports and law reform proposals

QR7.1 Sources covering both TSO and non-TSO publications [7.17–7.21]

— UKOP
  * **The best source for publications from 1980. Virtually the only source to cover both TSO and non-TSO publications.**
    — combines the data from TSO catalogues with Chadwyck-Healey's *Government Publications Not Published by TSO* (the latter remains available separately in hard copy with CD-ROM index)
    — available on the Internet (a subscription service) and also for the time being on CD-ROM
    — Internet version includes links to many documents in full text, including documents digitised specially for it
    — also includes publications of international organisations sold by TSO
— Stephen Richard *British Government Publications: an Index to Chairmen and Authors 1800–1982* (4 volumes)
  * **Indispensable as chairman the commonest identifying feature of government reports, though now out of date**
— Polis or Parlianet
  * **Not only for parliamentary publications; wide coverage of other official publications held by House of Commons Library**
    — Polis available free of charge on the Parliament website
    — Parlianet the more sophisticated commercial version available from Context
    — a bibliographical database, not full text, though Parlianet now has links to some full text material such as *Hansard*

Coverage is as follows:

Parliamentary Questions

House of Commons	October 1980
House of Lords	November 1981
Non-legislative debates and Early Day Motions	November 1981
Legislative debates	November 1982
House of Commons papers and Bills	May 1979
House of Lords papers and Bills	November 1981
Command papers	May 1979
Public General Acts	May 1979
Local and Personal Acts	November 1982
Statutory Instruments laid before the House	November 1982
Ministerial deposits in the Library	June 1983
Selected UK official publications	January 1982
EC legislative proposals	January 1983
Other selected EC documents	January 1984
Selected international official documents	January 1986
Pamphlets in the Libraries	January 1983
Books in the House of Commons Library	January 1985

— TSO Official Documents website

* **A very useful resource for official publications on the Internet**

— covers all documents published on the Internet by the Stationery Office, plus aims to collate those published on other government websites

— Government department websites

* **Increasingly unusual for departmental documents *not* to be made available on the Internet**

— the ukonline site will get you to the relevant departmental website

— or, as always, just do a Google search for the document (note as official documents are very often in pdf format, other search engines may not work for this)

— Badger or equivalent data on Westlaw UK

* **Generally excellent; if the document itself not indexed, press coverage may lead you to it**

— as well as parliamentary publications, Green Papers and other selected official publications it indexes selected government press releases and articles from the broadsheet newspapers, 1993–

— BOPCRIS (British Official Publications Collaborative Reader Information Service)

* **Index, with abstracts and some full text for about 23,000 selected key documents, Parliamentary and non-Parliamentary, 1688–1995**

— a new collaborative project being led by the Ford Collection of British Official Publications, University of Southampton Library

— initial data based on the hard copy *Ford Breviates and Select Lists of Parliamentary Papers*

— selective but free, so useful if you do not have eg the Chadwyck-Healey *Index to House of Commons Parliamentary Papers on CD-ROM 1801–*

Sources covering TSO publications only

QR7.2   All categories of TSO publications [7.17–7.25]

— The current Stationery Office on-line catalogue

    *   **TSO publications (and publications sold by TSO) currently in print**

        — TSO has a habit of revamping its websites; currently catalogue called clickTSO.com

— TSO monthly and annual catalogues

    *   **The main manual source if an approximate date is known; though recently falling into its bad old ways with regard to currency**

        — arranged in the following sequences

            — HL papers by session and number

            — HL Bills by session and number

            — HL *Hansard*

            — HC papers by session and number

            — HC *Hansard*

            — HC Bills by session and number

            — Command papers by number

            — All publications (except Bills, Acts and *Hansard*) alphabetically by department, body or committee

            — Alphabetical index to all of the above by keyword, chairman, or personal author

        — note that the annual catalogues are based on the calendar year so contain material from, and listed under, different parliamentary sessions

        — some parliamentary committees are numbered 1st, 2nd etc and are listed before the letter A in the main alphabetical list

        — some parliamentary committees are listed in the main alphabetical sequence under 'Select...' if that is their official title, eg Select Committee on Science and Technology, others directly under their name if that is their official title, eg Home Affairs Committee

        — do not include SIs

        — before 1966 annual catalogues grouped in five yearly volumes with continuous pagination and consolidated index

— TSO *Daily List*

    *   **For publications since the last monthly catalogue**

        — no cumulation or index, so no alternative but to read through every one

        — individual lists also batched together as the *Weekly List*

        — also on The Stationery Office website

QR7.3 Parliamentary papers [7.18–7.27]

— *Index to House of Commons Parliamentary Papers 1801–* on CD-ROM
   * **The most comprehensive source, except for very recent papers**
      — issued annually
      — does *not* include those House of Lords papers not also issued as House of Commons papers
      — references to the Chadwyck-Healey microfiche edition of the papers as well as the printed sets
      — data derived from the following two printed sources
— *Parliamentary Papers: General Alphabetical Index* 1900–49; 1950–1958/59; 1959/60–1968/69
   * **More convenient than looking through HMSO catalogues**
— Peter Cockton *Subject Catalogue of the House of Commons Parliamentary Papers 1801–1900* (Chadwyck-Healey, 1988, 5 volumes)
   * **Revolutionised finding nineteenth century papers; still valuable even if you have the CD-ROM above**
      — arranged by broad topics subdivided by narrower topics and within each sub-topic by Bills, reports of commissioners and accounts and papers
      — detailed subject index to main sequence in volume 5
      — gives full references to both printed version and Chadwyck-Healey microfiche edition
— *Parliamentary Papers: General Alphabetical Index* 1801–52; 1852–99
   * **A poorer alternative if the above is not available**
— Sessional indexes to bound sets of Parliamentary papers
   * **If papers kept in this form and date of relevant session known; will also translate an HC number or command number into volume and page reference in bound set**
— *General Index to the House of Lords Papers* 1859–70; 1871–84/85
   * **Only source for the period other than individual sessional indexes**
      — originally issued with the official papers
      — facsimile reprint (Dobbs Ferry, New York: Oceana, 1976)
— *Ford Breviates and Select Lists of Parliamentary Papers* (1696–1983)
   * **Selective and non-cumulative but abstracts provided**
      — for full bibliographical details of the nine volumes see the BOPCRIS website which is currently putting the data from them on the Internet (free of charge)

QR7.4 Parliamentary non-legislative debates and questions [7.27]

— For legislative debates see chapter 4
— Polis or Parlianet
   * **Probably the best source**
      — see QR7.1 above

— *Hansard* on CD-ROM (Commons 1988/89– , Lords 1992/93–)

    * **Quite good for this, though only one session can be searched at a time**

        — one disk per session with intermediate cumulating disks issued after Christmas and Easter recesses

— *Hansard* via the Parliament website (Commons 1988/89– , Lords, 1996/97–)

    * **Free**

— *Hansard*: fortnightly indexes, indexes to bound volumes and sessional indexes

    * **A long business unless you have a good idea of date to start with**

        — printed sessional indexes issued somewhat in arrears

— Contact the House of Commons Information Office

    * **Often the simplest solution, especially for recent material**

QR7.5　Common examples of Parliamentary papers and their categories [7.9]

Annual reports and accounts of public bodies and quangos – HC papers, TSO, the body itself, or not published at all

Charity Commissioners reports – HC papers

Criminal Injuries Compensation Board reports – command papers

Criminal Law Revision Committee reports – command papers

Criminal statistics – command papers

Crown Prosecution Service annual reports – HC papers

Green Papers – command papers (or TSO or department concerned)

Immigration Rules – HC papers

Judicial statistics – command papers

Law Commission reports – HC papers or command papers

Legal Services Ombudsman annual reports – HC papers

Monopolies and Mergers Commission reports – command papers

Ombudsman (Parliamentary Commissioner for Administration) reports – HC papers

Royal Commissions – command papers

Select Committee reports – HC or HL papers

Treaties – command papers

White Papers – command papers

QR7.6　Command paper series and abbreviations [7.10]

1833–1869	1 – 4222
1870–1899	C 1 – C 9550
1900–1918	Cd 1 – Cd 9239
1919–1956	Cmd 1 – Cmd 9889
1957–1986	Cmnd 1 – Cmnd 9927
1986 to date	Cm 1 – [Cm 5000 in 2001]

QR8   Law outside England and Wales

QR8.1   General comparative sources [8.6–8.15]

— *Statesman's Yearbook*
  * **For background on government and constitution, especially for far-flung or volatile parts of the world**
— *Oxford Companion to Law* (1980)
  * **For quick enquiries on foreign legal systems, though getting dated**
— General academic works on comparative law
  — eg Rene David *Major Legal Systems in the World Today*, Konrad Zweigert and Hein Kotz *An Introduction to Comparative Law*, Peter de Cruz *Comparative Law in a Changing World*
— *Modern Legal Systems Cyclopedia* (looseleaf)
  * **Detailed descriptions of legal systems, but bias towards needs of American lawyers**
— *Martindale-Hubbell International Law Digest* (annual)
  * **Very useful brief summaries of the laws of over 60 countries**
— *International Encyclopaedia of Laws* (looseleaf)
  * **Detailed account of laws world-wide in subject modules**
— *International Encyclopedia of Comparative law*
  * **Mainly for academic research; not yet complete; not updated**
— Collections of 'laws of the world' on various subjects
  * **Do not overlook; often a shortcut; some may provide full text translations of legislation**
— *Bibliography of Foreign and Comparative Law Books and Articles in English*
— *Index to Foreign Legal Periodicals*
  * **Articles mostly not in English**
— Thomas H Reynolds and Arturo A Flores *Foreign Law: Current Sources of Codes and Basic Legislation in Jurisdictions of the World* (3 volumes looseleaf)
  * **Invaluable guide to legislation (and also other sources of foreign law)**
    — also available, with numerous links, as an Internet subscription service Foreign Law Guide

— Blaustein *Constitutions of the Countries of the World* (looseleaf)

   *   **The standard hard copy source for the text of constitutions in English**

— University of Würzburg International Constitutional Law and University of Richmond Constitution Finder websites

   *   **Specialist constitutional websites; see also general websites below**

— general foreign law websites and gateways

   *   **Explore, if a general Google search does not get what you want; quite a number to choose from, including**

      — AustLII World Law (one of the best)

      — GLIN from the Library of Congress (texts from official sources)

      — Guide to Law Online 'Nations of the world' section (good set of links from the associated GLIN project)

      — Cornell Law Institute (generally impressive)

      — Eagle-I, SOSIG, Sarah Carter's Lawlinks (good sets of links, with the advantage of being UK-originated)

      — University of Washburn ForInt-Law, Maastricht Internet Law Library, Saarbrücken University Law-Related Internet Project

Other jurisdictions in the British Isles

QR8.2   Wales [8.16]

— Wales Legislation Online website

   *   **For details of devolved application of Acts**

QR8.3   Scotland [8.17–8.28]

— *The Laws of Scotland: Stair Memorial Encyclopaedia*

   *   **A first port of call**

QR8.4   Sources for the text of Acts of the Scottish Parliament [8.23]

— Queen's Printer copies of asps as passed
— HMSO website (as above)
— *Current Law Statutes*
— Butterworths Scottish Legislation Service
— Lawtel (links to the HMSO text as passed)
— Justis Statutes
— Westlaw UK Scots Law module (in consolidated form)
— Butterworths Scotland Direct
— *Parliament House Book* (looseleaf)

      — selection of legislative materials for the practitioner

QR8.5 Sources for the text of Westminster Acts applying only to Scotland [8.23]

— Public General Acts (Queen's Printer copies and HMSO bound volumes)
— HMSO website
— *Current Law Statutes* or *Scottish Current Law Statutes* 1949–90
— Lawtel (links to the HMSO text as passed)
— Justis Statutes
— Westlaw UK Scots Law module (in consolidated form)
— *Statutes in Force* (only updated to 1991)
— *Parliament House Book* (looseleaf)
    — selection of legislative materials for the practitioner

QR8.6 Finding-aids that cover Scottish Acts [8.23]

— electronic full text services as above
— *Current Law*: monthly parts and yearbooks 1991–
— *Scottish Current Law*: yearbooks 1948–90
— *Current Law Legislation Citator*
— *Chronological Table of the Statutes*
— *Is it in Force?*

QR8.7 Finding-aids that cover Scottish cases [8.24–8.27]

— *Current Law*: monthly parts, yearbooks and case citators, and Current Law Cases 1991–
— *Scottish Current Law*: monthly parts, yearbooks and case citators 1948–90
— *Green's Weekly Digest* 1986–
— *Scots Law Times* on CD-ROM
— *The Digest* (selected Scottish cases in the small print cases) and electronic version Case Search (but just name and citation not necessarily the summary at the moment)
— Lexis, full text of:

Reported cases

Session Cases	January 1950–
Scots Law Times	January 1950–
Scottish Criminal Case Reports	January 1981–
Scottish Civil Law Reports	February 1986–

Unreported cases

Scottish House of Lords decisions	July 1986–
All Inner House decisions	January 1982–
All Outer House decisions	January 1985–

— Westlaw UK Scots law module (includes full text cases from *Scots Law Times* 1930–)
— Butterworths Scotland Direct (digests of recent Scottish cases)
— Scottish Court Service website (transcripts of all cases 1998–)
— BAILII

Northern Ireland

QR8.8   Categories of primary legislation for Northern Ireland and where to find them [8.30–8.34]

Sources for the text as given below are as follows:

NI Statutes Revised = *Statutes Revised Northern Ireland* 2nd edn, text of statutes in force as amended as at 31 March 1981. Text also available on the Internet on BAILLI.

NI Statutes = Annual bound volumes as passed, either issued officially as bound volumes, or loose prints bound up with officially supplied title page and tables etc. Note that on the Northern Ireland Legislation part of the HMSO website these are available in full text from 1997, but if they are also UK SIs they are available on the UK part from 1987.

UK Statutes = Public General Acts of the Westminster Parliament available in the various ordinary sources as listed at QR3.1. Note that on the Northern Ireland Legislation part of the HMSO website these are available in full text from 1996, but they will also be available on the UK part from 1988.

UK SIs = Statutory Instruments that will only be available in hard copy as such if loose prints have been retained, and have not been bound as the NI Statutes. Not in the official TSO bound volumes of SIs. But are available in full text as made on the HMSO website from 1987.

— Acts of the Parliament of Ireland 1495–1800

   Text: *NI Statutes Revised* and, as originally passed, *The Statutes at Large Passed in the Parliaments held in Ireland* (20 volumes, 1765–1801)

— Acts of the Parliaments of England and of Great Britain 1226–1800

   Text: *NI Statutes Revised*, UK Statutes

— Acts of the United Kingdom Parliament 1801–1920

   Text: *NI Statutes Revised*, UK Statutes

— Acts of the Northern Ireland Parliament 1921–72

   Text: *NI Statutes Revised*, NI Statutes (with chapter numbers)

— Orders in Council under s 1(3) of the Northern Ireland (Temporary) Provisions Act 1972, 1972–73

   Text: *NI Statutes Revised*, NI Statutes (with NI numbers), UK SIs

— Measures of the Northern Ireland Assembly 1974

   Text: *NI Statutes Revised*, NI Statutes (with chapter numbers)

— Orders in Council under schedule 1 to the Northern Ireland Act 1974, 1974–99

   Text: *NI Statutes Revised* (to 1981only), NI Statutes (with NI numbers), UK SIs

—   Acts of the Northern Ireland Assembly 2000–

     Text: NI Statutes (with chapter numbers)

—   Orders in Council under the schedule to the Northern Ireland Act 2000 (during suspension of Assembly) 2000, (2001– ?)

     Text: NI Statutes (with NI numbers), UK SIs

—   Orders in Council under s 85 of the Northern Ireland Act 1998 (reserved matters), 2001–

     Text: NI Statutes (with NI numbers), UK SIs

—   Acts of the United Kingdom Parliament 1921–

     Text: UK Statutes

QR8.9 Law reports [8.35]

—   *Northern Ireland Law Reports*

     —   also on **Lexis** 1945–

—   *Northern Ireland Law Reports Judgments Bulletin*

     —   also on **Lexis** 1984–

—   a few cases so far, 1999– , on **BAILII**

—   some early cases in general Irish sources, eg *Irish Law Times Reports*

—   *Index to Northern Ireland Cases 1921 to 1997*

—   Cases in the *Northern Ireland Law Reports* also covered in the *Irish Digest* (to 1993, also on CD-ROM)

QR8.10 Finding-aids for legislation and law reports [8.34–8.35]

—   *Current Law*

—   *Bulletin of Northern Ireland Law*

—   **Badger,** indexes Northern Ireland Statutory Rules and Orders, 1993–

—   Statutory Rules and Orders on HMSO website 1998– , with selected items back to 1991

—   *Index to the Statutes* and *Chronological Table of the Statutes, Northern Ireland* (HMSO, Belfast)

—   *Index to the Statutory Rules and Orders of Northern Ireland*

QR8.11 Isle of Man [8.36–8.41]

—   Comparative works and journal articles on tax havens (examples at **8.36**)

—   Peter W Edge *Manx Public Law* (Isle of Man Law Society, 1997)

—   Edwards report (Cm 4109, 1998)

—   Bibliography of Manx legal literature in W Twining and J Uglow *Law Publishing and Legal Information: Small Jurisdictions of the British Isles* (1981)

—   Types of legislation:

     —   (1) Acts of Tynwald (which require Royal Assent)

— (2) United Kingdom statutes extended to the Isle of Man by Orders in Council (which are UK SIs)

— (3) Manx Statutory Documents (which are subordinate legislation made under 1 or 2)

— *Juta's Statutes of the Isle of Man* (Acts of Tynwald in consolidated form), regular hard copy editions + CD-ROM version

— *Isle of Man Orders in Council* (3rd edn, 2001)

— Isle of Man Government website: Acts of Tynwald 2001– , other materials eg consultation papers etc

— Tynwald website: progress of Bills (but not text), *Hansard* and other information

— *Subject Guide to the Acts of Tynwald including Alphabetical and Chronological Lists of the Acts* (annual)

— *Chronological Table of, Acts of Parliament Extending or Relating to the Isle of Man* (4th edn, 1998)

— *Subject Guide and Chronological Table to Subordinate Legislation* (1981)

— Central Reference Library, Government Buildings, Douglas, Isle of Man

    — for information on and copies of legislation

— *Manx Law Reports* 1952– (has cumulative tables and indexes)

— *A Book of Precedents: a List of Constitutional and Privy Council Judgments Affecting the Isle of Man from 1523 to 1991* (2nd edn, 1992)

— *Manx Law Bulletin* 1983–

QR8.12 Channel Islands [8.42–8.45]

— A G Chloros *Bibliographical Guide to the Law of the United Kingdom, the Channel Islands and the Isle of Man* (2nd edn, 1973)

— *Tolley's Taxation in the Channel Islands and the Isle of Man* (annual)

— Comparative works and journal articles on tax havens (see examples at **8.36**)

— Edwards report (Cm 4109, 1998)

— Types of legislation:

    — (1) United Kingdom statutes extended to particular islands by Orders in Council (which are UK SIs)

    — (2) Primary legislation passed by the legislatures on each island and then required to be sanctioned by Her Majesty by Orders in Council (which are *not* UK SIs)

    — (3) Legislation passed by the legislatures on each island under general powers granted by Orders in Council (Jersey) or under common law powers to legislate (Guernsey)

    — (4) Subsidiary legislation made on each island under powers delegated by 1, 2 or 3 above

QR8.13 Jersey [8.46–8.50]

— Stéphanie Nicolle *The Origin and Development of Jersey Law* (rev edn, States Greffe, 1998)

— Anthony Dessain and Michael Wilkins *Jersey Insolvency Law and Practice* (2nd edn, Key Haven, 2001)
— Paul Matthews and Terry Sowden *The Jersey Law of Trusts* (3rd edn, Key Haven, 1994)
— Paul Matthews and Stéphanie Nicolle *The Jersey Law of Property* (Key Haven, 1991)
— F de L Bois *A Constitutional History of Jersey* (1972)
— *Jersey Law Review* 1997– (indexed on Legal Journals Index)
— Series of legislation:
  — *Laws* (formerly *Recueil des lois*) ie category 2 above
  — *Regulations and Orders*, containing
    — regulations of three years duration (category 3 above)
    — regulations (or rules) of the States of indefinite duration (4 above)
    — acts (for eg commencements and treaties)
    — orders made by Committees of the States
— Jersey Legal Information Board website: legislation 1997– , consolidated court rules, practice directions 1979– , pre-legislative materials, *Jersey Law Review* pre-current years, and unreported judgments (full-text only to registered users) 1997–
— *General Index of Legislation* (annual)
— *Jersey Law Reports* 1985– (with cumulative tables and index, also covering *Jersey Judgments*)
— *Jersey Judgments* 1950–84
— *Table des décisions* 1884–1963; 1964–78
  — no recognised law reports or judgments in the English manner before 1950
  — 1884–1963 volumes a digest in French of the decisions filed at the Royal Court
  — 1964–78 volume a digest mostly in English of cases not reported in *Jersey Judgments*

QR8.14 Guernsey [8.51–8.53]

— Raymond Ashton *An Analysis of the Guernsey Law of Trusts* (Key Haven, 1998)
— Raymond Ashton *Guernsey Company Law* (Key Haven, forthcoming 2001)
— D E Thompson *Guernsey Company and Trust Law Handbook* (Guernsey Financial Services Commission, 1991)
  — reprints relevant legislation
— David Ehmann and Paul Le Pelley *A Guide to the Constitution of Guernsey* (Guernsey Press, 1993)
— Sir John Loveridge *The Constitution and Law of Guernsey* (Société Guernesiaise, 1975)
— G Rowland 'The Bailiwick of Guernsey' (1992) 23 *Law Librarian* 181–188

— J M Beaumont *The Constitution and Administration of Sark* (Guernsey Press, 1993)

— Series of legislation:

   — *Laws* (also called *Orders in Council*, formerly *Recueil d'ordres en conseil*) ie category 2 as described at QR8.12

   — *Ordinances* (formerly *Ordonnances*), containing both legislation made by the States under Laws and under common law powers

   — *Orders of the Royal Court*, containing rules of the Court and defence regulations

   — *Statutory Instruments* (*not* UK SIs) made by Committees (ie Ministries) of the States under Laws

— Alderney and Sark each have their own *Orders in Council* and *Ordinances*

— *Guernsey Law Journal* (1985–)

   — digest of legislation and cases (including Alderney and Sark) and occasional articles; a little tardy in coming out at the moment; indexed on *Legal Journals Index*

Other common law jurisdictions

QR8.15   Republic of Ireland [8.54–8.58]

— Thomas O'Malley *The Round Hall Guide to Sources of Law: and Introduction to Legal Research and Writing* (Round Hall Press, 1993)

— Textbooks published by Butterworths Ireland and Sweet & Maxwell Roundhall; Law Society manuals from Blackstone Press

— *Gazette of the Incorporated Law Society*, *Irish Law Times*, *Irish Jurist*

— Irish legal journals indexed on *Legal Journals Index* from 1993

— *Acts of the Oireachtas*

   — index 1922–86

   — chronological table to 1995

— Irish legislation (primary and secondary) as passed 1922–98 on CD-ROM, BAILII and the Attorney-General Office's website

— *Irish Current Law Statutes Annotated* 1984–

— *Statutory Instruments*

   — index 1922–79

— *Irish Reports* (also on CD-ROM from Context, 1919–), *Irish Law Reports Monthly*

— All written judgments of superior courts distributed 1976–

   — indexed in *Index to Irish Superior Court Written Judgments 1976–1982* and in 'pink lists' supplement to *Gazette of the Incorporated Law Society* to 1996; and from May 2001 from First Law

— electronic Irish Weekly Law Reports all reserved judgments July 1998–

— *Irish Digest* 1894–1993 (9 volumes, also on CD-ROM from Context 1919–)

— *The Digest* (selected Irish cases among small print cases)
— *Irish Current Law Monthly Digest* 1995–
— Irish Law Site from University College Cork

United States

QR8.16 Legal research guides [8.59]

— Morris L Cohen and Kent C Olson *How to Find the Law in a Nutshell* (7th edn, West, 2000)
— Robert C Berring and Elizabeth A Edinger *Finding the Law* (11th edn, West, 1999)
— J Myron Jacobstein, Roy Mersky and Donald J Dunn *Fundamentals of Legal Research* (7th edn, Foundation Press, 1998)
— annotated bibliography of research guides, 'Finding the law', on Cornell Law Library website

QR8.17 Internet resources: some starting points [8.61]

— Cornell Legal Information Institute
— FindLaw
— American Association of Law Libraries – links to the 13 mostly highly rated gateways
— American Bar Association Lawlink – annotated links
— SOSIG – annotated links

QR8.18 Textbooks and journals [8.63]

— Francis R Doyle *Searching the Law* (2nd edn, Transnational, 1999)
— Francis R Doyle *Searching the Law: the States: a Selective Bibliography of State Practice Materials in the 50 States* (3rd edn, Transnational, 1999)
— *Index to Legal Periodicals and Books*
— *Current Law Index* or Legaltrak
— University Law Review Project

QR8.19 Federal legislation [8.64]

— *United States Code*
    * **The official unannotated version, but commercially published annotated versions usually to be preferred:**
        — *United States Code Annotated* (West)
        — *United States Code Service* (Lawyers Co-operative)
— *Statutes at Large* (Public Laws)
    — equivalent of bound volumes of Queen's Printer copies of Public General Acts

—   *Federal Register*
     —   published daily containing the equivalent of SIs
—   *Code of Federal Regulations*
     —   consolidation of above
—   all the above available on GPO Access, the federal government printer's website

QR8.20   Law reports [8.66-8.73]

—   *United States Supreme Court Reports* (US)
     *   **The official edition, but commercially published annotated versions often to be preferred:**
       —   *Lawyers' Edition* (L Ed) (Lawyers' Co-operative)
       —   *Supreme Court Reporter* (S Ct) (West) from 1882 only
       —   US reports from 1893 on FindLaw; also from 1990 on US Supreme Court and Cornell (with selected earlier decisions)
—   *Federal Reporter* 1880–
     —   part of West's *National Reporter System*
—   *Federal Supplement* 1932–
     —   part of West's *National Reporter System*
     —   District Court reports, hived off from the above
—   *Federal Cases*
     —   reprint of pre-1880 federal nominate reports
—   *National Reporter*
     —   comprehensive collection of state reports arranged by region (with additional separate reporters for California and New York)
     —   likely to be the only (printed) source of state reports available
—   *National Reporter Blue Book*
     —   converts a state report citation to a *National Reporter* citation
—   *American Law Reports*
     —   selected cases only but commentary and annotations
     —   from 1969 state cases only
—   *American Law Reports Federal*
     —   as above for federal cases from 1969
—   Lexis or Westlaw
     *   **For text of all American law reports if printed copies not available; by far the best way to research American cases**
—   Most federal and state appellate court decisions on the Internet from 1990s: use both Cornell and FindLaw
—   Printed finding aids:
     —   *American Digest* and *General Digest* (West)
     —   *Corpus Juris Secundum*
     —   *American Jurisprudence*
     —   *Shepard's Citations*

QR8.21 Commonwealth in general [8.74–8.78]

— Donald Raistrick *Lawyers' Lawbooks* (3rd edn, Bowker Saur, 1997), includes selected Commonwealth textbooks

— *International Legal Books in Print* (Bowker Saur, 1994)

— *A Legal Bibliography of the British Commonwealth* (2nd edn, Sweet & Maxwell, 1955–64)

— Jerry Dupont *The Common Law Abroad: Constitutional and Legal Legacy of the British Empire: an Annotated Bibliography of Titles Relating to the Colonial Dependencies of Great Britain* (Rothman, 2001)

— *Commonwealth Legal Bulletin*

— Wallace Breem and Sally Phillips *Bibliography of Commonwealth Law Reports* (Mansell 1991)

— Institute of Advanced Legal Studies *Union List of Commonwealth and South African Law* (2nd edn, 1963)

— *Law Reports of the Commonwealth* 1980–

Australia

QR8.22 Legal research guides [8.79]

— Enid Campbell *Legal Research: Materials and Methods* (4th edn, LBC, 1996)

— Surendra Dayal *E-Law Research: Your Guide to Electronic Legal Research* (Butterworths, 2000)

— Deakin University School of Law Research Staff *Researching Australian Law* (LBC, 1997)

— Andrew D Mitchell and Tania Voon *Legal Research Manual* (LBC, 2000)

— Irene Nemes and Graeme Cross *Effective Legal Research* (Butterworths, 1998)

QR8.23 Textbooks and journals [8.80–8.81]

— *Halsbury's Laws of Australia* (Butterworths)

— *Laws of Australia* (LBC)

— Attorney General's Information Service (AGIS), the main journal indexing service (available on Lexis)

QR8.24 Legislation [8.82–8.84]

— AustLII

    — all Commonwealth statutes in the 1973 consolidation and passed since

    — all reprints of individual Commonwealth statutes

    — reprints of Statutory Rules 1989– and numbered Statutory Rules

    — reprints of consolidated legislation for all the states

    — numbered legislation as passed for some of the states

— Scaleplus
  — official site but generally does not have anything that AustLII does not, except surperseded reprints of Acts for the Commonwealth and some states
— *Acts of the Parliament of Australia*
  — consolidation to 1973
  — individual Acts as passed
  — reprints of individual Acts as amended
— *Statutory Rules*
  — consolidation to 1956
  — individual Rules as passed
  — reprints of individual Rules as amended
— *Federal Legislation Annotations* (Butterworths), three yearly with supplements
  — alphabetically by Act
  — includes all Acts in the 1973 consolidation and passed since 1973
  — annotations:
    — whether reprinted
    — amendments and repeals
    — operation dates
    — regulations made under Acts
    — case law
— *Commonwealth Statutes Annotations* (LBC)

QR8.25   Law Reports [8.85–8.89]

— AustLII
  — all High Court judgments 1947– plus title, citation, judges, list of cases cited only from *Commonwealth Law Reports* 1903–46
  — all state supreme court decisions from varying dates 1980s/1990s
  — various other tribunal decisions
— Scaleplus
  — AustLII has more; with only minor exceptions nothing on here that is not on AustLII
— *Australian Legal Monthly Digest* (Law Book Co)
— *Australian Digest*
— *Australian Case Citator* 1825–
— *Australian Current Law* (Butterworths)
— *Australian and New Zealand Citator to UK Reports*
  — see QR5.19
— *The Digest* (selected Australian cases in the small print cases)

Canada

QR8.26   Legal research guides [8.90]

— Douglass T MacEllven *Legal Research Handbook* (4th edn, Butterworths, 1998)
— Margaret A Banks *Banks on Using a Law Library* (6th edn, Carswell, 1994)
— Jacqueline R Castel and Omeela K Latchman *The Practical Guide to Canadian Legal Research* (2nd edn, Carswell, 1996)

QR8.27   Textbooks and journals [8.91]

— *Index to Canadian Legal Literature*
  — part of the *Canadian Abridgment*
  — books and articles
  — supplemented by *Canadian Legal Literature* issued as part of the *Canadian Current Law* service
— *Index to Canadian Legal Periodical Literature*

QR8.28   Legislation [8.92–8.93]

— University of Montreal LexUM
  — links to legislatures and government printers providing legislation on the Internet
— CanLII
  — so far consolidated federal statutes and regulations, statutes as passed 1995– ; no state material yet
— *Revised Statutes of Canada* (looseleaf, 1985–)
— *Canada Gazette*
  — statutes and regulations as passed
  — available in pdf format 1998–
— *Consolidated Regulations of Canada* (1978)
— *Canada Statute Citator*
  — federal statutes only
  — amendments, repeals, dates in force, and cases
— *Canadian Current Law: Legislation*
  — federal and provincial statutes
  — three sections:
    — progress of Bills
    — amendments, repeals, and entry into force
    — regulations by enabling Act
  — parts consolidated as the *Legislation Annual*

QR8.29   Law reports [8.94–8.96]

— LexUM
  — links to Supreme Court decisions 1985– , Federal Court decisions 1993– various provincial court decisions starting in the 1990s
— CANLII
  — does not yet have all there is; use individual sites through LexUM as well
— *Canadian Abridgment*
  — vast digest of case law
— *Canadian Current Law: Jurisprudence*
  — digest of federal and provincial cases by subject
  — includes many unreported cases
— *Canadian Current Law: Canadian Citations*
  — cases judicially considered
  — legislation judicially considered
— Quicklaw
  — main commercial database; to be made available in UK through Context

QR8.30   New Zealand [8.97–8.100]

— Margaret Grevill, Scott Davidson and Richard Scragg *Legal Research and Writing in New Zealand* (Butterworths, 2000)
  — appendix includes a bibliography of the main current legal texts
— Auckland District Law Society
  — good set of New Zealand law links
— *The Laws of New Zealand* (Butterworths), equivalent of *Halsbury's Laws*
— *New Zealand Law Journal*
— *Statutes of New Zealand*
  — consolidation 1957
  — statutes as passed
  — statutes as amended reissued in numbered bound volumes, *Reprinted Statutes of New Zealand*
— *Table of New Zealand Acts and Ordinances and Statutory Regulations in force* (annual)
— Knowledge Basket
  — statutes as passed in browsable but not searchable form
— Brooker's
  — New Zealand Court of Appeal decisions 1995–
— *New Zealand Case Law Digest* (Brooker's)
— *Butterworths Current Law*
— *Abridgment of New Zealand Case Law*
— Lexis: *New Zealand Law Reports* 1970–

Other Commonwealth countries

QR8.31 Africa [8.102]

— *Journal of African Law* (indexed on *Legal Journals Index*)
— Wits Law School
  — South African Constitutional Court judgments, and from 1999 Supreme Court judgments
— Parliament of South Africa
  — Acts as passed 1993–

QR8.32 India and Pakistan [8.103]

— *All India Reporter* (AIR)
  — includes legislation as well as cases
  — covers both central and state materials
— *All Pakistan Legal Decisions* (PLD)

QR8.33 Malaysia, Singapore and Brunei [8.104]

— *Halsbury's Laws of Malaysia*
— *Halsbury's Laws of Singapore*
— *Malayan Law Journal*
  — main series of law reports for Malyasia and, until 1991 Singapore, as well as articles
— *Singapore Law Reports* 1992–
— *All Malaysia Law Reports* 1992–
— *Mallal's Digest of Malaysian and Singapore Case Law* (4th edn, 1990–)
  — also lists main relevant legislation for each topic
— *Mallal's Current Law*
  — various titles back to 1987
  — covers both cases and legislation: similar to the English *Current Law*
— CLJ Legal Network
  — main on-line service, but subscribers only

QR8.34 Hong Kong [8.105–8.107]

— *Halsbury's Laws of Hong Kong*
— *Hong Kong Law Journal*
— *Laws of Hong Kong*
  — official looseleaf consolidation containing both primary and secondary legislation in English and Chinese
— *The Hong Kong Gazette*

— the official vehicle for promulgating legislation as past; available on the Internet as well as hard copy (full title *The Government of the Hong Kong Special Administrative Region Gazette*)

— BLIS (Bilingual Laws Information Service)

— the full text of the *Laws of Hong Kong*, fully searchable free of charge

— text up to date to within a few days; text to be amended marked with a 'pencil tick' within 24 hours of the publication of the *Gazette*

— provides point of time research for text no longer in the looseleaf edition

— *Annotated Ordinances of Hong Kong* (Butterworths)

— selected statutes in amended and annotated form

— *Hong Kong Law Reports and Digest*

— merger of *Hong Kong Law Reports* and *Hong Kong Law Digest* in 1997

— the official series

— two parts a month, first part reports, second part reports and digests of additional cases

— available on CD-ROM and online from 1903

— *Hong Kong Court of Final Appeal Reports*

— a spin off from HKLRD, in which the cases also appear

— LJAS – Latest Judgments Alert Service

— Westlaw International

— includes HKLR, HKLD and JLAS

— *Hong Kong Cases* 1991– (with retrospective coverage to 1946)

— also available on Lexis

QR8.35   Caribbean [8.108]

— a few student textbooks now available from Cavendish

— *Caribbean Law Review* 1992–

— Annual cumulative indexes to primary and secondary legislation in force in each of the Islands prepared by the West Indian Legislation Indexing Project based at the Faculty of Law, University of West Indies, Barbados (distributed by US publisher William Gaunt)

— *West Indian Reports* 1959– (also as a module on Butterworths LEXIS Direct)

— *Law Reports of the Bahamas* 1965–

— *Cayman Islands Law Reports* 1980–

— *Jamaica Law Reports*

— current series being published retrospectively with coverage from 1933, but still very incomplete

— law reports covering cases from the offshore jurisdictions, eg *Butterworths Offshore Service, International Tax Reports, Wills and Trusts Law Reports*

— some nascent websites, eg Supreme Court of Jamaica, Supreme Court of Trinidad and Tobago; also scattered legislation, for which use AustLII World Law

QR8.36 Pacific [8.109]

— Jacqueline D Elliott *Pacific Law Bibliography* (Pacific Law Press, 1990)
— Jennifer Corrin Care, Tess Newton and Don Patterson *Introduction to South Pacific Law* (Cavendish, 1999)
— Jennifer Corrin Care *Contract Law in the South Pacific* (Cavendish, 2001)
— University of the South Pacific School of Law
  — indexes to legislation (not full text yet); some recent court decisions
— PacLII
  — a prototype at the moment, being developed with the above by AustLII

QR8.37 European countries [8.110–8.116]

— Individually published translations of particular codes
  — only very selectively available
— *Commercial Laws of Europe*
  — monthly, translations of texts of legislation
— *European Commercial Cases*
  — monthly, translations of text of cases
— *International Litigation Procedure*
  — includes translations of cases from European countries; strong on Brussels Convention cases
— *European Current Law* 1992–
  — similar to the English companion
  — covers all European countries, not just EC member states
  — precursor: *European Law Digest* 1973–91
— Peter Kaye *European Case Law on the Judgments Convention* (Wiley, 1998)
— Lexis
  — French legislation from 1955
  — various French law reports from 1959
  — both of the above are in French!

C. List and Index of Websites and Web-based Services

Name	Address	Paragraph in main text
About	about.com	1.45
Adobe Acrobat Reader	www.adobe.com	1.45
All England Direct	www.butterworths.co.uk	5.9; 5.24; 5.26; 5.27; 5.28; 5.36; 5.73; 5.78; 5.114; 5.118; 5.126; 5.137
All ER (EC) *see* Butterworths EU Direct		
Altavista	uk.altavista.com	1.43; 1.45
American Association of Law Libraries	www.aallnet.org	8.61
American Bar Association's Lawlink	www.lawtechnology.org/lawlink/	8.61
American Society of International Law (ASIL)	www.asil.org	6.13; 6.16; 6.36
Aslib's Index to Theses *see* Index to Theses		2.35
Attorney-General's Office (Ireland)	www.irlgov.ie/ag	8.56
Auckland District Law Society	www.adls.org.nz	8.100
AustLII (Australian Legal Information Institute)	www.austlii.org	5.23; 6.16; 8.13; 8.15; 8.82; 8.83; 8.85; 8.86; 8.92; 8.94; 8.100; 8.108; 8.109
Australian Treaties Library	www.austlii.org/au/other/dfat/	6.16
Badger	www.sweetandmaxwell.co.uk	3.39; 3.40; 3.44; 3.46; 3.67; 3.69; 3.89; 3.91; 3.98; 3.101; 3.105; 3.131; 3.135; 3.170; 4.6; 4.60; 5.37; 7.20; 8.34
BAILII (British and Irish Legal Information Institute)	www.bailii.org	5.23; 5.24; 8.24; 8.33; 8.35; 8.56; 8.58; 8.94
Bar Council *see* General Council of the Bar		
Bar Directory	www.sweetandmaxwell.co.uk/bardirectory/website/	2.56
BLIS (Hong Kong Bilingual Laws Information Service)	www.justice.gov.hk/index.htm	8.106
BOPCRIS	www.bopcris.ac.uk	7.18
British Library catalogue	blpc.bl.uk	1.47; 2.13; 2.34

Name	Address	Paragraph in main text
Brooker's	www.brookers.co.nz/legal/judgments/	8.100
Butterworths All England Direct *see* All England Direct		
Butterworths CaseBase	www.lexislegal.com/aus/butterworths/ butterworths.asp	8.89
Butterworths Case Search	www.butterworths.co.uk	5.70; 5.78; 5.112; 5.125; 5.136; 8.26
Butterworths EU Direct	www.butterworths.co.uk	3.127; 5.38; 5.83
Butterworths Law Direct	www.butterworths.co.uk	2.25; 3.34; 3.40; 3.64; 5.24; 5.73; 5.78
Butterworths LEXIS Direct	www.butterworths.co.uk	2.2; 2.4; 3.26; 3.49; 3.58; 3.87; 3.98; 3.105; 5.7; 5.11; 5.26; 5.54; 5.130; 8.108
Butterworths Scotland Direct	www.butterworths.co.uk	8.21; 8.23; 8.27
Canada Gazette	canada.gc.ca/gazette/	8.92
CANLII (Canadian Legal Information Institute)	www.canlii.org	8.92; 8.94
Case Search *see* Butterworths Case Search		
CaseBase (Butterworths Australia) *see* Butterworths CaseBase		
Casebase (Smith Bernal)	www.casetrack.com/casebase	5.24; 5.114
Casetrack	www.casetrack.com	5.24; 5.29; 5.114
Celex; *see also* Butterworths EU Direct, Justis, Lawtel EU, Lexis, Lovdata, OJ Online, Westlaw (not UK)	europa.eu.int/celex/htm/celex_en.htm	3.121; 3.127; 3.128; 3.129; 3.133; 3.134; 3.135; 4.85; 5.38; 5.85; 6.17; 6.18
Chambers Guide to the Legal Profession	www.chambersandpartners.com	2.52; 2.58; 2.65
Charity Commissioners	www.charity-commission.gov.uk	7.4
CLJ Legal Network	www.cljlaw.com	8.104
Commission of the European Communities	europa.eu.int/comm/index_en.htm	4.87
Competition Commission	www.competition-commission.org.uk	7.11

Name	Address	Paragraph in main text
ConnectingLegal	www.connectinglegal.com	2.51
Constitution Finder *see* University of Richmond Constitution Finder		
COPAC	copac.ac.uk/copac	2.13; 8.78
Cornell Law Library	www.lawschool.cornell.edu/library	8.59
Cornell Legal Information Institute	www.law.cornell.edu	1.48; 6.16; 8.15; 8.61; 8.67; 8.69
Council of Europe	www.coe.int	6.19; 6.32
Council of the European Union	ue.eu.int/en/summ.htm	4.87
Council of the European Union Agreements Office	ue.eu.int/accords	6.18; 6.32
Court Service	www.courtservice.gov.uk	2.60; 5.24; 5.38; 5.24; 5.47; 5.104
Crawford's Online	www.crawfordsonline.co.uk	2.66
Current Law Cases	www.sweetandmaxwell.co.uk	2.21; 5.79; 5.81; 5.82; 5.114; 5.116; 5.120; 5.123; 5.124; 5.125; 5.126; 5.130; 5.135; 5.147; 5.149
Current Law Case Citator	www. sweetandmaxwell.co.uk	2.21; 5.68; 5.78; 5.112; 5.114; 5.116; 5.119; 5.120; 5.135; 5.136; 5.137; 5.139; 5.140; 5.143; 8.25
Current Law Legislation Citator	www. sweetandmaxwell.co.uk	3.56; 3.67; 3.105; 5.76; 5.143; 5.147; 8.82; 8.98
Current Law Statute Citator *see* Current Law Legislation Citator		
Current Legal Information	www. sweetandmaxwell.co.uk	1.37; 2.19; 2.21; 5.76
Current Legal Research *see* Institute of Advanced Legal Studies		
Daily List *see* TSO Daily List		
Daily Telegraph *see* Telegraph		

Name	Address	Paragraph in main text
Delia Venables' Legal Resources	www.venables.co.uk	1.48; 2.53; 5.24
Department for Education and Skills	www.dfes.gov.uk	7.11
Department for Work and Pensions	www.dwp.gov.uk	5.24
Department of Trade and Industry	www.dti.gov.uk	4.91
Department of Trade and Industry Single Market Legislation UK Contact List	www.dti.gov.uk/support/adm_coop.htm	4.91
Directory of Community Legislation in Force *see* EUR-Lex		
Dissertation Abstracts International	wwwlib.umi.com/dissertations	2.35
DTI *see* Department of Trade and Industry		
Eagle-I	ials.sas.ac.uk/links/eagle-i.htm	1.48; 6.16; 8.15
EG interactive *see* Estates Gazette interactive		
Electronic Law Journals Project	elj.warwick.ac.uk	2.28
electronic Irish Weekly Law Reports	www.firstlaw.ie	8.58
electronic Law Reports	www.context.co.uk	5.7; 5.123
Ellis (Celex) *see* OJ Online		
Employment Appeal Tribunal	www.employmentappeals.gov.uk	5.24
English Short-title Catalogue	www.rlg.org/estc.html	2.16
Estates Gazette interactive	www.egi.co.uk	5.11
EU Direct (Butterworths LEXIS Direct)	www.butterworths.co.uk	3.127
EUR-Lex	europa.eu.int/eur-lex/en/index.html	3.122; 3.127; 3.128; 3.129; 3.131; 3.133; 4.85
EUR-OP	eur-op.eu.int	3.127
Europa	europa.eu.int	2.32; 3.128; 4.87; 6.17
European Court of Human Rights	www.echr.coe.int	1.47; 5.47; 5.50; 5.51; 5.54; 5.55; 5.86; 5.120; 5.132; 5.147
European Court of Justice	europa.eu.int/cj	5.38; 5.85

Name	Address	Paragraph in main text
European Information Association	www.eia.org.uk	4.84
European Information Network in the UK	www.europe.org.uk	4.91
European Parliament	www.europarl.eu.int	4.87
European Parliament. London office	www.europarl.org.uk	4.91
Faculty of Advocates	www.advocates.org.uk	2.62
FCO *see* Foreign and Commonwealth Office		
Financial Journals Index	www.sweetandmaxwell.co.uk	2.18
Financial Services Authority	www.fsa.gov.uk	3.162
FindLaw	www.findlaw.com	2.28; 8.61; 8.67; 8.69
Fletcher School of Diplomacy	fletcher.tufts.edu	6.16
Foot and Mouth	www.defra.gov.uk/animals/diseases/fmd/default.htm	1.18
Foreign and Commonwealth Office	www.fco.gov.uk	6.10; 6.31; 6.32; 7.11
Foreign Law Guide	www.foreignlawguide.com	8.12
ForInt-Law *see* University of Washburn		
Gazette of Law Society of Ireland *see* Law Society of Ireland Gazette		
General Council of the Bar	www.barcouncil.org.uk	2.59
Global Legal Information Network *see* Library of Congress: Global Legal Information Network		
Google	www.google.com	1.1; 1.22; 1.45; 1.46; 1.47; 8.15
GPO Access	www.access.gpo.gov	8.64
Gray's Inn	www.graysinn.org.uk	2.59
Guide to Law Online *see* Library of Congress Guide to Law Online		
Hague Conference on Private International Law	www.hcch.net/e/index.html	6.16
Halsbury's Direct	www.butterworths.co.uk	2.2
Hammicks catalogue	www.hammickslegal.com	2.12
Hansard – Commons	www.parliament.the-stationery-office.co.uk/pa/cm/cmpubns.htm	4.49; 7.19

Name	Address	Paragraph in main text
Hansard – Lords	www.parliament.the-stationery-office.co.uk/pa/ld/ldhansrd.htm	4.49; 7.19
Hemscott Net	www.hemscott.net	2.66
HMSO	www.hmso.gov.uk	3.17; 3.18; 3.27; 3.46; 3.67; 3.87; 3.149; 8.23; 8.33; 8.34
Home Office	www.homeoffice.gov.uk	7.11
Hong Kong Cases	(via Lexis)	8.107
Hong Kong Department of Justice	www.info.gov.hk/justice	8.106
Hong Kong Gazette	www.info.gov.hk/pd/egazette	8.106
Hong Kong Law Reports and Digest	www.smlawpub.com.hk	8.107
House of Lords	www.parliament.uk	4.89
HUDOC *see* European Court of Human Rights		
Human Rights Commission (New Zealand)	www.hrc.co.nz/org/legal/index.htm	8.100
ICJ *see* International Court of Justice		
Index to Legal Periodicals and Books	www.hwwilson.com	2.27
Index to Theses	www.theses.com	2.35
Infolaw	www.infolaw.co.uk	2.53
Inner Temple	www.innertemple.org.uk	2.59
Inns of Court catalogues	www.smlawpub.jhc.net/inns.htm	2.13
Institute of Advanced Legal Studies	ials.sas.ac.uk	2.13; 2.35
International Constitutional Law *see* University of Würzburg		
International Constitutional Law		
International Court of Justice	www.icj-cij.org	6.36
International Labour Organization	www.ilo.org	6.32
International Law in Brief	www.asil.org.ilibindx.htm	6.36
International Law List	www.intl-lawlist.com	2.63
Irish Bar Council	www.lawlibrary.ie	2.62
Irish Law Site	www.irish-law.org	8.58

Name	Address	Paragraph in main text
Isle of Man Government	www.gov.im	8.39
Jersey Financial Services Commission	www.jerseyfsc.org	8.50
Jersey Law Review	www.jerseylegalinfo.je/publications/jerseylawreview	8.46; 8.50
Jersey Legal Information Board	www.jerseylegalinfo.je/	8.48; 8.50
Jordans	www.jordans.co.uk	5.11
Journal of Information Law and Technology	elj.warwick.ac.uk/jilt	2.28
Justis Celex	www.justis.com	3.127; 3.129; 3.133; 3.135; 4.91; 5.38; 5.85; 5.119
Justis European References	www.justis.com	2.32
Justis Human Rights	www.justis.com	5.54
Justis: law reports databases	www.justis.com	2.48; 5.7; 5.8; 5.11; 5.38; 5.81; 5.118; 5.146; 8.96
Justis Statutes	www.justis.com	3.24; 3.45; 3.46; 3.49; 3.50; 3.57; 3.77; 3.141; 3.155; 8.23; 8.33
Justis Statutory Instruments	www.justis.com	3.67; 3.87; 3.98; 3.103; 3.105
Justis Parlianet *see* Parlianet		
Knowledge Basket	www.knowledge-basket.co.nz	8.100
Latest Judgments Alert Service (Hong Kong)	www.smlawpub.com.hk	8.107
Law Commission	www.lawcom.gov.uk	4.6; 7.11
Law Direct *see* Butterworths Law Direct		
Law Society Directory *see* Solicitors Online		
Law Society's Directory of Expert Witnesses	www.expertsearch.co.uk	2.61
Law Society of England and Wales	www.lawsoc.org.uk	2.54
Law Society of Ireland	www.lawsociety.ie	8.55
Law Society of Ireland Gazette	www.lawsociety.ie/gaze.htm	8.55
Law Society of Scotland	www.lawscot.org.uk	2.62

Name	Address	Paragraph in main text
Lawlinks *see* Sarah Carter's Lawlinks		
Lawtel	www.lawtel.com	1.5; 1.37; 2.25; 3.27; 3.40; 3.44; 3.46; 3.87; 3.98; 3.100; 3.103; 3.105; 3.135; 5.27; 5.28; 5.36; 5.38; 5.54; 5.80; 5.114; 5.118; 5.126; 5.130; 5.137; 7.20; 8.23
Lawtel EU	www.lawtel.com	3.128; 3.136
Lawyer Locator (International and US) *see* Martindale-Hubbell		
Lawyer Locator (UK)	www.lawyerlocator.co.uk	2.51
The Legal 500	www.icclaw.com/l500/uk.htm	2.52; 2.58; 2.64
Legal Journals Index	www.sweetandmaxwell.co.uk	2.19; 2.22; 3.41; 3.75; 3.131; 3.170; 5.61; 5.82; 5.112; 5.126; 8.11; 8.55; 8.111
Legal Resources on the Internet *see* Delia Venables		
LegalTrac (via InfoTrac)	infotrac.galegroup.com	2.27
Legislation Direct *see* Butterworths LEXIS Direct		
Lexis (UK users linking from Butterworths)	web.lexis-nexis.com/professional	1.2; 1.24; 1.36; 1.37; 1.38; 2.25; 2.27; 2.28; 2.48; 3.26; 3.46; 3.49; 3.58; 3.87; 3.98; 3.105; 3.127; 3.150; 5.7; 5.8; 5.9; 5.11; 5.25; 5.26; 5.34; 5.38; 5.77; 5.79; 5.114; 5.118; 5.123; 5.137; 5.149; 6.13; 8.22; 8.23; 8.27; 8.35; 8.78; 8.81; 8.88; 8.96; 8.99; 8.107; 8.113; 8.116
Lexis (US users)	www.lexis.com	8.61; 8.67; 8.72; 8.73

Name	Address	Paragraph in main text
LexUM *see* University of Montreal LexUM		
Library of Congress: catalogue	www.loc.gov/homepage	2.13
Library of Congress: Global Legal Information Network (GLIN)	www.loc.gov/law/glin/GLINv1	8.15
Library of Congress: Guide to Law Online	lcweb2.loc.gov/glin/	8.15
Lincoln's Inn	www.lincolnsinn.org.uk	2.59
LJAS (Latest Judgments Alert Service) – Hong Kong	www.smlawpub.com.hk	8.107
Lord Chancellor's Department	www.lcd.gov.uk/	2.60; 7.11
Lovdata (Celex)	www.lovdata.no	3.127
Maastricht Internet Law Library	www.ub.unimaas.nl/mill/index.html	8.110
McGill Air and Space Law Institute	www.iasl.mcgill.ca/home.htm	6.16
Mannheim University *see* University of Mannheim		
Martindale-Hubbell's Lawyer Locator	www.martindale.com/locator/home.html	2.64
Middle Temple	www.middletemple.org.uk	2.59
National Conference of Commissioners on Uniform State Laws	www.law.upenn.edu/bll/ulc/ulc.htm	8.65
Nick Holmes' Infolaw *see* Infolaw		
Northern Ireland Court Service	www.nics.gov.uk	8.35
Northern Ireland Department of Social Development	www.dhsspsni.gov.uk	5.24
Northern Light	www.northernlight.com	1.45
Official Documents *see* TSO Official Documents		
OJ Online	www.ellispub.com	3.127
Organization of American States	www.oas.org	6.32
PacLII	www.paclii.org	8.109
Parliament	www.parliament.uk	1.37; 3.17; 3.40; 4.15; 4.50; 4.52; 4.55; 4.60; 4.81; 5.24; 7.14; 7.19
Parliament of South Africa	www.polity.org.za/govdocs/legislation/index.html	8.102

Name	Address	Paragraph in main text
Parlianet	www.parlianet.com	1.37; 3.67; 3.69; 3.165; 4.6; 4.64; 4.82; 4.87; 4.90; 7.19
Polis (*see also* Parlianet)	www.parliament.uk	4.81; 4.87; 7.19
Privy Council. Judgments	www.privy-council.org.uk/judicial-committee/jindex.htm	5.24
Privy Council. Secretariat	www.privy-council.org.uk/secretariat/index.htm	3.164
Quicklaw	www.quicklaw.com	8.92; 8.96
Saarbrucken University: Law-Related Internet Project	www.jura.uni-sb.de/english/	8.110
Sarah Carter's Lawlinks	library.ukc.ac.uk/library/lawlinks	1.48; 3.128; 5.24; 6.16; 8.15
SCAD *see* Europa		
Scaleplus	law.agps.gov.au	8.82; 8.83; 8.85
Scottish Court Service	www.scotcourts.gov.uk	8.24
Search Engine Showdown	www.searchengineshowdown.com	1.45
Search Engine Watch	searchenginewatch.com	1.45
SI-CD inc. SI Web	www.thestationeryoffice.com	3.38
Smith Bernal *see* Casebase; Casetrack		
Social Security Commissioners		5.24; 5.103
Unreported decisions:	www.hywels.demon.co.uk/commrs/decns.htm	
Starred decisions:	www.courtservice.gov.uk/tribunals/ossc_frm.htm	
Reported decisions:	www.dss.gov.uk/publications/dss/2000/commdecs	
Solicitors Online	www.solicitors-online.com	2.51
SOSIG Law Gateway	www.sosig.ac.uk/law	1.48; 8.15; 8.61
Standing Committee Debates	www.parliament.the-stationery-office.co.uk/pa/cm/stand.htm	4.52
The Stationery Office	www.the-stationery-office.co.uk	3.17; 7.21
Strasbourg *see* European Court of Human Rights		
Supreme Court of Jamaica	www.sc.gov.jm	8.108
Supreme Court of Trinidad and Tobago	www.ttlawcourts.org/Judgements/appeal.html	8.108

Name	Address	Paragraph in main text
Sweet and Maxwell	www.sweetandmaxwell.co.uk	2.24; 2.60
The Telegraph	www.telegraph.co.uk	5.14
The Times	www.thetimes.co.uk	5.14
TSO Daily List	www.clicktso.com	3.67
TSO Official Documents	www.official-documents.co.uk	7.21
Tynwald	www.tynwald.isle-of-man.org.im	8.39
ukonline	ukonline/gov.uk	7.21
Uniform Commercial Code *see* National Conference of Commissioners on Uniform State Codes		
United Kingdom Official Publications (UKOP)	www.ukop.co.uk	3.39; 3.67; 3.89; 4.6; 7.16; 7.17; 7.18; 7.28
United Nations. Treaty Collection	untreaty.un.org	6.13; 6.32
University College, Cork: Irish law *see* Irish Law Site		
University Law Review Project	www.lawreview.org	2.28; 8.63
University of California at Berkeley (EU resorces)	www.lib.berkeley.edu/GSSI/eu.html	3.129
University of London Union List of Serials	www.ull.ac.uk	8.78
University of Mannheim. Virtual Library of the European Documentation Centre	www.uni-mannheim.de/users/ddz/edz/edz/eedz.html	3.128; 3.129; 3.133; 5.38
University of Montreal LexUM	www.lexum.umontreal.ca/index_en.html	8.92; 8.94
University of Richmond: Constitution Finder	confinder.richmond.edu	8.13
University of the South Pacific, Vanuatu	www.vanuatu.usp.ac.fj	8.109
University of Washburn Forint-Law	www.washlaw.edu/forint/	8.102
University of Würzburg: International Constitutional Law	www.uni-wuerzburg.de/law/home.html	8.13
US Government Printing Office *see* GPO Access		
US State Department Private International Law Database	www.state.gov/www/global/legal_affairs/private_intl_law.html	6.16
US Supreme Court	www.supremecourtus.gov	8.66; 8.67
Wales Legislation Online	www.wales-legislation.org.uk/	8.16

Index